Corsica

Mark Zussman
Olivier Cirendini
Julien Fouin
Jean-Bernard Carillet
Christophe Corbel
Laurence Billiet
Tony Wheeler

LONELY PLANET PUBLICATIONS
Melbourne • Oakland • London • Paris

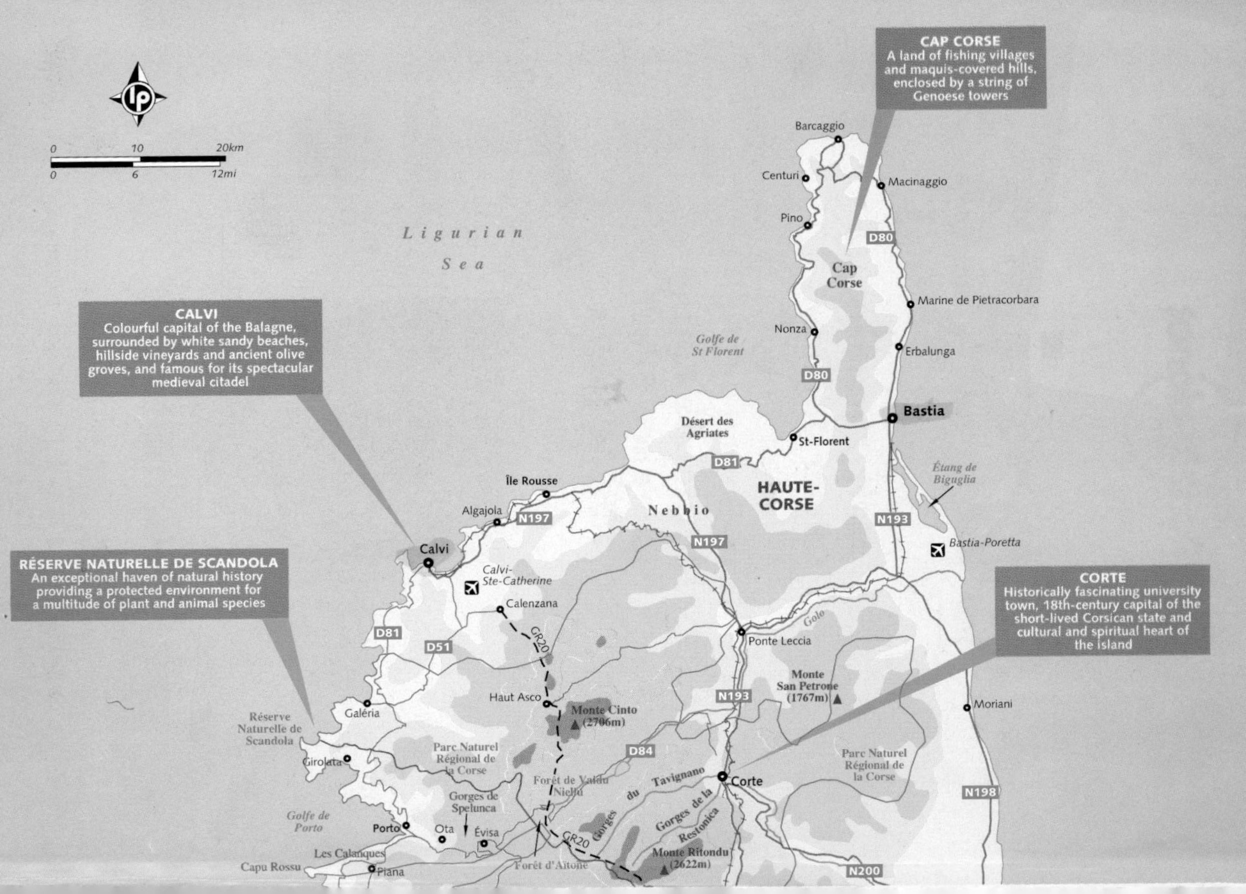
0
10
20km
0
6
12mi
Ligurian Sea
CAP CORSE
A land of fishing villages and maquis-covered hills, enclosed by a string of Genoese towers
CALVI
Colourful capital of the Balagne, surrounded by white sandy beaches, hillside vineyards and ancient olive groves, and famous for its spectacular medieval citadel
RÉSERVE NATURELLE DE SCANDOLA
An exceptional haven of natural history providing a protected environment for a multitude of plant and animal species
CORTE
Historically fascinating university town, 18th-century capital of the short-lived Corsican state and cultural and spiritual heart of the island
Barcaggio
Centuri
Macinaggio
Pino
D80
Cap Corse
Marine de Pietracorbara
Nonza
Golfe de St Florent
Erbalunga
Bastia
Désert des Agriates
St-Florent
D81
Étang de Biguglia
HAUTE-CORSE
Île Rousse
Algajola
N197
Nebbio
N193
Calvi
Calvi-Ste-Catherine
Bastia-Poretta
Calenzana
GR20
D51
Golo
Ponte Leccia
Monte San Petrone (1767m)
Haut Asco
Monte Cinto (2706m)
Galéria
Moriani
Réserve Naturelle de Scandola
Girolata
Parc Naturel Régional de la Corse
D84
Forêt de Valdu Niellu
Tavignano
Corte
Gorges du Tavignano
Gorges de la Restonica
N198
Gorges de Spelunca
Golfe de Porto
Porto
Ota
Évisa
Les Calanques
Capu Rossu
Piana
Forêt d'Aïtone
Monte Ritondu (2622m)
N200

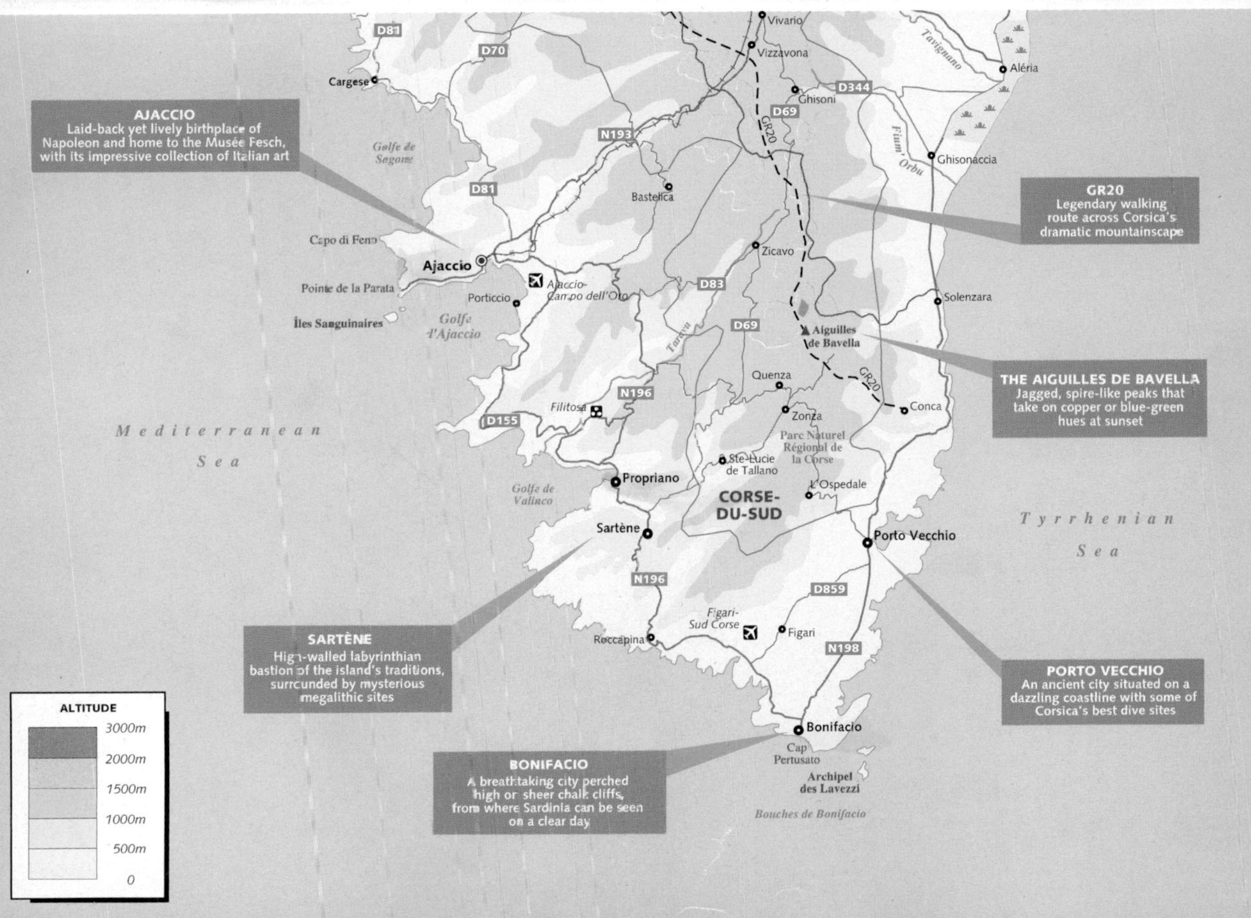
AJACCIO
Laid-back yet lively birthplace of Napoleon and home to the Musée Fesch, with its impressive collection of Italian art
GR20
Legendary walking route across Corsica's dramatic mountainscape
THE AIGUILLES DE BAVELLA
Jagged, spire-like peaks that take on copper or blue-green hues at sunset
PORTO VECCHIO
An ancient city situated on a dazzling coastline with some of Corsica's best dive sites
SARTÈNE
High-walled labyrinthian bastion of the island's traditions, surrounded by mysterious megalithic sites
BONIFACIO
A breathtaking city perched high on sheer chalk cliffs, from where Sardinia can be seen on a clear day
ALTITUDE
3000m
2000m
1500m
1000m
500m
0
Mediterranean Sea
Tyrrhenian Sea
Vivario
Vizzavona
Aléria
Tavignano
Cargese
D81
D70
D344
Ghisoni
D69
GR20
N193
Golfe de Sagone
Fium' Orbu
Ghisonaccia
Bastelica
Capo di Feno
Ajaccio
Zicavo
Pointe de la Parata
Ajaccio-Campo dell'Oro
Porticcio
D83
Solenzara
Îles Sanguinaires
Golfe d'Ajaccio
D69
Taravu
Aiguilles de Bavella
Quenza
N196
Filitosa
Conca
D155
Zonza
Parc Naturel Régional de la Corse
Ste-Lucie de Tallano
Propriano
L'Ospedale
Golfe de Valinco
CORSE-DU-SUD
Sartène
Porto Vecchio
N196
D859
Figari-Sud Corse
Figari
Roccapina
N198
Bonifacio
Cap Pertusato
Archipel des Lavezzi
Bouches de Bonifacio

Corsica
2nd English edition – July 2001
First published – August 1999
Translated from Lonely Planet's *Corse* (2nd edition)

Published by
Lonely Planet Publications Pty Ltd ABN 36 005 607 983
90 Maribyrnong St, Footscray, Victoria 3011, Australia

Lonely Planet Offices
Australia Locked Bag 1, Footscray, Victoria 3011
USA 150 Linden St, Oakland, CA 94607
UK 10a Spring Place, London NW5 3BH
France 1 rue du Dahomey, 75011 Paris

Photographs
Many of the images in this guide are available for licensing from Lonely Planet Images.
email: lpi@lonelyplanet.com.au

Front cover photograph
Gorges de la Restonica (Olivier Cirendini)

ISBN 1 86450 313 0

Printed by SNP SPrint (M) Sdn Bhd
Printed in Malaysia

Contents – Text

Contents – Maps

INTRODUCTION

FACTS ABOUT CORSICA

WALKING

DIVING

GETTING THERE & AWAY

GETTING AROUND

BASTIA & THE FAR NORTH

CALVI & THE BALAGNE

THE WEST COAST

THE SOUTH

THE EASTERN PLAIN

THE CENTRAL MOUNTAINS

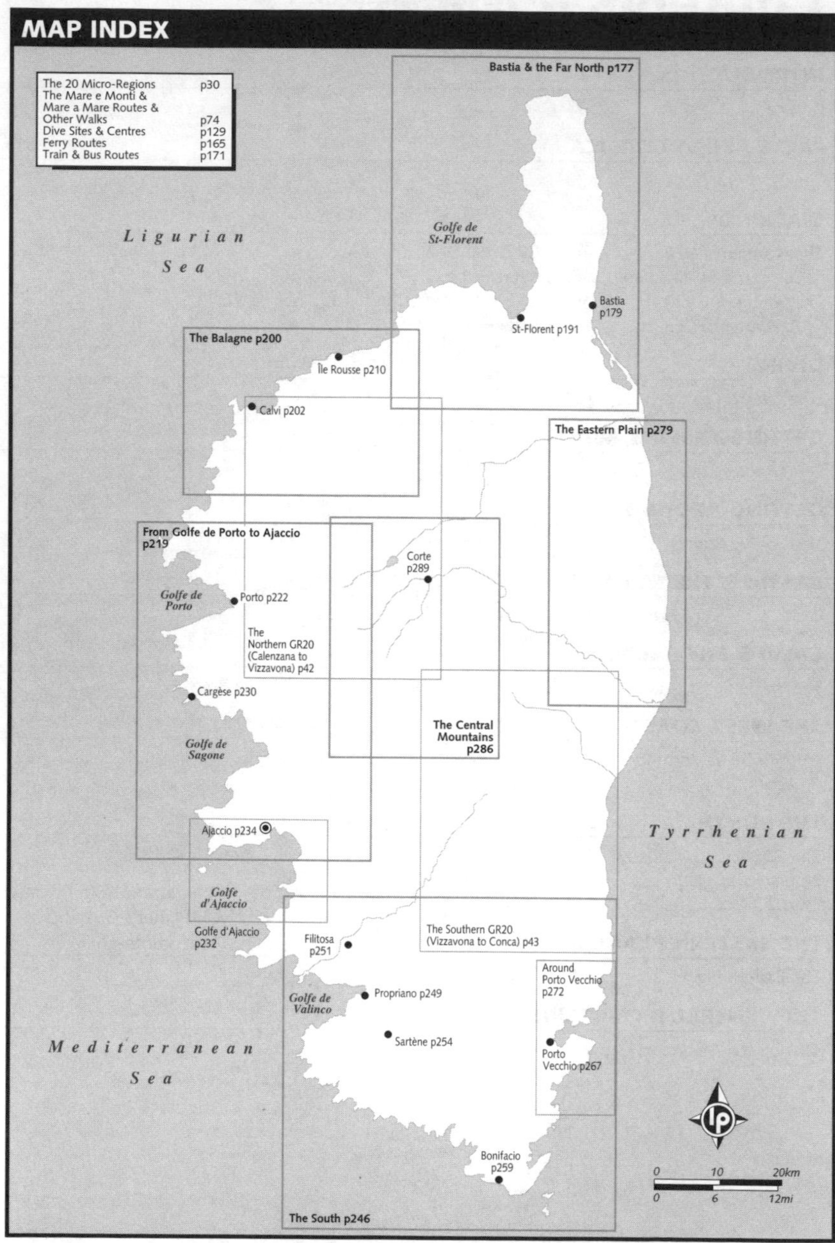
MAP INDEX
The 20 Micro-Regions p30
The Mare e Monti & Mare a Mare Routes & Other Walks p74
Dive Sites & Centres p129
Ferry Routes p165
Train & Bus Routes p171
Bastia & the Far North p177
Ligurian Sea
Golfe de St-Florent
Bastia p179
St-Florent p191
The Balagne p200
Île Rousse p210
Calvi p202
The Eastern Plain p279
From Golfe de Porto to Ajaccio p219
Corte p289
Golfe de Porto
Porto p222
The Northern GR20 (Calenzana to Vizzavona) p42
Cargèse p230
The Central Mountains p286
Golfe de Sagone
Ajaccio p234
Tyrrhenian Sea
Golfe d'Ajaccio
Golfe d'Ajaccio p232
Filitosa p251
The Southern GR20 (Vizzavona to Conca) p43
Around Porto Vecchio p272
Golfe de Valinco
Propriano p249
Sartène p254
Mediterranean Sea
Porto Vecchio p267
Bonifacio p259
The South p246
0 10 20km
0 6 12mi

The Authors

Mark Zussman & Barbara Lowenstein

Mark and Barbara are lifelong Francophiles. Once upon a time Mark lived and worked in Paris, while Barbara long commuted to Paris and to the Brittany coast. The couple have previously worked together on the French edition of the Lonely Planet guide to *New York City*, where they live. Mark, who did most of the word work on this new edition of *Corsica*, while Barbara worked on the maps, is now close to finishing a long-term project under the title *A Jane Austen We Can Really Use*. His next book after that will be called *The Brazilians Are Better Than We Are*. The couple's favourite spot in Corsica is the upper city of Bonifacio, with its seductive views over the straits to Sardinia. But, they say, there must be at least 100 close runners-up.

Olivier Cirendini

Although his surname evokes the fragrance of the Corsican maquis, Olivier was born in Paris. After studying English and journalism and spending time in London, he became a journalist, writing on subjects from frozen chips to manned space flights. He has travelled widely in his work and has assisted in writing Lonely Planet's *Jordanie et Syrie*, *Réunion et Mauritius*, *Louisiane*, *Madagascar* and *Côte bretonne et les îles*. Olivier loves black humour and red wine.

Julien Fouin

During his idyllic childhood in the countryside, Julien developed a penchant not only for the smell of hay, but also for travel and adventure. Studying both sociology and journalism he gave this up at the age of 21 to report on the Sommet de la Terre in Rio, and consequently travel in France and abroad. Crossing Burma by bike and the forest of Vancouver on foot are among his best memories. Foremost among all life's pleasures, Julien likes cooking, mountain-biking, doing up his house in Cantal and rummaging around markets. He's helped update Lonely Planet's *Guadeloupe et Dominique* and *Martinique, Dominique et Sainte-Lucie*.

Jean-Bernard Carillet

After studying international relations and translation at the Sorbonne Nouvelle, Jean-Bernard worked as an editor in Lonely Planet's French office for five years before becoming an independent author. A keen traveller and diving instructor, he will decamp for the sea at the slightest opportunity. Jean-Bernard has contributed to several Lonely Planet guides, including *Martinique, Dominique et Sainte-Lucie*, *Guadeloupe et Dominique*, *Tahiti et la Polynésie française*, *Marseille*, *Côte bretonne et les îles*, as well as *Guide de plongée Tahiti et la Polynésie française* and *Guide de plongée Mer Rouge*.

Christophe Corbel

Christophe was born in Paris in 1962, son of a Breton father and Alsatian mother. As a young man, he spent several years in industrial northern France before returning to the capital. After a stint in a communications firm, he then embarked on a promising career as a freelance journalist and became a master at using search engines and other tools of cyberspace. He's now one of the cornerstones of the Lonely Planet Web site.

Laurence Billiet

Originally from Lyon, Laurence emigrated to Melbourne to do an MBA. It was there that she came across Lonely Planet in 1993. The following year she returned to Paris and joined the staff at Lonely Planet's French office. Driven by a constant desire to travel, she has trekked over difficult terrain in Iceland, Réunion, Hawaii and now Corsica. She is fascinated by volcanoes, addicted to vanilla Danette and crazy about football. Laurence is now Lonely Planet's International Marketing Coordinator, based in Melbourne.

Tony Wheeler

Tony was born in England but spent most of his youth overseas. He returned to England to do a university degree in engineering, worked as an automotive engineer, returned to university to complete an MBA then dropped out on the Asian overland trail with his wife, Maureen. They've been travelling, writing and publishing guidebooks ever since, having set up Lonely Planet Publications in the mid-70s.

FROM THE AUTHORS

Mark & Barbara It was the team from Lonely Planet's Paris office that did all the really heavy lifting on this book – it was they who tramped the GR20 and the Mare a Mare Centre, dove the dives and inspected the dozens of hotels and out-of-the-way crêperies. For our part, we spent several weeks researching with a view to gearing the work of the French team towards the needs of an English-speaking audience. *Chapeau*, then – in English, that's a tip of the hat – to Laurence Billiet, Jean-Bernard Carillet, Olivier Cirendini, Christophe Corbel and Julien Fouin. Terrific work! Thanks also to Paul Bloomfield, Abigail Hole, David Wenk and the whole of the Lonely Planet staff in London for their invaluable support. Of the dozens of Corsicans who made our stay on the island pleasant and instructive, one deserves particularly to be singled out: Joseph Calloni of Bastia has a depth of knowledge of his native town, as well as an enthusiasm for it, that could serve as an inspiration for all of us.

Olivier As well as those who helped on the first edition, to whom this new edition still owes a big debt, I want to thank the readers, who helped build this work through their input. Equal thanks go to Carinne, Kamel and confederates (and their lemon liquor), Jean-François, Léo and Stéphane, Monique and Claude, the warden of the Haut-Asco refuge for his enthusiasm, Bertrand, who injected a breath of fresh air into certain parts of the text, and Marcel and Joséphine, in Calvi. In Paris, thanks to Sophie, Caroline, Corinne, Julien and Michel-U Mitchunu, who lent their polyphonic voices to the project with brilliance and good humour. Kind regards also to my friend Mark Zussman in New York. Finally to the Great Bear, my lucky star, and to my daughter Nina, who so likes the Corsican donkeys' long ears.

Julien The support of certain people made my travels through South and Central Corsica much easier, and I want to thank particularly Jean-Philippe Di Grazia and the tourist information offices for their excellent assistance. Many thanks for memorable moments spent in La Castagniccia, to La Ferme Auberge A Pignata, to the horse-riding centre in Sartène, to Christophe Pigeault, and to all those who help to preserve the beauty and heritage of Corsica through their work in the tourist industry. Finally, special thanks to Zoulie who once more agreed to accompany me on a not always entirely restful voyage.

This Book

Olivier Cirendini, Jean-Bernard Carillet, Christophe Corbel, Laurence Billiet and Tony Wheeler wrote the first French-language edition of *Corse*, translated into English as *Corsica* by Atlas Translations in London. The second edition of *Corse* was updated by Olivier and Julien Fouin. This second English-language version was revised and updated by Mark Zussman.

From the Publisher

This second English-language edition of *Corsica* was edited and proofed in Lonely Planet's London office by Abigail Hole, with assistance from Sally Schafer and Sam Trafford. Abigail, Paul Bloomfield and Tim Ryder compiled the index.

David Wenk was responsible for design, layout and mapping. The original maps were drawn in Lonely Planet's French office by Corinne Holst, helped by Caroline Sahanouk, and they were revised for this edition by David. James Ellis compiled the climate charts and Ed Pickard created the map legend. The front cover was designed by Sophie Rivoire and Lachlan Ross drew the back-cover map. Dominique Cordonnier drew the illustrations and the Walking chapter pictograms were supplied by Valérie Police. The photographs were sourced from Lonely Planet Images.

Much appreciation to Quentin Frayne for his linguistic expertise, Emma Sangster for her help with the Health section and Rachel Suddart for checking information in the Getting There & Away chapter. Thanks also to Andrew Weatherill for his exceedingly calm last-minute Quark assistance, and to Sara Yorke, Paul and Tim in the London office and Isabelle Lethiec in the French office for all their support and assistance during the production of this book. Olivier and Julien helped greatly by answering last-minute queries.

Thanks

Many thanks to the following travellers who used the last edition and wrote to us with helpful hints, useful advice and interesting anecdotes:

Alan Timmins, Alice Duke, Anne Smith, Ben Steel, Borend Thijsse, Christiane & Raymond Matthey, Claudio Marchesi, Cynthia McFarlane, David Morgan, David Snadden, Elaine Gallagher, Éva & Denis Dolne, Francine Brochard, Francis Mossay, Gilles Wagner, Isla Luke, John Martin, Jonathan Cook, Lee Douglas, Marcel Rost, Mark Pennington, Matthew Demonte, Michael Coffey, Michel Ollers, Michel-Pierre Bouisset, Mme Gontier Benziane, Moira Snadden, Nicola Connor, Olivia Marisol Segura, R Alvis, Ralph Mertens, Richard Hancock, Richard Luke, Sophie Campe, Suzanne Goulet, Sylvie Seguin, Theresa Raucci, V Crawford, Valerie Weston.

Foreword

ABOUT LONELY PLANET GUIDEBOOKS

The story begins with a classic travel adventure: Tony and Maureen Wheeler's 1972 journey across Europe and Asia to Australia. Useful information about the overland trail did not exist at that time, so Tony and Maureen published the first Lonely Planet guidebook to meet a growing need.

From a kitchen table, then from a tiny office in Melbourne (Australia), Lonely Planet has become the largest independent travel publisher in the world, an international company with offices in Melbourne, Oakland (USA), London (UK) and Paris (France).

Today Lonely Planet guidebooks cover the globe. There is an ever-growing list of books and there's information in a variety of forms and media. Some things haven't changed. The main aim is still to help make it possible for adventurous travellers to get out there – to explore and better understand the world.

At Lonely Planet we believe travellers can make a positive contribution to the countries they visit – if they respect their host communities and spend their money wisely. Since 1986 a percentage of the income from each book has been donated to aid projects and human rights campaigns.

Lonely Planet gathers information for everyone who's curious about the planet – and especially for those who explore it first-hand. Through guidebooks, phrasebooks, activity guides, maps, literature, newsletters, image library, TV series and Web site we act as an information exchange for a worldwide community of travellers.

Updates Lonely Planet thoroughly updates each guidebook as often as possible. This usually means there are around two years between editions, although for more unusual or more stable destinations the gap can be longer. Check the imprint page (following the colour map at the beginning of the book) for publication dates.

Between editions up-to-date information is available in two free newsletters – the paper *Planet Talk* and email *Comet* (to subscribe, contact any Lonely Planet office) – and on our Web site at www.lonelyplanet.com. The *Upgrades* section of the Web site covers a number of important and volatile destinations and is regularly updated by Lonely Planet authors. *Scoop* covers news and current affairs relevant to travellers. And, lastly, the *Thorn Tree* bulletin board and *Postcards* section of the site carry unverified, but fascinating, reports from travellers.

Correspondence The process of creating new editions begins with the letters, postcards and emails received from travellers. This correspondence often includes suggestions, criticisms and comments about the current editions. Interesting excerpts are immediately passed on via newsletters and the Web site, and everything goes to our authors to be verified when they're researching on the road. We're keen to get more feedback from organisations or individuals who represent communities visited by travellers.

Research Authors aim to gather sufficient practical information to enable travellers to make informed choices and to make the mechanics of a journey run smoothly. They also research historical and cultural background to help enrich the travel experience and allow travellers to understand and respond appropriately to cultural and environmental issues.

Authors don't stay in every hotel because that would mean spending a couple of months in each medium-sized city and, no, they don't eat at every restaurant because that would mean stretching belts beyond capacity. They do visit hotels and restaurants to check standards and prices, but feedback based on readers' direct experiences can be very helpful.

Many of our authors work undercover, others aren't so secretive. None of them accept freebies in exchange for positive write-ups. And none of our guidebooks contain any advertising.

Production Authors submit their raw manuscripts and maps to offices in Australia, USA, UK or France. Editors and cartographers – all experienced travellers themselves – then begin the process of assembling the pieces. When the book finally hits the shops some things are already out of date, we start getting feedback from readers, and the process begins again ...

WARNING & REQUEST

Things change – prices go up, schedules change, good places go bad and bad places go bankrupt – nothing stays the same. So, if you find things better or worse, recently opened or long since closed, please tell us and help make the next edition even more accurate and useful. We genuinely value all the feedback we receive. Julie Young coordinates a well travelled team that reads and acknowledges every letter, postcard and email and ensures that every morsel of information finds its way to the appropriate authors, editors and cartographers for verification.

Everyone who writes to us will find their name in the next edition of the appropriate guidebook. They will also receive the latest issue of *Planet Talk*, our quarterly printed newsletter, or *Comet*, our monthly email newsletter. Subscriptions to both newsletters are free. The very best contributions will be rewarded with a free guidebook.

Excerpts from your correspondence may appear in new editions of Lonely Planet guidebooks, the Lonely Planet Web site, *Planet Talk* or *Comet*, so please let us know if you *don't* want your letter published or your name acknowledged.

Send all correspondence to the Lonely Planet office closest to you:

Australia: Locked Bag 1, Footscray, Victoria 3011
USA: 150 Linden St, Oakland, CA 94607
UK: 10a Spring Place, London NW5 3BH
France: 1 rue du Dahomey, 75011 Paris

Or email us at: talk2us@lonelyplanet.com.au

For news, views and updates see our Web site: www.lonelyplanet.com

HOW TO USE A LONELY PLANET GUIDEBOOK

The best way to use a Lonely Planet guidebook is any way you choose. At Lonely Planet we believe the most memorable travel experiences are often those that are unexpected, and the finest discoveries are those you make yourself. Guidebooks are not intended to be used as if they provide a detailed set of infallible instructions!

Contents All Lonely Planet guidebooks follow roughly the same format. The Facts about the Destination chapter or section gives background information ranging from history to weather. Facts for the Visitor gives practical information on issues like visas and health. Getting There & Away gives a brief starting point for researching travel to and from the destination. Getting Around gives an overview of the transport options when you arrive.

The peculiar demands of each destination determine how subsequent chapters are broken up, but some things remain constant. We always start with background, then proceed to sights, places to stay, places to eat, entertainment, getting there and away, and getting around information – in that order.

Heading Hierarchy Lonely Planet headings are used in a strict hierarchical structure that can be visualised as a set of Russian dolls. Each heading (and its following text) is encompassed by any preceding heading that is higher on the hierarchical ladder.

Entry Points We do not assume guidebooks will be read from beginning to end, but that people will dip into them. The traditional entry points are the list of contents and the index. In addition, however, some books have a complete list of maps and an index map illustrating map coverage.

There may also be a colour map that shows highlights. These highlights are dealt with in greater detail in the Facts for the Visitor chapter, along with planning questions and suggested itineraries. Each chapter covering a geographical region usually begins with a locator map and another list of highlights. Once you find something of interest in a list of highlights, turn to the index.

Although inclusion in a guidebook usually implies a recommendation we cannot list every good place. Exclusion does not necessarily imply criticism. In fact there are a number of reasons why we might exclude a place – sometimes it is simply inappropriate to encourage an influx of travellers.

Maps Maps play a crucial role in Lonely Planet guidebooks and include a huge amount of information. A legend is printed on the back page. We seek to have complete consistency between maps and text, and to have every important place in the text captured on a map. Map key numbers usually start in the top left corner.

Introduction

For many people, Corsica will always be, first and foremost, the place that gave birth to world-conquering Napoleon Bonaparte. Beyond this, people may know that Corsica has a somewhat uneasy relationship with the Metropolitan France to which it belongs. Beyond this, many people outside of the immediate neighbourhood may not know very much at all. In the last year for which figures are available, British visitors accounted for barely 3% of the total, and visitors from Ireland, North America, the Pacific countries and South Africa were, unsurprisingly, even rarer.

Corsica nevertheless has recently become something of a holiday phenomenon. Every July and August, the months in which the French and the Italians vacation en masse, hundreds of thousands of these near neighbours head for Corsica's seashores and high inland mountains. They go because Corsica has preserved such a majestic and thinly populated primitiveness that, even at the beginning of the 21st century, the island could easily be mistaken for a great offshore nature park. A good third of it and more *is* a great national nature park.

The French and Italians go to lie in the sun, to swim, to scuba down to plane- and shipwrecks, eat mouth-watering home-cooked meals and drink the local liqueurs and wines, to bicycle, to climb amidst the spooky needles and moonscapes of the seemingly endless mountain ranges, to try their driving skill on the perilous mountain roads, to sail, to water ski, sometimes to snow ski, to watch the sun go down and not least of all to go walking. For a number of these French and

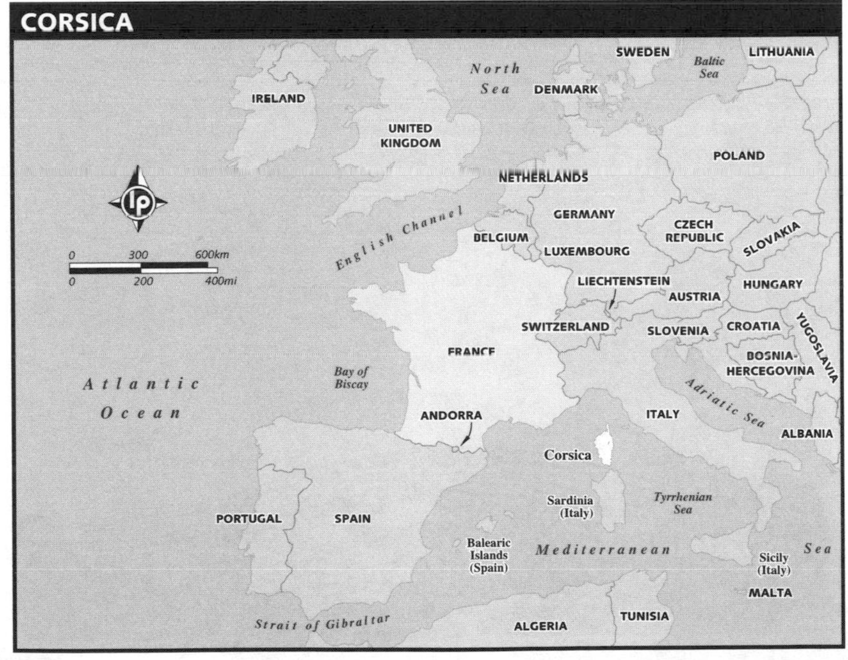

Italian visitors, Corsica is in effect an extension of the French and Italian Rivieras, while for others it is the anti-Riviera: It is the uncomplicated, unspoiled, earthy, casual holiday spot that the mainland seacoasts have long since buried under their tons of jewellery, designer evening wear and many other markers of conspicuous consumption and social competitiveness. Paradise? Near enough.

Non-French and non-Italian visitors to Corsica who've done a little reading may have some surprises. If you fill up your head with romantic images of noble bandits and vendettas enduring to the umpteenth generation, you will discover that they have ceased to exist. Perhaps not very long ago, but they have ceased to exist nevertheless. The mainland French will often see the island as an exotic escape from France, but Francophiles will be delighted to discover that Corsica is like one of those perplexing figure-ground perception puzzles that seems first one thing, then another. It's Corsica. But it's France. It's Corsica. But it's France. Fortunately no one is obliged to choose between the two. *Vive la Corse! Vive la France!* Corsica gives you both great destinations in one neat island package.

Facts about Corsica

HISTORY

World history is generally told without reference to Corsica at all, except, in passing, as the place that gave birth to world-bestriding Napoleon. Nevertheless, Corsica's history is a fascinating and turbulent one. Its strategic position long attracted the attentions of the major Mediterranean and European powers – at one point even the faraway Russian Empire considered making a bid for it. Pisa, Genoa, France, Spain and Britain, not to mention the Moors and the armies of the Roman and Holy Roman Empires, have all fought on Corsican soil. This long history of conflict reflects another battle – the islanders' struggle to assert their identity while dominated by a succession of foreign rulers.

Origins

It is likely that the island was inhabited in the Palaeolithic era, but the earliest signs of human existence – the skeletal remains of Bonifacio Woman, dating from 6570 BC – are from the early Neolithic era.

The first inhabitants of the island probably came from what we now call Tuscany, in Italy, and survived by hunting, gathering and fishing. Rock caves of the kind in which they lived can still be seen at Filitosa in the south.

Around 4000 BC the inhabitants of the island succumbed to the romance of big stones. At various sites, particularly in the south-western corner of the island, they erected great standing slabs of stone (menhirs) and shelter-like constructions (dolmens), in which two or more great standing stones support a huge slab of a 'roof'. At some point, the menhirs began to transmogrify into statuary, with carved warrior faces. In many instances, the figures can clearly be seen to be bearing swords.

In about 1100 BC an alien race arrived on the island, possibly originating from the eastern Mediterranean. Some historians have speculated that they were the mysterious Shardanes, who attacked and then were crushingly defeated by Ramses III of Egypt. These new islanders have come to be known as Torréens for their own seemingly indestructible signature edifices, the *torri*, or towers, that stand alongside or on the ruins of menhirs and dolmens. Evidence suggests that the Torréens routed their predecessors, the menhir and dolmen builders. Those artier folk, with less sophisticated weapons, appear to have migrated or fled to the north. Many of the Torréens, it seems, then headed south to Sardinia, where they built some of the first conical stone edifices, now called *nuraghi*.

The island's architectural development continued, and *castelli* (castles) are the outstanding vestiges of the settled, organised way of life that arose. The remains of two of these can be visited in the mountains between Porto Vecchio and Propriano.

Early 'Big-Name' Conquerors

Although no traces of their visits have been discovered, the adventurous Phoenicians of Asia Minor, the Etruscans of mainland Italy and the Carthaginians of what is today Tunis are all believed to have dropped anchor at one time or another in Corsican bays. In the 6th century BC, the Phocaean Greeks founded Alalia at what is now Aléria, on Corsica's flat eastern plain. Alalia thrived on trade and Corsica soon rose to fame.

For the cosmopolitan, seafaring peoples of the Mediterranean, however, the island was primarily a place for brief port calls. Nobody before Rome actually undertook to invest and dominate the island, and when Rome did step in it was above all for strategic reasons, to prevent Corsica falling into the hands of its enemies, the Carthaginians.

Rome conquered Alalia, renaming it Aléria, and set about imposing its manners on the islanders, exacting tributes, and even selling some of them into slavery. Rome, though, never went to any great pains to improve the island. In what was to become a recurrent pattern in Corsica, those islanders least willing to bend to invaders sought the protection of the unconquerable mountains.

Goths, Vandals & Other Invaders

After the collapse of the Western Roman Empire in AD 476, the distant Byzantine Empire (the Eastern Roman Empire, based in Constantinople) began to take an interest in former Roman territories such as Corsica. The collapse of Rome had initially left Corsica vulnerable to Rome's own despoilers – the Goths under Totila and the Vandals under Genseric. It's likely the latter sacked Aléria after laying waste to Gaul. Byzantium's equally bloody conquest of the island in the first half of the 6th century ended the brief dominion of the Germanic tribes.

Beginning in the early 8th century, Corsica was also increasingly subject to attack by the Moors (Saracens, or Muslims) from North Africa. Whether as organised states or as free-booting pirates, the Moors raided for slaves, and from time to time they took possession of a coastal village or a whole coastal region or even ventured inland. Between the 8th and 18th centuries, the islanders lived in perpetual fear of invasion.

It is known that Christendom responded to these attacks, but it is difficult to distinguish Corsican myth from reality, especially with regard to the 'crusades' mounted on the island's behalf. There is no doubt that Pépin le Bref, the father of Charlemagne, was involved and it is said that he promised Corsica to the papacy. A certain Ugo Colonna, at the very least a hero of legend, may have been charged by the pope with running the Moors off – and even to have succeeded, temporarily. In any event, by Charlemagne's time, the papacy was the leading Christian power in Corsica.

Lords, Popes & Pisans

The 10th century saw the rise to power of the nobility. Important seigniorial families, often of Tuscan or Ligurian origin, created fiefdoms on the island and ruled them with a rod of iron. Some historians date the predominance of so-called clans in Corsica from this time. Still, little is known of the period other than that the seigniorial families vied with one another. The one thing that is certain is that, at the request of certain Tuscan feudal lords, in 1077 the pope appointed the bishop of Pisa to oversee his Corsican interests.

The then-powerful Italian city of Pisa, continually at odds with its rival, Genoa, put commerce ahead of all other values, and its bishop served as a front man for its merchants. Corsica nevertheless also benefited from Pisan overlordship and this period was one of peace, prosperity and development, particularly for the Balagne and Cap Corse. Handsome Pisan-style churches were erected in the Balagne, the Nebbio, and on and around the north-eastern coast.

Pisa's good fortune in Corsica aroused Genoa's jealousy, and Genoese ambitions took a turn for the better when Pope Innocent II, in 1133, divided the island between the two Italian republics. From then on it was simply a matter of gaining ground for Genoa.

First, Genoa undermined its rival's supremacy by fortifying the town of Bonifacio, in the south. Genoese forces then ventured north, where they turned Calvi into a stronghold. By the 13th century, despite opposition from some island lords who remained loyal to Pisa, Genoa unmistakably enjoyed the upper hand. Pisa's defeat in the sea battle of Meloria, a small island near Livorno in 1284 marked the end of Pisan rule in Corsica.

Genoese Occupation

Before Italian unification in the second half of the 19th century, Genoa was one of the great early modern merchant states. A key port from Roman times, Genoa's commercial interests ranged from Spain to the Crimea, and if it had been more ambitious, Genoa rather than Spain might very well have been the first to discover and exploit the Americas; Columbus, after all, was Genoese, whether he was born in Genoa proper or, as some Corsicans would have it, in Genoese Calvi.

Genoa occupied and dominated Corsica for five centuries, during which time the island was turned into a fortress. A chain of watchtowers went up round the periphery of the island as complements to the high walls, first at Bonifacio, then at Calvi, followed by other important coastal population centres.

The Genoese had little sentiment for the Corsicans who were often evicted or excluded from towns, and put to work on the land to serve Genoa's commercial and economic interests and pay taxes. Those who disobeyed were punished severely.

The old feudal lords were particularly dissatisfied and Alphonse V, the king of Aragon, allied with Genoa's new arch-rival, Venice, promised to lend his support to the most powerful of the feudal lords, Vincentello d'Istria. In 1420 the Aragonese fleet, led by Alphonse himself, entered Corsican waters. The Genoese stronghold of Calvi was tricked into submission and an attack was launched on the other great stronghold, Bonifacio. However, Bonifacio was not so easily overcome, and after four months of unsuccessful siege the disheartened Aragonese fleet sailed away.

Left to his own devices, Vincentello d'Istria, continued to cause the Genoese grief for a good many years. He was finally captured and executed in 1434. In 1453, the Genoese turned to their powerful financial institution, the Banco di San Giorgio, to administer the fractious colony.

The new administration created towns and set the population to work at cultivating olive and chestnut trees, with a view towards turning Corsica into Genoa's bread basket. Taxes were raised and force used to curb opposition. Over several decades, during which thousands of summary executions occurred, nothing much was done to benefit the Corsicans themselves. But the island was 'pacified'.

By the mid-16th century, the Genoese believed they at last had Corsica under control. However, the island's strategic importance in Europe would soon prove a catalyst once again.

Sampiero Corso & the French

In 1552 Henri II, king of France, saw an opportunity to gain ground in Italy when the Sienese rose against the Spanish garrison in their city and called on France for protection. Corsica, because of its location, got caught up in the middle of the struggle. In 1553 an expeditionary corps reached Bastia under the command of the Maréchal de Termes and his second in command, the Turkish privateer Dragut, a French ally. The town was captured, shortly followed by others, and within a few days Corsica was declared French territory.

During this campaign, Sampiero Corso, a Corsican colonel in the French army, came to be renowned for his courage, and to symbolise the fight against the Genoese. Yet his popularity and determination were not enough to safeguard the French victory. The Genoese appealed to Charles V, the king of Spain and Holy Roman Emperor, for support, and Henri, after suffering a series of agonising defeats, signed the Treaty of Cateau-Cambrésis, which, in addition to ending 65 years of struggle between France and Spain for supremacy in Italy, recognised Genoese supremacy on the island.

After the breather under the French, the Corsicans found themselves again at the mercy of their familiar enemy and despite a favourable start, Sampiero Corso's independent effort to free the island from the Genoese in 1564 was short-lived.

Some historians have called the second period of Genoese rule the 'century of fire'.

Sampiero Corso 'the Fiery'

Born in 1498 near Bastelica, Sampiero Corso became known as 'the most Corsican of Corsicans'. He rose to fame on the mainland as a soldier in the French army. Despite his modest background, his military reputation made it possible for him to marry the noble Vanina d'Ornano, 35 years his junior. Vehemently anti-Genoese, Sampiero fought with great courage alongside the French army, in 1553, in a bid to reconquer his native island. Although this first attempt was unsuccessful, he refused to give up hope. He returned to the island with a band of partisans in 1564, having failed to obtain European backing, and managed to destabilise the Genoese but could not vanquish them. Three years later, Sampiero was assassinated.

One of the most tragic episodes of his life was when his hatred of the Genoese was directed at his wife. Believing that she had betrayed him to his sworn enemies, he killed her with his own hands before burying her with great pomp and ceremony.

The new Genoese governor had more watchtowers built to protect the island from the increasing number of Saracen raids, while the republic continued where it had left off, governing and suppressing the islanders, favouring the traditional Genoese strongholds and forcing the islanders to cultivate olives, chestnuts and vines. The island's inhabitants remained dissatisfied, especially since they reaped none of the fruits of their labours, and poverty was rife. Excluded from the management of their country's affairs, many Corsicans decided to emigrate.

Uprising & French Intervention

Corsica's Forty Years' War began in 1730, when an old peasant in a mountain village near Corte balked at paying tax to a Genoese tax collector. The effects of his action snowballed, with more and more Corsicans refusing to pay their taxes each day. The rebels grew bolder and organised themselves into a group, stealing weapons and gradually weakening Genoese rule. Bastia, Algajola and St-Florent were taken. With a revolt on their hands, the Genoese successfully appealed to the emperor of Austria for assistance and St-Florent and Bastia were subsequently recovered. The Genoese forces were defeated at the Battle of Calenzana (1732) but then regained control of the situation. It was a transient success, however: the revolt recovered momentum and at a meeting in Corte in 1735 the Corsicans drew up a constitution for an independent sovereign state.

A somewhat comical episode followed. In 1736, an eloquent, opportunistic German aristocrat named Theodor von Neuhof disembarked in Aléria. Seeing him as the leader for whom they had been looking, the rebels allowed this peculiar man to declare himself king of Corsica – though, to be sure, under a constitution. During his eight-month sojourn on the island, he handed out honorary titles and battle orders; then abandoned the throne on the pretext of going in search of money and reinforcements, which never arrived.

The battle continued in Theodor's absence and the Genoese grew so uneasy that in 1738 they accepted France's offer of assistance. Delighted to be involved in the island's affairs again, this time with Genoa's blessing, the French king, Louis XV, sent an expeditionary corps to Corsica, paid for by the Genoese, under the command of General de Boissieux. The general's mission was one of 'conciliation and arbitration', which only thinly disguised France's real designs. Boissieux took a bad beating at Borgo, south of Bastia, but his successor, the Marquis de Maillebois, did better. By the time the French left Corsica in 1741, 1000 Corsicans had gone into exile abroad. The rebellion appeared to be over.

Troubles, all the same, bubbled up again in 1748, and the Genoese again enlisted French help. The Marquis de Cursay succeeded in regaining administrative control of the island, and he juggled Corsican and Genoese interests as best he could. He was poorly rewarded for his labours: denounced by the Genoese as being too pro-Corsican, he was recalled to Paris and imprisoned. In 1753, when the last French regiments pulled out, Corsica was still under Genoese rule.

Theodor I, King of Corsica

Born in Cologne in 1694, Theodor de Neuhof sought a land where he could make a name for himself. His interest in Corsica had been awakened when he met some Corsicans in mainland Europe and was touched by their plight. He then raised money for his expedition among Greek and Jewish merchants in Tunis. Had he had more time and ampler resources, he may even have done the Corsicans some good but his military strategy was based on the interminable siege warfare that was still the main pillar of military doctrine in Europe. Theodor's Corsican troops were good for lightning strikes and guerrilla warfare, or nothing. Disenchantment was inevitable. When he left Corsica, he did actually crisscross Europe in an effort to rally support – but to no avail. He died in London, penniless, in 1756.

Pascal Paoli & the Revolt

In 1755 the troubles resurfaced with an insurrection led by Pascal Paoli. Educated and a product of the European Enlightenment, Paoli – despite the opposition of several important families – succeeded where everyone else before him had failed: he united the struggle against Genoa. Furthermore, he cobbled together a constitutional state – unique of its kind in that still dynastic and absolutist age – which, given time, might have ensured Corsica a happy independence. It was not to be.

In the aftermath of disastrous attempts by the Genoese to regain control of Corsica once again, France seized the opportunity it had been waiting for – the recent loss of a large chunk of its American colonial empire had redirected its sight-lines towards the Mediterranean. In 1764 France accepted Genoa's offer to occupy the strongholds of Bastia, Ajaccio, Calvi and St-Florent. The Treaty of Compiègne, which sealed the agreement, was, however, only the first stage: the Treaty of Versailles, four years later, formalised the Genoese cession of Corsica to France. Now France itself began acting less like a mediator and more like a ruler. The mobilisation of Paoli's supporters failed to reverse the situation. Their defeat at the Battle of Ponte Novo on the River Golo, north-east of Ponte Leccia, on 8 May 1769 marked the beginning of French rule of Corsica in earnest, and Paoli fled north to London.

Corsica Under French Rule

Once again Corsica had a military government of outsiders. In re-establishing law and order and taking control of the administration, the French followed the example of the Genoese, but without their brutality. They proclaimed a new set of laws, known as the Code Corse, particular to the island, and made some efforts to develop agriculture. The period was characterised by Corsica's increasing adaptation to a style of French governance that revolution was about to blow to smithereens.

The Moor's Head

It was Pascal Paoli who made the Moor's head Corsica's official emblem. Yet no one really knows for certain why. You see it everywhere – on beer-bottle labels, on the Corsican coat of arms that adorns public buildings and on Corsica's traditional flag. The Moors, or Saracens, in their incarnation as pirates from the Mediterranean's southern shores, were one of Corsica's traditional enemies. During the crusades, any crusader who had a victory over the 'infidels' could add the Moor's head to his personal coat of arms, suggesting that the Moor's head is a symbol of Corsica's victory over its enemies. The emblem could also represent both conquest of an oppressor and the strength to confront one's own destiny.

Why, though, does the Corsican Moor wear his bandanna around his forehead, whereas the four Moors on the Sardinian arms wear theirs as blindfolds as did the Moors so plentifully represented in Corsica before Paoli's time? The Corsican general, Ghjuvan Petru Gaffori, when he attacked the Genoese citadel in Bastia in 1745, was perhaps the first to reposition the cloth. 'Corsica at last has its eyes open', Gaffori said. And Paoli commented, 'Corsicans want to see clearly. Freedom must walk by the torch of philosophy. Could we say that we seem to fear the light?' Both of these remarks suggest that Corsica had come to identify with the Moor.

A latter-day incarnation of the Moor, in posters promoting the Corsican language against the French-language juggernaut, placed the bandanna, not over his eyes and not over his forehead, but over his mouth, as if gagged.

DOMINIQUE CORDONNIER

The Corsican emblem decorates many a bottle, belly or building.

Pascal Paoli – Pioneer

Paoli was born in 1725 in Morosaglia, in the Castagniccia region, and since 1889 his ashes have been buried there as well. He spent his youth in Italy with his father, who had gone into exile during the French occupation. In Naples, where he was educated, he read Montesquieu's *The Spirit of Laws*, Plutarch and Machiavelli. He was barely 30 when he returned to the island, and three months later he was named General of the Nation. He then proceeded to displace the Genoese from everywhere throughout the island but their six fortress towns. His military successes, never decisive, were not, however, his greatest claim to fame.

That title is assigned to his relentless constitutionalism. 'Wishing to give durable and constant form to its government', 'the felicity of the nation' – these are phrases from the first of his efforts at writing a framework for governance, and he penned them three decades and more before the Americans convened to try something along similar lines in Philadelphia. To be sure, not all the members of his parliament were elected democratically; a significant number – satraps, Corsican war heroes, surviving sons and brothers of war heroes – were simply appointed. But the 325 parliamentarians who were elected were elected by secret ballot. His efforts to root out criminality and in particular Corsica's trademark murderous vendettas were heroic, as also were his efforts to promote public education. The English religious reformer John Wesley called him 'as great a lover of his country as Epaminondas and as great a general as Hannibal'. In America, patriots on the outskirts of Philadelphia met in the General Paoli Tavern, in what was later to become the town of Paoli. (There are in fact now four towns in the US named Paoli). In Boston, patriots named their sons – and their sailing vessels – Paoli and Pascal Paoli. But his battle was not winnable, and he spent much of his life in exile in London, where he died.

The French Revolution was initially applauded by many Corsicans. For the impoverished islanders, it gave new voice to popular dissatisfaction and new hope. In 1789 a decree proclaimed that 'Corsica belongs to the French Empire and its inhabitants shall be governed by the same constitution as the rest of France'. An amnesty was granted, and Paoli returned to Corsica. But reconciliation between Corsica and France was not complete. In 1793, Paoli was blamed for the failure of the French revolutionary government's Sardinian expedition; he had committed fewer troops than the government had expected. He also sided with the moderate wing of the revolutionary movement (the Girondins) rather than the more radical forces (the Montagnards and Jacobins). The stern and irreconcilable Revolutionary Convention that had judged and executed Louis XIV and his queen Marie-Antoinette ordered Paoli's arrest for counter-revolutionary behaviour. He declared Corsica's secession, and requested help from Britain.

For Britain, this was an opportunity of the same kind that Genoa's mismanagement had been for France. Britain had held the island of Menorca on and off for about 70 years but, having recently lost it again, had no sovereign base east of Gibraltar from which to look after her own Mediterranean interests, and now Britain was being all but begged to establish one.

On its arrival in Corsica in 1794, the British fleet captured St-Florent, Bastia and Calvi (it was during a battle for the latter that Admiral Horatio Nelson lost the sight in his right eye). George III, king of England, was proclaimed sovereign in Corsica. Yet the British soon proved a disappointment to Paoli. He had believed Britain to be liberal and enlightened. But Britain did as little to benefit Corsicans as other rulers had. Paoli was passed over for the vice-royalty and again went into exile in London, where he died in 1807.

The Anglo-Corsican kingdom lasted just over two years. The signing of the Treaty of Paris between France and Sardinia soon undermined English security in the Mediterranean; in London an idea was mooted to cede the island to their then friends the Russians, who had already expressed a zealous interest but this came to nothing.

Following the English departure in 1796, the island's affairs came once again under the jurisdiction of the French and specifically of Napoleon Bonaparte, a Corsican by birth. His single ambition for the place was to make it French once and for all. The undertaking was not without difficulties. Immediately, Napoleon's enforcers bumped up against the clergy, and the conflict resulted in an anti-French insurrection in 1798. Mistrustful of Corsica's own political class, Napoleon excluded Corsicans from island administrative posts, and broke the island up into two departments. He still managed to make friends in Corsica, and paradoxically – as the island's most famous progeny – did more to Gallicise the island than any other individual.

Solidarity & Exceptionalism

In the 19th and 20th centuries, except for a brief period leading up to and during WWII,

Napoleon Bonaparte

As a young raw artillery officer, the future 'Emperor of the French' began but never finished a passionately pro-Corsican, anti-French novella that anticipated much of the romantic prose fiction set in Corsica in the 19th century. The story went roughly like this: An Englishman is shipwrecked on the little island of Gorgona (between the top of Cap Corse and Livorno). Before long he meets an aged Corsican and his lovely young daughter who inhabit a cave. Their chief sport is to kill the French who occasionally land or are shipwrecked there. A partisan of defeated Pascal Paoli, the aged Corsican had, it seems, kept up his resistance to the French on Corsican soil, even after their conquest of his native island.

Dorothy Carrington summarises the young Bonaparte's story in *Napoleon and His Parents*: Still in Corsica, the Corsican 'joined a band of 60 conspirators pledged to drive out the French, "enemies of free men". After some engagements, in which a hundred Frenchmen are taken prisoner, he reaches his village to find his father lying in his own blood, his mother mutilated and naked "in the most revolting posture" and his wife and seven sons hanging from trees…Soon he sets sail with some fellow rebels from "the accursed isle where tigers reigned"'. Even the Turkish pirates, who have kidnapped his daughter but later return her to him unharmed on Gorgona, are, it seems, less cruel than the French.

Despite this early expression of Corsican patriotic feeling, Napoleon grew to be extremely ambivalent about his native island, if not hostile to it. In his final exile on the island of St-Helena in the southern Atlantic, he was asked why he had never done more to help develop Corsica's economy. His answer: 'Je n'en ai pas eu le temps' – 'I didn't have time for it'. His mature policy towards Corsica was in fact altogether cold-blooded. Let the Corsicans keep their religion and their priests, he said, but let them love France and let them serve in her armies. A mere two roads, one between Ajaccio and Bastia, one between Bastia and St-Florent, should suffice, he said, for a people whose principal highway should be the sea. Native Corsicans, he decreed, were to be excluded from the administration of the island as they weren't trustworthy.

In 1814, the year of Napoleon's first definitive defeat, the people of Ajaccio threw a bust of Napoleon into the sea as the people of Bastia welcomed British troops. Resentment, however, seems to have passed with time. Ultimately, Napoleon was lionised as the homeboy who'd made good in the wider world and brought the island fame. All that remained was to plaster his face on T-shirts and coffee mugs!

DOMINIQUE CORDONNIER

when Mussolini tried to persuade the Corsicans that they were really Italian, Corsica ceased to be a pawn in the strategies of other powers. Although integrated into France, Corsica rejected some central government decisions. The clan structure endured and there was a propensity towards organised crime. Problems of poverty, development and agriculture remained unsolved.

Under Napoleon III's (son of Napoleon I's brother Louis) prosperous French Second Empire, real investment was made in Corsica's infrastructure for the first time. Corsicans took advantage of the greater employment opportunities available in France in enormous numbers and they filled many posts in the French empire. The sword, though, has cut both ways. Disproportionate numbers of Corsicans died on the battlefields of WWI.

Corsica fought bravely in WWII as well. In 1940, the island was occupied by more than 90,000 Axis troops and it was in Corsica that the term 'maquis' was coined for the whole of the French Resistance. Corsica was the first region of France to be liberated and, like its neighbouring islands in the Mediterranean, served as a forward base for the liberation of mainland Europe.

Significant investment in the island has also been made since WWII.

The Corsican Malaise

Corsica's latter-day difficulties date from the 1960s, when France came to be perceived as pursuing a colonialist policy in Corsica. A Corsican movement for autonomy began to take shape to combat it. One particular source of friction was France's use of Corsica's eastern plain for the resettlement of refugees from the French defeat in Algeria. Before WWII, mosquitoes and malaria had made the eastern plain all but uninhabitable. But with state investment in irrigation and other infrastructure, as well as the use of the insecticide DDT, the eastern plain became the most agriculturally advanced and prosperous region on the entire island. The people benefiting most roundly from the investments and incentives, however, weren't necessarily 'real' Corsicans.

In 1975, the powder keg went up when Corsican separatists, led by the Simeoni brothers, unearthed a scandal involving fraudulent wine-making practices in the eastern coastal town of Aléria. The *pieds-noirs* (literally 'black feet' – the name given to Algerian-born French people) winegrowers, along with the government, were accused of corrupt profiteering. The protesters occupied a building used to store wine, and an attempt by the police to resolve the situation ended in two deaths.

The *boues rouges* (red mud) affair, in which an Italian multinational was found to be dumping toxic waste off the coast of Bastia, served as a further catalyst for discontent. In 1976 this manifested itself in the creation of the Front de Libération Nationale de la Corse (FLNC). Talk of autonomy was increasingly talk of independence and plastic explosives went off at the rate of one a day. Tempers have not so much cooled in subsequent years as found other outlets.

By the 1990s, the FLNC had broken into any number of splinter groups, and many other independent groups had come into existence. From 1993 to 1996 these groups warred against each other every bit as furiously as they had previously against the perceived coloniser.

The French state, meanwhile, has tended towards its own sort of rudderlessness. One government tries repression and waves of often random arrests, another experiments with accommodationism. In the early 1980s two measures seemed designed to soothe the nationalists. First, a university was opened in Corte; for many years, after the French had closed down Pascal Paoli's university, higher education was only available on the mainland. Second, the Assemblée de Corse was created; previously, the island had belonged to the Provence-Alpes-Côte d'Azur region. The detente arising from these measures was short-lived, however, and in 1983 the government shut down the FLNC. They might just as well have ordered the wind to stop blowing. The nationalist movement pursued its militancy under the name of 'ex-FLNC'.

The quarrel continues in various arenas, from economic development policy to environment to language. Tourism is a focal point of the argument, as in Corsica it is intimately bound up with these three issues, as well as many others. Industry is virtually non-existent, and agriculture less than ideally productive. For central government ministries responsible for economic planning, land management and so on, the tourist industry has been perceived as the means by which Corsica is most likely to pay its own way. Yet some separatists criticise this obsession with tourism as despoiling the environment, forcing assimilation and turning the island into a carnival for two months of the year and a desert for 10.

For anyone beginning to wonder at this point whether a trip to Corsica is such a good idea after all, it's to be noted that separatists have maintained a strict hands-off policy with regard to tourists themselves.

Where Things Stand Now

The assassination of the regional prefect, Claude Érignac, on 6 February 1998 upped the separatists' ante considerably. Érignac was the highest representative of the French state on the island, and many close observers of Corsican affairs saw his murder as an announcement that the nationalist movement was back in business, and serious, despite its internal divisions and previous renunciation of violence.

As of this writing, no suspect has yet been charged with the crime. The murder sparked strong expressions of disgust among Corsicans themselves – as many as 40,000 of them took to the streets to demonstrate their horror at the violence. Shortly afterwards, a commission of 30 members of the French lower house led by Jean Glavany assessed the Corsican situation as a whole. The 600-page report they published six months later called Corsica's attitude towards democracy and law 'ambiguous'; it detailed the existence of organised gangs on the island, speaking of racketeering by some militant nationalists; it found the island to be 'immoderately' attached to firearms and expressed grave doubts as to whether the government would ever be able to pacify the nationalists with tax breaks, debt-forgiveness and amnesties. Before the year was out, Lionel Jospin's government launched a 'Clean Hands' operation, with a view towards re-establishing law and order on the island. This operation did not win the hearts and souls of Corsicans, who felt they had been demonised.

The stand-off took a turn both comic and grave when, in April 1999, a beach restaurant, Chez Francis, which had been constructed illegally on public property near Ajaccio, went up in flames, and the arsonists turned out to have been the police. There was a loud outcry. Bernard Bonnet, the zealous prefect who had replaced Claude Érignac, was identified as having called the shots, and he has since got to see the Santé prison from the inside. The island's very highest authority, it seems, had decided that the law was going to be respected, even if he had to take the law into his own hands.

There is a further twist. As this book goes to press, the French government, negotiating with Corsica's elected leaders, has been preparing to grant Corsica unprecedented legislative autonomy within the hitherto rigidly centralised French state system – as well as yet more explicit recognition of the Corsican *différence*. The negotiations have come to be known as the Matignon Process, the Matignon being the seat of the French prime minister, and for France as a whole the developments have been extremely controversial (and for some, traumatic), since they have raised the deepest questions about the future of France as France. What has troubled many French traditionalists is that, if Corsica is treated differently, the dam bursts. Jean-Pierre Chevènement, the Interior Minister, found the French government's conciliatory mood distressing enough to resign over it in mid-2000, arguing that any concessions to terrorists are indefensible, and that other regions with a strong sense of separate identity will inevitably claim the same privileges as Corsica.

GEOGRAPHY

The island of Corsica rises out of the sea 150km south of the Italian city of Genoa – the island's former master. The Italian port of Piombino, 90km to the east, is closer still, and the Italian island of Sardinia, almost three times as large as Corsica, is a mere 12km south of Bonifacio. Nice, the closest mainland French town, is 170km away.

In surface area, 8722 sq km, Corsica is around a fifth of the size of Switzerland; but represents only 1.6% of all French territory. The island's length from top to bottom is 183km and it spans 85km at its widest part. Cap Corse, the 40km-long peninsula that juts into the Gulf of Genoa at the northern end of the island, gives Corsica its distinctive shape.

The island is extremely mountainous. In many places, it no sooner rises above sea level than it rises into the clouds. The highest mountain is Monte Cinto (2706m). Other high peaks include Monte Ritondu (2622m), Paglia Orba (2525m), Monte Pedru (2393m), Monte d'Oro (2389m) and Monte Renoso (2354m).

It is on the western coast that the mountains rear out of the sea most dramatically. The Golfe de Porto, Golfe de Sagone, Golfe d'Ajaccio and Golfe de Valinco all allow for a little human habitation at sea level, but not a lot. The eastern coast is less dramatic. The long coastal plain of Aléria stretches back far enough to allow for some lowlands agriculture, and when the mountains rise up, they do so relatively gently.

In addition to its coastal waters, Corsica has several important lakes and rivers. The River Golo, which flows for 80km from the Valdu Niellu forest to south of the Étang de Biguglia, is the fastest moving. Other rivers include the Tavignano, which flows to Aléria, and, on the western side of the island, the Liamone, the Rizzanese and the Taravu. Corsica has 43 glacial lakes.

GEOLOGY

Geologists now believe that the massif formed by Corsica and Sardinia, the Corso-Sardinian micro-continent, broke away from Provence around 30 million years ago. The islands ended up in their current position after slowly rotating around an axis somewhere in the middle of the Gulf of Genoa.

The western and southern part of Corsica, from the Balagne to Solenzara, is composed of the original platform that broke away from mainland Europe. This ancient crystalline base consists of magmatic rock (igneous rock formed by magma rising within the earth's crust, which slowly crystallised as it rose), including granite, a hard rock containing feldspar, quartz and mica. This has been eroded to form such dramatic features as the rocky inlets near Piana and the Scandola nature reserve. The same phenomenon created *tafoni* (cavities), which can be seen in various places on the island.

The island's north-eastern fringe, including Cap Corse, bound to its west by Corte and to the south by Solenzara, has a different geological structure. This is composed of complex sedimentary and metamorphic rocks, such as schist. To give a simplified outline of the formation of Corsica's geology: two stages have been identified in the creation of this alpine, or schistose, scenery. First, a sedimentary platform was formed on the sea floor from deposits produced by the disintegration or alteration of existing rocks, and chemical or biological activity (shell particles, for example). Layer by layer, the platform was built up, eventually rising above sea level. The rocks then metamorphosed, their composition changing as a result of the heat and pressure during the formation of the Alps in the Tertiary era.

A rift zone divided the island in half at Corte, giving the island its herringbone mountain range and numerous east–west valleys. In the Quaternary era, glaciation modified the island's geology, creating a more alpine relief.

Corsica's mountainous make-up can be simplistically classified: into red rocks (the crystalline platform, in evidence around Piana and Scandola), white rocks (chalk, found near Bonifacio) and green rocks (ophite, a complex magmatic rock created during the major folding periods).

Corsica owes the existence of a variety of ornamental rocks and the rare orbicular diorite to geological upheaval. Diorite, an igneous rock, recognisable by its grey honeycomb structure, is found in Ste-Lucie de Tallano in the Alta Rocca.

CLIMATE

The Mediterranean climate, characterised by its summer droughts and sun, gives Corsica an average annual temperature of 12°C. The mountains are cooler, however, and the temperature drops significantly as you climb. Snow can be seen above 1600m from October to June. This means that some skiing is feasible, but visitors to Corsica are usually sun- rather than snow-seekers.

On average, the island has 2700 hours of sunshine each year. This is one and a half times the sun that Paris sees. Between June and September, average temperatures often exceed 25°C; in July and August temperatures can sizzle above 35°C. According to the French meteorological office in Ajaccio, temperatures climb over 30°C on average 12 days a year in Ajaccio and 32 days in Corte.

Spring and autumn are both fine, with average temperatures of around 15°C and maximum temperatures of around 20°C. Rainfall is highest during the last three months of the year, when there are often severe storms and flooding. In high summer, precipitation is minimal. The mountains often experience severe winters and some of the island's peaks are snow capped year round. Corte has on average 30 days of frost per year, compared with 11 in Ajaccio and three in Bastia. Corsica's climate is typically slightly warmer in the north than in the south.

The prevailing winds are the dry, gentle *libecci*, especially in Haute-Corse, and the *tramontane*, which comes down from the north in winter. The warm, moisture-bearing *sirocco* occasionally blows up from the south-east. Cap Corse and the Bouches de Bonifacio are the windiest points (in 1965 wind speeds hit 288km/h).

AJACCIO

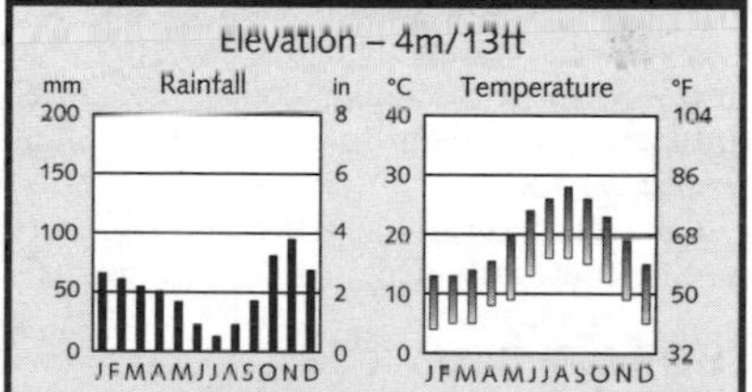

Source: Météo France Centre d'Ajaccio (average over 30 years)

CORTE

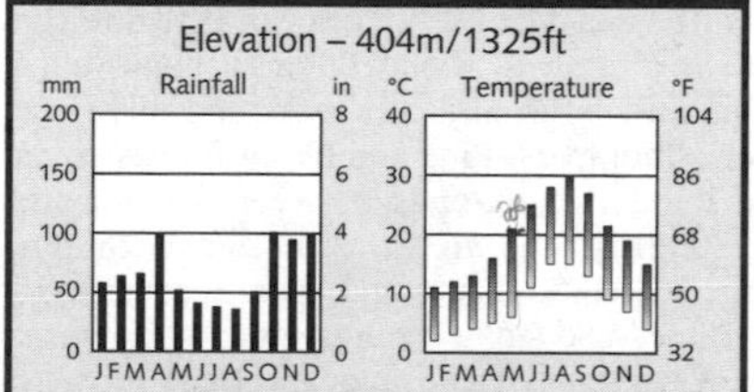

Source: Météo France Centre d'Ajaccio (average over 30 years)

ECOLOGY & ENVIRONMENT

For outsiders, Corsica's main attraction is its environment, which for a variety of reasons is remarkably well preserved. The Corsicans themselves are devoted to the ecological well-being of their island, and they react quickly when they feel it to be under threat. Exhibit number one is the popular uprising, in 1973, against off-shore toxic-waste disposal by an Italian multinational during the boues rouges affair. Corsican eco-nationalism, as it is sometimes called, has persisted, and the threat of bombings has kept property developers from lining the coastline with mega-hotels and fast-food outlets.

The creation in 1972 of the Parc Naturel Régional de Corse (PNRC; Corsican Nature Reserve), was yet another decisive step. The PNRC is a protected area totalling 350,500 hectares, and the PNRC administration actively promotes environmental consciousness throughout the island.

Unlike the national parks, which cover uninhabited areas, France's regional nature parks undertake to 'protect and stimulate' the survival of natural, cultural and human heritage. Hence the creation by the PNRC of approximately 2000km of signposted footpaths. This body has also encouraged the preservation of Hermann's tortoise, the mouflon and the osprey, and was responsible for the reintroduction of the Corsican red deer. The 75 agents of the PNRC also take an interest in the preservation of flora, in encouraging the cultivation of fruits not traditionally grown on the island, in breeding livestock and in fire prevention.

Corsica has four other nature reserves:

the Îles Finocchiarola, the Îles Lavezzi, the Îles Cerbicale and the Réserve Naturelle de Scandola, which is a UNESCO World Heritage site.

The Conservatoire de l'Espace Littoral et des Rivages Lacustres (Organisation for the Conservation of Coastal Areas and Lakeshores; more commonly known as Conservatoire du Littoral) works to protect the coastline. This public institution, created in 1975, buys land in order to save it. It has acquired coastal sites across the island, particularly in Roccapina, the Agriates, the Bouches de Bonifacio, the tip of Cap Corse and the islands of Finocchiarola, in Scandola, Cargèse, Piana and the Étang d'Urbino. These sites account for more than 15% of the 1000km of Corsican coastline. The Conservatoire has also gained recognition through its excellent books and brochures.

The Agence pour la Gestion des Espaces Naturels de Corse (AGENC; Office for the Management of the Natural Areas of Corsica) provides the Conservatoire du Littoral with technical and scientific support – ecological surveys, project management, monitoring – on all of its Corsican sites. The organisation also acts as an adviser to local authorities.

Half of the 28,000 hectares of forest on the island is managed by the Office National des Forêts (ONF; National Office for Forests). The ONF provides seasonal guided visits to the national forests of Bavella, Bonifatu, Marmaro, Chiavari, Valdu Niellu, Aïtone, Pineta, Fangu, Vizzavona and l'Ospedale.

However, as effective as they are, these organisations cannot fully protect Corsica from ecological damage. Fire is by far the biggest threat. Stubble-burning, a time-honoured custom among Corsican farmers, produces potash, which is used to improve soil quality. Fires are also the means by which shepherds have transformed expanses of *maquis* and forest into meadows for grazing; add careless tourists, property developers and the occasional pyromaniac to the mix and the results are devastating. Repeated fires can turn a verdant landscape into desert. The Désert des Agriates, formerly an agricultural area, is evidence of this.

In 1974, no fewer than 22,000 hectares went up in smoke, while, between 1980 and 1990, a total of 140,000 burned. Even now, as many as 20 fires may be reported on a single summer's day and, despite the deployment of sophisticated fire-fighting equipment, fire-fighters are often injured and sometimes killed. For information on what action to take if you see a fire starting, refer to the boxed text 'In the Event of Fire' in the Dangers & Annoyances section of the Facts for the Visitor chapter.

Tourism does its fair share of damage to the environment, fires aside. Though walkers are targeted in awareness-raising campaigns, many persist in strewing rubbish along the trails. The sharp peak in the island's population in summer months creates a rubbish-and-waste problem in the seaside resorts as well, and this is aggravated by undisciplined dumping in the countryside.

On the coast, tourist activity and overgrazing of livestock alike have contributed to the destruction of plants that stabilise the Roccapina and Barcaggio dunes. The Conservatoire du Littoral has happily come to the rescue by erecting protective barriers. Corsica's forests are damaged, meanwhile, as Corsican farmers continue, as they always have, to allow their livestock to range freely. Pigs in particular contribute to deforestation by disturbing the soil in their search for food.

An awareness among the island's visitors will help preserve Corsica's environment.

FLORA & FAUNA

Flora

The rich Corsican flora is divided over three platforms. The Mediterranean platform (up to an altitude of about 1000m) is home to the maquis, holm and cork oaks and olive and chestnut trees. Pine and beech forests cover a band that extends between 1000m and 1800m. In the alpine zone, above 1800m, the vegetation, low and sparse, consists of grasses and small mountain plants.

Citron, kiwi and avocado trees grow in the eastern lowlands.

Maquis It is said that when Corsican exiles finally returned home, they were able to smell the maquis while still several miles off the coast. Napoleon said he could catch whiffs of it on Elba. Covering about 200,000 hectares, it combines various species, generally sweet-smelling, which usually flower in the spring. The maquis is tough enough to survive the intense summer heat, and, though it is typically rather scrubby and short, some of its component species can attain heights of 5m, assuming that fire doesn't get them. The maquis plants burn quickly. They also regrow quickly after a fire. The following brief inventory of maquis plants is by no means exhaustive.

The most common species is the **rock rose**. One type of this shrub, the shoots of which secrete a sticky resin, can be recognised by its profusion of white flowers with yellow centres approximately 3cm in diameter. Another type has larger, pinkish-mauve flowers.

Treasured for its blue-black berries, which are used in some excellent liqueurs, **myrtle** flowers in June. Its white flowers give off a peppery aroma. **Tree heather** flowers at the beginning of the year. This often grows to 2m in height and its white flowers exude a honey-like scent. **Strawberry trees** are recognisable by their round, red fruit.

The **mastic tree** also bears red fruit, although these then turn black and exude a resin-like fragrance. **Asphodels**, which can reach up to 1.5m in height, produce groups of small white flowers with narrow petals. Some bear small fruit. Holm and cork oak (see the following sections) sometimes appear in the maquis as well.

Holm Oak Found below 500m, holm oak produces the acorns on which pigs feed. It can grow to around 15m, but fires often act as a brake on its growth and it's commonly found in bush form.

Cork Oak Between 15m and 20m in height, the *Quercus suber* is distinguished by its low, twisted branches and spongy, fissured bark. This bark is removed every eight to 10 years, primarily to fashion the cork stoppers for wine bottles. Wood from the cork oak is used for fuel and carpentry. Common in the south, around Porto Vecchio, this tree, which flowers in April or May, is found at the same altitude as the olive tree.

Chestnut The chestnut tree is as central to Corsica's identity as the palm tree is to tropical islands. Introduced by the Genoese, the chestnut soon came to be widely cultivated in the region to which it gave its name: La Castagniccia. The husks open in October, exposing the flavourful brown fruit, which is used in a variety of local dishes or ground down into flour. Chestnut-tree cultivation is now somewhat on the defensive from ink disease (caused by a mushroom), lack of plant regeneration and the damage caused by domestic pigs.

Pine The main constituent of the forests between 700m and 1500m is the laricio, or Corsican, pine. This is a tree that can grow to as high as 50m. As it ages, its foliage spreads horizontally, like a parasol, and some specimens on the island are thought to be as old as 800 years. The laricio pine is more resistant than the maritime pine, also found in Corsica, which does not live as long.

Olive Found on the coast below 600m, the olive tree flowers in June and can produce up to a million pollen-rich flowers. The tree is still cultivated for its oil, even if the number of trees on the island has declined precipitously since the Genoese period. The absence of frost in Corsica means that the fruit can be left on the trees until it falls naturally. This explains the long reproductive cycle of Corsica's olive trees; they produce fruit only every second year. The olive tree thrives on sunny slopes, particularly in the Balagne.

Barbary Fig The barbary fig was brought back from Central America by Christopher Columbus. A member of the *Cactaceae* family, it resembles a cactus, 20cm to 40cm long, with prickly, oval-shaped 'arms' and yellow flowers. It produces a sweet fruit with a thick pulp.

Fauna

Many of the land animals seen in Corsica today are domesticated ones – pigs, cows, goats, sheep and mules. But it's home to a number of endemic species too.

Walkers will be happy to learn that there are no snakes in Corsica. Small black rats, which used to be common all over Corsica, are now mainly seen on the little islands off the coast and in Scandola. Corsica is home to many varieties of insects, including 40 species of dragonfly, and 53 varieties of spider. A few of the spiders – rare ones – are venomous.

Mouflon The mouflon, Corsica's king of the mountains, is a type of short-fleeced sheep whose males are recognisable by their huge horns. Their horns become increasingly coiled with each passing year. Another characteristic of the species is their white facial markings (or 'face mask'), which also increase with age. At the beginning of the century, the mouflons numbered in the thousands. Their present population is estimated at between 400 and 600. The species, consequently, is protected. Since these herbivores do not like snow very much, they descend to valleys with a little southerly sun exposure in the months from December to February. In summer, they retreat to higher altitudes. Their habitat nowadays is confined more or less to the Bavella and Asco areas.

Wild Boar The maquis and the forests harbour a dark, silky-coated distant cousin of the domestic pig. This fierce omnivore mainly lives on acorns, chestnuts, roots and fruit. Occasionally, however, it will feed on worms and insects, which it unearths by rooting in the soil with its snout; in doing so, it causes extensive damage to the environment. Wild sows and their young live in groups, while males, which are surprisingly fast runners, are solitary creatures. Males also have short but fearsome tusks, which they use to fight other males during the rutting season in November and December. Hunting wild boar is a traditional winter activity throughout the island.

Corsican Red Deer Although it disappeared from the island in the 1960s, the Corsican red deer *(Cervus elaphus corsicanus)* was reintroduced in 1985 from Sardinian specimens. This inhabitant of the maquis lives on brambles, strawberry trees, acorns and chestnuts. The males often grow to over 1m (measured at the withers) and are recognisable by their antlers, which start growing from the age of one. The antlers are shed each spring and grow again in the summer, each time slightly larger. The specimens brought from Sardinia and their earliest descendants were initially confined to protective enclosures, under PNRC supervision, in Quenza, Casabianda and Ania di Fiumorbu. In 1998, 16 adults were at last released back into the wild. Since then fawns have been born in the wild.

Audouin's Gull This sea bird has disappeared from mainland Europe and is now only found on the shores of Mediterranean islands such as Corsica, Sardinia and the Balearics. It is smaller and more slender than the herring gull and can be recognised by its dark-red and black striped beak, which ends in a small yellow point. It nests among rocks, particularly in the Finocchiarola nature reserve.

Bearded Vulture The bearded vulture, or *altore*, with a wingspan of up to 3m, often resembles a falcon as it soars overhead. It is further recognisable by the black 'beard' under its beak, by the white or yellowish plumage that covers the lower part of its body and by the dark underside of its wings. A solitary bird, nesting in rocky niches in the mountainous massifs, it follows the herds and feeds on carrion. To get at the bone marrow essential to its diet, it drops bones onto rocks to break them open.

Osprey Thanks to sharp eyesight and talons capable of grasping the most slippery of prey, this enormous predator, with its white body and brown wings, is a formidable fisherman. In 1973 there were only three pairs on the entire island; a little more than a quarter century later, the population has grown to

The osprey, a fearsome fisher, has an enormous wingspan.

around 20. The osprey build their large nests on the rocky coasts and headlands of the Réserve Naturelle de Scandola; they breed in early summer. The osprey species includes several sub-branches found in North America, Africa, Asia and Australia.

Corsican Nuthatch One of the rare birds that is peculiar to the island, the Corsican nuthatch was discovered at the end of the 19th century. Only the most keen-sighted will spot it: the bird rarely exceeds 12cm in length. It is nevertheless recognisable by the white 'brow' across its head. The nuthatch is, generally speaking, sedentary; it feeds on pine seeds, which it finds in the conifer forests, and insects. It is able to cling to the most delicate of branches, because it is very light in weight and an agile climber.

Shag This web-footed bird, with its narrow head and black-green plumage, nests in colonies on Corsica's rocky coasts and islands. It is sometimes found on the Finocchiarola islands.

Hermann's Tortoise Formerly very common in France, Spain, Italy, the Balkan countries and Greece, this land tortoise remains relatively common in Corsica despite its diminishing numbers elsewhere. It has orange and black stripes and is about 19cm long. Typically, it inhabits the maquis, where it hibernates from mid-November until the end of February under piles of leaves. It has a life expectancy of 60 to 80 years.

GOVERNMENT & POLITICS

Corsica's mountainous landscape and its diversity of human cultures have given the small island around 20 geographic-cultural 'micro-regions'. These boundaries can vary from one map to another, if they appear at all. Furthermore, the old distinction between the Au delà des Monts (the far side of the mountains) and the En deçà des Monts (this side of the mountains) is still used. Au delà des Monts corresponds to a large region in the south and north-west, from Île Rousse to Solenzara. En deçà des Monts corresponds to the north-eastern part of the island. However, they are traditional, rather than political, boundaries.

Corsica differs from other French regions, which are governed by a conseil régional, or regional council. In 1991, the island was granted special status as the Collectivité Territoriale de Corse (Territorial Collective of Corsica), often referred to as 'Joxe status' after Pierre Joxe, the socialist minister of the interior who was a driving force behind the change. Corsica consequently has had more autonomy than other regions in areas such as economic and social development, education, culture (particularly where Corsican identity appears to be at stake) and the environment.

The island is governed by a regional prefect, appointed, like all other French prefects, by order of the president of the Republic. The most senior state representative on the island, the regional prefect is responsible for everything that impacts on the interests of the French nation as a whole, for administration and for law enforcement. The current prefect is Jean-Pierre Lacroix, who succeeded the disgraced Bernard Bonnet.

The Territorial Collective of Corsica has three consultative bodies that work with the prefect. The first is the Assemblée de Corse (Corsican Assembly) based in Ajaccio, whose 51 members, elected for six years by universal suffrage, are consulted on any relevant bills and decrees. The Assemblée is primarily deliberative, although its powers extend to proposing statutory changes to the prime minister. It also elects the executive body of the Territorial Collective of Corsica, the seven-member Conseil Exécutif (Executive Council). This body advises the prefect on law implementation. The Conseil Économique, Social et Culturel (Economic, Social and Cultural Council) advises the Conseil Exécutif.

The administrative division of Corsica is more traditional. Since 1975 Corsica has been split into two *départements* (departments; France is divided into 95 of these administrative divisions in all), Corse-du-Sud, with its administration in Ajaccio, and Haute-Corse, run from Bastia. Each comes under the authority of a departmental prefect, and each has a deliberative assembly, the Conseil Général (General Council), which implements legislation locally and oversees departmental services. The offices of regional prefect and departmental prefect of Corse-du-Sud are currently held by the same person.

Finally, Corsica is divided into 360 *communes* (districts); the basic administrative unit of local government. Each one of these districts is presided over by a *maire* (mayor).

The island's two departments, meanwhile, each elect two députés to the Assemblée Nationale, the lower house, in Paris and two senators to the Sénat, or upper chamber. These representatives, like the presidents of the general councils, have tended to be right of centre.

Corsica's administrative status is by no means settled. There is talk of a return to a single department. And the Matignon Process concerns, among other things, the possibility of granting the Assemblée de Corse increased legislative power.

To be sure, a different reading of Corsican politics says this is all just window-dressing, and government in Corsica is in reality based on cronyism and patronage. Critical observers claim this explains what they see as the island's stagnant civic life.

THE 20 MICRO-REGIONS

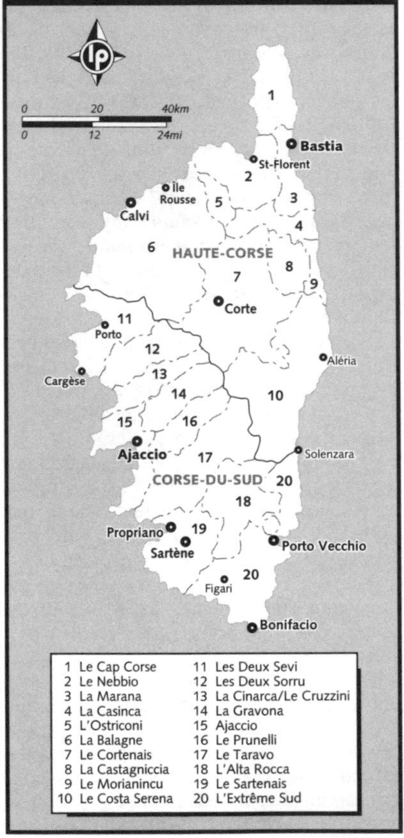
0
20
40km
0
12
24mi
1
Bastia
St-Florent
2
Île Rousse
5
3
Calvi
4
6
HAUTE-CORSE
8
7
9
Corte
11
Porto
12
Aléria
Cargèse
13
14
10
15
16
Ajaccio
17
Solenzara
CORSE-DU-SUD
20
18
Propriano
19
Sartène
Porto Vecchio
20
Figari
Bonifacio
1 Le Cap Corse
2 Le Nebbio
3 La Marana
4 La Casinca
5 L'Ostriconi
6 La Balagne
7 Le Cortenais
8 La Castagniccia
9 Le Morianincu
10 Le Costa Serena
11 Les Deux Sevi
12 Les Deux Sorru
13 La Cinarca/Le Cruzzini
14 La Gravona
15 Ajaccio
16 Le Prunelli
17 Le Taravo
18 L'Alta Rocca
19 Le Sartenais
20 L'Extrême Sud

Political Parties

Whatever impression Corsica's nationalist movement may give to the contrary, Corsica, in terms of the French national picture, has always leaned to the right. The main French parties represented on the island include, unsurprisingly, President Jacques Chirac's Rassemblement pour la République (RPR; Rally for the Republic), Le Parti Socialiste (PS; Socialist Party), L'Union Démocratique Française (UDF; French Democratic Union) and Le Parti Communiste Français (PCF; French Communist Party). Environmentalist parties are not represented in Corsica, however, and neither is the extreme right wing anti-immigration Front National (National Front). According to Corsican political analysts, these absences can be explained by the fact that the island's nationalist parties lobby for the protection of the environment and also channel protest votes.

Since the 'dissolution' of the FLNC in 1983, whole rafts of nationalist and separatist organisations have come into existence and then drifted away (see History earlier in this chapter). At the time of writing, the pre-eminent organisations of the stripe were A Cuncolta Naziunalista (Nationalist Assembly), Corsica Viva (Living Corsica), Accolta Naziunalista Corsa (ANC; Corsican Nationalist Assembly) and Unione di u Populu Corsu (UPC; Union of the People of Corsica), the separatist party of the Simeoni brothers (see History earlier in this chapter).

At the end of 1999, militants from A Cuncolta Naziunalista, from Corsica Viva, the ANC and, to a lesser degree, the Muvimentu per Autodeterminazione (MPA; Movement for Self-Determination), joined together under the new banner of Jean-Guy Talamonni's Unità. Corsica Nazione is an alliance of the nationalists serving in the Assemblée de Corse. The FLNC (in a new incarnation), FLNC Canal Historique, Fronte Ribellu (Revolutionary Front), Clandestinu and Armata Corsa are the armed branches of the nationalist movement.

The composition of the Assemblée de Corse by political tendency gives some idea of the kind of support that each enjoys. Right-of-centre parties occupy approximately 47% of the 51 seats, left-of-centre parties 31%, the nationalist Corsica Nazion group about 16%, and the independent Mouvement pour la Corse 6%.

ECONOMY

Corsica has few natural resources and no raw materials. Apart from agriculture, its main income comes from tourism, which not only provides jobs and revenue, but also is seen to boost other local economic activities, from construction to improving the island's traditionally flimsy transport infrastructure. But the 'tourism, tourism and more tourism' policy has repeatedly been criticised by articulate nationalists. Tourism generates jobs, yes, but many of them are low-skill, low-wage jobs. In addition, the shortness of the traditional tourist season in Corsica has resulted in a lack of equilibrium; for example, the jobs tourism generates are not only poorly paid and unskilled but they leave a majority of their incumbents idle for a full nine months of the year.

Industry occupies a mere 7% of Corsica's workforce, producing only 5% of island GDP. Some hesitant experimentation in the industrial-revolution-era with iron smelting and mining long ago collapsed. Today, Corsica's industrial sector consists of aeronautical engineering, industrial boiler-making, food processing and small-scale undertakings in the areas of cork and lumber. Only around 30 companies on the island employ more than 20 people and only one employs more than 100 people.

Most of Corsica's electricity is produced in two oil-fuelled power stations, one in Lucciana in the environs of Bastia, the other in Vazzio in the environs of Ajaccio. In addition, seven dams supply hydraulic power stations, notably near Calacuccia and on the Prunelli. Energy needs that these facilities are unable to meet have been taken care of via underwater cable from Italy. From the year 2000, Corsica has hosted 11 of the 55 French high-tech windmill sites as part of the Éole 2005 project.

Despite the high quality, and the renown, of Corsican agricultural products, from sausages to cheeses to honey, agriculture in Corsica has been another under-performer, and French and EU agricultural subsidies have sometimes done more to exacerbate the situation than to improve it. The EU's suckler-cow premium, for example, rewarded farmers for every calf that was born. It has become notorious both for engendering abuses such as fraudulent claims and also for increasing herds to such an extent that farmers have deliberately started numerous brush fires – to clear land for grazing – whose overall effect is devastating.

Traditionally, Corsican agriculture was a family affair, with each household virtually self-sufficient on its own little plot of land, and so to a large extent it remains. In recent years some larger scale production has at last been undertaken on the eastern plain but, since only 14% of the island is even susceptible to cultivation, the obstacles look considerably greater than the opportunities.

Agriculture currently represents just 2% of the island's GDP.

Services are at the inverse of Corsica's other economic sectors. Services currently provide 78% of the island's jobs and 80% of GDP. Government is the island's number one employer. In 1997, 30% of working Corsicans were employed by one or another government entity. Huge subsidies and tax breaks are further sources of help to the island, as are the pensions of Corsicans who have spent their working lives off of the island, returning only in their retirement.

POPULATION & PEOPLE

France's 1999 census gave Corsica a population of 260,000 of whom roughly 100,000 live in Ajaccio and Bastia. The record high measured was 276,000 inhabitants in 1884, while the record low was 170,000 inhabitants in 1955.

A 1990 study by the French National Institute of Economic and Statistical Information, suggested that more than 60% of the then population was born on the island. Throughout ancient, medieval and early modern times, Corsica assimilated untold numbers of Mediterranean peoples. Corsica opened its arms wide to immigrants in the 20th century as well. Italians settled in, as did many of the French who had abandoned their homes in Algeria at the end of the Algerian war of independence in 1962. The arrival of refugees from Algeria, most of them settling in Corsica's eastern lowlands, caused problems, however, and served as an important stimulus for the nationalist movements.

Since 1975, the flow of immigrants from outside France has diminished. The number of mainland French settling in Corsica – *pinzuti*, as the Corsicans call them – has increased. Non-French immigrants currently number around 22,000, or 8% of the total population, of whom 12,000 are Moroccan, 3000 Italian, 3000 Portuguese and 2000 Tunisians.

Corsica's birth rate is so low, meanwhile, that approximately 75 of its towns record more deaths than births. The exodus from the inland villages is also worrying. Between the 1960s and 1990s, the mountain communities lost around 15,000 inhabitants, and some regions have a population density approaching that of the Sahara. One in every three of the inhabitants of the island's mountain villages is over 60 years old. However, the island does much to keep its mountain culture alive and the PNRC (see Ecology & Environment earlier) encourages tourists to explore its mountainous regions.

Corsicans Abroad

From earliest times, Corsica has lost and acquired population. Population outflow explains the always-low population density of the island rather than a Corsican dislike of Corsica. One perennial Corsican phenomenon is the return of retirees on pensions and of yet others who've made large fortunes abroad, having left originally because economic opportunity on the island is too limited.

In the days of Genoese overlordship in Corsica, Corsicans may have made up half the enlisted men in the Genoese army. In the glory days of the French empire, when Corsicans represented only 0.5% of the total French population, they contributed, it has been estimated, as many as 20% of French administrative and military personnel in colonial outposts stretching across the globe from Cayenne to Niamey to Saigon and Bora Bora. To this day, there are large Corsican communities in the French mainland cities of Paris, Marseille, Lyon and Nice and yet more Corsicans in dozens of smaller mainland cities and towns.

Emigration, it seems, has always been particularly tempting to the outward-looking inhabitants of northern Corsica and especially to those of Cap Corse and the Balagne. Adventuresome Corsicans from those regions figured prominently among early explorers and settlers in the Americas, and Corsicans have subsequently come to form substantial communities in Puerto Rico, Mexico, Venezuela and Peru.

It has been estimated that, overall, 700,000 to 800,000 people have emigrated from Corsica over the years – in other words, some three times the island's present population.

SALLY DILLON

SALLY DILLON

SALLY DILLON

SALLY DILLON

SALLY DILLON

Savour the traditional flavours of Corsican *brocciu*, as well as the island's distinctive, chestnut-fragrant *charcuterie,* and fruit, vegetables and olives ripened in the intense Mediterranean sun.

JEAN-BERNARD CARILLET

OLIVIER CIRENDINI

OLIVIER CIRENDINI

JEAN-BERNARD CARILLET

Asphodels, cork trees and cacti are just a few elements of the heady mix of the *maquis*, which lent its name to the French Resistance.

To approach the Corsican people from a different angle, it's worth noticing that they tend to have Italianate surnames and French given names. As of this writing, the mayor of Bastia is Émile Zuccarelli, Marc Marangeli is mayor of Ajaccio, Corte's mayor is Jean-Charles Colonna, and Jean-Baptiste Lantieri bears the title in Bonifacio. Another point of interest is the disproportionate representation of Corsicans in the French government, bureaucracy and military. The mayor of Paris and numerous other high functionaries of Paris city government are Corsican and more than one Paris police commissioner has originated from the island. The editor of France's most respected newspaper, *Le Monde* (based in Paris, of course), is also a Corsican.

EDUCATION

As everywhere else in France, education on the island is compulsory for all persons between the ages of six and 16. *Lycée* (secondary school) studies are divided into two stages. The first stage, generally called *collège*, provides a general curriculum for persons between the ages of 11 and 15; the second stage, serving persons up to the age of 18, consists both of an academic track and a vocational track. Students in the academic track can take the *baccalauréat*, the university entrance exam.

In early modern times, privileged Corsicans pursued education at all levels in Italy. Pascal Paoli opened the first university in Corsica in 1765. Though it was financed by the church and the faculty consisted primarily of Franciscan friars, the curriculum was inspired by Enlightenment modernism. Carlo Maria Buonapate, a few years in advance of fathering the future emperor, enrolled there to take a course in ethics in the inaugural season – he subsequently earned a doctorate in law at Pisa. But when the French took over they closed Paoli's university, and for the next two centuries Corsicans seeking a higher education were obliged once again to leave the island for Italy or, as was increasingly the case, for the French mainland. The result was an epidemic brain drain. Corsica's best and brightest left the island to study and often they did not return.

The situation was only remedied in 1981 when the University of Corsica–Pascal Paoli opened for business in response to nationalist demand. Based in Corte, for its symbolic significance as much as for any practical reason, it has 3500 students and offers courses in the arts, languages (including a degree in the Corsican language), science, technology, law and economics. There are also technical institutes, or IUTs, on the island.

ARTS

Music

Corsica's haunting ancient music is undergoing a revival. The most frequently encountered of the traditional secular polyphonic forms is the *paghjella*, which combines three or four male voices in chants for purposes from satire to seduction. The men are usually dressed in black and each stands with a hand over one ear so as not to be distracted by the voice of the person next to him. This is critical, since each voice contributes a different harmonic element: the first provides the melody, the second provides the bass, while the third, more high-pitched, improvises on the theme.

The *voceru*, a women's art, is sung, mournfully, at wakes. The women sob and rock to and fro as if in a trance, and their singing is at once halting, monotonous and riveting. In the old days, during vendettas, the *voceri* were typically accompanied by cries for vengeance. In the *lamentu*, a gentler expression of the same general tendency, a woman bemoans the absence of a loved one never to return.

The *chjam'e rispondi* have a call and response form that is similar to that of spiritual or blues music. Since chjam'e rispondi are improvisational, they lend themselves to competitions.

Corsican vocal music is not of course necessarily performed a capella. Accompaniment might be by way of wooden or horn flutes, stringed instruments or percussion.

Groups that have recorded the traditional Corsican forms include Canta U Populu

Corsu, I Muvrini, A Filetta and I Chjami Aghjalesi. Petru Guelfucci, sometimes of the group Voce di Corsica, has become something of a household name throughout France, as a soloist – and has even developed a following beyond France.

Older recordings include a set of three LPs, dating from the period 1961 to 1963, under the title *Musique Corse de Tradition Orale*. This treasure, if you can find it, gives you an idea of how Corsican music must have sounded when it was still more expression than performance. (Some cuts feature the father of Jean-François Bernardini, the leader of I Muvrini.) Another curiosity is the *Canzone di i Prigiuneri Corsi in Alimania 1916–1917* (Songs of the Corsican Prisoners in Germany), distributed by the Corsican publisher La Marge; the recordings were made on wax rolls by German ethnomusicologists in WWI prisoner-of-war camps.

Tino Rossi, a pop crooner and balladeer, from his first recordings in the 1930s through to his death in 1983, simply *was* Corsica to mainland France and to much of the world beyond. In the course of his career, he recorded 1014 songs and sold 300 million records.

Literature

Native storytelling was for many centuries exclusively oral and Corsican has only been a written language for a century or so. Like much oral literature, it wavered between fantastic folk imaginings *(fola)* – talking animals, human-to-animal metamorphoses ('Once upon a time there was a father and a mother who had as a child a little red pig', begins one typical story) – and the more or less artful rendering of incidents from daily life. The stories were told around firesides on cold winter evenings; they were communicated by shepherds on their journeys from summer to winter pasture. Like much oral literature, they were often rendered in poetry or in song – from lovers' serenades to bandits' ballads – in part because it made them easier to remember.

Much of this oral literary heritage has been adopted by modern Corsican polyphonic groups (see Music earlier in this section). But there was never a great national epic, though collections have been assembled (for example, the 1979 French-language *Contes Populaires et Légendes de Corse* in the *Richesse du Folklore de France* series). These narratives resemble traditions elsewhere: the Corsican *Gendrillon* is the French *Cendrillon* and the equivalent tale in English, *Cinderella*.

For some centuries, literate Corsicans expressed themselves on paper in Italian. At the end of the 18th century they began to use French instead, and French is of course the language of literary expression today.

Corsica's two most prominent novelists of the 20th century, Angelo Rinaldi and Marie Susini, may be of interest to travellers competent in French; only Susini's *Les Yeux Fermés (With Eyes Closed)* appears to have been translated into English. Rinaldi, Bastia-born in 1940, meticulously describes post-war Corsican society in *Les Dames de France*, *La Dernière Fête de l'Empire*, *Les Jardins du Consulat* and *Les Roses de Pline*. Marie Susini looks sceptically at Corsican family structure and island insularity in *L'Île sans Rivage*, *Je m'appelle Anna Livia* and other works. Susini had a love-hate relationship with her native is-

Ex Marks the Spot

Antoine de Saint-Exupéry, that stoic swashbuckler of the air, is still beloved for his *The Little Prince, Night Flight, Wind, Sand and Stars* and half-a-dozen other prose romances from the days when to be a pilot still smacked of heroism and wasn't merely the airborne equivalent of driving a bus. In the last years of WWII, he flew reconnaissance missions over southern France, first from Sardinia, then, as of July 1944, from Bastia in Corsica. On the last day of July, he took off with six hours' worth of fuel in his tank. Cap Corse radar tracked him in the direction of the French Mediterranean coast. He never returned. Though no remains have ever been recovered, circumstantial evidence points to an encounter with the Luftwaffe.

land, and Corsica was only one of her themes.

Two contemporary crime writers have made something of a splash. Elisabeth Milleliri, a journalist with the Paris newspaper *Libération*, has published *Caveau de Famille* (1993) and *Comme un Chien* (1995), while Archange Morelli has written *La Maison Ardente* (1997), a detective story set in Corsica at the beginning of the 16th century.

Architecture

Corsica's greatest architectural treasure is ecclesiastical. Hundreds of small churches and rural chapels were built in the early Romanesque period (from the 9th to 11th centuries), but perhaps only 10 survive, and most of these are in ruins. There are more examples of the so-called Pisan Romanesque, a legacy of the end of the 11th century, when Pisa sent architects to Corsica with orders to build small cathedrals. Among the most impressive still standing are the Cathédrale de Mariana south of Bastia and San Michele de Murato in the mountains south of St-Florent, famous for their polychrome walls. Others can be found in the Nebbio, Castagniccia and Balagne regions.

The Baroque style of church architecture, with its sumptuously decorated interiors and facades featuring triangular or curvilinear pediments, was introduced to Corsica in the 17th and 18th centuries, during the period of Genoese domination. Many churches in the Balagne and Castagniccia were built in this style, which was very fashionable in northern Italy. Good examples are the churches and oratories of Bastia and the cathedrals of Ajaccio and Cervione out of a total inventory of about 150.

The island's rich military and defense architecture is outstanding and hard to miss. Of the Genoese watchtowers that girdle the coast, around 60 remain standing today. Some were extended by the French, such as the one in Corte. Citadels dominate numerous coastal towns from Bastia and Calvi all the way down to Bonifacio.

Largely without ornament and fortress-like, traditional Corsican houses bear resemblance to those found in provincial villages in France or Italy. They are usually constructed from granite, although shale was preferred in the chalky areas of Bonifacio and St-Florent; four- and five-storey houses are common. Small apertures in the facades keep the house warm in winter and cool in summer. The large narrow slates on the roofs vary in colour according to where they are from: grey-blue in Corte, green in Bastia and silver-grey in Castagniccia.

Corsica has some impressive 20th-century modernist architecture – the prefecture building and the Notre Dame des Victoires church in Bastia, the Lycée Laetitia in Ajaccio, the HLM (a low-cost public housing development) in Olmeto and numerous private villas at Pointe de Spérone are all in their own ways fascinating. A superb 38-page booklet, *Architectures Modernes en Corse*, will point enthusiasts in the right direction. (Available from some larger tourist offices, or contact Le Service du Patrimoine, Collectivité Territoriale de Corse, 22 Cours Grandval, BP 215, 20187 Ajaccio, ☎ 04 95 51 64 73, fax 04 95 51 65 05.)

Painting

As with architecture, Corsica has tended to import, or imitate, Pisan and Genoese painting rather than developing a school of its own. Ajaccio's Musée Fesch, the biggest museum in Corsica, houses the second-largest collection of Italian paintings in France after the Louvre. Assembled by Napoleon's uncle, Cardinal Joseph Fesch, the Italian commissioner for war and later an astute businessman, it contains dozens of early Italian works. These, by and large, are works that were looted from Italy during the Napoleonic wars.

In the 19th century, a handful of Corsican artists such as Charles Fortuné Guasco and Louis Pelligriniles, now all but forgotten, gained a small measure of recognition by studying and working in mainland Europe.

Corsica made a much more important contribution to the graphic arts as one of those many places continental innovators visited in the late 19th century and early 20th century in search of Mediterranean light. Matisse confided that 'it was in Ajaccio that I had my first vision of the South'. Fernand Léger, early in his career, made repeated visits to Corsica, as did Maurice Utrillo and his mother, the painter Suzanne Valadon. Paul Signac and the American James McNeill Whistler also visited.

Contemporary island painters such as Lucien Peri, François Corbellini, Pierre Dionisi and Jean-Baptiste Pekle are synonymous with Corsica's artistic reawakening after WWI. More often than not they have taken their inspiration from the island's stunning land- and seascapes.

SOCIETY & CONDUCT

Traditional Culture

A sense of honour is a particularly important legacy of the island's turbulent past. Injured pride has been the cause of many a bloody vendetta. The island has spawned a number of 'bandits of honour', outlawed and seeking refuge in the maquis, sometimes for years, after having avenged an offence by violent means. Weapons have always been an important part of Corsican culture – and not only for hunting.

An instance from a short story 'Mateo Falcone' by Prosper Mérimée – a keen observer of Corsican mores – further illustrates this principle. In the story, a man and his wife go out, leaving their son to watch over their house. While they are gone, a fleeing bandit begs the boy to hide him, offering him a 5FF piece. The boy accepts, but before long betrays him to the soldiers in pursuit of a more appealing bribe. When his father and mother return and learn what has happened, the boy's father pronounces him 'the first in his line to be guilty of a treason',

The Vendetta

The word vendetta actually comes from Italian; the Corsican language prefers *vindetta*. But it is with Corsica (more so even than with Sicily) that the vendetta will forever be identified. The reason, to a large extent, is that the stern and obsessed idea of justice it embodied captured the imagination of fiction writers of the stature of Balzac, Dumas, Mérimée and Maupassant.

Vendetta is the quarrel that never goes away. You kill my father – or, in the sometimes tenuous provocation, your pig trespasses on my little plot of land – and our families mobilise against each other for generations into the future. The vendetta, at its worst, did not pit one town against a neighbour town; it pitted one house against another in the same town. When a vendetta was at maximum pitch, children couldn't go out to school for fear of reprisals. Virtually no one went out. People lived as if under siege. For the vendetta was never the gentleman's quarrel fought under the level-playing-field rules of the classic sword duel. The vendetta rather was a matter of setting ambushes, waiting patiently, then shooting the adversary in the back. In the great era of the vendetta, in the 17th and 18th centuries, vendetta quarrels claimed perhaps as many as 900 lives annually in Corsica. They were unknown in Cap Corse and rare in the Balagne but their prevalence in the south goes a long way towards explaining why houses in a town like Sartène look so much like fortresses.

What gave the vendetta in Corsica much of its stark tragic quality was that the violence in response to an initial provocation was rarely spontaneous. Rather, it was brooded over, saved up, and feelings of vengefulness were cultivated and elaborated; they were not acted on, until passion had died and hatred had turned ice cold. Hence, the painful protractedness of the vendetta.

As represented in fiction, a son turned 'soft' by exposure to more civilised continental modes of behaviour might, moreover, have to be hectored into settling a score by a mother or sister. More or less disinterested townspeople or villagers, as the Corsican incarnation of an ancient Greek chorus, might further egg him on by giving the *rimbecco*. This was that under-the-breath background hum of a veiled and not-so-veiled insult: 'Coward! Your father – your brother – has not yet been avenged'.

Eventually, of course, 'soft' and civilised ways prevailed. The last of the vendettas supposedly came to an end around 1950.

Women in Corsican Society

Prosper Mérimée's exceptional short story 'Mateo Falcone' (1829) captures what must have been one aspect of time-honoured social arrangements: 'The woman advanced slowly under the weight of an enormous sack of chestnuts, while her husband took it loungingly, one rifle slung over his shoulder and a second rifle in his hand; it is undignified for a man to carry any other burden than his weapons'.

Despite suffering immemorial subordination, women were a powerful force of sorts in traditional Corsican society. In his *Guide de la Corse Mystérieuse* (1995), for example, Gaston d'Angélis reports that if a man was murdered, his wife would often visit the scene of the crime, where she would place her children's fingers in the bullet wound. She would then make the sign of the cross on their foreheads with their father's blood, before making them promise to avenge his death. Legend also has it that when Bonifacio was under siege in 1420, the townswomen gave mothers' milk to its soldiers. This was sometimes used to make cheeses, which were then used to bombard the assailants.

Corsican women today are not significantly different from women anywhere else in France in terms of the opportunities available to them. They pursue careers in business, medicine, the law and everything else in between.

In 1995, a group of Corsican women issued a Manifeste pour la Vie (Manifesto for Life) calling for an end to the island's traditions of macho violence. The document was immediately signed by 3000 others. The association known as 51 Femmes pour la Corse de l'An 2000 (51 Women for Corsica in the Year 2000) has focused primarily on economic issues.

takes him out to a ravine, invites him to say his prayers and shoots him dead.

The family is also important, and certain rules of inheritance have served to preserve its unity and continuity. The affiliation to a clan automatically provided an extended family, which also included members of a village community in a structure that was protective of its influence and authority.

However, Corsica isn't one big happy family; ties within families, clans and villages are matched by antipathy for those on the outside – other families, clans and villages.

Corsica's traditions, marked by a code of obligatory hospitality and often wildly disproportionate rough justice, have never been universal on the island or without dissenters. However, the response to the violent traditions has often itself been violent. Pascal Paoli, during the brief lifespan of independent republican Corsica in the mid-18th century, perhaps meant to help his countrymen rethink their antique and chilling conception of honour when he razed the homes of vendetta murderers and put up signposts to publicise the sometime occupants' crimes.

Napoleon went further in trying to bring his countrymen into the modern world: if a murderer could not be apprehended, he had four of his close kinsmen arrested and executed instantly.

Dos & Don'ts

The Corsica of vendettas and overheated ideas of honour has passed into history. Corsicans are accustomed to foreigners and are friendly and easy-going. You may want to punctuate any conversation you have with more than the usual fair number of 'monsieurs' and 'madames'. Instead of just a curt *merci*, be generous. Say *merci, monsieur* or *merci, madame*. You'll gain points for showing patience and more points still for taking your time at things rather than rushing. You'll also do well to introduce yourself in any conversation that goes beyond a mere exchange of niceties or simple commerce; Corsicans like to know who they are dealing with.

Should you happen to be invited into a Corsican home, there is no need to take your hosts a present. In Corsica, a bottle of wine extended as you cross the threshold may be thought to imply your uncertainty as to whether the house is able to provide.

In public drinking establishments, it is more customary to buy rounds than to attempt to divide up a bill.

RELIGION

France is notoriously lax about church attendance, and some observers have taken the position that the country is Roman Catholic in name only. Corsica, however, might be expected to be more conservative in this respect, although one source suggests – among respondents to a Corsican language-use survey – that 8% attend church regularly, 21% sometimes, 11% rarely, 44% only for social ceremonies and 16% never.

To be sure, religious enthusiasm manifests itself in Corsica in lavish Holy Week processions in towns such as Bonifacio, Sartène and Calvi; Corsica, for many centuries, belonged to the Pope's own diocese. Catholicism in Corsica coexists with vestiges of mystical and superstitious behaviours and beliefs, among them, for example, belief in the *spiritu* (the dead who return from beyond to revisit their terrestrial homes) and the belief that magic spells can cure illness.

LANGUAGE

French is Corsica's official and working language and the language in which Corsicans express themselves most of the time. Corsica is nevertheless impressively bilingual and even trilingual. Many older Corsicans and even some younger Corsicans express themselves quite eloquently in Corsican (Corsu) and even in Italian – not that the leap from Corsican to Italian is a very daunting one.

Spontaneous use of Corsican has been on the decline, but it has benefited from various forms of life support. It is now even taught in the primary and secondary schools. (This is a significant turnaround from the days when signs posted in Corsican village schools read: *Il est interdit de cracher par terre et de parler corse* – No spitting on the floor, no talking Corsican.) Young people can, moreover, now study Corsican at the university at Corte. Politicians have seen to it that Corsican enjoys equal status with French on road signs, although the French place names will often have been edited out with spray paint or bullets!

Walking

Arguably the best way to explore Corsica is on foot. It will slow you down and make it impossible not to savour the extraordinary landscapes and the fresh mountain air, and this is even before you calculate what it will do for your calves and your overall well-being.

The island, moreover, is criss-crossed with paths leading coast to coast and into otherwise inaccessible mountain redoubts. Walking options range from the most challenging two- or three-week hike to the easy afternoon stroll along the coast; there is something for all tastes, all levels of ambition and all abilities.

This chapter isn't an exhaustive inventory of walks, but rather provides some technical, practical and cultural information. All the routes described have been tested. The GR20 is included, as is the Mare a Mare Centre (central sea-to-sea) path, which is for intermediate-level walkers. The chapter concludes with descriptions of 14 short walks, half an hour to half a day in duration, which are easy and suitable for families. Details of accommodation, restaurants and other resources are given for the GR20 and Mare a Mare Centre walks.

Before embarking on any of the walks in this chapter make sure you are healthy and that the walk you have chosen is suitable for your level of physical fitness. For tips on health for walkers see the Health section of the Facts for the Visitor chapter.

The authors and the publisher cannot accept any responsibility for any loss, injury or inconvenience sustained by people using this book. Although they have done their utmost to ensure the accuracy of all information in this guide, they cannot guarantee that the tracks and routes described here have not become impassable for any reason during the interval between research and publication.

The fact that a trip or area is described in this guidebook does not mean that it is safe for you and your walking party. You are ultimately responsible for judging your own capabilities in the light of the conditions you encounter.

Walks for Everyone

- The GR20: a difficult hike for the exceptionally fit only. Duration: 15 days – or longer if you subdivide the stages.
- Five intermediate hikes: two Mare e Monti (sea-and-mountains) and three Mare a Mare (sea-to-sea) outings. Duration: five to 10 days.
- Fourteen easy circular routes: along seashores or starting from mountain or seaside villages. Duration: half an hour to half a day.

A number of companies offer guided walks in various parts of the island. For more information see the boxed text 'Organised Walks' under Activities in the Facts for the Visitor chapter.

The Parc Naturel Régional de Corse (PNRC; see the boxed text later in this chapter) is an excellent source of information for walkers. If you can access the French Minitel system, there's a Minitel service: 3615 Rando.

RESPONSIBLE WALKING

Walking seems like a harmless enough activity, but can put enormous pressure on any natural environment. Anyone who wants not just to enjoy but also to preserve the Corsican countryside should read the following closely.

Rubbish

Rubbish and other waste are a problem on the GR20 and other walks in Corsica. So as not to make things worse, follow these guidelines:

- Always carry your rubbish with you and dispose of it in the bins at the refuges at the end of the day: not only larger items, but also easily forgotten litter such as orange peel, cigarette butts, silver paper and plastic wrappers.

- Empty packaging weighs very little anyway; take it away with you in a rubbish bag. Make an effort to pick up rubbish left by others.
- Never bury your rubbish: digging disturbs soil and ground cover and encourages erosion. Buried rubbish will more than likely be dug up by animals, and animals may be injured or poisoned by it. It may also take years to decompose, especially at high altitudes.
- Minimise the waste you must dispose of by taking minimal packaging and taking no more food than you will need. If you can't buy in bulk, unpack small-portion packages and combine their contents in one container before your trip. Take reusable containers or stuff sacks.
- Don't rely on bought water in plastic bottles. Disposal of these bottles is creating a major problem in many countries. Fill up at refuges and springs indicated in the text or use iodine drops or purification tablets in water from other springs.
- Sanitary napkins, tampons and condoms should also be carried to the next bin despite the inconvenience. They burn and decompose poorly.

Erosion

Hillsides and mountain slopes, especially at high altitudes, are prone to erosion.

- Stick to existing tracks and avoid short cuts that bypass a switchback. If you blaze a new trail straight down a slope, it will turn into a watercourse with the next heavy rainfall and eventually cause soil loss and deep scarring.
- If a well-used track passes through a mud patch, walk through the mud: walking around the edge will increase the size of the patch.
- Avoid removing the plant life that keeps topsoil in place.

Washing

If you are washing or washing up outside:

- Don't use detergents or toothpaste in or near watercourses, even if they are biodegradable.
- For personal washing, use biodegradable soap and a water container (or even a lightweight, portable basin) at least 50m away from the watercourse. Disperse the waste-water widely to allow the soil to filter it fully before it finally makes it back to the watercourse.
- Wash cooking utensils at least 50m from watercourses using a scourer, sand or snow instead of detergent.

Cols & Boccas

Col is the French word and *bocca* the Corsican word for what English calls a mountain pass. In this guide, they've all been called cols for the sake of consistency. But don't be fooled. Corsican usage is extremely inconsistent. Particularly in the rustic interior, passes that you see here as cols will appear on signs as boccas and, more confusing still, a simple Col du Porc may appear in Corsican as Bocca di u Porcu. The Col de la Croix (of the cross) will also be known as the Bocca a Croce and so on. You won't have unwittingly stumbled across a border from a French to a Corsican-speaking region. All Corsicans speak French even if many also speak the vernacular language. Place names, not just in Corsica but throughout the world, tend simply to be stubbornly unchanging.

Human Waste Disposal

The lack of adequate sanitation facilities on the mountain trails means that particular care must be taken with human waste.

- Contamination of water sources by human faeces can lead to the transmission of hepatitis, typhoid and intestinal parasites such as giardia, amoebas and roundworms. It can cause severe health risks not only to members of your party but also to local residents and wildlife.
- Where there is a toilet, please use it.
- Where there is none, bury your waste. Dig a small hole 15cm deep and at least 100m from any watercourse. Consider carrying a lightweight trowel for this purpose. Cover the waste with soil and a rock. Use toilet paper sparingly and bury it with the waste. In snow, dig down to the soil; otherwise your waste will be exposed when the snow melts.

Low Impact Cooking

Refuges usually have cooking facilities; camp sites and bergeries usually do not. Lighting fires is strictly forbidden in any part of the PNRC.

Use a lightweight kerosene, alcohol or Shellite (white gas) stove for cooking and avoid those powered by disposable butane gas canisters.

Wildlife Conservation

Do not feed the wildlife. Animals quickly get dependent on hand-outs. They get diseases. Animal populations get unbalanced. Don't even leave food scraps behind. Place gear out of reach and tie packs to rafters or trees.

Do not pick any flowers: most of the species are protected.

The GR20

France has more than 120,000km of marked walking paths, of which the best known are the *sentiers de grande randonnée*. These are long-distance hiking trails, numbered in the way that national vehicular roads are and known for short as GRs. The Corsican route, the GR20, was created in 1972 and has since become an institution. It links Calenzana, in the Balagne, with Conca, just north of Porto Vecchio, and every year it attracts some 10,000 brave souls from all over Europe and even beyond.

Roughly speaking, the route follows a diagonal from north-west to south-east along the island's continental divide (hence its Corsican name – Fra Li Monti – which means 'between the mountains'). It's about 200km long, and is commonly divided into 15 stages of five to eight hours' walking each.

The route cuts directly through the heart of the Parc Naturel Régional de Corse (see the boxed text later in this chapter) and, as it does so, it traverses spectacular wilderness scenery at average altitudes of between 1000m and 2000m, peaking at 2225m.

Between one end and the other, the traveller will pass through deep forests of laricio pine and beech, along granite moonscapes, windswept craters, glacial lakes, torrents, peat bogs, maquis, snow-capped peaks, plains and stretches of frozen snow called *névés*. Nature lovers will be delighted, as will those in search of tranquillity. The route crosses only three little hamlets – Haut Asco, Vizzavona and Bavella. *Refuges* (mountain shelters) and *bergeries* (shepherd's huts) provide accommodation, and there are camping facilities.

Do not be fooled by the – relatively – low altitudes. The GR20 is a genuine mountain

North–South or South–North?

From which direction should you tackle the GR20? Nearly two-thirds of walkers opt to travel north–south, as does this guide. Reasons for this are various – access to Calenzana is easier than access to the southern terminus, north–south on the map looks like downhill, while south–north looks like an unrelenting climb. There's a strong case to be made though for south–north. First, the southern section between Conca and Vizzavona is easier, giving your body a chance to get used to the effort. Second, heading in this direction means not having to walk with the sun in your eyes.

What to Bring

- good-quality walking boots
- a 1:50,000 scale map
- a pair of trainers or flip-flops/thongs
- a comfortable, well-fitting rucksack
- a first-aid kit, including plasters for blisters and an anti-inflammatory cream
- a windcheater and plastic poncho
- a head cover for sun and rain
- sunglasses
- a pair of shorts
- washing essentials (soap, towel)
- spare underwear, T-shirts, socks
- sun cream
- long trousers (for hiking in scrub vegetation)
- a survival blanket
- a fleece jacket
- a torch
- supplies for several days (freeze-dried and high-energy foods)
- isotonic powder
- a penknife
- a flask and a supply of water (a plastic pouch containing 3L of water, for example)
- a sleeping bag
- a tent (in case beds are unavailable)
- a mobile phone (optional)
- toilet paper
- ear plugs (to ensure a good night's sleep)

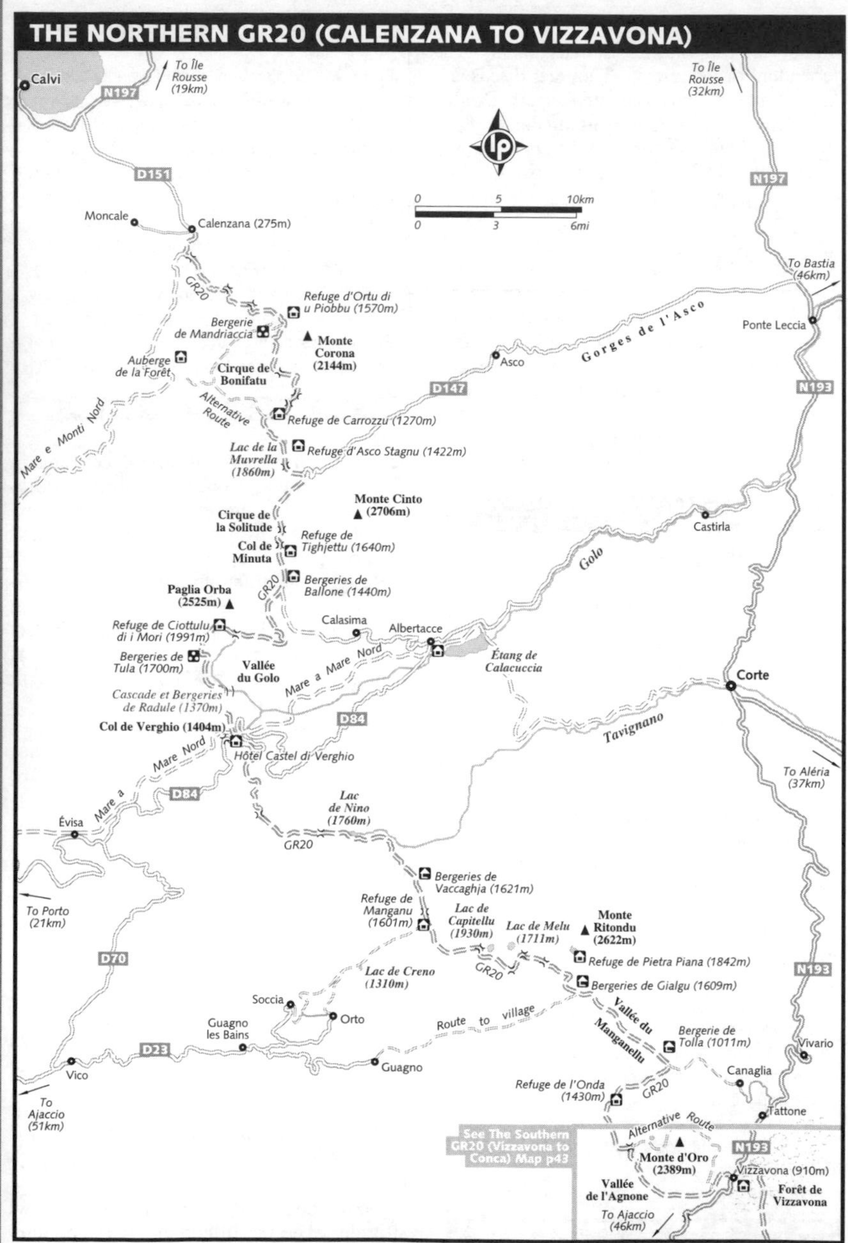
THE NORTHERN GR20 (CALENZANA TO VIZZAVONA)
Calvi
To Île Rousse (19km)
N197
To Île Rousse (32km)
D151
N197
0 5 10km
0 3 6mi
Moncale
Calenzana (275m)
To Bastia (46km)
GR20
Refuge d'Ortu di u Piobbu (1570m)
Bergerie de Mandriaccia
Monte Corona (2144m)
Ponte Leccia
Gorges de l'Asco
Auberge de la Forêt
Cirque de Bonifatu
Asco
D147
N193
Alternative Route
Mare e Monti Nord
Refuge de Carrozzu (1270m)
Lac de la Muvrella (1860m)
Refuge d'Asco Stagnu (1422m)
Monte Cinto (2706m)
Cirque de la Solitude
Castirla
Refuge de Tighjettu (1640m)
Col de Minuta
Golo
Bergeries de Ballone (1440m)
Paglia Orba (2525m)
GR20
Calasima
Refuge de Ciottulu di i Mori (1991m)
Albertacce
Bergeries de Tula (1700m)
Vallée du Golo
Mare a Mare Nord
Étang de Calacuccia
Corte
Cascade et Bergeries de Radule (1370m)
D84
Col de Verghio (1404m)
Tavignano
Hôtel Castel di Verghio
Mare a Mare Nord
To Aléria (37km)
D84
Lac de Nino (1760m)
Évisa
GR20
Bergeries de Vaccaghja (1621m)
To Porto (21km)
Refuge de Manganu (1601m)
Lac de Capitellu (1930m)
Lac de Melu (1711m)
Monte Ritondu (2622m)
D70
Refuge de Pietra Piana (1842m)
GR20
N193
Lac de Creno (1310m)
Bergeries de Gialgu (1609m)
Soccia
Orto
Route to village
Vallée du Manganellu
Guagno les Bains
Bergerie de Tolla (1011m)
Vivario
D23
Vico
Guagno
Canaglia
Refuge de l'Onda (1430m)
GR20
To Ajaccio (51km)
Tattone
Alternative Route
See The Southern GR20 (Vizzavona to Conca) Map p43
N193
Monte d'Oro (2389m)
Vizzavona (910m)
Vallée de l'Agnone
Forêt de Vizzavona
To Ajaccio (46km)

THE SOUTHERN GR20 (VIZZAVONA TO CONCA)

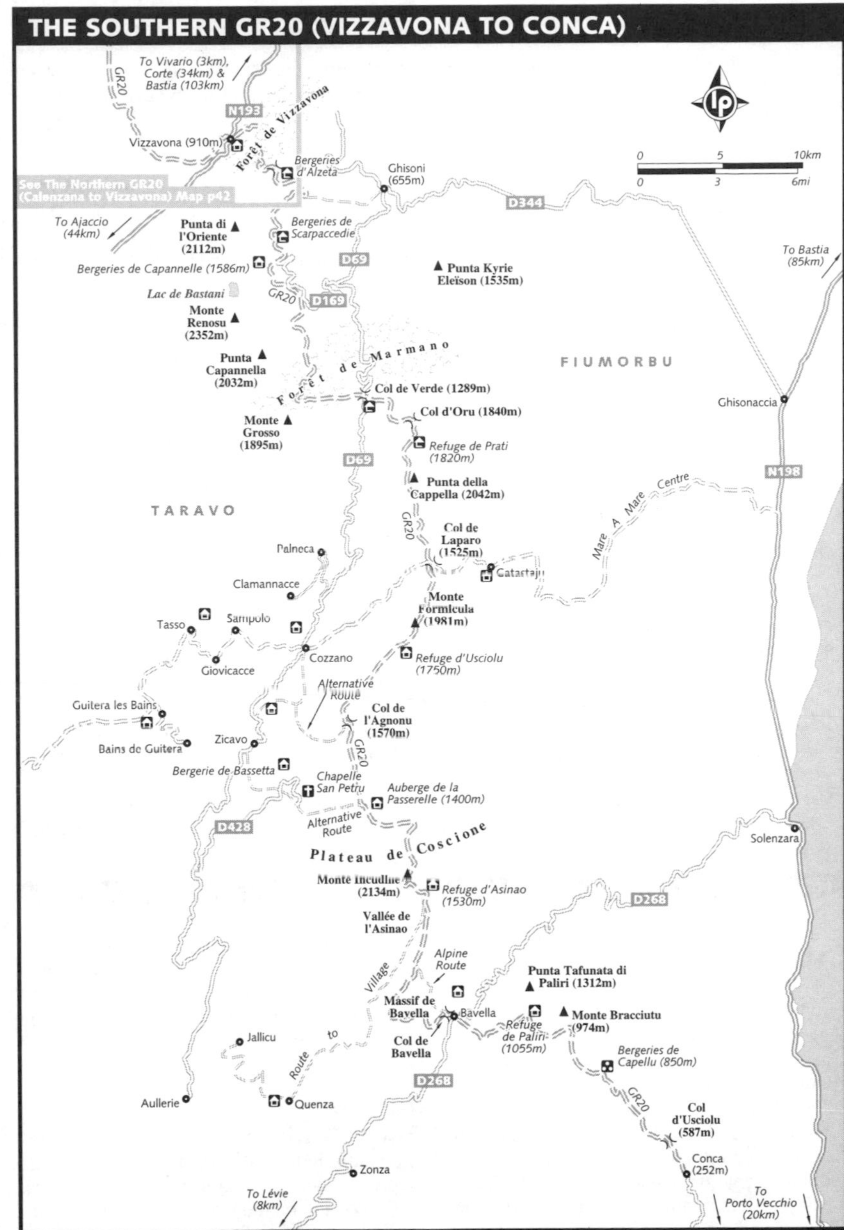
To Vivario (3km), Corte (34km) & Bastia (103km)
N193
Forêt de Vizzavona
Vizzavona (910m)
Bergeries d'Alzeta
Ghisoni (655m)
See The Northern GR20 (Calenzana to Vizzavona) Map p42
D344
To Ajaccio (44km)
Punta di l'Oriente (2112m)
Bergeries de Scarpaccedie
Bergeries de Capannelle (1586m)
D69
Punta Kyrie Eleïson (1535m)
To Bastia (85km)
Lac de Bastani
GR20
D169
Monte Renosu (2352m)
Punta Capannella (2032m)
Forêt de Marmano
FIUMORBU
Col de Verde (1289m)
Ghisonaccia
Col d'Oru (1840m)
Monte Grosso (1895m)
Refuge de Prati (1820m)
D69
N198
Punta della Cappella (2042m)
Mare A Mare Centre
TARAVO
Col de Laparo (1525m)
Palneca
Catastaju
Clamannacce
Monte Formicula (1981m)
Tasso
Sampolo
Cozzano
Refuge d'Usciolu (1750m)
Giovicacce
Alternative Route
Guitera les Bains
Col de l'Agnonu (1570m)
Zicavo
Bains de Guitera
Bergerie de Bassetta
Chapelle San Petru
Auberge de la Passerelle (1400m)
D428
Alternative Route
Plateau de Coscione
Solenzara
Monte Incudine (2134m)
Refuge d'Asinao (1530m)
D268
Vallée de l'Asinao
Alpine Route
Punta Tafunata di Paliri (1312m)
Route to Village
Massif de Bavella
Bavella
Monte Bracciutu (974m)
Refuge de Paliri (1055m)
Jallicu
Col de Bavella
Bergeries de Capellu (850m)
D268
Aullerie
Quenza
Col d'Usciolu (587m)
Conca (252m)
Zonza
To Lévie (8km)
To Porto Vecchio (20km)
0 5 10km
0 3 6mi

The GR20 at a Glance

This summary table includes the start and finish points of each stage with their altitudes, the average walking time for each stage, alternative routes, opportunities to do a half-stage or stop off in a village, and places to eat.

Stage 1: Calenzana (275m) to Refuge d'Ortu di u Piobbu (1570m); seven hours.

Stage 2: Refuge d'Ortu di u Piobbu (1570m) to Refuge de Carrozzu (1270m); 6½ hours. Refreshments at Refuge de Carrozzu. Alternative route via the Auberge de la Forêt (food and accommodation) in Bonifatu.

Stage 3: Refuge de Carrozzu (1270m) to Refuge d'Asco Stagnu (Haut Asco) and Le Chalet Haut Asco (1422m); six hours. Food at Le Chalet Haut Asco.

Stage 4: Refuge d'Asco Stagnu (1422m) to Refuge de Tighjettu or Bergeries de Ballone (1440m); seven hours. Food at Bergeries de Ballone.

Stage 5: Bergeries de Ballone (1440m) to Castel di Verghio (1404m); seven hours. Possible half-stage as far as Refuge de Ciottulu di i Mori (accommodation only). Optional stopoff in the villages of Calasima and Albertacce at the end of the stage. Food at Castel di Verghio.

Stage 6: Castel di Verghio (1404m) to Refuge de Manganu (1601m); 5½ hours. Optional stopoff in the villages of Soccia and Orto at the end of the stage. Food at Bergeries de Vaccaghja.

Stage 7: Refuge de Manganu (1601m) to Refuge de Pietra Piana (1842m); six hours.

Stage 8: Refuge de Pietra Piana (1842m) to Refuge de l'Onda (1430m); five hours. Optional stopoff in the villages of Canaglia and Tattone. Food at the Bergeries de Gialgu and at the Refuge de l'Onda.

Stage 9: Refuge de l'Onda (1430m) to Vizzavona (910m); 5½ hours. Alternative route via Monte d'Oro, to the north. Food in Vizzavona.

Stage 10: Vizzavona (910m) to Bergeries de Capannelle (1586m); 5½ hours. Optional stopoff in the village of Ghisoni. Food at the Bergeries de Capannelle.

Stage 11: Bergeries de Capannelle (1586m) to Col de Verde (1289m); five hours. Food at Col de Verde.

Stage 12: Col de Verde (1289m) to Refuge d'Usciolu (1750m); 7½ hours. Optional stopoff in the village of Cozzano. Refreshments at Refuge d'Usciolu.

Stage 13: Refuge d'Usciolu (1750m) to Refuge d'Asinao (1530m); eight hours. Optional stopoff in the village of Zicavo. Possible half-stage as far as Refuge de la Bergerie de Bassetta (accommodation and food). Refreshments at the Refuge d'Asinao.

Stage 14: Refuge d'Asinao (1530m) via the alpine route to Refuge de Paliri (1055m); 6¼ hours. Optional stopoff in the village of Quenza. Possible half-stage as far as Bavella (accommodation and food).

Stage 15: Refuge de Paliri (1055m) to Conca (252m); five hours.

route that requires real stamina and commitment; it is not a challenge to be undertaken lightly. The changes in altitude are unrelenting. In the course of the entire walk, the changes in altitude (both up and down) add up to about 10,000m. There are single-stage climbs – some of them steep – of as much as 800m. In addition, the path is rocky, weather conditions can be difficult and you have to carry enough equipment and supplies to be self-sufficient for a number of days. Top-notch physical condition, strong motivation and some advance training are a must.

Do not overestimate your capabilities, and do not be above using the resources close to the route, for example, villages where you can stop off and recuperate or restock, even after mid-stages; these resources are detailed in the text.

INFORMATION

Times & Distances

The times indicated in the text for each stage represent actual walking time only (that is, they do not include resting time) and are valid for walkers of average speed. Make allowance for the weight of your rucksack (average 15kg), your physical condition, your training, your interests (natural history, photography and so on) and how long you anticipate taking for rest. This means that a stage estimated here to take six hours could take somewhat less time; it could also easily take two to three hours longer.

The distances in kilometres are only a rough measure. A kilometre on level city pavement is one thing; a kilometre on rocky mountain terrain is something else. Time estimates in these pages are based on the assumption that an average walker will climb 250–300m in an hour.

Highlights

The GR20 will take grit and hard work, but the rewards are substantial as well. These are just a few entirely subjective highlights:

- The glorious Cirque de la Solitude (Stage 4)
- The pools in the Vallée du Golo (Stage 5)
- Magnificent glacial Lac de Nino (Stage 6)
- Sunrise over the Bergeries de Capannelle (Stage 10)
- The route along the ridge between Refuge de Prati and Refuge d'Usciolu (Stage 12)
- The *pozzines* on the high Plateau de Coscione (Stage 13)
- A wild-boar casserole washed down with Corsican wine in any of two dozen country eating places in villages along the route
- The alpine route crossing over the Aiguilles de Bavella (Stage 14)
- The cosy surroundings of the Refuge de Paliri (Stage 15)
- Scents of the maquis in the last stage, from Refuge de Paliri to Conca

When to Go

The best time of year to do the GR20 is May to October. Some parts of the route are partially covered in snow until June. July and August are the most popular months and accordingly the most crowded. The ideal months are June and September, just before and after the high season.

For details about weather forecasts, see the boxed text under Planning in the Facts for the Visitor chapter.

Accommodation & Supplies

A refuge stands at the end of each of the 15 stages of the GR20, and very nearly all of the refuges are managed by the PNRC. Though they are open year round, they tend to be staffed only between May or June and September or October.

Each refuge has grounds for campers alongside it. In 2000 a night in a refuge cost 55FF; campers paid 20FF, collected by the warden, or caretaker. The dormitory itself is equipped with fairly primitive bedding. An adjacent communal room is stocked with useful equipment such as a table, benches, gas heaters, cooking utensils and a fire or stove in winter. As a rule, 20FF campers do not get to share in these amenities. Outside there's a water point, generally with toilets (though frequently too few of them) and showers (not always hot).

Refuges work on a first-come, first-served basis. Bearing in mind that the capacity is limited (between 20 and 50 places), you are wise to set out early in the day if you seek the (relative) luxury of a refuge, and you should take a tent with you, just in case. Bear in mind also that the condition of the refuges depends on the individual wardens. Some, consequently, are impeccable. Others are not.

Food is another potential sore point. There will be no feasting in these establishments, though some do offer light meals of *charcuterie*, cheese, eggs and drinks. Food services have gradually been improving, and a slight relaxation of PNRC policy now allows the wardens to engage in a little sideline grocery business. Before you set out, the PNRC may be able to help you identify those refuges where food services will be a bit less barebones minimal. There are a few private guesthouses and bergeries along the route, or close to it, where you can get a better quality night's sleep than in a refuge and a properly cooked meal. Within reach in the valleys are actual villages – two to four hours' walk off the GR20 along marked paths.

GR20 ELEVATION CHART – STAGES 1 TO 7

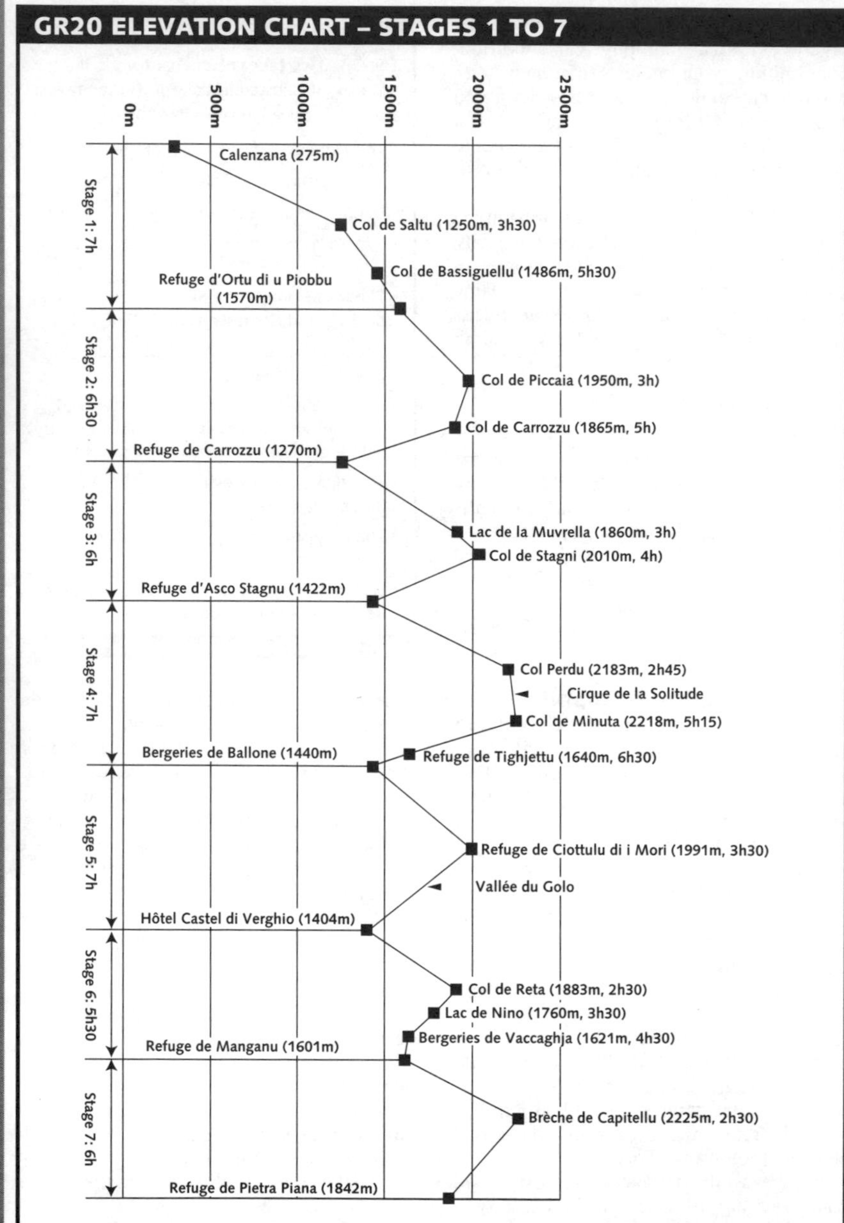
0m
500m
1000m
1500m
2000m
2500m
Stage 1: 7h
Calenzana (275m)
Col de Saltu (1250m, 3h30)
Col de Bassiguellu (1486m, 5h30)
Refuge d'Ortu di u Piobbu (1570m)
Stage 2: 6h30
Col de Piccaia (1950m, 3h)
Col de Carrozzu (1865m, 5h)
Refuge de Carrozzu (1270m)
Stage 3: 6h
Lac de la Muvrella (1860m, 3h)
Col de Stagni (2010m, 4h)
Refuge d'Asco Stagnu (1422m)
Stage 4: 7h
Col Perdu (2183m, 2h45)
Cirque de la Solitude
Col de Minuta (2218m, 5h15)
Refuge de Tighjettu (1640m, 6h30)
Bergeries de Ballone (1440m)
Stage 5: 7h
Refuge de Ciottulu di i Mori (1991m, 3h30)
Vallée du Golo
Hôtel Castel di Verghio (1404m)
Stage 6: 5h30
Col de Reta (1883m, 2h30)
Lac de Nino (1760m, 3h30)
Bergeries de Vaccaghja (1621m, 4h30)
Refuge de Manganu (1601m)
Stage 7: 6h
Brèche de Capitellu (2225m, 2h30)
Refuge de Pietra Piana (1842m)

GR20 ELEVATION CHART – STAGES 8 TO 15

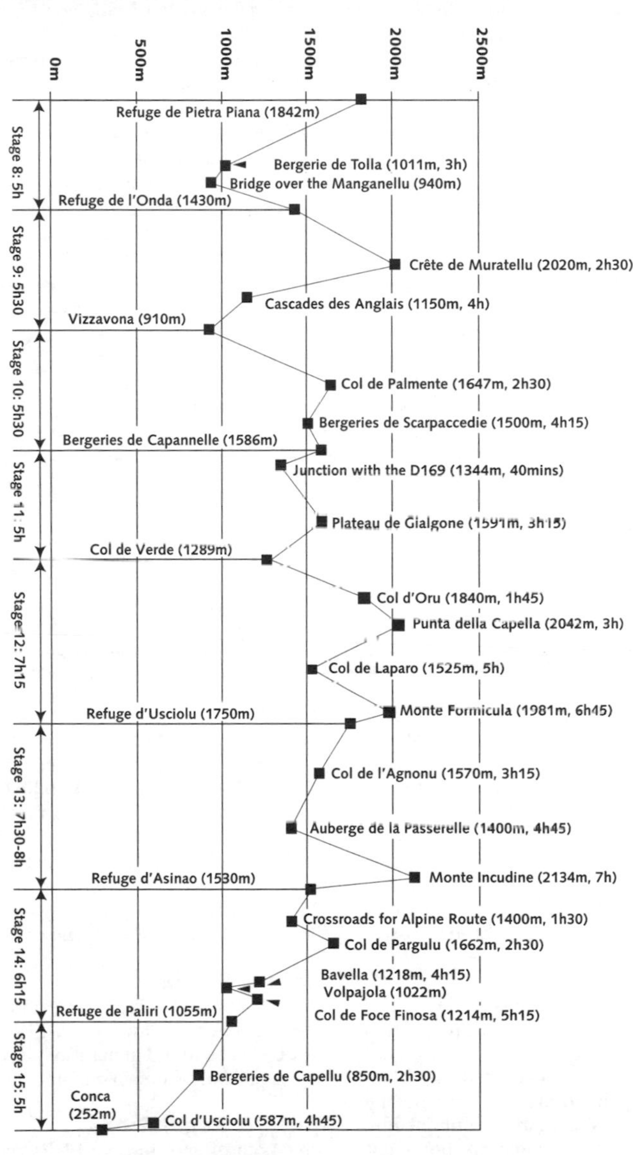

0m
500m
1000m
1500m
2000m
2500m
Stage 8: 5h
Refuge de Pietra Piana (1842m)
Bergerie de Tolla (1011m, 3h)
Bridge over the Manganellu (940m)
Refuge de l'Onda (1430m)
Stage 9: 5h30
Crête de Muratellu (2020m, 2h30)
Cascades des Anglais (1150m, 4h)
Vizzavona (910m)
Stage 10: 5h30
Col de Palmente (1647m, 2h30)
Bergeries de Scarpaccedie (1500m, 4h15)
Bergeries de Capannelle (1586m)
Stage 11: 5h
Junction with the D169 (1344m, 40mins)
Plateau de Gialgone (1591m, 3h15)
Col de Verde (1289m)
Stage 12: 7h15
Col d'Oru (1840m, 1h45)
Punta della Capella (2042m, 3h)
Col de Laparo (1525m, 5h)
Monte Formicula (1981m, 6h45)
Refuge d'Usciolu (1750m)
Stage 13: 7h30-8h
Col de l'Agnonu (1570m, 3h15)
Auberge de la Passerelle (1400m, 4h45)
Monte Incudine (2134m, 7h)
Refuge d'Asinao (1530m)
Stage 14: 6h15
Crossroads for Alpine Route (1400m, 1h30)
Col de Pargulu (1662m, 2h30)
Bavella (1218m, 4h15)
Volpajola (1022m)
Col de Foce Finosa (1214m, 5h15)
Refuge de Paliri (1055m)
Stage 15: 5h
Bergeries de Capellu (850m, 2h30)
Conca
(252m)
Col d'Usciolu (587m, 4h45)

Making the Most of the GR20

Assuming you actually are walking the GR20 (and not reading this on a lazy beach) you'll encounter many sorts of walkers on the trail, from the super-organised (they'll have calculated their rations of freeze-dried food, for example, to the nearest gram), to the spontaneous who've undertaken the trek virtually on a whim. Figures show that, of the 10,000-odd people who take up the challenge every year, more than half fail to finish.

Needless to say, the experience of the GR20 can be extremely exhilarating, with an enormous sense of accomplishment if you finish it, or even merely make a stalwart effort. The following tip is offered in the hope that it might make some wanderers' experience just that little bit richer.

Though the main text on the GR20 details villages that you can go off to along the route, it is not a good idea to make these detours at every opportunity. That breaks the rhythm too much. On the other hand, you should from time to time take a day to escape the rigours of the unrelenting forward march, the monotony of freeze-dried food and the overcrowded refuges, and simply recharge your batteries. The traditional villages situated in the valleys below the GR20 are veritable oases of camaraderie. They have comfortable bed-and-breakfast accommodation, often family-run, out of whose kitchens come local delicacies to revive even the weariest of walkers.

Your best bet is probably to go down once between Calenzana and Vizzavona (first week, northern GR20) and a second time between Vizzavona and Conca (southern GR20). When preparing your trip, think about including these detours in your itinerary and make up your own GR by using these little side paths. It will also mean that your rucksack is lighter, as you can stock up in the villages.

Even a couple of brief forays into Corsica's mountain valleys will give you a taste of a traditional way of life that those who restrict their stay to the seaside will be at pains to discover. In any event, don't blindly follow those who go straight to Calenzana from the airport, swallow up the route and then, as soon as they arrive in Conca, take the plane home on the same day. They'll have done the GR20 but they'll have missed much of Corsica.

DOMINIQUE CORDONNIER

The villages all have comfortable bed-and-breakfast facilities and well-stocked shops, and some of them are served by public transport, which makes them good places to join or leave the GR20.

Though you can generally count on withdrawing cash against a credit card (with some form of identification) at post offices in Corsica, there are not many along the route, so be sure to start out with adequate cash on you.

Maps & Signs

Signs marking the GR20 consist of two horizontal lines, one red and one white, painted onto tree trunks and rocks. Cairns (small mounds of stones) are also used in certain places where painted signs would not be visible. The path is regularly maintained by the park wardens and navigation should not be a problem, though the painted sign markings could, at some points along the way, come at somewhat closer intervals.

A detailed map is highly recommended. Best are Didier Richard's 1:50,000 *(Corse du Sud and Corse du Nord)*, and the 1:25,000 IGN products (Top 25, blue series).

The paths linking the GR20 to the villages below are marked with yellow painted lines. On some of the less frequently used paths, the markings can be inadequate or confusing.

Flora & Fauna

A description of the main flora and fauna of Corsica, much of which you will see on the GR20, can be found under Flora & Fauna in the Facts about Corsica chapter.

Rules & Regulations

Take note of and observe PNRC rules and regulations. It can't be repeated often enough that the lighting of fires is strictly forbidden, as is camping outside the designated areas near the refuges. There are notices to remind you of these points at various strategic intervals along the route. See also the Responsible Walking section earlier in this chapter.

STAGE 1

Calenzana (275m) to Refuge d'Ortu di u Piobbu (1570m)

Distance: 10km
Standard: Difficult; very little shade
Average Duration: Seven hours
Highest Point: 1570m

Summary: You are confronted with the rigorous conditions of the GR20 from the outset. This stage is one long ascent across a series of ridge lines with hardly any downhill breaks at all. There's no assured source of water either, so bring at least the recommended 2L per person. The other vital necessity is sunscreen: in summer the sun is unrelenting and there are many long stretches with not much shade.

The walk starts by winding up to the top of the village, then the path starts to climb steadily through ferns, with good views back to Calenzana and Moncale, another hillside village. Farther up, Calvi and the sea come into view. The path climbs into pine forests. At the well-signposted Carrefour de Sentiers (550m), less than an hour from Calenzana, the Mare e Monti Nord route (see the Mare e Monti & Mare a Mare section later in this chapter) splits from the GR20. Soon after, the trail reaches the rocky Col de Ravalente at 616m.

At the pass, there is a view of a wide terraced valley. The path then skirts the valley and fords a few small streams; these usually dry up towards the end of the season. There is then a relatively gentle climb to 820m, the easy stretch, before the trail begins to climb steeply and zigzags uphill to another pass, the **Col de Saltu** (1250m). About 3½ hours from the Calenzana starting point, this may appear the perfect spot to stop for a picnic. Beyond the ridge, on the northeastern face of Capu Ghiovu, the trail starts to climb even more steeply; at times you'll have to clamber over rocks – good practice for the rock climbs you'll encounter a few days farther along. About halfway along this stretch there's a stream that is sometimes a good source of drinking water but it tends to dry up as the summer peaks.

The climb becomes less steep before reaching its highest point, about 5½ hours into the walk. The grassy expanse at the **Col de Bassiguellu** (1486m) is dotted with shady pine trees and makes another good place for a rest stop. From here the trail crosses a rather rocky and unsheltered stretch but stays fairly level. The refuge comes into view across a valley. From this point it will look as if the final bit will push you to the limit, but it's actually not as bad as it appears. A final short climb brings the day to an end.

This first day's walk has been almost continuously uphill – with each successive ridge line only marking the start of the climb to the next ridge. Walkers just starting the GR20 may wonder what they've got themselves into, and the lack of water resources, particularly later in the season, can make it even harder.

Walkers who still feel strong may want to climb nearby **Monte Corona** (2144m); a trail, marked by cairns and flashes of paint, goes up the slope directly behind the refuge to the **Col de Tartagine** (1852m). From there head south and climb the rocky ridge line until you catch sight of the rounded summit, which is covered in loose stones and marked by a cairn. A spectacular view stretches from the refuge below to the northern coast. Allow 2½ to three hours to get to the summit and back.

Places to Stay

Refuge d'Ortu di u Piobbu (1570m) has 30 beds and plenty of camping space both on the slopes below the building and among the trees behind it. There's just one rather primitive toilet and shower but there is an alternative water source about 200m beyond the refuge on the GR20 itself.

Beds in the refuge cost 50FF; camping costs 20FF per person.

STAGE 2

Refuge d'Ortu di u Piobbu (1570m) to Refuge de Carrozzu (1270m)

Distance: 8km
Standard: Difficult
Average Duration: 6½ hours
Highest Point: 2020m

Note: There are two possible routes: the more traditional route cuts right across a range of mountains; the other avoids the mountains by skirting them to the west, via Bonifatu.

Summary: A varied day's walk starts with a short ascent and descent followed by a long and arduous climb to an altitude of 2020m. There's then a rocky and often spectacular traverse before a long and seemingly endless descent to the refuge. There is only one relatively reliable water source, about two hours into the walk. Supplies may be available at the refuge.

The day's walk starts with a gentle ascent through a pine forest to a ridge line (1630m) with a very disheartening view. In front of you is a sharp drop to the valley bottom and then a long, steep ascent to a much higher ridge line on the other side.

The trail quickly descends to the valley floor, passing the ruined **Bergerie de Mandriaccia** (1500m) and the Mandriaccia stream, then starts the long climb up the other side. About halfway up the unrelenting ascent there's a spring that's usually a reliable source of good drinking water; it may be the only such source you'll come across all day.

Eventually, about three hours from the start, you'll get to the **Col de Piccaia** (1950m), a climb of 500m from the valley bottom. Be warned there's very little shade along this stretch, which makes the climb particularly tough in the heat of the day. At the top there's a dramatic change in scenery. Over the other side of the crest stretches out a landscape of precipices and bare rock punctuated by thrusting rocky spires – a marked contrast to what was already a quite steep and rocky slope on the northern side, and one of many occasions when you'll notice the ridges along the GR20 herald abrupt changes in topography.

The trail does not cross the ridge line immediately but for a time cleaves to its northern side at a height of around 2020m, before crossing to the other side and gently descending to the **Col d'Avartoli** (1898m). The trail then traverses the southern and western faces of the next ridge line, dropping steeply, then climbing again sharply to the next pass. Now it follows the eastern side of a ridge, then crosses to the western side at the **Col de Carrozzu** (1865m) five hours into the walk.

From here the route commences the long, somewhat tedious descent to the refuge. At first the trail is rather loose and slippery, but at the start of the descent it's worth looking back to see where you've been in the past couple of hours. The views are magnificent. Not until well down this descent do trees offer some welcome shade. A short distance before the Refuge de Carrozzu the trail crosses a stream.

There is an alternative low-level route for this stage that skirts the mountain range that the main route crosses. It leads off to the west from the Refuge d'Ortu di u Piobbu. Two kilometres on, it meets a forest road that it then follows for about 5km down the valley to the village of **Bonifatu** (540m), with its Auberge de la Forêt (see the section on Bonifatu in the Calvi & the Balagne chapter). From Bonifatu the route goes back up the road for 1.5km before climbing to rejoin the GR20 at the Refuge de Carrozzu.

Places to Stay & Eat

Refuge de Carrozzu (1270m) is in a magnificent setting. It is hedged in by sheer rock faces on three sides but with an open terrace looking down the valley to the west. It sleeps 26 and there are plenty of camping spots in the surrounding woods. The standard 55/20FF charges for dormitory/camping apply.

This refuge offers soup, sausage, cheese, cake, drinks (nonalcoholic and alcoholic alike) and other foods and supplies.

The shower isn't much but a steep path down from the refuge brings you to a stream that at a couple of points widens out enough to allow you to swim a few strokes.

STAGE 3

Refuge de Carrozzu (1270m) to Haut Asco (1422m)

Distance: 6km
Standard: Average
Average Duration: Six hours
Highest Point: 2010m

Summary: This stage is slightly easier than the first two, consisting of a short ascent and descent, the bridge over the River Spasimata and a long and often spectacular rocky ascent to Lac de la Muvrella. From there it's only a short climb to a final ridge, the Col de Stagni (2010m) before the long descent to the ski resort of Haut Asco. Allow an extra hour to climb the Muvrella peak. Once you've left the Spasimata there is little water; but the hotel at Haut Asco has a restaurant and a bar and food supplies are plentiful.

The day starts with a short, rocky zigzag up through the forest to a ridge line, then a slightly longer drop to the River Spasimata at 1220m. You'll cross it on a shaky suspension bridge that's not for the faint-hearted. The trail then edges along above the river, crossing long sloping slabs of rock. At some points plastic-coated cables offer reassuring hand holds. These rocky stretches can be dangerously slippery, however, if it rains.

Leaving the river and its tempting rock pools, the trail next starts a long, rocky ascent of three to 3½ hours to **Lac de la Muvrella** (1860m). As you approach the lake, be sure to look back. You'll still be able to make Calvi out on the northern coast. The lake water, unfortunately, is not safe to drink.

Beyond the lake it's only a short scramble to the next knife-edge ridge, but you'll want to hold on with your hands wherever you can. After a short drop on the other side, the trail soon starts to climb again, skirting around the side of Muvrella peak and making its way to the **Col de Stagni** (2010m). Just before the pass there's a sign indicating that the walk down to the River Spasimata, now behind you, takes 2½ hours. Coming the other way, from the River Spasimata, uphill, will have taken around four hours.

From the pass, the route used to continue to Refuge d'Altore, but the refuge was ravaged by fire in the mid-1980s. Now at the pass the route begins a 600m descent to Haut Asco, already visible in the distance. If you are walking in one of the warm months, Haut Asco will look like any ski resort off season – bare, dusty and forlorn – but it's a haven for walkers after the Spartan conditions of the last couple of days.

A one-hour detour from the Col de Stagni, if you still have the energy, will take you to the summit of **Muvrella peak** (2148m). Alternatively, you can climb to the summit from Lac de la Muvrella and then rejoin the GR20 at the Col de Stagni. The advantage of the first detour option is that you can leave your rucksack at the pass, climb without all the load and then pick it up again on your way back. Minus the detour, the day will have been distinctly less taxing than the previous two.

Haut Asco

Refuge d'Asco Stagnu (1422m) has 30 beds in rooms for two, four or six persons (55FF). It also has hot showers, a kitchen and dining area and a sun terrace. There's camping space aplenty on the grassy ski slopes (20FF per person).

Ski lodge ***Le Chalet Haut Asco*** *(☎ 04 95 47 81 08)* is another lodging option. A double with shower and toilet en suite costs from 250FF in May and June and 300FF from July to September. Half-board runs from 200FF to 240FF depending on the season. The hotel has a popular bar and a huge outdoor terrace. In the evening, its restaurant offers the spectacle of hoards of ravenous walkers shovelling down tremendous quantities of simple food, washed down with equivalent quantities of local wine. The hotel and the restaurant both accept credit cards. There's a public telephone in the ski-lodge bar and a phone box across from the refuge, at the foot of the ski lift. It also operates a ***gîte d'étape*** (mountain lodge) with beds for 40FF per person or 160FF at half-board. Showers in the gîte cost extra.

A ***shop*** sells such cross-country walking essentials and luxuries as freeze-dried food, sausage, cheese, bread, energy bars, chocolate, cereals and fresh fruit.

Since Haut Asco is accessible along the D147, which meets the N197 2km north of Ponte Leccia, it's a good spot at which to join or leave the GR20 if you're not planning to do the hike in its entirety.

STAGE 4

Refuge d'Asco Stagnu (1422m) to Bergeries de Ballone (1440m)

Distance: 8km
Standard: Difficult; technical climbs in the Cirque de la Solitude; little shade
Average Duration: Seven hours
Highest Point: 2218m

Summary: The fact that the altitudes at the beginning and the end of this stage are practically identical could lead you to think it an easy section – it is not. Generally held to be the most spectacular of the GR20's 15 separate segments, it starts with a long climb from Haut Asco ski resort followed by the crossing of the Cirque de la Solitude. After this exhilarating rock climb there's a long descent to the Refuge de Tighjettu and the Bergeries de Ballone. There is water at the otherwise disused Refuge d'Altore, and from there to the bergerie the trail follows a mountain stream. The bergerie has a cafe, bar and food supplies.

From Haut Asco the trail starts off on the left (southern) side of the ski run, and it's easy to lose the trail temporarily as it abandons the ski run for the trees. This is nothing to worry about: you will easily find the official route again when it starts to climb above the valley and the ski slopes to cross the glacial moraines. The views over the valley and Haut Asco are stunning.

Allow about two hours to reach the site of the old **Refuge d'Altore** at 2000m. From the small lake at the site, a steep 45-minute climb takes you to the **Col Perdu** (Lost Pass; Bocca Tumasginesca), at 2183m. From the pass the Cirque de la Solitude falls dramatically away beneath your feet. For most walkers this is the highlight of the entire GR20, and one's first reaction is probably sheer amazement that it's possible to descend the steep side of the hanging valley and climb up again on the other side. A close inspection of the equally sheer-looking walls on the other side of the valley, however, will reveal tiny figures scaling the rock face. In two or three hours you will be there yourself.

The descent and ascent of the **Cirque de la Solitude** (a steep-sided basin formed by the erosive action of ice) is more of a rock climb than a walk. However, there are chains bolted into the rock face to make the climb easier. In any event, since other walkers will often be almost vertically beneath you, you must take great care not to dislodge rocks or stones. Typically it takes about 2½ hours to cross the cirque but since much of the route is strictly single file, a single cautious or hesitant walker can slow the entire column down.

From the Col Perdu it's 200m down to the scree-covered valley floor, where many walkers pause for lunch. On the other side of the valley, the route crosses rock slabs – there are cables to help you – and then makes a series of steep, rocky ascents before emerging into an equally steep gully carpeted with loose rocks and stones. Towards the top, the climb becomes a little gentler before emerging 240m above the valley floor at the **Col de Minuta** (2218m), the second highest point on the GR20.

Past the ridge the scenery becomes dramatically wider and more open. The trail makes a long and at times steep descent down the **Ravin de Stranciacone**. Initially, the surface may be somewhat crumbly and hence slippery but it soon becomes rockier before reaching the Refuge de Tighjettu about 1¼ hours beyond the Col de Minuta.

Places to Stay & Eat

Refuge de Tighjettu (1640m) charges the standard 55FF for one of its 48 beds and 20FF for camping. As space near the refuge is scarce, however, many campers prefer to pitch their tents lower down, by the river.

It's only another half-hour walk down the valley to the ***Bergeries de Ballone*** (1440m), open June to October. The trail descends less steeply as it approaches the old farm, the trees and vegetation become more dense and there is a pretty little river, which sparkles as it snakes down the valley. There are lots of good spots to camp or bivouac around the bergerie and there's no charge. Beds in a large tent cost 10FF.

The bergerie has a more than satisfactory restaurant and bar. A three-course Corsican meal is available for about 80FF, and you can get beer and wine. Breakfast is served in the

Parc Naturel Régional de Corse

The PNRC was created in 1972 and today covers more than one-third of the island, including many of the most beautiful areas. These include the Golfe de Porto, the Réserve Naturelle de Scandola (a UNESCO World Heritage Site) and the highest peaks on the island, including the Aiguilles de Bavella. The PNRC's mission is twofold: protection of the environment and development.

With respect to protection, the PNRC seeks to preserve all the island's endangered animal and plant species, such as the native wild sheep (the mouflon) and the Corsican stag. It is also active in protecting such sensitive and imperilled attractions as the *pozzines* and the highland lakes (see the boxed text later in this chapter).

Its aim in the areas of development is to give a boost to Corsica's traditional ways of life. Walkers will notice how superbly maintained the facades of the bergeries are: In order to help keep high-altitude livestock farming alive, the PNRC undertook to restore the mountain bergeries some 20 years ago. Many mills and hundreds of *casgili* (cheese cellars) have also been restored.

Since, moreover, to the PNRC's way of thinking, the best way to develop the central areas of the island is by way of tourism, more than 1500km of hiking and walking paths have been created. There are about 100 people responsible for maintaining the paths, clearing the scrub and providing information to the public.

The Maison d'Information Randonnée du PNRC (PNRC Walking Information Office; ☎ 04 95 51 79 10, fax 04 95 21 88 17), 2 rue Sergent Casalonga, Ajaccio, publishes a wealth of information about the park in English and Spanish, as well as in French, along with a number of walking guides – those, mostly in French. It also provides sensible advice on the opportunities for walking, hiking and camping. It opens 8.30 am to noon and 2 to 6 pm (to 5 pm on Friday) Monday to Friday. The PNRC Web site is at www.parc-naturel-corse.com. Yet more – and different– information is to be found at the site for all French regional parks at www.parcs-naturels-regionaux.tm.fr/lesparcs/corseh.html

In summer (June to September) walk-in help is provided not just at the Ajaccio office but at half a dozen remote information offices as well:

Maison de Calvi
(☎ 04 95 65 16 67) Office de Tourisme, 20260 Calvi

Maison de Corte
(☎ 04 95 46 27 44) La Citadelle, 20250 Corte

Maison d'Évisa
(☎ 04 95 26 23 62) Peasolu d'Aïtone, 20126 Évisa

Maison de Moltifao
(☎ 04 95 47 85 03) Village des Tortues, 20218 Moltifao

Maison de Porto
(☎ 04 95 26 15 14) La Marine, 20150 Porto

Maison de Porto-Vecchio
(☎ 04 95 70 50 58) Rue du Colonel-Quenza, 20137 Porto-Vecchio

morning, and food and other supplies are for sale. After the exhilarating crossing of the Cirque de la Solitude, a cold beer on the bergerie's terrace, overlooking the pretty forested valley with the sun sinking behind the mountain ridge, may be just what's needed to make the day perfect.

STAGE 5

Bergeries de Ballone (1440m) to Castel di Verghio (1404m)

Distance: 13km
Standard: Average; partially shady route
Average Duration: Seven hours
Highest Point: 2000m

Note: Optional half-stage if you stop at the Refuge de Ciottulu di i Mori; access to the villages of Calasima and Albertacce

Summary: A varied walk which ascends through forest before the path becomes steep and rocky as it approaches a pass below Paglia Orba. The walk then circles the southern side of Paglia Orba before dropping down to follow an enticing river that descends into the forested Vallée du Golo and on to the ski resort of Castel di Verghio. There are plentiful supplies of water, because much of the walk follows the course of streams. Hôtel Castel di Verghio has a bar and restaurant and sells food supplies.

The day begins with a gently undulating ascent through pine forests, with streams tumbling down the hills to the west to join the River Viro at the valley floor. Across the valley to the east you can see the road up from **Albertacce** to **Calasima**, the highest village on the island at 1100m. The trail finally turns west around the eastern slope of Paglia Orba and then emerges from the forest for the steep and rocky three-hour slog up to the Col de Fogghiale (1962m).

On the other side of that pass a wide valley opens out to the south but the route continues to the west, crossing the slopes of Paglia Orba and climbing slightly to reach the Refuge de Ciottulu di i Mori (see Places to Stay & Eat later in this section).

Paglia Orba (2525m), the third highest peak in Corsica rises directly behind the refuge. If you do make a halt at the refuge here, you may want to undertake the three-hour round-trip to the summit via the Col des Maures, but the final stretch includes some reasonably challenging rock climbing. This is not an ascent for beginners.

The hike continues around to the western slope of the Vallée du Golo, descending slightly to 1907m before dropping steeply down to the river at 1700m, just below the ruins of the **Bergeries de Tula**. The final two hours of the day's walk take you along the impressive, rocky ravine of the **River Golo**; a series of rocky basins filled with clear water tempt some walkers on this stretch to take a break to sunbathe or swim. For centuries, farmers used the path tracing the lower part of the valley to drive livestock to summer pastures. As the trail descends you'll meet casual walkers who've joined the GR20 from the Fer à Cheval bend on the D84.

The valley narrows before the trail reaches the **Cascade de Radule** (1370m) and the **Bergeries de Radule**, after what will now have been a hike of five to six hours (more if you've indulged in a swim). For the final hour you walk through the beech forests of the Valdu Niellu, passing the signposted turn-off to the Fer à Cheval bend and crossing the Mare a Mare Nord trail before finally emerging on the D84 just 100m west of Castel di Verghio (1404m). The ski slopes are on the other side of the road.

Places to Stay & Eat

Mid-stage At ***Refuge de Ciottulu di i Mori*** (1991m) standard rates are charged: 55FF for one of 26 beds or 20FF to camp or bivouac. Along one side of the building there's a terrace looking out over the valley below.

End-stage Not the most seductive of lodgings, ***Hôtel Castel di Verghio*** *(☎ 04 95 48 00 01)* has 29 rooms, each with a shower and sink (toilets on the landing), for 250/350/400FF per double/triple/quadruple. Half-board in a double room runs to 250FF per person. Lodging gîte d'étape-style is available for 80FF per person (half-board 170FF). Camping costs 30FF per person.

In the evening, the hotel's restaurant offers a 100FF *menu* that attracts hordes of hungry walkers. The hotel bar sells a range of basic foodstuffs as well. Credit cards are not accepted and there is only one phone line.

A bus service linking Corte and Porto passes by here once daily in each direction.

Calasima (1100m) & Albertacce (840m)

You can get to Calasima in 1½ hours via another route from the Bergeries de Ballone. About 2km before the village you pass a memorial to three fire-fighters killed in an aircraft crash during a forest fire in 1979. Bar du Centre is the only business in Calasima. But it's only another 5km downhill to Albertacce, on the D84, where there are various shops, cafes, bars and restaurants.

STAGE 6

Castel di Verghio (1404m) to Refuge de Manganu (1601m)

Distance: 14km
Standard: Average; partially shady route
Average Duration: 5½ hours
Highest Point: 1760m

Note: Access to the villages of Soccia and Orto at the end of the stage

Summary: Here at last is an easy day! It starts with a forest stroll followed by a pleasant little climb to the Col de Reta (1883m) before it drops down to the beautiful Lac de Nino. From there it's mainly downhill, past a bergerie to the night's stop. Water is available at a spring in a shrine just above Lac de Nino. After the lake the walk follows a stream most of the way to the night's stop.

After crossing the D84, the GR20 runs gently through pine and beech forests, dropping very slightly to 1330m before making a sharp turning to the west and climbing to the small shrine at the **Col de St-Pierre** (Bocca San Pedru; 1452m). The walk to this point will have taken about 1½ hours.

The route then continues to climb, following the carefully laid stones of an ancient mule path. There are great views off to the east of range after range of hills, while to the north the view takes in the hotel and ski runs at Castel di Verghio and the Vallée du Golo up to Paglia Orba. With binoculars it's easy to pick out the Refuge Ciottulu di i Mori. The trail climbs to a ridge, drops off the ridge, climbs back on to it and eventually reaches the **Col de Reta** (1883m). It then descends to **Lac de Nino** (1760m), about 3½ hours from the start. Surrounded by grassy meadows, the lake makes a wonderfully tranquil spot to stop for a picnic. There's even a little fountain in a chapel just above the lake.

The trail continues east now along the course of the Tavignano stream, which drains the lake. It crosses meadows and the remains of an abandoned refuge and then little patches of beech forest to arrive at the **Bergeries de Vaccaghja** (1621m).

The Refuge de Manganu (see Places to Stay & Eat), moreover, will now be visible in the distance. The trail drops gently from the bergerie to **Col d'Acqua Ciarnente** (1568m). Finally it makes a short, sharp ascent, crosses a bridge over the Manganu stream and delivers you to the refuge door. This last stretch of trail should take less than an hour to walk.

Places to Stay & Eat

The ***Bergeries de Vaccaghja***, one to 1½ hours beyond the lake, sells wine, cheese and bread.

Pleasant ***Refuge de Manganu*** (1601m) has 26 beds, good showers and toilets, plenty of grassy camping space around the building and easy access to swimming in the Manganu stream. The prices are no surprise: 55FF for a bed and 20FF per person to camp.

Lac de Creno (1310m), Soccia (750m) & Orto (700m)

The day's workout having been relatively easy, walkers who have not spent too much time lazing beside Lac de Nino may want to consider a little supplementary hike down to Lac de Creno. The lake is particularly pretty,

Highland Lakes & *Pozzines*

Corsica's 40-odd highland lakes, formed from the glaciers that used to cover the mountains, have been subjected to some danger both by rooting pigs and careless hikers. The PNRC has therefore implemented a programme whereby seasonal workers collect the rubbish summer visitors leave behind at the most popular lakes – Melu, Nino and Creno – and at the same time enforce the camping bans. As a further precaution, the GR20 has been diverted from the grassy areas around Lac de Nino. Walkers should not have to be reminded to respect the rules: no fires, no rubbish and no heedless tramping.

The *pozzines* (from the Corsican *pozzi*, meaning pits), another fragile environment, are threatened by intensive pasturage. Pozzines are little water holes that are linked together by small rivulets over an impermeable substratum – they're like peat bogs, in other words.

They feel underfoot like a carpet of cool moss. They are found near Lac de Nino and on the Plateau de Coscione, between the GR20 and the Refuge de la Bergerie de Bassetta.

set amid pine trees. Many travellers do it simply as a short stroll down from the mountain village of Soccia (see the Strolls & Country Walks section later in the chapter).

Hikers on the GR20 will turn west just before the Refuge de Manganu; the descent takes about an hour. For those who feel the pull, it's a further hour's walk to a car park, then a tedious 30 minutes down the road to Soccia, where there's a church with a 15th-century triptych.

Resources for the walker are relatively limited. The ***Hôtel U Pease*** *(☎ 04 95 28 31 92, fax 04 95 28 35 19)* offers single/double rooms for 195/295FF in low season and 220/330FF from mid-July to the end of August. Reduced rates are available for stays of three nights or longer. Breakfast costs 35FF.

The bar ***Chez Louis*** on the main square is the place to meet after night falls; snack foods, short of real dinner dishes, are available. Just below the square, the ***Restaurant A Merendella*** *(☎ 04 95 28 34 91)* also proves very popular because it is the only establishment in town serving full meals, other than a pizzeria open in high season only. There are no shops for reprovisioning in Soccia; however, a baker's truck passes through every morning and a grocery van passes through several times a week.

Just beyond the Lac de Nino, another trail turns off to the village of Orto, at the foot of a steep-sided valley. Each house looks as if it is almost overhanging the one below. Orto is even more out of it than Soccia; the bar ***Chez Titou*** is the village's unique business enterprise.

STAGE 7

Refuge de Manganu (1601m) to Refuge de Pietra Piana (1842m)

Distance: 10km
Standard: Difficult
Average Duration: Six hours
Highest Point: 2225m

Note: It is possible to climb Monte Ritondu (2622m) at the end of the stage.

Summary: Almost as spectacular as the Stage 4 crossing of the Cirque de la Solitude, the walk starts with a taxing climb to the narrow pass that is the highest point along the GR20. From there the walk teeters vertiginously around a spectacular mountain face high above two glacial lakes, and only at the end does it drop down to the refuge. Water is available from streams during the first ascent and from another stream on the final descent to the refuge.

After crossing the bridge from the refuge, the GR20 immediately begins to climb, emerging onto a small meadow after 30 minutes, climbing again to another brief, horizontal break at around 1970m and then ascending even more steeply up a rocky gully. There then commences a scramble to the **Brèche de**

Capitellu (2225m), a spectacular small slot through the spiky ridge line of peaks. Around 2½ hours from the refuge, this crossing is the highest point on the GR20 and the view to the east, over **Lac de Capitellu** (1930m) and beyond it **Lac de Melu** (1711m), is breathtaking. It's not immediately obvious that the two lakes are at such different levels.

The trail bends round to the south-east and edges around the ridge's eastern face, high above the lake. Later, looking back towards this ridge, it seems impossible that there could be a trail there, the slope seems to drop so steeply down to the lake. There's often snow on the path well into the walking season, so take great care; it's a long way down.

Just before another small pass at 2000m, where the GR20 crosses to the southern side of the ridge, a secondary trail diverges off to the east and drops down to Lac de Capitellu. It's possible to continue down from there to Lac de Melu and then climb back up to the main trail at the Col de Soglia. The main route climbs slightly to reach the **Col de Soglia** (2052m), about an hour's walk from the Brèche de Capitellu. Far below you can see cars on the D623. Lots of day-trippers drive into the valley from Corte to walk up to the lakes. In the other direction the village of Guagno is clearly visible to the south-west.

The trail then bends round to the north-east, high above Lac de Melu and climbs to the gentle little Col Rinosa (2150m). From there it passes Lac de Rinosa and continues on to the Col de la Haute Route (Bocca Muzzella, 2206m), about five hours from the start of this stage. From here it's less than an hour, downhill all the way, to the Refuge de Pietra Piana (see Places to Stay later).

Despite the tough climb at the start of the day and the spectacular walk above the two lakes, this is not a really difficult day and strong walkers may want to consider climbing **Monte Ritondu** (2622m), the second highest peak in Corsica. Though the 800m ascent may be a little tiring at the end of the day, it is not a technically difficult climb. The round-trip from the refuge takes about three to four hours.

Cairns mark the route to a meadow and dried-up lake just above the refuge. The trail then zigzags uphill before crossing the ridge line at 2260m, to the south of the peak. Don't descend from the ridge towards the small lakes below – instead, continue north along the eastern side of the ridge, crossing patches of frozen snow until the large **Lavu Bellebone** lake comes into view. The trail drops down to the extreme southern end of the lake and then edges around the south-eastern side of the lake before beginning to ascend the narrow and rocky sloping corridor that leads to the spiky rock marking the Col du Fer de Lance. From here the trail turns west and climbs to a small metal-roofed shelter just below the summit. There are superb views in all directions from the summit.

Places to Stay

The small, 28-bed ***Refuge de Pietra Piana*** (1842m) is nicely situated on the edge of a ridge with a nice view south into the Vallée du Manganellu. The facilities are good, and there's plenty of grassy camping space. As usual, the beds cost 55FF, with camping and bivouacs for 20FF per person.

STAGE 8

Refuge de Pietra Piana (1842m) to Refuge de l'Onda (1430m)

Distance: 10km
Standard: Easy; route mostly shady
Average Duration: Five hours
Highest Point: 1842m

Note: Refreshments available at the Bergeries de Gialgu and Bergerie de Tolla; possible detour to the villages of Canaglia and Tattone

Summary: An easy day's walk that starts with a fairly steep descent past a bergerie, following an ancient shepherds' route into the Vallée du Manganellu. The Bergerie de Tolla is a pleasant place at which to stop and have lunch or just a drink before the final ascent to the night's refuge. The walk follows streams almost all day so water is no problem; you can supplement it with beer and wine at the lunch stop.

After the dramatic ascents and descents of previous days, this stage of the walk is gentle and for the most part downhill. As soon as the trail leaves the refuge there's a choice between following the main GR20 through the Vallée du Manganellu or taking an alternative high-altitude route, marked in yellow, which follows ridge lines to the Refuge de l'Onda. The high-altitude route is quicker but less interesting.

The main GR20 starts to drop almost immediately and soon reaches the Bergeries de Gialgu (1609m; see Places to Stay & Eat later). The trail then winds down the hill to the Manganellu stream at 1440m along an ancient mule track of neatly laid stones. It continues, through often dense forest, to the Bergerie de Tolla (1011m), about three hours from the start (see Places to Stay & Eat later).

Just below the bergerie a bridge crosses the Manganellu stream (940m), and from here, if you choose, you can make a detour off the GR20 to the villages of Canaglia and Tattone (see the end of this section).

If you stick with the GR20, you'll turn upstream from the bridge and almost immediately come on the Goltaccia, which flows into the Manganellu. Do not cross the bridge here but instead continue upstream and uphill beside the Goltaccia. Eventually the trail crosses the river and climbs away to the northern side, soon reaching the busy Bergeries de l'Onda, a hive of activity next to the Refuge de l'Onda's grassy camping site.

Places to Stay & Eat

Mid-stage Bread, cheese and wine are available at ***Bergeries de Gialgu*** (1609m).

Bergerie de Tolla (1011m) is a pleasant little haven, which sells the usual supplies and also serves food. The classic Corsican omelette of *brocciu* and mint can be ordered, along with a glass of wine or a cold beer, and the really famished may be tempted by a full meal.

End-stage The ***Refuge de l'Onda*** (1430m) overlooks the bergerie and camp site, and it is surrounded by fencing to keep out the many pigs poking around nearby. It charges the usual 55FF for a bed and 20FF to camp or bivouac, and it also sells bread, cheese, sausage and wine.

Canaglia & Tattone (600m)

It's about an hour's easy walk from the Manganellu bridge on the GR20 to the pretty village of Canaglia. Walkers appreciate the wide track running alongside the river and the string of little pools that are good for a swim. Canaglia's small restaurant, the ***Osteria u Capitan Moru,*** specialises in trout, and has a telephone.

From Canaglia it's 4km by road to Tattone. For a taxi call Alain (☎ 04 95 47 20 06, 06 07 89 16 10) in Vivario. Tattone is on the Bastia–Vizzavona–Ajaccio railway line; Tattone–Vizzavona (see Stage 9) by train takes seven minutes and costs 8FF.

The ***Bar du Soleil Camping*** *(☎ 04 95 47 21 16)*, near the train station, charges 24FF per person plus 10FF for a tent. The camp site has a snack bar and supplies and also runs a shuttle bus. There's another camp site, ***Camping Savaggio***, 2km beyond Tattone.

STAGE 9

Refuge de l'Onda (1430m) to Vizzavona (910m)

Distance: 10km
Standard: Average
Average Duration: 5½ hours
Highest Point: 2159m

Note: Alternative route via Monte d'Oro to the north

Summary: The walk to Vizzavona, traditionally the mid-point of the GR20, starts with an arduous ascent over rock. There then follows a descent over a barren terrain before reaching the woods around the series of waterfalls and pools known as the Cascades des Anglais. There are plentiful supplies of water during the long descent and Vizzavona, with its train station, hotels, restaurants and cafes, is the best-equipped stop anywhere along the GR20.

The route sets off northwards, following the high-level alternative route to the Refuge de Pietra Piana, but soon doubles back to head south – climbing – to the **Crête de Muratellu** (2020m). From this bleak and windy height, some two to 2½ hours out, the balance of the day's walk is a long descent downhill.

The first stretch of this descent is steep and rocky into the upper heights of the Vallée de l'Agnone. Then, as the trail drops below the 1600m mark, the descent becomes less steep and the environment greener. At 1500m you pass the remains of an abandoned refuge. Then, about four hours into the day's march, you pass a high waterfall – part of the **Cascades des Anglais** (1150m). As the trail continues on through pine forests, you'll share it for a time with day walkers. To the north-east, Monte d'Oro, Corsica's fifth highest peak, broods over the scene.

A snack bar and a **bridge** over the Agnone hint now at the proximity of civilisation, and from here into Vizzavona the walking path metamorphoses into a track quite suitable for cars. There are several turnings, several bridges and what seems like an interminable trudge – and then suddenly you're right in the middle of the village of Vizzavona and only a short distance from the train station.

An alternative route, marked only by stone cairns, along this ninth segment, continues up from the aforementioned Crête de Muratellu and turns slightly north-east to the **Col de Porc** (2159m). Then it turns south-east to climb to the summit of **Monte d'Oro** (2389m), which you would otherwise only pass beneath. There are stretches of difficult rock climbing on this route; it should not be undertaken by the inexperienced. This alternative route finally rejoins the main GR20 just before Vizzavona and adds about three hours to the day's exertions.

What a Waste

You wouldn't really expect it out here in the wilderness, but there's plenty of litter along the GR20. This includes empty tins – especially sardine tins – paper tissues, cigarette ends and, last but not least, toilet paper.

The problem is exacerbated, regrettably, by the lack of sanitation facilities along the route. Camping is restricted to the areas around the refuges and a few of the bergeries. The bergeries do not, as a rule, have any toilets at all, and the toilets at the refuges – about one for every 100 campers – are famously inadequate, if they work at all. Walkers should do their best not to make things any worse than they have to be.

Vizzavona (910m)

Vizzavona is a tiny health spa at the foot of the massive Monte d'Oro, and traditionally represents the pivot point between the northern and southern sections of the GR20. It's a welcome breath of civilisation to those who tackle the whole of the GR20, an opportunity to reprovision, have a decent meal and a good night's sleep in a hotel. It's advisable to book somewhere to stay in advance. Vizzavona is situated at the heart of one of Corsica's prettiest forests, which is mainly made up of laricio pines and beech trees, and provides an excellent setting for a number of well-marked forest walks.

There's a telephone box and a post box next to the station, and another phone box next to Hôtel Monte d'Oro.

Recommended ***Hôtel I Laricci*** *(☎/fax 04 95 47 21 12)*, with its look of a big Swiss chalet, has 12 spacious, renovated rooms that cost 450FF for two at half-board and 340FF for a single. Half the rooms have a spectacular view of Monte d'Oro. Book ahead, though, if you can; the hotel is much in demand. Fortunately, there's also an annexe with three six-bed dormitories where 145FF buys a bed, hot shower and an evening meal. To do your wash will cost an additional 50FF. The dinner *menu*, not on the half-board plan, goes for 85FF. The food is simple and portions are generous. The owners also provide good advice on exploring the area on foot, and credit cards are welcome. It opens from early April to late October.

The ***Resto Refuge de la Gare*** *(☎ 04 95 47 22 20)*, just opposite the train station, is home to a restaurant and two clean, simple, renovated dormitories housing six persons each at 75FF per night or 175FF at half-board. Board, however, is not obligatory. There's a *menu* for as little as 70FF but no self-catering facilities. This very friendly, family-run establishment opens from the beginning of June to the end of September; exact dates depend on how busy it is.

Hôtel Monte d'Oro *(☎ 04 95 47 21 06, 04 95 47 23 44, fax 04 95 47 22 05)* is an old hotel full of nooks and crannies, 3km to the west of the village, in the hamlet of Foce, just before the Col de Vizzavona. To get there, you can leave the GR20 at the Cascades des Anglais and come via the N193. Alternatively, the hotel will send a shuttle to pick you up if you ring from Vizzavona station. In season, singles/doubles cost 230/300FF with shared toilet, 300/410FF with shower and toilet and 340/460FF with bath. They're less expensive out of season. Half-board (840FF for two in season) is yet another option. The hotel also has a refuge in which a bed goes for 90FF per person or 190FF at half-board.

At the northern entrance to the town, above the N193, ***Casa Alta*** offers bed and breakfast for two at 300FF, which can be a good alternative to Hôtel I Laricci (often full) and Hôtel Monte d'Oro (some way from the centre).

Campers tend to pitch their tents on a flat piece of land behind the station, but while it is free to camp, there are no toilets or washing facilities and in summer it is often full to bursting.

You can do some serious stocking up at ***Épicerie Rosy***, which is in the station itself and run by Mme Zagnoli. It opens from 7.30 am daily, including Sunday and public holidays, and sells everything walkers could want at reasonable prices: bread and other food staples, freeze-dried foods, Corsican speciality foods, cold drinks, films, batteries, gas refills and first aid equipment. Mme Zagnoli won't take credit cards, though. It closes after the last Saturday in September.

Restaurant-Bar l'Altagna, next door to the grocery, has *menus* for 70FF and 95FF. Local specialities, including a Corsican platter at 60FF, and snacks are served all day.

The train between Ajaccio and Bastia stops at Vizzavona four times daily in each direction. Two of the services continue beyond Bastia to Île Rousse and Calvi.

From Vizzavona, tickets cost 8FF to Tattone, 39FF to Ajaccio, 26FF to Corte, 102FF to Calvi, 82FF to Bastia, 86FF to Île Rousse and 46FF to Ponte Leccia.

STAGE 10

Vizzavona (910m) to Bergeries de Capannelle (1586m)

Distance: 13.5km
Standard: Average
Average Duration: 5½ hours
Highest Point: 1647m

Note: Access to the village of Ghisoni

Summary: This section of the walk is punctuated by magnificent views as you approach the Monte Renoso ski resort against a background of laricio pine and beech trees.

From the station in Vizzavona, follow the marked route for the GR20 Sud. You will pass in front of Hôtel I Laricci and cross the access path to the GR20 Nord on the right. Then you will cross a little bridge and climb for 15 minutes or so to reach the N193 and the ONF (Office National des Forêts; National Office for Forests) facility. A sign tells you that Bergeries de Capannelle is 4½ hours off, but this is rather optimistic. From here, you will follow a dirt track that ascends gently through the woods. Here and there you will come across holly bushes several metres high, quite lost among the pine trees. After a while you'll come to a fork. The right spur leads off to a spring about 450m distant; you'll take the left. You will catch your first glimpse of the **Forêt de Vizzavona** and Monte d'Oro behind you and you'll still be able to hear the faint rumble of the waterfalls of the Cascades des Anglais.

The route quickly leaves the dirt track behind and makes a twisting ascent up to a high-voltage power cable, which marks the start of a long, flat trek through undergrowth. The pleasant shade of the beech trees is gone.

The path then turns steep again and leads off to a junction from which the GR20 goes off to your left. But take the time to detour 100m down the right fork for a wonderful view of Monte d'Oro and Vizzavona below.

Back on the GR20, the path soon emerges from the undergrowth into a bare, almost lunar landscape from where you can see the **Col de Palmente** (1647m) ahead. Pay attention to the markings and the junction where the GR20 turns right to arrive at the pass. If you're careless and you don't make the turning, you'll end up at the Palmente spring, about 200m from where you want to be.

After a 15-minute climb, there's a cairn to indicate that the pass is now near. The dark silhouette of Monte d'Oro is behind you at this point; ahead is the Oculo ridge in the foreground and behind it the Cardo ridge and little **Monte Calvi** (1461m).

The path goes downhill now towards the **Bergeries d'Alzeta**, then continues flat. After about 30 minutes a hairpin bend marks the left turn-off that leads to Ghisoni (see the end of this section).

From the turn-off to Ghisoni, the GR20 continues along the hillside and goes through a forest of laricio pines, some of which are of an impressive size. About 1¼ hours later it reaches the three charming **Bergeries de Scarpaccedie** whose sanitation facilities and electricity are no small surprise.

A short distance on, the route bears off to the right. It might be a good idea to take a few deep breaths at this point, as the next stretch involves a change in altitude of 150m and a good 20 minutes of solid effort. There's a reward, though, in the wonderful view you'll have of **Monte Renoso** (2352m). The route then follows an asphalt road uphill for about 100m before coming to a sign detailing the services available at the **Bergeries de Capannelle**: the Gîte U Renosu, straight ahead, boasts of its hot showers, while the Gîte U Fugone, to the left, counters with the delights of its draught beer. The two gîtes are 300m apart and your best bet is to go left, as the U Renosu often shuts in the summer.

Although there is only one remaining shepherd, the bergeries to which you are headed, 20 minutes ahead at the foot of the Ghisoni ski lifts, were kept by local families for holiday-making and hunting. They were once lost amid beech forests, but the trees were cut down to clear the ski slopes. When the snow melts, the water washes away everything in its path, which explains why the slopes look so desolate in summer.

From the Bergeries de Capannelle, there is a signposted walk of about 2½ hours to Lac de Bastani. It is even possible to climb Monte Renoso from the lake.

Water? BYO!

Though there's water enough at every refuge along the GR20, this is not the case in the long intervals between the refuges. What water sources are available are detailed in the main text. But they are few, so you must carry water with you – 2L per person is the absolute minimum. As far as water from streams is concerned, safety is not guaranteed: do not use it unless strictly necessary and, if possible, treat it with water purification tablets.

Places to Stay & Eat

The ***PNRC refuge*** is on your path just before the Gîte U Fugone. Made of stone, its comfort level is less than optimal, but a recent coat of paint has at least made it look clean. Wooden planks hold up some 10 mattresses. A gas stove by the entrance allows for some light cooking. A night costs 30FF, collected by the warden of the Gîte U Fugone, where it is possible to shower. Whether you stay here or not, it's worth having a look at any notice posted by the PNRC as to conditions farther along the GR20.

Gîte U Fugone *(☎ 04 95 57 01 81)*, run by Paul Maurizi and his wife, is much better value. It's large, with dormitories for three to five people, toilets and hot showers. Half-board – bed, dinner and breakfast – will set you back 165FF. The restaurant also offers *menus* of Corsican products for 68FF, 80FF and 110FF. There is a little grocery too. It opens mid-May to September.

The *Gîte U Renosu*, 300m away, generally only opens in winter.

Ghisoni (665m)

The way down to the village of Ghisoni is marked with yellow lines. It leads first to the Bergeries de Cardo, where there is a building that can serve for crude shelter, then crosses a plain. Follow the winding path to the left of the plain and ignore the yellow and blue markings off to the right. Your path continues through a little forest of maritime pines and meets up with a canal that was used to irrigate Ghisoni's gardens back in the 19th century. Before long, you will come to the D69, which, if you turn right, leads to the village. Allow 1½ to two hours to get down to the village and three hours to climb back up again. The change in altitude is 850m.

Ghisoni is a peaceful little village at the foot of **Punta Kyrie Eleïson** (1535m). It's dead in winter. But it seems to turn almost lively in summer when its errant sons and daughters return from where they go to earn a living, namely Bastia, Ajaccio and even the mainland. As you walk amid the pretty stone houses, it is easy to imagine what Ghisoni was like in its glory days before WWII. Back then, there were no fewer than three dance halls, 12 cafes and 1800 permanent inhabitants; today's summer population is 3000, falling to 200 in the winter. In the good old days, Ghisoni's income came primarily from chestnut flour and from exploiting forest products, in particular the laricio pine.

Shops here can be found along the D344, the village's main street.

Ghisoni's post office opens 8.50 am to noon and 1.50 to 4.30 pm Monday to Friday and Saturday morning. There are also two telephone boxes in town.

There are two options for walkers wishing to spend the night: ***Camping Municipal***, at the intersection of the D69 and the D344 – only a sloping piece of land with sanitation limited to the communal wash house just below – and ***Hôtel Kyrie*** (☎ *04 95 57 60 33, fax 04 95 57 63 15*), which has 30 slightly old-fashioned but clean rooms with showers and toilets. Rooms for two, three and four range in price from 250FF to 300FF. The hotel opens from the end of April to 10 October and has a restaurant with *menus* for 100FF or 150FF.

Pizzeria Guy (☎ *04 95 57 60 74*) at the bottom of the village serves good pizzas for 40FF to 50FF and a Corsican platter for 60FF. There's a little terrace that makes it possible to enjoy a view of the river; the service is friendly. It opens year round. The ***Libre-Service Micheli*** (☎ *04 95 57 60 39*), with the Super JP/Tabac sign, next to the old church, is a grocery selling tinned food, fresh produce, Corsican specialities and supplies for walkers (but no freeze-dried foods). It opens 9 am to noon and 4.30 to 7 pm daily except Sunday year round.

There are no bus services from Ghisoni. To connect with public transport, you have to hitch to Ghisonaccia (28km south-east) or Vivario (21km north-west).

STAGE 11

Bergeries de Capannelle (1586m) to Col de Verde (1289m)

Distance: 11.5km
Standard: Average
Average Duration: Five hours
Highest Point: 1591m

Summary: This stage is relatively short and easy. It skirts the Monte Renoso massif to the east but mostly remains on a plateau at an average altitude of 1500m, eventually reaching the Col de Verde. This is the last stopoff point before a series of ridges.

The route begins at the foot of the ski lift and then quickly enters a forest of beech trees; the forest seems a kind of witness to how idyllic the Bergeries de Capannelle area must have been before the construction of the ski resort.

It will take you about 40 minutes to reach the **Bergeries de Traggette** (1520m) and the D169 (1344m). Fifty metres farther on there is a sign to the 'Bocca di Verdi' (Col de Verde) and the route heads uphill again. There are views over the Fiumorbu region and the Kyrie Eleïson range before the path penetrates a thick forest of pine and beech trees; this forest, to judge by the large numbers of spent cartridges on the ground, is frequented by both wild boar and their hunters.

After 45 minutes in the undergrowth, the GR20 rounds a hairpin bend to the right. When the snow is melting you will have to cross a string of streams here, which may require a few acrobatics. Forty-five minutes later there's a second hairpin bend, this time in the open.

You are now halfway through the day's walk, right next to **Punta Capannella** (2032m) and below the Lischetto stream, which cascades down in a profusion of little waterfalls; its source is the little Lacs de Rina (1882m). These little torrents from the eastern face of Monte Renoso converge a few kilometres downstream to form the River Fiumorbu.

Once you have crossed the **Lischettu**, it will not take more than 30 minutes to get to the **Plateau de Gialgone** (1591m); from here is an inspiring view over the Col de Verde. In front of you is **Monte Grosso** (1895m) and, at the edge of the plateau, a wooden sign directs you to the Pozzi, a magnificent grassy plain – it's a two-hour detour there and back.

The GR20 itself forges straight on towards Col de Verde and begins an impressive descent that delivers you, some 30 minutes later, at a little wooden bridge straddling the Marmano stream, which flows into the Fiumorbu.

A few metres on, a simple wooden sign on the ground draws your attention to a giant fir tree that rises to the amazing height of 53.2m. The path remains flat and enters the undergrowth of beeches before turning to the right and widening out in the middle of a forest of fir trees. After about 20 minutes the trail reaches a large picnic area.

From here, a path through the forest to the right leads to the village of Palneca; a path to the left leads to the Col de Verde after about 300m.

Places to Stay & Eat

Relais San Pedru di Verdi *(☎ 04 95 24 46 82)*, better known as the Refuge du Col de Verde, is in a lush green setting on the edge of the D69. It's a wooden cottage with bunk beds, clean toilets, a couple of hot showers and a little kitchen area if you want to prepare your own meals. A bed will set you back 60FF, while camping, with access to a shower, costs 25FF. For 10FF more you can rent a tent. One of the best things about this refuge is its lovely terrace, where you can treat yourself to generous salads (35FF), sandwiches (25FF), lamb chops (49FF), wood-fire pizzas (45FF) and drinks (13FF); a *menu* goes for 89FF. Half-board costs 170FF. The refuge opens 1 May to the end of September.

STAGE 12

Col de Verde (1289m) to Refuge d'Usciolu (1750m)

Distance: 14km
Standard: Difficult; not much shade; very steep sections and sometimes high winds on the ridges
Average Duration: 7½ hours
Highest Point: 1981m

Summary: This long stage could be called the 'ridge route'. From the Col de Verde, the trail climbs up to a ridge and then continues along it at heights between 1500m and 2000m almost as far as the Refuge d'Usciolu. At the Col de Laparo (1525m) it cuts across the Mare a Mare Centre walk. There are spectacular – almost aerial – views over Fiumorbu to the east and Taravo valley to the west.

After crossing a local road, the trail climbs gently up into a pine forest. But the honeymoon period doesn't last long: 10 minutes out, the GR20 turns off to the left and begins the assault on the mountain. It will take 20 minutes of sustained effort to reach an intermediate plateau, the end of the first segment. From here, if you look down to the bottom of the valley, you'll have a view of the village of Palneca. A stream marks the start of a second steep stretch, though now at least you'll enjoy the shade of beech trees for a while. After 20 minutes you'll see clearly where you're headed.

A further 35 minutes of hard climbing up a steep, rocky and unshaded path delivers you to the **Col d'Oru** (1840m), and an excellent view over the eastern plain. If you turn around, you'll see a line-up of Monte Ritondo, Monte d'Oro and Monte Renoso, and you'll be able to survey the distance you've covered.

A very pleasant walk then leads, after about 15 minutes, to the handsomely sited **Refuge de Prati** (1820m), reconstructed now after the lightning fire that destroyed it in 1997 (see Places to Stay & Eat later).

From the refuge, a path to the left, marked out in yellow, leads down to the village of Isolacciu di Fiumorbu, 1km below to the east. The GR20 turns right and heads straight on to the ridges. The stretch of very steep slope only lasts about 20 minutes, but the path afterwards remains rocky and challenging. There is a breathtaking bird's-eye view of the villages of Palneca, Ciamannacce and Cozzano, more than 1km below. To the left (east), meanwhile, you can clearly see the village of Prunelli di Fiumorbu, perched up high, and Ghisonaccia down on the plain.

Make the most of the view because you will need all your strength to climb up over the large rocks on the next stretch of trail. This stretch, happily, takes only about 30 minutes, but can be quite nerve-wracking to walkers who don't like heights, and can also be dangerous in bad weather – so take care. The next 1¼ hours of trail is rocky and difficult as well, and at times comes within whispering distance of some fairly frightening precipices.

Once past **Punta della Cappella** (2042m), the trail skirts round the Rocher de la Penta before quitting the ridge for a little forest that makes an ideal spot for a picnic. From here it's less than half an hour to the **Col de Laparo** (1525m), where the route crosses the Mare a Mare Centre (Ghisonaccia to Porticcio) walk. There's a sign to a spring and near this is a very basic refuge (no warden; closed at the time of research).

The path from the Col de Laparo to **Cozzano** (about 2½ hours of walking) forms part of the Mare a Mare Centre route; see the section on this walk, which also details the tourist resources available in Cozzano, later in this chapter.

After the pass, the trail continues along the ridge, this time climbing steadily up to **Monte Formicula** (1981m), the highest point of the day; it's a little less than 500m above Laparo. The climb takes between 1¾ and two hours. As the altitude increases, vegetation gradually thins out, and the landscape becomes scarred and barren.

Now the route follows the eastern side of the ridge for a while; then it crosses to the windier western side. Once past Monte Formicula, it's only another 30 to 45 minutes to the Refuge d'Usciolu and, after what you've come through, rather like a Sunday afternoon stroll; it's downhill all the way. The path returns to the eastern side, overlooking a vast grassy plain – pasture land – dotted with heaps of stone. It continues along the line of the ridge before tackling the descent itself, first towards this plain, then finally to the Refuge d'Usciolu.

Places to Stay & Eat

Mid-stage A night at the ***Refuge de Prati*** costs 55FF, and you can fill up on a big bowl of pasta. If you continue on be sure to fill up your flask at the refuge's water fountain, as there are no other water sources for the rest of the stage and there's still a long way to go.

End-stage Leaning against the mountain, the ***Refuge d'Usciolu*** has a bird's-eye view south over the whole valley; the valley is dominated by the majestic Monte Incudine (2134m), which seems close enough to reach out and touch. The refuge has 32 beds (55FF per night) and is clean and well-maintained. The camp site is just below the refuge (20FF per person). Excellent meals and light refreshments – ewe's milk cheese (40FF), drinks (13FF), sausage, chocolate and hard-boiled eggs are on offer.

SALLY DILLON

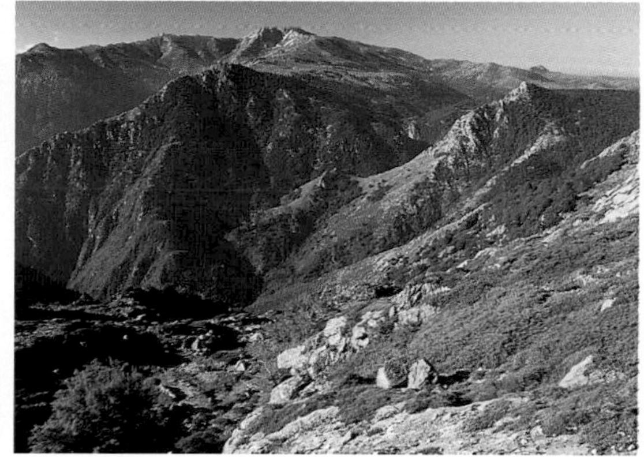

JEAN-BERNARD CARILLET

TONY WHEELER

TONY WHEELER

TONY WHEELER

SALLY DILLON

Exchange the rat race for a rock face: the exhilarating GR20 takes in pine forests, glacial craters and lakes and granite massifs at an average altitude of 1500m.

JEAN-BERNARD CARILLET

Take the plunge at Lavezzi.

GEORGES ANTONI

The *girelle* is the most tropical of Corsica's fish.

GEORGES ANTONI

Unfortunately for red coral, it's considered a precious stone and has suffered intense harvesting.

GEORGES ANTONI

Face to fish-face in Mérouville: the grouper in the area are famed for their friendliness.

STAGE 13

Refuge d'Usciolu (1750m) to Refuge d'Asinao (1530m)

Distance: 14.5km
Standard: Average
Average Duration: 7½ to eight hours
Highest Point: 2134m

Note: It's possible to do this stage over two days, with a detour to the village of Zicavo or a stopoff at the Bergeries de Bassetta; in this event, the climb up Monte Incudine is saved for the second day.

Summary: The stage begins with a kind of skywalk, since you keep to the ridge line for at least two hours before descending to the crossroads at the Col de l'Agnonu. From there the trail crosses the undulating Plateau de Coscione before starting the climb up Monte Incudine (2134m), the highest point on the southern section of the GR20. This is followed by a steep descent to the Refuge d'Asinao.

A short, steep path from the refuge leads back up to the ridge. There's a sign to Cozzano, where it is possible, but not very practical, to stop off. From here it's a tightrope walk along the **ridge**, which is particularly steep at this stage, for a good two hours. Monte Incudine looms ahead of you.

The altitude now never varies a great deal from 1800m, but a series of tiny ups and downs make the going very hard. At times you also have to squeeze through blocks of rock and heaps of knife-like granite. There's no shade, and the signs are not always easy to find in this desolate landscape. However, the views over the Taravo valley to the west, the pastures on the plain to the east and, of course, Monte Incudine ahead to the south are sublime.

Eventually, the trail passes a distinctive U-shaped gap, then climbs down towards a cluster of beeches on the western side of the ridge. Vegetation appears again. The shrubs and heather are gradually replaced by yet more beech trees.

After about three hours you'll reach a wonderful, huge clearing – an ideal spot for a picnic. It is surrounded by little streams and the trunks of trees struck down in storms, along with majestic beech trees, which provide some very welcome shade. The pastoral setting is in stark contrast to the barren austerity of the route along the top of the ridge. There's also a spring; it's signposted. About 10 minutes from here the trail reaches the crossroads at the **Col de l'Agnonu**, about 3¼ hours from the start of this stage.

At the crossroads is a sign for Asinao. The phrase '*Ravitaillement, gîte, camping à 1 heure*' (Refreshments, accommodation, camping – one hour) has been painted below, in red. This reference is to the Auberge de la Passerelle, but the time is an underestimate.

From Col de l'Agnonu, you can leave the GR20 and make a detour to the village of Zicavo (see the end of this section) in the Taravo valley, a walk of less than three hours.

If you don't turn off to visit Zicavo, you continue along the GR20 among beech trees beyond Col de l'Agnonu for about 20 minutes to an overhang from where there's a wonderful view over the Coscione and, in the background, the imposing spectacle of Monte Incudine. The trail then leaves the beeches behind and fast passes onto the hilly plain, dotted with groves, grassy moors and rock outcroppings. You'll also come on a number of little streams that have to be forded. The route is easy until it reaches the foot of Monte Incudine. So make the most of this because Incudine, which looms ever nearer, is the main item on the day's agenda. After about an hour the trail reaches the junction with the route back from Zicavo and the **Refuge de la Bergerie de Bassetta**, 1½ hours' walk to the west (see Places to Stay & Eat later).

A short distance beyond the path off to the Bergerie de Bassetta, the GR20 crosses a rickety wooden footbridge over the Casamintellu stream and then begins its ascent towards Monte Incudine. As you climb the slope, the beech trees thin out and the landscape becomes more barren. After climbing for about 30 minutes, you reach the ***Aire de Bivouac I Pedinieddi***. The

A Jewel Set in the Mountains

Between the Col de l'Agnonu and Monte Incudine, the GR20 crosses a section of the Plateau de Coscione, and this is actually a mosaic of environments so different one from another as to give the area a special personality all its own. There are beech groves here, streams, pozzines, moors, meadows and heaps of fallen rocks, one right after another at an average altitude of 1400m. In August, when the monkshood is in bloom, the Plateau de Coscione is painted with patches of violet.

The topography of the plateau, with its gentle oscillations, its terraces and its little valleys, is in stark contrast to the rest of the GR20, where the relief is much less friendly. Walkers tend to think of the walk across the Plateau de Coscione as a welcome intermission before the ascent of Monte Incudine.

The Plateau de Coscione is not just a pleasant pastoral scene, though. It is also important in socioeconomic and even mythic terms. In the early 20th century nearly 600 people lived on the plateau. As recently as a few decades ago, shepherds would come here from all over southern Corsica to graze their flocks in summer. Those days are long gone. The last real Coscione shepherd died in 1997. True, you will see your share of pigs, cattle, sheep and goats on the plateau even today. But the shepherds who own these animals are of a different breed from their predecessors. Today's shepherds bring their livestock up to the plain in cattle trucks, and then they return to inspect them every week in 4WDs. One tradition that has nevertheless endured is the annual shepherds' fair in the village of Zicavo, at the beginning of August. Once it would have attracted more than 1000 people. Today far fewer come. But livestock is still blessed by a priest.

In winter the plateau is frequented by cross-country skiers, although they do not always find as much snow as they might wish for.

If you really want to appreciate the Plateau de Coscione, it is worth taking the alternative route via Zicavo and the Chapelle San Petru, or making a detour to the Refuge de la Bergeries de Bassetta, about 1¼ hours to the west of the GR20. This will give you the opportunity to set foot on the *pozzines* (see the boxed text 'Highland Lakes & *Pozzines*' earlier in this chapter), the water-filled peat bogs that make you feel as if you are walking on a fine English lawn.

Refuge de Pedinieddi, which used to stand on this little plateau, was destroyed by lightning. But there is a water supply here, and it's still possible to bivouac. After this plateau, the climb continues, often passing through heaps of broken rocks. Behind you is a magnificent view over the Coscione and the little valleys that overlap it.

About one hour's walk from the footbridge, you reach the **Col de Luana** (1800m), on a ridge. The route then turns to the right and begins to climb the ridge leading on to the summit. To the left (east) you can see down to the rocky, wild valley through which the Tremoli flows. The climb is quite difficult, but there is a flat bit off to the west that gives you a 15-minute breather. After just over two hours of climbing, you'll catch sight of the cross on the summit of Monte Incudine. It is not uncommon for there to be névés at this altitude in the month of June.

All that's left now is the descent to the refuge. The first quarter of an hour is an easy walk along the ridge. The trail reaches a junction and you can see what lies ahead: a drop down to the refuge 500m below. The slope really is impressive, and your joints and muscles will feel it.

The path follows the ridge to the east before diving to the south and then twisting its way down to the refuge. Allow 1¼ to 1½ hours before you get to set your rucksack down.

Places to Stay & Eat

Mid-stage The ***Refuge de la Bergerie de Bassetta*** *(☎ 04 95 25 74 20, 06 87 44 04 08)* can be reached, from the GR20, in a walk of about 1½ hours, with only slight change in altitude. This is a private refuge in an old bergerie, run impeccably by Toussaint Franceschi and his wife, and, if you haven't made the detour via Zicavo, it is well worth the walk in order to see the wonderful setting the bergerie enjoys in the most rural part of the Plateau de Coscione.

A night costs 70FF in the bergerie or slightly more in one of the new little chalets. Sanitation facilities are outstanding. Excellent meals, with high-quality house charcuterie, cost 110FF, the daily special costs 55FF and sandwiches cost 25FF. Half-board costs 170/180FF for a bed in the refuge/chalet. Meals are served in a big communal room, with a fireplace decorated with photographs of old Corsica.

End-stage There is room for only 20 people at ***Refuge d'Asinao*** (1530m). A bed costs 55FF (camping 20FF). The refreshments available – charcuterie, honey, cheese, beer and wine – are basic and may not be available at the end of the season. From the refuge you can see the Bergeries d'Asinao below; they are still used and bivouacking is not allowed here.

Zicavo (750m)

To get to Zicavo, turn off at the sign and follow the yellow markings. The route is pleasant, downhill and for the most part shaded. The shape of this detour is a big S and it is not particularly difficult, but you have to pay attention because the signs and the path are not always clear. About two-thirds of the way down (about two hours into the walk) the trail emerges onto a variant of the Mare a Mare Centre route (orange markings), which it joins. The main Mare a Mare Centre route is described later in this chapter.

Zicavo is a pretty village stretching out along the mountainside. For a long time it relied on agricultural and pastoral activities and served as a base for the shepherds going up to the Plateau de Coscione (see the boxed text 'A Jewel Set in the Mountains' on the previous page). Those days are gone and Zicavo now relies on ecotourism.

The history of the village is intimately linked to the Albatucci family, many members of which (including a general) were close to the two Napoleons. The main road through the village is cours Albatucci, and you are sure to be able to find someone who will show you the family home. The village is full of imposing grey granite buildings, and the feeling of past greatness and fallen nobility remains tangible today.

Zicavo is an oasis for walkers. The hotels are excellent and the little shops well stocked. For those wishing to linger here, there are walks – to hot springs and nearby villages – that make it possible to discover the Haut Taravo valley in more depth. A very pretty little waterfall, about 1km beyond the village in the direction of Aullène (go left at the level of the bridge), is a good spot for a dip on a warm day.

A Funtana, a little gîte d'étape at the GR20 end of the village, has five rooms and charges 150FF for two persons. The nearby ***Hôtel-Restaurant du Tourisme*** *(☎ 04 95 24 40 06)* offers comfortable singles/doubles/triples for 170/200/240FF. The restaurant offers *menus* for 80FF, 100FF and 120FF.

Gîte Le Paradis *(☎ 04 95 24 41 20)*, five minutes away on the D69 towards Cozzano, just beyond Chapelle St-Roch, offers individual rooms, with or without bathroom, for 180FF to 200FF. Sharing a room with one, two or three other people can lower the cost per night to as little as 70FF. For 25FF, you can camp in the garden. Louise Pirany, the former schoolteacher who runs this establishment, cooks up some good Corsican dishes, and offers a nice myrtle liqueur. Dinner goes for 75FF, breakfast for 25FF.

Hôtel Le Florida *(☎ 04 95 24 43 11)*, about 100m farther on, is a comfortable establishment with double rooms for 200FF and *menus* for 90FF and 120FF. Half-board is good value at 200FF. Die-hard campers can pitch their tents in the shade of chestnut trees at José Fratini's ***camp site*** *(☎ 04 95 24 40 87)*, 1km beyond the village in the direction of Cozzano. The charge is 25FF per person, and there are hot showers.

Pacifique Sud *(☎ 04 95 24 41 37)*, a bar-restaurant-pizzeria, south on the D69, just beyond the grocery, offers pizzas (30FF to 42FF) and a *menu* for 70FF. Some evenings the bar gets agreeably crowded.

Le Prestige Club *(☎ 04 95 24 42 13)*, next door to Hôtel-Restaurant du Tourisme, serves pizzas for 40FF to 55FF, pasta starts at 55FF and meat and fish dishes at 60F. There's a little terrace with a nice view.

A well-stocked little ***grocery*** opens 7 am to 12.30 pm and 3 to 7.30 pm daily, mid-May to mid-September, and Jacques Lusinchi, the owner, does everything he can to help out walkers. There's also a ***bakery*** and a post office.

Autocars Santini provides a service between Ajaccio and Zicavo daily except Sunday (70FF).

To return to the GR20, you do not have to retrace your steps. A good alternative route takes you south via the small Chapelle San Petru and then over the best part of the Plateau de Coscione (the section of the GR20 between Col de l'Agnonu and the junction with this route is less spectacular). From Zicavo, follow the D69 southwards for 1.5km until the path turns off to the left.

Simpler still is to get a lift to the Refuge de la Bergerie de Bassetta (see Places to Stay & Eat earlier), which is accessible by road (the D69, then the D428). Ask Jacques the grocer, who goes up there almost every day with supplies, or Toussaint-Franceschi, the owner of the Refuge de la Bergerie de Bassetta, who also makes the 14km journey frequently. This will save you a 600m change in altitude that takes several hours to walk and is not particularly interesting.

From Bassetta, follow the D428 for 1.5km as far as the **Chapelle San Petru**, a good picnic spot. The trail, marked with yellow lines and cairns, runs off here from behind the chapel and climbs up in about 20 minutes to meet a path wide enough for a 4WD. It continues to the Refuge de Matalza (very basic: no warden, no water) before reaching the most interesting section of the Coscione.

From here, the path turns due east to rejoin the GR20 after another 1¼ to 1½ hours of easy walking. You will now be roughly one hour south of Col de l'Agnonu. But watch carefully for signs along the way. Otherwise, you are liable to make any number of wrong turnings.

STAGE 14

Refuge d'Asinao (1530m) to Refuge de Paliri (1055m), via Alpine Route

Distance: 13km
Standard: Difficult (tricky sections on alpine route); lack of shade when crossing the Bavella massif
Average Duration: 6¼ hours
Highest Point: 16 62m

Note: Optional half-stage at the Col de Bavella; access to the village of Quenza; alternative route which skirts around the Bavella massif

Summary: One of the most beautiful stages of the southern GR20, the highlight of which is the Aiguilles de Bavella, which can be crossed on the alpine route. Under tree cover, the path continues southwards, above the Vallée de l'Asinao, then turns east to the Bavella massif and leads to the path of the same name (1218m). It then continues eastwards and reaches a little depression (1022m) before crossing a mountainous ridge, behind which is the refuge. You will pass from green surroundings to a granite lunar landscape.

Do not expect to pass the Bergeries d'Asinao, which are below the refuge to the south. The trail heads west first, then only gradually changes direction towards the south on its way to the ravine the Asinao passes through. It's a good half-hour walk before you ford the river. The gradual descent passes through a wooded section dominated by pine trees.

The shape of the Vallée de l'Asinao can be clearly made out; downstream, towards Quenza, the valley widens out, while upstream it seems more boxed-in. A sign upstream indicating the path to Quenza, three to four hours distant, will now be about 10 minutes behind you (see later in this section).

On the other side of the River Asinao the path climbs gently and then later evens out along the side of the mountain at an average altitude of 1300m. You'll see various plants and trees, including alders, pines, arbutuses, violets, bracken and, for the first time on the GR20, silver birches. The route, as it follows a ledge above the Asinao for about an hour, is easy and pleasant. There are spectacular views downstream and of the opposite bank, where the rounded valley-side has been etched with deep scars by the ravines running down it. There is also a marked difference in the vegetation on either side; the opposite side of the valley is rocky, while the side you're on is much greener. A number of little streams cross the path. In places you can catch glimpses through the foliage of the towering foothills of the Bavella massif.

After about 1½ hours of walking you come upon a crossroads. Straight ahead, the GR20 trunk route will follow the flank of the mountainsides by a south-westerly route. To the left, the **alpine route**, marked out in yellow, heads for the heart of the massif. The two branches meet up again a little in advance of the Col de Bavella.

The alpine route is unquestionably more technically difficult and physically taxing than the main route. It takes you through areas of fallen rocks and stones and in one section you have to use your hands to get across a rock slab. If you're susceptible to vertigo, you may want to avoid this test. You may also want to avoid it in the wet; there's a real risk of losing your footing. The alpine route is nevertheless one of the highlights of the GR20, and it is definitely the preferred route if you're up to it.

The path for the alpine route turns off at 90° to the normal path and tackles the mountainside directly. The climb is very

Climbing in Bavella

The Bavella massif is popular not only with walkers but also both novice and expert climbers. Coming along the GR20 from the Refuge d'Asinao, just before you get to the Col de Bavella you'll see the training surfaces, which are signposted on the slopes themselves. These slopes, ranging in height from 40 to 90m, are ideal for beginners. There are more technical climbs farther up in the massif, between Punta di l'Acellu and Punta di u Pargulu (accessible via the alpine route of the GR20). The level of difficulty ranges from 3 to 8a on the French climbing scale and there are a good number of slopes that are classified as 4 or 5, making them suitable for climbers of medium ability.

If you continue south-east, heading for the Refuge de Paliri along the GR20, you will see other possible climbs, especially on the Punta Tafunata di Paliri, which has a distinctive hole in its summit. The Refuge de Paliri nestles at the foot of this mountain, on the slopes of which is a *via ferrata* (see the boxed text 'Via Ferrata: Climbing with a Handle' in the Calvi & the Balagne chapter) consisting of some 70m of cables and about 20 bars, suitable for anyone who doesn't suffer from vertigo. You can get to it from the Refuge de Paliri (two hours there and back) zor make a day of it from the Col de Bavella.

If you would like to know more and you can make out French, consult Jean-Paul Quilici's *Petra di Luna*, which is Corsica's first mountain-climbing guidebook. Alternatively, contact a qualified guide, such as Quilici himself (☎ 04 95 78 64 33), Didier Micheli (☎ 04 95 25 54 24) or Jacques Andreani (☎ 04 95 70 51 93).

DOMINIQUE CORDONNIER

Needles, teeth or horns? The Bavella rock formations defy description.

The Mule Makes a Comeback

The PNRC regularly uses a helicopter to re-provision its refuges and also to remove trash and garbage, but this is expensive and noisy, so it is now contemplating switching over to old-fashioned, low-tech mules.

This option would allow the PNRC to get to higher altitudes and do a better job of sanitation. Walkers might profit from the introduction of mules in yet other ways. In some places it is already possible to hire a mule to carry camping equipment, and an enlarged herd might help people if they wanted to take their children along.

For more information contact the Fédération Nationale Ânes et Randonnées (☎ 04 95 61 80 88, ⓔ balagnan@mygale.org).

steep and snakes its way between silver birches and pines, which thin out as the altitude increases and as you go farther south-west.

You get about 10 minutes' relief here, then the path leaves the woods and continues its climb towards the **Col de Pargulu** (1662m); it's about an hour's work to get there. Towards the end, the knife-edge rock faces really begin to take a toll. But when you get to the top and see the panoramic views, you'll feel duly rewarded: opposite you are mountains stretching out in parallel to the range you are on; between the two ranges is a valley, the pass and the village of Bavella; and to the east is the sea. Amid this jagged landscape you can make out peaks that look like huge sharp teeth – these are the Aiguilles de Bavella (Bavella Needles; see The South chapter later in the book).

From here the path descends steeply through a stony gully for about 30 minutes until reaching the famous chain across a smooth, steep slab, about 10m in width. After another half-hour's tricky progress along rocky slopes you reach a pass, where you have a wonderful view of the Aiguilles and the village of Bavella, close by to the east. The path to the village plunges through a deep gully of pink granite.

From here, you'll see the rocks used to teach rock climbing (see the boxed text 'Climbing in Bavella' on the previous page). The markings along this difficult descent are sometimes less than adequate, however. Roughly four hours after you set out, the path rejoins the normal route of the GR20. It's then only a 10-minute stroll through a pine forest to the Col de Bavella car park.

Go past the Madone des Neiges (a statue of the Virgin Mary) and take the tarmac road (one of the few concessions to civilisation on the GR20) to the left for about 300m. This leads into the village of **Bavella** (see the end of this section) where it may be worth stopping off, as the Refuge de Paliri does not provide refreshments. Some walkers, moreover, choose to leave the GR20 at this point. But, if you've come all the way from Calenzana, you should stick it out if you have the time; the last part of the walk is particularly lovely.

The Col de Bavella marks a real change in the character of the GR20. The green, wooded setting is in distinct contrast to the barren ruins of the Aiguilles de Bavella and the route along the ridges.

If, at the Col de Bavella, you wish to continue directly on to the Refuge de Paliri, allow another 2¼ hours. The only difficult section will be around the Col de Foce Finosa.

When you reach the Auberge du Col de Bavella (see under Bavella later in this section), take the turning off to the right, which changes into a forest track some 50m farther on. This bit is level, pleasant and easy, and the pine trees and silver birch keep you company for a good 15 minutes. The path then narrows before forking to the left and descending to a small stream. About 10 minutes later you come to another forest track – follow it to the right for 50m. Turn left at the fork and cross the **Volpajola** stream on the small masonry bridge.

Opposite you to the east is a long range of mountains, which you will cross via the Col de Foce Finosa. Five minutes beyond the stream, the path forks to the right to begin the ascent. It takes a good 45 minutes to cover the 200m altitude change to the **Col de**

Foce Finosa (1214m). But once you reach the pass there are views towards the sea in the south-east and the Aiguilles de Bavella the other way.

The last section of the route is the one-hour walk to the refuge down the eastern face of the range. The descent starts off sharply, before turning towards the north-east and becoming gentler as it follows the contour line. A small rise just before you reach the Refuge de Paliri (1055m) marks the end of this long stage of more than six hours.

Places to Stay & Eat

Given that it was constructed out of the stones and on the site of a former bergerie, the little 20-bed ***Refuge de Paliri*** actually has some personality. It is also in a magnificent setting. The surroundings include the Punta Tafunata di Paliri, the Anima Damnata, the Punta di Paliri and a strip of green land to the south-east. You can also make out the towering peaks of the mountain range to the south-west, and on a clear day you can see all the way to Sardinia.

A bed costs 55FF (camping 20FF). There are toilets and a kitchenette but this refuge does not sell any food, and the showers are cold.

Quenza (813m)

The village of Quenza is no farther than a four-hour walk from the GR20, with a descent of roughly 500m. The access route, marked in yellow, may be long, but it is also easy; two-thirds of the path is forest track. Quenza lies square on the Mare a Mare Sud trail. The tourist resources are first class and the village itself, at the heart of a region with its own unique character, is a real gem.

The village has an excellent reputation as a base for leisure pursuits such as walking, horse riding and canyoning.

Corse Odysée *(☎ 04 95 78 64 05, fax 04 95 78 61 91)*, to the north of the village, operates between the end of May and the end of September as a gîte d'étape with rates of 190FF per person for the obligatory half-board; campers pay 20FF per person and 5FF per tent. Dinner alone costs 100FF, a packed lunch costs 45FF. The establishment also provides qualified guides for day-long walks (200FF), canyoning (350FF per person) and canoeing (350FF).

If you prefer more luxurious accommodation, head for ***Hôtel Sole e Monte*** *(☎ 04 95 78 62 53, fax 04 95 78 63 88, e sole.e.monti@wanadoo.fr)*, at the eastern end of the village, on the main road from Porto Vecchio and Zonza (D420). In high season, a double room costs 400FF to 450FF per person (half-board obligatory). Alone, you'll pay a 200FF supplement. It has a good restaurant where you can choose between a variety of *menus* (from 150FF) and an extensive game-oriented a la carte menu.

Chez Pierrot, in the isolated hamlet of Jallicu about 5km north-west of Quenza, is an unusual, horsey sort of establishment in an interesting setting. The rooms, functional and clean, sleep four, six or eight persons

The Return of the Corsican Red Deer

The Corsican red deer *(Cervus elaphus corsicanus)* first came to the island in ancient times and quickly found its way around – several place names, including Cervioni and Punta di u Cervu, bear witness to this. However, under pressure of poaching, the deer disappeared from the island in the 1960s.

In 1985 the PNRC went to neighbouring Sardinia, where the species still lives in the wild, collected two stags and two does and brought them back to a protected enclosure in Quenza. The animals reproduced, and there are now more than 100 of them on Corsican soil, residing in three enclosures.

On 3 February 1998, a first contingent was released into the wilderness, and since then several fawns have been born. The organisers of the project are optimistic about their survival. However, poaching plainly remains a threat to the fully grown animals, and the fawns are vulnerable to wild boars, foxes and even stray dogs.

for a rate of 195FF per person (20FF extra for sheets) at half-board. An evening meal of good country dishes, without the bed, will cost 150FF. Pierrot is a horse breeder and horse riding costs 120FF an hour. Half- and full-day outings can be arranged.

The village has two ***groceries*** where you can stock up, as well as a post office and two telephone boxes. In the tourist season, Autocars Balesi buses stop once daily, except Sunday, in each direction, on their Ajaccio to Porto Vecchio line.

Bavella (1218m)

Near the Madone des Neiges, ***Les Aiguilles de Bavella*** *(☎ 04 95 57 46 06)* charges 70FF for a bed in a room for four (half-board 180FF), or 210FF for a double room and 90FF for an extra bed. There is also a kitchen corner if you want to prepare your own meals. The restaurant provides Corsican meals for 65FF, including *raviolis au brocciu* and home-made charcuterie. Corsican soup costs 35FF. It opens 1 April to 15 October.

About 300m closer in towards the village, on a hairpin bend, is the ***Auberge du Col de Bavella*** *(☎ 04 95 57 43 87)*, which has an excellent reputation, especially for its food. You can choose between three Corsican *menus* (69FF, 99FF and 130FF) or an extensive a la carte menu featuring mixed salads, home-made specialities such as Corsican ham-bone soup (50FF), or a wonderful chestnut tart (40FF). A bed in a six-person dormitory costs 80FF and half-board costs 180FF. This gîte opens April to October. Credit cards are welcome.

Le Refuge *(☎ 04 95 57 40 26)*, next door, another refuge-restaurant-bar, rents rooms for up for four persons for 150FF. The restaurant does pizza (40FF to 55FF), sandwiches (25FF) and omelettes (35FF); *menus* cost 65FF or 120FF. It opens May to September.

Opposite the Auberge du Col de Bavella, there's a ***grocery***, but it's not particularly well stocked.

In high season, an Autocars Balesi bus stops once daily, except Sunday, on its route between Ajaccio and Porto Vecchio.

STAGE 15

Refuge de Paliri (1055m) to Conca (252m)

Distance: 12km
Standard: Average
Average Duration: Five hours
Highest Point: 1055m

Summary: The final stage is sometimes left out, but this is unfortunate, because it's spectacular, and in addition contrasts sharply to the previous day's trajectory. Once the trail quits the southern section of the Bavella massif, it returns at long last to the intoxicatingly fragrant maquis, which, after all the barren rocks along the previous days' hikes, you may have forgotten. Towards the end of the stage, the sea figures increasingly on the horizon.

From the refuge the path descends briefly before coming to the heart of a superb forest of maritime pines and silver birch. On the left is the imposing spectre of the **Anima Damnata** (Damned Soul) at 1091m, with its distinctive sugar-loaf shape that becomes all the clearer when you emerge from the forest. After a short walk along a ledge, you can easily make out the Monte Bracciutu massif to the east and Monte Sordu about 25 minutes off to the south-east. The path then follows a ridge that curves north-east around a cirque, in the middle of which are the peaks of the **Massif du Bracciutu**.

To the north-east you can see the hole that rather resembles a bull's-eye in the Punta Tafunata di Paliri, the line of mountains that extends from the north-east to the south-west, with the Refuge de Paliri at its feet. The vegetation is now maquis rather than shrubs. Follow the unshaded ledge for about 30 minutes until you reach the **Foce di u Bracciu** (917m). At this point the trail turns to head due south.

The vegetation here is made up of arbutuses, rock rose, lavender and heather. The trail follows the contour line for about 10 minutes before tackling the ascent of the **Col de Sordu** (1065m). It takes 30 minutes of difficult climbing to reach the pass, with its distinctive masses of fallen rock. The view from here stretches as far as the sea.

Just after the pass you climb down across a vast granite slab covering about 50m; it's relatively steep and, in the wet, it could easily turn into a natural slide. This leads to a sandy path that slices through a pine forest. Five to 10 minutes later it emerges at a little plateau dotted with granite domes and strangely shaped rock piles. The setting now consists of maquis, a few maritime pines and the trunks of trees destroyed by forest fires. After about 15 minutes in this environment the path starts to descend. The relief becomes gentler; the mountainous part of the day's walk draws to an end. The **Bergeries de Capellu** (850m), in ruins, are still about 2½ hours ahead of you. A spring – signposted – is about 300m off to the left of the main path. It's a good place to stop for a picnic.

About 15 minutes on from here, you come to a little shelf from which you can admire the distinctive sugar-loaf shape of the Punta Balardia to the north-east.

The main trail continues steadily down towards the **Punta Pinzuta** stream, which you'll hear before you see it, as it's hidden by rows of pine trees that have somehow escaped the general devastation. Scorched trunks everywhere else bear witness to the violent forest fires that have passed through here. The atmosphere is ghostly.

The trail eventually fords the stream, then follows the course of the stream for a while before crossing back at a large bend. A little 20-minute climb then takes you out of this steep-sided valley and up to a pass. The path continues along the mountainside, almost on the level, and for about another 45 minutes describes long curves on a ledge through the maquis. At last you come to the **Col d'Usciolu** (587m), a narrow U-shaped passage through a wall of granite. From the other side of the pass you can clearly see **Conca** (252m), the end of the whole GR20, in the valley below. To the south there's a pretty little cove.

The 20- to 30-minute descent into the village passes through thick undergrowth, emerging at a tarmac road. Turn left, follow the road to a crossroads and then take the road leading down. You will soon be able to see the main road. For information about the end of the route, see the section on Conca in The South chapter.

The Mare e Monti & Mare a Mare

The Mare e Monti and Mare a Mare routes are five PNRC paths – Sea and Mountain and Sea to Sea – that transect or cut into the island both north and south. Less publicised than the GR20, they are also not as mountainous or as long, which makes them more accessible. They can serve as a good test, or a training ground, for those who might want to try their luck with the GR20 at some later date. They also offer more comfort than the GR20 in that walkers will find numerous gîtes, hotels and places to eat along or near the trails. This means there are more options to split the walks up. The routes are also less crowded than the GR20.

The differences between these walks and the GR20 translate into a different kind of tourism too. The GR20 runs across the high mountains, and passes through only two villages. By contrast, the Mare e Monti and Mare a Mare walks pass through some of the island's prettiest villages. The various stages of these walks are designed to start you in one village and deliver you to another, providing you with an excellent opportunity to explore not only the island's natural landscape but also its human side.

This section gives a detailed description of the Mare a Mare Centre walk and general descriptions of each of the others, along with details of the villages through which they pass. More information on some of the villages can be found in the regional chapters, together with descriptions of places to stay and eat.

Accommodation & Supplies

There are fewer logistical problems on the Mare e Monti and Mare a Mare walks than on the GR20. There is a gîte at the end of

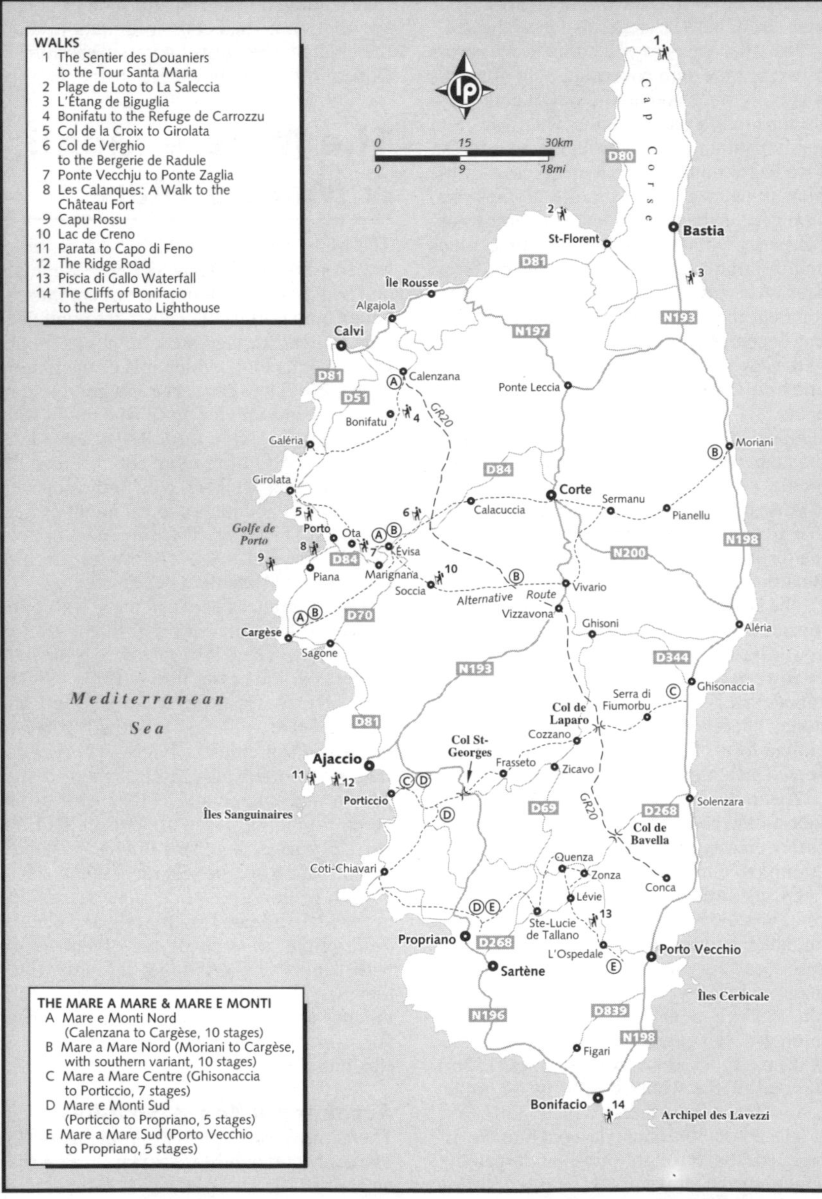
THE MARE E MONTI & MARE A MARE ROUTES & OTHER WALKS
WALKS
1 The Sentier des Douaniers to the Tour Santa Maria
2 Plage de Loto to La Saleccia
3 L'Étang de Biguglia
4 Bonifatu to the Refuge de Carrozzu
5 Col de la Croix to Girolata
6 Col de Verghio to the Bergerie de Radule
7 Ponte Vecchju to Ponte Zaglia
8 Les Calanques: A Walk to the Château Fort
9 Capu Rossu
10 Lac de Creno
11 Parata to Capo di Feno
12 The Ridge Road
13 Piscia di Gallo Waterfall
14 The Cliffs of Bonifacio to the Pertusato Lighthouse
THE MARE A MARE & MARE E MONTI
A Mare e Monti Nord (Calenzana to Cargèse, 10 stages)
B Mare a Mare Nord (Moriani to Cargèse, with southern variant, 10 stages)
C Mare a Mare Centre (Ghisonaccia to Porticcio, 7 stages)
D Mare e Monti Sud (Porticcio to Propriano, 5 stages)
E Mare a Mare Sud (Porto Vecchio to Propriano, 5 stages)
0 15 30km
0 9 18mi
Cap Corse
Bastia
St-Florent
Île Rousse
Algajola
Calvi
Calenzana
Ponte Leccia
Bonifatu
GR20
Galéria
Girolata
Moriani
Corte
Calacuccia
Sermanu
Pianellu
Golfe de Porto
Porto
Ota
Évisa
Piana
Marignana
Soccia
Alternative Route
Vivario
Vizzavona
Ghisoni
Aléria
Cargèse
Sagone
Mediterranean Sea
Ghisonaccia
Serra di Fiumorbu
Col de Laparo
Cozzano
Col St-Georges
Frasseto
Zicavo
Ajaccio
Porticcio
Îles Sanguinaires
Solenzara
Col de Bavella
Quenza
Zonza
Conca
Coti-Chiavari
Lévie
Ste-Lucie de Tallano
Propriano
L'Ospedale
Porto Vecchio
Sartène
Îles Cerbicale
Figari
Bonifacio
Archipel des Lavezzi
D80
D81
N193
N197
D51
D84
N198
N200
D70
D344
D69
D268
N196
D839

each stage, and it is generally better run and more comfortable than a normal refuge. The gîtes are generally divided into small dormitories (four to 10 people), and offer hot showers and blankets and sometimes sheets. The atmosphere and quality of the services is very much dependent on the wardens, often a local family. Some invest a great deal in upkeep and have earned a good reputation, especially for their food.

You can choose between accommodation only (about 65FF), half-board (sometimes obligatory, about 170FF), *table d'hôte* (traditional meal; about 100FF) and packed lunch, and even camping in some cases. A few provide kitchen facilities. Opening times vary from one gîte to another and many close in low season (from November to April). It is worth telephoning in advance. In high season you will have to make a reservation. You can pay by cash or travellers cheque.

Some of the villages you pass through will even have hotels. And there's also no chance that you will go short of food: in addition to the food at the gîtes there are groceries, self-service shops and even restaurants. Many of the villages have post offices. Be forewarned, though: opening times can be eccentric.

Maps & Signs

The routes are marked out in orange (a painted line on tree trunks or rocks), though on some stretches the visibility and frequency of the markings leaves something to be desired. Be suspicious, accordingly, if you have seen no markings for more than 100m. Always retrace your steps and find the last marking.

The Didier Richard maps of *Corse du Nord* and *Corse du Sud* at a scale of 1:50,000 and the IGN maps at 1:25,000 (Top 25, blue series) are clear, and useful to the point of being indispensable.

The Mare e Monti Routes

As the Corsican name suggests, these are paths between the sea and the mountains.

Mare e Monti Nord This is a superb (and not especially difficult) walk which links Calenzana in the Haute Balagne region to Cargèse, south of the Golfe de Porto. It is divided into 10 stages of four to seven hours each, and its highest point is 1153m. It passes through several exceptional natural sites, such as the Forêt de Bonifatu, the Réserve Naturelle de Scandola and the Gorges de Spelunca, and it also passes through several charming villages, including Galéria, Ota and Évisa. There are gîtes in Calenzana, Bonifatu, Tuarelli (☎ 04 95 62 01 75), Galéria (☎ 04 95 62 00 46), Girolata, Curzu (☎ 04 95 27 31 10), Serriera (☎ 04 95 26 10 67), Ota, Évisa, Marignana, Revinda-E Case (☎ 06 08 16 94 90) and Cargèse. Names, addresses and phone numbers for yet more lodgings in some of the larger of these villages will be found in the regional chapters.

The Mare e Monti Nord is passable year round, but the periods before and after the main season (May to June and September to October) are preferable so as to avoid the worst of the heat. The path crosses the Mare a Mare Nord at Évisa and Marignana.

Mare e Monti Sud This path runs between the bays of two well-known seaside resorts in the south-west of Corsica – Porticcio and Propriano. It's divided into five stages of five to six hours and ascends to a maximum height of 870m. There are stops in Bisinao, Coti-Chiavari (which towers above the two bays), Porto Pollo and Olmeto. The walk ends in Burgo (7km north of Propriano).

There are only two gîtes on the route: in Bisinao (☎ 04 95 24 21 66) and Burgo (☎ 04 95 76 15 05). In the other villages you can either stay in a hotel or at a camp site, or try the ***Ferme Équestre de Baracci*** *(☎ 04 95 76 19 48)*.

The route is characterised by its views over the bays, Genoese towers and the beaches at Cupabia and Porto Pollo. Like its northern counterpart, this path is not very difficult and passable year round, though at its best in spring and autumn. The path meets the Mare a Mare Sud in Burgo.

The Mare a Mare Routes

There are three Mare a Mare (sea to sea) paths, which link the island's western and eastern coasts via the central mountains.

Mare a Mare Nord From Moriani, south of Bastia, on the eastern coast, to Cargèse in the west, this path traverses strikingly contrasting regions in 10 stages of from four to six hours each. The maximum altitude is approximately 1600m. For the final section of the walk, between Évisa and Cargèse, the route merges with that of the Mare e Monti Nord.

You will see something of Corte (fourth day), the Bozio (a remote area famous for its chapels and frescos) and the Tavignano before climbing to the Col de Verghio (where the path crosses the GR20). After this the path passes through forests and continues to Évisa and Cargèse. There are gîtes in Pianellu (☎ 04 95 39 60 74), Sermanu (☎ 04 95 48 67 97), Corte, Calacuccia, Albertacce, Casamaccioli (☎ 04 95 48 03 47) and then, after the merger with the Mare e Monti Nord, in Évisa, Marignana, Revinda-E Case and Cargèse, as already mentioned.

On the fourth day, you can take an alternative route. From Sermanu, follow the trail south to Vivario via Poggio di Venaco, then turn west and find your way through L'Onda, Pastricciola, Guagno, Guagno les Bains (the Guagno region is famous for its thermal waters) and Renno. You will join the Mare e Monti Nord route at Marignana.

Because of the altitudes along this route, some portions may be snow-covered in the months from November to April. Take care.

Mare a Mare Centre This route is described in detail in the next section.

Mare a Mare Sud This is a famous, easy walk linking Porto Vecchio in the south-east to Propriano in the south-west. It is passable year round, and is divided into five stages whose average walking time is five hours. Maximum altitude is 1171m. A stone's throw from the Aiguilles de Bavella and Monte Incudine, it crosses through the magnificent region of Alta Rocca and many of the island's most beautiful villages. You stop in Cartalavonu, Lévie, Serra di Scopamena and Ste-Lucie de Tallano and pass through the wonderful village of Quenza. There is an alternative route via Zonza (for this allow one extra day).

The Mare a Mare Centre

The Mare a Mare Centre merits a detailed description because, though it is not the best known or most popular of the routes, it's neither too easy nor too difficult. Moreover, between its starting point in Ghisonaccia and end in Porticcio, it runs through the little-known districts of Fiumorbu and Taravo, with their charming villages, and then the hinterland of Ajaccio. Landscape is spectacular and flora is rich and abundant.

The Mare a Mare Centre breaks down into seven stages of three to seven hours each. Many sections are in the shade. The route reaches an altitude of 1525m at the Col de Laparo, meaning that it is passable mainly between April and November.

STAGE 1

Ghisonaccia to Serra di Fiumorbu (460m)

Markings: Yellow
Standard: Average; long climb near the end
Average Duration: 2¾ to 3¼ hours
Highest Point: 460m

Access: Rapides Bleus buses (☎ 04 95 70 10 36) from Bastia and Porto Vecchio, twice daily except Sunday

Summary: This stage takes you away from the sea and into the foothills of the interior. The route is divided into two parts: the first is a stroll across flat farmland; the second is a straightforward climb up to Serra di Fiumorbu.

The starting point for the Mare a Mare Centre is on the N198, 4.5km south of Ghisonaccia and 1km south of the hamlet of Casamozza, just beyond the bridge over the **Abatescu** and to the right. The start of the walk is marked with a PNRC sign indicating that it is three hours to Serra di Fiumorbu, seven hours to Catastaju (the second stage) and 11 hours to the Col de Laparo.

The first, flat part of the walk follows a little tarmac road that heads due east towards the foothills of the mountains. It passes through fields of farmed chestnut trees, a reminder that the Fiumorbu is a rich and fertile agricultural region. After less than 30 minutes, you'll approach the village of **Asprivu**. Watch carefully here, because the markings are somewhat confusing. As you enter the hamlet, you'll see a fork with a pebbly path to the right Do not take this path, but continue along the tarmac road for another 100m and then take the path off to the right, towards the farm shed. The yellow marking is on the electricity pylon (if you are facing the pylon, take the path to the left).

The trail now goes through a countryside of cultivated hedgerows and shrub vegetation. After 20 minutes, it reaches the **River Fiumorbu** and follows the course of the water for about 100m along first a narrow ledge, then a wider track. Gradually, the fields give way to trees, notably oak, and maquis; it begins to feel something of a wilderness.

The next village is **Suartellu**. Go past the little house called Le Palmier, follow the tarmac road for about 800m until you reach a crossroads, cross the road and follow the sign to the left. This tells you that you are one hour from Serra di Fiumorbu. In fact, it is more like 1½ hours.

After this, you're in for your first challenge. About 200m after the first bend, you leave the road for a little path (signposted) that dives into the vegetation. The climb that follows is of the take-no-prisoners variety so start with a deep breath. After 45 minutes you'll reach a tarmac road; turn left here and follow the road for about 20m before rejoining the path up the mountainside to the left; although there are orange markings they are not easy to spot.

After another (25-minute) climb you meet the tarmac road again. This time, follow it to the right towards the village of **Serra di Fiumorbu**, which you will see nestling on the mountainside at an altitude of 457m. As you come into the village you have a wonderful view over the whole of the plain.

Some walkers, because they deem this stage to be of limited interest, simply skip it. They start from Serra di Fiumorbu. Others continue on past Serra di Fiumorbu and spend their first night at Catastaju.

Serra di Fiumorbu

The ***gîte d'étape*** *(☎ 04 95 56 75 48, 06 81 04 69 49)*, a granite building on the left at the edge of the village, is run by a Mme Guidicelli and sleeps 25 in several dormitories for 60FF per person or 150FF for half-board.

A ***cafe-grocery***, at the centre of the village, opens according to the owner's whim in July and August. Consequently, don't count on it for your supplies. You'll be better off asking Mme Guidicelli to make you a packed lunch for the following day. There's a telephone box opposite the cafe.

STAGE 2

Serra di Fiumorbu (460m) to Catastaju (523m)

Markings: Orange
Standard: Easy; no shade on the first part of the route
Average Duration: 4½ to five hours
Highest Point: 957m

Summary: This route alternates between ridges, maquis and pine forests and takes you into the heart of the mountains. It starts with a long flat walk along a ridge, continues by way of several fairly steep climbs, and finishes with a shady descent towards the hamlet of Catastaju, in a steep-sided valley.

About 500m out of Serra di Fiumorbu there's a sign for, among other places, Col de Juva. Follow this trail up to the right. The route follows along a broad ridge, oriented to the south-west, that rises in a measured way and at the same time offers magnificent views over a mountain range and the vast depression of Fiumorbu to the west. The vegetation is largely maquis, with rock rose, bellium, purple foxglove and bracken. There is little or no shade. The villages nestling at the bottom of the valley could almost have been rendered by an impressionist.

The ridge continues to rise, although it barely feels as if you are climbing. The path continues in the open, but there are several tracks where you could go wrong and the markings are less than useful when you need them most. First, you come to a fork with three paths: take the left one. Then you come to another junction: this time take the right-hand option, which follows a steep path up the slope (there are markings on a rock).

After about 1¾ hours the trail reaches a pass, from which there's a stunning view over another valley, and then continues along the ridge for about 200m to a crossroads. To the left is a sign for Bovile and Ventiseri and straight ahead is Col de Juva, two hours away. The climb gets steeper now and the path leads through thick undergrowth. Then you come to another little valley and the landscape changes. It's not so barren now; there are pine trees and bracken.

The climb continues for about 10 minutes until you reach a patch of dense undergrowth, where once again you're in danger of losing track of the markings and of the trail itself.

The path curves to the left and then climbs steeply again for another 10 minutes until it reaches a peak; you're now roughly 2¾ hours into the walk. The trail then begins to descend through spectacular scenery, surrounded by mountains. You go through a pine forest, then reach the crossroads at the **Col de Juva** (866m), where there's a sign to Ania and Catastaju to the right. From here the descent through the pines is gentle and steep by turns.

Just over one hour after the Col de Juva (3¾ hours into the walk) the trail crosses a stream, then climbs for 50m before reaching another crossroads. Don't go straight ahead towards Ania (the orange signpost is more than a little confusing here); instead, turn left and aim for Catastaju.

Presently you'll come to another signpost, and this time you'll turn right for Catastaju. You'll know you're almost there when you begin to hear the sound of the River Abatescu. You'll then climb down the slope to meet it. The gîte is across the footbridge, on the right. A swim in the clear, refreshing waters of the Abatescu is a great way to relax from your day's efforts.

Catastaju

The ***gîte d'étape*** *(☎ 04 95 56 70 14/74 97)*, 3km upstream from the village of San Gavinu di Fiumorbu, overhangs the Abatescu, a stone's throw from the Mare a Mare trail. Formerly, it was a hydroelectric power station but, believe it or not, it has been comfortably renovated. It sleeps 27 in dormitories. Mme Paoli here will give you a warm welcome, and her generous meals of traditional Corsican dishes for 50FF to 100FF are unbeatable; they'll revive even the most exhausted of walkers. A night costs 60FF (70FF with sheets), half-board costs 180FF and a packed lunch goes for 50FF. Drinks (around 10FF) and light meals are also available. It opens year round. You can also camp next to the stream for 10FF.

If you wish to do just a section of the walk, with Catastaju as your starting or finishing point, you can, through the gîte, arrange for a car to take you from Ghisonaccia (150FF), Bastia-Poretta airport (300FF) or Cozzano (400FF).

There's a ***grocery*** in San Gavinu di Fiumorbu, as well as a telephone box.

STAGE 3

Catastaju (523m) via Col de Laparo (1525m) to Cozzano (727m)

Markings: Orange
Standard: Average; significant change in altitude (1000m) over the first section; markings sometimes confusing
Average Duration: Six to 6½ hours
Highest Point: 1525m

Summary: This long stage is varied and shady; the highlight is the crossing of the Col de Laparo, the highest point on the Mare a Mare walks. This pass forms a natural boundary between the regions of Fiumorbu and Taravo. Flora is varied on this part of the trail.

A schematic profile of the stage would resemble an upside-down 'V' shape: first there's a steady ascent towards the pass, then a long descent into the Cozzano valley.

From the gîte, follow the tarmac road uphill for 300 to 400m, then turn right towards Col de Laparo. Say goodbye to the tarmac and prepare for a gradual but uncompromising ascent to the pass.

The first 30 minutes is uneventful. The climb is slow and regular and follows the Macini stream towards its source. Don't let your attention lapse, though, because you don't want to miss the hairpin fork on the right, at about the same level at which the stream spills over a waterfall. Pay attention to the markings on the ground.

After 45 minutes the trail comes to a ledge from which the whole of the Macini valley is visible. This leads, after another 30 minutes, to a crossroads: the path to the right goes to San Gavinu di Fiumorbu; you want to follow the sign to Col de Laparo, straight ahead. A few minutes later the trail fords a stream, which it then follows uphill along a ridge. A 10-minute climb follows and you cross back over a stream, using large rocks as stepping stones. At this point the markings are barely visible, but there are little cairns and orange markings on the trees on the other side.

From here the path tacks back and forth through the pine forest, among large rocks and roots. As you progress you'll notice the pines gradually give way to beech trees. After a while you come to a point at which your apparent direction is blocked by branches on the ground and you have to turn left. The marking, on a little stone, is not visible at first glance.

After about two hours of walking the trail comes to a pass in the form of a little clearing, where you will see the ruins of the **Bergeries de la Scanciatella**. The views are great here, and you won't find a better spot for a picnic. If you face the valley with the beech forest behind you, you'll find the continuation of the path to the right.

A little higher up there is another little bergerie, which has been renovated. About 50m after this the trail enters the beech forest again and follows the contour line. After 15 minutes you cross a little stream. Continue walking through the beech forest until you come to a small cairn indicating that you need to turn left. There is an orange line painted on a tree trunk, but the marking is not particularly easy to spot.

The trail arrives at the **Refuge de Laparo** 3¼ hours after you set off. It's a permanent building with no warden, but you can sleep here, on a basic sort of mattress, for 20FF. There's a gas stove and a water pipe below if you want to quench your thirst.

To continue, turn left just before the refuge. The trail follows the face of the mountain, then takes a 90° turn uphill. A 15-minute climb leads to a clearing where the signs are a little confusing. Follow the yellow marking on the rock uphill.

Note that the route via the Refuge de Laparo is optional. It will add no more than 10 minutes to the day's walk, but it can be cut out, if you head directly for the Col de Laparo at the junction where you can just make out the word 'Laparo' on a stone (the word 'refuge' is on a sign that has come away from a tree).

After the clearing, climb for 15 minutes to reach the **Col de Laparo** (1525m), where the path intersects the north–south GR20 at a right angle. There are views over the region of Taravo to the west, where you will be headed. You're now 3½ to four hours from Catastaju.

DOMINIQUE CORDONNIER

From the Col de Laparo, the trail descends for about 20 minutes before entering a splendid forest of laricio pine and leading to a forest track. Turn left and before long you will pass a rapidly flowing stream. A natural spring awaits you on the edge of the path about 200m farther on. Follow the path, which becomes much wider, until you see a sign for Cozzano pointing towards a little path that seems to disappear into the forest.

Half an hour later the trail joins a newly built forest road, which it follows for about 300m, before turning off to the left on a bend and following the course of a dry river bed. You now see the first chestnut trees. The path keeps crossing the forest road, so keep looking out for the orange markings.

After about 30 minutes of this criss-crossing, you come first to a wooden gate and then, a few metres on, to a broad stream, and finally to a tarmac road. Turn left and it'll take you into the centre of **Cozzano**. The Auberge A Filetta is on the right-hand side.

Cozzano

The ***Auberge A Filetta*** *(☎ 04 95 24 45 61, fax 04 95 24 47 05)*, at the edge of Cozzano on the road to Guitera les Bains, offers warm, comfortable, modern rooms for 180FF. In August it's often extremely busy, so it's worth making a reservation. There's a *menu* for 80FF or specials for 50FF; breakfast costs 25FF. Service is in the dining room or on the terrace. The auberge opens from the end of April to the beginning of October.

On the other side of Cozzano, towards Palneca (to the north), a large building houses the ***Gîte Rural Bella Vista*** *(☎ 04 95 24 41 59)*, with its six dormitories for six people each (65FF per person) and three double rooms (160FF per room). You can also camp in the garden for 30FF and there is a kitchen if you want to cook for yourself. If you don't feel like cooking, an evening meal here costs 75FF; breakfast 30FF. The Bella Vista indeed has a nice view overlooking Cozzano.

The Cozzano chemist (☎ 04 95 24 40 40) is the only one in the area, so, if you need anything, this is your chance. The shop is in the main square and opens 9 am to 12.30 pm and 3 to 7.30 pm daily except Sunday. The main square also contains a petrol station and a well-stocked grocery; these both open 9 am to noon and 3 to 7 pm Monday to Saturday and on Sunday morning.

The post office opens 9 to 10 am and 1.45 to 3.45 pm Monday to Friday and on Saturday morning. Two bars, the ***Central Bar*** and the ***Snack Bar Terminus***, welcome the thirsty, and a baker's van passes through the village daily except Monday at about 8 am.

Autocars Santini buses run between Cozzano and Ajaccio Monday to Saturday.

STAGE 4

Cozzano (727m) to Guitera les Bains (620m)

Markings: Orange
Standard: Average
Average Duration: Six hours
Highest Point: 955m

Note: Villages along the way offer services

Summary: Unfortunately, this rather long stage is probably the least well-marked on the entire route. On the other hand, it is dotted with little villages that offer a unique opportunity to see something of rural Corsican culture. It culminates in a long climb down to Guitera les Bains past a number of spectacular lookouts.

The trail leads off the vehicular road to Guitera les Bains at a chestnut tree 50m before the Auberge A Filetta. It's about 1½ hours from here to Sampolo, the first village. After going downhill for about 10 minutes, you come to the **Taravo**, the river that gives its name to the whole region. It is the same Taravo that provides the warm waters for the baths in Guitera les Bains, a few kilometres downstream.

Cross the bridge, follow the D28 for about 300m and you'll see a wooden sign pointing to Sampolo on the left. The trail leaves the road and, 100m later, starts up a steep, poorly maintained path that rapidly turns into a narrow gully lined with rocks.

This section of the Mare a Mare Centre is sometimes covered in thick vegetation. If the PNRC has not cleared it, you will have to look very carefully for the orange markings until you reach Sampolo. They are usually on tree trunks at about eye level. You go through a wooden gate and then navigate your way through a veritable labyrinth of little paths until you reach two pretty houses overhanging the valley.

The path turns to the left and, after a short descent, climbs steeply until it reaches a grave just before a house. Continuing, it joins the D28, which leads into **Sampolo** 200m downstream.

This pretty little village used to be frequented by shepherds moving their flocks to summer pastures but now has a winter population of only about 20. It's a real godsend for walkers: it has a ***grocery*** (the last one before Porticcio), open 9 am to noon and 4 to 7 pm. There's also a very nice bar-tobacconist, the ***Bar des Amis***, which has been welcoming locals and visitors alike since 1900. It opens daily. A map on one of the walls inventories all the former walking paths through the Haut Taravo region.

It will take less than 30 minutes to get to Giovicacce, the next village along the route. The trail goes through Sampolo and arrives at a fork, where it continues along the D28. It passes several little cemeteries, some of which are rather overgrown. The third cemetery is on a bend and here the path leaves the road and heads off to the left. It roughly follows the route of the stone wall before descending into a river bed.

When you get to a crossroads in the open, turn left and you will come to two little wooden bridges in a state of disrepair. Shortly afterwards the path turns right towards **Giovicacce**, where it rejoins the main road (at a telephone box). Follow this road for about 500m until you reach a bridge where a PNRC sign tells you that Tasso is half an hour away.

Here the path runs in and out of the undergrowth along a stream. You will notice black plastic pipes – these have long been used instead of traditional open channels to irrigate the terraces around villages. The sophisticated water distribution system in Corsica made it possible for the villages to grow vegetables and fruit trees in the 19th century, but this declined after WWI.

The trail crosses a tarmac road twice. The second time it does so, climb up to **Tasso** on the road rather than try to find the path, which is very badly marked.

Tasso is a good stop-off point for those who would prefer to split the fifth stage of the walk in two. The ***gîte d'étape*** *(☎ 04 95 24 52 01)*, run by the aptly named M and Mme Tasso, sleeps up to 22 in dormitories for four to six people. A whole floor of this large house is reserved for walkers, and there is a common room, a washing machine and a well-equipped kitchen. The rate is 70FF (half-board 180FF). It opens year round.

Auberge de Tasso *(☎ 04 95 24 50 54)*, also open year round, is a pleasant, modern building with a shady terrace and four smart double rooms for 250FF, including breakfast. Guests pay 100FF for dinner, non-guests 150FF.

It's a 2½ hour walk from Tasso to Guitera les Bains. The trail starts along a tarmac road about 50m from the gîte. It passes several little cemeteries before coming to a group of houses with a spring, which is an excellent source of refreshment. The road then begins to climb up the mountainside before the path branches off it to the left.

It takes nearly an hour to reach a large, flat, open area (955m) at which several paths cross. Take the path opposite you, which descends 350m within 30 minutes. Through the gaps there are some sublime views of Zicavo on the valley's opposite slope. In the background you will be able to make out the Col de Laparo and the ridges of the GR20. When you reach a tarmac road, turn left towards the centre of **Guitera les Bains**.

The gîte d'étape is at the bottom of the village, past a spring and a stone wash house. You can walk or hitch from Guitera les Bains to the **Bains de Guitera**, a small, natural warm-water pool 5km away.

Guitera les Bains

The ***gîte d'étape*** *(☎ 04 95 24 44 40)* is in an old stone house, and is run by Paul-Antoine Lanfranchi. A bed in a dormitory for four will cost you 70FF (half-board 180FF). The terrace is a lovely cool haven and the food is among the best in the region. Dinner costs 85FF to 120FF. Camping in the garden is permitted.

STAGE 5

Guitera les Bains (620m) to Quasquara (721m)

Markings: Orange
Standard: Easy
Average Duration: Three to four hours
Highest Point: 1048m

Summary: Most of this short, pleasant walk is shady. It passes through the village of Frasseto, where you can stop for a while before tackling the steep climb to Quasquara. This is an excellent way to stretch your legs in preparation for the longer walk tomorrow.

Climbing back up towards the centre of the village, you pass the Café l'Archia and the village hall, where you will want to note the period letter box. Carry on until you get to a sign for Frasseto, 3½ hours away. After a 30-minute climb up a rocky track, the trail rounds a hairpin bend, the first in a series of twists and turns. Don't miss the path: it turns off to the left into the forest.

The path comes to a large clearing and turns left, after which there is a fallen tree across the path. You will be able to see holly as the trail continues to wend its way through the undergrowth for another 20 minutes to the **Col de Lera** (1048m), the highest point of the day. Once you reach it, ignore the path to Tasso to the right and you will come to a sandy clearing where there's a sign for Frasseto, 1¾ hours away. The following descent is pleasant, regular and shady, and emerges at another large clearing where it heads towards Frasseto to the right.

The descent alongside a chestnut grove reveals a magnificent view of the crest of **Punta di Forca d'Olmu** (1646m), just 3km away as the crow flies. Heather and oak trees line the rest of the route, which leads to a tarmac road after less than 45 minutes. Turn left and you will soon be in **Frasseto**, a pretty hamlet, whose large stone houses indicate a more glamorous and glorious past.

Chez Jean et Pierrette *(☎ 04 95 25 79 60)* is a cafe-restaurant – the only business in Frasseto – whose charm lies equally in the simplicity of the location and the friendliness of its owners. It opens May to the end of October and serves as a meeting place for the villagers, who come here for lunch or for a pastis at the bar. For walkers it's an ideal place at which to stop for lunch or a break. The garden is pleasant and you can camp there (with permission). If you warn her in advance, Pierrette will also prepare you a meal to take with you.

From Frasseto, it will not take more than 30 minutes to get to **Quasquara**. Walk down Frasseto's main road to the Chiova stream, and be careful not to miss the little turn-off to the right, 300m after the bridge. The poorly maintained path starts to climb immediately. After about 15 minutes it gets to a cemetery and then begins to descend just past the first houses in the village.

Quasquara

The ***gîte d'étape*** *(☎ 04 95 53 61 21)* is a little farther on along the main road, just after the old communal oven. It opens year round and sleeps up to 33 people in dormitories. The setting is spacious and pleasant and there are the added bonuses of a well-equipped kitchen and bathrooms with bathtubs. A night's sleep goes for 95FF and half-board for 180FF. A *menu* is available

St-Georges Water

St-Georges water comes from a spring about 1km from the Col St-Georges at the endpoint of the sixth stage of the Mare a Mare Centre walk. The water was first bottled in 1980 by two private entrepreneurs, M Livrelli and M Colonna d'Ornano. Initially they were probably the only ones with any faith in the enterprise, and the early years were difficult. But now nearly nine million bottles a year are sold, chiefly in Corsica and to some extent on the mainland. The bottling facility employs 18 people. You can visit the premises if you telephone the Société des Eaux du Col St-Georges (SECG; ☎ 04 95 25 71 64) in advance. The bottle currently in use was designed by Philippe Starck.

for 85FF and a takeaway lunch sells for 30FF. Pierre et Valérie Yvars, your host and hostess, will greet you warmly. They'll also get you to Col St-Georges for 200FF or to Porticcio for 300FF by car. In addition, they rent apartments for four to eight travellers farther up in the village.

Opposite the town hall is the ***Association Socio-Culturelle de Quasquara***, known as 'le chalet' for reasons that are obvious on seeing the building. It serves drinks and has a television. A village pool opens to the public starting in July. There's also a little circuit of local walking paths marked with arrows.

STAGE 6

Quasquara (721m) to Col St-Georges (757m)

Markings: Orange
Standard: Average; little shade on the route
Average Duration: Five to six hours
Highest Point: 1150m

Summary: Early on, this stage scales the heights of the south-westerly mountain ridge, along which Punta d'Urghiavari stands out prominently, and it does not really leave the ridge for the rest of the day. At the Col St-Georges you come back to earth with a bump as you cross the very busy N196 leading to Ajaccio.

Make sure you fill up your flask before setting off because there is no water anywhere on this stage. You start by climbing up through the village – there are even steps for some of the way. Once you reach the last communal oven, follow the sign that says 'Col St-Georges six hours'. The stage now properly begins with a sustained climb of about 1½ hours in duration. If you look back, you will see the village of Bicchisano on the opposite slope.

When you reach a first open area, you can look with satisfaction at the distance you have covered from Frasseto, nestling below you. There is a magnificent view across the peaceful valley. The trail continues for another 30 minutes before reaching the highest point of the day, the **Col de Foce** (1150m), from where you have a view over both sides of the ridge.

The path follows the ridge for about 30 minutes, then descends to the level of the **Punta d'Urghiavari** and reaches a wooden gate. Here the path turns off immediately to the left and, a few hundred metres farther on, arrives at the **Col de Sant'Antone** (907m). You can clearly make out the sea and the runways at Ajaccio airport for the first time.

It will take nearly 45 minutes to zigzag through the maquis that crowns this pass. Then you're up against a tough 20-minute climb in the sun until you reach **Punta Maggiola** (1082m). With the views stretching out towards the village of Santa Maria Siché below you, Propriano to the south and the highest peaks on the island to the north, this is an ideal place at which to stop for a picnic.

After this the trail begins a long, 30-minute descent though oak trees. When you reach a dirt track, follow it for about 20m; the path then turns sharply to the right. Strangely, there are no trail markings for another 100m. Go through a metal gate and you'll get to a crossroads in a clearing. Take the left path, which will take you to the **Col St-Georges** (727m) in 30 minutes.

Col St-Georges

The spacious, brand-new ***gîte d'étape*** in Col St-Georges seems more like a four-star hotel than like the general run of walkers' refuges. It has five rooms of four bunk beds, a well-equipped kitchen, showers and a pretty, shady terrace – all for 75FF per person per night or 240FF at half-board.

The ***Auberge du Col St-Georges*** *(☎ 04 95 25 70 06; fax 04 95 53 61 47)* has seven modern and comfortable double rooms, which will set you back 300FF or 650FF for two at half-board. The restaurant is one of the best in the region, and very popular with the locals. The gastronomic *menu* costs 160FF. A la carte it'll cost at least 200FF (dishes include lamb chops, wild-boar stew or any number of other Corsican and Continental specialities). Cheapest are omelettes at 35FF. The auberge is on the road between Ajaccio and Bonifacio and it opens year round but closes on Monday in the low season.

STAGE 7

Col St-Georges (757m) to Porticcio

Markings: Orange
Standard: Easy
Average Duration: Five to six hours
Highest Point: 890m

Summary: This dazzling finale takes you from the heights of Col St-Georges to the beaches of Porticcio, a refreshing haven and a well-deserved reward for the week's hard work. On a clear day the spectacular views along the descent towards the sea add to the thrill of this final stage, which all too often walkers leave out.

This stage of the route begins a few metres beyond the auberge, on the right, and climbs through green oaks before turning left and starting a climb of no more than 10 minutes. The vegetation becomes more interesting, and is gradually replaced by superb fields of asphodel.

A sign to Porticcio marks the start of a flat road leading to a solid-looking house, a few metres beyond which the road splits. Here you want to take the right-hand fork, even if you cannot see any signs. After 300m there's a small path to the right (keep a look out because it's easy to miss) that follows a stone wall through oak trees.

You will come to an electricity pylon after which there's a short steep climb to a signposted turning for Bisinao. Ignore this and continue until you come to a second turning for Bisinao; at this fork the Mare a Mare Centre merges with the Mare e Monti Sud. There follows a descent of around 40 minutes, along the whole of which you will enjoy superb views over Ajaccio and the Tour de l'Isolella on the coast.

When you reach the D302, turn right and follow the road for nearly 2.5km as far as the sign for Buselica. Here the trail turns off to the left and joins a second tarmac road for 150m before leaving it again to head for the ruins of a tower.

The path goes steadily downhill, crossing a maze of junctions on its way, but the route is well marked so you won't get lost. The views of the sea are spectacular but all too fleeting. If you're tired out, you may find it ironic that the municipal cemetery in Porticcio marks the official end of the Mare a Mare Centre walk.

To get to the town centre, turn left onto the road that goes past the Pierre residence and Vacances Terra Bella. Go straight ahead at the first crossroads and continue until you come to a roundabout. Head in the direction of Porticcio and you will get to the sea in less than 10 minutes.

For details of places to stay and eat in Porticcio, see that section in The West Coast chapter.

Strolls & Country Walks

Walking in Corsica is by no means limited to the GR20 and the Mare a Mare and Mare e Monti walks. There's every bit as much, and perhaps more, for those who would prefer an easy walk of a single day, half a day or less.

The PNRC (see the boxed text earlier in this chapter) can provide brochures on easy 'country walks' it has designed around the villages of Alta Rocca, Bozio, Fiumorbu, Niolu, Taravo, Venachese and Giussani, in interior parts of the island that visitors don't often see. These walks, all round-trips, three to seven hours in length, are perfectly suited to casual walkers and even to families.

The additional 14 walks detailed in the Strolls & Country Walks section of this chapter also require no special experience, prowess or training. Unless otherwise specified, they, too, are all suitable for families. Their points of interest, meanwhile, are diverse: from waterfalls to Genoese forts.

SENTIER DES DOUANIERS TO TOUR SANTA MARIA

Access & Location: Plage de Tamarone, Macinaggio (Cap Corse)
Markings: Green logo and yellow paint
Standard: Easy; accessible to all; take protection against the sun in summer
Duration: Two hours there and back
Change in Altitude: Minimal

Summary: A walk along a protected stretch of coastline amid the fragrant maquis of Cap Corse to an exceptional Genoese tower.

To reach the Plage de Tamarone from Macinaggio, head for Camping U Stazzu on the northern edge of town. A not very good road continues for about 1km beyond the camp site to the beach. Turn north along the beach until you come to a junction at which you can either turn left to reach the inland path to the Chapelle Santa Maria or right for the Sentier des Douaniers (Customs Officers' Route). Take the second option; this will take you onto a path that is well marked out with wooden stakes with a green logo on them and yellow paint markings on the ground.

The path then enters the maquis in the protected area of Capandala, which belongs to the Conservatoire du Littoral, a coast conservation society (see Ecology & Environment in the Facts about Corsica chapter). The green of the maquis and the turquoise of the sea here are equally stunning. Continuing, you'll see a sign to the Chapelle Santa Maria, which is 45 minutes away.

Fifteen minutes later a Genoese tower on a little islet comes into view and the path begins to descend towards the area around the Îles Finocchiarola. These three tiny islands were classified as a nature reserve in 1987 and they are now an important animal sanctuary. Access to the islands is forbidden between 1 March and 31 October.

As the path then climbs up to the left, you will see Île de la Giraglia to the north and the superb Tour Santa Maria. The path now leads down towards the tower, passing the little Chapelle Santa Maria on the way. Standing as if it's been placed on the water, it is one of the most beautiful towers along the Corsican coastline.

If you continue past the tower you come to two secluded little coves with sandy beaches that are ideal for bathing; you can also continue walking from the Tour Santa Maria to Barcaggio, in the middle of the northern coast. From the Chapelle Santa Maria, you can return to your starting point along a wide inland path that is lined with vines.

PLAGE DU LOTO TO SALECCIA

Access & Location: In the Agriates; access is by boat from St-Florent
Markings: None
Standard: Easy
Duration: 1½ there and back
Change in Altitude: Imperceptible

Summary: A circular jaunt through the Agriates 'desert', sea and land side alike, between two exceptional beaches.

For information on reaching the Plage du Loto by boat, see the St-Florent section in the Bastia & the Far North chapter.

The broad track begins at the southern end of the beach with a short ascent, then makes its way into the fragrant maquis of the Désert des Agriates. After about 25 minutes, look out for a way through to the little wooded area on the right. This route leads to the northern end of the superb Plage de Saleccia, at the same time showing that the Agriates is not exactly the Sahara. Alternatively, stay on the main path, which leads directly to the edge of the camp site at the southern end of the beach. To return to your starting point, take the path along the seafront. It begins among the rocks at the extreme northern end of Plage de Saleccia and follows a stretch of beautiful little rocky inlets. There's a small wood, then a group of residences – you're back at your starting point.

ÉTANG ET RÉSERVE NATURELLE DE BIGUGLIA

Access & Location: A few kilometres south of Bastia on the Plage de la Marana; the path starts at the beach parking area behind the Réserve Naturelle sign
Markings: None, but there's no getting lost
Standard: Very easy
Duration: 30 minutes
Change in Altitude: None

Summary This short stroll along Corsica's largest inland body of water will particularly delight bird lovers.

It was the Conseil Général de Haute-Corse that commissioned this discovery path that cuts through the Étang et Réserve Naturelle de Biguglia, and the walk offers no worse challenges than humidity and mosquitoes. The 2km path, with water on one side and the road on the other, provides an opportunity to observe at least some of the 120 or more bird species that live or periodically pass through here. These include herons, egrets, coots, teals and many others. Half-way along the path there's an observation facility. For more information about the reserve itself, stop at the information booth (☎ 04 95 33 55 73) on the main road, about 6km beyond where the path starts. Guided visits are sometimes organised. A bicycle path runs the entire length of the Plage de la Marana.

BONIFATU TO THE REFUGE DE CARROZZU

Access & Location: 20km from Calvi on the N197 and D251 towards Calvi-Ste-Catherine airport, then farther along the D251 as far as the Auberge de Bonifatu
Markings: Yellow, then red and white
Standard: Average
Duration: Two hours there, 1½ hours back
Change in Altitude: 700m

Summary: A flirt with the GR20 against the scenic backdrop of the Cirque de Bonifatu.

Although this walk is not technically difficult it can still be challenging because so much of it is uphill. It is nevertheless an opportunity to discover the marvellous stone formations of the Cirque de Bonifatu. The trail joins the GR20 route and follows it as far as the Refuge de Carrozzu, near which there are natural pools where you can swim. You will need good walking shoes. For more information on the cirque see under Forêt & Cirque de Bonifatu in the Calvi & the Balagne chapter.

After you've reached the Auberge de Bonifatu (536m) by road, take the Sentier du Mouflon (Mouflon Path) at the far end of the car park. This very accessible broad forest track leads you in 20 minutes to a junction, from which you continue straight ahead towards the Refuge de Carrozzu (the path to the left crosses the river before climbing up to the Refuge d'Ortu di u Piobbu). Follow the yellow markings and begin the climb in the shade of the forest. After 15 minutes or so, you'll have views to the left of a striking rocky landscape. Half an hour more, and the trail crosses over the River Figarella, then continues to climb, with the splendid peaks of the cirque in the background. The trail crosses the river again, this time on a little suspension bridge, and continues as far as a little stone altar and a shelter, where it joins the GR20 with its red and white markings.

At this point, there is a sign pointing right to the Lac de la Muvrella and Asco, and left to the Refuge de Carrozzu, which is 100m away. These 100m offer the most spectacular view over the sharp peaks of the cirque, with their strange red and blue-green hues. In summer you can quench your thirst at the refuge.

If you're willing to invest a little more time, retrace your steps and take the turning to Asco and the Lac de la Muvrella and you will come to a suspended footbridge, under which the river forms pools where you can swim. The trail of a few hundred metres takes you across slabs of rock, but there are cables to help you avoid slipping. It is an impressive stretch and, provided you don't hot-dog it, you shouldn't have any trouble.

COL DE LA CROIX TO GIROLATA

Access & Location: At the Col de la Croix, 22km from Porto on the D81 heading for Galéria; SAIB buses (☎ 04 95 22 41 99) from Porto to Calvi provide service from mid-May to mid-October
Markings: Vague traces of white paint; reasonably marked path
Standard: Average
Duration: Three hours there and back
Change in Altitude: 250m

Summary: This walk leads to an idyllic hamlet and bay that cannot be reached by road.

The trail from the Col de la Croix (Bocca a Croce) sets off on a clear path down a gentle slope through dense maquis. After about 15 minutes you pass a pretty pebbled fountain. Fifteen minutes later you reach a fork; take the left path, which leads down to the Tuara cove. Theoretically, this cove should be idyllic but the charm can sometimes be spoiled when the tide carries in gravel and rubbish. Don't spend too much time here; instead walk round to the northern end of the beach. In the maquis, you'll make out a path to the left that follows the line of the coast and a second, to the right, that heads up the hill. Take the path to the right; there's a 20-minute climb to the junction with the Mare e Monti Nord (orange markings).

DOMINIQUE CORDONNIER

Girolata is only accessible on foot or by boat.

Once there, you have a stunning view over Girolata and the Baie de Girolata, havens of tranquillity guarded by a small Genoese fort. To the south-west is Capo Senino and on the other side, to the north-east, is Punta Muchillina (on the edge of the Réserve Naturelle de Scandola). Descending to Girolata from here takes about 30 minutes.

Girolata, unfortunately, tends to get overcrowded in summer, and the beach is disappointing. There are a few good restaurants on the seafront, though (see Girolata in The West Coast chapter). And you might have the pleasure of spotting Guy Ceccaldi, the postman, with his distinctive white beard, who goes from the hamlet to the Col de la Croix in double-quick time every day to deliver the post.

You can return by a slightly different route. Cross back over the beach in Girolata and follow the path you came on for about 20m. Then, instead of continuing up, take the path to the right, which follows a ledge around the coast as far as the Tuara cove.

COL DE VERGHIO TO THE BERGERIES DE RADULE

Access & Location: Col de Verghio, 12km beyond Évisa on the D84
Markings: Yellow
Standard: Easy; some pebbly sections; wear good walking shoes
Duration: 40 minutes (one way)
Change in Altitude: 100m

Summary: A lovely path through the forest and the mountains.

The path starts from behind the statue that by tradition marks the border between Haute-Corse and Corse-du-Sud, and it is marked out in yellow. This walk is a spectacular one, among mountain-tops and forests, and it is not very difficult. The Bergeries de Radule are on the GR20; make sure on your way back that you follow the yellow markings, and not the red and white route of the GR20.

The bergeries are a few little stone shepherds' huts and sheep pens clinging to the side of the mountain and it is very difficult to make them out against their barren background. A shepherd lives here during the summer months. A few minutes' walk from here, where a natural stone basin catches water flowing over some small falls, you might think you have stumbled on heaven on earth.

PONTE VECCHJU TO PONTE ZAGLIA

Access & Location: Via the D124; between Porto and Évisa, 2km beyond Ota
Markings: Orange
Standard: Very steep section at the end of the walk
Duration: One hour there and back; return along the same route
Change in Altitude: Minimal

Summary: A foray into the spectacular Gorges de Spelunca to discover a remarkably well-preserved Genoese bridge.

The path starts at the edge of the double bridge – on the left if you are coming from Ota. It's a former mule track which links the villages of Ota and Évisa through the Spelunca canyon and, for at least part of the way, along the Porto stream. This is actually a section of the Mare e Monti Nord between Calenzana and Cargèse. It passes two outstanding Genoese bridges. Ponte Vecchju is the first of these, and it is about 300m downstream from the start of the path and can be seen from the D124.

The rocky path now climbs rapidly up the left face of the valley, but green oaks provide a substantial amount of shade. After 30 minutes you come to Ponte Zaglia, the second magnificent Genoese bridge, which is located in the depths of the vegetation. You can refresh yourself in any number of pools close by the bridge.

It is worth noting that you can also start this walk in Ota (just past the Chez Felix restaurant), but it is not as interesting.

LES CALANQUES: A WALK TO THE CHÂTEAU FORT

Access & Location: Starts 3.5km from Piana in the direction of Porto
Markings: Blue; blue circles in a white rectangle
Standard: Easy; accessible to all
Duration: 20 to 30 minutes (one way)
Change in Altitude: Negligible

Summary: A short walk with beautiful views over the Golfe de Porto.

This short path leads off from the Tête de Chien (Dog's Head), which is a distinctively shaped rock signposted on a large bend in the D81, 3.5km from Piana on the way to Porto. If you happen to be coming from Porto, the reason for the rock's name will actually make some sense. The trail is roughly marked but you are unlikely to get lost because there are always lots of people around in the summer. Avoid wearing sandals because the path, although easy, is rocky.

Twenty to 30 minutes into the walk, you reach a natural platform known as the Château Fort (Fortress), from which the view over the Golfe de Porto and the deep rocky inlets of Les Calanques (see The West Coast chapter) is stunning. It's even better at sunset.

CAPU ROSSU

Access & Location: From Porto or Cargèse, take the D81 to Piana, then follow the D824 towards Plage d'Arone for about 5km; a snack bar at a turning marks the start of the walk
Markings: Obvious path; sections marked with cairns
Standard: Steep path at the end; no shade
Duration: 2½ to three hours there and back
Change in Altitude: 300m

Summary: One of the most beautiful walks in Corsica, culminating in breathtaking views.

From the road you can clearly make out the haughty silhouette of the Tour de Turghiu as it rises above Capu Rossu to the west. The pebbly path, lined initially with low stone walls, descends steadily through the maquis for 20 minutes to a point at which you will see a little bergerie to the left.

A bit farther on, there's a spectacular view to the left over the cove and the white sand of Plage d'Arone. The path skirts around to the south of the rocky escarpment on which the Tour de Turghiu stands before coming to a second bergerie. Note how the granite here takes on different shades of grey and pink. The path then turns right (northwards) to tackle the climb to the tower. Watch the small cairns that mark the tight bends up to the summit. Allow about 30 minutes. Though there's no shade whatsoever, the effort will seem worthwhile when you reach the Tour de Turghiu. At your feet, there's a 300m sheer drop of cliff to the sea beneath. The views of the Golfe de Porto and the Golfe de Sagone are fantastic. Bivouacking is permitted here.

LAC DE CRENO

Access & Location: About 35km north-east of Sagone; take the D70 as far as Vico, then the D23 to Soccia
Markings: Yellow (orange on the section from Soccia to Orto)
Standard: Easy
Duration: Two hours there and back
Change in Altitude: 300m

Summary: The walk takes you to a tranquil glacial lake perched at an altitude of 1310m in the heart of the forest.

Those with their own transport can drive to the car park on the far side of Soccia and pick up the path there; you'll be spared an uninteresting 3km walk from the village itself. There's a small cafe by the parking area, too.

From the car park, the path climbs the southern side of the valley, rising high above the river on the northern slopes of Monte Sant'Eliseo (1511m). Allow about an hour to walk from the car park to the pretty little lake, which covers 2.4 hectares and remains frozen for three or four months of the year. According to legend, the lake was the result of either a hammer blow from the devil or a kick from a horse. Science, predictably prosaic, traces the formation of the lake to the last ice age.

An alternative is to walk from Soccia itself, to the little village of Orto, close by, before continuing to the lake. This is an alternative route on the Mare a Mare Nord (orange markings), but is often overgrown and the markings are difficult to see. There's also a good deal of evidence of the pigs that dug out the path. The views of Orto, nestling in a very narrow, steep-sided valley, are wonderful, however. Just above Orto, a steep path marked in yellow climbs up to the ridge through a magnificent chestnut forest, then joins the path from the Soccia car park to the Lac de Creno.

PARATA TO CAPO DI FENO

Access & Location: D111 (Route des Sanguinaires) or No 5 bus (Frati stop)
Markings: None
Standard: Average; take water with you
Duration: 1½ hours (one way)
Change in Altitude: Negligible

Summary: This is a fairly easy walk along a shelf overlooking the sea, with wonderful views over the Îles Sanguinaires.

The walk starts from the foot of a small eucalyptus forest opposite La Parata motel, on the way into Parata.

When you get to a large eucalyptus tree in the very middle of the path, the route forks to the left and winds gently up the hill. The eucalyptus gradually give way to pines and then to maquis. The path meets a tarmac road and passes an upright stone slab before emerging onto a dirt track just above some tennis courts and opposite the Îles Sanguinaires. Take the dirt track to the right and continue northwards along the sea.

Less than an hour later the path reaches two large coves of crystal clear water at the foot of Capo di Feno. You'll find a couple of snack bars open in season.

THE RIDGE ROAD

Access & Location: About 15 minutes walk from the centre of Ajaccio, through the Bois des Anglais; continue along the cours Grandval and ave du Général Leclerc as far as the Grotte Napoléon, then skirt round to the right on ave Nicolas Piétri; alternatively, take bus No 7 (Empereur) to the Bois des Anglais stop
Markings: Practically non-existent
Standard: Average; passable year round, except (for risk of fire) when there are high winds in the summer; take water with you
Duration: Three to four hours one way (return by bus)
Change in Altitude: 300m

Summary: A stone's throw from Ajaccio, this walk allows you to explore the countryside to the north of the Golfe d'Ajaccio.

The walk starts just opposite the Bois des Anglais (English Woods) bus stop near Ajaccio. There's a sign reminding you of the basic safety rules and telling you that the path is marked out with blue arrows, not that these arrows are really visible anymore.

The dirt track quickly narrows in order to wind its way through an arid landscape of cactus and aloe. As the markings are almost non-existent and there are numerous crossroads, the easiest thing to do is keep on climbing until you reach a wide forest track; depending on how you go, this will take anywhere between 15 and 40 minutes.

The forest track you'll have found is known as the Chemin des Crêtes (Ridge Road); it looks down over the town of Ajaccio and the Golfe d'Ajaccio, and it even affords an interesting perspective on Monte d'Oro, which begins to take shape inland at the bottom of the Vallée du Gravone. Follow this path away from the town centre as it snakes through the maquis and eucalyptus bushes and alongside large, eroded rock formations. You'll have wonderful views all the way over a whole string of beaches and inlets. After you've walked for about two hours, you'll clearly make out the Îles Sanguinaires.

The path then descends for about 30 minutes to the sunny resort of Vignola and the Route des Sanguinaires (D111), which goes along the coast to the west starting from the No 5 bus stop opposite the Hôtel Week-End.

At the end of this walk, the beaches, the snack bars and restaurants are plentiful, and you can return to Ajaccio on the No 5 bus (every hour between 7.30 am and 7.30 pm, daily during high season).

PISCIA DI GALLO WATERFALL

Access & Location: Via the D368 between Porto Vecchio and Zonza; about 25km from Porto Vecchio and 1km after the Barrage de l'Ospedale
Markings: Cairns with pictograms
Standard: Very steep section at the end of the walk
Duration: 1½ hours there and back; return along the same route
Change in Altitude: 80m

Summary: The trail leads to a natural curiosity nestled in the heights of Porto Vecchio's hinterland, at the very heart of the wonderful wooded Ospedale massif.

The start of the walk, marked by a signpost, is near a couple of snack bars beside the D368. The first part of the route slopes down gently through the middle of a splendid forest of maritime pines. The path then fords two streams before ascending to a bald little plateau, where the coast becomes visible to the west. Next, the trail follows along a ridge that overhangs a steep-sided canyon with a fast-flowing stream running through it to the right; it's the same one that will flow over the falls somewhat farther on. You then get to a little pass with panoramic views over the coast and the Golfe de Porto Vecchio. The pink granite massifs, left and right, form a gorge that appears to narrow in the direction of the coast.

The path then descends across the maquis, here consisting chiefly of arbutus and heather, and winds between massive lumps of rock. You can clearly hear the sound of the waterfall at this stage, and a sign informs you of the end of the trail markings and warns of danger. If you want to see the Cascade de Piscia di Gallo (Chicken Piss Waterfall!), you have to descend through a very steep rocky gully and use your hands to steady yourself until you reach a little ledge. This perch gives a good view of the water crashing down onto a rocky outcrop and dividing into two streams. But this last section is not advisable if you have small children with you or if there's wet weather – you risk slipping.

Although you cannot bathe under the waterfall, on the way back up you'll come to a pine tree beside which, on the left, a path leads down to some inviting pools.

THE CLIFFS OF BONIFACIO TO THE PERTUSATO LIGHTHOUSE

From the starting point, a ramp of paving stones climbs to the top of the cliffs. When you get there, follow the path along the cliffs towards the south-east. There is low-growing maquis on your left; to the right, a sheer drop down to the sea.

After no more than 30 minutes the path joins the D260, which leads to the signal station and lighthouse. Follow this little road as it veers away from the cliff edge for a short distance. The path passes a farm, then curves around low and then starts back up again past some old military bunkers to the signal station. The walk to this point will have taken about 45 minutes.

After the signal station, the road follows a long hairpin-shaped indentation in the coast to the lighthouse. Notice that, 50m before the lighthouse, a path leads down to a cove edged with golden sand and to Île St-Antoine.

On the way out, your view is dominated by chalk cliffs shaped and eroded by the sea, while on the return journey you'll have leisure to admire the old town of Bonifacio balanced atop its promontory, and you'll also have excellent views of Sardinia to the south. But it's wise to avoid the hottest parts of the day, as there is no shade and nowhere to get water.

Access & Location: In Bonifacio, on the road to the upper town; turn left at the bend
Markings: Information point at the start
Standard: Little shade; children must be supervised because the path is close to the cliff edge, especially at the beginning of the walk
Duration: 2½ hours there and back; return along the same route
Change in Altitude: Minimal

Summary: Away from the hustle and bustle of tourism in Bonifacio's centre, this walk follows the line of the cliffs to the east of the town and affords excellent views of the spectacular Bouches de Bonifacio (Straits of Bonifacio) between Corsica and Sardinia

Facts for the Visitor

SUGGESTED ITINERARIES

Some visitors to Corsica choose to stay in one place and make day trips to the rest of the island. It's small enough that a day trip will get you a long way. Visitors who want merely to get an overview of the island can cover a lot of ground in a week, if travelling by car. A second week will fill in the details, and in a month, it should be possible to see just about everything.

The following itineraries, starting in Bastia and ending in Ajaccio, are easier, admittedly, by car. If travelling by public transport, you will have to fit your plans around straitjacket train and bus schedules. The routes suggested are also highly arbitrary. Many visitors with a week, two weeks, or even a month to spend will want to explore only a corner of Corsica.

Walking itineraries are described in the Walking chapter.

One Week

Start off in Bastia, cross the Col de Teghime to St-Florent and go on to spend the night in Île Rousse. Next, go on to Calvi, stop in Galéria, and finish up in Porto. Visit Les Calanques before going on to Corte. Drive southwards through Ghisoni, Zicavo, Aulléne, Quenza, Zonza and l'Ospedale, and stay the night in Porto Vecchio. Explore Bonifacio, visit the prehistoric site of Cauria, and then head for Sartène. Have a look at Propriano and the prehistoric site at Filitosa. Finally, explore Ajaccio and its surroundings and take it easy. You've earned some rest.

Two Weeks, Three Weeks and Four Weeks

First, slow down the whistle-stop pace of the one-week itinerary. Stay in Bastia a day or two, and drive down to see the Étang de Biguglia. Then instead of following the short, easy route from Bastia to St-Florent via the Col de Teghime, take the long way around via the Cap Corse coast road. Give Cap Corse several days. From St-Florent, take time to explore the Désert des Agriates. Visit some of the little villages of the Balagne interior from Île Rousse and Calvi. From Porto, spend a day on a boat on the coast of the Réserve Naturelle de Scandola. You can also consider a detour beyond Piana to Cargèse. Explore the mountain interior, perhaps using Corte as a base. As you head south, don't miss the archaeological sites around Lévie or the Aiguilles de Bavella. Explore the beaches around Porto Vecchio. Use Bonifacio as a base for discovering the Pointe de Spérone, the Îles Lavezzi and the Bouches de Bonifacio. Take time to visit the archaeological sites of the Sartenais. Explore the coast from Propriano up to Ajaccio.

An Itinerary by Train and Bus

Visitors planning to use public transport would be wise to go with the flow of train and bus routes rather than to fight them. Start in Bastia. Take the train to Île Rousse and Calvi. From Calvi take the train to Corte, then to Ajaccio; and continue to Bonifacio by bus.

PLANNING

When to Go

The vast majority of visitors to Corsica go in July and August. The water temperature in July, August and September is favourable for water sports. Around this time, however, prices are higher and there are likely to be crowds. Some of the island's most idyllic sights – Girolata, the Désert des Agriates, Bonifacio, Cap Corse, the GR20 and any number of little seashore coves and inlets – may even be pushed beyond capacity. High

Weather Forecasts

The French meteorological office (Météo France) provides seven-day forecasts for each department. This service is available on ☎ 08 36 68 08 08. Calls are charged at 2.23FF per minute. The forecasts are updated three times a day.

The Minitel 3615 Météo server provides special bulletins for coastal and mountainous regions for the same price.

If you would like an idea of the weather in Corsica before you leave home, look up www.wunderground.com, the Web site for the Weather Underground, which provides data for Ajaccio, Bastia and Calvi. La Chaîne météo at www.lachainemeteo.com (French only) provides data for Ajaccio, Bastia, Calvi, Corte, Figari and Solenzara.

summer is the period during which hotel prices peak.

Walkers on the GR20 and other routes may prefer the less sweltering months of May, June and September. Some travellers may even prefer the island at its emptiest – in early spring, late autumn or winter.

Bear in mind that, if you travel in low season, a significant number of hotels, camp sites, restaurants, transport and sports facilities will either have shut down completely or be operating at only half steam.

Maps

Michelin road map No 90, at a scale of 1:200,000 (1cm = 2km) and the two IGN 'green series' maps (No 73 for the north and No 74 for the south) at a scale of 1:100,000 (1cm = 1km) are excellent for motoring.

For the more detailed maps required for walking see the Walking chapter.

What to Bring

If you plan to travel by public transport or to walk, you'll want to take as little as possible. Start off with too little rather than too much, as virtually anything you could possibly need is available locally.

Even if your only walking will be from the hotel to the train, a backpack is the most practical option.

A basic checklist for walkers appears in the Walking chapter.

Travellers in need of medical supplies or toiletries should anticipate not finding a pharmacy at every turn and should bear in mind that opening hours are shorter than in cities.

TOURIST OFFICES

Local Tourist Offices

There are tourist offices and information centres in the main towns and tourist sites on the island. The staff are generally competent, often speak English and/or Italian, and almost always provide brochures and maps.

L'Agence du Tourisme de la Corse (ATC; ☎ 04 95 51 00 00, fax 04 95 51 14 40, ⓔ info@visit-corsica.com), at 17 blvd du Roi Jérôme BP 19, 20180 Ajaccio, can provide a wealth of planning information. Access the ATC Web site at www.visit-corsica.com (French only as of writing) or the Minitel service at 3615 Corse Info.

Tourist Offices Abroad

French government tourist offices, usually called Maisons de la France, where you live, can also be helpful, though typically they are shakier on Corsica than on other parts of France. They include:

Australia
(☎ 02-9231 5244, fax 9221 8682, ⓔ ifrance@internetzy.com.au) 25 Bligh St, 22nd floor, Sydney, NSW 2000

Canada
(☎ 514-876 9881, fax 845 4868, ⓔ mfrance@attcanada.net) 1981 McGill College Ave, Suite 490, Montreal, Quebec H3A 2W9

Germany
(☎ 069-580 131, fax 745 556, ⓔ maison_de_la_france@t-online.de) Westendstrasse 47, 60325 Frankfurt

Ireland
(☎ 01-679 0813, fax 679 0814, ⓔ frenchtouristoffice@tinet.ie) 10 Suffolk St, Dublin 2

Italy
(☎ 166 116 216, fax 02 5848 622, ⓔ entf@enter.it) Via Larga 7, 20122 Milan

Netherlands
(☎ 0900 112 2332, fax 020-620 3339, ⓔ informatie@fransverkeersbureau.nl) Prinsengracht 670, 1017 KX Amsterdam

Spain
(☎ 91 541 8808, fax 91 541 24 12, ⓔ info.francia@mdlfr.com) Plaza de España 18, Torre de Madrid 8, 28008 Madrid

UK
(☎ 09068 244 123, fax 020-7493 6594, ⓔ piccadilly@mdlf.co.uk) 178 Piccadilly, London W1V 0AL

USA
Los Angeles: (☎ 310-271 6665, fax 276 2835, ⓔ fgtola@juno.com) 9454 Wiltshire Blvd, Suite 715, Beverly Hills, CA 90212-2967
New York: (☎ 212-838 7800, fax 838 7855, ⓔ info@francetourism.com) 444 Madison Ave, 16th floor, New York, NY 10022-6903

VISAS & DOCUMENTS

Passport

By law, everyone in France, including tourists, must carry some sort of ID on them at all times. For foreign visitors, this means a passport (if you don't want to carry your passport for security reasons a photocopy should do, although you may be required to verify your identity later) or, for citizens of those European Union (EU) countries that issue them, a national ID card.

Visas

Tourist EU nationals have no entry requirements, and citizens of Australia, the USA, Canada, New Zealand and Israel do not need visas to visit France as tourists for up to three months. Except for people from a handful of other European countries (including Switzerland and Poland), everyone else needs a Schengen visa, named after the Schengen Agreement that abolished passport controls between Austria, Belgium, Denmark, Finland, France, Germany, Greece, Italy, Luxembourg, the Netherlands, Portugal, Spain and Sweden. A visa for any of these countries should, in theory, be valid throughout the area, but it always pays to double-check with the embassy or consulate in the country you intend to visit.

Visa fees depend on the current exchange rate, but a transit visa should cost about UK£6.50, a visa valid for stays of up to 30 days around UK£16, and a single/multiple-entry visa of up to three months about UK£19 /22.50. You will need your passport (valid for a period of three months beyond the date of your anticipated departure from France), a return ticket, proof of sufficient funds to support yourself, two passport-size photos and the visa fee in cash. You may also be asked for proof of pre-arranged accommodation. South African visas take two days to process.

If all the forms are in order, your visa will be issued on the spot at the French consulate closest to you in your home country. You can also apply for a French visa after arriving in Europe – the fee is the same, but you may not have to produce a return ticket. If you enter France overland, your passport may not be checked for a visa at the border, but, if you don't have one, major problems can arise later on (for example, at the airport as you leave the country).

Long-Stay & Student Citizens of EU countries and Switzerland wishing to stay in Corsica for longer than 90 days must apply for a residence permit from the nearest town hall or from the *service des étrangers* (foreigners' department) of the Corsican prefecture.

Préfecture Corse-du-Sud (☎ 04 95 11 12 13, fax 04 95 11 10 28), Palais Lantivy, cours Napoléon, BP 401, 20188 Ajaccio

Préfecture Haute-Corse (☎ 04 95 34 50 00, fax 04 95 34 06 82), vallée du Fango, 20401 Bastia

Citizens of Australia, Canada and the USA are limited to two stays of 90 days each per year. Those wishing to extend their stay must apply for an extended residence permit from the French embassy or consulate in their own country.

Non-EU nationals wanting to work or study in France or stay for over three months should apply to their nearest French embassy or consulate for the appropriate *long séjour* (long-stay) visa. Unless you live in the EU, it is extremely difficult to get a visa allowing you to work in France. For any sort of long-stay visa, begin the paperwork in your home country several months before you plan to leave. Applications cannot usually be made in a third country nor can tourist visas be turned into student visas after you arrive in France. People with student visas can apply for permission to work part-time (inquire at your place of study).

Carte de Séjour A non-EU national with a long-stay visa valid for six or more months will probably have to apply for a *carte de séjour* (residence permit) within eight days of arrival in France. Apply at the foreigners' department of the prefecture in Ajaccio (see the Long-Stay & Student section).

Visa Extensions Tourist visas will not be extended except in emergencies (for example, medical emergencies). Again, apply at the foreigners' department of the prefecture in Ajaccio (see the Long-Stay & Student section).

If you don't need a visa to visit France, you'll almost certainly qualify for another automatic three-month stay if you leave and then re-enter France. The fewer recent French entry stamps you have in your passport the easier this is likely to be. If you needed a visa the first time around, one way to extend your stay is to go to a French consulate in a neighbouring country and apply for another one there.

People entering France by rail, road or even air often don't have their passports looked at, much less stamped. Fear not: you're in France legally, whether or not you had to apply for a visa before arriving (though at some point, to show your date of entry, you may be asked to produce the plane, train or ferry ticket you arrived with). If you prefer to have your passport stamped (for example, if you expect to have to prove when you last entered the country), be insistent – politely.

Travel Insurance

Travel insurance can protect you against not only emergency medical and repatriation costs, but also forced cancellations, forced curtailments, delays, lost tickets and luggage. Cover depends on your insurance and type of airline ticket.

Remember that airlines will themselves compensate you to a limited extent should *they* be responsible for losing your luggage. Paying for an airline ticket with a credit card will often provide some additional protection; for example, it may make it possible for you to get reimbursed if an operator fails to deliver. In the UK institutions issuing credit cards are required by law to reimburse consumers if a company goes into liquidation and the amount in dispute is more than UK£100. Credit card issuers may also cover expensive car hire insurance. If you are in doubt as to what your credit card issuer provides, ask.

EU citizens are eligible for free emergency medical treatment if they have an E111 certificate. See Predeparture Planning under Health later for more details.

Driving Licence & Permits

Driving licences issued by member states of the EU allow you to drive in France, as do those from the USA and Canada and numerous other countries (provided they are written in the Roman alphabet).

Though numerous non-EU drivers' licences are valid in France, many people like to arm themselves with an International Driving Permit (IDP) anyway. It can be obtained for a small fee from your local automobile association – bring along a valid driver's licence issued in your own country, and one or two passport photos.

When you travel, do not leave your normal licence behind. The IDP is not a substitute; it merely provides a multilingual translation of its details.

Hostel Cards

There is one Hostelling International (HI) *auberge de jeunesse* (youth hostel) in Corsica at Poggio Mezzana, and another non-HI-affiliated youth hostel at Calvi. An HI card is necessary at the Pozzio Mezzana hostel. If you don't pick one up at home, you can buy one at official French hostels for 100FF (those aged under 26, 70FF). One-night membership (where available) costs between 10FF and 19FF, and a family card costs 100FF.

Carte Jeunes

A Carte Jeunes (120FF for one year) is available to anyone under 26 who has been in France for at least six months. It gets you discounts on things like air tickets, car hire, sports events, concerts and movies. In France, details are available from ☎ 08 03 00 12 26; by Minitel key in 3615 CARTE JEUNES.

Copies

All important documents (passport data page and visa page, credit cards, travel insurance policy, air/bus/train tickets, driving licence etc) should be photocopied before you leave home. Leave one copy with someone at home and keep another with you, separate from the originals.

There is another option for storing details of your vital travel documents before you depart – Lonely Planet's on-line Travel Vault. Storing details of your important documents in the vault is safer than carrying photocopies. Your password-protected travel vault is accessible on-line at anytime. You can create your own travel vault for free at www.ekno.lonelyplanet.com. However, its usefulness in Corsica will be limited until Internet access is more prevalent there.

If you do lose your passport, you should of course immediately notify the police to get a statement, and contact your nearest consulate.

EMBASSIES & CONSULATES

Your Own Embassy

It's important to realise what your embassy can and can't do to help you if you get into trouble. Generally speaking, it won't be much help in emergencies if the trouble you're in is remotely your own fault. Remember that you are bound by the laws of the country you are in. Your embassy will not be sympathetic if you end up in jail after committing a crime locally, even if such actions are legal in your own country.

In genuine emergencies you might get some assistance, but only if other channels have been exhausted. For example, if you need to get home urgently, a free ticket home is exceedingly unlikely – the embassy would expect you to have insurance. If you have all your money and documents stolen, it might assist with getting a new passport, but a loan for onward travel is out of the question.

French Embassies & Consulates

French diplomatic offices overseas include:

Australia
Embassy: (☎ 02-6216 0100, fax 6216 0127, e embassy@france.net.au) 6 Perth Ave, Yarralumla, ACT 2600
Consulate: (☎ 03-9820 0944/0921, fax 9820 9363, e cgmelb@france.net.au) 492 St Kilda Rd, Level 4, Melbourne, Vic 3004
Consulate: (☎ 02-9262 5779, fax 9283 1210, e cgsydney@france.net.au) St Martin's Tower, 31 Market St, Sydney, NSW 2000

Canada
Embassy: (☎ 613-789 1795, fax 562 3735) 42 Sussex Drive, Ottawa, Ont K1M 2C9
Consulate: (☎ 514-878 4385, fax 878 3981, e fslmral@cam.org) 26th floor, 1 place Ville Marie, Montreal, Que H3B 4S3
Consulate: (☎ 416-925 8041, fax 925 3076, e fsltto@idirect.com) 130 Bloor St West, Suite 400, Toronto, Ont M5S 1N5
Web site: www.ambafrance-ca.org (links to all three sites).

Germany
Embassy: (☎ 030-206 39000, fax 206 39010, e presse.berlin@diplomacie.fr) Kochstrasse 6–7, D-10969 Berlin
Web site: www.botschaft-frankreich.de
Consulate: (☎ 030-885 90243, fax 885 5295) Kurfürstendamm 211, 10719 Berlin
Consulate: (☎ 089-419 4110, fax 419 41141, e info@consulfrance-munich.de) Möhlstrasse 5, D-81675 Munich
Web site: www.consulfrance-munich.de

Ireland
Embassy: (☎ 01-260 1666, fax 283 0178) 36 Ailesbury Rd, Ballsbridge, Dublin 4
Web site: www.ambafrance.ie

Italy
Embassy: (☎ 06 686 011, fax 06 860 1360, e france-italia@france-italia.it) Piazza Farnese 67, 00186 Rome
Consulate: (☎ 06-6880 6437, fax 6860 1260, e consulfrance-rome@iol.it) Via Giulia 251, 00186 Rome
Web site: www.france-italia.it

Netherlands
Embassy: (☎ 070-312 5800, fax 312 5854) Smidsplein 1, 2514 BT The Hague
Web site: www.ambafrance.nl
Consulate: (☎ 020-530 6969, fax 530 6968/61, e consulfr@euronet.nl) Eertse Weteringdwarsstraat 107, 1000 HA Amsterdam
Web site: www.consulfrance-amsterdam.org

New Zealand
Embassy: (☎ 04-384 2555, fax 384 2577, e consul.france@actrix.gen.nz) 34–42 Manners St, Wellington

Spain
Embassy: (☎ 91 423 8900, fax 91 423 8901) Calle de Salustiano Olozaga 9, 28001 Madrid
Consulate: (☎ 91 700 7800, fax 91 700 7801, e creire@consulfrance-madrid.org) Calle Marqués de la Enseñada 10–3, 28004 Madrid
Consulate: (☎ 93 270 3000, fax 93 270 0349, e info@consul-france.org) Ronda Universitat 22, 08007 Barcelona
Web site: www.ambafrance.es

UK
Embassy: (☎ 020-7201 1000, fax 7201 1004, e press@ambafrance.org.uk) 58 Knightsbridge, London SW1X 7JT
Consulate: (☎ 020-7838 2000, fax 7838 2018) 21 Cromwell Rd, London SW7 2EN
Visa section: (☎ 020-7838 2051) 6a Cromwell Place, London SW7 2EW. Dial ☎ 09065 508940 for visa information.
Web site: www.ambafrance.org.uk

USA
Embassy: (☎ 202-944 6000, fax 944 6166, ⓔ visas-washington@amb-wash.fr) 4101 Reservoir Rd NW, Washington, DC 20007
Consulate: (☎ 212-606 3600, fax 606 3620) 934 Fifth Ave, New York, NY 10021
Visa section: (☎ 606 3680, ⓔ visa@france consulatny.org) 10 East 74th Street, New York, NY 10021
Web site: www.consulfrance-newyork.org
Consulate: (☎ 310-235 3200, fax 312 0704) 10990 Wilshire Blvd, Los Angeles, CA 90024
Other consulates are located in Atlanta, Boston, Chicago, Houston, Miami, New Orleans and San Francisco.

Embassies & Consulates in France

All foreign embassies can be found in Paris, although some countries also have consulates in other major French cities.

Only a few countries, Italy among them, have any kind of diplomatic representation in Corsica.

Australia
Embassy: (☎ 01 40 59 33 00) 4 rue Jean Rey, 15e, Paris. The consular section opens 9.15 am to noon and 2 to 4.30 pm weekdays.

Canada
Embassy: (☎ 01 44 43 29 00) 35 ave Montaigne, 8e, Paris. Consular services are available 9 am to noon and 2 to 5 pm weekdays.

Germany
Embassy: (☎ 01 53 83 45 00, ⓔ ambassade@amb-allemagne.fr) 13–15 ave Franklin D Roosevelt, 8e, Paris
Consulate: (☎ same) 34 ave d'Iéna, 16e, Paris

Ireland
Embassy: (☎ 01 44 17 67 00, 01 44 17 67 67 after hours, Minitel 3615 IRLANDE) 4 rue Rude, 16e, Paris. The chancellery opens 9.30 am to noon weekdays or by appointment.

Italy
Embassy: (☎ 01 49 54 03 00) 51 rue de Varenne, 7e, Paris
Consulate: (☎ 01 44 30 47 00) 5 blvd Émile Augier, 16e, Paris
Consulate: (☎ 04 95 31 01 52, fax 04 95 32 56 72) rue St-François Prolongée, 20200 Bastia

Netherlands
Embassy: (☎ 01 40 62 33 00) 7 rue Eblé, 7e, Paris

New Zealand
Embassy: (☎ 01 45 01 43 43) 7 ter rue Léonard de Vinci, 16e, Paris. Consular services are available 9 am to 1 pm and 2 to 5.30 pm weekdays (8.30 am to 2 pm on Friday in July and August).

Spain
Embassy: (☎ 01 44 43 18 00) 22 ave Marceau, 8e, Paris

UK
Embassy: (☎ 01 44 51 31 00, 01 42 66 29 79 (emergencies), ⓔ ambassade@amb-grandebretagne.fr) 35 rue du Faubourg St-Honoré, 8e, Paris
Consulate: (☎ 01 44 51 31 02) 18 bis rue d'Anjou, 8e, Paris. The consulate opens 9 am to noon and 2.30 to 5 pm weekdays.

USA
Embassy: (☎ 01 43 12 22 22, ⓔ ambassade@amb-usa.fr) 2 ave Gabriel, 8e, Paris
Consulate: (☎ 01 43 12 23 47, 01 43 12 49 48 for emergencies, Minitel 3614 ETATS-UNIS) 2 rue St-Florentin, 1er, Paris. The American Services section opens 9 am to 3 pm weekdays (except French and US public holidays).

The following countries are represented on the island by honorary consulates:

Belgium & the Netherlands
(☎ 04 95 20 89 99, fax 04 95 23 56 44) c/o Air Fret Service, aéroport Campo dell'Oro, 20090 Ajaccio

Germany
(☎ 04 95 33 03 56) RN 193, zone industrielle Furiani, 20600 Bastia

Switzerland
(☎/fax 04 95 20 80 34) 2 ave Pascal Paoli, 20000 Ajaccio

CUSTOMS

The following items can be brought into France, hence into Corsica, duty free from non-EU countries: 200 cigarettes, 50 cigars or 250g of loose tobacco; 1L of strong liquor or 2L of liquor which is less than 22% alcohol by volume; 2L of wine; 500g of coffee or 200g of extracts; 50g of perfume and 0.25L of eau de toilette.

Do not confuse duty-free allowances with duty-paid items (including alcohol and tobacco) bought at normal shops and supermarkets in another EU country and brought into France, where certain goods might be more expensive. Then the allowances are more generous: 800 cigarettes, 200 cigars or 1kg of loose tobacco; and 10L of spirits (more than 22% alcohol by volume), 20L of fortified wine or apéritif, 90L of wine or 110L of beer. There are no duty-free shopping facilities in Corsican airports.

Note that your home country may have strict regulations regarding the import of meat, dairy products or plants.

In the unlikely event that you will be arriving on the island by boat from outside the EU – few visitors do – you must present yourself to the port authorities when you disembark. Customs authorities will usually want to board the boat.

MONEY

Currency

Until the euro is introduced (see the boxed text 'Bonjour Euro, Adieu France') the national currency is the French franc, abbreviated in this book to the letters FF. One franc is divided into 100 centimes.

French coins come in denominations of five, 10, 20 and 50 centimes (0.5FF) and 1FF, 2FF, 10FF and 20FF; the two highest denominations have silvery centres and brass edges. Coins not only tend to accumulate in your pockets until you get used to them, they're useful for laundrettes, vending machines and parking meters. Banknotes are issued in denominations of 20FF, 50FF, 100FF, 200FF and 500FF. It can often be difficult to get change for a 500FF bill.

Exchange Rates

country	unit		franc
Australia	A$1	=	3.74FF
Canada	C$1	=	4.71FF
euro	€1	=	6.56FF
Germany	DM1	=	3.35FF
Italy	L1000	=	3.39FF
Japan	¥100	=	5.98FF
Netherlands	f1	=	2.98FF
New Zealand	NZ$1	=	3.00FF
Spain	100 ptas	=	3.94FF
UK	UK£1	=	10.54FF
USA	US$1	=	7.29FF

Bonjour Euro, Adieu Franc

You'll come across two sets of prices at hotels, restaurants, department stores and so on while visiting France. Since 1999 both the franc and Europe's new currency – the euro – have been legal tender, and businesses must now by law list prices in both currencies. Along with the franc, the currencies of 10 other EU members are being phased out to complete Europe's monetary union. The advent of the cash euro will end the 642-year reign of the franc, which began in 1360 when King Jean le Bon struck coins to signify that his part of France was *franc des anglois* (free of English domination).

Euro coins and banknotes will be introduced in January 2002; before that time payment in euros can only be made by credit card or cheque. Both the euro and the franc will remain in circulation until 28 February 2002, when the franc will be withdrawn and prices displayed in euros only.

The scheme is open to abuse; a restaurant might, for example, print euro prices more prominently on the menu than franc prices during the period of coexistence. Check your bill carefully, too – your total might have the amount in francs, but a credit card company may bill you in the euro equivalent.

Fortunately, the euro has many benefits – cross-border travel will become easier, and prices in the 11 'euro-zone' countries will be immediately comparable. Also, once euro notes and coins are issued, you won't need to change money when travelling within most of the EU. Indeed, even EU countries not participating (such as the UK) may price goods in euros and accept cash euros over shop counters.

The EU has a dedicated euro site, http://europa.eu.int/euro, and you can also check the currency converter at www.oanda.com for the latest rates.

country	unit		euro
Australia	A$1	=	€0.57
Canada	C$1	=	€0.72
France	1FF	=	€0.15
Germany	DM1	=	€0.51
Japan	¥100	=	€0.91

country	unit		euro
New Zealand	NZ$1	=	€0.46
Spain	100 ptas	=	€0.60
United Kingdom	UK£1	=	€1.60
United States	US$1	=	€1.11

Exchanging Money

At banks and bureaux de change, you can tell how good the rate is by checking the spread between the rates for *achat* (buy rates, that is what they'll give you for foreign cash or travellers cheques) and *vente* (sell rates, that is the rate at which they sell foreign currency) – the greater the difference, the further each is from the interbank rate (printed daily in newspapers, including the *International Herald Tribune*).

Banks, exchange bureaux and post offices often give a better rate for traveller cheques than for cash. However, a low exchange rate might not be the bargain it appears if you end up paying a hefty commission.

If you are carrying cash and happen to be passing through mainland France before you get to Corsica, you will do well to change your money there. Paris in particular, but many provincial cities as well, will give you rates with low or no commission, and you're not likely to encounter this on the island.

Cash Hard cash, despite its advantages, is generally not a very good way to carry money. Not only can it be stolen, but in France you don't get an optimal exchange rate. Nevertheless, it can be a good idea to bring the equivalent of about US$100 in low-denomination notes, so that you can change a small sum when the rate is poor or you need just a few francs. Because of counterfeiting, it may be difficult to change US$100 notes.

Credit Cards Credit cards will by and large prove the cheapest and easiest way to pay for major purchases in Corsica; the only problem with relying on credit cards is that you will often be tempted to eat the more expensive meal that you don't really want at the restaurant that accepts your card rather than that at the modest cafe that doesn't. In Corsica, as throughout France, Visa (Carte Bleue) and MasterCard (Eurocard) are the cards most widely accepted by hotels, restaurants and stores. American Express cards are mainly recognised in upmarket establishments, but do allow you to get cash at certain ATMs. In general, all three cards can be used to pay for air, train and sea-ferry travel.

Though the credit card companies usually charge you at home in your own currency at a favourable exchange rate, watch out for soaring foreign currency transaction fees. One Visa or MasterCard issuer might charge no more than the credit card company's own 1% fee. Another might charge total fees of as much as 3%. You might want to check what your credit card issuer charges before leaving home.

If your Visa card is lost or stolen, call Carte Bleue on ☎ 02 54 42 12 12 (24 hours). To get a replacement card you'll have to deal with the issuer.

Report a lost MasterCard or Eurocard to Eurocard France at ☎ 01 45 67 53 53 and, if you can, to your credit card issuer back home (for cards from the USA, call ☎ 314-275 6690).

If your American Express card is lost or stolen, call ☎ 01 47 77 70 00 or 01 47 77 72 00 (24 hours). In an emergency, Amex card holders from the USA can call collect on ☎ 202-783 7474 or 677 2442. Amex should now be represented on the island by Corsicatours at ☎ 04 95 34 11 12, 1 ave Maréchal Sebastiani, Bastia.

A lost Diners Club card should be reported on ☎ 01 47 62 75 75.

ATMs Known in French as DABs *(distributeurs automatiques de billets)* or *points d'argent*, ATMs (automated teller machines) will let you draw on your home account or get a cash advance on a credit card, at a favourable rate of exchange. Visa, MasterCard or Cirrus are accepted widely.

Watch out, though: some non-US ATMs won't accept PIN codes with more than four digits. If this is a potential problem for you, consult your bank before you leave home, and while you're at it find out about withdrawal fees and daily limits. If you normally remember your PIN code as a string of letters, translate it back into numbers, as keypads abroad may not show letters.

Many Corsican towns now have at least one ATM machine. However, the ATM is still not nearly as widespread in Corsica as they are elsewhere.

Cash Advances & Debits Whether you take a cash advance against your Visa or MasterCard credit account or you debit a debit account, your issuer charges a transaction fee and/or finance charge. With some issuers, the fees can be as high as US$10 plus interest per transaction, however small, so learn the facts up front from your card issuer before leaving home or risk unpleasant surprises. Again, you may also want to enquire as to limits on the amounts you may withdraw. Know that the French bank whose ATM you use will likely impose an additional commission on your transactions.

If you are taking a cash advance against a credit rather than a debit card, you can avoid paying interest (which normally accrues from the moment you receive the cash, not from the end of the billing period) if you deposit covering funds in your credit card account before you leave home, turning your credit card account into a bank account and your credit card into a debit card.

If you get a cash advance through a bureau de change, make sure that the charge to your card will be in French francs and not dollars or pounds. Your object is to take advantage of your credit card company's favourable rate of exchange. You do not want to pay a fee and perhaps other costs to your credit card company, then have to convert to francs at the bureau de change's rate of exchange and pay their exchange commission as well.

Travellers Cheques & Eurocheques If you don't want to carry large amounts of cash and if plastic isn't the right solution for you either, you may want to carry at least some of your money in the form of travellers cheques and, unless you are afraid of having more money than you are likely to use, you will do better to buy travellers cheques denominated in French francs than in either US dollars or British pounds. Travellers cheques denominated in French francs, as long as face values are not disproportionate to the amount of your purchase, are as good as money almost everywhere in Corsica. Travellers cheques denominated in dollars or pounds as well as Eurocheques lead to the same problems of exchange rates and commissions that you will have with any non-French currency. American Express, Thomas Cook and other issuers of travellers cheques provide cheques in French francs at a favourable, if not the best, rate of exchange, and the charge is generally a maximum of 1% of the total transaction.

If you lose your American Express (Amex) travellers cheques in France, or they are stolen, call the 24-hour toll-free number ☎ 08 00 90 86 00. If you lose your Thomas Cook cheques, call the company's toll-free customer service bureau on ☎ 08 00 90 83 30.

Commercial Banks The typical charge per foreign currency transaction at a commercial bank is between 35FF and 50FF. The rates vary, so where there are choices it may pay to compare. Bank hours vary as well; sometimes they may be eccentric. It is hoped that the hours given in the Money sections for the various towns are accurate, but they cannot be guaranteed. Bear in mind, moreover, that exchange services may end half an hour before the bank's official closing time.

Bureaux de Change Rare in Corsica, bureaux de change will often charge inflated commissions for the convenience of their shorter lines and longer hours. If your object is to get the best possible rate, you will almost always be better off at a bank.

Post Offices Many post offices in Corsica change foreign currency and some travellers cheques at middling rates. In some villages, the post office may be the only place where you can change a foreign currency.

International Transfers In Corsica telegraphic transfers are not very expensive but, despite their name, they can be slow. Be sure to specify the name of the bank and the address of the branch where you'd like to pick the money up.

It's quicker and easier to have money wired via American Express (US$50 for US$1000). Western Union's Money Transfer system (☎ 01 43 54 46 12) and Thomas Cook's MoneyGram service (☎ 01 47 58 21 00) are also popular.

Costs

Corsica is not an expensive destination. However, if you come from a country where sleeping is expensive and eating is cheap, it's well to remember that the French tend to spend less on lodging and more on food than other nationalities. You can economise by travelling in low season and/or by doing at least some self-catering. The interior of the island is also significantly cheaper than the coast. There's little competitive conspicuous consumption in Corsica; if you happen to run into any, you can get away from it fast. Naturally if you are planning to indulge in diving, horse riding, boating and so on, this will up your costs.

As a general rule, you can expect to pay at least 200FF to 250FF for a decent double room in high season (often more in August if you like your creature comforts) You will have to pay the same minimum rates if you are on your own, as there are very few single rooms.

Cut costs by renting lodgings on a weekly or monthly basis rather than by the night, or camping. Sites charge an average of 30/12/12FF per person/tent/car.

Most restaurants offer tourist *menus* for about 80FF. However, it is often better to choose a good restaurant and have one good course rather than a mediocre complete meal. The island has quite a large number of good restaurants where you can have an excellent meal for about 120FF. A number of pizzerias open during high season, and although they're not always good, they are a relatively economical choice.

Bus travel (often seasonal as well) is generally quite expensive if you consider the actual distances travelled (Ajaccio to Bonifacio, 140km, 120FF; Calvi to Bastia, 93km, 80FF). The journey from Ajaccio to Bastia (153km) comes to 124FF if you go by train. Hiring a car will cost you about 1700FF per week with unlimited mileage and comprehensive insurance. The monthly rate (5000FF) is good because there is little demand for it.

Perhaps the cheapest and most rewarding way to experience Corsica is to spend a couple of weeks on the GR20 or one of the other celebrated island hikes. Then you are bound to sleep in gîtes or in refuges (about 55FF per night along the GR20) or to camp, and transport is of course free!

Tipping & Bargaining

French law requires that restaurant, cafe and hotel bills include the service charge (usually 10 to 15%), so a *pourboire* (tip) is neither necessary nor even expected. If you want to leave something extra that's up to you.

If you take a taxi from or to an airport, the meter fare or the prescribed flat rate is sufficient, though you may want to round up modestly. If you happen to want to use taxi services for sightseeing, negotiate the fare in advance.

Bargaining is rare in France, except at flea markets.

Taxes & Refunds

France's VAT (TVA) is 19.6% on most goods except food, medicine and books, for which it's 5.5%; it goes as high as 33% for such items as watches, cameras and video cassettes. Prices that include VAT are often marked TTC (*touts taxes comprises*; all taxes included).

If you are not a resident of the EU, you can get a refund of most of the VAT provided that you're over 15 years of age, you'll have spent less than six months in France, you purchase goods (not more than 10 of the same item) worth at least 1200FF (tax included) at a single shop and the shop offers *vente en détaxe* (duty-free sales).

Present your passport at the time of purchase and ask for a *bordereau de détaxe* (export sales invoice); some shops may refund 14% of the purchase price rather than the full 17.1% you are entitled to in order to cover the time and expense involved in the refund procedure.

As you leave France or another EU country, have all three pages (two pink and one green) of the bordereau validated by customs officials at the airport or at the border. Customs officials will take the two pink sheets and the stamped self-addressed envelope provided by the store; the green sheet is your receipt. One of the pink sheets will then be sent to the shop where you made your purchase, which will then send you a *virement* (transfer of funds) in the form you have requested it, such as by French-franc cheque or by direct transfer into your bank account. Be prepared for a long wait.

POST & COMMUNICATIONS

There are almost 180 post offices on the island of Corsica, including some in tiny hamlets. In addition to providing customary mail services, they will also often send and receive faxes and perhaps cash travellers cheques and perform other modest banking services. They mostly survive either by selling postcards or by doubling as tobacconists. There are often public telephones either in or near the office.

Postal Rates

Domestic letters up to a weight of 20g cost 3FF. Postcards and letters up to 20g cost 3FF within the EU, 3.80FF to most of the rest of Europe and some of North Africa, 3.90FF to the rest of Africa, 4.40FF to the USA, Canada, Mexico and the Middle East, 4.90FF to Asia and Central and South America and 5.20FF to Australia and New Zealand. Aerograms cost 5FF to all destinations.

It will cost 35FF (or 20FF economy rate) to send a parcel weighing up to 500g to EU countries or Switzerland, 52FF (25FF economy) to send it to North America and 72FF (42FF economy) to send it to Australia or New Zealand.

Sending Mail

All mail to Corsica must include the five-digit postcode, which begins with 20, the number of the department.

Mail to France should be addressed as follows:

SMITH John
8, rue de la Poste
20000 Ajaccio
FRANCE

Street Numbers

When a building in France, Corsica included, goes up in a location in which there's no consecutive street number to be assigned, a new address is formed by adding a *bis* (twice), a *ter* (thrice) or, rarely, a *quater* (four times) to the last previous street number. Thus, the street numbers 17 bis and 89 ter are the equivalent of 17A or 89B.

The surname (family name) should be written in capital letters. As you'll see, the French put a comma after the street number and don't capitalise 'rue', 'ave', 'blvd' (boulevard) and similar abbreviations. CEDEX after a city or town name simply means that mail sent to that address is collected at the post office rather than delivered to the door.

Receiving Mail

Poste Restante To have mail sent to you via poste restante (general delivery), available at all French post offices, have it addressed as follows:

SMITH, John
Poste Restante
Poste Principale d'Ajaccio
Cours Napoléon
20185 Ajaccio RT
FRANCE

Since poste restante mail is held alphabetically by last name, it is vital that you follow the French practice of having your surname or family name *(nom de famille)* written first and in capital letters. In case your friends back home forget, always check under the first letter of your first name *(prénom)* as well. There's a 3FF charge for every piece of poste restante mail you pick up weighing less than 20g; for anything between 20g and 100g, the fee is 4FF. It is usually possible to forward *(faire suivre)* mail from one poste restante address to another. To collect poste restante mail, you'll need your passport or national ID card.

Poste restante mail not addressed to a

particular branch goes to the town's *recette principale* (main post office) whether or not you include the words Recette Principale in the address. If you want it sent to a specific branch office, include the street address.

Post is generally kept for about two weeks.

Telephone

Mobile Phones Mobile phone reception is poor because of the relief of the island.

Corsica uses GSM 900/1800, which is compatible with the rest of Europe and Australia but not with the North American GSM 1900 or the totally different system in Japan (though some North Americans have GSM 1900/900 phones that do work here). If you have a GSM phone, check with your service provider about using it in Corsica, and beware of calls being routed internationally (very expensive for a 'local' call).

International Dialling To call Corsica, or anywhere else in France, from outside France, dial your country's international access code, then 33 (France's country code), then omit the 0 at the beginning of the 10-digit local number.

To call someone outside France, dial the international access code (00), the country code, the area code (without the initial 0 if there is one) and the local number. International Direct Dial (IDD) calls to almost anywhere in the world can be made from public telephones, of which there are a reasonable number on the island. Useful country codes include:

Australia	☎ 61
Belgium	☎ 32
Canada	☎ 1
Germany	☎ 49
Ireland	☎ 353
Japan	☎ 81
Monaco	☎ 377
Netherlands	☎ 31
New Zealand	☎ 64
UK	☎ 44
USA	☎ 1

If you don't know the country code *(indicatif pays)* and it doesn't appear on the information sheet posted in most telephone booths, consult a telephone book or dial ☎ 12 for directory inquiries.

To make a reverse-charge (collect) call (*en PCV*, pronounced '**pey-sey-vey**') or a person-to-person call (*avec préavis*, pronounced 'ah-**vek** preh-ah-**vee**'), dial 00, and then 33 plus the country code of the place you're calling (for the USA and Canada, dial 11 instead of 1). There won't be a dial tone after you've dialled 00, so don't wait for one. Don't be surprised if you get a recording and have to wait a while. If you're using a public phone, you must insert a *télécarte* (see Public Phones later in this section) or, in the case of public coin telephones, 1FF to place operator-assisted calls through the international operator.

For directory inquiries concerning subscriber numbers outside France, dial 00 then 3312 and finally the relevant country code (again, 11 instead of 1 for the USA and Canada). You often get put on hold for quite a while. In public phones, you can access this service without a télécarte, but from home phones the charge is 7.30FF per inquiry.

Most of the toll-free 1-800 numbers in the USA and Canada can be called from phones in Corsica, but you will be charged at the same international rates as for any other call.

International Rates From Corsica a call to an EU country costs 1.85FF per minute (1.45FF off-peak). A minute to the USA or Canada costs 2FF (1.60FF off-peak). Off-peak rates apply between 7 pm and 8 am on weekdays and from 7 pm on Friday to 8 am on Monday.

Country Direct Services Country Direct lets you phone your home country (or elsewhere) by billing the long-distance carrier you use at home or by billing another long-distance carrier that can charge you on a credit card. Country Direct can be dialled from public phones without inserting a phonecard; with some models, you're meant to dial even if there's no dial tone. The following numbers will connect you, free of charge, either with a Country Direct automatic dialling menu or with an operator:

country	carrier	toll-free numbers
Australia	Telstra	☎ 08 00 99 00 61
	Optus	☎ 08 00 99 20 61
Canada		☎ 08 00 99 00 16
		☎ 08 00 99 02 16
Ireland		☎ 08 00 99 03 53
New Zealand		☎ 08 00 99 00 64
UK	BT	☎ 08 00 99 02 44
	Mercury	☎ 08 00 99 09 44
USA	AT&T	☎ 08 00 99 00 11
	MCI	☎ 08 00 99 00 19
	Sprint	☎ 08 00 99 00 87
	Worldcom	☎ 08 00 99 00 13

Domestic Dialling France has five telephone dialling areas. To make calls within any region or between regions, just dial the 10-digit number. The five regional area codes are:

Paris region	☎ 01
north-west	☎ 02
north-east	☎ 03
south-east (including Corsica)	☎ 04
south-west	☎ 05

If you want France Telecom's directory inquiries or assistance service *(service des renseignements)*, dial ☎ 12. Don't be surprised if the operator does not speak English. The call is free from public phones but costs 3.71FF from private lines.

It is not possible to make a domestic reverse-charge call. You can, though, ask the person you're calling to ring you back (see under Public Phones later).

Domestic Tariffs Local calls are quite cheap, even at the peak tariff: one calling unit (0.81FF with a télécarte) is good for three minutes. For calls over greater distances (to the other side of Corsica, to the border with Belgium or Germany) one calling unit will be good for anywhere from 72 seconds down to just 21 seconds.

Tarif rouge (red tariff) rates apply during the hours of heaviest business use between 8 am and 12.30 pm Monday to Saturday and between 1.30 and 6 pm Monday to Friday. *Tarif blanc* (white tariff), in effect 12.30 to 1.30 pm Monday to Saturday and 6 to 9.30 pm Monday to Friday, gives you a 30% discount. The rest of the time, you enjoy 50% off with the *tarif bleu* (blue tariff), except between 10.30 pm and 6 am, when the *tarif bleu nuit* (blue-night tariff) gives you a 65% discount.

Note that numbers beginning with 08 36 are always billed at 2.23FF per minute, regardless of the day or the time.

Toll-Free Numbers Two-digit emergency numbers, Country Direct numbers and *numéros verts* (green numbers; toll-free numbers that have 10 digits and begin with 08 00) can be dialled from public telephones without inserting any payment.

Public Phones Most public telephones in Corsica require a *télécarte* (telephone card), which can be purchased at post offices, tobacconists *(tabacs)*, supermarket check-out counters and anywhere you see a blue sticker reading *télécarte en vente ici*. Cards worth 50/120 units cost 40.60/97.50FF.

To make a domestic or international phone call with a télécarte, follow the instructions on the LCD display. It should first read *décrochez* (if it says *hors service* it's out of order). If the phone has a button displaying two flags linked with an arrow, push it for the explanations in English. If not, when you see the words *introduire carte ou faire numéro libre* (insert the card or dial a toll-free number), insert the card chip-end first with the rectangle of electrical connectors facing upwards. *Patientez SVP* means 'please wait'.

When the top line of the display tells you your *crédit* or *solde* (how many *unités*, or units, you have left), the bottom line of the LCD screen will read *numérotez* (dial). When you key in the number you want, it, too, will appear, digit by digit, on the display.

After you dial, you will hear a rapid beeping followed by long beeps (it's ringing) or short beeps (it's busy). When your call is connected, the screen begins counting down your card's value. To redial, you may have to pull your card out and reinsert it.

If, for any reason, something goes wrong in the dialling process, you'll be asked to *rac-*

crochez SVP (please hang up). *Crédit épuisé* means that your télécarte has run out of units.

It's possible to replace a used-up télécarte with a new one in the middle of a call – an especially useful feature with overseas calls – but only if you follow the instructions exactly. When the screen reads *crédit = 000 unités – changement de carte*, press the green button, wait for the message *retirez votre carte* and then take out the old télécarte. When you see the words *nouvelle télécarte* (not before!), insert a fresh card.

You will occasionally come across phones that take coins (1FF for a local call) rather than télécartes. Most such phones give you a dial tone immediately, even before you insert a coin, but with the very oldest models – the ones with windows down the front and no slot for 2FF pieces – you have to deposit your money first.

In remote regions, you may still find old-style phones for which you pay at the counter after you've made your call.

Many cafes and restaurants have privately owned, coin-operated telephones – intended primarily for the use of their clients – known as Point Phones. Point Phones require that you deposit 2FF to dial, but you can get half of that back if you make a short call and use two 1FF pieces rather than one 2FF coin. To make another call with your left-over credit (which is shown on the LCD screen), press the *reprise crédit* button.

You cannot get the international operator from, or receive calls at, a Point Phone, but you can dial emergency numbers (no coins needed) and use Country Direct services (insert the 2FF – you'll get it back at the end). To find a Point Phone, look for blue-on-white window stickers bearing the Point Phone emblem.

All public phones except Point Phones can receive both domestic and international calls. If you want someone to call you back, just give them France's country code, the area code (04 for Corsica) and the number, usually found after the words *Ici le* or *No d'appel* on the tariff sheet or on a little sign inside the phone box. When there's an incoming call, the words *décrochez – appel arrivé* will appear in the LCD window.

Minitel A very useful telephone-connected computerised information service, Minitel can be expensive to use. The most basic Minitels, equipped with a black and white monitor and a clumsy keyboard, are available for no charge to telephone subscribers. Newer models have colour screens, and many people now access the system with a home computer and a modem.

Minitel numbers consist of four digits and a string of letters. Home users pay a per-minute access charge, but consulting the *annuaire* (directory) is free. Most of the Minitels in post offices are also free for directory inquiries (though some require a 1FF or 2FF coin), and many of them let you access pay-as-you-go on-line services.

eKno Communication Service

Lonely Planet's eKno global communication service provides low-cost international calls – for local calls you're usually better off with a local phonecard. eKno also offers free messaging services, email, travel information and an on-line travel vault, where you can securely store your important documents. You can join on-line at www.ekno.lonelyplanet.com, where you will find the local-access numbers for the 24-hour customer-service centre. Once you have joined, always check the eKno Web site for the latest access numbers for each country and updates on new features.

Fax

Fax services are often available in post offices. Details are included under the appropriate towns throughout this book.

Email & Internet Access

Cybercafes are still rare in Corsica. Where we have found one, we mention it under Post & Communications in the relevant chapter. You should be under no illusion, however, that you will have an easy time collecting or sending email while you are on the island.

Similarly, there are very few hotels on the island where the telephone system is sufficiently modern to allow you to connect to the Internet from your room with a modem.

INTERNET RESOURCES

The amount of information available on the World Wide Web continues to increase at an absolutely breathtaking rate. You can use the Web to research your travels, hunt down bargain air fares, book hotels, check on weather conditions or chat with locals and other travellers about the best places to visit (or avoid!).

One of the best places to start your Web explorations is the Lonely Planet Web site (www.lonelyplanet.com). Here you'll find succinct summaries on travelling to most places on earth, postcards from other travellers and the Thorn Tree bulletin board, where you can ask questions before you go or dispense advice when you get back. You can also find travel news and updates to many of our most popular guidebooks, and the subWWWay section links you to the most useful travel resources elsewhere on the Web.

Though Corsica is hardly the world leader in electronic information, it's coming up from nowhere fairly fast. Useful Web sites on Corsica in English include:

Corse Matin Tomorrow's news and weather today: Corsica's leading daily newspaper (French only)
www.corsematin.com

CorseWeb Smashing pictures, useful links to numerous local tourism authorities, notes on history, food, language, etc
www.internetcom.fr/corsica/uk/home.htm

Corsica Isula The most exhaustive of Web sites about Corsica in English – and perhaps in any language! Be sure to scroll down to the 'Hot List of Corsican Web Sites' and also don't miss the copious links to other useful sites under 'Travel to Corsica'.
www.corsica-isula.com

Corsica Nazione Nationalist politics made easy (almost)
www.corsica-nazione.com

CorsicaWeb From lodging to travel information to calendar events
www.corsicaweb.fr

L'Agence du Tourisme de la Corse More good practical information, this time from the island's official tourism board
www.visit-corsica.com

Quel avenir pour la Corse? Dossier of articles from leftish Paris daily that looks on Corsican nationalism with extreme scepticism (French only)
www.liberation.fr/corse/archives.html

BOOKS

Most books are published in different editions by different publishers in different countries. As a result, a book might be a hardback rarity in one country while it's readily available in paperback in another. That said, many of the books about Corsica in English are out of print, and a big library or a second-hand bookseller may be your best bet for tracing these.

Lonely Planet

Lonely Planet's *France*, with a chapter on Corsica, is an exhaustive guide to the whole country. *Walking in France* has a chapter devoted to Corsica. *Western Europe* and *Mediterranean Europe* may be useful if Corsica is going to be just one component of a much longer trip you're planning. Other useful companions are the *French Phrasebook* and *World Food France*. On a more general note, *Travel with Children* has lots of handy tips, and *Travel Photography: A Guide to Taking Better Pictures* is written by internationally renowned travel photographer, Richard I'Anson. It's full colour throughout and designed to take on the road. These are all, of course, widely available.

Travel

Dorothy Carrington's 1971 *Granite Island: a Portrait of Corsica*, also known as *Corsica: Portrait of a Granite Island*, is a travel book only in the sense that it is structured around the author's comings and goings around the island. Its learning and passion for Corsica is immense. It is possibly the finest book about Corsica in any language. Unfortunately, it is out of print on both sides of the Atlantic. You can find it, however, in many libraries and occasionally in a second-hand book shop.

Carrington's 1995 *The Dream Hunters of Corsica*, expanding on a chapter of her first Corsica book, describes the women – *mazzeri* – who, in Corsica of yore, foresaw the deaths of their kinsmen and neighbours in prophetic dreams. Good luck on finding this one, too! Her *Napoleon and His Parents* makes brilliant use of archival material available only on the island. Carrington,

English by birth, lives on the outskirts of Ajaccio. It is her announced intention to be buried in Bonifacio.

James Boswell's *An Account of Corsica, The Journal of a Tour to That Island, and Memoirs of Pascal Paoli* is no more merely a travel book than Carrington's books are. Boswell already knew Dr Johnson when he went to Corsica in 1765, but this book was his first sustained exercise in hero worship. In a sense the book made Boswell; it was also largely responsible for the Paoli and Corsica craze in England – and elsewhere in Europe ('Foolish as we are,' a Whig parliamentarian said, 'we cannot be so foolish as to go to war' – with France, he meant – 'because Mr Boswell has been to Corsica'). After the book was published in Glasgow in 1768, it was all but immediately translated into Italian, French, German and Dutch.

Edward Lear (nonsense poet – author of 'The Owl and the Pussycat') wrote an extremely interesting *Journal of a Landscape Painter in Corsica* (1870). Finding this may also be a challenge.

Literature

How exotic Corsica must have seemed to continental writers when they began to discover it in the 19th century, perfect for the purposes of swashbuckler fiction. If you search hard, you may be able to find an old edition of Alexandre Dumas' *The Corsican Brothers*, of Guy de Maupassant's Corsica stories, of Honoré de Balzac's story 'La Vendetta' and of Prosper Mérimée's still almost credible novel *Colomba* or his superb short story 'Mateo Falcone'. Unsurprisingly, they all deal with honour, murder, implacable hatreds and revenge, exploring an insular value system through the tinted glass of a more 'civilised' mainland value system.

For details on Corsican authors, see the Arts section in the Facts about Corsica chapter.

History & Politics

If you are determined to be learned about Corsica (in English only), you will have to turn to academic monographs. Among the best of them, Stephen Wilson's 1988 *Feuding, Conflict and Banditry in Nineteenth-Century Corsica* examines the reality behind what was typically glamorised by romantic novelists and short-story writers.

Desmond Gregory's 1985 *The Ungovernable Rock* looks into British involvement in Corsica during the revolutionary wars. The theme of Alexandra Jaffe's 1999 *Ideologies in Action: Language Politics on Corsica* is self-explanatory (this book will be of interest not just to people on their way to Corsica but anyone with an interest in the survival of 'small' languages). In the context of these others, Peter Thrasher's 1970 biography *Pasquale Paoli* comes closest to popular reading.

Walking

Lonely Planet's *Walking in France* provides detailed coverage of the GR20. *The Corsican High Level Route – Walking the GR20*, by Alan Castle, also offers concise details of the famous trail. *Landscapes of Corsica*, by Noel Rochford, lists a number of shorter walking excursions on the island as well as tours suitable for visitors with their own transport.

French-Language

Travellers with a good reading knowledge of French will have access to much richer resources. Robert Colonna d'Istria's *L'Histoire de la Corse*, informed throughout by the premise that Corsica *is* French and that's the end of it, is one good introduction. Another is Roger Caratini's *Histoire du Peuple Corse*, where he takes the position that the centuries of Genoese rule were Corsica's golden age, while the French long pursued a policy of cryptocolonialism.

Nicolas Giudici's *Le Crépuscule des Corses* is a brilliant and pessimistic analysis of Corsica's prospects in the world (*crépuscule* means twilight). Hélène Masson-Maret's *La Personnalité Corse* attempts – with some success – to get beneath Corsican skin. Six-volume *La Mémorial des Corses* is a veritable encyclopedia of Corsican themes.

The island's flora is detailed in Marcelle Conrad's *Plantes et Fleurs Recontrées. Roches et Paysages de la Corse* from the Parc Naturel Régional de Corse (PNRC) describes

Corsica's geology and also recommends some geological walks.

La Corse Sous-marine, with photographs by Georges Antoni, will make you want to go diving even if you have never felt the urge before (*sous-marine* means underwater).

Films

Lonely Planet's videotape *Corsica, Sicily & Sardinia* is an excellent introduction to Corsica and its neighbouring islands.

In the 1941 film version of Alexandre Dumas' *The Corsican Brothers*, swashbuckler Douglas Fairbanks, Jr plays both of the Corsican twins separated at birth. It's available in some video libraries, and is good for a laugh – but has virtually nothing to do with the island you're going to.

NEWSPAPERS & MAGAZINES

The two main daily newspapers are regional editions of newspapers based in mainland France. *Corse Matin* is based on *Nice Matin* and has a circulation of around 40,000. *La Corse* is partially edited by Marseille-based La Provence group, and has a circulation of around 16,000. If you read French, you'll get through either one of them almost as fast as if you don't read French. This doesn't mean that there isn't occasionally an amusing item or even an illuminating one.

Le Journal de la Corse proclaims itself the 'weekly newspaper that has been defending the interests of the island since 1817'. *U Ribombu*, the scathing voice of A Concolta Indipendentista, expounds the demands of the main Corsican nationalist movement. *Arriti*, the oldest of the nationalist weeklies, still chugs along too, and there are others.

The main French newspapers are widely available on the island, and English newspapers and magazines – for example, the *Independent* and *Times*, and *Time* – are available here and there, particularly in summer.

RADIO & TV

Corsica's mountains serve as an effective barrier to radio signals, though even on a car radio in the very most rugged parts of the island you will sometimes find yourself, surprisingly, picking up Italian stations. Unless you're spending time in just one place, your best bet is simply to cruise the dial from time to time, where you'll find a variety of French stations, for example, France Info is at 105.5Mhz FM.

The BBC World Service transmits on short-wave only; the frequency varies over the course of the day. The Voice of America can be picked up in the Ajaccio area at 96Mhz FM.

A television will be found in many hotel rooms or else in the lobby or common room. Usually, though, this television will pick up only a few local channels. Hotels receiving any English-language channel by cable are few and far between, and expensive.

VIDEO SYSTEMS

French TV broadcasts are in SECAM *(système électronique couleur avec mémoire)* and non-SECAM TVs won't work in France. French videotapes can only be played on video recorders and TVs that have a SECAM capability.

PHOTOGRAPHY & VIDEO

Film & Equipment

Colour film (C41) can be developed for a reasonable price in the larger towns within a few hours. Developing slides (E6) is more expensive and time-consuming because the film is sent off to mainland France.

Standard colour film is easy to come by in Corsica, but it tends to be expensive. Slide film or black and white film is harder to find, as is highly sensitive or specialist film, and it, too, tends to be expensive. Always check the use-by date on the box and never buy film that has been exposed to heat.

You'll find blank video tapes in supermarkets in the larger towns, but make sure you buy the correct format. It is usually worth buying at least a few cartridges duty-free to start off your trip.

Technical Tips

Corsica is exceptionally photogenic. However, the sun – which wipes out contrast – and the strong light can represent a problem in summer. Hence, it's just as well not to shoot when the sun is way up in the sky. It's pointless to use very sensitive film – 100 ASA will be more than sufficient. A polarising filter may help.

Lonely Planet's *Travel Photography: A Guide to Taking Better Pictures*, by acclaimed photographer Richard I'Anson, is a useful companion on the road.

Restrictions

Photography is rarely forbidden, except in museums and art galleries. Of course, taking snapshots of military installations is not appreciated in any country.

Photographing People

When photographing people, it is basic courtesy to ask permission. If you don't know any French, smile while pointing at your camera and they'll get the picture – as you probably will.

Video

Properly used, a video camera can give a fascinating record of your holiday. But video cameras have very sensitive microphones, and you might be surprised how much sound is picked up. This can also be a problem if there is a lot of ambient noise – filming by the side of a busy road might seem OK when you do it, but viewing it back home might simply give you a cacophony of traffic noise. For beginners, one good rule is to try to film in long takes, and don't move the camera around too much. If your camera has a stabiliser, you can use it to obtain good footage while travelling on various means of transport, even on bumpy roads.

Make sure you keep the batteries charged and have the necessary charger, plugs and transformer.

Finally, remember to follow the same rules regarding people's sensitivities as for still photography – always ask permission first.

Airport Security

Be prepared to have your camera and film run through x-ray machines at airports and the entrances to sensitive public buildings. The machines are supposedly film-safe up to 1000 ASA, and laptops and computer disks appear to pass through without losing data, but there is always some degree of risk.

The police and gendarmes who run x-ray machines often seem to treat a request that they hand-check something as casting doubt on the power and glory of the French Republic. Arguing almost never works, and being polite is only slightly more effective unless you can do it in French. You're most likely to get an affirmative response if you are deferential and your request is moderate: request that they hand-check your film, not your whole camera (which could, after all, conceal a bomb). They are usually amenable to checking computer disks by hand. You might also want to invest in a lead-laminated film-shielding pouch.

TIME

Corsica uses the 24-hour clock, with the hours separated from the minutes by a lowercase 'h'. Thus, 15h30 is 3.30 pm, 21h50 is 9.50 pm, 00h30 is 12.30 am, and so on.

Corsica is on the same time as the rest of France, that is, on Central European Time, which is one hour ahead of (later than) GMT/UTC. During daylight-saving time, which runs from the last Sunday in March to the last Sunday in October, France is two hours ahead of GMT/UTC.

Without taking daylight-saving time into account, when it's noon in Paris it's 3 am in San Francisco, 6 am in New York, 11 am in London, 8 pm in Tokyo, 9 pm in Sydney and 11 pm in Auckland.

The time difference to Melbourne and Sydney is complicated because daylight-saving time in Australia takes effect during the northern hemisphere's winter. The Australian eastern coast is between eight and 10 hours ahead of France.

ELECTRICITY

Voltages & Cycles

The electricity supply in Corsica is 220V at 50Hz AC. You will need a transformer if you are coming from a country where the voltage is different.

While the usual travel transformers allow appliances to run in Corsica, they cannot alter the Hz rate, which determines – among other things – the speed of electric motors. As a result, tape recorders not equipped with built-in transformers may function poorly.

There are two types of transformers: mixing them up will destroy either the transformer or your appliance, so be warned. The 'heavy' kind, usually designed to handle 35W or less (see the tag) and often metal-clad, is designed for use with small electric devices such as radios, tape recorders and razors. The other kind, which weighs much less but is rated for up to 1500W, is for use only with appliances that contain heating elements, such as hair dryers and irons.

Plugs & Sockets

Old-type wall sockets, often rated at 600W, take two round pins. The new kinds of sockets take fatter pins and have a protruding earth (ground) pin.

Adapters to make new plugs fit into the old sockets are said to be illegal but are still available at electrical shops.

WEIGHTS & MEASURES

Metric System

Corsica, like the rest of France, uses the metric system. For a conversion chart, see the inside back cover of this book.

Numbers

For numbers with four or more digits, the French use full stops or spaces where writers in English would use commas: one million therefore appears as 1.000.000 or 1 000 000. For decimals, on the other hand, the French use commas, so 1.75 appears as 1,75.

LAUNDRY

Most of the large and medium-size coastal towns on the island have laundrettes. A load costs anywhere from 25FF to 40FF.

To find a *laverie libre-service* (an unstaffed, self-service laundrette), see the relevant town section in this book or ask at your hotel or hostel.

In general, you deposit coins into a *monnayeur central* (central control box) – not the machine itself – and push a button that corresponds to the number of the machine you wish to operate. These gadgets are sometimes programmed to deactivate the washing machines an hour or so before closing time.

Except with the most modern systems, you're likely to need all sorts of peculiar coin combinations – change machines are often out of order, so come prepared. Coins, especially 2FF pieces, are handy for the *séchoirs* (dryers) and the *lessive* (laundry powder) dispenser.

You can choose between a number of washing cycles:

blanc – whites
couleur – colours
synthétique – synthetics
laine – woollens
prélavage – prewash cycle
lavage – wash cycle
rinçage – rinse cycle
essorage – spin-dry cycle

TOILETS

Public toilets, signposted *toilettes* or *WC*, are rare on the island, but you can use the toilets in most restaurants and bars. Simply ask, *Est-ce que je peux utiliser les toilettes, s'il vous plaît?*

Generally, toilets are clean and the mechanisms intelligible though, in remote areas, you may still now and again encounter a Turkish-style toilet *(toilette à la turque)*. This is a squat toilet, with a high-pressure flushing mechanism that will soak your feet if you don't step back in time!

Travellers will often not find convenient toilet facilities at beaches, and obviously the more remote the beach the greater the likelihood that there will be no toilet facilities at all. Hikers will find a few chemical toilets near PNRC refuges but none, of course, along the trails.

It goes without saying that beachgoers and hikers alike should be careful not to leave toilet paper behind them.

HEALTH

Once malaria was wiped out in Corsica's eastern lowlands 50-odd years ago, the island ceased to present any unusual threat of infectious diseases. Health problems nevertheless can arise as the result of walking, mountain climbing and diving accidents, excessive sun exposure and change of climate. Information on how to locate medical services will be found in the town sections of this guide. The best medicine remains prevention.

Predeparture Planning

Health Insurance Travellers should be sure they have adequate health insurance. See Travel Insurance in the Visas & Documents section earlier in this chapter for details.

Citizens of EU countries are covered for emergency medical treatment throughout the EU on production of an E111 certificate, though charges are likely for medication, dental work and secondary examinations, including x-rays and laboratory tests. Ask about the E111 at your local health services department or travel agency at least a few weeks before you travel. In the UK you can get the form from post offices.

Immunisations No particular jabs are required for Corsica, but it's recommended that all travellers be up to date on basic vaccinations (such as polio, tetanus, and diphtheria) irrespective of where they are going.

You should seek medical advice at least six weeks before travel; some vaccinations require more than one injection, while some should not be given together. Note that some vaccinations should not be given during pregnancy or to people with allergies – discuss this with your doctor.

Condoms All pharmacies in France carry condoms *(préservatifs)*, and a few, even in Corsica, may have 24-hour condom vending machines outside the door. So may some bars, discos and petrol stations.

Condoms that conform to French government standards are always marked with the letters NF *(norme française)* in black on a white oval inside a red and blue rectangle on the packet.

Travel Health Guides Lonely Planet's *Travel with Children* includes advice on travel health for younger children.

There are also a number of excellent travel health sites on the Internet. From the Lonely Planet Web site there are links at www.lonelyplanet.com/weblinks to the World Health Organization and the US Centers for Disease Control & Prevention.

Other Preparations A trip to the dentist before you leave is never a bad idea and if you wear glasses take a spare pair and your prescription.

If you require a particular medication take an adequate supply, as it may not be available on the island. Take part of the packaging showing the generic name, rather than the brand, which will make it easier to refill the prescription. It's also a good idea to have a legible prescription or letter from your doctor to show that you legally use the medication to avoid any problems.

Medical Treatment

Major hospitals are indicated on the maps in this book, and their addresses and phone numbers are mentioned in the text. Tourist offices and hotels will almost always be able to recommend a doctor or dentist – and perhaps one who speaks your language. You can also contact SAMU *(Service d'Aide Médicale Urgente)* at ☎ 15 to find out the address of the closest hospital or doctor.

Public Health System Anyone (including foreigners) who is sick, even mildly, can receive treatment in the *service des urgences* (casualty ward or emergency room) of any public hospital. Hospitals try to have people who speak English in the casualty wards, but this is not done systematically. If necessary, the hospital will call in an interpreter. It's an excellent idea to ask for a copy of the diagnosis – in English, if possible – for your doctor back home.

Getting treated for illness or injury in a public hospital costs much less in France, and thus Corsica, than in many other western countries, especially the USA: being seen by a doctor (a *consultation*) costs about 150FF (235FF to 250FF on Sunday and holidays, 275FF to 350FF from 8 pm to 8 am). Seeing a specialist is a bit more expensive. Blood tests and other procedures, each of which is billed at a standard rate, will increase this figure. Full hospitalisation costs from 3000FF per day.

Hospitals usually ask that visitors from abroad settle accounts immediately after receiving treatment, while residents of France are sent a bill in the mail.

Dental Care Most major hospitals offer dental services.

Pharmacies French pharmacies are usually marked by a green cross that is lit up when the pharmacy's open. Pharmacists *(pharmaciens)* can often suggest treatments for minor ailments. If you are prescribed medication, make sure you understand the dosage, and how often and when you should take it. It's a good idea to ask for a copy of the prescription *(ordonnance)* for your records.

Pharmacies co-ordinate their days and hours of closure so that a town or district isn't left without a place to buy medication. For details of the nearest on night/weekend duty *(pharmacie de garde)*, consult the door of any pharmacy.

For sundries such as toothpaste, shampoo and soap, prices will be much more reasonable at a general merchandiser such as Monoprix on ave de la Libération in Bastia or at 33 cours Napoléon in Ajaccio.

Basic Rules

Food There is an old colonial adage which says: 'If you can cook it, boil it or peel it you can eat it...otherwise forget it'. Vegetables and fruit should be washed with purified water or peeled where possible.

If a place looks clean and well run and the vendor also looks clean and healthy, then the food is probably safe. In general, places that are packed with travellers or locals will be fine, while empty restaurants are questionable. The food in busy restaurants is cooked and eaten quite quickly with little standing around and is probably not reheated.

Water Tap water in Corsica is safe to drink. However the water in most fountains is not drinkable and – like the taps in some public toilets – may have a sign reading *eau non potable* (undrinkable water).

Many people do not hesitate to drink water from streams during their walks. However, given all the free-ranging livestock and other animals, this water is not necessarily safe.

The simplest way of purifying water is to boil it thoroughly. Note, however, that at high altitude water boils at a lower temperature, so germs are less likely to be killed. At high altitude, you'll need to boil water longer than at sea level.

Simple filtering will not remove all dangerous organisms, so if you can't boil water it should be treated chemically. Chlorine tablets will kill many pathogens but not some parasites such as amoebic cysts and giardia. Iodine is more effective in purifying water and is available in tablet form (such as Potable Aqua). Follow the directions carefully and remember that too much iodine can be harmful.

It's very easy not to drink water in sufficient quantities, especially on hot days or at high altitudes, and you can easily dehydrate yourself without even feeling particularly thirsty. Not needing to urinate or very dark-yellow urine is a danger sign.

Bites & Stings

Jellyfish stings are generally just rather painful. Antihistamines and analgesics may reduce the reaction and relieve the pain. Scorpion fish and weevers can also sting if you touch them; although the stings are not serious, you may need to see a doctor. There are no poisonous snakes on Corsica.

Environmental Hazards

Fungal Infections More common in hot weather, fungal infections are usually found on the scalp, between the toes (athlete's foot) or fingers, in the groin and on the whole body (ringworm). You get ringworm (which is a fungal infection, not a parasite) from contact with infected animals or other people, for example by walking in damp places such as showers.

To prevent fungal infections wear loose, comfortable clothes, avoid artificial fibres, wash frequently and dry yourself thoroughly. Keep your flip-flops on in showers you don't completely trust. If you do get an

Medical Kit Check List

Following is a list of items you should consider including in your medical kit – consult your pharmacist for brands available in your country.

- ☐ **Aspirin** or **paracetamol** (acetaminophen in the US) – for pain or fever.
- ☐ **Antihistamine** – for allergies, such as hay fever; to ease the itch from insect bites or stings; and to prevent motion sickness.
- ☐ **Antibiotics** – consider including these if you're travelling well off the beaten track; see your doctor, as they must be prescribed, and carry the prescription with you.
- ☐ **Loperamide** or **diphenoxylate** – 'blockers' for diarrhoea; **prochlorperazine** or **metaclopramide** for nausea and vomiting.
- ☐ **Rehydration mixture** – to prevent dehydration, eg due to severe diarrhoea; particularly important when travelling with children.
- ☐ **Insect repellent**, **sunscreen**, **lip balm** and **eye drops**.
- ☐ **Calamine lotion**, **sting relief spray** or **aloe vera** – to ease irritation from sunburn and insect bites or stings.
- ☐ **Antifungal cream** or **powder** – for fungal skin infections and thrush.
- ☐ **Antiseptic** (such as povidone-iodine) – for cuts and grazes.
- ☐ **Bandages**, **Band-Aids (plasters)** and other wound dressings.
- ☐ **Water purification tablets** or **iodine**.
- ☐ **Scissors**, **tweezers** and a **thermometer** (note that mercury thermometers are prohibited by airlines).
- ☐ **Cold** and **flu tablets**, **throat lozenges** and **nasal decongestant**.
- ☐ **Multivitamins** – consider for long trips, when dietary vitamin intake may be inadequate.

infection, wash the infected area at least daily with a disinfectant or medicated soap and water, and again rinse and dry it thoroughly. Apply an antifungal cream or powder. Try to expose the infected area to air or sunlight as much as possible. Change all towels and underwear regularly, wash them in hot water and let them dry in the sun.

Hay Fever Sufferers should be aware that the pollen count in Corsica is especially high in May and June.

Heat Exhaustion & Prickly Heat Dehydration and salt deficiency can cause heat exhaustion. In high-temperature environments, take time to acclimatise, drink sufficient liquids and do not do overexert yourself physically.

Salt deficiency is characterised by fatigue, lethargy, headaches, giddiness and muscle cramps; salt tablets may help, but adding extra salt to your food is better.

Prickly heat is an itchy rash caused by excessive perspiration trapped under the skin. It usually strikes people who have just arrived in a hot climate. Keeping cool, bathing often, drying the skin and using a mild talcum or prickly heat powder may help, as may a good dose of air-conditioning.

Heatstroke This serious, occasionally fatal, condition can occur if the body's heat-regulating mechanism breaks down and the body temperature rises to dangerous levels. Long, continuous periods of exposure to high temperatures and insufficient fluids can leave you vulnerable to heatstroke. Avoid alcohol and exhausting activities when you arrive in a hot country.

The symptoms are feeling unwell, not sweating very much (or at all) and a high body temperature (39 to 41°C or 102 to 106°F). Where sweating has ceased the skin becomes flushed and red. Severe, throbbing headaches and lack of co-ordination will also occur, and the sufferer may be confused or aggressive. Eventually the victim will become delirious or convulse. Hospitalisation is essential, but in the interim get victims out of the sun, remove their clothing, cover them with a wet sheet or towel and then fan continually. Give fluids if they are conscious.

Sunstroke Prolonged exposure to the sun can result in sunstroke. The symptoms are nausea, hot skin and headaches. If sunstroke occurs, rest in the dark, apply a compress of cold water and take aspirin.

Health for Divers

Decompression Sickness Corsica is perfect for two activities that it is *not* a good idea to try in the same day: diving and mountain walking. Always avoid climbing at altitude straight after diving; this will allow your body to get rid of the residual nitrogen that it has stored up. Climbing as little as 1500m can prove dangerous if you have been diving only a few hours earlier, and so can air travel. As a rule of thumb, wait at least 12 hours after resurfacing for either.

The hospital in Ajaccio (☎ 04 95 29 90 90), 27 ave de l'Impératrice Eugénie, has a decompression chamber.

Health for Walkers

Head Injuries & Fractures A serious fall, resulting in head injuries or fractures, is always a possibility when walking, especially if you are on steep slopes.

If a person suffers a head injury but is conscious, they are probably OK but should be closely monitored for at least 24 hours for any deterioration in their condition. If a person is unconscious, check the airway and breathing immediately and position the casualty in the recovery position. Bleeding from the nose or ear may indicate a fractured skull. If this occurs, lay the victim so the bleeding ear is downwards and avoid carrying them if at all possible. Seek medical attention urgently.

Indications of a broken bone are pain, swelling, loss of function in a limb or irregularities in the shape of the bones. Fractures in unconscious victims may be detected by gently attempting to bend each bone in turn. If the bone moves it is broken and you should not try to move it any further except to try to straighten out obviously displaced fractures.

Immobilise a non-displaced or straightened fracture by securing one limb to an adjacent one or by applying a splint. Fractures associated with laceration of the skin require more urgent medical treatment, as there is a risk of infection.

Hypothermia Too much cold can be just as dangerous as too much heat, especially if it results in hypothermia. The conditions in the Corsican mountains can be surprising. There can be frost above 2000m on the GR20, even in summer, and at this altitude the temperature and wind and storm conditions are often alpine. In Corsica, the weather can also change quite abruptly. Cold, then, in Corsica, is potentially as big a problem for walkers as heat.

Hypothermia occurs when the body loses heat quickly and the core temperature of the body falls. It is surprisingly easy to progress from very cold to dangerously cold due to a combination of wind, wet clothing, fatigue and hunger, even if the air temperature is above freezing. It is best to dress in layers; silk, wool and some of the new artificial fibres are all good insulating materials. A hat is also important, as a lot of heat is lost through the head. A strong, waterproof outer layer is essential. Carry basic supplies, including food containing simple sugars to generate heat quickly and plenty of fluid to drink.

Symptoms of hypothermia are exhaustion, numb skin (particularly toes and fingers), shivering, slurred speech, irrational or violent behaviour, lethargy, stumbling, dizzy spells, muscle cramps and violent bursts of energy. Victims of hypothermia will sometimes think they are warm and try to take their clothes *off*.

To treat mild hypothermia, first get the sufferer out of the wind and/or rain, remove their clothing if it's wet and replace it with dry, warm clothing. Give them hot liquids – not alcohol – and easily digestible high-calorie food. This should be enough to treat the early stages of hypothermia. Do not rub victims, nor place them near a fire, and do not change their clothes when they are exposed to the wind. If possible, make them take a hot bath.

Sprains Ankle and knee sprains occur commonly when walking, particularly in rugged areas. If you expect such conditions make sure you have all-leather boots with adequate ankle support. Ultra-light, low-cut walking boots are glorified tennis shoes and not suitable.

Mild sprains should be wrapped immediately with a crepe bandage to prevent swelling. Often a day spent resting and elevating the leg will allow you to continue the walk without too much pain. For more serious sprains when the victim is unable to walk, seek medical assistance.

Infectious Diseases

Diarrhoea Simple things such as a change of water, food or climate can cause a bout of diarrhoea. Dehydration is the main danger with any diarrhoea, particularly in children and the elderly. Therefore the first treatment is to drink lots of fluids: ideally you should mix eight teaspoonfuls of sugar and one of salt in 1L of water. Otherwise weak black tea with a little sugar, or soft drinks allowed to go flat and diluted 50% with purified water are recommended. In the case of severe diarrhoea, a rehydrating solution is excellent for replacing lost minerals and salts. When you feel better, continue to eat lightly.

Gut-paralysing drugs such as loperamide or diphenoxylate can be used to bring relief from the symptoms, although they do not actually cure the problem. Only use these drugs if you do not have access to toilets, for example, if you *must* travel. Note that these drugs are not recommended for children under 12 years. Antibiotics can be useful for severe diarrhoea, especially when it is accompanied by nausea, vomiting, stomach cramps or a slight fever. Three days of treatment are generally sufficient, and some improvement is normally seen within 24 hours. However, if the diarrhoea persists for more than 48 hours or if there is blood in the stools, you should consult a doctor.

Viral Gastroenteritis This is caused by a virus rather than by bacteria. Symptoms include stomach cramps, diarrhoea and sometimes vomiting and/or a slight fever. The only treatment is to rest and drink lots of fluids.

Hepatitis There are several different viruses that cause hepatitis (a general term for inflammation of the liver) and they differ in the way that they are transmitted. The symptoms are similar in all forms of the illness, and include fever, chills, headache, fatigue, feelings of weakness and aches and pains, followed by loss of appetite, nausea, vomiting, abdominal pain, dark urine, light-coloured faeces, jaundiced (yellow) skin and yellowing of the whites of the eyes. People who have had hepatitis should avoid alcohol for some time after the illness, as the liver needs time to recover.

Hepatitis A is transmitted by contaminated food and drinking water. You should seek medical advice, but there is not much you can do apart from resting, drinking lots of fluids, eating lightly and avoiding fatty foods. Hepatitis E is transmitted in the same way as hepatitis A; it can be particularly serious in pregnant women.

Hepatitis B is spread through contact with infected blood, blood products or body fluids, for example, through sexual contact, unsterilised needles and blood transfusions or contact with blood via small breaks in the skin. Other risk situations include shaving, tattooing or body piercing with contaminated equipment. Hepatitis C and D are spread in the same way as hepatitis B.

There are vaccines against hepatitis A and B, but there are currently no vaccines against the other types of hepatitis. Following the basic rules about food and water (hepatitis A and E) and avoiding risk situations (hepatitis B, C and D) are important preventative measures.

HIV & AIDS Infection with the human immunodeficiency virus (HIV) may lead to acquired immune deficiency syndrome (AIDS), which is a fatal disease. Any exposure to blood, blood products or body fluids may put the individual at risk.

The disease is often transmitted through sexual contact or dirty needles – vaccinations, acupuncture, tattooing and body piercing are potentially as dangerous as intravenous drug use. It is therefore essential to use condoms and to avoid sharing needles in any way.

HIV can be transmitted through infected blood transfusions, but blood used for transfusions in European hospitals is screened for HIV and should be safe.

Sexually Transmitted Diseases HIV/AIDS and hepatitis B can be transmitted through sexual contact – see the relevant sections earlier for more details. Other STDs include gonorrhoea, herpes and syphilis; sores, blisters or rashes around the genitals and discharges or pain when urinating are common symptoms. In some STDs, such as wart virus or chlamydia, symptoms may be less marked or not observed at all, especially in women. Chlamydia infection can cause infertility in men and women before any symptoms have been noticed.

The only way to prevent STDs is always to use condoms during sexual encounters. The treatment of gonorrhoea and syphilis is with antibiotics. The different sexually transmitted diseases each require specific antibiotics.

Women's Health

Gynaecological Problems Antibiotic use, synthetic underwear, sweating and contraceptive pills can lead to fungal vaginal infections when travelling in hot climates. Fungal infections are characterised by a rash, itch and discharge. The infection can be treated with a vinegar or lemon-juice douche with yoghurt, or ask a pharmacist for nystatin, miconazole or clotrimazole pessaries or a vaginal cream. Good personal hygiene and wearing loose-fitting clothes and cotton underwear may help prevent these infections.

Some women experience an irregular menstrual cycle while travelling because of the upset in routine. Your doctor can give you advice about this.

Pregnancy It is not advisable to travel to some places while pregnant as some vaccinations normally used to prevent serious diseases are not advisable during pregnancy (eg, yellow fever). In addition, some diseases are much more serious for the mother (and may increase the risk of a stillborn child) in pregnancy (eg, malaria).

Most miscarriages occur during the first three months of pregnancy. Miscarriage is not uncommon and can occasionally lead to severe bleeding. The last three months should also be spent within reasonable distance of good medical care. A baby born as early as 24 weeks stands a chance of survival, but only in a good modern hospital. Pregnant women should avoid all unnecessary medication, although vaccinations and malarial prophylactics should still be taken where needed. Additional care should be taken to prevent illness and particular attention should be paid to diet and nutrition. Alcohol and nicotine, for example, should be avoided.

WOMEN TRAVELLERS

Attitudes Towards Women

Something of the traditional role of women in Corsican society has been mentioned in the boxed text 'Women in Corsican Society' in the Facts about Corsica chapter. Twentieth century economic change, the influence of modern mass media, the relentless travel of Corsicans abroad and the explosive growth of the tourism industry in Corsica itself have of course changed everything. In Corsica, women travelling solo, or with one or more other women, will experience no particular inconveniences.

Safety Precautions

Physical attack is unlikely, but it does happen. As in any country, the best way to avoid being assaulted is to be conscious of your surroundings and aware of situations that could be potentially dangerous: deserted streets, lonely beaches, dark corners of large train stations and so on.

France's national rape-crisis hotline (☎ 08 00 05 95 95) can be reached toll-free from any telephone without using a phone card. Staffed by volunteers from 10 am to 6 pm Monday to Friday, it's run by a women's organisation called Viols Femmes Informations. In an emergency, you can also always call the police (☎ 17).

GAY & LESBIAN TRAVELLERS

Contrary to what you might expect, homosexuality does not seem to pose a problem to this conservative and traditional society.

The Web site Corsegay at http://corsegay.free.fr, by its own account Corsica's first gay Web site, lists various meeting places, including the quai Tino Rossi and Le Curieux Bar-Discothèque (☎ 04 95 21 14 40, 2 rue des Halles) in the Ajaccio area, in the Bastia area Plage de la Marana, Plage de St-Restitut beyond Camp de Légionnaire at Calvi, the north of Plage d'Algajola in the Île Rousse area, and Santa Julia, opposite the Moby Dick bar, in Porto Vecchio.

DISABLED TRAVELLERS

The Ajaccio branch of the Association des Paralysés de France (☎/fax 04 95 20 75 33), ave du Maréchal Lyautey, 20090 Ajaccio, publishes the details of places in Corsica (hotels, restaurants, cultural sites and so on) that are accessible to disabled people. These details can also be obtained from the tourist office in Ajaccio (☎ 04 95 51 53 03, fax 04 95 51 53 01), 3 blvd du Roi Jérôme.

Airlines ensure that there are no access problems for disabled travellers on aeroplanes or at the airports. The traditional ferries *Napoléon Bonaparte*, *Île-de-Beauté*, *Danièle Casanova*, *Monte d'Oro* and *Paglia Orba* all have some cabins that are accessible to wheelchair users, as do the NGVs, the new high-speed ferries. However, in all cases you must contact the companies in question before travelling. For their details see the Getting There & Away chapter.

The town centres of Bastia, Ajaccio, Bonifacio, Porto Vecchio, Propriano and, to a lesser extent, Sartène are completely accessible, as are most of Corsica's museums.

The following hotels, all figuring elsewhere in this book, are singled out by the Association des Paralysés de France as having rooms accessible to disabled people:

Ajaccio
Hôtel Mercure
Bonifacio
Hôtel Caravelle
Hôtel-Restaurant du Centre Nautique
Calvi
Hôtel Le Rocher
Erbalunga
Hôtel Castel Brando
Propriano
Hôtel Loft
St-Florent
Hôtel Tettola
Sartène
La Villa Piana
Vallée de la Restonica (Corte)
Hôtel Dominique Colonna
Vizzavona
Hôtel Monte d'Oro

See the sections on individual towns or villages for more details of these hotels.

SENIOR TRAVELLERS

The Corsican climate, particularly in the shoulder seasons, the drama and majesty of the scenery and slow pace may all appeal strongly to senior travellers. They might – like many younger travellers – be reluctant to undertake the GR20, and for good reason, but there are any number of less punishing walks around the island.

Discounts to which senior travellers in Corsica are entitled are listed in the text as appropriate.

TRAVEL WITH CHILDREN

Corsica has a relatively low birth rate, but the family is highly valued in Corsica, and young children are often cooed over. There are no particular dangers on the island to watch out for, and there is a wide range of sporting activities to occupy kids on the water, the shore (schools for diving, windsurfing and so on) and in the mountains.

Many hotels provide additional beds for children and most car-hire companies can provide you with child seats.

Nappies, milk for babies up to six months old and between six and 12 months of age, mineral water and a range of medicines are also readily available. Discounts for children are common.

In summer, you should make sure that children are not overexposed to the sun: you should use barrier cream and reapply it several times daily, and make sure that they wear a hat. Try to ensure that they drink lots of water as well. The Lonely Planet title *Travel with Children* gives plenty of other tips.

DANGERS & ANNOYANCES

When Corsica makes the headlines, it's often because nationalist militants seeking Corsican independence have engaged in some act of violence, such as bombing a public building, robbing a bank or murdering the prefect. But the violence has never been targeted at tourists, and there's no reason for visitors to fear for their safety from this particular quarter.

The main peril in Corsica is the winding roads which follow narrow precipices and the sometimes blind turnings, combined with the impatience of Corsican drivers, and the tendency for livestock and other animals to appear suddenly and without warning in the right of way.

Motorists do not go off to certain death on Corsican roads; the majority of motor vehicle accidents indeed appear to involve local young people on their way home from clubs in the early morning. Keep your eyes on the road. If you want to admire the scenery, stop at a lay-by.

It must also be noted that some Corsicans are racist, especially against North Africans, who represent a relatively large community on the island.

EMERGENCIES

If you need an ambulance in Corsica or anywhere else in France, dial ☎ 15. For police assistance, dial ☎ 17. For fire, dial ☎ 18. All these numbers are toll free. Information on hospitals and clinics can be found in the sections relating to specific towns and villages later in the book.

LEGAL MATTERS

Police

Thanks to the Napoleonic Code (on which the French legal system is based), the police can pretty much search anyone they want to at any time – whether or not there is probable cause.

France has two separate police forces. The Police Nationale is under the command of the prefects of the individual departments and includes the Police de l'Air et des Frontières (PAF) – the border police. The Gendarmerie Nationale, a paramilitary force under the control of the Ministry of Defence, handles airports, borders and so on.

The dreaded Compagnies Républicaines de Sécurité (CRS), riot police heavies, are part of the Police Nationale. You often see hundreds of them, equipped with the latest riot gear, at strikes or demonstrations.

Police with shoulder patches reading Police Municipale are under the control of the local mayor.

In the Event of Fire

Fire destroys hundreds or even thousands of hectares of Corsica's precious pine forests every year. This is in spite of the use of sophisticated aerial fire-fighting equipment (surveillance aircraft, helicopters, Canadair waterbombers), and the positioning of firefighters at the edge of critical wooded areas on days on which intense heat, low humidity and wind conspire to increase the likelihood of forest fires.

If you see a fire, telephone ☎ 18 (or ☎ 112 from a mobile phone) and, as best you can, give details of:

- precise location (road, distance from road etc)
- type of vegetation (maquis, forest etc)
- accessibility (track, road etc)

If asked a question, the police are likely to be correct and helpful but no more than that (though you may get a salute). If the police stop you for any reason, be polite and remain calm. They have wide powers of search and seizure and, if they take a dislike to you, they may choose to use them. The police can, without any particular reason, decide to examine your passport, visa, residence permit and so on.

French police are very strict about security, especially at airports. Do not leave baggage unattended: they're serious when they warn that suspicious objects will be summarily blown up.

Drinking & Driving

As elsewhere in the EU, the laws are very tough when it comes to drinking and driving, and for many years the slogan has been: *Boire ou conduire, il faut choisir* (Drink or drive, you have to choose). The acceptable blood-alcohol limit is 0.05%, and drivers exceeding this amount face fines of up to 30,000FF, plus up to two years in jail. Licences can also be immediately suspended.

Drugs

Importing or exporting drugs can lead to a jail sentence of between 10 and 30 years.

The fine for possession of drugs for personal use can be as high as 500,000FF.

Smoking

Laws banning smoking in public places do exist in France, but they are not strictly adhered to. If you ask for a non-smoking table in a restaurant, you are likely to be told, 'Anywhere you like'.

Litter

The fine for littering is about 1000FF.

BUSINESS HOURS

Many businesses remain open continuously between 8 am and 8 pm – and sometimes even later – for every last one of the seven days of the week in July and August. Others, notwithstanding the once-a-year opportunity to replenish the till, continue to close for a couple of hours in the early afternoon, not for a siesta, but because the owners and the staff believe in their God-given right to eat a proper lunch, and frankly they cannot believe that anyone can fail to want to spend an hour or two over lunch.

In other months of the year, businesses tend to open between 8 am and noon and between 2 and 6 pm from Monday to Friday or Saturday. Even many food businesses such as bakeries, pastry shops, butchers and greengrocers shut down between these hours.

The opening times displayed outside shops are not always adhered to.

PUBLIC HOLIDAYS & SPECIAL EVENTS

The following are public holidays in Corsica:

New Year's Day 1 January
Easter Sunday & Monday March or April
Labour Day 1 May
Victoire 1945 (VE) Day 8 May
Ascension 40th day after Easter
Pentecost/Whit Sunday & Monday 8th Sunday & Monday after Easter
Bastille Day 14 July
Assumption Day (Napoleon's birthday) 15 August
All Saints' Day 1 November
Armistice Day 11 November
Christmas 25 December

Some of the events below are celebrated outside Corsica as well; others are entirely local.

January

Île Danse This festival of Mediterranean dance welcomes 13 dance companies for 10 days in Ajaccio and Propriano. Information: ☎ 04 95 22 09 01

February

A Tumbera: Foire du Porc Coureur Festival and competition of a characteristically Corsican variety of mountain pig, in Renno on the first weekend of the month. Information: ☎ 04 95 26 65 35

Rencontres du Cinéma Italien de Bastia The Bastia Italian film festival celebrated its 12th anniversary in 2000. Information: ☎ 04 95 31 12 72

March

Fête de l'Olive The olive festival takes place in mid-March in Ste-Lucie de Tallano. Information: ☎ 04 95 78 80 13

La Passion A major Corsican-language event retracing the Passion of Christ, in Calvi during Holy Week in March or April. Information: ☎ 04 95 65 23 57

Pâques Orthodoxe (Orthodox Easter) Celebrated in Cargèse.

Processions de la Semaine Sainte The most famous processions are those in Bonifacio (Procession of the Five Colleagues) and Sartène. Calvi, Corte, Erbalunga, La Castagniccia and Bastia also celebrate Holy Week fervently, from late March to early April.

Rencontres du Cinéma Espagnol de Bastia Bastia's Spanish film festival. Information: ☎ 04 95 31 12 72

April

A Merendella in Castagniccia This fair featuring local farm products takes place in Piedicroce at Easter weekend. Information: ☎ 04 95 35 81 26

Salon de la Bande Dessinée This celebration of the art of cartooning takes place in Bastia for three days at the beginning of the month. Information: ☎ 04 95 32 12 81

Journée du Brocciu At the end of the month in Piana, everything you want to know about Corsica's world-famous cheese. Information: ☎ 04 95 27 82 05

May

A Fera di u Casgiu This cheese fair takes place in Vénaco. Information: ☎ 04 95 47 00 15

Festimare d'Île Rousse Dating from 1998, this now annual celebration of the pleasures of the sea is aimed at young people. Information: ☎ 04 95 60 04 35

Nautival A one-day festival also focused on the sea, in Macinaggio, at the end of the month. Information: ☎ 04 95 35 40 34

Semaine du Film Britannique Yes, a week of British film, in Bastia. Information: ☎ 04 95 55 96 96

June

Calvi Jazz Festival In the middle of the month, featuring big names from the international jazz scene. Information: ☎ 04 95 65 16 67/00 50

Fête de St-Jean de Corse Day of lectures and concerts staged at the Musée de la Corse in the citadel at Corte. Information: ☎ 04 95 45 25 45

St-Érasme In Ajaccio, Bastia and Calvi, the fishing boats are blessed on 2 June.

Cavall'in Festa In the middle of the month, this is an equestrian fair in Corte. Information: ☎ 04 95 16 19 14

Journées Médiévales de Bonifacio A medieval fair on Whit Sunday weekend. Information: ☎ 04 95 73 00 15

La Foire de la Mer In the middle of the month in Solenzara, this fair celebrates the people who earn their living from the sea, the sea's pleasures and sea ecology. Information: ☎ 04 95 57 48 94

July

Festivoce A festival of music and song in the Balagne, along the stretch from Île Rousse to Calvi. Information: ☎ 04 95 61 77 81

Foire du Livre Corse de l'Île Rousse A book fair. Information: ☎ 04 95 60 27 03

Foire de l'Olivier In mid-month, this celebration of the olive tree takes place in Montemaggiore, in the Balagne. Information: ☎ 04 95 62 81 72/72 78

Foire de Vin de Luri The island's leading annual wine event, on Cap Corse. Information: ☎ 04 95 35 06 44/04 17

Les Estivales d'Ajaccio A music and dance festival, from the end of July to the beginning of August. Information: ☎ 04 95 50 40 80

Les Musicales d'Ajaccio Classical music reigns supreme for the first two weeks of the month (started 1995). Information: ☎ 04 95 50 40 80

Nuits de la Guitare de Patrimonio Big names from the worlds of classical, jazz and flamenco guitar meet in the Théâtre de Verdure in mid-month. Information: ☎ 04 95 37 12 15

Relève des Gouverneurs On 11 July, this costume pageant retraces the arrival of the Genoese governors in Bastia. Information: ☎ 04 95 31 09 12.

Foire Artisanale This crafts fair takes place in Lumio. Information: ☎ 04 95 60 61 45

Santa Severa A festival of the sea and night-time carnival at Luri harbour. Information: ☎ 04 95 35 06 44

August

Festival de Film de Lama Open-air festival of European film focusing on rural life, since 1993, in the Nebbio. Information: ☎ 04 95 48 21 60

Festival de Musique d'Erbalunga Light music, jazz and guitars echo over Cap Corse in the first week of the month. Information: ☎ 04 95 33 20 73/30 19 68

Fêtes Napoléoniennes d'Ajaccio Parades, shows and fireworks, culminating on 15 August, the birthday of the city's leading native son. Information: ☎ 04 95 51 53 03

Foire du Pratu On the first weekend of the month, at the Col de Pratu in Castagniccia. Information: ☎ 04 95 39 20 07/61 10 48

Pèlerinage de Notre Dame des Neiges Pilgrimage, 5 August, at the foot of the Aiguilles de Bavella.

Rencontres Culturelle de Nonza Opera, concerts and plays in this event dating from 1998. Information: ☎ 04 95 37 82 82

Festa Antica Your chance to immerse yourself in Corsican antiquity. In Aléria, the first week of the month. Information: ☎ 04 95 57 01 51

Rencontres Théâtrales de Haute-Corse More than a dozen shows are presented in Vallée de Giussani. Information: ☎ 04 95 61 93 97

Porto Latino Three days of throbbing South American music in St-Florent. Information: ☎ 04 95 31 22 24

Foire de l'Amandier Fair consisting of competitions, exhibitions and concerts in Aregno. Information: ☎ 04 95 61 79 42

September

Fêtes de Notre Dame à Bonifacio A religious festival, on 8 September, and also a chance to try stuffed aubergines made the Bonifacio way.

Foire du Niolo
Fair taking place in early September in Casamaccioli. Information: ☎ 04 95 48 03 01

Foire de Porto Vecchio Fair in Porto Vecchio. Information: ☎ 04 95 70 67 33

Rencontres de Chants Polyphoniques de Calvi Takes place in mid-month in the fantastic setting of the citadel. Information: ☎ 04 95 65 23 57

Rencontres Européennes de Plongée Sous-Marine d'Ajaccio Exhibition of beautiful underwater images at the end of the month. Information: ☎ 04 95 25 12 58

Settembrini di Tavagna International music in five villages in this tiny region. Information: ☎ 04 95 36 91 94

Mosaicales In the first week of the month, classical music concerts throughout southern Corsica. Information: ☎ 04 95 70 09 58

Journées Napoléoniennes d'Ajaccio If you didn't have enough of Napoleon in August. Information: ☎ 04 95 21 85 62

Mele in Festa A honey festival in Murzo at the end of the month. Information: ☎ 04 95 22 67 39

October

Festival de Vent A celebration of wind in art, sport and science, in Calvi at the end of the month. Information: ☎ 04 95 65 16 67/01 53 20 93 00 Web site: www.le-festival-du-vent.com

Musicales de Bastia Jazz, classical music, light music, dance and theatre. Information: ☎ 04 95 32 75 91

November

Festival du Film des Cultures Méditerranéennes de Bastia This important festival of Mediterranean film dates from 1982. Information: ☎ 04 95 32 08 32/08 86

Fête du Marron d'Évisa Honouring chestnuts and mushrooms. Information: ☎ 04 95 26 20 09

Open International d'Échecs de Corse A chess tournament, dating from 1998, in Bastia. Information: ☎ 04 95 31 59 15

Journées de la Pomme et des Produits Naturels In honour of the apple and other fruits of nature's bounty, in Bastelica. Information: ☎ 04 95 28 71 83

December

Foire à la Chataigne The oldest and most important fair in Corsica honours the chestnut. It takes place mid-month in Bocognano. Information: ☎ 04 95 27 41 76

ACTIVITIES

There are separate chapters in this book dedicated to walking and diving, but the sporting activities available don't stop there.

Cycling

Cycling is popular in Corsica, and you can hire out mountain bikes (*VTTs* or *vélos tout terrain* in French) throughout the island. Look for details in the sections on Activities and Getting Around for various individual towns. Lonely Planet's *Cycling in France* will also help steer you along the best routes. Bear in mind, though, that the combination of hills and heat can make cycling in Corsica a trying experience.

Skiing

Skiing facilities on the island are still limited, although there are resorts in Èse and at the Col de Verghio.

Climbing & Canyoning

The area surrounding the Col de Bavella provides opportunities for climbing and canyoning. You can sign up at the tourist information centre in Porto Vecchio (☎ 04 95 70 09 58) or at the Auberge du Col de Bavella (☎ 04 95 57 43 87), which is where you meet the local guides.

The Association Sportive et Culturelle du Niolu (☎ 04 95 48 05 22) can provide you with information on the possibilities for climbing, canyoning and canoeing offered by the Niolo region.

Water Sports

In the summer, you can find companies hiring out windsurfers, dinghies and sports catamarans on some of the island's beaches (including Porticcio, around Porto Vecchio and St-Florent). These operators are detailed in the sections for those towns.

Details of the companies hiring out boats are included in the sections on the relevant towns.

Horse Riding

You will find a large number of riding centres in Corsica, and some of them are included in this book (for example, see the sections on the Désert des Agriates, Calvi, Île Rousse and Porticcio). The riding centre at Baracci (☎ 04 95 76 08 02, fax 04 95 76 19 48) near Propriano is a good example: it can organise your rides from one centre to the next, meaning that you can cover almost the entire island on horseback. The Association Nationale du Tourisme Équestre (National Association of Equestrian Tourism) has a Corsican branch (☎/fax 04 95 46 31 74, ⓔ arte.corse@wanadoo.fr) at 7 rue de Colonel Feracci, BP 58 Corte.

Organised Tours

Altore (☎/fax 04 95 37 19 30 or ☎ 06 83 39 69 06), résidence Ste-Anne, 20217 St-Florent, has a reputation for its paragliding, adrenaline sports and off-piste skiing. Contact them for a brochure.

At Objectif Nature (☎/fax 04 95 32 54 34 or ☎ 06 13 86 47 47, ⓔ objectif-nature@wanadoo.fr), 3 rue Notre Dame de Lourdes,

Organised Walks

For visitors to Corsica who would like to do some serious high-mountain walking, but not necessarily alone, a number of companies will offer either organised tours or private guides or both. Some of them will even carry your luggage from one stage to the next.

A Muntagnola, Quenza
☎ 04 95 78 65 19, fax 04 95 78 73 02

Alta Strada, Moltifao
☎/fax 04 95 47 83 01

Altore, St-Florent
☎/fax 04 95 37 19 30 or ☎ 06 83 39 69 06)
Web site: www.altore.com

Association Sportive et Culturelle du Niolu, Calacuccia
☎ 04 95 48 05 22, fax 04 95 48 08 80

Compagnie des Guides de Haute Montagne
Jean-Paul Quilici: ☎ 04 95 78 64 33
Pierre Grisgelli: ☎ 04 95 44 04 50
Pierre Piétri: ☎ 04 95 32 62 76
Didier Micheli: ☎ 04 95 25 54 24

Compagnie Régionale des Guides et Accompagnateurs en Montagnes de Corse, Calacuccia
☎ 04 95 48 05 22

Cors'Aventure, Bastellicaccia
☎ 04 95 23 80 00, fax 04 95 23 80 96

Corse Odyssée, Quenza
☎ 04 95 78 64 05, fax 04 95 78 61 91

Corsica Trek, Marignana
☎ 04 95 26 21 21

In Terra Corsa, Ponte Leccia
☎ 04 95 47 82 69, fax 04 95 47 60 01

Muntagne Corse in Libertà
☎ 04 95 20 53 14, fax 04 95 20 90 60
Web site: www.montagne-corse.com (French only)

Objectif Nature, Bastia
☎/fax 04 95 32 54 34
Web site: http://obj-nature.ifrance.com (French only)

Paesolu d'Aïtone, Évisa
☎ 04 95 26 20 39, fax 04 95 26 21 83

Bastia, you can arrange guided cycling, walking, horse-riding and fishing trips to the island's interior (for example, along parts of the GR20) as well as sea kayaking, diving and paragliding.

In Ajaccio, contact the Maison d'Information Randonnée of the Bureau d'Information du Parc Naturel Régional de Corse (see Information in the Ajaccio section) or Muntagne Corse in Libertà (☎ 04 95 20 53 14, fax 04 95 20 90 60) at 2 ave de la Grande Armée.

WORK

The tourist season generates thousands of seasonal jobs in hotels, in restaurants and in numerous other enterprises catering to visitors. But, given the Lilliputian size of most Corsican enterprises, finding a job won't necessarily be easy. If this doesn't put you off, you can write letters, knock on doors, or put a good Internet search engine such as Google to work on 'corse emploi ete'. *Emploi* means job, *été* means summer. Not everyone, however, even qualifies to work in Corsica legally.

Permits

To work legally in Corsica you must have a residence permit known as a carte de séjour. Getting one is almost automatic for an EU national and almost impossible for anyone else except full-time students (see under the Visas & Documents section earlier in this chapter).

Non-EU nationals cannot work legally unless they also obtain a work permit *(autorisation de travail)* before arriving in France. Obtaining a work permit is no easy matter, because a prospective employer has to convince the authorities that there is no French – and, increasingly these days, no EU – citizen who can do the job being offered to you.

ACCOMMODATION

There is very little luxurious, but a great deal of adequate and even comfortable, accommodation in Corsica. The majority of the clientele are French, whose main concern is often the quality of food available.

Reservations

Advance Reservations A good way to avoid the hassle of having to search for a place to stay each time you pull into a new town is to make a reservation in advance, and they're especially useful if you're travelling by public transport or due to arrive in a place in the evening. In the high summer, advance reservation may even be the difference between your sleeping in a bed or on the beach.

Tourist Offices Many tourist offices will help people who don't speak French make local hotel reservations, usually for a small fee. In some cases, you pay a deposit that is later deducted from the first night's bill. They will not help by phone, though – you have to go in to the office.

By Telephone Cheap international phone calls make it feasible to call or fax a hotel in Corsica from anywhere in the world to find out if they can accommodate you. If your French isn't good, faxing obviously reduces the chances for misunderstanding. If you phone, double-check to make sure the hotelier understands the date and estimated hour of your arrival, and make sure you know what is expected in terms of a deposit or written confirmation. It is unfair to make hotel reservations by telephone and then not show up. If you won't be able to arrive as planned, call the hotel and inform them as soon as possible. A small number of hotels in Corsica can now be reached by email, but these are still few and far between.

Deposits Many hotels, particularly budget ones, accept reservations only if they are accompanied by a deposit (*des arrhes*; pronounced 'dez **ar**') in French francs. Some places, especially those with two or more stars, don't ask for a deposit if you give them your credit card number or send them confirmation of your plans by letter or fax in clear, simple English.

French francs may be crucial. You may make a deposit by Eurocheque, but you shouldn't be surprised if, because of the high exchange commission, the hotel holds onto it until you arrive, then returns it to you in exchange for cash.

Post in Corsica usually takes only a couple of days, so, after you have arrived on the island, deposits can easily be sent on ahead of you by money order. After you've made your reservations by phone, go to any post office and purchase a *mandat lettre* (money order) for the amount agreed upon and make it payable to the hotel.

Same-Day Reservations A hotel that didn't have a room when you first got in contact may, as a result of no-shows, have one on the day you need it. If you call, they will perhaps be willing to hold it for you until 6 or 7 pm, with no deposit. If you are running late, let them know, otherwise they're liable to rent out the room to someone else.

Camping

Corsica has dozens, maybe even hundreds, of camp sites, ranging in quality from extremely basic to deluxe – with restaurants, bars, mini-golf courses and swimming pools. Most sites fall somewhere in between the two extremes.

The majority of camp sites in Corsica open only from June to September. *Camping sauvage* (literally 'wild camping', or camping outside recognised camp sites) is prohibited; this, in large part, is to reduce the chances of forest fires (especially in the maquis). In remote areas walkers can bivouac in *refuge* (mountain shelter) grounds for a nominal fee.

Refuges & Gîtes d'Étape

Refuges, located in the remote mountain areas of Corsica, offer basic dormitory accommodation exclusively to walkers. Gîtes d'étape, similarly located, offer dormitory accommodation and shared bathroom facilities mainly to walkers; but, because they are not only close to walking routes but to roads as well, these facilities also open to non-walkers, who will normally have to opt for half-board. The Maison d'Informations Randonnées of the Parc Naturel Régional de Corse provides lists of refuges and gîtes d'étape along the GR20 and other walking trails.

A night's accommodation in one of the park refuges costs 55FF. Nightly rates in a gîte d'étape may be slightly lower or slightly higher, while half-board is likely to cost anything up to 200FF.

Hotels

For a directory of approximately 20 distinctly superior Corsican hotels, contact Logis de France (☎ 01 45 84 70 00, fax 01 45 83 59 66, ⓔ info@logis-de-france.fr) at 83 ave d'Italie, 75013 Paris, whose Web site is at www.logis-de-france.fr.

The majority of Corsica's hotels are small and independent, and often family-run. Rooms are impressively clean and frequently have rooms with balconies or a terrace, a view of mountains or of the sea. At the budget level, Corsica's hotels are said to be more expensive than budget hotels on the mainland, but by international standards they are reasonable at all levels, and in low season they are frequently discounted.

Rental Accommodation

You can enjoy anything from a bargain-basement to an ultra-luxurious Corsican holiday by renting by the week or by the month. Several companies rent villas. One of them, Maison des Îles (☎ 04 95 28 44 00, fax 04 95 28 44 81) at 20117 Suarella, offers about 40 different luxury villas in the Porto Vecchio area, mostly with swimming pools, for 10,000FF to 20,000FF per week in July or August.

A more economical option is to rent out a simple but comfortable *gîte rural* (a self-catering cottage in the country), at a price as low as 1000FF to 2200FF per week in low season. For 50FF, you can buy a brochure detailing all the *gîtes ruraux* in Corsica from the Ajaccio branch of Gîtes de France (☎ 04 95 51 72 82, fax 04 95 51 72 89, ⓔ Corsica.gites.France@wanadoo.fr) at 1 rue du Général Fiorella, BP 10, 20181 Ajaccio Cedex 01. See also their informative Web site at www.gites-de-france.fr. For summer accommodation by the week or month, in a villa *or* in a gîte, advance booking is essential.

Other appealing options for one-week-minimum rentals can be found through tour operators in your own country or by searching 'village vacances corse' on a good Internet search-engine such as Google.

FOOD

Whatever the characteristics of Corsican cuisine, Corsica is a region of France, and certain habits die hard. First of all, food in Corsica is of enormous importance. It is not eaten on the run, and is generally eaten at certain specified hours of the day. Between noon and 2 or 3 pm, many businesses shut their doors so that employees can eat a proper lunch. Portions are smaller than in many other countries, but courses are more numerous. Lunch and dinner are usually accompanied by wine.

But start with breakfast. Corsican *petit déjeuner* consists of *croissants*, *pain au chocolat* (bread with chocolate filling) and *tartines* (pieces of French bread slathered with butter) – one of these, not all at once. Coffee is generally *café crème* or *café au lait* (coffee with lots of hot milk).

At *déjeuner* (lunch) and *dîner* (dinner), you generally begin with an *entrée* or *hors d'oeuvre* (starter or appetizer), followed by a main dish, and finish with a dessert or cheese and finally coffee. You can, to be sure, short-circuit this ritual by ordering just a main dish a la carte or by eating at a cafe.

Veal with Olives

To make this typical Corsican dish, cut the veal into small pieces and brown it in a little olive oil until it is golden. Then sauté some white or red onions in a casserole dish with one clove of chopped garlic. Add a little tomato juice, a glass of white or rosé wine, a pinch of salt, some pepper and a few bay leaves.

Allow to simmer for half an hour, then add some stoned green olives. Continue to cook on a medium heat for half an hour and serve with fresh tagliatelle.

The ingredients that make Corsican cuisine distinctive are above all the regional *charcuterie* (pork meats), chestnut, pork and wild boar products, local seafood and *brocciu* (fresh sheep or goat cheese, also spelled *bruccio* and *brucciu*).

Of the various charcuterie, *figatellu*, a liver sausage, is Corsica's pride, but also watch out for *lonzu*, *coppa*, *salamu*, *salciccia* and *prizuttu*. If among these you think you recognise cognates of more familiar salami and prosciutto you will not be mistaken. But Corsican charcuterie has a distinctive flavour, because the meat generally comes from *cochons coureurs* (free-ranging pigs), which feed primarily on chestnuts and acorns. The *assiette de charcuterie* you will see as a starter on many a *menu Corse* will consist of a sampling of thin slices of four or five of these. If you want to know which is which, ask your server.

Main courses, generally speaking, will answer to your idea of French cookery, but look out for the local speciality of veal with olives, and of *sanglier* (wild boar) particularly in long-simmering stews called *civets* in French or *tiani* (*tianu* in the singular) in menu Corsican.

Dishes of local seafood include sardines stuffed with brocciu. (See the boxed text 'A Fishy Business' in the Diving chapter; the swimming creatures you see through your diving goggles are the same ones you may later see on your table.)

Be sure to try an omelette of brocciu too. The cheese combines particularly harmoniously with mint, with which it will almost always be paired in an omelette. You can also enjoy brocciu in pasta dishes such as canneloni and lasagna or stuffed into vegetables.

Crepes can be made either of *froment* (wheat) or *sarrasin* (buckwheat). If you are offered a choice between crepes and galettes, you have fallen among purists for whom a crepe will always be made of wheat, whereas, if it's buckwheat flour that's used, you've got a galette. Two distinctively Corsican crepe fillings are brocciu cheese with mint, and chestnut.

The 'sandwich corse', or Corsican sandwich, you will see on many cafe menus, is a *panino* (a grilled toasty – the term is Italian) of charcuterie and cheeses. Varieties include the Libecciu, the Stellu – according to the menu, 'the most Corsican of *panini*' – the Velacu, the Astu. Merenda, the company that assembles and distributes these little masterpieces throughout the island, tells us that in earlier times these are what shepherds ate for a midday meal in their pastures.

For dessert, try the wonderful *fiadone*, a light flan made with brocciu, lemon and eggs, brocciu fritters or *canistrelli*, biscuits made with almonds, walnuts, lemon or aniseed. Corsican jams (made with oranges, figs, chestnuts and so on) are also delicious.

Recipe for *Fiadone*

If you liked it in Corsica, you can make it at home. Finely grate the zest of one lemon, and mix this in with 500g of brocciu (or ricotta, if you can't find brocciu), six beaten eggs and 350g of superfine sugar in a bowl. Beat until you have a smooth paste. Then turn this mixture into a buttered flan dish and cook at a medium heat until the surface of the *fiadone* is golden in colour (between 45 minutes and one hour).

Vegetarian Cuisine

Though there are no vegetarian restaurants per se in Corsica, this doesn't mean that vegetarians will go hungry. Staples will be salads, soups, pizzas, pastas, crepes, omelettes, cheeses, bread products and, if you are not averse, fish. Dishes such as stuffed aubergines and courgettes are common, and though a vegetable platter might strike some Corsican restaurateurs as a novelty, they do serve vegetables as side dishes and might be willing to assemble a plate of several vegetable side dishes for you. Certainly don't be afraid to ask.

DRINKS

Nonalcoholic Drinks

Soft drinks and fruit juices are all but universally available.

There are also some excellent mineral waters from springs in Zilia in the Balagne and in St-Georges in the region of Ajaccio. Orezzo water is a sparkling water from La Castagniccia.

Alcoholic Drinks

Two breweries on the island produce eight different beers. La Pietra is an amber beer whose ingredients include chestnut flour from La Castagniccia. Enthusiasts contend that, even though the beer doesn't taste of chestnuts, its flour is nevertheless largely responsible for the beer's unique characteristics. Serena is a lighter product of the same brewery; the label bears a Corsican Moor's head. Colomba, launched in 1999, is flavoured with maquis herbs. The Tribbiera brewery uses mountain spring water to make Dea, Prima, Apa (with Corsican honey), Ambria and Mora (Mora is a dark beer).

Corsican wines, red, white and rosé, from vineyards that can be visited, notably in the Nebbio and on the eastern coast (see the relevant chapters for details), can be bought in stores for as little as 30FF a bottle (or even less), and the mark-up in restaurants is not scandalous. These are not necessarily the most distinguished of wines but, unless you're celebrating a golden wedding anniversary, they'll be better than good enough. Cap Corse is a local wine-based aperitif that might do something for you and then again might not. Casanis is a pastis, and although not strictly from Corsica (it's from Marseille), it was developed by a Corsican with the good Corsican name of Casabianca, and the label still has the Corsican Moor's head on it. You won't be shot for asking for a Ricard or a 51, but ask for a Casa anyway and pronounce it ca-**zah**.

The *eaux de vie* (brandies) for consumption after dinner are particularly good when based on a citrus fruit the Corsicans call *cédrat* (for all practical purposes a lemon) or on myrtle or other maquis plants. These are generally home-made. If at the end of your dinner, your server puts down a little plate with a couple of sugar cubes on it and an unlabelled bottle, you are to pour a little of the contents of the bottle over the sugar cubes and suck them. This is a very old custom and a very good one.

Corsican Wine in Numbers

About 48% of Corsican wines are red, 29% are rosés, 23% are whites. Approximately 413 different producers on the island bottle some 347,000hl annually. Of the total, something more than 91,000hl are of *Appellations Contrôlées*, or, as we might say, of sufficient quality to justify a kind of trademark protection. More than 181,000hl are *vin de pays*, or high-quality table wines. Seventy-six thousand hectolitres are simple table wines. À votre santé!

ENTERTAINMENT

If your happiness hinges on a rich nightlife – beyond dinner and then a coffee and a nightcap on a cafe terrace – Corsica may not be the place for you. Discos can, to be sure, be found in or near Bastia, St-Florent, Calvi, Ajaccio, Porticcio and Propriano, but they may not answer to everyone's standards. There are cinemas in Ajaccio and Bastia, and some towns on the coast (such as Calvi and Porto) have open-air cinemas in the summer months.

Festivals of one kind or another, often featuring music, dance and theatre, are meant to give visitors something to hang their hat on (see Public Holidays & Special Events earlier in the chapter), a handful of festivals even exist for locals more than for tourists. For gamblers, there's the casino in Ajaccio.

There are reasons for Corsica's scarcity of nightlife beyond mere thinness of population and predominantly rural, as opposed to urban, traditions. Until recently, Corsica found its solace almost exclusively in the family. When night fell, families withdrew into themselves.

Best in Corsica is not to fight it. Sample the range of outdoor activities during the day, linger over a long Corsican-French dinner in the evening, and enjoy the peace.

SPECTATOR SPORTS

Several large sporting events are held in Corsica in the course of the summer. For tickets phone the following numbers:

Corsica Raid Adventure This gruelling competition, taking place over eight days in mid-May, combines various activities, including mountain races, mountain biking and canyoning. It has been held since 1998, and it opens to amateurs. Information: ☎ 04 95 23 83 00

Fita Star Kallisté The best archers from around the world compete in Biguglia in April. Information: ☎ 04 95 32 25 70

Inter-Lac This two-stage walking competition, in July, covers 28km around the mountain lakes near Corte. Information: ☎ 04 95 46 12 48

Mediterranean Trophy This international sailing competition, in July, opens to vessels greater than 9m in length. Information: ☎ 04 95 23 89 00

Ripcurl This competition counts as the French national windsurfing championship and is held in Bonifacio in May. Information: ☎ 04 95 73 11 59

Tour de Corse Automobile This three-day competition is regarded as the rally world championship. The Tour de Corse takes place on the roads (but you should see the roads!) at the end of September each year. Information: ☎ 04 95 23 62 60

Also worth mentioning are the Route de Sud (a cycling event held in May, ☎ 04 95 25 08 13); the Kyrnea Jump (a show-jumping event held in August in Ajaccio, ☎ 04 95 22 28 35); La Paolina (a 72km race on foot starting at Île Rousse in September, ☎ 04 95 25 05 99/98 89) and the Six Jours Cyclotouristes de l'Île de Beauté (a six-day 600km cycling event, in September, ☎ 04 95 21 96 94).

SHOPPING

You could easily pass through Corsica without buying anything to take home. In the souvenir shops, what will astonish you above all is the number of useful and nearly useful objects that can either be tortured into the shape of or imprinted with an image of the island. The shop Aux Délices du Palais at 62 rue du Cardinal Fesch in Ajaccio sells sublimely kitsch decorations – of ribbon, lace and sweets – in the shape of the island of Corsica. In Ajaccio in particular, numerous items will also be found bearing the image of a little plumpish man with his hand in his waistcoat.

The best items to take home from Corsica are consumable rather than durable. Hams, sausages, chestnut products, little bags of a biscuit called *canistrelli* (honey-flavoured, lemon-flavoured, aniseed-flavoured), olive oils flavoured with bits of aromatic maquis herbs, honeys, wines and liqueurs (some, admittedly, in bottles in which a flattened-out Bonifacio constitutes the base and Cap Corse constitutes the neck) – all of these pack well, travel well, and have the capacity for reawakening vivid memories of Corsica even if they don't last forever.

Recordings of traditional Corsican polyphonic and contemporary Corsican pop music, and books on Corsica are of interest. Visitors may also want to remember that they are, after all, in France. You won't find everything in the way of clothing and perfumes that you'd find in Paris, but at least in the two major towns, Ajaccio and Bastia, you will find plenty of designer names. Given the fondness many Corsicans have for hunting gear, this is also a good place to stock up on your basic camouflage wardrobe, multipurpose and speciality knives and other militaristic clothing and equipment.

Diving

If you're a diver, Corsica will show you about as good a time as you'll find anywhere in Mediterranean waters. The coastline runs nearly 1000km. The inlets and beaches are numerous. The dramatically rugged landscape on the dry side of the shoreline continues underwater in the form of yet more mountains and canyons, needles, sharp peaks, rocky masses and scree. The onshore maquis scrub, meanwhile, transforms underwater into a handsome carpet of yellow flowering anemone, red coral and gorgonian. The underwater swimmers include grouper, brown meagre and dentex. There are a number of easily accessible wrecks. In summer, the clarity and temperature of the water are such that, despite the latitude, the feel of this underwater world borders on the tropical.

A further plus is that Corsica's underwater kingdom has been remarkably well preserved thanks to the careful management of two internationally renowned marine nature reserves (the Réserve Naturelle de Scandola and the Réserve Naturelle des Bouches de Bonifacio), the absence of an intensive commercial fishing industry and an almost total lack of polluters and pollution.

Corsica's Remarkable Wrecks

Porto Vecchio The *Pecorella* (5m to 12m) and the *Toro* (20m)
Golfe de Valinco The yacht on the Sec du Belge (24m) and the *Tasmania* (14m to 19m)
Golfe d'Ajaccio The *Meulière* (5m to 15m)
Golfe de Sagone The *Girafe* (18m) and the *Canadair* wreck (30m)
Golfe de Porto The collier at Punta Muchillina (20m to 30m)
Calvi The B-17 bomber (27m)
From Calvi to Île Rousse The *Grand Cerf* (25m)
St-Florent *L'Aventure* (10m) and the *Ça Ira* (18m)
Bastia The Heinkel-111 (33m), Thunderbolt P-47 (22m) and *Canonnière* (40m to 45m)

Corsica's roughly 30 diving centres, finally, have first-rate personnel and excellent facilities, and the opportunities for *après*-dive are abundant.

DIVE SITES

Diving Conditions

In winter, water temperature in Corsica hovers around a rather chilly 13°C to 14°C. In May, it rises to around 17°C and in June from 20°C to 21°C. Water temperature peaks in August at around 25°C. In September, it remains pleasant at roughly 23°C and it remains very bearable in October at about 20°C. These temperatures, though, are as measured at the surface. Temperatures will be lower farther down. In order to stay warm, you will do well to wear a wet or dry suit with a hood.

The clarity of Corsican waters is legendary. In summer, average visibility runs to 25m, although in August, in good weather, visibility sometimes runs as high as 40m. The wind, particularly the southwesterly *libecciu*, can, on the other hand, produce a heavy sea swell that will roil the waters in some of the less protected gulfs and inlets. Underwater sites by headlands and rocky overhangs are particularly vulnerable. But don't worry, in less favourable conditions the diving centres will generally make use of sheltered areas inside the bays.

Corsica is largely lacking in a continental shelf; the peaks and valleys of the mountains on the island's surface continue right on beneath the waves, and the result, on the western coast in particular, is that the water can get very deep quickly: in the Golfe de Porto, for example, it soon reaches a depth of 800m. At the same time, many *secs*, or shallows, take form in the shape of miniature lagoons with a range of depths. On the eastern coast, particularly around Bastia, the underwater landscape is totally different. Expect a sea bed of sand and silt dotted with rocky masses sloping off gently from the shore.

DIVE SITES & CENTRES

DIVING CENTRES

1. CIP La Palanquée; Hippocampe (La Chiappa); Kalliste (Palombaggia)
2. Atoll; Barakouda; Kalliste
3. Campomoro Plongée
4. Valinco Plongée; U Levante
5. Porto Pollo Plongée
6. Maeva (Marines de Porticcio); Club Subaquatique d'Agosta; Corse Plongée (Isolella Peninsula)
7. GSC; E Ragnole; Bulle Bleue; Les Calanques
8. Squale Plongée (Lava)
9. Le Grand Bleu; Nautica Sub (Calcatoggio)

DIVING CENTRES (continued)

10. Centre Subaquatique de Sagone
11. Centre de Plongée du Golfe de Porto; Génération Bleue
12. L'Incantu
13. École de Plongée Internationale de Calvi; Calvi Plongée Citadelle; JMB Diving; STARESO
14. Subcorsica (Sant'Ambrogio); Algajola Sport Nature
15. Beluga Diving; École de Plongée de l'Île Rousse
16. CESM; Actisub; Aquado
17. Thalassa Immersion; Club Plongée Bastiais
18. Aquatica Club (Santa Severa)
19. Capi Corsu Diving; Thalassoma

Beginners should try not to feel intimidated by the shallows and chasms or even the abysses. It is rare that a drop shoots straight down like the side of a tall building. They are usually criss-crossed by faults and small plateaus and ridges so the sites are spread out over several different levels.

The number of dive sites around Corsica runs into the hundreds, and the descriptions that follow only provide a rudimentary idea guide to some of the more popular ones. Bear in mind that the names of sites are often quite arbitrary, and may vary from one diving centre to another. The fish most commonly observed are also listed, but fish can never be counted on to keep an appointment. Ask any fisherman.

Although the authors and publisher have done their utmost to ensure the accuracy of all information in this guide, they cannot accept any responsibility for any loss, injury or inconvenience sustained by people using this book. The fact that a dive is described in this guidebook does not mean that it is safe for you and your diving party. You are ultimately responsible for judging your own capabilities in the light of the conditions you encounter.

Environmentally Aware Diving

To minimise the effects of diving on Corsica's fragile marine ecosystem, visitors should try to adhere to the following guidelines.

- Don't feed the fish, especially with food that is not part of their normal diet. This could disorder their metabolism or give rise to unnatural behaviour, particularly in the case of grouper, which lose their instinctive fear of human beings when fed (believe it or not) boiled egg; this turns them into easier targets for predators and makes them more likely to swallow objects such as plastic bags.
- Control your buoyancy and stability to avoid accidentally kicking the sea bed. If you touch sessile (nonmoving) organisms, particularly sponges and gorgonian, you can easily damage them.
- Don't linger in the caves: bubbles from your regulator will get trapped under the roof, exposing organisms such as encrusted sponges to the air and causing them to decompose.
- Don't remove shells and other fauna from anywhere on the French coastline. This is strictly forbidden.

Around Porto Vecchio

A dozen or so dives can be taken in this area, mainly in the vicinity of the Îles Cerbicale. The small island of **Le Toro** (The Bull), at the south-eastern end of this archipelago, is ideal for all abilities because it has a number of protected little coves and shallows with a maximum depth of around 40m. Its small canyons reach a similar depth, carpeted with encrusted sponges, and there is an abundance of fallen rocks and caves. Comber, rainbow wrasse, bogue and conger eel animate the scene, and sometimes a few dentex join in, attracted by the current.

Farther out to sea, the **Danger du Toro** is one of the wildest sites in this area. Three shallows begin several metres below the surface before dropping to 40m. Carved into canyons decorated with gorgonian, they are frequented by grouper, dentex, rainbow wrasse and, near the surface, by schools of damselfish.

La Vacca (The Cow), an islet to the east of the archipelago, has a similar configuration to that of Le Toro and a depth of approximately 20m to 25m. Farther out to sea lies the **Danger de la Vacca**, where shallows descend in terraces from 3m to 40m. When it's windy or there's a strong current these two sites are exposed and you should keep to the sheltered areas of Le Toro and La Vacca islets.

Experienced divers will enjoy **Les Arches**, between Le Toro and La Vacca, when the sea is calm. This is a huge rocky peak, covered in gorgonian, which extends from 19m to 37m. At 35m, where a plateau opens up, divers can pass beneath arches thronged with grouper, moray eel, brown meagre and predators such as dentex and leerfish.

Of the two wrecks to be visited in the area, the more famous is the *Pecorella*, a 45m-long cement carrier, which sank in a storm in 1967. The vessel rests on its keel at the northern end of the Golfe de Porto Vecchio on gravel just 5m to 12m below the surface in the middle of a Poseidonion bed (see the boxed text 'A Fishy Business' later in this chapter). The state of preservation of this wreck is remarkable, and its bridge and helm, gangways, engine room, cement holds and chain lockers can all be explored safely. Though there are few fish in the area apart from a handful of brown meagre and some red scorpion fish, organisms such as red coral and sea anemones decorate the vessel's hull. The site is regularly used for introductory dives, night dives and underwater photography.

The *Toro* wreck, near the islet of the same name, is a wooden coaster that once carried marble and other construction materials. It seems to have sunk around 1910–20, and its entire superstructure, which lies at 20m, at the foot of a shallows that rises to 8m, has disintegrated. Red scorpion fish, moray eel and conger eel are often found nearby.

Bonifacio

The waters around Bonifacio are the most dived in Corsica, and there's a reason: the Réserve Naturelle des Bouches de Bonifacio (see the boxed text 'Corsica's Marine Reserves'), about 20 minutes south-east of the coast, offers a stunning stage set and exceptional conditions for divers of all abilities. The turquoise-green water, among chiselled granite rocks, is reminiscent of more tropical climes. The small inlets seem to have been designed for novice divers, and the more renowned sites – some of them quite famous – provide thrills for more experienced divers. In general, the underwater topography here differs from that of Corsica's western coast. Drops are rarer, and the underwater relief is less disorderly.

Corsica's most popular dive site, **Mérouville**, is in the Îles Lavezzi to the east of the archipelago. Here a platform of rocks drops off from 17m to a sandy floor at about 30m. The main attraction though, is not the underwater architecture, but the dozens of friendly brown grouper. These uniquely friendly fish, some up to 1.2m long, are accustomed to the presence of divers. They will sidle up to you, watching hopefully for titbits, but you should not oblige. Provided you don't make any sudden or uncoordinated movements, you may remain exceedingly close to the fish.

In addition to commercialised Mérouville, which has to an extent been the victim of its own success (see the boxed text 'Mérouville Mon Amour'), the Îles Lavezzi are host to a number of other more secluded and wild sites, rich in marine invertebrates. True, the grouper are less approachable here than at Mérouville, but their furtive movements are fascinating in their own right. Near the main island of the Îles Lavezzi, the **Est du Phare** has interesting rock passageways at depths of 3m to 20m but there are few fish. **Dahbia 1**, **Dahbia 2** and **Dahbia 3**, to the south-west, are different again. The first is a drop of 10m to 23m, cloaked in gorgonian and inhabited by moray eel, sea spider, brown meagre and grouper; the second, between 19m and 40m, is a mass of fallen rocks and rock fragments; and the third, between 12m and 30m, is the most beautiful gorgonian-covered drop in the Îles

Mérouville Mon Amour

The success of the Mérouville site has been a double edged sword. Divers flock here to swim among the friendly grouper and scavenging rainbow wrasse and sargo but the site is overexploited in summer, when it is not unusual to find several dozen boats from Corsica and Sardinia moored here at once. The sea bed has suffered as a result. Also, many divers feed the grouper boiled eggs, bread or salami, and this not only plays havoc with grouper physiology, it risks serious adverse effects on nature's equilibrium.

The diving centres in Bonifacio are trying to find a compromise between demand and the site's capacity, and the Parc Marin International des Bouches de Bonifacio (the Bouches de Bonfacio International Marine Park; ☎ 04 95 50 45 44) has drawn up a circular requesting divers neither to touch nor feed the fish and also to be careful that they avoid harming the sea bed with their anchors.

Lavezzi. Grouper, moray eel and red scorpion fish are plentiful.

West of these sites and farther out to sea, a real treat is in store at the **Écueil des Lavezzi**, a vast rocky plateau marked by a tower that peaks at 5m of depth and gradually descends to 50m. When conditions are good here, you can find wild grouper, brown meagre, dentex, moray eel, rockfish, shoals of silver bream and masses of flourishing marine invertebrates. The **Tête de Cheval** (Horse's Head), extending from 16m to 50m, is a rock that juts out from the drop, complete with gorgonian, caves and rocky passages.

To the north-west, the **Tête d'Homme** (Head of a Man), another rocky pile descending from 6m to 40m below the surface, is named for the shape of its rocky summit. It's accessible to level 1 divers. Gorgonian grows on its side from a depth of 13m and grouper, dentex and brown meagre patrol the environs.

The **Écueil de Sperduto** to the east of the Île de Cavallo is a rock visible above the surface of the waves and marked by a kind of turret. This site is suitable for divers of all levels, provided the sea is calm. Sargo, moray eel and damselfish can all be found here and you may even come face to face with a barracuda.

Diving in the Îles Lavezzi is not always a picnic, however. Situated right in the middle of the Bouches de Bonifacio, between Sardinia and Corsica, the archipelago is exposed to winds from all directions, particularly westerlies, and to strong currents. The sea can sometimes be capricious and boat trips to the sites a little bumpy. Visit them in fine weather if you can.

Not all of the diving centres in the area run dives around Bonifacio's chalky cliffs but **Les Grottes**, at the entrance to the harbour, is accessible come rain or shine. A number of caves and passages honeycomb the cliff. But, even though the water depth is less than 10m, this is a site best reserved to divers with experience. Cardinalfish, squad lobster, flat lobster and conger eel occasionally appear in this biotope.

To the east of Bonifacio, the Cap Pertusato

Corsica's Marine Reserves

The preservation of the marine kingdom is not taken lightly in Corsica – hence the island's two large underwater nature reserves.

The **Réserve Naturelle des Bouches de Bonifacio** (the Bouches de Bonifacio Nature Reserve), created in September 1999, in the far south between Corsica and Sardinia, replaces the old Réserve Naturelle des Îles Lavezzi and constitutes the French contribution to the Parc Marin International (International Marine Park) whose Italian component is the Maddalena archipelago off of Sardinia. Though Île de Cavallo, nicknamed Millionaires' Island, and Îlot de San Baïnsu have somehow strangely escaped the protected zone, some 80,000 hectares do fall within it, and 12,000 of those are very strictly protected. Twelve hundred hectares are off limits to divers with oxygen cylinders.

The **Réserve Naturelle de Scandola** on the western coast, dating from 1975, covers 919 hectares on the land side and 1000 hectares at sea, between Punta Muchillina in the south (at the northern entrance to the Golfe de Porto) and Punta Nera in the north. Four hundred and fifty different species of seaweed have been identified in the area, and 125 species of fish. Regulations prohibit underwater hunting, line fishing, any removal of marine flora or fauna, scuba diving, mooring for more than 24 hours and the dumping of rubbish. Scandola is listed as a Unesco World Heritage Site.

Since the early 1990s, a plan has been postulated to make the Scandola reserve the basis for a new national marine park. This ideally would protect 125km of coastline between Pointe de la Revellata in the north all the way down to Capu Rossu to the south of the Golfe de Porto. But the project's supporters have not had an easy task of it so far and there is no certainty that they will ever prevail. Diving clubs, anglers, yachting enthusiasts and local people all have agendas that sometimes overlap, sometimes diverge.

region contains a number of diving locations such as **Pertusato**, extending from 3m to 20m, and, slightly farther east, **Supertusato**. These two sites, teeming with small rockfish, are ideal for an introductory dive. For the more experienced diver, a shallow in the form of a vertical drop between 32m and 46m lies just off Cap Pertusato.

Golfe de Valinco

The Golfe de Valinco is treasured by divers for its underwater relief – even more dramatic than that of other parts of the western coast – with depths of up to 800m. It's home to an abundance of sessile organisms such as gorgonian, parazoa and the jewel of the Mediterranean, red coral. The density of the fauna increases as you approach the wilderness around the mouth of the gulf, and the most appealing dives are over rocky mounts close by the shore at the northern and southern entrances to the gulf. For beginners there are sheltered inlets closer to Propriano.

Red Canyon on the southern side of the gulf, halfway between Propriano and Campomoro, is a huge rock split open on one side to create a gully rich in red coral (at a depth of about 25m) and other marine organisms. Slightly farther west is the **Sec du Belvédère**, a rocky peak extending from 9m to 30m, famous for the gorgonian and caves adorned with red coral near its base. **Le Tonneau** is a remarkably complex configuration. This huge rock begins at a depth of 6m. Down at 23m you'll find an arch, at 47m a cave, and at 41m a path from which you can re-emerge at 33m. Your companions will be grouper and rock lobster. This, though, is a site for experienced divers only.

Monica is the name of a series of three peaks along the shore at the eastern entrance to the Baie de Campomoro at the bottom of the Golfe de Valinco. The first of these peaks extends from 6m to 22m, the second from 7m to 40m and the third from 14m to 40m. A coral cavern is found between 27m and 35m, and at 12m there is a tangle of tubes several metres in diameter, lost from a ship, which gives the site the feel of a playground.

At the entrance to the gulf at the western end of the Baie de Campomoro, about level with the Genoese tower, the **Sec de Campomoro** consists of several rocky platforms, one of which just breaks the surface of the water, bottoms out at 40m. This site, suitable for divers of all levels, is heavily fissured, and gorgonian (at a depth of about 25m), bogue, sargo, rock lobster, dentex, forkbeard and occasionally grouper populate the scene. Behind the Punta Campomoro, the wreck of a yacht lies on the **Sec du Belge** at 24m. This site teems with rock lobster.

Centres in Propriano also arrange dives at yet wilder and little-visited fishy sites beyond the gulf, particularly around Cap Senetosa to the south. **Senetosa**, just off the cape of the same name, is a shallow extending from 13m to 40m; grouper abound. Nearer the coast, the **Tombant de Conca**, suitable for divers of all abilities, falls away sharply from 8m to 47m.

Valinco Plongée (see under Diving Centres later in the chapter) pushes as far as the Réserve des Moines, out at sea south-west of the Tour d'Olmeto, for visits to the wreck of the *Tasmania*. The *Tasmania* is a 142m-long steamer that sank en route to Marseille in 1887. It lies at a depth of between 14m and 19m, and you can still make out the smokestacks, winches, propeller and stern.

On the northern side of the Golfe de Valinco, the sites are mainly concentrated around the Punta di Porto Pollo. Most famous is undoubtedly **Les Cathédrales**, a short distance from the small harbour of Porto Pollo. To picture the scene, imagine a scaled-down underwater version of the Aiguilles de Bavella (south-west of Solenzara). Extending from 12m to 40m, its peaks, faults, shelves and arches (at 37m) are home to a variety of sea creatures that attract marauding predators. Other evocatively named sites – **La Vallée** and **Le Colorado** – can be found slightly farther west.

Golfe d'Ajaccio

Dozens of sites can be found along the scalloped border of the Golfe d'Ajaccio, from the surprisingly little-visited Îles Sanguinaires in the north to Capu di Muru in the south. **Le Tabernacle**, at the north-western end of the gulf, is the main site on this part of the coast. It's ideal for beginners, with a plateau descending from 3m to 22m as if along paving stones. Forkbeard, rock lobster, brown meagre, sargo and even grouper are the sea life here.

At a distance of 300m from the coast, the closer **Guardiola** suits beginners and more experienced divers alike. The rather sharp drop is down to 40m. The sea-life attractions include gorgonian, rock lobster, grouper and red scorpion fish.

The most spectacular dives in this area are found mainly in the southern section, between the Tour de l'Isolella (also known as the Punta di Sette Nave) and Capu di Muru. There are several unusual sites around the Pointe de l'Isolella though they tend to get somewhat crowded in summer. At the **Punta di Sette Nave** enormous rocks covered in organisms such as gorgonian descend in terraces from 4m to 45m; the rocks are riddled with small passages and tunnels.

Near the coast, **La Campanina** scores high ratings with both beginners and advanced divers, and the same is true of the **Tête de Mort** (Dead Man's Head), where a plateau opens out at a depth of 15m to 20m, a mount tops out at 6m, a chimney and cave can be found at 17m and another cave at 10m. There are also brown meagre, sargo, rock lobster, dentex and even leerfish and barracuda, and sessile organisms abound. A short distance from La Campanina is the **Sec d'Antoine** with similar features. The Punta di Sette Nave and the Tête de Mort are often used for introductory dives.

The wilderness Punta di a Castagna also offers several sites for underwater forays, including the *Meulière*, a minesweeper that sank during WWII; it rests now at a depth of between 5m and 15m. Two sites are reserved for experienced divers. The first is the **Tombant du Corailleur**, several miles out into the ocean beyond the gulf; the sec-

The Last of the Underwater Miners

Red coral is actually an animal species *(Corallium rubrum)*, which lives on rocks as deep down as 300m below the surface of the sea. But because it has a hard red skeleton, it looks like a stone – and a particularly pretty one at that. Consequently, it's much valued by jewellers and by people who buy jewellery.

Harvesting coral, meanwhile, is more than just a job, it is part of the history of the Mediterranean. Corsica currently has about 15 coral divers who descend to depths of up to 100m to extract the so-called 'red gold', which ancient mythology identified fancifully as the blood that flowed when Perseus cut off the Medusa's head. The diver dresses in a wetsuit of up to three layers, he wears a dive computer on his wrist and he carries two large oxygen cylinders, a diving torch, a basket for collecting the coral and an axe-like tool for detaching the coral.

Like all other deep-sea divers, coral divers face two principal hazards: failure to decompress when resurfacing and nitrogen narcosis, or 'rapture of the deep', at the bottom. Most divers now use new air/helium mixes in their cylinders to eliminate the risk of nitrogen narcosis, and they have recompression chambers on their boats. They make their ascents slowly, in stages. Before modern diving tools were developed, coral was harvested in a rather hit-or-miss fashion; for example, boats might drag a contraption of wooden beams and nets along the sea bottom.

At the end of each season (which extends from May to November) the harvest is sold at Torre del Greco near Naples, where a kilo of Corsican coral, among the world's most colourful, can fetch between 1000FF and 4000FF, depending on quality, size and thickness. It is then worked in special cutting shops and sold on to jewellers all over the world to be incorporated into necklaces, bracelets, rings, earrings and pendants.

The coral divers' days are nevertheless numbered in Corsica waters: the pickings are increasingly slim. Corsican coral divers, some of whom have already moved to Tunisia, now have their eyes on Libyan and Albanian shores.

ond, the **Grotte à Corail** off Plage d'Agosta, south of Porticcio. The latter, with depths ranging from 25m to 57m, is a chimney festooned with gorgonian and coral.

Golfe de Lava

Because of its relative inaccessibility north of the Îles Sanguinaires, the Golfe de Lava tends not to be visited much, yet it boasts one of Corsica's most stunning dive sites – the **Banc Provençal**, out in open sea towards the Golfe de Liscia. This is a memorable dive, only for the initiated, and in calm seas. The rocky mass, consisting of a twin summit divided by a fault, extends from 17m to 80m in depth. One side is plateau; the other side, rocky shelves that pile up on top of one another like platforms. The whole, with its blanket of multicoloured sponges, gorgonian and flowering anemones, serves as home to brown meagre, forkbeard, rock lobster, moray eel, swallow-tail sea perch, damselfish and a family of grouper living in a cave at 37m.

At the south-western entrance to the Golfe de Lava, the **Sec de Pietra Piombata**, ranging in depth from 3m to 60m, hosts gorgonian and coral. Because it is near the open sea it attracts predators: you may find yourself face to face with dentex, brown meagre or barracuda.

Golfe de Sagone

This huge gulf boasts several exceptional dives. On the southern shore, towards the Golfe de Liscia (a kind of suburb of the Golfe de Sagone), experienced divers can have fun with the series of drops at **Castellaci**. Nearby the plateau extends out from the coast in a series of wide steps (15m to 30m, 30m to 50m) honeycombed with caves.

Similar architecture can be found at **Punta Paliagi**, farther east, where small plateaus start at a depth of 3m. At **Punta Palmentoju**, level with the Tour d'Ancone in the Golfe de Liscia, a dozen peaks fall away sharply from 3m to 50m. This spectacular scenery is home to moray eel, gorgonian, rock lobster, brown meagre, dentex and even barracuda. At the nearby **Langue de Feu** (Tongue of Fire), red coral blankets a cavern at around 30m.

Studying Marine Life

The most unusual diving club in Corsica is the oceanographic centre Stareso (Station de Recherches Sous-marines et Océanographiques; Submarine and Oceanographic Research Station) at Pointe de la Revellata west of the Baie de Calvi. Founded in 1972, it permits novice and experienced divers alike to rub shoulders with marine experts in a friendly and informal setting. Revenue from tourism helps the centre to continue operating.

Stareso offers an introductory dive for 220FF, exploratory dives for between 180FF and 220FF, level 1 instruction (5–7 dives plus 250FF for a licence) and a marine biology course. The most frequently used sites are Pointe de la Revellata, Punta Bianca and the Sec du Lion, all less than 15 minutes away. There are occasional trips to the wreck of the B-17 bomber.

Accommodation options include a comfortable double in the research centre. Full board and one dive per day costs 550FF, and the same with two dives per day costs 650FF. The price is the same for a room in the lighthouse itself. Lunch for daytime visitors costs 80FF.

To reach the centre, take the D81 4km to the west of Calvi in the direction of Galéria, then turn onto a stony track riddled with potholes for another 4.5km. Don't worry about signs; there aren't any. Just keep your eyes on the lighthouse.

Stareso (☎ 04 95 65 06 18, 06 12 95 57 51, fax 04 95 65 01 34, ⓔ stareso@stareso.com) opens daily and arranges two excursions daily. Visit their Web site at www.stareso.com for more information.

If sheer drops are more your thing, you'll enjoy **Punta Capigliolo**, north of the Golfe de Liscia. The rock drops vertically from the surface down to 130m. Farther north, **Punta San Giuseppe** stands out due to its huge rectangular megaliths (around 20m long and several metres high) at a depth of 20m, from which level masses of fallen rocks descend to 40m.

The Anse de Sagone is the final resting place of two wrecks. The *Girafe*, a

Napoleonic store ship that transported Corsican pine for shipbuilding, was scuttled hereabouts by its own crew in order to keep it from falling into the hands of its British tormentors. What's left of its hull, as well as cannons and cannonballs, is at a depth of 18m. It's a good site for beginners.

Slightly farther out to sea, at the mouth of the cove, the wreck of a Canadian **firefighting plane** can be visited by seasoned divers. The carcass of the plane, which crashed in 1971 after accidentally veering off course, now lies upside down on a sandy bed at 30m.

Golfe de Porto

The Golfe de Porto, with its granite walls plunging fast to abysses 800m beneath the surface, is Corsica's jewel. Yet the dozen sites between Punta Muchillina in the north and Capu Rossu in the south are exploited by only three diving centres. Although the area is glorious, diving here is complicated by two problems. Boat trips to the best sites, close to the northern and southern edges of the gulf, are sometimes made difficult if not impossible by the westerly wind; and diving is prohibited within the fauna-rich Réserve Naturelle de Scandola just above the gulf.

As sites for introductory dives and instruction, clubs in Porto have the **Porte d'Aix**, an inlet on the northern shore five minutes from the harbour, **Castagne** in the south, accessible by road or sea, and the **Sec du Château**, also in the south but slightly farther away, consisting of several little shallows near the surface.

Farther west along the southern shore you'll come to **Figajola**, where two headlands descend from 5m to around 35m. They are rich in sessile organisms and often visited by dentex and brown meagre. This site is suitable for both beginners and experienced divers.

Continuing towards Capu Rossu, the delightful **Vardiola** is a sugar-loaf mountain breaking the surface of the waves and encircled by a deep gash at 10m to 30m. Red coral abounds at the lowest level here; a higher plateau is populated by brown meagre, dentex, forkbeard, rock lobster and grouper.

Between Vardiola and Capu Rossu, the **Pitons de Vardiola** are rocky summits that plunge from 8m to 50m. Experienced divers can see the magnificent gorgonian covering the rock face between 30m and 40m.

Facing the open sea, **Capu Rossu** is the outermost point on the southern side of the gulf. Two massive rocks that break the surface of the waves descend in a series of plateaus on the land side and in more dramatic tumbles on the side exposed to the open sea. Faults are numerous. The proximity of the open sea means you may well encounter large fish such as tuna, barracuda and leerfish. Beginners do well here.

The northern side of the gulf, close to the Réserve Naturelle de Scandola and culminating in **Punta Muchillina**, pleases divers at all levels of proficiency by virtue of its teeming marine life. The stunning **Voûte à Corail** (coral cavern), 26m below the surface, is a favourite spot for introductory dives and instruction. It's just five minutes from Porto harbour, at Monte Rosso; fish are abundant.

Punta Scopa, halfway from Porto to Punta Muchillina, is a drop frequented by predators such as dentex and brown meagre. It's suitable for divers of all abilities. At **Seninu**, the site at the next headland, shallows top out at 1.5m, then tumble down on one side to 50m. The faults are numerous, and there is a dense array of sessile organisms, including splendid gorgonian. Grouper, dentex, moray eel, brown meagre, rock lobster and forkbeard may keep you company. This site, too, is suitable for divers of all abilities.

Punta Mucchilina, at the edge of the Réserve Naturelle de Scandola, is by some accounts the single most thrilling site on the entire Corsican coast. Near the shoreline, a two-headed shallows, separated by a basin, just 1m or so below the surface descends on the southern side to a depth of 50m. There are gorgonian, parazoa, rock lobster, brown meagre, dentex and even barracuda. On the eastern side, 20m to 30m down, you can check out the machinery room, propeller and boilers of an old collier, along with other debris.

Around Galéria

There is only one diving centre in the village of Galéria, and the sites in nearby waters, from Capu di a Morsetta, to the north, and the northern boundary of the Réserve Naturelle de Scandola, to the south, have an appealing, wild quality.

Heading north from Galéria, the first site you come to is **Ciuttone**, level with the headland of the same name at the eastern end of the Baie de Galéria. This site is accessible to all divers. Red coral is found from a depth of 20m. The **Roche Bleue** (Blue Rock), farther north, between Ciuttone and Capu di a Morsetta, is a sugar-loaf mountain ornamented with gorgonian, 30m to 50m in depth. It's for experienced divers only.

Farther north, the islet of **Morsetta** offers a spectacular underwater architecture of drops, faults, valleys and loose rock debris. The rocks take their colour from sessile organisms – such as gorgonian, which becomes denser as you descend. Habitués of this miniature mountain mass are forkbeard, rock lobster and moray eel; and grouper and brown meagre regularly look in. The site is suitable for divers of all abilities.

Le Tunnel, south of Morsetta, is an L-shaped corridor about 50m long and 2m to 3m across. You enter at a depth of 17m carrying a torch provided by the club to light your way. Though the dive is suitable for beginners, going deep into the cliffs can be frightening for claustrophobes. Inside, the rock is fairly bare and the cowries that once crowned the walls have disappeared; the beam of a torch, though, will almost always surprise forkbeard lurking in crevices. You come out of the gully at 12m. Not far away, **La Faille** gully goes back into the rock face for about 30m, and at one point you find yourself in an air chamber full of stalactites.

Yellow Seaweed

Every year, the increasing temperatures of early summer give rise to a tide of yellow seaweed that quickly covers both rock and nonmoving fauna. This is a perfectly natural phenomenon, and, though it is not pretty, it is not caused by pollution as many divers think. Currents gradually cause this rather unsightly moss to disappear.

As you get closer to the Réserve Naturelle de Scandola, to the south, the sites feel increasingly wild. The islet of **Porri**, a series of parallel rocky ridges with depths of between 15m and 40m, is of such appeal as to have served as a backdrop for the Mediterranean Underwater Photography Championship.

Around Calvi

The many contrasts in the area around Calvi make it attractive to divers. The southern part of the bay is admittedly nothing to write home about, but the wilderness around the Pointe de la Revellata, to the west, is extraordinary, and the Baie de Calvi contains one of the most highly rated sites in all Corsica in

A Lucky Escape

In 1944, as Germans and Americans fought it out relentlessly over the Mediterranean, a B-17 bomber was hit by a Messerschmitt during an air raid on Verona, Italy. The pilot attempted to reach Calvi, the nearest base with an airport, but was forced to splash down in front of the citadel. Four crew members survived.

Now lying under 27m of seawater at a distance of 200m out to sea from the citadel, the B-17 is a major attraction for experienced divers. This imposing metal hulk, about 30m wide, is truncated at the front and rear (the nose and tail were destroyed on landing) but the central part of the fuselage (including the cabin and bomb bay), a section of the landing gear, the wings and four engines with twisted blades are still intact. Don't expect to encounter much fauna: the metal structures are only partially colonised by sponges, and fish seem to stay away from the site.

the wreck of a **B-17 bomber** (see the boxed text 'A Lucky Escape'). The bomber is for experienced divers only, because of the depth at which it lies, though centres in Calvi are currently taking level 1 divers to where they can at least see it from a distance.

La Bibliothèque (The Library), so called because its rocky massifs resemble piled-up books, less than 20m deep in the Baie de Calvi, is used for introductory dives, as is the **Pointe St-François**, behind the citadel, on the way out of Calvi.

To the north-west of Calvi, on the edge of a fishing zone just below the lighthouse, **La Revellata** is a sprawl – exposed to the open sea – of rocky valleys, scree, miniature drops, canyons and faults, to a depth of 40m. It's a spectacular setting, and provides a chance to sample all of Corsica's underwater treasures. You'll find sponges, gorgonian and flowering anemones and, from a depth of 30m down, red coral. You will probably run into grouper, sargo, brown meagre, dentex, leerfish and shellfish. The site is accessible to divers at all competence levels.

Even farther west, experienced divers will enjoy **Mezzu Golfu** (also known as the Sec du Clocher), which has something of the appearance of a flattened ball. Its depth is 27m to 50m, and it is riddled with faults and caves and covered with gorgonian. You may see grouper and dentex. **Punta Bianca** has rather sharp drops that descend in terraces from 10m to 42m and are covered in gorgonian and red coral. Dentex, conger eel, forkbeard, rock lobster and brown meagre are in more or less permanent residence.

From Calvi to Île Rousse

The area between Punta Spano, west of the Marine de Sant'Ambrogio, and Algajola, to its east, offers unusual sites suitable for beginners and experienced divers alike. The most famous is the **Danger d'Algajola**, just off Algajola, which is in complete contrast to the type of dive site normally associated with Corsica. Around 1.5 nautical miles out to sea, the peaks and drops give way to an immense rocky plateau more than 1km long and 400m wide and dropping via landings from 1m to 40m in depth. The size of this formation, with its nooks and crannies, gorges, small peaks, jagged ridges and miniature valleys, makes it an ideal playground for rock-dwelling and pelagic fish, and it also suggests a variety of different dives. Divers may find themselves moving through shoals of damselfish and bogue, startling moray or conger eels, bumping into grouper, dentex or brown meagre, surprising octopus or coming nose to nose with barracuda. The top part of the plateau is devoid of gorgonian but coral can be found farther down.

Subcorsica (see under Diving Centres later in this chapter) runs dives at **Pietra Eramer**, which is an extension of the Punta di Sant'Ambrogio formed by masses of fallen rocks extending from 27m to 43m. Gorgonian provides a beautiful setting for grouper, sargo, dentex, crayfish and lobster.

Kalliste, with its abundance of caves, pinnacles and rocky passages between 23m and 45m, is a site for experienced divers. Brown meagre, sargo, forkbeard, moray eel and rock lobster often appear here, and gorgonian and coral are both found below 30m. What's left of the *Grand Cerf*, shipwrecked in the 19th century, lies at 25m; the ribs and derrick are still visible.

Cala Stella is an inlet near the Tour de Spano that fishermen formerly used for shelter; here, in 12m of water, beginners can swim alongside tiny rock fish between faults and canyons. **Pedra Mule**, an islet near the promontory west of Algajola, serves nicely for introductory dives on its eastern side. On its western side, which is deeper (15m), there is a slight drop inhabited by moray eel and damselfish.

Around Île Rousse

There are few sites in the Baie de l'Île Rousse, but the handful that do exist – rocks rising from a sandy floor and cloaked with magnificent gorgonian – might well be pronounced the most beautiful anywhere in Corsican waters.

Le Naso, the most famous of the Île Rousse sites, is a huge rock descending from 13m to 32m and distinguished by the concentration of conger and moray eel in the crevices around its base; the area is also home to brown meagre and dentex. The site is appropriate for divers at all levels of proficiency. The nearby **Petit Tombant**, between 16m and 42m, has similar features, and shoals of dentex and leerfish swim past its gorgonian-covered surface.

The Petit Tombant stretches out into the **Grand Tombant**, a plateau at a depth of 20m which, on the side facing the open sea, plunges down to 39m. The vertical rock face is colonised by striking encrustations of gorgonian and sponges, while the plateau is home to sargo and octopus.

Less than 200m from the Grand Tombant in the direction of the open sea, the **Trois Vierges** are three rocks hosting some striking specimens of brown meagre and dentex, and sometimes tuna or grouper. The depth of the water (between 25m and 42m) makes the site appropriate only for experienced divers. This is also the case with **Monlouis**, farther out to sea, which descends in terraces from 30m to 47m and is particularly resplendent with gorgonian. To the east, the **Tour de Saleccia**, aligned with its namesake on land, cascades down from 25m to 50m. Very much exposed to the current, these shallows are adorned with gorgonian; and sea bream, rock lobster and skate are often sighted.

Golfe de St-Florent

The Golfe de St-Florent boasts about a dozen regularly visited sites between the Désert des Agriates, to the west, and the low chalky cliffs, to the east, that beneath the waves turn as holey as a Swiss cheese. The **Grotte aux Pigeons** is one such location. Starting a few metres below the surface, the cliff face is gouged out in crevice upon gash upon crevice. Farther out to sea, the **Sec des Pigeons** is a rocky plateau from 25m to 30m deep and criss-crossed by small faults where grouper, brown meagre and octopus live.

Leaving the gulf and heading west you'll come to the area around Punta Mortella, near the lighthouse of the same name. **Le Gendarme** (The Policeman) is a large boulder that peaks at 17m and descends to 43m; it's home to grouper, conger eel, moray eel and rock lobster. Slightly to the west of Mortella, a rock resembling a **sphinx** juts above the water and drops to 17m.

Near the bottom of the gulf, in the Anse de Fornali, two rows of protruding rocks form a site known as **Les Cormorans**. The modest depth of the water (8m) makes this a good site for introductory dives and instruction.

Two wrecks can be found near the citadel in St-Florent: *L'Aventure*, at 10m, and the *Ça Ira*, at 18m. The latter, a hospital ship dating from the Napoleonic era, has been closely studied by an archaeological group.

The **Sec de la Citadelle**, a small rocky mount with an abundance of rock masses and hollows in only 6m of water, is perfect for beginners.

Bastia

Diving enthusiasts have tended to disdain Corsica's eastern coast. True, this side of the island lacks peaks and canyons and dramatic drops plunging down towards abysses, and gorgonian and red coral are also rare. On the other hand, the gently sloping sand-and-silt sea bed is strewn with rocky outcrops, which provide refuge for a whole range of creatures. And those divers who particularly like to explore disaster sites will really be in their element here. Wrecks can be found up and down the coast from Bastia harbour to the Tour de l'Osse on Cap Corse to the north. Be forewarned, though, that different diving centres call these wrecks by different names.

The nearest wreck to the town is that of a Heinkel-111, a German bomber, which lies upside down at a depth of 33m, a short distance from the breakwater of the new harbour. The plane's tail is broken and the engines have come away, but the landing gear is still in place. You can even swim inside the cockpit.

Slightly farther north, the **Roche du 14 Juillet** consists of small cliffs, extending from 17m to 38m, where shoals of sargo, grouper, moray eel and red scorpion fish swim. The **Roche à Mérous** has similar features, at a depth of between 22m and 34m. The **Rocher de Cinquini** consists of overlying rock strata at a depth of between 24m and 36m. This honeycombed rock, with its permanent carpet of sessile organisms, also

A Fishy Business

You won't be alone down there in the deep. The following is a list of some of the living creatures that'll keep you company.

Fish

Barracuda This predaceous fish, which sometimes grows to nearly 2m in length, is both swift and powerful. It visits coastal waters only occasionally and fleetingly.

Bogue One of the few vegetarian fish, this species lives in shoals above Poseidonion beds and feeds on the leaves. It is silver in colour with horizontal golden markings. Born male, specimens grow into females.

Brown meagre A favourite target for hunters, this fairly large predator (40cm to 80cm long) is often seen in shoals near the rocky sea floor or above Poseidonion beds. It is recognisable by its silvery-grey markings and arched back.

Cardinalfish Also known as 'king of the mullet', the cardinalfish is about 15cm long and lives near the entrances of caves or beneath overhangs. It is recognised by its red colouring and large black eyes.

Comber The most famous variety is the **painted comber**, which owes its name to the patterns on its head. It has vertical black stripes and a blue mark on its underbelly, and tends to live in the Poseidonion beds.

Conger eel Also known as the sea eel, the conger is greyish in colour and can grow to more than 2m in length. By day it hides in holes, between rocks and in wrecks, poking its head out when a diver passes. It leaves its den at night to hunt.

Damselfish These fish congregate in compact, slow-moving schools relatively near the water's surface and close to shallows. A maximum of 10cm in length, they have grey and black markings and scissor-shaped tails.

Forkbeard This brown fish prefers the shade of caves and overhangs. It is recognised by the two forked barbels under its chin.

Grouper The thickset darling of scuba divers, sometimes growing to 1.5m in length, is distinguished by its enormous thick-lipped mouth and by the whitish flecks on its brownish scales. It spends most of its time in holes but will let divers approach it, particularly if offered food – but you should not do so (see the boxed text 'Environmentally Aware Diving'). Born female, specimens change sex when they get older (this is also the case with rainbow wrasse and swallow-tail sea perch).

John Dory This fish has superb stripes on its dorsal fin, but it owes its French name, St-Pierre, to the legend that the black spot on its flank was left by the Father of the Church himself, when Jesus instructed him to catch the fish and remove the gold coin from its mouth.

Labridae This family's colourful representatives include the inescapable **rainbow wrasse**, the most 'tropical' fish in the Mediterranean, which sometimes approaches divers for food. A maximum of 20cm long, it is found near the surface and has remarkable turquoise and red mottled markings.

Moray eel This fierce predator waits in crevices, from which only its mouth is visible. Growing to 1.5m, it is distinguished by its speed, its sharp teeth and its dark, sometimes yellow-flecked markings.

Red scorpion fish Known locally as capon, the red scorpion fish lies in wait for its prey on the sea floor, using its camouflage skills to blend in with its surroundings. Its body is covered in poisonous spines and outgrowths.

Sargo Extremely common, sargo swim alongside divers who go near the rocky sea floor or beds.

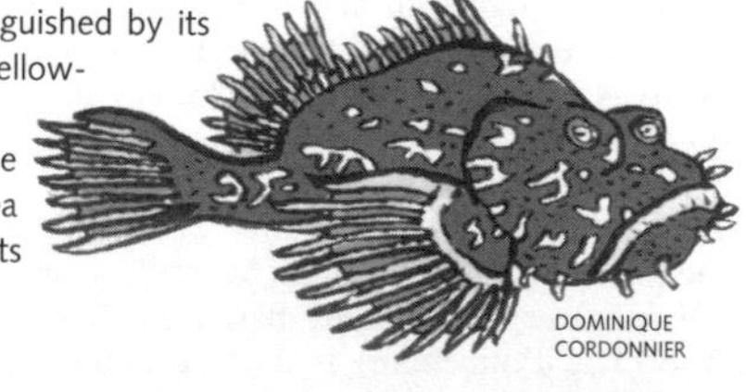

The venomously spined red scorpion fish

A Fishy Business

The most widespread variety is the silvery **white bream** (around 40cm long), which has two characteristic black marks on its gills and tail. In the same family, the **dentex** is a formidable carnivore that can grow to 1m in length, but its appearances are only fleeting.

Swallow-tail sea perch Usually found at the entrances to caves or wrecks, away from the light, this is a small, graceful, orange-red fish.

DOMINIQUE CORDONNIER

Make the most of the chance to mingle with marine life.

Sessile Organisms & Invertebrates

The most common sessile organisms are **sponges**, which form wide coloured patches on the surfaces of rocks and filter-feed on phenomenal quantities of water. Glance under the roofs of caves or overhangs to see **yellow anemones** covering the rocks. These colonies of tiny 'flower-animals' resemble gold buttons with yellow tentacles.

Coral, often scarlet in colour and covered with white polyps, lives on rocks, well away from the light, and feeds on suspended particles. **Red gorgonian** (blue if you're not using a torch) blooms in the form of a candelabra or as ramified bushes up to 1m wide. It has a supple skeleton, unlike the calcified coral, and it decorates the walls of drops in vast fields that are a photographer's favourite.

Ascidians resemble soft tubes and grow in a range of colours, usually violet, red or black. They are sometimes transparent, as in the case of **claveline** and the elegant **Neptune's lace**, which forms bushes of pink calcified petals, and the **sea rose**, which is hard and crumbly with pinkish convolutions.

With a bit of luck you'll see a **sabella** (or **spirographe**), part of the worm family. It lives in calcareous tubes 10cm to 30cm long attached to rocks or buried in the sand. From there it extends long multicoloured plumes to filter water.

Mediterranean crustaceans include **crab**, **lobster**, with its enormous pincers, **crayfish**, with its long antenna, and the **hermit crab**, which uses a shell as a squat. The **flat lobster**, a protected species that clings beneath overhangs, and the **squad lobster**, which is reddish with pretty blue stripes, are less well known. Crustaceans live in holes and caves.

The mollusc family includes **cuttlefish**, which propels itself backwards and emits a black fluid at the slightest threat; the **octopus**, with eight sucker-covered tentacles (it usually lives in a hollow but it allows itself to be stroked by divers); the **large pearl**, a protected species that can grow to up to 1m and stands upright in the sand near the beds; and **scallop**.

There are also minute creatures such as **dori** and **flabellinidae**, which look like slugs and are less than 5cm long. The dori (of which there are a number of species, including the Dalmatian variety with black markings on a white background) are brightly coloured, while the gracious flabelline is mauve and covered in papulae.

The prickly echinoderms include various types of **sea urchin**, with its characteristic quills, **starfish**, able to turn its stomach inside out to digest particularly large prey, and the **sea cucumber**, or holothurian, which resembles a large black pudding lying on the sand or among the rocks.

Underwater Flora

There are several varieties of **seaweed** in the Mediterranean; brown, green or red, hard or soft. The calcified varieties can have superb mineral formations. The infamous ***Caulerpa taxifolia***, which has proliferated along the Côte d'Azur, destroying everything in its path, has so far spared Corsica.

Endemic to the Mediterranean, the Poseidonion (from Poseidon, the god of the sea) is a green plant that forms vast meadows on the sand. Divers generally spurn these grassy beds but they form a choice biotope, home to numerous species of fish seeking shelter or spawning in the foliage.

The Return of the Grouper

After decades of unregulated fishing, the grouper, prized for its meat, had virtually disappeared from the western shores of the Mediterranean. On 2 April 1993 it was declared a protected species, and the population is now growing, particularly around Corsica. Its young are seen with increasing frequency at the dive sites.

attracts shellfish, particularly squad lobster, flat lobster and crayfish, as well as grouper, forkbeard and moray eel. Dentex and sargo can also be seen.

The **Roche des Minelli** comprises three ascents extending from 8m to 22m. Bogue, octopus, red scorpion fish, grouper and moray eel are found among the masses of fallen rocks. Nearby, the **Pain de Sucre**, a sugar-loaf mountain that extends from 28m to 42m, opens out onto a honeycombed plateau at depths of between 36m and 42m, providing an ideal breeding ground for grouper, forkbeard and swallow-tail sea perch.

Farther north, 20 minutes by boat from Bastia, is the **Ancre Perdue**, a series of sugar-loaf mountains separated by sandbanks; the deepest reaches 42m, the most shallow 24m. The **Roche de Miomio** is a 150m-long sculptured massif that's ideal for beginners.

Continuing northwards, you will come to two wrecks. A Thunderbolt P-47, a small British fighter plane, still in good condition, lies on seaweed in 22m of water. The *Canonnière*, off of Pietracorbara still farther to the north, is a 45m-long vessel that went to the bottom in 1943. It is at a depth of 40m to 45m so can only be visited by experienced divers. The hull, a section of the deck, the propeller and engine, as well as a cannon are all still relatively intact. The site teems with grouper, lobster, brown meagre, conger eel and swallow-tail sea perch.

DIVING CENTRES

There are diving centres in nearly all the gulfs as you travel clockwise from Porto Vecchio around to St-Florent.

They are virtually all affiliated with the Fédération Française d'Études et de Sports Sous-Marins (FFESSM; French Federation of Submarine Studies and Sports) and welcome all divers, regardless of their training. Invariably there are one or two instructors who speak English. Most centres have no specific diving itinerary but instead take into account the weather conditions and divers' experience when deciding which sites to visit on a given day.

Like most leisure activities and tourist facilities in Corsica, diving is highly seasonal. Of some 30 centres on the island, only a handful open year round, and some only open on demand or at the weekend. Most open at the end of April and close at the end of October, but in April, May and October they really just tick over. The season proper starts in June and reaches its peak in July and August.

The number of daily outings is also influenced by seasonal demand. A centre may organise two outings daily in June (at 8.30 am or 9 am and at 2 pm or 3 pm) and four or five in July and August, especially if it opens seven days per week and employs a substantial number of instructors. Go in June, before it gets busy, or in September, when it gets quieter again. At the height of the season the staff are more in demand and the whole experience becomes much less personal.

Whatever time of year you go, always book at least a day in advance – or even longer if you are able. The centres are not always staffed when the boats are out so, unless you're calling on the phone to book, plan your visit for either a good half-hour before a departure time or at the end of the morning or afternoon.

Costs & Facilities

Corsica's diving centres offer a wide range of services, such as introductory dives (for children and adults), night dives, exploratory dives and training for diving qualifications. The price of an introductory dive includes equipment hire, while the price of an exploratory dive varies according to how much equipment you need to borrow. Ex-

Learning to Dive

If you're going to continue beyond the introductory dive, theoretical and practical training are mandatory. Several organisations or federations are authorised to provide such training and to issue certificates. These include FFESSM, PADI, CMAS, SSI and NAUI. To the uninitiated, these abbreviations can be confusing. In practice, it does not matter which body you train with, since they all offer similar courses and everybody accepts everybody else's certificates. Get qualified by any one of them and you will be able to dive all over the world.

In France, the main organisation is the Fédération Française d'Études et de Sports Sous-Marins (FFESSM), which offers training in four stages. Level 1 (CMAS; three to five days, around six dives at sea or in a pool, learning basic techniques and safety rules) allows you to dive accompanied by an instructor down as far as 20m; level 2 (two weeks) consists of more detailed theoretical and technical training. You can then dive with another diver of the same level as deep as 20m without an instructor, and with an instructor as far as 40m. From level 3, you can dive on your own with other divers of the same level. The more professional level 4 is instructor training.

In England the equivalent of the FFESSM is the British Sub-Aqua Club (BSAC). BSAC-certified divers should be welcome at centres internationally.

The US-based Professional Association of Diving Instructors (PADI) system, widely used in English-speaking countries outside Europe (and increasingly within Europe), works along the same lines. After the 'Discover Scuba' introductory dive, trainees go on to the Open Water Diver, Advanced Open Water Diver, Rescue Diver and Divemaster levels.

Other well known international organisations are Scuba School International (SSI) and the National Association of Underwater Instructors (NAUI). If you want to learn to dive in your own country, ask the diving centre which organisation it's affiliated with.

pect to pay 100FF to hire all the equipment. If you are planning to make repeated dives it might be cheaper to bring your own.

Generally clubs have a price for 'equipped divers' (those with their own gear, often including an air cylinder), a 'semi-equipped' price (for those who have some gear) and an 'unequipped price'. This explains why there is a range of prices in the centre listings that follow. Packages of three, five or 10 dives are invariably cheaper than the same number of dives purchased individually. Night dives, which are usually more expensive, are arranged either subject to demand or on certain programmed nights.

When it comes to training, only the cost of level 1 instruction is given in our listings because this is the most popular. An indication of the charge for level 1 instruction for the PADI Open Water qualification is given for those centres that offer it (see the boxed text Learning to Dive). You should make sure the charge includes theoretical and practical instruction as well as administrative fees (such as the licence, diving log, diving pass and certificate). Only a handful of centres accept credit cards so bring along cash or travellers cheques.

The boats used to take divers to the sites may be aluminium barges, small semi-rigid 10-seat vessels, large covered 30- or 40-seat launches with all the equipment on board, or even old trawlers or converted tugboats.

Choosing a Centre

Like a hotel or restaurant, each diving centre has its own personality and style. Some people may be more comfortable with the intimacy and slightly seat-of-the-pants feel of one or another of the smaller establishments; others will prefer the well oiled machinery, the logistics and the no-nonsense professionalism of a larger American-style centre. Some divers will feel reassured only if an instructor is strict and methodical; others will prefer an instructor with a relaxed, flexible approach.

Getting Started

With its reassuringly shallow inlets and crystalline, warm waters, Corsica offers ideal conditions for novice divers, so if you've always fancied scuba diving but never taken the plunge, now's your chance. Arrange an introductory dive to give you a feel for the experience; a preliminary session lasts about 20 minutes in a safe location under the watchful eye of an instructor. In some centres, instructors spend half their time taking the uninitiated out on introductory dives, so there's no need to feel embarrassed or nervous.

Since it's essential that you have confidence in your instructor, call or visit a few clubs, ask questions and listen to your gut instinct. There are no formalities other than that those aged under 18 need permission from a parent. However, you shouldn't dive if you have acute ear, nose or throat problems, a serious medical condition such as epilepsy or heart disease, a cold or sinusitis, or if you are pregnant. If you are uncertain as to whether some medical condition should keep you on the sidelines, ask.

Your one-to-one introductory dive will begin on dry land, where the instructor will run through basic safety procedures (the use of sign language to indicate that everything is 'OK' or 'not OK' and ear equilibration techniques) and show you the equipment. Special equipment means that children aged over eight years can also learn to dive.

You'll practise breathing with the regulator above the surface before going underwater. When you do go under, to a depth of 3m to 5m, the instructor will hold your hand and guide your movements. Some centres offer free instruction for apprehensive divers in waist high water in a hotel swimming pool.

If you enjoy your introductory dive you might like to undergo novice training for a certificate that will allow you to dive anywhere in the world (see the boxed text 'Learning to Dive').

Other factors that may influence your decision include the setting (is there a beach nearby so a nondiving companion will have something to do?), price, schedules, facilities (such as the availability of hot showers or the degree of comfort on the boats), the range of services (such as full day trips and special training), the friendliness of the staff, accessibility and whether there are any little extras (are you offered a drink after the dive? Do you have to maintain your own cylinder?). If you are unsure about a centre, go somewhere else, and be wary of word of mouth: each centre has its admirers and critics, especially when there are several centres in one area.

All of the centres listed below are authorised diving centres. They employ qualified instructors, have modern, well maintained equipment and observe strict safety regulations. The list, however, is not exhaustive.

Snorkelling in Corsica

The best place for snorkelling in Corsica is the Îles Lavezzi. Several firms in Bonifacio, including two diving centres (Kalliste and Atoll), can take you out to swim in the archipelago's turquoise waters.

Snorkelling is the ideal activity for those reluctant to dive. The best places are inlets or rocky promontories, where small fauna is most abundant, but make sure to consult local diving centres for information on currents, and do not swim alone.

Rules & Regulations

No special procedures apply for an introductory dive but minors are required to have parental consent. If you are already qualified, you will be asked to produce your certificate and diving card. All divers are welcome, whether they trained with PADI, FFESSM or another body.

If you have not dived for a while, you may be asked to do a refresher dive so that your diving ability and technical skills can be assessed. A medical certificate attesting to your fitness to dive is mandatory for instruction and strongly advised (sometimes compulsory) if you intend to dive regularly with one centre. It can be issued on the spot for the price of a medical consultation.

As for insurance, the situation varies. Some centres require you to obtain an FFESSM licence (around 160FF), which includes insurance; others have civil liability insurance for their customers. Make sure your travel insurance covers medical treatment and transport home in case of a diving accident. If it doesn't, you can take out supplementary insurance with the centre.

What Diving Doesn't Mix With

You should wait at least 12 hours after a dive before climbing or flying. The reduction in pressure that occurs when you gain altitude could interfere with your body's disposal of dissolved nitrogen, with adverse effects ranging from nausea to paralysis of the limbs or even, in the most extreme cases, death. For more on decompression sickness see the Health for Divers section in the Facts for the Visitor chapter.

Accommodation & Transport

Several of the diving centres are affiliated with a hotel, while others can recommend places to stay for a range of budgets, sometimes at a special rate. Some even offer diving packages that include flights, transfers, accommodation and meals.

If you are travelling by public transport, see the Getting There & Away and Getting Around chapters earlier in this book.

Around Porto Vecchio

CIP La Palanquée This centre (☎ 04 95 70 16 53, fax 04 95 70 64 48), with more than 20 years of service to its credit, is 400m from the town harbour on the road to Bonifacio. It's in a large building on the right, 100m before you get to the Casino supermarket.

The price for a single dive ranges from 200FF to 285FF. But expect to pay 1140FF for a six-dive package (excluding equipment hire). The introductory dives (usually at the wreck of the *Pecorella*) cost 280FF. Level 1 instruction costs 2100FF.

Alain Desogère, a national FFESSM trainer, has a team of up to 10 instructors in high season, and diver training represents 75% of the centre's activity. The dives are conducted in the area between the Golfe de Porto Vecchio and the Îles Cerbicale, 20 to 50 minutes away by one of the centre's two boats, one of which, a pilot boat, has been adapted to seat 30. The divers meet at the club; they're driven to the harbour by van.

The centre opens year round, except on Sundays, and runs excursions at 8.30 am and 2.30 pm. Credit cards are accepted.

Hippocampe This small centre (☎/fax 04 95 70 56 54, e dive@hippocampe.de), with just three instructors, links diving with naturism. It's owned by a German couple, and its headquarters are on naturist beach La Chiappa, south of the Golfe de Porto Vecchio. Follow the main road towards Bonifacio and, as you leave Porto Vecchio, turn left towards Palombaggia. Continue on this road for 7km, then bear left towards Chiappa, 2.5km away. The drive from the town centre takes roughly 20 minutes. After you leave your vehicle in the car park, you will hand over some ID at the reception desk. But divers get in free.

An introductory dive off the beach costs 200FF; from the boat it costs 300FF. An exploratory dive costs between 160FF and 250FF. A package of 10 dives costs 1450FF to 2050FF. Level 1 instruction costs 1800FF, and instruction for the Open Water certificate costs 2300FF.

The sites, between Golfe de Porto Vecchio and the Îles Cerbicale, are less than 15 minutes away by one of the centre's two semirigid boats. A baby-sitting service is available at the naturist camp (ask at reception).

The centre opens daily from mid-May to mid-October and runs from two to five daily outings, subject to demand. The two certain starts are at 8.30 am and 2 pm.

Kalliste This centre (☎/fax 04 95 70 44 59, 06 80 11 71 54) is about 13km from the centre of Porto Vecchio, on picturesque Palombaggia beach. To get there, take the main road in the direction of Bonifacio and, as you leave the town, turn left towards Palombaggia.

Introductory dives (in an inlet in the Îles Cerbicale) cost 330FF. Exploratory dives cost between 210FF and 265FF. A package of six dives costs from 1140FF to 1440FF. Level 1 instruction costs 2250FF and instruction for the PADI Open Water certificate costs 3200F.

Divers opting for a diving package and those on an instruction course can use facilities both here and at the sister centre in Bonifacio harbour.

The 10 instructors on duty in the high season will take you to the sites between the Golfe de Porto Vecchio and the Îles Cerbicale. Getting to the jump-off point takes about a quarter of an hour in a 20-seat boat.

Open daily from April to November, the centre runs two daily excursions at 8 am and 2 pm, increasing to four subject to demand.

Bonifacio

Atoll This operation (☎ 04 95 73 02 83/53 83, fax 04 95 73 17 72), probably the most famous in Corsica, is part of the Auberge A Cheda about 2km from the town marina on the Porto Vecchio road. It also operates a welcome centre on the marina itself, close to the terminal for ferries to Sardinia.

Atoll employs as many as 12 instructors at the height of the season, yet it strives to maintain the friendliness of a smaller-scale enterprise. Its dynamism, professionalism and high level of organisation are, on the other hand, reflected in its expansive pricing. Introductory dives in the Îles Lavezzi or at Cap Pertusato will set you back 345FF (with the option of a free introductory session in the hotel swimming pool). An exploratory dive costs between 235FF and 295FF. Three dives cost 705FF to 825FF and six dives will set you back 1135FF to 1495FF. Level 1 instruction costs 2465FF. Atoll is also a PADI-approved centre; expect to pay 3170FF for the Open Water certificate. Photography courses are available as well.

The club's pride and joy is its bespoke 43-seat diving boat, with all diving equipment on board. Divers are taken to sites in the Bouches de Bonifacio and the Îles Lavezzi, 20 minutes away. An outing to Mérouville takes place on Tuesday, Thursday and Sunday mornings. A day trip to Sardinia is organised every Friday (you pay for two dives plus an extra 100FF for lunch on board). Be aware that Atoll's instructors do not condone the feeding of grouper.

Atoll opens year round and there are daily departures at 8.15 am and 2.15 pm. Credit cards are accepted.

Barakouda This centre (☎ 04 95 73 13 02/19 02) is 1km before Atoll on the road from Bonifacio to Porto Vecchio. Look for it on the left. If you come to the large roundabout, you've gone 200m too far. Established in 1971, Barakouda is in every way unconventional. It has a den-like headquarters and the director, Gérard Arend maintains an informal atmosphere.

Prices are reasonable: an introductory dive costs 240FF, an exploratory dive between 150FF and 240FF and a set of five dives from 720FF to 1140FF. Level 1 instruction, including five dives, costs 1470FF.

The centre's three boats, including a trawler that can carry 40 divers, depart from the beach at Pietranella, with minibus transfer service from the club HQ. Arend, who prides himself on having single-handedly domesticated the Mérouville grouper, will only take you to sites in the Îles Lavezzi, which he knows like the back of his hand. In high season Mérouville is on the itinerary every day at 11.15 am and also on Tuesday and Sunday at 8.15 am. Here divers may feed the grouper.

The centre opens daily year round, subject to demand. In high season, there are three excursions at 8.15 am, noon and 2.30 pm daily. Credit cards are not accepted.

Kalliste This beautifully maintained centre (☎ 04 95 73 53 66) is the twin of the one with the same name in Porto Vecchio (see Around Porto Vecchio earlier), and its prices are identical. As you enter Bonifacio from the direction of Porto Vecchio, take the small road on the right just after the Esso petrol station. The centre is situated a few metres back from the harbour, just in front of the Hôtel Résidence.

On board an ultramodern glass-bottomed boat able to carry 40 passengers and store all equipment, Michel Rossi and his team will take you out to dive in the neighbourhood of the Îles Lavezzi, 20 minutes away, as well as in the Bouches de Bonifacio. Mérouville is on the itinerary twice per week. For 200FF you can be filmed while diving. (Nondivers pay 70FF.) The program also includes a weekly excursion to the wreck of the *Angelica* in Sardinia, and from time to time Rossi will take divers down to wrecks that only he seems to know about.

Open April to November, the centre runs two excursions at 8 am and 2 pm daily. Credit cards are accepted.

Golfe de Valinco

There are two centres at the foot of the gulf in Propriano and one either side of its entrance in two small seaside resorts.

Campomoro Plongée This small, friendly establishment (☎ 04 95 74 23 29, 06 09 95 44 43) is located in the magnificent Baie de Campomoro, a peaceful seaside resort, 15km from Propriano at the southern end of the gulf. The office is on the beach opposite the church. An introductory dive costs 230FF and an exploratory dive costs between 170FF and 215FF. Four dives cost between 560FF and 740FF, but the fifth then costs only 130FF. Level 1 instruction costs 215FF (and 30FF for a theory lesson) per dive.

Yann Lemoël uses two 12-seat boats to take you out to the Sec de Campomoro in the west, and Le Tonneau or the Sec du Belvédère in the east. Those diving for the first time will be taken to the western end of the bay, near some small islands just off a Genoese tower, or to the east, near the shore.

Open daily from Easter to the end of October, the centre runs two to four excursions daily, subject to demand. Times vary.

Valinco Plongée This centre (☎ 04 95 76 31 01, fax 04 95 76 24 78), in a large yellow prefabricated building next door to the tourist office, at the marina, charges 230FF for an introductory dive at Cala Muretta, an inlet near Portigliolo, or in a cove across from the marina on the northern shore. An exploratory dive costs from 160FF to 200FF. A five-dive package costs from 750FF to 950FF and level 1 instruction costs 1600F.

Valinco Plongée also uses sites such as Le Tonneau, Les Cathédrales and the Sec de Campomoro on the southern and northern shores near the mouth of the gulf. There are also occasional trips out to the Réserve des Moines, with a dive down to the wreck of the *Tasmania* (200FF) and a picnic (additional charge) in an inlet near Capu di Senetosa.

Depending on demand, there are up to five daily excursions between 8 am and 4 pm. The centre opens April to October.

U Levante This centre (☎ 04 95 76 23 83, fax 04 95 74 03 00, ⓔ u-levante-plongee@wanadoo.fr) is also housed in a prefabricated building, only 20m away from Valinco Plongée. Expect to pay 155FF to 195FF for an exploratory dive, 440FF to 560FF for three dives, 725FF to 925FF for five dives, 1600FF for training or level 1 instruction and 3200FF for the PADI Open Water certificate.

Beginners can go on the usual introductory dive for 195FF; it takes place in an inlet on the southern shore near Portigliolo beach or on the northern shore across from the harbour. Or they can opt for instruction in a hotel swimming pool followed by an introductory dive in the sea, at a cost of 250FF.

Divers are taken to sites in the gulf on one of two aluminium launches or a 17-seat inflatable. Outings to Les Cathédrales take place on Sundays or on demand. Day trips north or south of the gulf with a picnic lunch in an inlet take place once weekly (500FF).

The centre opens April to November and runs two to five trips daily. At the height of the season, up to nine instructors may be on duty. Their Web site can be found at http://perso.wanadoo.fr/ulevante (French only).

Porto Pollo Plongée At the northern tip of the gulf, in the village of Porto Pollo, this centre (☎/fax 04 95 74 07 46, 06 87 20 55 42, ⓔ portopolloplongee@wanadoo.fr) has a relaxed family atmosphere. Headquartered in a prefabricated building overlooking the small marina, it charges some of the most competitive rates on the island. An introductory dive in an inlet at the mouth of the Baie de Porto Pollo costs 180FF, an exploratory dive 150FF to 210FF, three dives 420FF to 600FF, six dives 825FF to 1185FF and level 1 instruction an all-inclusive 1776FF.

Porto Pollo Plongée tailors its program to individual customers. On board an old tugboat or a 10-seat barge, you will explore sites which are less than 15 minutes away in the northern part of the gulf. The star attractions, such as Les Cathédrales and Les Aiguilles, are barely five minutes from one another. Porto Pollo is also the only operator to take divers to a site known as Le Jardin, with its magnificent black coral.

The centre opens year round and runs excursions at 9 am and 3 pm daily during the height of the season. Its Web site (http://perso.wanadoo.fr/portopolloplongee) has more information.

Golfe d'Ajaccio

Maeva In this centre (☎ 04 95 25 02 40/10 84, ⓔ maeva-plongee@wanadoo.fr) at the Marines de Porticcio, opposite the Elf garage, you'll pay 230FF for an introductory dive, 170FF to 250FF for an exploratory dive, 910FF to 1385FF for six dives and 1850FF for level 1 instruction. The sites on offer are at Pointe de l'Isolella and Punta di Porticcio, and you get to them on a 20-seat covered vessel or in an inflatable boat.

The centre opens daily from April to mid-October. Departures are at 8.30 am and 2 pm.

Club Subaquatique d'Agosta In the Agosta Plage motel, at Agosta, overlooking a superb white-sand beach, this centre (☎ 04 95 25 40 26/25 58 22, 06 11 57 77 63), with more than 20 years' experience, caters primarily to seasoned divers. The morning deep-dive excursions are organised expressly for experienced divers, and the afternoon is reserved for instruction.

An exploratory dive will cost you 130FF to 210FF, or you can buy six dives for between 760FF and 1200FF. Level 1 instruction costs 1950FF. Dive sites are between Pointe de l'Isolella and Capu di Muru.

The centre opens daily from the beginning of May to mid-October. There are departures at 9 am and 2 pm.

Corse Plongée The clubhouse (☎ 04 95 25 50 08, 06 07 55 67 25, fax 04 95 25 46 30) is located on the Isolella Peninsula just south of Porticcio. An introductory dive costs 250FF, an exploratory dive 160FF and 240FF, and six dives go for 900FF and 1410FF. Level 1 instruction costs 2000FF and there's a charge of 2400FF for the PADI Open Water certificate.

Corse Plongée operates between Capu di Muru in the south and Punta di Porticcio in the north. The sites are a maximum of 40 minutes away via a covered 40-seat launch that has all the equipment on board, or in a smaller semi-rigid vessel. The itinerary includes all of the famous sites – the wreck of the *Meulière*, the Tête de Mort and the Grotte à Corail – but Nicolas Caprili, director, diver and skipper, prides himself on having several other 'private' sites up his sleeve. The centre also offers night dives at 360FF, diving cruises (see the boxed text 'Diving Cruises') and diving day trips that include lunch in a traditional fishermen's tavern at 250FF per dive.

Corse Plongée opens from April to the end of October, with daily departures at 9 am and 3 pm.

GSC The only club in the centre of Ajaccio proper, specifically in the Tino Rossi marina, GSC (☎ 06 03 58 93 00) is a small establishment that charges 200FF for an introductory dive (those aged under 14, 150FF), 130FF to 200FF for an exploratory dive and 750FF to 1100FF for six dives. A Thursday evening dive is offered for 250FF. The program includes the most popular sites in the gulf, with the exception of the Îles Sanguinaires. Introductory dives take place in an inlet at Pointe de l'Isolella.

The centre opens daily mid-May to the end of September. There are two trips at 8.30 am and 2.30 pm daily, and there may be a third, depending on demand. GSC also runs a squid-fishing sail on Saturday evenings at 50FF per person.

E Ragnole This centre (☎/fax 04 95 21 53 55) is part of the Anthinéa fitness club, and the team of young instructors give it a particularly relaxed atmosphere. Look for it about 2km from the centre of Ajaccio on the beach side of the Route des Sanguinaires, just after the Champion supermarket. Rates are 200FF for an introductory dive in the sea (or 150FF on the beach), 140FF to 200FF for an exploratory dive and a mere 1300FF for level 1 instruction. PADI Open Water instruction costs 3200FF. The instructors use several sites, including a nice coral reef, close to the centre but also take their customers out to sites in the southern part of the gulf near Pointe de l'Isolella.

The centre opens daily May to October and at weekends in low season. In July and August, there are daily outings at 8 am, 9 am, 2.30 pm and 6 pm. Transportation is a pair of 14-seat inflatables.

Bulle Bleue In the basement of the Hôtel Stella di Mare, on the route des Sanguinaires 8km from Ajaccio centre, this small establishment (☎ 04 95 52 01 68, 06 11 89 01 11, fax 04 95 52 08 69) offers introductory dives in front of the hotel for 240FF or a little beginners' course starting in the swimming pool and then moving out to sea for 300FF. Exploratory dives cost 210FF to 250FF, a six-dive package costs 1150FF to 1350FF and level 1 instruction costs 1500FF.

Bulle Bleue (Blue Bubble in English) usually visits sites on the northern side of the gulf between Ajaccio and the Îles Sanguinaires. It also organises weekend diving cruises (see the boxed text 'Diving Cruises').

The centre opens year round, and programs outings every day.

Diving Cruises

In Corsica, it's possible to combine the joys of diving with those of sailing. Here are three options for divers with a minimum level 2 qualification:

- A full-day excursion aboard a 12m vessel along the north-western coast between Porto, Capu Rossu, Girolata and the Réserve de Scandola, at an all-inclusive price of 600FF per person, is available from Bulle Bleue, just outside Ajaccio (☎/fax 04 95 52 01 68). This club also offers diving cruises of several days in length and a snorkelling program within the magnificent Réserve de Scandola for 400FF (snorkelling is permitted there, if diving isn't).
- A tailor-made diving cruise on request only, preferably out-of-season, can be arranged with Nicolas Caprili, the director of the Corse Plongée centre in Isolella (☎ 04 95 25 50 08, 06 07 55 67 25, fax 04 95 25 46 30).
- A week-long diving cruise to the most beautiful locations on Corsica's western coast, between Girolata and Propriano, is offered by the Centre Subaquatique de Sagone at Hôtel Cyrnos in Sagone (☎ 04 95 28 00 01, 04 95 21 09 97, fax 04 95 28 00 77). Specific dive sites, 12 in all, include the Golfe de Valinco, Golfe d'Ajaccio, Golfe de Sagone, Golfe de Porto and Golfe de Girolata. Courses operate from April to October, and the price of 3390FF to 3990FF, depending on specific departure date, includes all meals and all dives. There is a maximum of eight participants. The skipper is an instructor at the centre and has been diving around the island for almost 20 years.

Les Calanques This centre (☎ 04 95 52 09 37, fax 04 95 51 10 88) is located in the Hôtel des Calanques on the right-hand side of the road from Ajaccio, a little beyond Bulle Bleue. It charges 240FF for an introductory dive, 190FF to 260FF for an exploratory dive, 1100FF to 1400FF for six dives and 1850FF for level 1 instruction.

The centre is owned by the Nouvelles Frontières group and is run by Jean-Pierre Malamas, author of several reference works on diving. The Nouvelles Frontières Group also owns the centre in Le Grand Bleu hotel in the Golfe de Liscia (see under Golfe de Liscia/Golfe de Sagone later in this section), so the six dives can be taken at one centre or split up between the two. The club in the Ajaccio area visits around 10 sites on the northern side of the gulf between Ajaccio and the Îles Sanguinaires.

The centre opens daily from the beginning of May to the end of September, except for Saturdays in July and August. In high season, there are four excursions daily between 8 am and 4 pm.

Golfe de Lava

Squale Plongée This small centre (☎ 06 09 72 69 77), in a smart chalet on Lava beach about 20km north of Ajaccio, makes a special point of conviviality and hospitality. To get here, head towards Mezzavia, then take the D81 towards Cargèse and Porto. After 10km or so bear left on the D381. An introductory dive, conducted at Pietra Piombata, at the southern entrance to the gulf, costs 230FF. An exploratory dive costs 165FF to 220FF, six dives cost 910FF to 1170FF and level 1 instruction 1950FF.

A semi-rigid 16-seat vessel takes divers to otherwise little-visited sites in the Golfe de Lava, notably the aforementioned Pietra Piombata, as well as in the Golfe de Liscia to the north. It is also ideally placed for access to the renowned Banc Provençal, about 10 minutes north of headquarters.

The centre opens April to the end of September. There are two to four outings daily in summer, with exploratory dives in the morning and introductory dives and training in the afternoon.

Golfe de Liscia/Golfe de Sagone

Le Grand Bleu In the hotel of the same name in the town of Calcatoggio, about 30km north of Ajaccio, this centre (☎ 04 95 52 24 34, fax 04 95 51 10 88) – like Les Calanques on the outskirts of Ajaccio – is owned by the Nouvelles Frontières Group. From Ajaccio, follow the signs to Mezzavia and Cargèse. At the entrance to the Golfe de Liscia, take the small road on the left that leads to the Tour d'Ancone. Le Grand Bleu is 400m along the beach.

Prices and products are identical to those offered by Les Calanques (see Golfe d'Ajaccio – Northern Shore). A free introductory dive in the hotel swimming pool takes place once or twice weekly.

Look out for the special course (between the introductory dive and level 1) available to those who are pressed for time; it includes a pool lesson, a theory lesson, a slide show on fauna and flora and two dives to between 5m and 10m (650FF in season). The sites used are about 10 minutes away on the southern shores of the Golfe de Liscia and the Golfe de Sagone, between Punta Palmentoju and the Banc Provençal.

The centre opens Easter to the end of October but closes on Saturday. There are two fixed outings at 8.30 am and 4 pm daily and up to two outings more, as required.

Nautica Sub About 900m along the beach from Le Grand Bleu, Nautica Sub (☎ 04 95 52 27 11) is a straightforward little establishment employing a maximum of four instructors and charging 200FF for an introductory dive in an inlet or on the beach, 140FF to 200FF for an exploratory dive, 740FF to 1080FF for six dives and 1400FF for level 1 instruction.

A semi-rigid 12-seat boat takes divers to sites in the Golfe de Sagone and the Golfe de Lava, including the popular Banc Provençal, Pietra Piombata and a wreck of a fire-fighting aircraft, the *Canadair*.

Open May to October, the centre runs up to four excursions daily in summer. Their Web site is at www.chez.com/nauticasub.

Centre Subaquatique de Sagone This medium-size centre (☎ 04 95 28 00 01, fax 04 95 28 00 77, ⓔ hotelcyrnos@free.com), located in the Hôtel Cyrnos in Sagone, across from a superb beach, charges 170FF to 200FF for an exploratory dive and 850FF to 1000FF for a package of six.

A covered 20-seat launch that used to belong to the customs authorities will take you to sites 15 to 20 minutes away in the Golfe de Sagone, between Punta Paliagi in the south and the Rocher de Marifaga in the north. The *Canadair* and *Girafe* wrecks are a short distance out to sea between the two.

The centre opens daily from May to the beginning of October. It operates two daily departures. Credit cards are accepted. Rates including lodging can be worked out.

Golfe de Porto

Centre de Plongée du Golfe de Porto

This centre (☎/fax 04 95 26 10 29, 06 84 24 49 20, ⓔ guy.lannoy@wanadoo.fr), under the management of Sylvie Lannoy, is at the back of the store called Lannoy Sport at the entrance to Porto as you arrive from Piana. Look for it across from Les Oliviers camp site just after the bridge over the River Porto. Or, in season, go into the welcome centre in the little bungalow by the mini-golf on the left bank of the river. Prices run to 250FF (children 220FF) for an introductory dive at Castagne, the Sec du Château or Capu Rossu (with one instructor per learner), 160FF to 250FF for an exploratory dive, 1900FF for level 1 instruction and 2400FF for the PADI Open Water certificate, including six dives. Expect also discounts of 5/10% below the regular exploratory dive rate for packages of six/10.

In high season the 12 instructors use two boats to carry you to the key sites between Punta Mucchilina in the north and Capu Rossu in the south, five to 35 minutes away. In May, June and September a day trip is organised once or twice weekly to include a dive at Punta Muchillina on the edge of the Réserve Naturelle de Scandola, a lunch at Girolata, then a second dive at Capu Seninu or Punta Scopa. The rate is that for two dives plus 150FF. In July and August, there are half-day excursions to Punta Muchillina once or twice weekly, depending on the weather. Transfers between the centre and the landing stage are by van, and the centre is looking into the possibility of eventually making use of a building right on the harbour. A baby-sitting service is available if you book in advance.

The centre opens Easter to October. It runs four excursions daily in season and credit cards are accepted. Its Web site at www.plongeeporto.com has more information.

Génération Bleue This centre (☎/fax 04 95 26 24 88, 06 07 43 21 28, ⓔ pascal.juppet@wanadoo.fr) is run by Pascal Juppet, who in winter doubles as a ski instructor. It employs up to six instructors at the height of the season and is right on the marina. The centre charges 230FF for an introductory dive at Castagne or Capu Rossu, 170FF to 230FF for an exploratory dive, 800FF to 1100FF for five dives and 1700FF for level 1 instruction. The charge for a night dive is 280FF.

The program is identical to that of the Centre de Plongée du Golfe de Porto, and both tend to lower their fees as the season begins

Diving Equipment

Above water, diving equipment is heavy and bulky; underwater, you'll feel it very much less. During an introductory dive your instructor will control and adjust your equipment, the components of which are explained here.

- The **regulator** controls the flow of air from the oxygen cylinder to the diver's mouthpiece.
- The **cylinder**, usually of steel construction, contains 12L to 15L of compressed air; sometimes a diver will carry more than one. Special mini-cylinders with capacities of 6L to 8L are available for children.
- The **suit** comes in a variety of sizes and thicknesses (from 3mm to 7mm) and serves as a second skin both for warmth and for protection against getting cut or scratched by the coral.
- The **weight belt** compensates for the buoyancy of the suit. Without it, the diver would float to the surface.
- The inflatable **stabilising jacket**, or stab-jacket, connected to the cylinder, provides comfort and security by allowing divers both to adjust their buoyancy while underwater and to resurface effortlessly at the end of a dive.
- The **manometer** indicates the pressure in the cylinder, measured in bars, as well as showing how much air is left.
- The **mask** enables divers to see clearly underwater. Short-sighted divers can wear masks adapted to their special needs, and contact lenses may also be worn.
- **Flippers** provide propulsion.
- A **depth gauge**, **dive computer** (worn on the wrist), **knife** and **torch** complete the gear.

to wind down. A day trip to Punta Muchillina with lunch at Girolata and an afternoon dive at Capu Seninu is organised in the summer (July and August excepted), subject to demand. Punta Muchillina is also a half-day excursion in summer, subject to demand; there's an additional charge of 50FF. Transportation is aboard two semi-rigid vessels of 7.4m with a capacity for 20 divers each.

The centre opens May to the end of October, conducting two outings daily. You can visit the Web site at www.generation-bleue.com.

Galéria

L'Incantu Perched above Galéria, 300m from the church, in the hotel with which it shares its name, this centre (☎ 04 95 62 03 65, fax 04 95 62 03 66) manages to maintain its status as the largest on the entire island, without making you feel that you're just another in a long line of customers. It's a good balance: efficient yet relaxed. One part of the trick is that the club limits its excursions to two daily even at the height of summer, which is unusual for Corsica. Another is that the range of options is particularly broad: introductory dives, unsupervised dives (140/200FF), supervised dives (180/240FF), a six-dive package costing from 780FF for an unsupervised diver with his or her own equipment to 1320FF for a diver desiring supervision and club equipment, and level 1 instruction for 2040FF. You can also train for the PADI Open Water certificate here.

The 15 summer instructors, including Jo Vrijens, a veteran of the French Foreign Legion, take divers to sites between Punta Morsetta, north of the Golfe de Galéria, and the southern edge of the Réserve de Scandola. This centre is practically the only one that uses these sites. Transport is aboard two covered 20-seat launches.

Among other innovative 'products', L'Incantu has inaugurated a June week of jazz and diving in conjunction with the Calvi jazz festival; it also offers courses in marine biology.

The centre opens year round and has daily excursions at 9 am and 3 pm. Credit cards are accepted, and lodging can be arranged.

Calvi

École de Plongée Internationale de Calvi EPIC (☎ 04 95 65 43 90, fax 04 95 65 42 23) is a family-run centre whose headquarters are a prefabricated building at the entrance to the marina. You'll pay 220FF for an introductory dive at Pointe St-François or Punta Spano, 170FF to 210FF for an exploratory dive, 800FF to 1000FF for five dives and 1700FF for all-inclusive level 1 instruction. Prices, though, may be slightly higher in July and August.

A rigid boat or 25-seat covered launch takes divers to the area between the western side of Pointe de la Revellata and the eastern end of the Baie de Calvi, where there's a B-17 bomber close to the citadel.

The centre opens from April to November. There are departures daily at 9 am and 2.30 pm.

Calvi Plongée Citadelle You'll find this high-calibre centre (☎/fax 04 95 65 33 67), which employs 10 instructors in summer, in an office just downstairs from the tourist office. An introductory dive in a rocky inlet at Pointe St-François, west of the citadel, or at Punta Spano, east of the Baie de Calvi, costs 220FF. An exploratory dive costs between 160FF and 220FF, five dives cost between 750FF and 950FF. Level 1 instruction is offered at an all-inclusive price of 1750FF. The centre is also PADI-approved, and instruction for the PADI Open Water certificate costs 2250FF.

The sites on offer are spread out between the Sec du Lion, west of Pointe de la Revellata, and Punta Spano, to the east just before you come to Algajola.

The centre opens daily May to September, and there are up to four daily excursions. Rates that include lodging can be arranged.

JMB Diving This family-run centre (☎ 04 95 65 12 07/29 37, fax 04 95 65 39 71) is temporarily housed in a chalet on the beach in Calvi, at the eastern edge of the town. To get there, head in the direction of Île Rousse, pass La Camargue disco, then turn left down the small road that leads to the beach. Or take the tram and get out at the stop called Club Olympique. The price of an introductory dive is 220FF. An exploratory dive costs 160FF to 190FF, 10 dives 1450FF to 1750FF and level 1 instruction 1750FF.

Divers are taken on a 10-seat aluminium or a 12-seat plastic barge to sites 15 to 20 minutes away in the Golfe de Calvi and around Pointe de la Revellata.

Open year round, the centre runs two to three excursions daily in summer.

From Calvi to Île Rousse

Subcorsica This largish centre (☎ 04 95 60 75 38, 06 81 70 46 25, fax 04 95 60 79 66), established in 1980, is in Sant'Ambrogio marina, about 15km east of Calvi. An introductory dive in an inlet next to the harbour costs 220FF, an exploratory dive costs 150FF to 230FF. The centre also offers five-dive packages and level 1 instruction as well as a four-session post-starter course.

Subcorsica visits the quiet area between Algajola to the east (including le Danger d'Algajola) and Punta Spano to the west, accessible in 10 to 45 minutes on a 17m boat. The instructors' favourite sites include the wreck of the *Grand Cerf*, Pietra Eramer and Kalliste. The area around la Revellata, west of the Baie de Calvi, and the B-17 bomber are occasionally included in the itinerary (at a slight additional charge).

The centre opens May to October and runs excursions daily from June to September.

Algajola Sport Nature Right on the superb Algajola beach, Algajola Sport Nature (☎ 06 08 21 09 51, 06 80 04 65 17, fax 06 08 37 35 33) adjacent to L'Escale restaurant. Rates run to 170FF for an introductory dive right off the beach, 220FF for an introductory dive at Pedra Mule, a little island at the edge of the bay, 170/200FF for an exploratory dive, 750/850FF for five dives and 1550FF for level 1 instruction. This convivial establishment is run by Ange Benedetti and employs eight instructors at the height of the season. Divers are taken to quiet sites near Algajola, including the popular Danger d'Algajola, accessible in less than 10 minutes on one of two aluminium boats. The program also includes the wreck of the *Grand Cerf*, Pedra Mule and the sites on the Baie de Calvi, including the B-17.

The centre opens April to the end of October with up to three outings, at 9 am, 2 pm and 4 pm daily except Sunday when it is closed. Check out the Web site at http://perso.wanadoo.fr/escale.algajola.

Île Rousse

Beluga Diving In a wing of Hôtel La Pietra, to the side of the ferry terminal near the Genoese tower, this centre (☎ 04 95 60 17 36/52 25, fax 04 95 60 42 75) caters mainly to experienced divers. It is in fact the only centre in Corsica to offer Nitrox dives (with a higher percentage of oxygen through special compressors), for which prices start at 175FF, excluding equipment hire. An exploratory dive costs between 145FF and 231FF and level 1 instruction costs 1550FF.

Hans Berz and his eight instructors lead divers to the spectacular underwater landscape west of Île Rousse in a covered 20-seat launch or a semi-rigid vessel. Regularly featured on the program are Le Naso, the Grand Tombant, the Petit Tombant and the Tour de Saleccia. Day trips are organised once or twice weekly to the Baie de Calvi, 1¼ hours away, with dives down to the B-17 bomber and around la Revellata (for an additional charge of 180FF, which includes a meal). From time to time there are day trips to the small island of Centuri, just off the north-western tip of Cap Corse.

The club also offers an introductory course in marine archaeology and underwater photography at 3000FF per week, lodging not included.

The centre opens from March to December daily except Sunday. There are two outings daily.

École de Plongée de l'Île Rousse In a prefabricated building near the ferry terminal, Jean and Véronique Escales (☎ 04 95 60 36 85, fax 04 95 60 45 21) specialise in diving for children, although they cater for all ages. An introductory dive in an inlet below the lighthouse costs 220FF while an exploratory dive costs from 150FF to 200FF, with a 10% discount available for 10 dives. All-inclusive level 1 instruction costs 1800FF.

Sites in the Golfe de l'Île Rousse, such as Le Naso and the Grand Tombant, are reached in 10 minutes on board a 20-seat semi-rigid covered vessel or a smaller 10-seat boat.

The centre opens year round and runs from two to three outings daily in summer. Fixed departures are at 9 am for experienced divers and at 3 pm for beginners and instruction.

St-Florent

CESM This establishment (☎ 04 95 37 00 61, fax 04 95 37 09 60) is located in the water sports facility of La Roya. From the centre of St-Florent, head in the direction of Oletta. As you leave the town, turn right after the Shell petrol station towards Île Rousse and, when you've crossed the small bridge, turn right immediately into the road to La Roya beach. About 500m later you'll come to CESM, which is part of the sailing school. It has a warm atmosphere, although like the beach itself it's not much to look at.

Charges are 200FF for an introductory dive at Les Cormorans, near Fornali lighthouse west of the gulf. An exploratory dive costs 200FF (children 170FF), a set of five dives costs from 850FF (children 700FF), and level 1 instruction costs 1160FF, including 10 dives. A night dive costs 200FF.

Instructors will take you to the Golfe de St-Florent and Punta Mortella to the west and to Nonza to the north-east on board a 10-seat semi-rigid vessel or a 14-seat aluminium barge.

Open from mid-June to mid-September, the centre runs a minimum of two excursions, at 9 am and 2 pm, daily except Sunday and sometimes one or two more.

Actisub This little outfit (☎/fax 04 95 39 06 62), which you'll find at Sun Folie's on the beach at La Roya, offers an introductory dive for 230FF, exploratory dives for 180FF to 210FF and courses for adults and children.

An ABC of Diving

Thinking of introducing the kids to diving in Corsica? Nothing could be easier: there are small, reassuring inlets with clear, warm water and small rock fauna, and children are guaranteed a warm welcome.

Under French law diving centres can accommodate children starting as young as eight years of age, provided they have parental consent. Most clubs take young people from holiday camps or schools during the summer so they're familiar with their needs. Nearly all of the centres have special equipment such as 'bibs', miniature stab-jackets and small mouthpieces and suits.

After the introductory dive kids can go on to obtain special bronze, silver and gold awards.

Aquado This club (☎ 04 95 37 27 43, fax 04 95 37 25 12) is in town on the edge of the Aliso Rive. A dive costs 120FF if you have your own equipment and you can take care of yourself, 150FF with your own equipment and club supervision or 200FF with club equipment and supervision. Aquado's strong point is the interest it takes in marine biology.

Bastia

Thalassa Immersion This centre (☎ 04 95 31 78 90, 06 86 37 60 14, e thalassa@club-internet.fr), brilliantly run by three dynamic young instructors, is in a well equipped, luxurious building about 1.5km north of Bastia town centre. Follow the signs for Cap Corse and, after the port of Toga, look out for the Elf petrol station on the left. The centre is opposite the petrol station, down on the beach.

An introductory dive at a site rich in marine life nearby costs 200FF, an exploratory dive costs 150FF to 180FF, and eight dives cost 1040FF to 1280FF. There is an all-inclusive charge of 1480FF for level 1 instruction.

The club uses the area between the Heinkel-111 wreck, near the port of Bastia in the south, and the wreck of the *Canon-*

nière, just off Pietracorbara in the north. The latter takes about an hour to get to by launch, and therefore it is generally offered as a day trip, with lunch at Erbalunga and a second dive in the afternoon.

Bookings can be made at the Thalassa diving shop, 2 rue St-Jean, near the old port. Credit cards are accepted.

The centre opens year round but closes on Sunday morning. It runs from two to four excursions daily. They have a Web site at http://tibastia.free.fr.

Club Plongée Bastiais This centre (☎ 04 95 33 31 28/30 56 64, 06 14 62 56 14) has no fixed roof, strictly speaking: Divers report directly to the entity's boat, the *Mykonos*, in the old port of Bastia, 20m from the harbour master's office. An introductory dive in the Anse de Ficajola near the harbour costs 190FF (children aged eight to 12, 150FF). An exploratory dive costs between 150FF and 190FF, or buy 10 dives for 1300FF to 1700FF. Level 1 instruction costs 1850FF. On Friday there's an evening dive followed by a light meal for 270FF.

The sites visited are the same as those used by Thalassa Immersion, between the Heinkel-111 and the *Canonnière* wreck.

The centre opens daily except Sunday afternoon, July to September and at weekends the rest of the year. There are two outings per day.

Cap Corse

Aquatica Club This low-key club (☎ 04 95 35 01 06/02 86, fax 04 95 35 01 06), in the marina at Santa Severa on the eastern side of the Cape, offers dives throughout the area, an impressive airplane wreck included. The introductory dive costs 200FF. Exploratory dives cost 150/190FF with/without equipment, with discounts after five dives. Level 1 instruction costs 1800FF. The operation functions from May to the end of September with lodging available in the hotel in which the office is located.

Capi Corsu Diving This club (☎/fax 04 95 35 48 57) in the village of Macinaggio, open only since June 2000, conducts dives around Île de la Giraglia, the Sec de Ste-Marie, the Petit and the Grand Danger and several wrecks. There are two daily outings aboard a 6.7m semi-rigid vessel. An introductory dive will cost from 230FF (children 180FF) and an exploratory dive from 200FF (children 150FF), depending on equipment. Level 1 instruction costs 1800FF.

Thalassoma This little setup (☎ 06 20 04 14 83), also at the Macinaggio harbour, offers dives, in season, in the area between Macinaggio and the Île de la Giraglia, a few wrecks included. The introductory dive costs 230FF, the exploratory dive costs 170/200FF with/without equipment.

Getting There & Away

Corsica is not on any of the international trunk routes, and is not the easiest place in the world to get to, unless of course you're hopping over from one of its neighbours. But part of Corsica's charm is that even though the island is practically within eyeballing distance of Italy and not much further from mainland France, it has an air of exotic isolation.

AIR

Air fares mentioned in this section are as quoted by airlines and tour operators at the time of writing. They are approximate – fares change fast, and none is to be understood as constituting a recommendation of any particular airline.

Airports & Airlines

There are airports at Ajaccio, Bastia, Calvi and Figari. (Figari serves Corsica's deep south, notably the towns of Porto Vecchio, Bonifacio and Propriano.) They are all modern enough and serviceable.

Air France, Corse Méditerranée, Air Liberté, Air Littoral and Nouvelles Frontières affiliate Corsair provide the vast majority of flights in to Corsica from airports around the French mainland. Crossair has begun to fly in four times weekly in high season from Basel-Mulhouse.

No noncharter carrier not based in France currently flies in to Corsica. So, wherever your starting point is, you won't (except by charter) arrive by air in Corsica without changing planes somewhere in continental France.

Because many scheduled non-French carriers do fly, however, into Nice-Côte d'Azur airport (the most heavily trafficked in France outside of Paris) and also into Marseille, Milan and Pisa, you may be tempted to book air fare only as far as one of those destinations and make the final approach to Corsica by ferry. (Note, moreover, that not only the high-profile international carriers fly to the French and Italian airports on Corsica's doorsteps, but also budget airlines easyJet (to Nice), Ryanair (to Pisa) and Buzz (to Marseille).

Buying Tickets

World aviation has never been so competitive, making air travel better value than ever. But you have to research the options carefully to make sure you get the best deal. The Internet is an increasingly useful resource for checking air fares.

Full-time students and those aged under 26 (under 30 in some countries) sometimes have access to better deals than other travellers. You have to show a document proving your date of birth or a valid International Student Identity Card (ISIC) when buying your ticket.

Generally, there is nothing to be gained by buying a ticket direct from the airline. Discounted tickets are released to selected travel agents and specialist discount agencies, and these are usually the cheapest deals going.

The days when some bad-seed bucket shops and travel agencies absconded with their clients' money are, happily, almost over, but it's still worth being cautious. Paying by credit card generally offers protection, as most card issuers provide refunds if you can prove you didn't get what you paid for. Similar protection can be obtained by buying a ticket from a bonded agent, such as one covered by the Air Travel Organiser's Licence (ATOL) scheme in the UK. Agents who only accept cash should hand over the tickets straight away and not tell you to 'come back tomorrow'.

For good deals on tickets, try on-line: the expanding number of 'no-frills' carriers, which only sell direct to travellers, offer competitive prices, and you might also try the airlines' own Web sites. Many travel agencies around the world have Web sites, which can make the Internet a quick and easy way to compare prices. There is also an ever-increasing number of on-line agents such as www.travelocity.com, www.travelocity.co.uk

Air Travel Glossary

Alliances Many of the world's leading airlines are now intimately involved with each other, sharing everything from reservations systems and check-in to aircraft and frequent-flyer schemes. Opponents say that alliances restrict competition. Whatever the arguments, there is no doubt that big alliances are the way of the future.

Courier Fares Businesses often need to send urgent documents or freight securely and quickly. Courier companies hire people to accompany the package through customs and, in return, offer a discount ticket which is sometimes a bargain. However, you may have to surrender all your baggage allowance and take only carry-on luggage.

Fares Airlines traditionally offer 1st class (coded F), business class (coded J) and economy class (coded Y) tickets. These days there are so many promotional and discounted fares available that few passengers pay full fare.

Lost Tickets If you lose your airline ticket, an airline will usually treat it like a travellers cheque and, after inquiries, issue you with another one. Legally, however, an airline is entitled to treat it like cash and if you lose it then it's gone forever. Take very good care of your tickets.

Onward Tickets An entry requirement for many countries is that you have a ticket out of the country. If you're unsure of your next move, the easiest solution is to buy the cheapest onward ticket to a neighbouring country or a ticket from a reliable airline which can later be refunded if you do not use it.

Open-Jaw Tickets These are return tickets where you fly out to one place but return from another. If available, this can save you backtracking to your arrival point.

Overbooking Since every flight has some passengers who fail to show up, airlines often book more passengers than they have seats. Usually excess passengers make up for the no-shows, but occasionally somebody gets 'bumped' onto the next available flight. Guess who it is most likely to be? The passengers who check in late. If you do get 'bumped', you are normally offered some form of compensation.

Reconfirmation Some airlines require you to reconfirm your flight at least 72 hours prior to departure. Check your travel documents to see if this is the case.

Restrictions Discounted tickets often have various restrictions on them – such as needing to be paid for in advance and incurring a penalty to be altered or cancelled. Others are restrictions on the minimum and maximum period you must be away.

Round-the-World Tickets RTW tickets give you a limited period (usually a year) in which to circumnavigate the globe. You can go anywhere the carrying airlines go, as long as you don't backtrack. The number of stopovers or total number of separate flights is decided before you set off and they usually cost a bit more than a basic return flight.

Ticketless Travel Airlines are gradually waking up to the realisation that paper tickets are unnecessary encumbrances. On simple one-way or return trips, reservations details can be held on computer and the passenger merely shows ID to claim their seat.

Transferred Tickets Airline tickets cannot be transferred from one person to another. Travellers sometimes try to sell the return half of their ticket, but officials can ask you to prove that you are the person named on the ticket. On an international flight, tickets are compared with passports.

and www.deckchair.com, which operate only on the Internet.

On-line ticket sales work well if you are doing a simple one-way or return trip on specified dates. However, on-line super-fast fare generators are no substitute for a travel agent who knows all about special deals, especially if you're travelling to Corsica from a considerable distance.

Travellers with Specific Needs

If they're warned early enough, airlines can often make special arrangements for travellers such as wheelchair assistance at airports or vegetarian meals on the flight. Children under two years travel for 10% of the standard fare (or free on some airlines) as long as they don't occupy a seat. They don't get a baggage allowance. 'Skycots', baby food and nappies should be provided by the airline if requested in advance. Children aged between two and 12 can usually occupy a seat for half to two-thirds of the full fare, and do get a baggage allowance.

The disability-friendly Web site, www.everybody.co.uk, has an airline directory that provides information on the facilities offered by various airlines.

Taxes

Airport taxes are quite expensive in Corsica; they vary slightly from airport to airport, but can add up to 190FF. Remember to ask about the taxes in any ticket price that's quoted to you in order to avoid any nasty surprises later.

Mainland France

Wherever you're coming from in the world, you're unlikely to reach Corsica by air without passing through an airport in mainland France first.

Air France's lowest return fare to Corsica from Nice costs 710FF, year round, while from Paris, fares start at 1170/1065FF in high/low season. Both fares are before taxes and have restrictions. Air France can be reached at ☎ 08 20 82 08 20 (France), ☎ 0845 084 5111 (UK), ☎ 01-605 383 (Ireland), ☎ 800 237 2747 (USA), ☎ 800 667 2747 (Canada) and ☎ 1300 361 400 (Australia), or check out its Web sites at www.airfrance.fr (French only), www.airfrance.co.uk (UK) or www.airfrance.com (USA).

Compagnie Corse Méditerranée (☎ 04 95 29 05 00, fax 04 95 29 05 05), with a Web site at www.ccm-airlines.com, operates three or four flights daily between Nice and Ajaccio and the same number between Nice and Bastia in low season; five or six flights daily on each of those two routes in summer; and their flights are even more numerous between Marseille and Ajaccio or Bastia. CCM fares are the same as Air France's. If you are starting your journey outside France arrangements to travel via CCM should be made through Air France.

Air Liberté (☎ 08 03 80 58 05), an airline chiefly owned by Swissair, flies from Nice (1168FF return, daily in summer, three times weekly in winter), Marseille (1247FF return, daily) and Paris Orly (1755FF to 2010FF return, daily in summer, three times weekly in winter) to Figari-Sud Corse. All taxes are included. Air Liberté is fairly easy to reserve with over the Internet, if you're patient. Its Web site is at www.air-liberte.fr (French only).

The regional airline Air Littoral (☎ 08 03 83 48 34) flies to all four of the Corsican airports from Marseille, Nice and Montpellier (where they are based) daily, but, since Air Littoral uses those three towns as hubs, they in effect also provide daily service from Nantes, Strasbourg, Bordeaux, Lyon and Toulouse. Air Littoral prices are in line with Air Liberté prices.

Paris travel agencies specialising in bargain flights include Go Voyages (☎ 01 53 40 44 29, Minitel 3615 GO), French student travel company OTU (☎ 01 40 29 12 12), Usit Connect Voyages (☎ 01 42 44 14 00), Voyageur du Monde (☎ 01 42 86 16 00) and Franco-Belgian company Wasteels (☎ 08 25 88 70 70).

Charter Flights The charter flight season to Corsica falls between April and October and during the Christmas holidays.

Nouvelles Frontières/New Frontiers (☎ 08 25 00 08 25 in France, ☎ 020-7637 2488 in the UK, ☎ 888-277 6058 in the USA,

☎ 514-871 3060 in Canada) is France's leading budget-minded travel agency. From May to October, its air-carrier subsidiary Corsair operates about 10 flights per week from Paris into one or another of the four Corsican airports and still more from the French provincial cities (including Lille – much closer to Calais than Paris is) and Brussels. From Paris, the return fare starts at 1090FF in June and from late September to late October, rising to a peak of 1650FF at the end of July and the beginning of August, with two intermediate fares in between. All fares are plus taxes. Lille fares start *and* peak lower than the Paris fares, and Brussels fares are only small change higher than the Paris fares.

Corsair can get you in to Orly to connect with its Corsica flights from four North American gateways – New York, Montreal, Los Angeles and Oakland. For more information on these flights, see the section on the USA and Canada later in this chapter. For detailed information on Corsair in general, the best place to start is the Corsair Web site at www.corsair-int.com.

Ollandini Voyages (☎ 04 95 23 92 20/93, fax 04 95 23 92 80/83), a Corsica-based travel products company that first opened its doors in 1890, offers Saturday flights from the very end of March to early October from Paris, Brest, Caen, Lyon, Nantes, Toulouse and Quimper and a slightly shorter season of Saturday departures from Bordeaux, Lille and Strasbourg. Since a good half of these continental gateways are in the north of France and Strasbourg sits directly on the German border, imaginative planners in the UK, Ireland, the Netherlands, Scandinavia and Germany might want to get out their maps and start looking for angles of approach. (Again, notice that Lille, for example, is much closer to Calais than Paris is.) Return fares between Paris and Ajaccio run from 1135FF to 1785FF (taxes included); return fares between Lille and Ajaccio run from 1387FF to 1737FF (taxes included). The fares vary according to the season.

Though Ollandini is currently in transition to new intermediaries in the UK, the USA and Germany, bookings can be made through Vacances Air Transat (ⓔ information@airtransat.com) in Canada, Arke Reizen (☎ 053-4880 622) in the Netherlands, Opus Tours (☎ 012-955 533, ⓔ opus@rbm.ch) in Switzerland, and Rhomberg in Austria, which has a Web site at www.rhomberg.at.

The UK & Ireland

Cheap fares appear in the weekend editions of the national British papers and, in London, in *Time Out*, the *Evening Standard* and *TNT* (a free magazine available from bins outside underground stations). Trailfinders (☎ 020-7937 5400) and Flightbookers (☎ 020-7757 2000) are reliable travel agencies, with Web sites at www.trailfinders.co.uk and www.ebookers.com respectively.

Air France can get you from 10 different airports in the UK and Ireland to Corsica with a stop in Paris. However, connection in Paris is slow – a minimum of 2¼ hours – as you have to transfer from Charles de Gaulle to Orly Airport. Air France's fares between London and Corsica can start at as low as UK£199, plus taxes, year round.

British Airways flies to Marseille, Nice, Montpellier, Genoa and Pisa, British Midland flies to Nice, and Aer Lingus flies from Dublin, Shannon and Cork to Paris. All of these airlines will arrange onward flights directly into Corsica.

Nonstop charter flights between the UK and Corsica run on Sundays from the weekend before Easter, to around the last weekend of October. In high season, there may be up to 10 Sunday flights per week: Heathrow–Ajaccio, Gatwick–Ajaccio, Gatwick–Bastia, Birmingham–Bastia, Manchester–Bastia, Gatwick–Calvi, Stansted–Calvi, Edinburgh–Calvi, Gatwick–Figari and Stansted–Figari. Most operators to Corsica, notably Corsican Places (reservations ☎ 01903-748180, brochure ☎ 748145), with a Web site at www.corsica.co.uk, VFB Holidays Ltd (☎ 01242-240310) whose Web site is at www.vfbholidays.co.uk and Voyages Ilena (☎ 020-7924 2244) with a Web site at www.voyagesilena.co.uk, prefer to sell a charter fare as part of a package with accommodation and, in some cases, hire car. For details on the programs, see Organised Tours at the end of this chapter.

Holiday Options (reservations ☎ 01444-244411, fax 242454) Martlet Heights, 49 The Martlets, Burgess Hill, West Sussex RH15 9NJ, is the exception; they *will* gladly sell flights only to Corsica. Gatwick–Calvi in early May, for example, starts at UK£199 return; Birmingham–Bastia in late May costs from UK£230 return. GR20 walkers will be happy to know that Holiday Options will even sell open-jaw tickets, flying in to Calvi or Figari – each close to either end of the GR20 – and out from the other, though seats are limited. Air-only bookings to Corsica are available for stays of one, two, three or four weeks. Their Web site is at www.holidayoptions.co.uk.

For charter 'air only', you could try Simply Corsica (☎ 020-8541 2205), which sometimes quotes extremely low fares. Check out the Web site www.simply-travel.com.

The fast-multiplying 'no-frills' airlines, meanwhile, won't get you from the UK to Corsica nonstop the way the charter carriers will, but they can get you to Corsica quite cheaply if you're willing to fly into Marseille, Nice, Genoa or Pisa and take either Corse Méditerranée, Air Liberté, Air Littoral or a ferry over the last distance. Buzz (☎ 0870 240 7070 in the UK) flies London Stansted to Marseille twice on weekdays and once daily at the weekend for a return fare of UK£99, including tax. Its Web site is at www.buzzaway.com. Rival easyJet (☎ 0870 600 0000) flies nonstop from London Luton and Liverpool to Nice and from Gatwick, Stansted, Belfast and Edinburgh to Nice with a stop either in Amsterdam or Geneva for fares as low as UK£30 in each direction, taxes not included, but with a discount of UK£2.50 for booking on-line. (easyJet's fare structure is complicated. Fares can be higher.) Its Web site is at www.easyjet.com. Ryanair (☎ 0870 156 9569) flies twice daily from London Stansted to Genoa and twice daily to Pisa for 'regular' fares as low as UK£29.50 in each direction, taxes not included, but with a discount of UK£2.50 for booking on-line. The Web site is at www.ryanair.com. In addition, Virgin Express (☎ 020-7744 0004) flies to Nice through Brussels. Check out its Web site at www.virginexpress.com.

To work out the real cost of getting to Corsica via one of these no-frills airlines, you must obviously add the fare of your second air carrier or your ferry line to that of your initial carrier, and, if the alternatives come out close, don't forget that you may also have to get back and forth between airports and ferry terminals, which will add to the cost.

Continental Europe

In addition to Air France, any one of the continental European carriers – Lufthansa, with a Web site at www.lufthansa.com; KLM, whose Web site's at www.klm.nl; SAS, with a Web site at www.scandinavian.net; CSA Czech Airlines, on-line at Web site www.csa.cz; or Lot Polish Airlines, with a Web site at www.lot.com – will gladly sell you a through ticket to any of the Corsican airports but, as is the case with any international carrier other than Air France, sooner or later they're going to have to link up with Air France, Corse Méditerranée, Air Liberté or Air Littoral. As for those travelling from the UK, the alternative is to take a flight as far as Nice, Marseille or Genoa and catch a ferry for the last distance.

Other options are the charter flights that pop up here and there around mainland Europe. Numerous charter flights operate between Brussels and Corsican airports. At the time of writing, Transavia Airlines intended to begin operating between Amsterdam and Corsica and Crossair between Geneva and Corsica. The Frantour Travel Agency (☎ 41 22 906 41 00, fax 738 74 72) in Geneva, which is marketing the flight, even offers a free rail ticket from any railroad station in Switzerland to Geneva airport, should you, for example, find it easier to make your way to Zurich or Basel than to Geneva.

In addition, budget airline easyJet operates between Amsterdam and Nice, while Virgin Express flies from Brussels to Nice (see under The UK & Ireland for contact details). Maersk Air operates between Denmark and Norway and Paris and Milan.

In Germany, anyone with an itch to get to Corsica might do well to look in at one of the 27 branches of STA Travel (☎ 069-703 035 in Frankfurt, ☎ 030-311 0950 in Berlin).

A similar agency in Berlin is SRS Studenten Reise Service (☎ 030-283 3094). In Amsterdam, you might try the official student travel agency, NBBS Reizen (☎ 020-620 50 71) with a Web site at www.nbbs.nl.

The USA & Canada

Between New York and Ajaccio (via Paris) Air France low-season return fares start at US$338 (with some restrictions), while high-season fares cost from US$758 (students US$652). Between the West Coast USA and Paris, low-season fares start at US$478, and high-season fares at US$1042 (student US$894); none of these quotes includes taxes. A stopover in Paris is going to cost at least US$60 extra; if you want to stop in Paris, check that your deal allows you to break the journey, otherwise you may only see Paris from the Air France bus that shuttles you from Charles de Gaulle down to Orly.

Air France does not fly nonstop to Nice from anywhere in the Americas, but its codeshare partner Delta operates between New York and Nice daily, and offers a mouthwatering low-season fare of US$288 (plus taxes) on that route. Ask Delta to quote a return fare New York–Ajaccio by way of Nice, however, and fares start at US$629 plus tax.

Nouvelles Frontières (New Frontiers; ☎ 888-277 6058 in the USA, ☎ 514-871 3060 in Canada) sells tickets between Los Angeles or Oakland and Paris Orly on weekly flights of their subsidiary Corsair; their prices start at US$398 return plus taxes in the low-season. Fares rise to at least US$498 in the shoulder season and to US$798 plus taxes for most of July and August; flights are twice weekly from Los Angeles and Oakland in the high season, three times weekly from New York, as many as four times weekly from Montreal. New York midweek fares start at US$498 return, the weekend fares from US$568.

For budget-minded travellers, it is always worthwhile to read the small ads in the weekend travel section of *The New York Times*, *Los Angeles Times*, *Chicago Tribune*, Toronto *Globe & Mail* and *Vancouver Sun* and also in the so-called 'alternative' newspapers along the lines of the New York *Village Voice*. Ticket consolidators are almost always able to beat the major airlines' best published fares between any two remote points on the map.

Two reliable sources of cheap tickets in the USA are STA Travel (toll-free ☎ 800 777 0112), with a Web site at www.statravel.com, and Council Travel (toll-free ☎ 800 226 8624) with a site at www.counciltravel.com; both have offices throughout the country.

Canada's best bargain-ticket agency is Travel CUTS (toll-free ☎ 800 667 2887) with a Web site at www.travelcuts.com.

Australia & New Zealand

Qantas and Air France have flights from Australia to Ajaccio, via Paris, starting at around A$2902/3659 low/high-season return (plus taxes). AOM French Airlines fly the same route for about the same price.

Airlines from New Zealand also fly to Corsica via Paris. Low-season return fares from Auckland start at around NZ$3134 – for example, Thai Airways International has a flight from Auckland to Paris and on to Ajaccio with Air France. Similar deals are available with a dozen other airlines.

Budget-minded travellers should also check the travel agencies' advertisements in the Yellow Pages and the weekly travel sections of the *Sydney Morning Herald*, *The Age* in Melbourne and the *New Zealand Herald*.

STA Travel (☎ 131 776 in Australia, ☎ 09-309 0458 in New Zealand) specialises in cheap air fares. Check out the Web site at www.statravel.com.au. Flight Centre (☎ 131 600 in Australia, ☎ 09-309 6171 in New Zealand) has similar good deals, with a Web site at www.flightcentre.com.au. The companies have offices all over both countries.

Asia

Most Asian countries offer fairly competitive air-fare deals with Bangkok, Singapore and Hong Kong being the best places to shop around for discount tickets. Hong Kong's travel market can be unpredictable, but some excellent bargains are available if you are lucky.

Khao San Rd in Bangkok is the budget traveller's headquarters. Bangkok has a number of excellent travel agents, but there are also some suspect ones; ask the advice of other travellers before handing over your cash. STA Travel (☎ 02-236 0262), 33 Surawong Rd, is a good and reliable place to start.

In Singapore, STA Travel (☎ 65-737 7188) is located at 35a Cuppage Rd, Cuppage Terrace. Check its Web site at www.statravel.com.sg. STA offers competitive discount fares for Asian destinations and beyond. Singapore, like Bangkok, has hundreds of travel agents, so you can compare prices on flights. Chinatown Point shopping centre on New Bridge Rd has a good selection of travel agents.

Hong Kong has a number of excellent, reliable travel agencies and some not-so-good ones. A good way to check on a travel agent is to look it up in the phone book: fly-by-night operators don't usually stay around long enough to get listed. Phoenix Services (☎ 2722 7378, fax 2369 8884) Room B, 6th floor, Milton Mansion, 96 Nathan Rd, Tsimshatsui, is recommended. Other agencies to try are Shoestring Travel (☎ 2723 2306) Flat A, 4th floor, Alpha House, 27–33 Nathan Rd, Tsimshatsui, and Traveller Services (☎ 2375 2222), Room 1012, Silvercord Tower 1, 30 Canton Rd, Tsimshatsui.

Africa & the Middle East

Since there are no nonstop or direct flights, scheduled or chartered, from Africa or the Middle East to Corsica, you won't get to Corsica without passing through a European centre first. Though Corsica is French, the fastest and most efficient routing for you may well be via Italy. From Rome, it is a relatively short train ride to the ferry embarkation port of Piombino. From Milan, it is a still shorter distance to Genoa. From Pisa to Livorno, you might almost be tempted to walk.

LAND

Bus

Eurolines With the increase in availability of low air fares, buses are no longer the cheapest means of transport around Europe, but are an option if you can't find a cheap flight or if you prefer to stay on the ground to watch the landscape slide past. The easiest way to book tickets is through Eurolines, a consortium of coach operators with offices all over Europe. Eurolines' coaches are fairly comfortable, with reclining seats, on-board toilets and sometimes air-conditioning. They stop for meals. In summer, it's a good idea to book at least several days in advance.

The following are a small handful of some 200 Eurolines offices across Europe:

Amsterdam
Eurolines Nederland
(☎ 020-560 8787, fax 560 8766)
Rokin 10, and Amstel Bus Station,
Julianaplein 5, Amsterdam
Web site: www.eurolines.nl

Frankfurt
Deutsche Touring/Eurolines
(☎ 069-790 350)
Mannheimerstrasse 4
Frankfurt-am-Main
Web site: www.deutsche-touring.com

London
Eurolines
(☎ 0870 514 3219, fax 01582-400694)
4 Cardiff Rd, Luton LU1 1PP
Web site: www.eurolines.co.uk

Madrid
Eurolines Peninsular
(☎ 91 063 360, fax 91 063 365)
Estación Sur de Autobuses, Madrid
Web site: www.eurolines.es

Paris
Eurolines France
(☎ 08 36 69 52 52, fax 01 49 72 51 61)
Gare Routière Internationale de Paris,
28 ave du Général de Gaulle, Bagnolet
Web site: www.eurolines.fr

Florence
Eurolines Italy
(☎ 055 35 71 10, fax 055 35 05 65)
Via Mercadante 2/b, 50144 Florence
Web site: www.eurolines.it

The Web site at www.eurolines.com will link you to yet more Eurolines sites. In the USA, the Eurolines agent is National Express (☎ 540 298 1395).

London–Marseille starts at UK£63/104 single/return (those aged under 26 and seniors £57/93). The journey takes about 20 hours with a change of bus at Lyon. London–Nice costs from UK£66/109 single/return (those aged under 26 and seniors £99 return). It takes about 23 hours, changing at Lyon.

Train

CFC, the Corsican rail system, operates independently of SNCF, the French continental rail system. If travelling around Europe on a European rail pass, your pass entitles you to a 50% discount on CFC routes, and a 30% discount on SNCM ferry crossings as well (see the Sea section later in this chapter).

Mainland France A second-class fare, Paris–Marseille starts at 379/758FF single/return. First class costs more, as does travelling in peak hours. The return fare may start at 360FF for those aged between 12 and 25 years or over 60, and there are reductions for other classes of passenger too. These are TGV (high-speed train) fares. TGV can get you from Paris to Marseille in as little as four hours 21 minutes. With the new TGV Mediterranée operational from 10 June 2001, the Paris–Marseille journey can take a mere three hours. (You might think that the 10½ hour milk train between Paris and Marseille would be cheaper than the TGV, but it's pricier.)

The train between Paris and Nice, meanwhile, takes a couple of hours longer than Paris–Marseille and is also somewhat more expensive. But, if you plan to travel directly on to Corsica, you'll make up those extra hours easily on the NGV (the fast ferry) from Nice – there is no fast ferry from Marseille – and Marseille–Corsica is more expensive than Nice–Corsica (see the Sea section later in this chapter).

UK Rail Europe, owned principally by SNCF, will sell some good through rail fares from London to the French Mediterranean coast (see the next section), but is in business to sell rail passes rather than to sell individual tickets. If you just want to buy a ticket from Paris to Marseille or Nice, one-way or return, you will probably do better to buy it from SNCF directly.

In France, SNCF has a nation-wide telephone number (☎ 08 36 35 35 35 in French, ☎ 08 36 35 35 39 in English) or you can visit their Web site at wwww.sncf.com. In the USA, Rail Europe can be contacted at ☎ 800 4-EURAIL; and in Canada, at ☎ 800 361-RAIL. Or log on to the Rail Europe Web site at www.raileurope.com or www.raileurope.com/canada. For information on contacting Rail Europe in the UK see the next section.

The UK At the time of writing, Rail Europe in the UK (☎ 0870 584 8848) was offering Eurostar service between London and Paris and then ongoing fast-train service from Paris to either Marseille or Nice for a return standard/first-class fare of UK£125/200 (children aged under 11 UK£90/150). Rail Europe also operates a walk-in travel store at 179 Piccadilly, London W1, with a Web site at www.raileurope.co.uk. You can book direct with Eurostar (☎ 0870 518 6186) or look on the Web site at www.eurostar.com.

If your object is less comfort, speed and efficiency than to reduce expenses to the bare minimum (or if you simply prefer to experience distance rather than to vaporise it) take a normal British train to Dover or Folkstone, take a cheap ferry across, then connect with SNCF on the other side.

Continental Europe For links to most other major European rail Web sites and a host of unofficial sites you can try: http://mercurio.iet.unipi.it/misc/timetabl.html. In Germany check out the Web site www.bahn.hafas.de/bin/query.exe/en.

Information appears at www.ns.nl for the Netherlands, www.fs-on-line.com for Italy, www.sbb.ch for Switzerland and for Spain at www.renfe.es.

Car & Motorcycle

Documents All drivers are required by French law to carry a national ID card or passport; a valid driving permit or licence *(permis de conduire)*; car ownership papers, known as a *carte grise* (grey card); and proof of insurance, called a *carte verte* (green card). If you're stopped by the police and don't have one or more of these documents, you risk a hefty on-the-spot fine. Never leave your car ownership or insurance papers in the vehicle.

For information on getting an International Driving Permit, see under Visas & Documents in the Facts for the Visitor chapter.

If you've rented a car anywhere in France, you're unlikely to have any trouble taking it across to Corsica on one of the ferries. After all, it's all the same country. If you've rented a car in Italy and you're planning to carry it across to Corsica on one of the ferries, check the procedure first. If you're driving your own motor vehicle and it's registered in a country other than France, you must display a sticker identifying its country of registration (for example, GB for Great Britain, IRL for Ireland, NL for the Netherlands and so on).

For more information on motoring on the island, see Road Rules under Car & Motorcycle in the Getting Around chapter.

Equipment A reflective warning triangle, to be used in the event of breakdown, must be carried in the car. Recommended accessories are a first-aid kit, a spare bulb kit and a fire extinguisher. In the UK, the RAC (☎ 0990 275 600) or the AA (☎ 0990 500 600) can provide advice on these items.

A right-hand drive vehicle brought to France from the UK or Ireland must have deflectors affixed to the headlights to avoid dazzling oncoming traffic.

The UK & Mainland France It's 1224km from Calais to Nice. If speed is of the essence, avoid the Paris area. Take the A26 from Calais to Troyes and Dijon, then continue on south to Lyon and the coast.

Eurotunnel (reservations ☎ 0870 535 3535 in the UK) runs a 24-hour service that will get you from Folkestone to Calais in 35 minutes. The return fare per car ranges from as low as UK£99 to as high as UK£280, depending on season, time of day and so on. The fare includes as many passengers as your vehicle is legally permitted to carry. Look up the Web site at www.eurotunnel.co.uk.

Among the ferry companies, P&O Stena Line (☎ 0870 600 0600) has up to 35 crossings daily in each direction between Dover and Calais. Fares for a car and up to nine passengers run to UK£179. You can save UK£5 by booking on-line: their Web site is at www.posl.com.

SeaFrance (☎ 0870 571 1711) with a Web site at www.seafrance.co.uk, has fewer sailings, but it's slightly cheaper.

Hoverspeed's (☎ 0870 240 8070) return fares start at UK£155 for two passengers and a car. Its Web site is at www.hoverspeed.com.

If you want to save your driving for Corsica itself, you might also want to look into Motorail south from Paris to Nice. You put your car on a train and sleep in a berth. For information as to price and schedules, contact Rail Europe at ☎ 0870 584 8848.

If you want to compare driving with other options as regards expense you have to factor in the heavy price of fuel. And though the principal route from Calais to Nice is mercifully gentle as to tolls, watch out if you stray far afield of it. Tolls between Paris and Nice, for example, can increase your costs by 360FF for a car, 489.50FF for a car and caravan. So unless you're planning to be in the south of France and in Corsica for many months, you'll almost surely save money by flying and renting a car.

Bicycle

Bicycle is a great way to get around Corsica, provided you don't mind some strenuous uphill climbing. You can carry your bicycle by air. Either take it apart and put it in a bike bag or box, or, easier still, wheel it to the check-in desk, where it should be treated as a piece of baggage. Details should probably be checked even before you pay for your ticket. If going by ferry, SNCM, to give just one example, charges only 91FF to carry your bike across from any of the three French ports.

If you are planning to cycle in Corsica, you would also do well to go over your bike with a fine-tooth comb and fill your repair kit with every imaginable spare part before you leave home. That crucial gismo you need to keep on going will probably not be available at any roadside stall as the sun sets over the D420 between Zonza and Quenza.

SEA

Approaching Corsica by sea is a great experience in its own right, whether you do it on a new fast boat, one of the great floating palaces, a funkier older ferry, or even a private yacht. It will also underscore for you, as nothing else can, the island's singular position – remote from the continent, and until modern times somewhat isolated.

By sea, Corsica is accessible from the ports of Nice, Marseille and Toulon in France and from Genoa, Livorno, Savona and Piombino in Italy. There is also a service that links Corsica and the Italian island of Sardinia.

Ferry Companies

The sea transport market is divided among five ferry companies. Société Nationale Corse Méditerranéenne (SNCM) Ferryterranée, the largest of the carriers, sails from Marseille, Nice and Toulon.

SNCM also manages two subsidiaries, the Compagnie Méridionale de Navigation (CMN) and Corsica Marittima, which sails from the Italian ports of Genoa and Livorno. French-owned company Corsica Ferries sails from Nice and the Italian ports, and Moby Lines sails from the Italian coast only. For their contact details see the boxed text 'Ferries to Corsica' on the next page.

Over the last few years, sea transport to Corsica has changed considerably. The introduction of the NGV (high-speed ferry) service has about halved the journey time between Corsica and the mainland. For example, whereas normal car ferry service between Nice and Bastia takes as long as nine hours, the NGV service crosses in as little as 3½ hours.

Don't assume, however, that a fast crossing in an NGV is necessarily the best way to go. A night in a berth in an older boat has a romance all its own. And a crossing in the SNCM's flagship *Napoleon Bonaparte*, with its four restaurants, 11m x 5m swimming pool, disco, 555 cabins and four lounges is the cruise experience you would never have expected in a journey that takes 20 minutes by air. One nice solution, then, is to take a slow boat in one direction and an NGV in the other.

What follows is only an outline of service and prices. SNCM and Corsica Ferries both

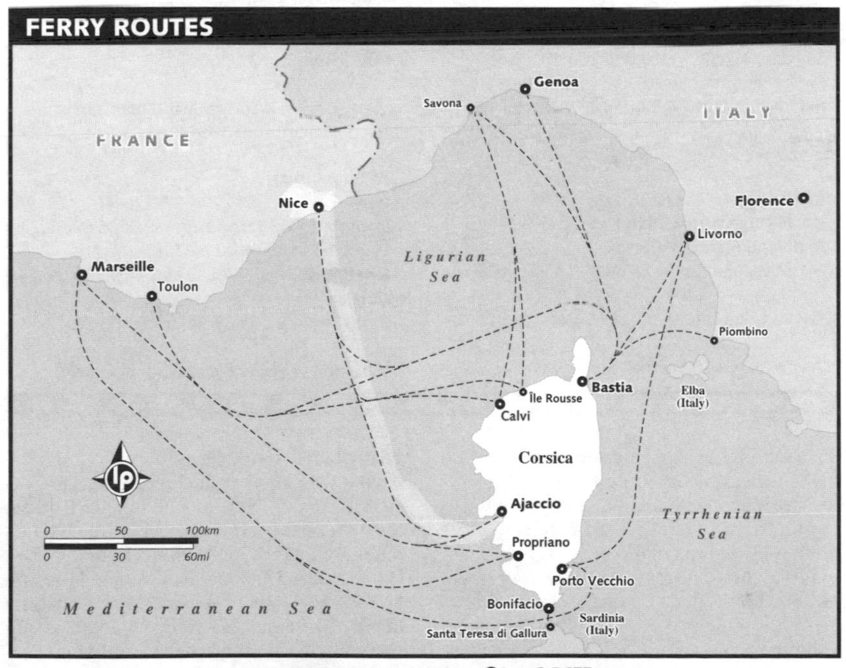

Ferries to Corsica

The following are the contact details for the ferry companies operating between ports in mainland France and Italy and ports in Corsica. All five of the companies have highly evolved Web sites. Attempt to secure detailed information from them in any way other than over the Internet and you risk high telephone charges and acute frustration.

Société Nationale Corse Méditerranéenne (SNCM)

Mainland France
Marseille: ☎ 04 91 56 32 00, fax 04 91 56 36 36
Nice: ☎ 04 93 13 66 99, fax 04 93 13 66 89
Toulon: ☎ 04 94 16 66 66, fax 04 94 16 66 68
Corsica
Ajaccio: ☎ 04 95 29 66 99, fax 04 95 29 66 77
Bastia: ☎ 04 95 54 66 66, fax 04 95 54 66 69

For other SNCM offices in Corsica (such as those in Calvi, Île Rousse, Propriano and Porto Vecchio), see the respective regional chapters of this book. Agents in other European countries can be reached as follows:

UK: ☎ 020-7491 4968, fax 7491 3502
Germany: ☎ 619-642 911, fax 648 3015
Sweden: ☎ 402-10050, fax 10059
Switzerland: ☎ 313-709 085, fax 709 091
Italy: ☎ 0586 21 05 07, fax 0586 21 05 15

Web site: www.sncm.fr

Compagnie Méridionale de Navigation (CMN)

Mainland France & Corsica
Marseille/Ajaccio/Bastia: ☎ 08 10 20 13 20

SNCM ticket offices also sell CMN tickets.

Web site: www.cmn.fr

Corsica Ferries

Mainland France & Italy
Nice: ☎ 04 92 00 43 76
Livorno: ☎ 0586 88 13 08, fax 0586 89 61 03
Savona: ☎ 019 216 00 41, fax 019 216 00 43
Corsica
Bastia: ☎ 04 95 32 95 95, fax 04 95 32 14 71

Web site: www.corsicaferries.com

Corsica Marittima

Italy
Livorno: ☎ 0586 210 507, fax 0586 21 05 46
Genoa: ☎ 010 58 95 95, fax 010 58 95 93
Corsica
Bastia: ☎ 04 95 54 66 95, fax 04 95 32 69 09
Porto Vecchio: ☎ 04 95 70 06 03, fax 04 95 70 33 59

Web site: www.corsica-marittima.com/fr (French only)

Moby Lines

Italy
Livorno: ☎ 0586 82 68 23, fax 0586 82 68 24
Piombino: ☎ 0565 22 52 11
Genoa: ☎ 010 254 15 13, fax 010 254 39 16
Corsica
Bastia: ☎ 04 95 34 84 94, fax 04 95 32 17 94

Web site: www.mobylines.it (Italian only)

have extremely sophisticated Web sites that make it possible not only to pin down sailing dates and fares in precise detail but also to purchase your tickets and receive confirmation by return email.

It may be advisable to reserve your ticket in advance during the high season; this is especially true if you are planning to take a vehicle.

Mainland France

Nice is the closest of the French ports to Corsica. By NGV, Nice to Calvi or Île Rousse, the two island ports closest to the French mainland, takes only three hours, Nice–Bastia takes 3½ hours (six to nine hours on a slow boat) and the Nice–Ajaccio trip is about the same. Marseille–Ajaccio is not served by NGV; it takes 9½ to 13 hours.

In high season the ports are well served by various companies, to and from mainland France. There is usually at least one NGV from Nice to Corsica every day year round (the number of boats per day rises slowly to four daily in summer). There's also at least one ferry a day from Marseille to Corsica. However, boats from Toulon only operate during the summer.

From Nice, SNCM fares run from 225FF to 255FF depending on the day and time; from Marseille or Toulon, they range from 265FF to 300FF. If you want overnight cabin accommodation, you can pay anywhere from a surcharge of 66FF (for a berth in a shared cabin) to 592FF per person for a stateroom suite for two. There are discount fares – for children, for young people, for holders of SNCF passes and for disabled veterans. There are also supplements – for taking a car along, for dragging a caravan (by the metre), and so on. Corsica Ferries tends to be somewhat cheaper, though their top deluxe cabins are pricier – but, then, Corsica Ferries also has what they call 'jackpot' deals, for example, a return for 750FF (two persons and a car). There are taxes on all of these fares.

Italy

The distances are even shorter from Italy. From Livorno (close to Pisa and Florence) it's only two hours to Bastia by Corsica Marittima NGV. Ferries leave about twice daily in both directions in high season, but do not operate in winter. From Piombino to Bastia, it's 3½ hours with Moby Lines. (Bastia is closer to Piombino than Livorno, but Moby Lines doesn't run NGVs.) Genoa to Bastia takes 6½ hours (Moby Lines), while the journey from Livorno lasts four hours (Moby Lines and Corsica Ferries). Savona to Bastia takes six hours, to Calvi takes two hours longer (Corsica Ferries). Moby Lines only operate between May and September, but Corsica Marittima sail year round.

Predictably enough, fares from Livorno and Piombino are lower than from mainland France, and the difference can be considerable if you're travelling by car and towing a few children, a caravan or a motor boat or some combination of these.

Ferry crossings between Corsica and Sardinia are covered under Bonifacio in The South chapter.

ORGANISED TOURS

The UK

A number of UK operators offer Corsican packages.

Corsican Places (reservations ☎ 01903-748180, brochure ☎ 748145) 27–31 West St, Storrington, West Sussex RH20 4DZ
A one-week package that includes a private villa with a swimming pool (or a village house or an apartment or, for that matter, a room in a hotel), air transportation from London, Manchester or

Corsica Brought Closer to France for 950 Million Francs

If it were possible, France would probably like to build a bridge to Corsica from some place such as Nice. Then the Corsicans might feel a little more as if they really belonged to the republic, and the die-hard separatists might find themselves with a less receptive audience. However, the best the state has been able to do is subsidise transport links like crazy so as to create the next best thing. The first agreement between the state and various ferry companies dates from 1948, but the fares and inadequate number of crossings, especially in the peak season, continually provoked criticism. In 1976, the system was remodelled and new agreements signed. In return for increased subsidies, the carriers undertook to run more ships and to stick to fares pegged to the French rail system's rate per kilometre. In 1979, the system was extended to airlines. In 1991, negotiations passed into the hands of the Collectivité Territoriale de Corse, which is now responsible for the system. The state's role is now solely that of a fairy godmother; it shells out subsidies on the order of 950 million francs per year. Further action in the development of the transportation infrastructure seem to be subordinate to the politics of the Matignon Process, which is deciding the future of the governmental relationship between Paris and the island.

Edinburgh, the use of a car in Corsica (or, if you prefer, airport transfers) begins at UK£341 for four adults sharing. The Web site is at www.corsica.co.uk.

VFB Holidays Ltd (☎ 01242-240310) Normandy House, Lower High St, Cheltenham GL50 3FB
VFB will sell you a comparable one-week package including a private villa with a pool, air transportation from London, Manchester or Birmingham, and the use of a car in Corsica, for UK£346 per person based on four adults sharing. It also offers eight-day group tours (air transportation from the UK, accommodation in Corsica and motor coach excursions) for prices starting at UK£799 per person. Check out its Web site at www.vfbholidays.co.uk.

Voyages Ilena (☎ 020-7924 2244) 1 Old Garden House, The Lanterns, Bridge Lane, London SW11 3AD
This company also makes a speciality of self-catering villas. A touring alternative provides air fare from the UK, the use of a car on the ground in Corsica and accommodation at mid-range hotels, plus breakfast, in different parts of the island. The one-week version costs from UK£655 per person; the two-week version from UK£875 per person. For more details see the Web site www.voyagesilena.co.uk.

Simply Corsica (☎ 020-8541 2205) Kings House, Wood St, Kingston upon Thames, KT1 1SG
Simply Corsica offers very much the same sort of product at a very similar price, with a Web site at www.simply-travel.com.

Holiday Options (reservations ☎ 01444-244411, fax 242454)
As well as arranging cheap flights (see the Air section earlier in the chapter), this company puts out a 59-page Corsica brochure and offers as many rental properties as anyone else. Check out its Web site at www.holidayoptions.co.uk.

France

Of the many French tour operators selling themed tours to Corsica, two are outstanding.

Nouvelles Frontières (☎ 08 25 00 08 25 in France, ☎ 353 1679 1233 in Ireland, ☎ 888-277 6058 in the USA, ☎ 514-871 3060 in Canada)
In addition to providing its Corsair charter flights, this company arranges land accommodation, tours, car hire and sports activities on the island. Corse Gourmande et Culturelle, a seven-day itinerary that, as the name suggests, emphasises Corsican culture and feasting, starts at 2990FF to 3430FF, depending on the time of year. Bear in mind that, if you sign up for it, you'd better brush up on your French pluperfect and subjunctives, as your travelling companions will be predominantly French-speaking. The Liberté package provides a self-drive car and a list of hotels from which customers stitch together their own itineraries at prices starting from around 2185FF to 2490FF, depending on the time of year. It has Web sites at www.nouvelles-frontieres.fr and www.newfrontiers.com.

Ollandini Voyages (☎ 04 95 23 92 90, fax 04 95 23 92 80)
Corsica's own leading tour operator offers a wide variety of special programs. One sample package includes camping vehicles for two to four people, flights between Paris and Ajaccio and 1300 free kilometres on the ground in Corsica for 4535FF to 4955FF per person. A weekend with a professional fragrance expert teaches you to identify asphodel, woodruff, mastic tree, hellebore and other maquis plants and costs from 2510FF per person. The program Bienvenue à la Ferme (Welcome to the Farm) provides return flights from Paris, a car for a week and nights at traditional small farms and half-board farm dinners. Packages start at 6262.50FF per person.

Other Countries

American tour operators specialising in Corsica tend to focus on outdoor activities of one sort or another.

Backroads (☎ 800 GO ACTIVE), 801 Cedar St, Berkeley, CA 94710-1800
Backroads offer six annual departures for a six-day hiking and biking tour of Corsica and Sardinia. Its Web site is at www.backroads.com.

Ciclismo Classico (☎ 800-866 7314 or 781-646 3377, fax 641 1512), 30 Marathon St, Arlington, MA 02474
This company also promotes hiking and biking tours, and some of their tours also combine Corsica and Sardinia.

British Travel International (☎ 800-327 6097)
BTI always offers nice villas and apartments in Corsica among its many other listings. See its Web site at www.europeapartments.com.

There are no major tour operators in Australia and New Zealand offering tours to Corsica – travellers in those countries will do best to work with an operator in the UK or France.

WARNING

The information in this chapter is particularly vulnerable to change: Prices for international travel are volatile, routes are introduced and cancelled, schedules change, special deals come and go, and rules and visa requirements are amended. Airlines and governments seem to take a perverse pleasure in making price structures and regulations as complicated as possible. You should check directly with the airline or a travel agent to make sure you understand how a fare (and ticket you may buy) works. In addition, the travel industry is highly competitive and there are many lurks and perks.

The upshot of this is that you should get opinions, quotes and advice from as many airlines and travel agents as possible before you part with your hard-earned cash. The details given in this chapter should be regarded as pointers and are not a substitute for your own careful, up-to-date research.

Getting Around

AIR

Though there are four civilian airports on Corsica, there is no scheduled commercial air service between any two of them.

BUS

Bus companies in Corsica serve all the major towns and many of the little ones in between. However, even if you happen to be in Corsica at the height of the tourist season, you may discover that there is only one departure per day on what looks like a major trunk route and no departure at all if it's a Sunday or a public holiday. Secondary routes may only have service on alternate days or only once or twice a week, and in the low season, when demand is low, some passenger routes may be combined with school or postal services.

It's not that Corsican buses fail to make good time, but that the frequencies and schedules on a particular route do not necessarily coincide with when you want and where you want to travel. Using public transport you will have to build your itinerary around route maps and schedules. To try to follow your own priorities will be to court frustration.

If you are debating whether to use Corsican public transport or rent a car, you will want to consider how much distance you want to cover, the flexibility that comes with a car, and to compare costs. Car hire in Corsica, particularly out of season, can be quite cheap, while bus fares, by contrast, may be relatively high considering how much distance is covered.

Dependence on public transport may also leave you with no easy way to get around once you reach your destination. That said, Ajaccio and Bastia, the island's two principal towns, have central bus stations, and in other places the bus stops for different companies are detailed in the relevant regional sections.

As a rule, you do not have to worry about buying tickets in advance. You can buy your ticket on any particular route, or leg of a route, from the driver.

The main bus routes and companies are as follows:

Ajaccio–Corte–Bastia
Eurocorse (☎ 04 95 21 06 30)
Daily except Sunday and public holidays
Ajaccio–Bastia (110FF), Bastia–Corte (55FF), Ajaccio–Corte (65FF)

Ajaccio–Ste-Marie Sicche–Olmeto–Propriano–Sartène–Roccapina–Bonifacio–Porto Vecchio
Eurocorse (☎ 04 95 21 06 30)
One to four daily in summer, daily except Sunday and public holidays in winter
Ajaccio–Bonifacio (120FF, three hours)

Ajaccio–Porto Vecchio, through mountains via Aullène, Quenza, Zonza, Bavella, L'Ospedale
Balési Évasion (☎ 04 95 70 15 55)
Daily except Sunday and public holidays from July to August, Monday and Friday only the rest of the year
Ajaccio–Porto Vecchio (110FF), Porto Vecchio–Zonza (35FF)

Ajaccio–St-Georges–Olmeto–Propriano–Sartène–Ste-Lucie de Tallano–Lévie–Zonza (plus Bavella in summer)
Autocars Ricci (☎ 04 95 76 25 59) or Eurocorse (☎ 04 95 21 06 30)
One or two daily
Ajaccio–Sartène (70FF, two hours), Ajaccio–Zonza and Bavella (100FF, 3¼ hours)

Ajaccio–Bastelica
Transports Bernardi (☎ 04 95 28 07 82)
Daily except Sunday and public holidays (50FF)

Ajaccio–Pisciatello–Porticcio–Isolella–Mare e Sole
Transports Casanova et Santini (☎ 04 95 25 40 37/21 05 17)
Daily in summer
Ajaccio–Porticcio (15FF)

Ajaccio–Tiuccia–Sagone–Vico–Renno–Évisa–Marignana
Autocars Ceccaldi (☎ 04 95 21 38 06)
Two or three daily except Sunday and public holidays
Ajaccio–Évisa (75FF)

Ajaccio–Porto Pollo
Autocars Ricci (☎ 04 95 51 08 19)
Monday, Wednesday and Saturday

Ajaccio–Tiuccia–Sagone–Cargèse–Piana–Porto–Ota
Transports SAIB (☎ 04 95 22 41 99)
Two to three daily
Ajaccio–Porto (70FF), Ajaccio–Cargèse (50FF)

Bastia–Ponte Leccia–Île Rousse–Algajola–Calvi
Les Beaux Voyages (☎ 04 95 65 15 02/11 35)
Two daily
Bastia–Calvi (80FF, 2¼ hours)

Bastia–Aléria–Ghisonaccia–Solenzara–Porto Vecchio
Les Rapides Bleus (☎ 04 95 31 03 79)
Two daily
Bastia–Porto Vecchio (115FF)

Bastia–Canari
Transports Saoletti (☎ 04 95 37 84 05)
Wednesday (40FF)

Bastia–Pino–Luri–Cagnano
Transports Luchesi (☎ 04 95 35 10 67)
Monday, Wednesday and Friday (45FF)

Bastia–Macinaggio
Transports Saladini (☎ 04 95 35 43 88) and STIB (☎ 04 95 31 06 65)
Daily (35FF)

Bastia–Moriani
STIB (☎ 04 95 31 06 65)
Several departures daily (35FF)

Bastia–St-Florent
Transports Santini (☎ 04 95 37 04 01)
Daily except Sunday and public holidays (30FF)

Bastia–Solenzara
Transports Tibéri (☎ 04 95 57 81 73)
Daily except Sunday and public holidays (80FF)

Bastia–Vescovato–Venzolasca
Autobus Casinca (☎ 04 95 36 70 64)
Daily except Sunday and public holidays (26FF)

Bastia–Erbalunga–Macinaggio–Centuri–Canari–Nonza–St-Florent–Oletta–Bastia (a complete tour of Cap Corse starting and finishing in Bastia)
Transports Micheli (☎ 04 95 35 64 02)
(110FF, high season)

Calvi–Calenzana
Les Beaux Voyages (☎ 04 95 65 15 02/11 35)
Two daily except Sunday and public holidays in July and August (30FF plus 5FF for luggage, 30 minutes)

Calvi–Galéria
Les Beaux Voyages (☎ 04 95 65 15 02/11 35)
Daily except Sunday and public holidays in July and August (35FF and 5FF for luggage, one hour)

Calvi–Porto via Col de la Croix
Transports SAIB (☎ 04 95 22 41 99)
Seasonal service from mid-May to 10 October, daily in August (110FF, three hours)

Corte–Aléria
Autocars Cortenais (☎ 04 95 46 02 12)
Daily in summer (55FF, one hour 10 minutes)

Corte–Calacuccia–Évisa–Porto
Autocars Mordiconi (☎ 04 95 48 00 04)
Daily except Sunday and public holidays from July to mid-September (110FF)

TRAIN & BUS ROUTES

Corte–Ponte Leccia–Bastia
Autocars Cortenais (☎ 04 95 46 02 12)
Monday, Wednesday and Friday year round
Corte–Bastia (60FF, 1¼ hours)

Porto Vecchio–Bonifacio
Eurocorse (☎ 04 95 21 06 30)
Four daily in summer, two in winter (40FF)

Porto Vecchio–Santa Giulia
Eurocorse (☎ 04 95 21 06 30)
Shuttle service in summer

See Getting There & Away in the sections on individual towns for more information.

TRAIN

The Corsican rail network – Chemins de Fer de la Corse (CFC; ☎ 04 95 32 80 57, 04 95 32 80 61) – is relatively limited in the destinations it serves. The principal line runs between Bastia and Ajaccio via Corte – and numerous other intermediate points. A spur runs from the Ponte Leccia junction between Bastia and Corte to the Balagne towns of Île Rousse and Calvi. Yet another line used to connect Bastia and Porto Vecchio along the flat east coast of the island. But it was badly damaged in German bombing raids in 1943, and for all the talk over the years of restoring it, no one has yet lifted a hammer.

The Corsican rail network is nevertheless more than just a way of getting between two points. It was constructed in a heroic age of railroad building, the 1880s and 1890s, and to this day it represents one of the great triumphs of man over topography. With 38 tunnels (one of them 4km in length), 34 viaducts and 12 bridges (one of them a Gustave Eiffel masterpiece), it is one of the world's great scenic rail lines. The scenery of course is spectacular, speeds are such – slower than buses – that you can enjoy the scenery; the train will occasionally have to stop for animals on the track. Prices are reasonable.

The main lines are as follows:

Bastia–Ajaccio via Corte (Bastia–Furiani–Biguglia–Casamozza–Ponte Nuovo–Ponte Leccia–Francardo–Corte–Vénaco–Vivario–Vizzavona–Bocognano–Mezzana–Ajaccio)
From June to September, trains leave Bastia at 7.15 am, 9.05 am, 2.25 pm and 3.50 pm; and Ajaccio at 7 am, 9 am, 2.30 pm and 4.35 pm (124FF, four hours 20 minutes). Ajaccio–Vizzavona (46FF), Ajaccio–Vivario (49FF) and Ajaccio–Corte (66FF). There are slightly fewer trains in winter.

Bastia–Corte
In summer only, there's an extra train between Bastia and Corte, stopping at all stations en route. The train departs Bastia at 6.10 pm and Corte at 7.05 am, except Sundays (59FF, 1½ hours).

Ponte Leccia–Île Rousse–Algajola–Calvi
In summer, trains leave the Ponte Leccia junction on the mainline at 10 am and at 6 pm; they leave Calvi in the other direction at 6.10 am and 2.10 pm year round. Ajaccio–Calvi (128FF, four hours 50 minutes to five hours 25 minutes depending on the layover at Ponte Leccia), Bastia–Calvi (95FF, three hours).

Tramways de Balagne

On the same right of way that the CFC uses, these little two-car trains shuttle back and forth all day long, April to October, on the relatively short stretch of coast between Calvi and Île Rousse. The approximately 20 intermediate stops include Lumio, Sant' Ambrogio, Algajola and Davia. Wherever you happen to be along the line, a train will pass in each direction approximately once an hour. To ride the length of the line and back costs 46FF.

Discounts

CFC offers a discount of 25% on return tickets covering more than 200km except during July and August. Groups of more than 10 people are eligible for a 30% discount (children aged under four, free; under 12, half price).

Passes

None of the major rail passes – InterRail, Eurail, Eurorail or even the France Railpass – provides for unlimited free travel on the CFC system; CFC operates independently of SNCF, the French national rail line. The major rail passes will, however, all earn you a 50% discount on CFC fares as well as a 30% discount on SNCM ferries to Corsica from the French Mediterranean ports of Marseille, Toulon and Nice.

In addition, the CFC sells its own rail pass – La Carte Zoom – for seven days of unlimited travel throughout the CFC network. La Carte Zoom costs 290FF. It can be purchased at any CFC station year round. It includes a free left-luggage service (maximum 20kg).

CAR & MOTORCYCLE

While there is no bridge between the continent and Corsica, the fleet of car ferries operating between French and Italian ports are nearly as good. (See Ferry Companies under Sea in the Getting There & Away chapter.)

Cars can of course be rented in Corsica, or on the French or Italian mainland and ferried to Corsica.

There are three categories of road in Corsica. Routes Nationales, whose names begin with the letter N, are major trunk routes overseen and maintained by the French central government. The N198, for example, runs along the flat eastern coast from Bastia to Bonifacio; as a measure of what it means, Corsicans themselves think nothing of travelling the length of it and back in a single day. The N193, meanwhile, makes a mockery of the distance and dramatic relief between Bastia, Corte and Ajaccio. Routes Départementales, whose names begin with the letter D, are secondary and tertiary local roads overseen and maintained by the two Corsican departments.

Routes Communales, whose names begin with the letter C or with nothing, are overseen and maintained by the smallest unit of government in rural areas, the *commune*.

The most beautiful and dramatic of the roads in Corsica include the D81 between Calvi and Porto, the D84 between Porto and Francardo (via Évisa, the Forêt d'Aïtone and the Scala di Santa Regina), and the D69 from just below Vivario to Ghisoni. But the most beautiful roads in Corsica are inevitably also the most hair-raising. Roads are narrow, indeed frequently too narrow for two vehicles to pass each other without pulling over onto a shoulder (if there is one). Hairpin bends are often blind, and rocky outcrops sometimes keep you from seeing oncoming traffic until it's on top of you – or from seeing livestock or other animals until you're on top of them. So use your horn to announce your presence. In addition, drops off the right of way may be sheer, guard rails nonexistent and locals impatient.

A last problem: The towns tend to be small and they were not really designed for cars. Finding a parking spot can be expensive, time-consuming or both, and at the height of the tourist season you may sometimes find yourself, even in a tiny hamlet, in a jam or a bottleneck.

The Michelin 1:200,000 map No 90 is all but indispensable to drivers.

ROAD DISTANCES (KM)

	Ajaccio	Bastia	Bonifacio	Calvi	Corte	Porto	Porto Vecchio	Sartène
Ajaccio	---							
Bastia	153	---						
Bonifacio	140	170	---					
Calvi	163	94	228	---				
Corte	83	70	150	96	---			
Porto	83	135	207	76	88	---		
Porto Vecchio	130	143	27	213	120	215	---	
Sartène	84	178	54	243	152	167	62	---

Road Rules

Motoring in Europe, published in the UK by the RAC, gives an excellent summary of road regulations in each European country, including the parking rules. Motoring organisations in other countries have similar publications. Unless otherwise indicated, a speed limit of 50km/h applies in built-up areas; on intercity roads you must slow to 50km/h the moment you pass a white sign with red borders on which a place name is written in black or blue letters. This limit remains in force until you arrive at the other edge of town, where you'll pass an identical sign with a red diagonal bar across the name.

Outside built-up areas, speed limits are 90km/h (80km/h if it's raining) on single carriageway N and D roads and 110km/h (100km/h if it's raining) on dual carriageways. You are nevertheless more likely in Corsica to fall short of the speed limit than to exceed it. Local drivers will consequently close to within a few metres of your rear bumper. They'll flash their lights impatiently. Don't let them rile you. Fines for speeding or driving through a red light range from 1300FF to 50,000FF, and the police can make tourists pay up on the spot. Motorists with a blood-alcohol concentration in excess of 0.05% (0.50g per litre of blood) – after two glasses of wine for a 75kg adult – are subject to fines of 500FF to 8000FF.

Priorité à Droite For overseas visitors the most confusing – and dangerous – traffic law in France is the notorious *priorité à droite* (give way to the right) rule, under which any car entering an intersection (including a T-junction) from a road on your right has right of way no matter how small the road it's coming from. To put it another way: if you're turning right from a side road onto a main road, you have priority over vehicles approaching from your left. If you're turning left, though, you have to wait for cars coming from your right.

At most larger roundabouts priorité à droite has been suspended so that the cars already in the roundabout have right of way. This is indicated by signs reading either *vous n'avez pas la priorité* (you do not have right of way) or *cédez le passage* (give way) or by yield signs displaying a circle made out of three curved arrows.

Priorité à droite is also suspended on *routes à caractère prioritaire* (priority roads), which are marked by a yellow diamond with a black diamond in the middle. Such signs appear every few kilometres and at intersections. Priorité à droite is reinstated if you see the same sign with a diagonal bar through it.

Rental

For a walk-in customer in high season, a Category A vehicle (the cheapest option: three doors, four seats, radio, tape deck, no air-conditioning) with unlimited mileage, could cost as much as 500FF per day, 1600FF to 1800FF per week and 4500FF to 5000FF per month. Attention North American visitors: the shift will be standard, not automatic.

Taxes add 19.6% more to the total, and a registration fee of 12.54FF per day is charged for the first four days on any hire. Most companies – though not, at the time of this writing, Avis – charge a stiff fee for picking a car up at one location and dropping it off at another. Some companies will impose a 'seasonal' surcharge for high-season bookings. Some companies will impose a surcharge (of around 100FF) for pick-ups and drop-offs at airports rather than in town centres. Full insurance can be almost as expensive as the base rate of the rental itself. If you want to make a realistic estimate of the total cost you have to consider fuel and other expenses.

Advance bookings will usually be cheaper than walk-in bookings. With some research you may be able to find something for as little as 1400FF per week or less, all-inclusive. The daily rate for weekly or monthly rents will normally work out cheaper than that for a single day. Special promotions are available from time to time, and you can also take advantage of discounts for on-line bookings. There are also substantial discounts available outside the short high season.

Most companies require that you be at least 21 (or, in some cases, over 25) and have had a driver's licence for a minimum of one year. Some may also require that you have a credit card. *Kilométrage illimité* means that there's no limit on how many kilometres you can drive.

The details of the main car-hire companies are as follows:

Ada
(☎ 04 95 23 56 57, fax 04 95 23 56 58)
Ajaccio-Campo dell'Oro airport
(☎ 04 95 54 55 44)
Bastia-Poretta airport

Avis
(☎ 04 95 23 56 90, fax 04 95 23 56 96)
Ajaccio-Campo dell'Oro airport
(☎ 04 95 54 55 46, fax 04 95 54 55 47)
Bastia-Poretta airport

Budget
(☎ 04 95 23 57 21, fax 04 95 23 57 23)
Ajaccio-Campo dell'Oro airport
(☎ 04 95 30 05 05, fax 04 95 36 32 72)
Bastia-Poretta airport

Europcar
(☎ 04 95 23 57 01, fax 04 95 23 57 03)
Ajaccio-Campo dell'Oro airport
(☎ 04 95 30 09 50, fax 04 95 30 09 59)
Bastia-Poretta airport

Hertz
(☎ 04 95 23 57 04/05, fax 04 95 23 57 06)
Ajaccio-Campo dell'Oro airport
(☎ 04 95 30 05 00, fax 04 95 36 14 92)
Bastia-Poretta airport

National-Citer
(☎ 04 95 23 57 15, fax 04 95 23 57 16)
Ajaccio-Campo dell'Oro airport
(☎ 04 95 36 07 85, fax 04 95 36 18 31)
Bastia-Poretta airport

Sixt
(☎ 04 95 23 57 00, fax 04 95 23 56 99)
Ajaccio-Campo dell'Oro airport
(☎ 04 95 54 54 70, fax 04 95 23 56 99)
Bastia-Poretta airport

See Getting Around under individual town sections for car-hire companies elsewhere. There are also companies at Calvi and Figari airports.

BICYCLE

The summer heat may be a deterrent to some cyclists; spring and autumn are probably better times to tackle the hills. See Cycling in the Facts for the Visitor chapter and the regional chapters for details about renting mountain bikes in Corsica. Many cyclists who want to see something of Corsica's mountainous interior begin by taking the train to Corte or some other starting point already high in the mountains.

HITCHING

Hitching is never entirely safe in any country in the world, and we don't recommend it. Travellers who decide to hitch should understand that they are taking a small but potentially serious risk. People who do choose to hitch are safer if they travel in pairs and let someone know where they're planning to go.

BOAT

There is no regular scheduled commercial boat service between any two Corsican ports. This said, you could try to persuade one of the tour-boat companies making daily excursions out from one Corsican town to another and back to sell you a one-way ticket. You might also be able to persuade them to allow you to go out one day and back another but don't expect bargains. Tourist boats ply the waters between Calvi and Girolata, Calvi and Ajaccio, Ajaccio and Bonifacio and Bonifacio and Porto Vecchio.

Sailors with their own boats can find information about harbour facilities in Getting There & Away under individual coastal towns.

LOCAL TRANSPORT

Most towns in Corsica are small enough to get around on foot. Ajaccio and Bastia, the island's two largest towns, both have local bus services. Elsewhere, you may find yourself to some degree dependent on taxis, and if you're on your own, taxis can be expensive. Approximate fare prices are given in the text, as are prices for short tours for which you might want to hire a taxi.

Taxis in Corsica have a 'Taxi' sign on the roof; the cars can be any colour. Look for details of taxi companies in Getting Around under individual towns.

ORGANISED TOURS

Various companies offer bus tours, half a day to two days in length, in different corners of the island. Most of the tours take place in high season, departing from Ajaccio, Bastia or Calvi, and have to have a minimum number of passengers subscribe before they'll set off. See Organised Tours under individual towns for more details. Or get in touch with L'Agence du Tourisme de la Corse (see Tourist Offices in the Facts for the Visitor chapter) for a complete list of the island's tour operators.

Bastia & the Far North

Corsicans have tended to prefer a pastoral existence, away from the water's edge, to seafaring. But the people of the Cap Corse peninsula have been an exception to this rule. The coast is dotted with tiny fishing ports between maquis-covered headlands. The Nebbio region to the west of Cap Corse is a landscape of vineyards, superb expanses of sand and an amazing desert. Bastia was for many long centuries Corsica's number one urban centre – until, in the time of Napoleon I, the balance began to tilt towards Ajaccio. It is an exciting, bustling town with an air of mystery.

Highlights

- Savour the narrow streets and odd byways of Bastia, Corsica's leading commercial town
- Stroll through the maquis-covered hills of the Cap Corse peninsula
- Explore the stunning barren landscape of the Désert des Agriates

Bastia

postcode 20200 • pop 38,000

Bastia may rank second to Ajaccio among Corsica's population magnets, but it is Ajaccio's equal as capital of one of the island's two departments. Economically it is probably more dynamic than Ajaccio, especially in areas not hinging on tourism and, for passenger traffic through its port, it ranks second in France only to the English Channel port of Calais. In 1999 the sum total of passengers in and out of Bastia hit the 1.8 million mark, and, as the Bastiais like to observe, when the colossal ferry *Napoleon Bonaparte* sits in its berth, it is far and away the biggest building in town. Many of the passengers arriving by sea in Bastia are, to be sure, heading elsewhere, and Bastia has long wished it could persuade more of them to linger. At last, it has succeeded. In the summer of 2000, Bastia was at times obliged to house its overflow visitors in convents! Travellers who did linger were not disappointed.

History

Although there were settlements in the area of what is now Bastia as far back as Roman times, Bastia was not founded officially until 1372. The Genoese governor of the time, residing in the poorly defended Château de Biguglia in a malaria-infested area several kilometres away, decided to build a fortress (or *bastiglia* – hence Bastia) on the only really significant rocky headland on a coastline that was otherwise rather featureless. The site thus became recognised as strategically important.

In 1452 the fortress became the provincial capital of Corsica under Genoese rule and, as such, the seat of the governors. The Terra Nova quarter grew up around the fortress.

Freedom-minded Corsicans, meanwhile, tended to see the fortress, or citadel, as the prime symbol of Genoese oppression, and on several occasions villagers came down from the mountains and sacked the town in protest over Genoese taxes. Despite instability Bastia kept building. The high apartment blocks, reminiscent of those in any number of secondary Italian cities, with their steep interior stairs, visible from the street, date from the 17th and 18th centuries.

In 1764 Bastia passed suddenly into the hands of the French but without suddenly becoming French. Before the century was out, the great British admiral, Horatio Nelson, conquered the town after a two-month siege and the British remained in the driver's seat for the next two years. Under Napoleon, revolts in the town were brutally suppressed and in 1811 Bastia lost its status as capital to Ajaccio. In 1943, in what has to have been

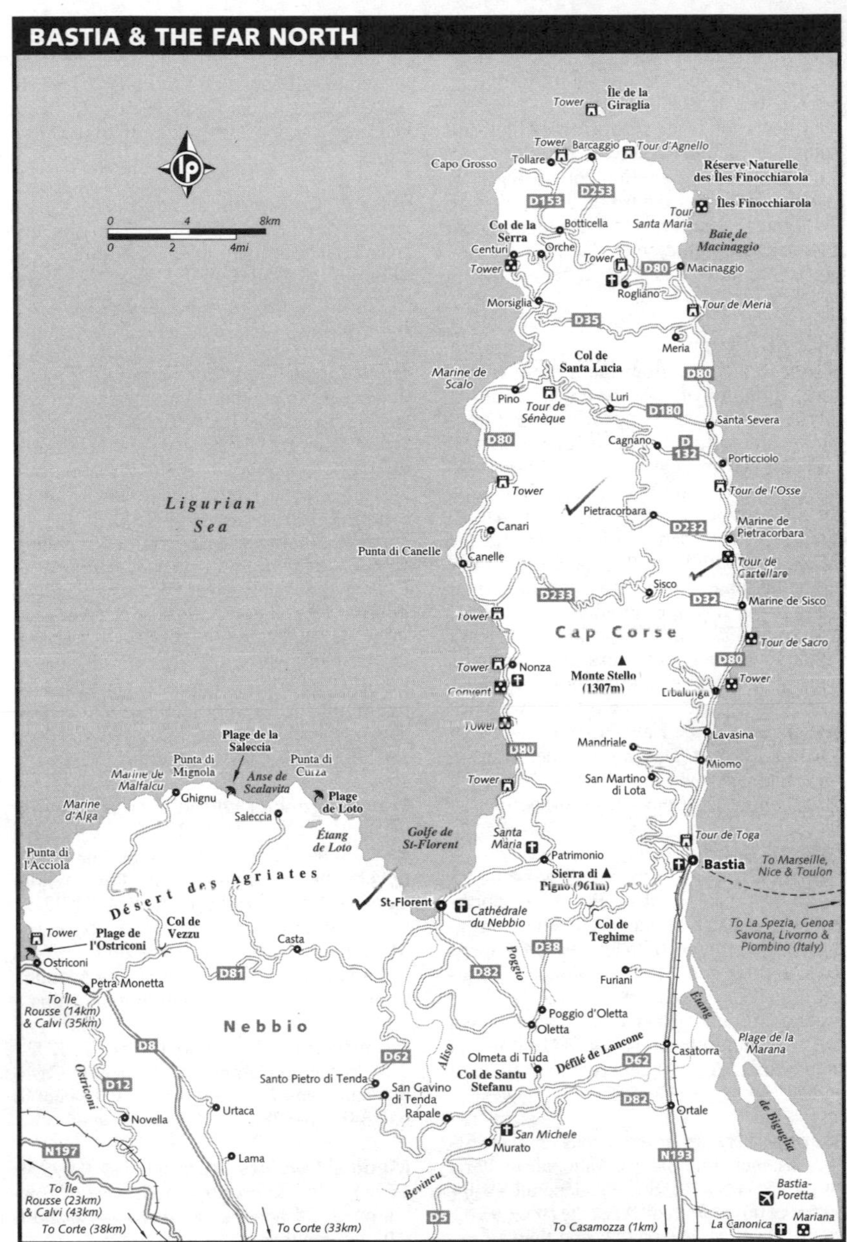
BASTIA & THE FAR NORTH
Île de la Giraglia
Tower
Barcaggio
Tour d'Agnello
Capo Grosso
Tollare
Réserve Naturelle des Îles Finocchiarola
Îles Finocchiarola
Tour Santa Maria
Baie de Macinaggio
Col de la Serra
Botticella
Centuri
Orche
Macinaggio
Rogliano
Morsiglia
Tour de Meria
Meria
Col de Santa Lucia
Marine de Scalo
Pino
Tour de Sénèque
Luri
Santa Severa
Cagnano
Porticciolo
Tour de l'Osse
Ligurian Sea
Pietracorbara
Marine de Pietracorbara
Canari
Punta di Canelle
Canelle
Tour de Cartellare
Sisco
Marine de Sisco
Cap Corse
Tour de Sacro
Nonza
Monte Stello (1307m)
Convent
Erbalunga
Lavasina
Mandriale
Miomo
San Martino di Lota
Plage de la Saleccia
Punta di Mignola
Punta di Curza
Marine de Malfalcu
Anse de Scalavita
Ghignu
Plage de Loto
Marine d'Alga
Saleccia
Étang de Loto
Golfe de St-Florent
Santa Maria
Patrimonio
Tour de Toga
Bastia
To Marseille, Nice & Toulon
Punta di l'Acciola
Désert des Agriates
Sierra di Pigno (961m)
St-Florent
Cathédrale du Nebbio
Col de Teghime
To La Spezia, Genoa Savona, Livorno & Piombino (Italy)
Plage de l'Ostriconi
Col de Vezzu
Casta
Ostriconi
Poggio
Furiani
Petra Monetta
To Île Rousse (14km) & Calvi (35km)
Nebbio
Poggio d'Oletta
Oletta
Étang
Plage de la Marana
Aliso
Olmeta di Tuda
Défilé de Lancone
Casatorra
Col de Santu Stefanu
Santo Pietro di Tenda
San Gavino di Tenda
Rapale
Ortale
de Biguglia
Urtaca
Novella
San Michele
Murato
Lama
Bevincu
Bastia-Poretta
To Île Rousse (23km) & Calvi (43km)
To Corte (38km)
To Corte (33km)
To Casamozza (1km)
La Canonica
Mariana
D253
D153
D80
D35
D180
D132
D232
D233
D32
D38
D81
D82
D8
D12
D62
N197
N193
D5
0 4 8km
0 2 4mi

one of the cruellest mistakes of WWII, US Air Force bombers savaged the town even after the last Axis troops had withdrawn. Several townspeople, joyously celebrating their liberation in the streets, were killed and numerous buildings were destroyed.

In the post-war period the strength of Bastia's port has contributed, happily, to the town's resurgence as the island's most dynamic economic pole. The Haute-Corse prefecture moved its headquarters to Bastia in 1975.

Orientation

If you're arriving from the airport, to the south of the town, the first thing you'll notice is the imposing citadel quarter (Terra Nova). Travelling by car or bus, you will probably go through the tunnel hollowed out of the town's rocky crags and pass along the old port before emerging into place St-Nicolas in the heart of Bastia. Behind the square and parallel to the sea are two busy shopping streets, blvd Paoli and rue César Campinchi. If you're in your own vehicle, it is a good idea to leave it in the car park underneath place St-Nicolas, to your left as you exit the tunnel; parking above ground is scarce. If you are arriving by sea, the place St-Nicolas will be right in front of you as you exit the port. The car-hire operations in the centre of town are all close by in the neighbourhood of the square St-Victor.

Information

Tourist Offices The tourist office (☎ 04 95 54 20 40, fax 04 95 31 81 34), on the northern side of place St-Nicolas, opens 8 am to 8 pm daily in summer. In low season it opens 9 am to noon and 2 to 6 pm Monday to Saturday and on Sunday morning. A range of brochures is available, including a town plan and a brief introduction to Bastia in English. In summer, the office organises themed walking tours (see Organised Tours later).

Money There are several banks on place St-Nicolas, including Banque Nationale de Paris (☎ 04 95 34 83 70), Société Générale (☎ 04 95 55 19 00) and Crédit Agricole (☎ 04 95 32 96 00). They all have ATMs and they all exchange money. You can also exchange money at the post office and in the ferry terminal in summer. Banque de France (☎ 04 95 32 82 00), 2 bis cours Henri Pierangeli, opens 8.45 am to noon and 1.45 to 3.30 pm Monday to Friday.

Post & Communications Bastia's main post office (☎ 04 95 32 80 70) is on ave Maréchal Sébastiani. It opens 8 am to 7 pm Monday to Friday, but closes 12.30 and 1.30 pm on Wednesday, and 8 am to noon on Saturday.

Bookshops Maps, Corsica walking books and other more general volumes are on sale in the Librairie Jean-Patrice Marzocchi (☎ 04 95 34 02 95), 2 rue du Conventionnel Salicetti. It opens daily 9.30 am to 2 pm and 2.30 to 7 pm except Sunday and Monday morning. Terra Nova (☎ 04 95 32 25 11), 12 rue Napoléon, is strong on works about Corsica and, needless to say, stronger in French than in English. It opens 9 am to noon and 2 to 7 pm Monday to Saturday. Le Point de Rencontre (☎ 04 95 31 23 10), on the corner of blvd Général Giraud and la montée Ste-Claire, makes a speciality of exhibitions and author readings and discussions. It opens 9 am to 12.30 pm and 1.30 to 7.30 pm Monday to Saturday.

Travel Agencies Ollandini Voyages (☎ 04 95 31 11 71, fax 04 95 32 66 77), 40 blvd Paoli, sells charter flights to the mainland, tickets for sea crossings and tours within Corsica. Nouvelles Frontières (☎ 04 95 32 01 62) is across from the post office on rue Maréchal Sébastiani. It opens 9 or 9.30 am to noon and 2.30 to 6 or 6.30 pm Monday to Friday as well as on Saturday morning.

Laundry Lavoir du Port (☎ 04 95 32 25 51), 25 rue du Commandant Luce de Casabianca, opens 7 am to 9 pm daily. Expect to pay 34FF for 7kg.

Medical Services The hospital (☎ 04 95 59 11 11), a few kilometres south-west of Bastia, opens 24 hours a day. Bus Nos 1 and 2 will get you there.

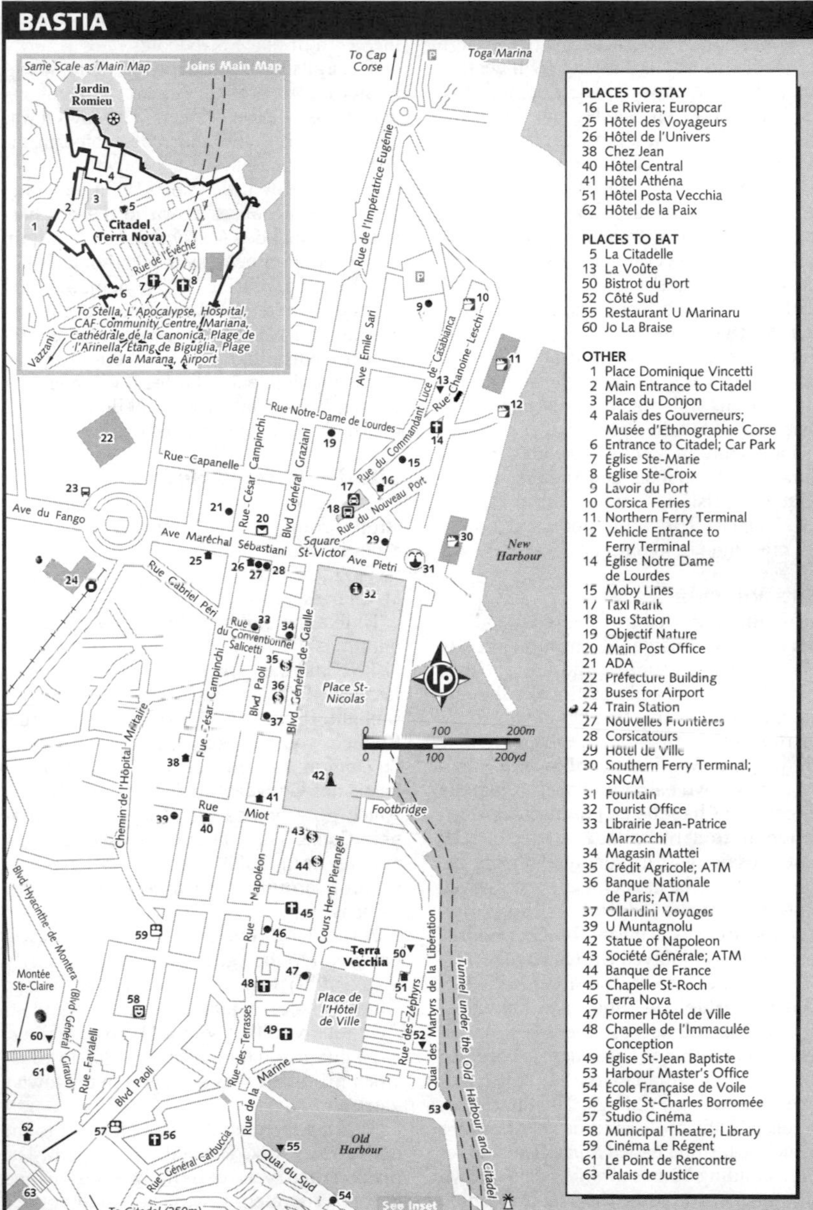
BASTIA
Same Scale as Main Map
Joins Main Map
Jardin Romieu
Citadel (Terra Nova)
Rue de l'Evêché
To Stella, L'Apocalypse, Hospital, CAF Community Centre, Mariana, Cathédrale de la Canonica, Plage de l'Arinella, Étang de Biguglia, Plage de la Marana, Airport
Vazzani
To Cap Corse
Toga Marina
Rue de l'Impératrice Eugénie
Ave Emile Sari
Rue du Commandant Luce de Casabianca
Rue Chanoine Leschi
Rue Notre-Dame de Lourdes
Rue Capanelle
Rue César Campinchi
Blvd Général Graziani
Rue du Nouveau Port
Ave du Fango
Ave Maréchal Sébastiani
Square St-Victor
Ave Pietri
New Harbour
Rue Gabriel Péri
Rue du Conventionnel Salicetti
Blvd Paoli
Blvd Général de Gaulle
Place St-Nicolas
Chemin de l'Hôpital Militaire
Rue Miot
Footbridge
Rue Napoléon
Cours Henri Pierangeli
Terra Vecchia
Place de l'Hôtel de Ville
Rue des Zéphyrs
Quai des Martyrs de la Libération
Tunnel under the Old Harbour and Citadel
Blvd Hyacinthe de Montera (Blvd Général Giraud)
Montée Ste-Claire
Rue Favalelli
Rue des Terrasses
Rue de la Marine
Old Harbour
Quai du Sud
Rue Général Carbuccia
To Citadel (250m)
See Inset
0 100 200m
0 100 200yd
PLACES TO STAY
16 Le Riviera; Europcar
25 Hôtel des Voyageurs
26 Hôtel de l'Univers
38 Chez Jean
40 Hôtel Central
41 Hôtel Athéna
51 Hôtel Posta Vecchia
62 Hôtel de la Paix
PLACES TO EAT
5 La Citadelle
13 La Voûte
50 Bistrot du Port
52 Côté Sud
55 Restaurant U Marinaru
60 Jo La Braise
OTHER
1 Place Dominique Vincetti
2 Main Entrance to Citadel
3 Place du Donjon
4 Palais des Gouverneurs; Musée d'Ethnographie Corse
6 Entrance to Citadel; Car Park
7 Église Ste-Marie
8 Église Ste-Croix
9 Lavoir du Port
10 Corsica Ferries
11 Northern Ferry Terminal
12 Vehicle Entrance to Ferry Terminal
14 Église Notre Dame de Lourdes
15 Moby Lines
17 Taxi Rank
18 Bus Station
19 Objectif Nature
20 Main Post Office
21 ADA
22 Préfecture Building
23 Buses for Airport
24 Train Station
27 Nouvelles Frontières
28 Corsicatours
29 Hôtel de Ville
30 Southern Ferry Terminal; SNCM
31 Fountain
32 Tourist Office
33 Librairie Jean-Patrice Marzocchi
34 Magasin Mattei
35 Crédit Agricole; ATM
36 Banque Nationale de Paris; ATM
37 Ollandini Voyages
39 U Muntagnolu
42 Statue of Napoleon
43 Société Générale; ATM
44 Banque de France
45 Chapelle St-Roch
46 Terra Nova
47 Former Hôtel de Ville
48 Chapelle de l'Immaculée Conception
49 Église St-Jean Baptiste
53 Harbour Master's Office
54 École Française de Voile
56 Église St-Charles Borromée
57 Studio Cinéma
58 Municipal Theatre; Library
59 Cinéma Le Régent
61 Le Point de Rencontre
63 Palais de Justice

Place St-Nicolas

Palm trees and cafe terraces line the western side of this nearly 300m-long 19th-century square that is the town's focal point. There is a flea market on Sunday mornings and rollerbladers are out almost every evening. The square also boasts an imposing **statue of Napoleon** with whom Bastia has never had a very easy relationship. His powerful torso is draped in a Roman emperor's tunic and his eyes are peering out to sea in the direction of Elba, the island of his first exile, which is less than 50km to the east. The **Magasin Mattei** (☎ 04 95 32 44 28), 15 blvd Général de Gaulle, at mid-point on the commercial western side of the square, not only sells its celebrated brand-name Cap Corse apéritif but the shop window also contains a display of spin-off products such as ashtrays, bottle labels and posters, and its antique furnishings are a feast for the eyes. It opens 9.30 am to noon and 2.30 to 7.30 pm Monday to Saturday.

Terra Vecchia

This is the oldest part of the town and has always been considered an authentically Corsican quarter, unlike the Terra Nova, which is higher up and traditionally thought of as Genoese, a label that has connotations of arrogance.

From place St-Nicolas, follow rue Napoléon past the two baroque chapels, **Chapelle St-Roch** and **Chapelle de l'Immaculée Conception**. In front of the latter, notice the Genoese mosaic with its sun symbolising the glory of God. The chapel itself once served as the seat of the Anglo-Corsican parliament. Its throne was meant for King George III and its organ played *God Save the King*.

Beyond the chapels, the street leads into **place de l'Hôtel de Ville**, also known as place du Marché because there is a market there every morning. The square is bordered by some rather dilapidated but still handsome four-storey buildings. The bluish coloration of their roofs is to be ascribed to a unique local stone called *lauze*. The one restored building here is a *hôtel de ville* (town hall) annexe primarily used as a wedding palace. The new town-hall building, the most important building in town, is just to the north of place St-Nicolas.

The **Église St-Jean Baptiste**, in the southwestern corner of the square, is recognisable by its twin bell-towers. The church was completed in 1666 and redecorated in the Baroque style in the 18th century. From the square, narrow little streets wind their way between tall houses down to the **old harbour** and **quai des Martyrs de la Libération**. The buildings nearest the harbour took a bad battering during WWII bombing missions designed to drive out Axis occupiers. The quarter behind the square is better preserved, particularly as you climb up towards the **Église St-Charles Borromée**. It is hidden behind tall narrow buildings, some of which have been recently restored.

Citadel & Terra Nova

From the southern quay of the old harbour, stroll through **Jardin Romieu** (open 8 am to 8 pm in summer and 8 am to 5 pm in winter) to the citadel via the steps of the **rampe St-Charles**.

Unlike the buildings in Terra Vecchia, the buildings in Terra Nova have been refurbished, and the ochre, red, yellow and green facades of the narrow streets gleam in the sunlight. If you are approaching from Jardin Romieu, you will enter the citadel via **place du Donjon**. Immediately on your right is the **Palais des Gouverneurs** (Governors' Palace), which now houses the **Musée d'Ethnographie Corse**. The museum is closed for renovations until 2002 but it is still possible to stroll around the palace courtyard and gardens.

A wander through the narrow streets will bring you to the **Église Ste-Marie** (formerly a cathedral) with its imposing yellow and white facade. A plaque on a house to its right tells you that Victor Hugo lived there as an infant and toddler (from 1803 to 1805) when his father was a general in the town's garrison.

Skirting the church, you will come to the **Église Ste-Croix**. The ceiling is superb. The **black crucifix** is extremely unusual and deeply venerated. It was supposedly pulled from the sea by fishermen in 1428. Be sure to notice the elegant entrance square of green and white stones.

Activities

Objectif Nature (☎/fax 04 95 32 54 34 or ☎ 06 13 86 47 47, e objectif-nature@wanadoo.fr), 3 rue Notre Dame de Lourdes, a stone's throw from the bus station, can provide information on sporting opportunities throughout Corsica: canyoning in the Bavella massif or the Gravona or Golo valleys (approximately 300FF), sea-kayaking along the Désert des Agriates (250FF per day), horse riding, night fishing, sailing, diving or even parapenting. Objectif Nature opens 8 am to 7 pm Monday to Saturday and on Sunday morning in the high season. You can get more information at http://obj-nature.ifrance.com (French only).

The École Française de Voile (☎ 04 95 32 67 33), in the old harbour, runs excursions in catamaran or kayak. It operates 8.30 am to 12.30 pm and 2 to 6 pm in high season.

Courses

The association Esse (☎ 04 95 30 12 00) arranges classes in the Corsican language. These classes are taught in the CAF community centre, route Impériale, Paese Novo, 20600, near the hospital.

Organised Tours

In summer the tourist office organises guided tours (around 35FF), some in English, on themes such as Baroque Bastia, Genoese Bastia, Bastia under Napoleon III and Bastia in Literature. Ask at the office on place St-Nicolas. They'll also tell you about other associations offering similar tours.

Micheli (☎ 04 95 35 64 02) offers a full-day bus tour around Cap Corse from the beginning of July until the beginning of September. The route takes in Erbalunga, Macinaggio, Centuri, Canari, Nonza, St-Florent and Oletta. It costs about 110FF. Ask at the bus station or at the tourist office.

Special Events

Each autumn Bastia hosts two major events. The Musicales de Bastia (☎ 04 95 32 75 91), with its five days of Baroque music, symphony, blues and popular song, is in October. The Festival du Film et des Cultures Méditerranéennes (☎ 04 95 32 08 86) is in November. The city also sponsors English-, Italian- and Spanish-language film festivals (see Public Holidays & Special Events in the Facts for the Visitor chapter). If you understand French, you'll find the latest information on cultural events in Bastia on Radio Corse Frequenza Mora at 101.7MHz FM.

Places to Stay

Even if Bastia has not traditionally been a principal tourist destination in Corsica, finding a room here is increasingly difficult, especially in summer. Advance booking is strongly recommended.

Places to Stay – Budget

The ***Camping du Bois de San Damiano*** *(☎ 04 95 33 68 02, fax 04 95 30 84 10)* is at Plage de la Marana 8km south of the tunnel under the old port (but north of the airport). Expect to pay 32/12/12FF per person/tent/car. The facility, right at the edge of the beach, includes a bakery, a pizzeria and a mini-golf course. You can also rent a bungalow here on a weekly basis. A shuttle bus connects with the port of Bastia twice daily. The closest railroad station is at Furiani, 4km away. ***Les Plages Rouges*** *(☎ 04 95 33 36 08)*, at Plage de l'Arinella, is less seductive but closer to town. It costs 22/10/15FF per person/tent/car.

Across from the post office, ***Hôtel de l'Univers*** *(☎ 04 95 31 03 38, fax 04 95 31 19 91, 3 ave Maréchal Sébastiani)* has singles/doubles, with common shower and toilet, for 180/190FF. More comfortable rooms, with shower en suite, air-conditioning, cable TV and telephone go for 300/350FF. Breakfast costs 35FF however you sleep. ***Chez Jean*** *(☎ 04 95 31 50 13, 19 rue César Campinchi)* has long boasted the cheapest rooms in town but the owner has been making serious noises about retirement. If you think it's worth your while, phone first.

Places to Stay – Mid-Range

Looking out to sea from a privileged location between place St-Nicolas and the old port is ***Hôtel Posta Vecchia*** *(☎ 04 95 32 32 38, fax 04 95 32 14 05, quai des Martyrs de la Libération)*. In low season, count on paying 220FF to 330FF for a single and 250FF to 370FF for a double, depending on size and amenities. In high season you'll pay 30FF to 40FF more but it's still exceptional. The whole hotel has been renovated recently; rooms have bathroom, TV and telephone and sometimes a little refrigerator.

Hôtel des Voyageurs *(☎ 04 95 34 90 80, fax 04 95 34 00 65, 9 ave Maréchal Sébastiani)*, renovated in 1998, offers tastefully decorated rooms with shower or bath, air-conditioning, TV and telephone for 285/410FF, or slightly less in low season. Note that the hotel closes between 20 December and 15 January.

Hôtel de la Paix *(☎ 04 95 31 06 71, fax 04 95 58 96 02, 1 blvd Général Giraud)*, not far from the Palais de Justice (law courts), is a small, clean, attractive and family-run. A double with en-suite bathroom, TV and telephone costs 280FF to 350FF and a triple costs 350FF to 450FF; prices depend on the season.

Hôtel Central *(☎ 04 95 31 71 12, fax 04 95 31 82 40, 3 rue Miot)* has basic rooms, pleasant though somewhat battle-scarred, for 200FF to 250FF a single and 250FF to 380FF double. It's a good choice for single travellers. The more elaborate rooms, with balcony, TV and telephone, cost 300FF to 350FF. For 400FF to 450FF, you can have a kitchenette. ***Hôtel Athéna*** *(☎ 04 95 34 88 40, fax 04 95 31 26 41, 2 rue Miot)*, notable for its quietness, rents spick-and-span little rooms from a low of 250FF.

Le Riviera *(☎ 04 95 31 07 16, fax 04 95 34 17 39, 1 bis rue du Nouveau Port)*, undergoing renovations at last visit, offers particularly nice doubles for 320FF in summer and 280FF out of season.

Places to Eat

Jo La Braise *(☎ 04 95 31 36 97, 7 blvd Hyacinthe de Montera)*, two minutes from the Palais de Justice, is a small, rather unimpressive-looking restaurant that nevertheless serves delicious, well prepared food. Jo, the owner, and his wife both work in the kitchen, which communicates directly with the dining room. The menu has been the same for 30 years: *charcuterie* from the owners' village of origin in La Castagniccia (see The Eastern Plain chapter), *tourtes* (rather busy little pies) dressed up with herbs or fromage frais and excellent wood-fire pizzas for 35FF to 40FF. Finish off your meal with one of the house speciality desserts such as banana flambée (35FF) or *fiadone*.

Slightly more chic is ***Restaurant U Marinaru*** *(☎ 04 95 32 45 99)*, on the old harbour. It is valued by the Bastiais themselves for its fish dishes. The daily special, which might, if you're lucky, be a seafood pot-au-feu, goes for 68FF. The restaurant opens daily except Sunday.

La Voûte *(☎ 04 95 32 27 82, 6 rue du Commandant Luce de Casabianca)* is a pleasant restaurant with quality food in a quiet street just behind the harbour. There is a 130FF *menu* and pizzas cooked over a wood fire cost 50FF.

Bistrot du Port *(☎ 04 95 32 19 83)*, just opposite the entrance to Hôtel Posta Vecchia, is an excellent little restaurant, a touch shabby of appearance but all the same pleasant and intimate. There is no *menu* but there is a wide range of imaginative a la carte dishes. The restaurant opens daily except Sunday.

Côté Sud *(☎ 04 95 31 67 73, quai des Martyrs de la Libération)* is an intimate restaurant, open daily except Wednesday and Saturday lunchtime. The *menu* costs 120FF.

La Citadelle *(☎ 04 95 31 44 70, 6 rue du Dragon)*, unsurprisingly within the citadel itself, is Bastia's most prestigious restaurant. Chef François Mattei offers a 180FF *menu*. La Citadelle opens daily except Sunday; it also does not serve a Saturday lunch.

For those who like to get up early, local traders and producers set up their stalls in the market place (place de l'Hôtel de Ville) each morning. You can stock up on local produce such as honey, fruit, charcuterie and wine, or simply treat yourself to a *brocciu* pastry.

Entertainment

Bars & Discos There is plenty of cafe-terrace activity around Bastia's old port of a summer evening, but of the kind of nightlife that hinges on pulsing rhythms and unbridled amplification there is little or none. Forget about it. Curiously, there are two discos in the town, ***Velvet*** *(☎ 04 95 31 01 00)*, near the old harbour, just next to the steps leading to the citadel, and ***Stella*** *(☎ 04 95 58 06 94)*, on the Plage de l'Arinella. But they both close in summer due to the competition from open-air establishments in nearby seaside resorts such as St-Florent. In the immediate vicinity, the one serious open-air disco is ***L'Apocalypse*** *(☎ 04 95 33 36 83)* at Plage de la Marana south of Bastia. Anyone desperate for animation might also have a look around the sailing harbour of Toga north of the ferry harbour, particularly at the bars called ***Macarana*** and ***Noche de Cuba***.

Cinema On rue César Campinchi is a multiscreen cinema, ***Le Régent*** *(☎ 04 95 31 30 31)*. ***Studio Cinéma*** *(☎ 04 95 31 12 94)* is in rue Miséricorde, near the Palais de Justice.

Shopping

One noteworthy store, U Muntagnolu (☎ 04 95 32 78 04), 15 rue César Campinchi, sells charcuterie, cheese (with sealed packaging to keep in the odour), wine, liqueurs and honey. It opens 9 am to 12.30 pm and 3 to 8 pm except Sunday. They'll post purchases anywhere. See also place St-Nicolas earlier.

Getting There & Away

Air Bastia-Poretta airport (☎ 04 95 54 54 54), with its new terminal in the shape of a flying saucer, is 24km south of the town. The terminal building has an ATM, car-hire agencies, several shops and a bar.

Bus The bus station (a grand term for a little parking area, with no ticket sales counters) is at the bottom of rue du Nouveau Port to the north of place St-Nicolas but certain buses leave from the train station or from ave Maréchal Sébastiani or ave Pietri. Details of destinations and operators follow.

Ajaccio Eurocorse (☎ 04 95 21 06 30)
Departs daily except Sunday and public holidays from bus station, 110FF

Calvi Les Beaux Voyages (☎ 04 95 65 15 02)
Departs twice daily from train station, 80FF

Canari Transports Saoletti (☎ 04 95 37 84 05)
Departs Wednesday from bus station, 40FF

Corte Autocars Cortenais (☎ 04 95 46 02 12)
Departs Monday, Wednesday and Friday from bus station, 60FF

Macinaggio Saladini (☎ 04 95 35 43 88) or STIB (☎ 04 95 31 06 65)
Departs daily from bus station (Saladini) or place St-Nicolas (STIB), 35FF

Pino, Luri, Cagnano Transports Lucchesi (☎ 04 95 35 10 67)
Departs Monday, Wednesday and Friday from bus station, 45FF

Porto Vecchio Les Rapides Bleus-Corsicatours (☎ 04 95 31 03 79)
Departs twice daily except Sunday and holidays out of season, from opposite the post office (ave Maréchal Sébastiani), 115FF

St-Florent Transports Santini (☎ 04 95 37 04 01)
Departs daily except Sunday and public holidays from bus station, 30FF

Vescovato & Venzolasca Autobus Casinca (☎ 04 95 36 70 64)
Daily except Sunday and public holidays, departs from bus station, 26FF

Train The train station (☎ 04 95 32 80 61) at the western end of ave Maréchal Sébastiani opens 6.15 am to 8.20 pm daily in summer. There is a left-luggage window.

There are two trains daily in summer from Bastia to Calvi (95FF, three hours). There are several trains daily to Corte (59FF, 1½ hours), Casamozza (20FF, 30 minutes) and Ajaccio (124FF, four hours).

Car Most of the car-hire firms have branches both in Bastia and at the airport. But don't even think of finding a car in high season if you haven't booked in advance. In town, ADA (☎ 04 95 31 48 95), 35 rue César Campinchi, opens 8 am to noon and 2 to 5 pm Monday to Friday, as well as on Saturday morning. Europcar (☎ 04 95 31 59 29), 1 rue du Nouveau Port, opens 7 am to 8 pm Monday to Saturday in summer.

At the airport try ADA (☎ 04 95 54 55 44), Avis (☎ 04 95 54 56 46), Budget (☎ 04 95 30 05 05), Europcar (☎ 04 95 30 09 50), Hertz (☎ 04 95 30 05 00), National-Citer (☎ 04 95 36 07 85) or Sixt (☎ 04 95 54 54 20).

Boat There are two ferry terminals in Bastia – the northern and the southern – a few hundred metres apart. The southern terminal appeared to be busier and the northern undergoing works at the time of writing. Tickets are sold for same-day travel inside the terminals in the harbour and ticket offices open a few hours before the ships arrive. The terminals also have a bureau de change. If you want to buy a ticket to travel on a different day, you will need to go to one of the carriers' offices:

SNCM (☎ 04 95 54 66 99, fax 04 95 54 66 54) commercial port southern terminal
Services from Bastia to Toulon, Marseille, Nice, Elba, Genoa and Livorno. Open 8 am to 6.30 pm Monday to Friday and on Saturday morning.

CMN (☎ 08 10 20 13 20, fax 04 95 32 37 01) commercial port northern terminal
Service from Bastia to Marseille. Open 8 am to noon and 2 to 6 pm Monday, Wednesday and Friday; to 7 pm Tuesday and Thursday; and 8 am to noon and 4 to 6 pm Saturday.

Corsica Ferries (☎ 04 95 32 95 95) 5 bis rue Chanoine Leschi
Service from Bastia to Toulon. Open 8.30 am to noon and 2 to 6.30 pm Monday to Friday and on Saturday morning.

Moby Lines (☎ 04 95 34 84 94, fax 04 95 32 17 94) 4 rue du Commandant Luce de Casabianca
Services from Bastia to Genoa and Livorno. Open 8 am to noon and 2 to 6 pm Monday to Friday and on Saturday morning.

Visiting sailing boats have a choice between the old harbour in Bastia (☎ 04 95 31 31 10, fax 04 95 31 77 95), right in the centre of town, and the new Toga marina (☎ 04 95 34 90 70, fax 04 95 34 90 71) just beyond the northern edge of Bastia in Pietrabugno. The former has more than 250 berths and the latter more than 350. Both have refuelling points, toilets, showers and maintenance facilities.

Getting Around

To/From the Airport The airport bus (50FF) leaves from in front of the entrance to the Préfecture building, which is on the roundabout in front of the train station. The times are posted at the bus stop and timetables are available from the tourist office. The No 1 bus also goes to the airport (7.50FF) from the Toga marina via blvd Paoli and the citadel area. A taxi to the airport (☎ 04 95 36 04 65) will cost you 200FF to 210FF or up to 280FF at night, on Sunday and on public holidays.

Bus The No 1 bus that goes to the airport may be a useful link.

Taxi Taxis Radio Bastiais (☎ 04 95 34 07 00), place St-Victor, operate 24 hours per day. Rates, for up to four passengers, are 250FF to St-Florent, 340FF to Macinaggio and 100FF to Erbalunga. Rates increase after 7 pm, at weekends and holidays. You can also call Taxis Bleus (☎ 04 95 32 70 70) or ABC Taxi Bastiais (☎ 04 95 55 82 25).

Bicycle Objectif Nature hires out mountain bikes for 100FF per day, 240FF for three days and 500FF per week. For more details, see Activities earlier.

AROUND BASTIA

Étang et Réserve Naturelle de Biguglia

This vast lagoon – more than 11km long and 2.5km across, with a total surface area of 1450 hectares – is the largest closed body of water in Corsica. Declared a nature reserve in 1994, it is an important stopping-off point for birds migrating between Europe and Africa, and the coot, the egret, the bittern, the heron and the marsh harrier are among the more than 100 species of bird that can be observed here. Eel and mullet are farmed in the waters. Though sailing and bathing are prohibited, a footpath, described in the Walking chapter, follows the northern and eastern shore. An information kiosk (☎ 04 95 33 55 73) opens during the summer on the eastern side.

Plage de la Marana is a narrow stretch of coastline more than 10km long between the Étang de Biguglia and the sea. Much of the area is devoted to tourism, with shops and businesses, residential areas, camp sites (see Places to Stay under Bastia earlier), discos and even a riding centre. The beach is nothing special but at least you will have room to spread out your beach towel. As you approach from Bastia you come to a car park alongside the beach. After this the road heads inland slightly and parking and beach access both become something of a problem. A track bordering the lake on its eastern side is frequently used by rollerbladers, cyclists and pedestrians.

Getting There & Away Numerous buses ply the route between the Bastia bus terminal and the Plage de la Marana and Étang de Biguglia every day. If you're going that way, look for buses marked Marana. You can also catch the Casamozza train as far as Rocade. The Étang de Biguglia is 200m to the east.

Mariana & Cathédrale de la Canonica

At the southern end of the Étang de Biguglia, a short distance from Bastia-Poretta airport, you'll find the archaeological site of Mariana, with its remains of a Roman baths, and the Cathédrale de la Canonica, consecrated at the beginning of the 12th century by the archbishop of Pisa. The strange little menagerie of animals on the decorative arched moulding over the western entrance is definitely worth a look. The Église de San Parteo, closer to the airport runways and perhaps even a mite older than the Cathédrale de la Canonica, is worth a look as well.

Cap Corse

Often described as an 'island within an island', the maquis-covered Cap Corse peninsula, 40km long and around 10km wide, sticks out from the rest of Corsica like a sore thumb, a geographical fact that has also shaped the area's unique history.

For many long years, the Cap Corse peninsula was ruled by important noble families from the city and republic of Genoa and surrounding Liguria, the coastal region of Italy closest to the border with France. As these families prospered on trade in wine and oil, Genoa and the Ligurians became accustomed to considering Cap Corse as an ally, and history rarely proved them wrong. This part of Corsica also has a long maritime tradition. Apart from Bonifacio, it is the only area within Corsica where the inhabitants have made a living from fishing.

The only merchants and sailors on an island of mountain dwellers (who were closed to an outside world that was often considered threatening), the inhabitants of Cap Corse eventually came to feel the need to broaden their horizons; and they have always been prominent in the Corsican diaspora. The aperitif bearing the region's name became a mascot for the émigrés and a symbol of their nostalgia for their homeland. Many of them won renown in the French colonies in North Africa and the Americas. Once they had made their fortune, many returned to Corsica, where some of them had unusual colonial-style houses built. Some of these 'American homes' can still be seen in the region today, particularly in Sisco and Canelle.

Girdled by numerous old watch towers built under the Genoese to protect the vulnerable peninsula from Saracen raiders, the cape is dotted with fishing villages and small communities perched precariously in the hills. The western coast, wilder in appearance than the eastern coast, is undoubtedly the more spectacular scenically.

The following description of the region starts in Bastia and follows the coastline round to St-Florent. Don't be surprised if you find that some villages have more than one name. The main hamlet of each commune is often also known by the name of the commune itself. Morsiglia is thus also known as Baragona, Botticella as Ersa and so on.

INFORMATION

The Cap Corse tourist office (☎ 04 95 32 01 00, fax 04 95 31 77 79) is in the Maison du Cap Corse across from Toga Marina in Pietrabugno, just north of Bastia. It opens 9 am to noon and 2 to 7 pm Monday to Friday and 10 am to noon and 3 to 7 pm on Saturday in summer. The times vary in winter. Brochures and programs for the region's cultural events are available here.

Note that the only ATM on the peninsula is outside the post office in Macinaggio. Theoretically, all the post offices change travellers cheques, but ever since the ATM

Genoese Towers

Around 60 of the 85 Genoese towers that the Banco di San Giorgio built in Corsica in the 16th century remain standing today. Mostly round but occasionally square, these fortified structures are about 15m high and are particularly common in Cap Corse.

The towers were supposedly intended to protect the island from Saracen raiders, but you can't help thinking that in building them Genoa also sought to protect its strategic and commercial interests in Corsica from European challengers. Placed around the coastline so that each was visible from the next, the towers formed a vast surveillance network. A system of signals enabled a message to circle the island in one hour.

On Cap Corse, Marine de Scalo, Pino, Erbalunga and the Sentier des Douaniers (which takes you to the lovely Santa Maria tower) all have Genoese towers. Outside of Cap Corse, particularly impressive Genoese towers can be inspected at Porto, Campomoro and Calvi.

DOMINIQUE CORDONNIER

was installed they've been extremely reluctant to advance cash against a credit card.

GETTING THERE & AWAY

The firm Micheli (☎ 04 95 35 64 02) organises coach tours around Cap Corse from July to the beginning of September. The itinerary starts and finishes in Bastia and takes in Erbalunga, Macinaggio, Centuri, Canari, Nonza, St-Florent and Oletta. The complete tour costs about 100FF but it is also possible to do just one or more segments of the complete tour. Visit the tourist office in Bastia, the Maison du Cap Corse in Pietrabugno or get in touch with the operator for schedule information.

Other companies provide a service to Cap Corse from Bastia the rest of the year. Transports Saoletti (☎ 04 95 37 84 05) runs buses to Canari (40FF) on Wednesday. Saladini (☎ 04 95 35 43 88) and STIB (☎ 04 95 31 06 65) can between them get you to Macinaggio (35FF) any day of the week. Transports Lucchesi (☎ 04 95 35 10 67) travel to Pino, Luri and Cagnano (45FF) on Monday, Wednesday and Friday.

ERBALUNGA

postcode 20222

Little of Erbalunga, around 10km north of Bastia, reveals itself as you pass through on the main road. It's worth stopping to explore, particularly the narrow streets that form a tight network around the tiny fishing harbour with its handful of colourful boats. A Genoese tower adds the finishing touch to the scene. The town is known for its processions during Holy Week (the week preceding Easter Sunday).

You will find several grocery stores and a post office (☎ 04 95 33 98 18) in Erbalunga but no bank or ATM.

Places to Stay

The only hotel in Erbalunga is three-star ***Castel Brando*** *(☎ 04 95 30 10 30, fax 04 95 33 98 18)*. The building has been charmingly restored, the swimming pool is pleasant and the welcome warm. The light, spacious, comfortable rooms all have air-conditioning, TV and telephone. Doubles cost 380FF in April, October and November, 450FF in May, at the end of September and in October and 630FF at the height of the season. Rooms constructed as recently as the year 2000, just above the swimming pool, cost 650FF, and suites are available for 1050FF. You can visit the Web site at www.castelbrando.com for more information.

Hôtel Les Roches *(☎ 04 95 33 26 57)*, in Lavasina, a few kilometres south of Erbalunga, is cheaper. Its spartan double rooms on the 'garden' side cost 250FF; its doubles on the beach side, across the street, cost 350FF. The latter are plainly better. The village church becomes a pilgrimage destination in early September.

Château Cagninacci *(☎ 04 95 31 69 30)*

is a 17th-century convent on a height overlooking the sea at San Martino di Lota, about halfway between Bastia and Erbalunga. People who like quiet and aren't afraid of solitude will find four spacious rooms here, each with antique furnishings, for 430FF to 470FF depending on the season. Do not be intimidated by the *'propriété privée'* (private property) sign at the entrance.

Places to Eat

A Piazetta *(☎ 04 95 33 28 69)* is the cheapest place to eat in Erbalunga, with pizzas for 45FF and daily specials at around 70FF. The restaurant, in the main square, is open every day but Tuesday. ***Le Pirate*** *(☎ 04 95 33 24 20)* is a lovely restaurant in the small harbour; you can eat lunch or dinner here with the little waves virtually lapping at your feet. The a la carte menu includes pasta with *pistou* (the basil and garlic concoction that is the Niçois equivalent of Italian pesto) for 70FF. The restaurant opens daily April to October.

ROGLIANO (RUGLIANU)

postcode 20247 • pop 480

Farther up Cap Corse and a few kilometres inland from Macinaggio, Rogliano (also called Bettolacce) had its heyday when the village was home to the powerful Da Mare family. Rogliano's hour of maximum glory came in 1869, when the ship carrying Empress Eugénie home from Egypt was forced to take shelter in the port of Macinaggio, the empress and her retinue climbed up to the village and, according to legend, the empress went to gather her thoughts at the **Église Sant'Agnello**. Behind its beautiful facade, the 16th-century church has a high altar made from Carrara marble.

Rogliano's other claim to fame is the array of wind energy collectors that have appeared since spring 2000. The overall project to which they belong is called Éole 2005; it is designed to test the feasibility of 'greener' energy for France as a whole. Rogliano is one of 11 pilot sites in Corsica of a total of 55 throughout France.

Wine-growers in the vicinity include the Gioielli and Pietri estates. An annual wine festival is held in nearby Luri at the beginning of July.

A shuttle between Macinaggio and Rogliano operates free of charge in summer.

Places to Stay & Eat

Pretty ***U Sant'Agnellu*** inn *(☎/fax 04 95 35 40 59)*, open April to October, has light, pleasant double rooms costing from 350FF to 370FF depending upon the season. The first-rate 90FF *menu* builds on local products. The panoramic view is superb and the tranquillity borders on the Olympian.

MACINAGGIO (MACINAGHJU)

postcode 20247

The harbour here has been reputed to be the best mooring in Cap Corse since time immemorial. In Pascal Paoli's time it was a naval base (to the extent of Corsica's abilities) and today it is treasured by sailing enthusiasts. Facilities include refuelling points, water, ship dealers, bars, restaurants and a bureau de change. Showers and weather forecasts are available at the harbour master's office (*capitainerie*; ☎ 04 95 35 42 57).

Macinaggio further prides itself on its lovely **Plage de Tamarone**, undoubtedly the most stunning beach in the region, which is north of the village centre. In summer you will find a refreshment stall there with a reasonably priced menu. There are no toilets.

The **Sentier des Douaniers** (Customs Officers' Route) leads away from the beach and up through fragrant maquis before dropping down to the protected shore that runs alongside the Îles Finocchiarola and the Capandula reserve, where the wonderful Genoese Tour de Santa Maria rises out of the shimmering water. See the Walking chapter for more on this path.

A little tourist office (☎ 04 95 35 40 34) is to be found above the Macinaggio harbour master's office. It opens 9 am to noon and 3 to 6 pm Monday to Friday and on Saturday morning in high season. The Macinaggio post office (☎ 04 95 35 42 67), to the left on the way out of town in the direction of Centuri, is the only place you'll find an ATM on the entire cape.

Wine enthusiasts can sample Corsica's

renowned white wine at Le Clos Nicrosi (☎ 04 95 35 41 17), which is both shop and tasting facility, opposite the post office. It opens 9.30 am to noon and 4 to 7 pm Monday to Saturday between mid-May and the end of September.

The *San Paulu* (☎ 04 95 35 07 09), tied up in the harbour, carries passengers out on sightseeing expeditions along the protected coastline in season. An hour's sail costs 55FF.

Cap Corse Location (☎ 04 95 35 45 19), next door to the post office, rents mountain bikes for 80FF per day between April and October. A horse-riding centre is adjacent to the Camping U Stazzu (see Places to Stay and Eat). For diving options, see the Diving chapter.

Places to Stay & Eat

Heading towards Centuri ***Camping U Stazzu*** *(☎ 04 95 35 43 73)* is signposted 800m on the right as you leave the village. It charges 27/16FF per person/tent. The site is near both the beach and the village; there's shade, and the washrooms pass muster. It opens April to September.

Hôtel des Îles *(☎ 04 95 35 42 03)*, directly on the harbour, has proper rooms with en-suite bathrooms from 280FF. It opens year round, and visitors are made to feel welcome. ***U Ricordu*** *(☎ 04 95 35 40 20, fax 04 95 35 41 88)*, at the northern edge of the village, is equipped with both a swimming pool and a sauna in addition to 54 comfortable rooms, each with air-conditioning, a balcony or terrace and TV. A single costs 320FF to 640FF depending on the season; a double costs 400FF to 720FF. Breakfast is included.

BARCAGGIO (BARCAGHJU)

postcode 20275

From Botticella, the lovely but rather narrow D253 winds its way through the maquis for 10km before reaching Cap Corse's (and Corsica's) northernmost village. In its far-flung location, Barcaggio seems eternally lost in silent contemplation of the remote Île de la Giraglia and its signal station, which was 10 years in the making. Don't look for public transportation in or out, though; there isn't any.

From the beach at Barcaggio, if you get there, you can nevertheless join the Sentier des Douaniers (see Macinaggio earlier in this section, and the Walking chapter). The trail begins behind the wooden fencing around the beach and runs to the Tour d'Agnello before continuing on to Santa Maria and Macinaggio. The fencing was erected at the instigation of the coastal conservancy authority to combat the loss of the dune grass and bindweed that stabilise the sand dunes. Tourism and overgrazing have both been taking their toll.

Capo Grosso, to the west of Barcaggio and of the hamlet of Tollare, has stunning views. Follow the rutted road off the D153 for 2.5km. It's not marked, but it's the only tarmac road to the west before Tollare.

Places to Stay & Eat

Hôtel La Giraglia *(☎ 04 95 35 60 54, fax 04 95 35 65 92)* takes advantage of the lack of any local competition to charge somewhat inflated rates for its unspectacular rooms. A double with toilet goes for 410FF; add a shower and the price goes up to 460FF. Credit cards are not accepted. It opens April to September.

U Pescadore *(☎ 04 95 35 64 90)*, Barcaggio's only restaurant, opens daily in high season. The surroundings are simple and unpretentious. The fish and the traditional Corsican dishes are reasonably priced.

Tents and caravans are prohibited in this area, except in the few designated parking areas.

CENTURI

postcode 20238 • pop 200

Nestling below Col de la Serra, the tiny port of Centuri keeps up the local tradition of rock-lobster fishing. Established by the Romans as Centurium, the village was once a busy trading centre. It was also used as a military base, as is evident from the old cannons converted into mooring posts in the harbour. In the 18th century Pascal Paoli based part of his naval fleet here, such as it was.

Nowadays, tourism is probably the village's major industry, and at the height of the season the village may even be said to get overcrowded. It remains nevertheless a charming and even soulful spot and a highlight of the entire region.

Above the village, the Moulin Mattei flaunts the merits of 'Mattei Cap Corse, an exquisite citrus liqueur' from Col de la Serra. Liqueur aside, this point offers a superb panorama over Île de la Giraglia and the Cap Corse mountains.

The nearest post office is in Orche, 4km from the harbour. It opens 9 am to noon and 1.30 to 4 pm Monday to Friday and also on Saturday morning.

Places to Stay

One and a half kilometres from Centuri harbour on the D35 to Morsiglia, ***Camping L'Isulottu*** *(☎ 04 95 35 62 81)*, is a pleasant place with proper sanitary facilities, a mini-market and a snack bar, and also a small shingle beach 10 minutes' walk away. Expect to pay 81FF for two people, a tent and car. The site opens March to December.

Hôtel-Restaurant du Pêcheur *(☎ 04 95 35 60 14)* is a pretty pink building directly on the harbour and very hard to miss. Its simple, but not uncharming, rooms cost 250FF to 300FF but then drop to 200FF outside of the high season. The hotel opens April to October. ***Hôtel-Restaurant Le Vieux Moulin*** *(☎ 04 95 35 60 15, fax 04 95 35 60 24)* is Centuri's most prestigious lodging but with reasonable enough prices: 290FF for a pretty double room with a shower, TV and telephone. Bungalow accommodation for two to three people, terrace included, costs 350FF. The restaurant serves a good 145FF *menu* and another *menu* whose highlight is grilled lobster (245FF), as well as less expensive snacks. An on-site disco, supposedly the oldest on the island, has been in business since 1960 and is in a vaulted room that was once a warehouse when Centuri thrived on trade. Le Vieux Moulin opens April to October.

Places to Eat

A Macciotta *(☎ 04 95 35 64 12)*, alongside Hôtel-Restaurant du Pêcheur, serves simple but satisfying cuisine. The restaurant offers 90FF and 120FF *menus*, daily specials at 60FF and grilled lobster in season.

The Best Views on Cap Corse

A number of sites offer fine viewing points over Cap Corse. In addition to **Capo Grosso** and the **Moulin Mattei** (see under Barcaggio and Centuri), there is the **Tour de Sénèque**, which dominates the hills above Pino on the western coast of the peninsula and offers views of both coasts.

Half a kilometre from Pino (where Église Santa Maria Assunta houses a 15th-century triptych attributed to the Florentine painter Fra Bartolomeo and classified as a historic monument), follow the D180 for around 6km. Once you reach the Col de Santa Lucia look out for the small road on the right next to the chapel. After 1km this brings you to a cluster of abandoned buildings where you can leave your car. There is a steep 15-minute climb to the tower along a path signposted in red.

Le Snack Cavalu di Mare, across from Agostini (below), sells the usual grab bag of hamburgers, sandwiches, omelettes and salads at modest prices. There is a small eating area outside. ***Mini-Market Agostini*** takes care of self-caterers daily in summer and also sells newspapers. It's close to the Hôtel-Restaurant Le Vieux Moulin.

NONZA

postcode 20217

This village, dating from medieval times, was built at least in part atop a spectacular rocky crag on the summit of which stands a Genoese tower, more than 150m above the shingle beach.

Nonza is particularly noted for its 16th-century **Église Ste-Julie**, whose ochre facade rises right from the edge of the road. Inside, you can admire the Baroque altar in polychrome marble (constructed in Florence in 1693), a painting of St Julie on the cross and painted and sculpted walls and ceiling.

Across the road, narrow, steep streets lead up to the Genoese **tower**. Though built in the 16th century, its moment of glory came in 1768, when it was, besieged by the French, to whom the Genoese had just ceded

Corsica. One lone villager, a certain Jacques Casella, so skilfully managed his firearms that his adversaries mistook him for a few dozen defenders. Eventually Casella surrendered, and the French were flabbergasted. Now the tower serves as a superb vantage point for views over the village, the gulf and the beach below.

Back at Église Ste-Julie, a path descends to the supposedly miraculous **Fontaine Ste-Julie**. A memorial plaque dedicated to Corsica's patron saint on the pediment of the white chapel there recalls that in AD 303:

> St Julie was martyred and crucified for her Christian beliefs. After her death, her breasts were cut off and hurled against the rock, whence this miraculous spring arose.

Below the fountain the path drops sharply down to the **beach**. Be careful: in summer when it is swelteringly hot the climb back up is murderous. You can also get to the beach by car by going north for about 2km to a narrow paved road, which takes you down to the shore in a couple of minutes.

Nonza has a small grocery shop and post office (☎ 04 95 37 82 14). The post office opens 9 am to noon and 2 to 5 pm Monday to Friday and 9 to 11.30 am on Saturday.

Places to Stay & Eat

In the main square ***L'Auberge Patrizi*** *(☎ 04 95 37 82 16, fax 04 95 37 86 40)* rents pleasant doubles, all with bathroom, in various stone buildings around the village for 300/400FF in low/high season, breakfast included. The inn also offers appealing daily specials and *menus* starting at 65FF at midday. Service is under a charming bower.

At ***Le Café de la Tour***, just down from L'Auberge Patrizi, you can have a drink in the shade of the chestnut trees and a statue of Pascal Paoli. A small shop opposite the cafe sells pizza slices and sandwiches. ***L'Auberge du Chat Qui Pêche*** *(☎ 04 95 37 81 52)*, about 10km north of Nonza on the D80, is a pretty stone house with rooms with bathroom for 200FF. The inn offers a 130FF *menu* of Corsican specialities assembled from excellent local products. In high season half-board is mandatory. The view from the terrace can be breathtaking.

The Nebbio

This small region is remarkable for its diversity – from the old Pisan churches to the vineyards of Patrimonio, the Désert des Agriates, the seaside town of St-Florent and one of the most beautiful beaches on the entire island.

St-Florent is served by buses from Bastia and there are numerous options for travel into the Désert des Agriates. A circuit by car will let you see parts of the eastern Nebbio but the area is not served by public transport.

ST-FLORENT (SAN FIURENZU)

postcode 20217 • pop 1450

As you leave the maquis and the mountains of Cap Corse, the landscape becomes more gently undulating and agriculture more a visible presence. St-Florent, 23km across the southern end of the peninsula from Bastia, is both the principal town in the Nebbio region and, thanks to the high quality of its bay, its beach, its marina and its other facilities, a good place to spend a few days and explore around.

History

More would be known about the town's past if the base of the Cathédrale du Nebbio were excavated, for this fine example of religious architecture was built on the site of a still older Roman city. Why the town is called St-Florent depends on whom you talk to: some speak of a St Florent, an African bishop, who was exiled to Corsica by the Vandals in the 15th century; others tell of a Roman soldier who converted to Christianity and paid for his beliefs with martyrdom.

The town flourished during the period of Pisan overlordship, but its strategic position as a safe harbour across the waters from the military port of Toulon made it a pawn in the struggle against the Genoese. After Genoa's conquest of the island, the town was neglected, and little was heard of it until the new harbour and the development of tourism made it popular once again.

Orientation

The main road from Patrimonio skirts the north-easterly side of the town and leads into place des Portes, St-Florent's nerve centre. The narrow streets of the old town stretch westwards. Crossing the River Poggio, the road continues south towards Plage de la Roya, accessible from the beach road on the right just after the bridge over the River Aliso.

Information

Tourist Offices The friendly staff in the tourist office (☎ 04 95 37 06 04) are professional and experienced. The office is in the Centre Administratif (Civic Centre), which also houses the post office and town hall, opposite Hôtel Madame Mère on the main road. The tourist office provides useful information on the town, the Nebbio region and the Désert des Agriates. It opens 9 am to noon and 3 to 6 pm Monday to Friday and also on Saturday morning.

Money Société Générale (☎ 04 95 37 04 35), on the main road, exchanges currency and travellers cheques. An ATM outside accepts Eurocard, MasterCard and Cirrus. The bank opens 9 am to noon and 1.45 to 4.30 pm

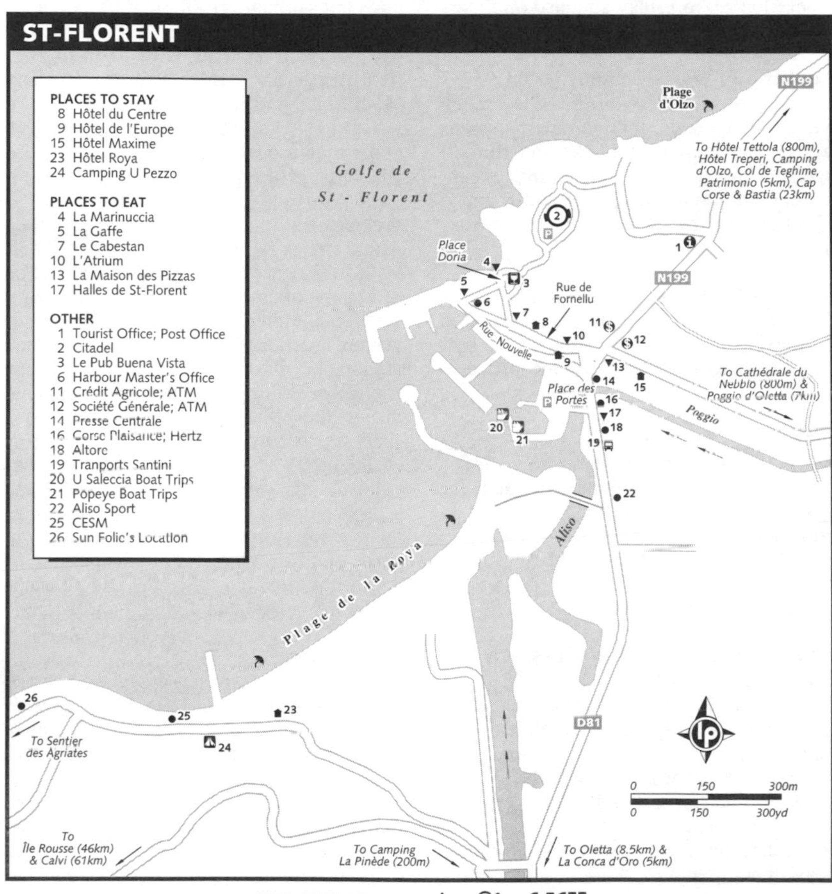

Monday to Friday. Across the road, Crédit Agricole (☎ 04 95 37 40 00) also has an ATM and will exchange currency and travellers cheques. It opens 8.10 to 11.55 am and 1.35 to 4.50 pm Monday to Friday. The post office cashes foreign currency travellers cheques free of charge and those denominated in French francs for a commission of 25FF or 2%, whichever is greater.

Post & Communications The post office (☎ 04 95 37 00 39) is in the Centre Administratif, along with the tourist office and the town hall. It opens 9 am to noon and 2 to 5 pm Monday to Friday and also on Saturday morning.

Bookshops Presse Centrale (☎ 04 95 37 13 79), on place des Portes, sells French and, in high season, foreign newspapers as well as a selection of books and film. It opens 7.30 am to 8.30 pm daily except Sunday afternoon in summer and 8 am to 12.30 pm and 2 to 7 pm daily except Sunday afternoon in the low season.

Medical Services The nearest hospital is 23km away in Bastia. Contact information for the doctor on call in town is posted outside the tourist office when the office is closed.

Citadel

Perched above the harbour, the sandy-coloured citadel built under the Genoese looks strangely like a Moroccan kasbah. Its ramparts no longer stand. It is generally closed to the public but in summer 2000 it was the site of an exhibition of contemporary art for the first time.

Cathédrale du Nebbio (Église Santa Maria Assunta)

Built in the 12th century by the Pisans, this fine example of religious architecture is a reminder that in the 4th century St-Florent became the seat of the bishopric of the Nebbio. It sits about 800m east of the town centre on the site of the ancient Roman city. Reliefs on the facade represent snakes and a strange beast that resembles a lion without quite being a lion. In his *Guide de la Corse Mystérieuse*, Gaston d'Angélis relates that the bishops of Nebbio were entitled by their office to 'carry a sword and to officiate with two pistols on the altar'. Ask at the tourist office if the church is open. If it's not, they'll lend you the keys. Admission is free.

Plage de la Roya

This long ribbon of sand around 2km southwest of the town centre gives you a lovely view over the town and the Nebbio hills. From June to September Sun Folie's Location (☎ 04 95 37 11 51 or 06 09 54 19 39) hires out sailboards (80FF/350FF per hour/day), catamarans (180FF/900FF per hour/day), inflatable boats with 6HP engines (600FF per day), three-seat sea scooters (450FF per half-hour) and any number of water toys. Sun Folie's will also put you under a parasol with two comfortable deck chairs for 150FF per day.

Activities

Altore (☎/fax 04 95 37 19 30 or ☎ 06 83 39 69 06), résidence Ste-Anne, next to Halles de St-Florent, offers courses in canyoning, parapenting, climbing and other fair-weather adventure sports, and also skiing and snowshoe trekking in winter. The operation opens April to October but can be contacted by telephone during the other months. The company's Web site is www.altore.com. Aliso Sport (☎/fax 04 95 37 03 50), a little distance beyond the big Corse Plaisance store (which sells spare parts for boats and fishing equipment among other things), heading south, rents mountain bikes for 100FF per day or 250FF for three days. See the Diving chapter for information on diving in the area.

Boat Trips

In season, two companies organise boat trips to the superb Plage du Loto on the edge of the Désert des Agriates and an easy 30 minutes' walk from the equally superb Plage de Saleccia. The *Popeye II* (☎ 04 95 37 19 07), an old fishing boat recognisable by virtue of the Rolling Stones mouth painted on its prow, leaves the quay three to five times daily in summer. The ride to Plage du Loto

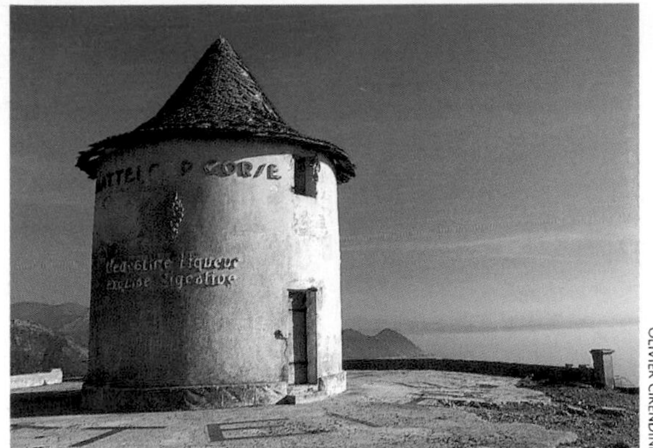

OLIVIER CIRENDINI

The Mattei windmill offers citrus liquor and stunning views.

OLIVIER CIRENDINI

A Centuri sailor looks the part.

OLIVIER CIRENDINI

The Cap Corse hills are dotted with small villages, nestling among the *maquis* and the vines.

OLIVIER CIRENDINI

A Genoese tower near Bastia

OLIVIER CIRENDINI

Centuri's traditional lobster-fishing industry still thrives.

OLIVIER CIRENDINI

Notre Dame de la Serra has superb views.

OLIVIER CIRENDINI

Relaxing in the sun is a primary Calvi concern.

OLIVIER CIRENDINI

More peaceful now – from 1758 to WWI, Île Rousse was a thriving trade centre.

takes around 30 minutes and costs 55FF return (30FF for children). You can hire diving masks, snorkels and parasols (25FF) on board. The launch *U Saleccia* (☎ 04 95 36 90 78) also makes several round trips daily in summer; the fare is identical.

Places to Stay – Budget

On the northern outskirts of the town ***Camping d'Olzo*** *(☎ 04 95 37 03 34)* is a three-star camp site with quiet, shady pitches. You will pay 31/17/10FF per person/tent/car. The camp site opens 1 April to 30 September. ***Camping La Pinède*** *(☎ 04 95 37 07 26)* is a pleasant, shady site, with a swimming pool, on the southern side of town in the direction of Plage de la Roya. Turn off the main road just after the metal bridge, and continue on to the camp site on the banks of the River Aliso. Rates are 26/10/14FF per person/tent/car. ***Camping U Pezzo*** *(☎ 04 95 37 01 65)*, opposite the sailing school right alongside Plage de la Roya, has proper pitches and facilities but it's crowded in summer. Expect to pay 20/12/11/8FF per person/tent/car/motorbike. It opens April to October.

Hôtel du Centre *(☎ 04 95 37 00 68, rue de Fornellu)* a stone's throw from the harbour in the old town, is an inexpensive, and worthy, family hotel. The 10 impeccable rooms with bathroom, TV and telephone cost between 230FF and 350FF for a double, depending on the time of year. The hotel opens year round. ***Hôtel de l'Europe*** *(☎ 04 95 37 00 03, place des Portes)* offers doubles starting at 250FF out of season, 300FF in July and in the 420FF to 450FF range in August. The hotel opens April to September.

Places to Stay – Mid-Range & Top End

Rising above the River Poggio, ***Hôtel Maxime*** *(☎ 04 95 37 05 30, fax 04 95 37 13 07)*, at the beginning of the road leading to the cathedral, has light, comfortable doubles with TV, telephone and mini-bar for 360FF in July, 400FF in August and 280FF in the other months of the year. Parking is available.

Hôtel Treperi *(☎ 04 95 37 40 20, fax 04 95 37 04 61)*, hidden among the vineyards north of the town, has 18 rooms, each with a terrace and a view over the gulf and vineyards, and also a swimming pool and tennis courts. Expect to pay anything from 280FF to 480FF for a double room, depending on the time of year. The owners have produced a leaflet with a dozen or so ideas for walks in the area. Meals in the hotel's restaurant cost 100FF or so. As you head out of town, look for the sign just after the Elf garage on the right. ***Hôtel Tettola*** *(☎ 04 95 37 08 53, fax 04 95 37 09 19)*, also on the northern outskirts of town, stands close by the beach and has a swimming pool as well. Doubles start at 450FF out of season and 580FF in summer; the more popular rooms overlooking the sea are more expensive. The hotel has a warm and friendly atmosphere. It closes in November, January and February.

Hôtel Roya *(☎ 04 95 37 00 40, fax 04 95 37 11 29, Plage de la Roya)* has an appealing ochre facade and private access to a pretty corner of the beach. As a member of the British Mark Warner hotel group, it has also been a favourite haunt of Anglo-Saxons with English more the working language than French. Things may alter, however, with the imminent change in management.

Places to Eat

Budget At ***La Maison des Pizzas*** *(☎ 04 95 37 08 52)*, on the main roundabout, wood-fire pizzas start at 42FF. In July and August, you'll get service until 11 pm or midnight. Those who want to shop for their food can head for the ***Halles de St-Florent*** supermarket just south of the River Poggio. It opens daily except Sunday afternoon.

Mid-Range & Top End In the heart of the old town, ***Le Cabestan*** *(☎ 04 95 37 05 70, rue de Fornellu)* offers an excellent 99FF *menu*. Wines start at 80FF. The restaurant opens daily for lunch and dinner from around Easter to mid-November.

La Gaffe *(☎ 04 95 37 00 12)*, on the harbour, is a good seafood restaurant that serves a tasty seafood tagliatelle (51FF), an excellent monkfish stew over tagliatelle (105FF) and a 130FF *menu*. The Patrimonio wines are priced reasonably. The restaurant opens daily except Tuesday.

L'Atrium *(☎/fax 04 95 37 06 09)*, in a corner of the main square, has customers who come only for the bouillabaisse-style braised shellfish and rockfish in pastry crust for 130FF. The restaurant opens daily in season but only Friday to Sunday in winter.

La Marinuccia *(☎ 04 95 37 04 36, place Doria)*, on a terrace by the water, invites you to enjoy the pleasure of a glorious sunset over dinner. There is a 105FF *menu*. The restaurant opens daily in season.

Entertainment

La Conca d'Oro *(☎ 04 95 39 00 46)* disco opens in summer, and is 5km from town on the road to Oletta. ***Le Pub Buena Vista*** *(☎ 04 95 37 10 83, place Doria)*, a musical sort of bar, gets going at around 10 pm also just in summer.

There are open-air screenings of films in July and August, details of which are available at the tourist office.

Getting There & Away

Bus Transports Santini (☎ 04 95 37 02 98), just after the bridge over the Poggio on the main road, runs a bus service (30FF) from St-Florent to Bastia. Buses usually leave twice daily except on Sunday and public holidays.

Car The small Hertz agency (☎ 04 95 37 16 19) opens during the summer season in a corner of Corse Plaisance just south of the River Poggio.

Boat The harbour master's office (☎ 04 95 37 00 79, fax 04 95 37 11 37) is next to Église Ste-Anne. The marina itself, large and attractive, reserves around 120 berths for visitors. Expect to pay from 88FF to 151FF to moor a 9m boat, depending on the time of year. Showers (15FF), chandlery supplies, water, fuel and weather reports are all available.

Getting Around

You can get around the town on foot but transport is useful if you want to go to the beach. Corse Plaisance (☎ 04 95 37 00 58) rents motorbikes for 300FF per day. It opens 9 am to noon and 3 to 7.30 pm Monday to Saturday.

PATRIMONIO

postcode 20253 • pop 650

The tall 16th-century Église St-Martin, with its half-moon pediment and stone scrolls, overlooks this peaceful little village 6km outside St-Florent in the direction of Cap Corse. Most visitors come for the wine, primarily muscat, and the area as a whole was the first in Corsica to be granted an *appellation d'origine contrôlée* (AOC) seal. Around 600 hectares are cultivated hereabouts by some 35 growers, and many of them invite visitors in for tastings. If you have a car, a tour of the vineyards is a must.

As you leave St-Florent and head for Cap Corse you'll come to the locally renowned **Domaine Gentile** on your left (☎ 04 95 37 01 54). A few kilometres farther along on the right is the white headquarters building of **Domaine Orenga de Gaffori** (☎ 04 95 37 45 00). The estate's Cuvée du Gouverneur (55FF) is one of the best red wines produced on the island. You can taste and buy it in season. Once you get to the village (signposted to the right at the roundabout), stop off at **Clos Marfisi** (☎ 04 95 37 01 16), where tastings are held daily in the summer months and by appointment the rest of the year. **Clos de Bernardi** (☎ 04 95 37 01 09), above the road to the church, offers tasting tours for small groups in a lovely stone house. The congenial M de Bernardi produces a good red wine, and so does the **Domaine Leccia** (☎ 04 95 37 11 35). As you leave the village, pause to visit **Domaine Lazzarini** (☎ 04 95 37 13 17), which in summer even receives coach parties. In addition to an excellent muscat, you can sample and/or purchase orange and peach wines and table wines.

With one or two exceptions, the wines in the Patrimonio area are not aged, nor are they meant to be. But this may change.

COL DE TEGHIME

High up on the island's raised backbone, Col de Teghime (536m), midway between Bastia and St-Florent, offers breathtaking views in two directions. To the east you can see to Bastia and the Étang de Biguglia and, on clear days, as far as the island of Elba.

To the west you can make out the Patrimonio vineyards, the Golfe de St-Florent and the Désert des Agriates.

From Bastia town centre follow the signs towards Calvi and then towards St-Florent. Just before you get to the pass, you'll see a large open-air rubbish tip that attracts seagulls and birds of prey. It's about 10km from Bastia.

From the pass itself, you can get to the summit of the **Sierra di Pigno** (961m) on a narrow paved road (bear right as you come from Bastia). The 4.5km climb, very pleasant on foot, will afford you a yet more magnificent view to east and west and also over Cap Corse. The windy summit itself is somewhat disfigured by radio masts and a small military area.

DÉFILÉ DE LANCONE

The Défilé de Lancone in the Massif du Monte Pinzali was sculpted by the River Bevincu, which becomes a torrent here before flowing downhill into the Étang de Biguglia. From the Col de Santu Stefanu roundabout two roads overhang the narrow gorges: the D82 joins the N193 at Ortale, while the more spectacular D62 goes to Casatorra. The D62 is narrow, however, and becomes difficult if traffic is heavy.

Oletta & Poggio d'Oletta

postcode 20232 • pop 900 & 150

The villages Oletta and Poggio d'Oletta cling to the hillside between St-Florent and Bastia to the south of Col de Teghime, and the road that joins them offers another superb view over the Golfe de St-Florent.

In summer, a stroll through the narrow streets of Oletta will take you to the workshops and cellars of local artisans.

In Poggio d'Oletta two small churches in a superb location below the town hall merit at least a passing glance. Of the two, the Église de San Cervone is the better restored, and opens to the public. If it's not open, ask at the town hall for the key. The choir dates from 1145 but the largest part of the building as we see it today dates from the 18th century. The clock tower was added in the 19th century.

Places to Stay & Eat At the northern entrance to Oletta ***L'Auberge A Magina*** *(☎ 04 95 39 01 01)* serves the best food in either village and the view from the dining room is spectacularly panoramic. *Menus* are 115FF and 150FF. A la carte, duck in maquis honey for 90FF is outstanding. L'Auberge A Magina also rents rooms in a pretty stone house that overlooks the road. Expect to pay 220FF for a room with a bathroom and small garden. In July and August half-board will be urged on you, but it is not compulsory. It opens Tuesday to Sunday April to October.

At ***Bar-Restaurant U Lampione*** *(☎ 04 95 39 02 97)*, near the church in the centre of Oletta, service is at tables under trees. From 15 August (when the wild-boar season opens) hunters come here on Sunday for an aperitif and to compare their trophies.

There is a small ***grocery shop*** near the Église d'Oletta and a ***mini-market*** at the southern end of the village as you head towards Olmeta di Tudda.

Murato

postcode 20239 • pop 560

Murato is a large village with pretty houses and an unusual church, south of Oletta. During Corsica's brief independence in the 18th century, Murato was the seat of the mint in which the coins of the new state were struck. The village is also the birthplace of Giuseppe Fieschi and of the father of Raúl Leoni (see the boxed text 'The President & the Terrorist' on the next page). There are a few bar-restaurants and a disco.

Église de San Michele de Murato The green and white Romanesque Église de San Michele de Murato rises out of a meadow surrounded by rocky crags above the tranquil Vallée de St-Florent and the Désert des Agriates. The white (chalk) came from St-Florent and the green (ophite) was taken from the bed of the nearby River Bevincu. The colours are laid out first in horizontal stripes, then in an irregular patchwork. Local legend has it that the church was built in a hurry in just one night. What is certain is that it dates from around 1140. It was restored in the Baroque style and visited by the French author Prosper Mérimée, who wrote about and sketched it, during his sojourn in Corsica as inspector of historical monuments. To see the frescoes inside get the key from Murato village hall.

Around Murato

After visiting the Église de San Michele, it's possible to get back to St-Florent via the villages of Rapale, San Gavino di Tenda and Santo Pietro di Tenda. Rapale is a charming village with several cafes. You can also walk from here to the ruins of a church that resembles the Église de San Michele de Murato in its patterning of colours. The path is signposted from behind the cemetery a short distance beyond the Rapale church.

Corsican Buffalo (☎ 04 95 37 61 78), a horse-riding centre, is 6km south of Murato in the direction of Corte.

The President & the Terrorist

At the age of 58 Raúl Leoni was voted president of Venezuela in the December 1963 elections. His Murato-born father Clément Leoni had left Bastia for Caracas at the age of 22 to try his luck in the South American republic about a decade before the future president was born there. Raúl Leoni made his first and only visit to Corsica in 1970, but father and son are both now heralded as symbols of successful Corsican migration. Leoni's opponent in the 1963 election, Arturo Uslar Pietri, a distinguished man of letters, was also, interestingly, of Corsican descent.

Born in Murato in 1790, Giuseppe Fieschi was yet another kind of emigre. A sometime shepherd, sometime solider, he organised an attempt on the life of the Orleanist citizen king of France, Louis-Philippe, and the royal family during the fifth-anniversary celebration of the July 1830 revolution that overthrew the last Bourbon monarch, held in Paris. The daring assassination attempt failed but 19 people were killed and many more injured. Fieschi and his accomplices were condemned to death and they were executed a year later. Fieschi is better remembered in Murato than Raúl Leoni is.

DÉSERT DES AGRIATES

Between St-Florent and the mouth of the Ostriconi lie 30km of arid landscape known as the Désert des Agriates, with its low chalky mountains and a maquis so sun-scorched that even the plants seem rocklike. It's hard to believe this area was once used to grow food for Genoa. Yet, until the 20th century, life in the area was governed alternately by seasonal livestock grazing and sowing. In October shepherds from the Nebbio highlands and the Vallée d'Asco would bring their goats and sheep down for the winter. In June farmers arriving by boat from Cap Corse would take over the area. The region was even famous for its olive groves. *Écobuage* (cultivation on burnt stubble) and fires fanned by the prevailing winds are mainly to blame for transforming the fertile soil into a stony desert.

The Agriate coast, by contrast, has boasted a radiant appearance since time immemorial. Its highlight is undoubtedly the outstanding **Plage de Saleccia**, which stretches for nearly 1km and ranks with the best of what any tropical island can offer. The smaller but equally stunning **Plage du Loto** and **Plage de l'Ostriconi**, at the western end of the Agriates, are also superb. Some partisans claim that the latter has the finest sand in all of Europe.

Almost 5000 hectares (bought by the Conservatoire du Littoral), together with the adjoining common land, make up the protected natural site of the Désert des Agriates, managed by the Syndicat Mixte Agriate (Joint Agriate Association; ☎ 04 95 37 09 86). The entity is in the hamlet of Casta, 700m beyond the sign announcing the place as you arrive from St-Florent. Its job is to protect this area of outstanding interest and beauty, including bird, butterfly and plant species, and the staff also gladly propose walks to visitors. The office opens 9 am to noon and 2 to 6 pm Monday to Friday.

Off-road motor vehicles, fires and camping are prohibited in the Agriates as is, of course, the dumping of rubbish.

Exploring the Désert des Agriates

Boat The easiest and probably the most pleasant way of getting to the Agriates is by boat. See Boat Trips under St-Florent.

Car Two roads descend into the Agriates from the D81. Both are around 12km long. The first starts in the village of Casta, the second from Col de Vezzu, 10km from Casta in the direction of Île Rousse. Don't be taken in by the little bit of tarmac starting at Col de Vezzu – it doesn't last long. The roads are both rough and stony, and they're worse when rain has dug deep ruts in the ground and the ruts have then been baked hard by the sun. In summer, plenty of people try it by car, but the option is really not to be tested unless you have four-wheel drive.

Walking There's a coastal path into the Agriates from St-Florent (Plage de la Roya), and you can walk to Plage de l'Ostriconi at the other end of the Agriates in three days. The walk is divided into three stages: St-Florent to Saleccia (around 5½ hours); Saleccia to Ghignu (around 2¾ hours); and Ghignu to Ostriconi (around 6½ hours). The route is passable year round and not very hard-going but you should take plenty of water with you.

The extremely difficult walk to Saleccia from Casta is not to be undertaken in summer. The walk between the two beaches of Loto and Saleccia is described in the Walking chapter.

Cycling This is certainly one of the sportier ways of getting in to the Agriates. The sandy coastal path (see Walking earlier) won't give you adequate traction, but the 12km-long track from the village of Casta will. The track from Casta will also give you the chance to explore the interior of the Désert des Agriates. The negatives are that the hard, stony ground makes the descent extremely bumpy, hence quite difficult for novices, and the expression 'blazing sun' takes on brutal meaning here in summer.

If you remain undeterred, be sure, no matter what, to have plenty of water, a hat, sun cream and time. You might also consider attempting the descent early in the morning so that you get to spend the hottest part of the day at the beach rather than on the road. The dusty track, however, does take you through breathtaking scenery, and the maquis here is fragrant. A last warning: allow 1½ to two hours for the difficult climb back up to Casta and expect to get off the bike and push it for much of the way.

You can hire mountain bikes from Relais de Saleccia (☎ 04 95 37 14 60) in Casta, about 100m before the track. Expect to pay 90FF per day; the price includes the loan of an instant puncture sealant. It opens April to October. It's also possible to hire mountain bikes in Île Rousse and St Florent. See under Activities in the appropriate chapters.

Horse Riding Arbo Valley (☎ 04 95 60 49 49) organises half-day rides around the Agriates for 300FF, including a meal, as well as trips lasting several days to other, more distant corners of the island. The centre is approved by the Association Nationale du Tourisme Équestre (National Association of Equestrian Tourism; see under Activities in the Facts for the Visitor chapter). It is signposted on a bend 4km from Île Rousse on the D81: follow the rough track for 800m to the pretty valley in which it is located. In summer the centre also runs a remote station at Village de l'Ostriconi (see under Places to Stay & Eat later in this section).

Sea Sun Folie's Location (see Plage de la Roya under St-Florent earlier) organises outings on three-seat sea scooters along the

Posidonia Oceanica

The long brownish leaves that often carpet Corsica's sandy beaches (and upset some swimmers) are one of the most important elements of the Mediterranean marine ecosystem. Often mistaken for seaweed, they are part of the aquatic plant *Posidonia oceanica* – Poseidonion in English – that grows as far down under the surface as 35m. The underwater meadows of it produce oxygen and hence serve as a breeding ground as well as a source of food for small marine fauna. At the same time, they cushion the effect of the waves and thereby help to protect the sandy beaches. In Corsica, *Posidonia oceanica* is a protected species.

Agriates seashore. Objectif Nature provides information on sea-kayaking (see Activities under Bastia).

Places to Stay & Eat

Relais de Saleccia *(☎ 04 95 37 14 60)* in Casta has 12 lovely double rooms for 250FF to 320FF depending on the season, and for 30FF extra you can get a private terrace with an unobstructed view over the Agriates. The hotel's restaurant serves a good-value Corsican *menu* at 80FF but also sandwiches, salads, grilled meats and cannelloni with brocciu (48FF). It opens April to September.

Camping U Paradiso *(☎ 04 95 37 82 51)* is at the end of the track from Casta to Plage de Saleccia, 12km from the D81. This worthy camp site charging 20/15/10/5FF per person/tent/car/motorbike has a small grocery store, public telephones, a bar, a billiard table and a children's play area. The site, around 100m from Plage de Saleccia, also has a few pretty stone bungalows for 250FF per person at half-board. These are often booked up well in advance. The restaurant opens June to September and the 90FF dinner *menu* changes daily. At lunchtime you can order salad or a daily special.

Ferme-Auberge de Pietra Monetta *(☎ 04 95 60 24 88)* is on the D81 from St-Florent towards Île Rousse, not far from River Ostriconi. This lovely stone building has four rustic double rooms with bathroom (but shared toilet) for 300FF, including breakfast. There is a 120FF *menu* at the restaurant. Half-board, mandatory in July and August, costs 250FF per person.

Village de l'Ostriconi *(☎ 04 95 60 10 05, fax 04 95 60 01 47)*, on the D81 close to Plage de l'Ostriconi, has camping facilities for 36/18/15/15FF per adult/child/tent/car, a swimming pool, a grocery store and tennis courts. Double rooms are available for 180FF and 275FF, and functional bungalows with kitchenette for four to five people go for 230FF to 410FF depending on the time of year.

Calvi & the Balagne

The Balagne is a secluded territory in the north-west of Corsica with the Désert des Agriates to the north-east and the foothills of Monte Cinto to the south and south-east. It is one of the island's largest micro-regions (sometimes called the 'orchard of Corsica') and its landscape has a gentleness that distinguishes it from the turbulence of so much of the island's other topography. Its success may be ascribed to the fertile soil that supports citrus-fruit plantations and olive groves, to its strategically positioned ports and its proximity to mainland France. The Balagne was also one of the first regions on the island to open up to tourism. Calvi in particular has attracted numbers of holiday-makers since between the two world wars. Ferries from mainland Europe to both Calvi and Île Rousse as well as air service into Calvi-Ste-Catherine airport have kept the area popular and even fashionable.

Highlights

- Ride the Tramways de Balagne train along the beautiful coastline between Calvi and Île Rousse
- Wander through the Forêt de Bonifatu and breathe the pure air as you watch the sun set over the cirque
- Feast your eyes on the endless groves of olive trees on Balagne hillsides

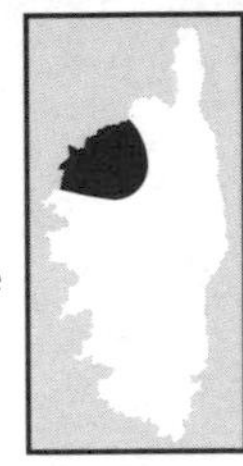

The Coast

CALVI

postcode 20260 • pop 4900

Calvi, the 'capital' of the Balagne, is a thriving little town that stretches lazily along its bay under the watchful eye of two giants: the citadel and Monte Cinto (2706m). It is the island town closest to the Mediterranean coast of metropolitan France, and in many respects it resembles any number of the smaller towns along the French Riviera itself. Calvi, accordingly, has attracted more holiday-makers than any Corsican destination other than Porto Vecchio and the Ajaccio area, and some visitors will perhaps turn up their noses at what they take to be another tacky holiday town in the making. Others, of course, will see the same evidence only as a liveliness that they miss in other corners of the island. You will have to decide for yourself if this is your place – or a place to be avoided.

History

It was in the 1st century AD that the Romans laid the foundations of the town of Calvi, although the Golfe de Calvi has been a port of call for sailors since even earlier. Later laid to ruin by Saracen raiders, Calvi got back on its feet under the Pisans between the 11th and the 13th centuries. Rivalries between local lords, especially those from Cap Corse, led the population finally to turn to Genoa for protection in 1278. The then powerful republic on the Italian mainland could not have asked for better luck and wasted no time in turning the inhabitants of Calvi into good Genoese citizens. Using Calvi as a base, along with the southern town of Bonifacio (which it already controlled) it was able to exert its power over the rest of the island.

Calvi came to be so utterly identified with its loyalty to Genoa that many other Corsican communities considered Calvi, rather than Genoa, the oppressor. The finger is in fact still sometimes pointed at Calvi, even today. In any event, under Genoese influence, Calvi built its citadel and fortified itself, and in due course Genoa began to use the Banco di San Giorgio (a financial institution that administered the island) to make Calvi's fortune. Over the centuries of Genoese overlordship, Calvi was nevertheless twice put sorely to the test.

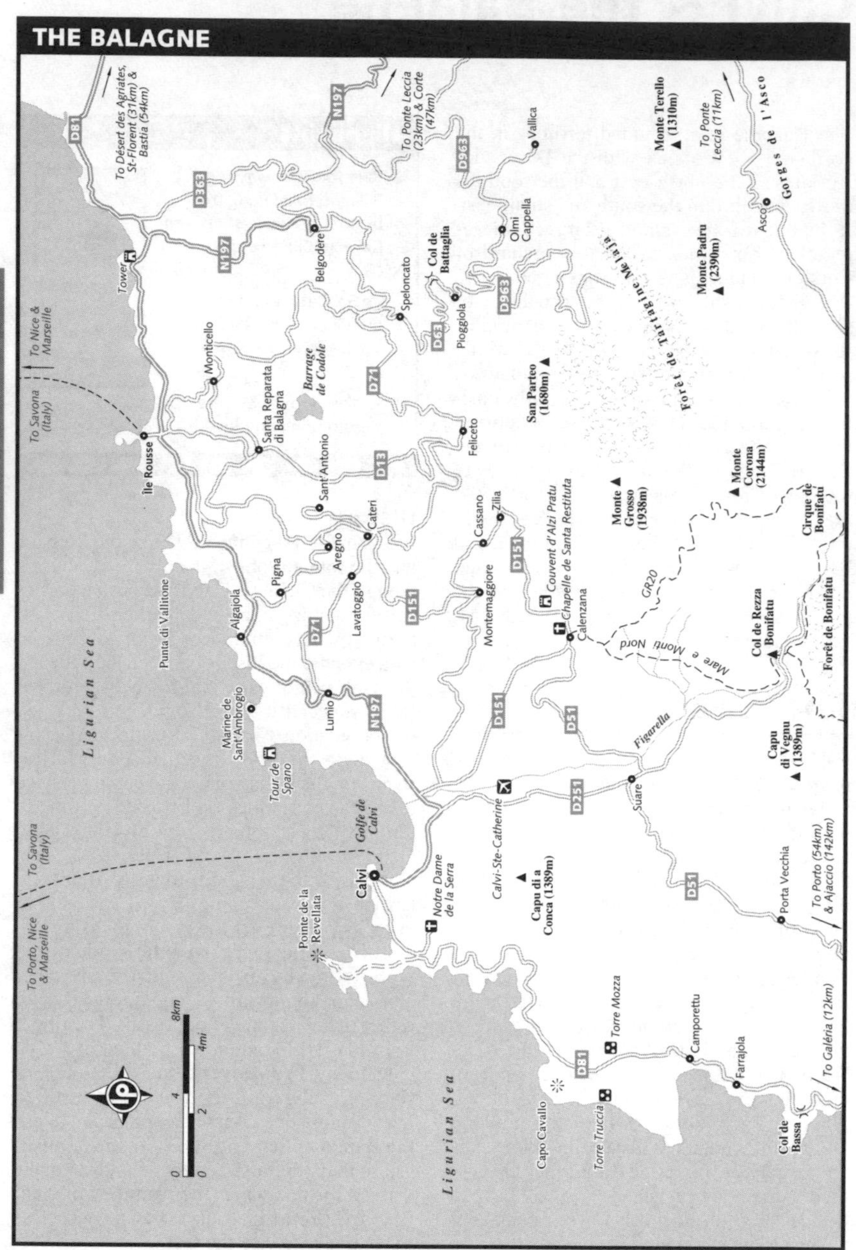
THE BALAGNE
To Désert des Agriates, St-Florent (31km) & Bastia (54km)
To Ponte Leccia (23km) & Corte (47km)
To Ponte Leccia (11km)
To Nice & Marseille
To Savona (Italy)
To Porto, Nice & Marseille
To Porto (54km) & Ajaccio (142km)
To Galéria (12km)
Ligurian Sea
Ligurian Sea
D81
N197
D363
D963
D63
D71
D13
D151
D51
D251
Tower
Belgodère
Vallica
Olmi Cappella
Col de Battaglia
Speloncato
Pioggiola
Monticello
Barrage de Codole
Santa Reparata di Balagna
Île Rousse
Sant'Antonio
Feliceto
San Parteo (1680m)
Forêt de Tartagine Melaja
Monte Padru (2390m)
Monte Terello (1310m)
Asco
Gorges de l'Asco
Monte Grosso (1938m)
Monte Corona (2144m)
Cirque de Bonifatu
Zilia
Cassano
Cateri
Aregno
Pigna
Lavatoggio
Montemaggiore
Couvent d'Alzi Pratu
Chapelle de Santa Restituta
Calenzana
GR20
Mare e Monti Nord
Col de Rezza Bonifatu
Forêt de Bonifatu
Punta di Vallitone
Algajola
Lumio
Marine de Sant'Ambrogio
Tour de Spano
Figarella
Suare
Capu di Vegnu (1389m)
Golfe de Calvi
Calvi
Calvi-Ste-Catherine
Capu di a Conca (1389m)
Notre Dame de la Serra
Pointe de la Revellata
Porta Vecchia
Torre Mozza
Camporettu
Farrajola
Capo Cavallo
Torre Truccia
Col de Bassa
0 4 8km
0 2 4mi

In the mid-16th century Corsica got caught up in the rivalry between Henri II of France and Charles V of Spain (king of Spain and also Holy Roman Emperor). In 1553 France dispatched a squadron made up of French troops, supporters of Sampiero Corso (see the boxed text 'Sampiero Corso the Fiery' in the Facts about Corsica chapter) and Turkish forces under the command of the Turkish privateer Dragut. This fleet captured Bastia, St-Florent and Bonifacio but failed to take Calvi. It was on this occasion that Genoa gave the town its motto in recognition: *Civitas Calvi Semper Fidelis* (ever-faithful city of Calvi).

The second episode was less glorious for Calvi. In 1794 the town, which Genoa had ceded to France in 1764, came under attack from the British army and separatist forces led by Pascal Paoli. It was heavily bombarded and largely destroyed during the fighting, which also cost Admiral Nelson his right eye. Calvi eventually capitulated. The Anglo-Corsican kingdom was short-lived, however, and Calvi returned to French control in 1796.

Orientation

The citadel – also known as the upper town *(haute ville)* – is built on a promontory to the north-east of the lower town *(basse ville)*. Most activity is centred around quai Landry (along the marina), ave de la République, blvd Wilson and, to a lesser extent, ave Christophe Colomb. A section of the lower town to the east of blvd Wilson is pedestrianised. There's a long beach stretching out to the south-east of the marina.

Information

Tourist Offices The tourist office (☎ 04 95 65 16 67, fax 04 95 65 14 09) is in the marina, above the harbour master's office *(capitainerie)*. It can provide you with a variety of brochures and information about the town (and also the leaflet concerning the Balagne Craft Road, see the boxed text of that name later). The office opens 9 am to 8 pm daily in July and August; 9 am to 7 pm daily, June and September; and 9 am to noon and 1.30 to 5.30 pm Monday to Friday, the rest of the year. The staff speak English, Italian and German as well as French.

Money There's a branch of Société Générale (☎ 04 95 65 05 38) on blvd Wilson, right by the post office; it changes money 8.30 to 11.30 am and 2 to 4.30 pm. Eurocheques are not accepted. Crédit Agricole (☎ 04 95 65 90 20), 8 ave de la République, opposite the *sous-préfecture* (local government office), has an ATM. The bank opens 8.15 to 11.50 am and 2 to 5 pm Monday to Wednesday, to 4.50 pm Thursdays and Fridays. There's also an ATM at the post office.

Post & Communications The post office (☎ 04 95 65 00 40) on blvd Wilson opens 8.30 am to 5.30 pm (longer during July and August) Monday to Friday and Saturday morning. Poste restante mail should be addressed to Bureau de Poste de Calvi, blvd Wilson, 20260 Calvi, Corsica. Café de l'Orient (☎ 04 95 65 17 43), on the harbour, will give you an Internet connection for 10FF plus 0.70FF per minute.

Bookshops Press'Infos (☎ 04 95 65 17 43), ave de la République, has a large range of French and foreign newspapers and magazines. It opens 7 am to 10 pm (sometimes later) daily, in summer; 7.30 am to 12.30 pm and 2 to 7.30 pm, the rest of the year.

Originally just a record shop, Black 'n' Blue (☎ 04 95 65 25 82), 20 blvd Wilson, now also sells a choice of foreign-language books, some a cut above the usual offerings. It opens 9 am to noon and 2.30 to 5 pm Monday to Saturday, year round; and also Sunday morning in summer.

Laundry There is a laundrette in the car park of the Super U supermarket on ave Christophe Colomb. It opens 8 am to 10 pm and a load costs 34FF plus 25FF for 30 minutes of drying.

Medical Services Although there is no hospital in Calvi, there is an emergency medical centre (☎ 04 95 65 11 22, fax 04 95 65 10 15) in route du Stade, off route de Santore, a few minutes walk below the town centre. It's attached to the hospital in Bastia and opens 24 hours. The centre only handles emergencies, but the staff will be

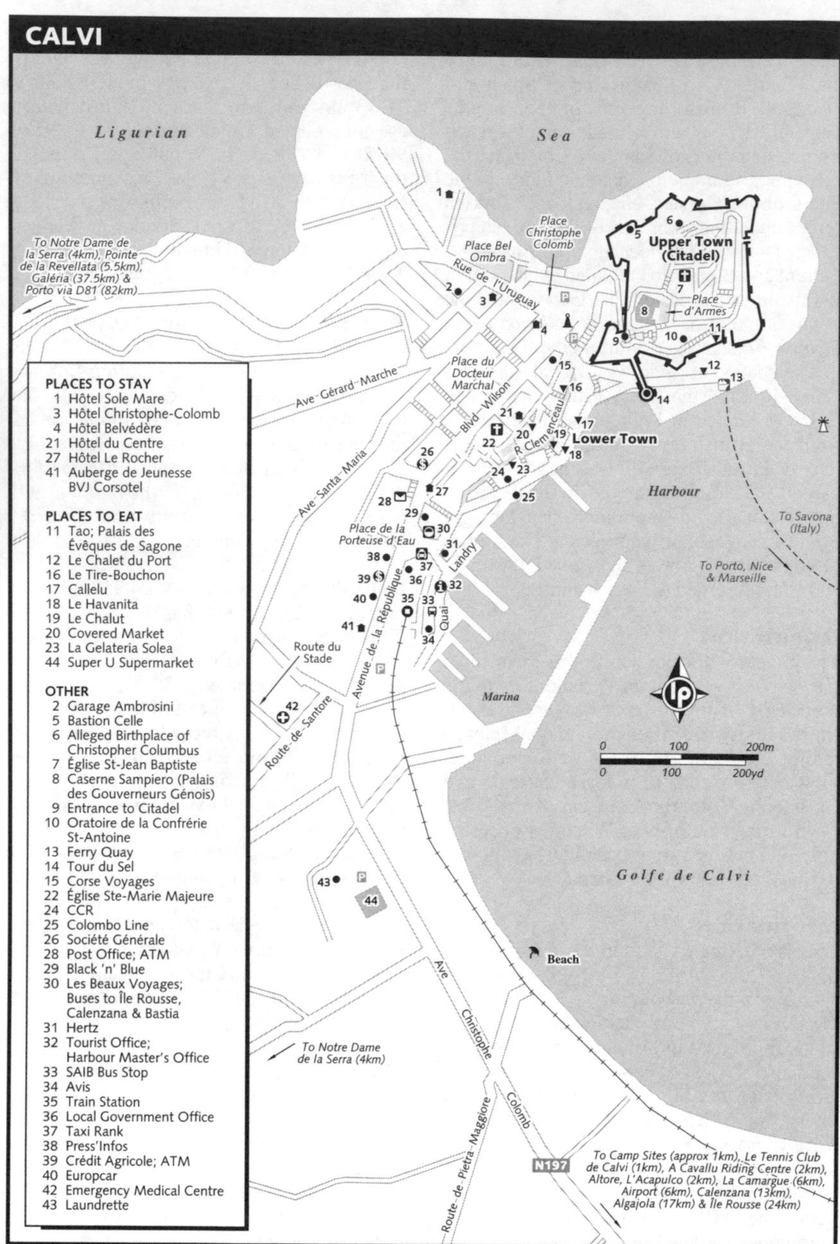

CALVI
Ligurian
Sea
To Notre Dame de la Serra (4km), Pointe de la Revellata (5.5km), Galéria (37.5km) & Porto via D81 (82km)
Place Christophe Colomb
Place Bel Ombra
Rue de l'Uruguay
Upper Town (Citadel)
Place d'Armes
Ave Gérard Marche
Place du Docteur Marchal
Blvd Wilson
R Clemenceau
Lower Town
Harbour
Ave Santa Maria
Place de la Porteuse d'Eau
Landry
Quai
Avenue de la République
Route du Stade
Route de Santore
Marina
To Savona (Italy)
To Porto, Nice & Marseille
Golfe de Calvi
Beach
To Notre Dame de la Serra (4km)
Ave Christophe Colomb
Route de Pietra Maggiore
N197
To Camp Sites (approx 1km), Le Tennis Club de Calvi (1km), A Cavallu Riding Centre (2km), Altore, L'Acapulco (2km), La Camargue (6km), Airport (6km), Calenzana (13km), Algajola (17km) & Île Rousse (24km)
0 100 200m
0 100 200yd
PLACES TO STAY
1 Hôtel Sole Mare
3 Hôtel Christophe-Colomb
4 Hôtel Belvédère
21 Hôtel du Centre
27 Hôtel Le Rocher
41 Auberge de Jeunesse BVJ Corsotel
PLACES TO EAT
11 Tao; Palais des Évêques de Sagone
12 Le Chalet du Port
16 Le Tire-Bouchon
17 Callelu
18 Le Havanita
19 Le Chalut
20 Covered Market
23 La Gelateria Solea
44 Super U Supermarket
OTHER
2 Garage Ambrosini
5 Bastion Celle
6 Alleged Birthplace of Christopher Columbus
7 Église St-Jean Baptiste
8 Caserne Sampiero (Palais des Gouverneurs Génois)
9 Entrance to Citadel
10 Oratoire de la Confrérie St-Antoine
13 Ferry Quay
14 Tour du Sel
15 Corse Voyages
22 Église Ste-Marie Majeure
24 CCR
25 Colombo Line
26 Société Générale
28 Post Office; ATM
29 Black 'n' Blue
30 Les Beaux Voyages; Buses to Île Rousse, Calenzana & Bastia
31 Hertz
32 Tourist Office; Harbour Master's Office
33 SAIB Bus Stop
34 Avis
35 Train Station
36 Local Government Office
37 Taxi Rank
38 Press'Infos
39 Crédit Agricole; ATM
40 Europcar
42 Emergency Medical Centre
43 Laundrette

able to put you in touch with the town's GPs and specialist doctors if necessary.

Citadel

Built at the end of the 15th century by the Genoese, Calvi's citadel still towers over the town from atop its rocky promontory. A handful of cafes and restaurants set out tables in the shadow of its ochre walls. Unlike its Bonifacio counterpart, it is not an integral part of the town, and the majority of its buildings are closed to the public. Still, the citadel is definitely worth a visit for its remarkably peaceful atmosphere, its interesting religious edifices and the spectacular view it offers over the Golfe de Calvi.

Crossing place Christophe Colomb, you reach the citadel through a porch over which the town motto is inscribed. Little alleyways then lead to the place d'Armes, with the former **Palais des Gouverneurs Génois** (Genoese Governors' Palace) on the left. This imposing building, which has been renamed Caserne Sampiero, was built by the Genoese in the 13th century and extended by the Banco di San Giorgio. It now houses a French Foreign Legion officers' mess.

The **Église St-Jean Baptiste** is on the other side of the place d'Armes, halfway up a little alley. Built in the shape of a cross, this 13th-century church narrowly escaped complete destruction when an adjacent powder store exploded in 1567. It was rebuilt three years later and consecrated as a cathedral in 1576. The dome is superb and the interior boasts a high altar of polychrome marble dating from the 17th century, to the right of which is the *Christ des Miracles*. This ebony statue has been venerated since the town was besieged in 1553. According to legend, the ships of the besieging forces simply sailed back out to sea after the population of Calvi carried the statue in a procession through their streets. The *Vierge du Rosaire* (Virgin of the Rosary), a large statue also in this church, has three different robes: a black one for Good Friday, a purple one for the Wednesday after Palm Sunday and a rich brocade one for use in processions. She was supposedly donated to the city by a Calvian who brought her back from Peru but others maintain that she is Spanish in origin. She is dressed, unsurprisingly, only by women.

If you retrace your steps to the place d'Armes and take a little street to the left, you will come to the **Oratoire de la Confrérie St-Antoine** (Oratory of the St Antoine Brotherhood), a charitable institution that has been active in Corsica since the 14th century. Behind the ornate facade of the building, which features a slate lintel depicting the abbot St Antoine, are walls covered in frescoes from the 15th and 16th centuries (some badly timeworn, unfortunately) and an ivory Christ attributed to the Florentine sculptor Jacopo d'Antonio Tati, known as 'Le Sansevino'.

You can also have a look at the **Palais des Évêques de Sagone**, the former palace of the bishops of Sagone, which now houses the Tao restaurant and piano bar (see Places to Eat and Entertainment later in this section).

The citadel has five **bastions**, erected one after another and now providing wonderful views. To the north-west is the Bastion Celle, flanked by a stone sentry box suspended over the ramparts to keep an eye on the surroundings. Nearby is a plaque marking the alleged birthplace of Christopher Columbus (see the boxed text 'A Calvian Called Columbus?' on the next page). It's also worth seeing the **Tour du Sel** (salt tower), a pretty round tower on quai Landry (outside the ramparts) once used to store the town's salt.

The tourist office rents audio guides for self-guided tours of the citadel for 35FF. Guided tours are available for groups of at least 11 people at 25FF per person but must be booked in advance.

The best picture-postcard views of the citadel are from the marina's eastern sea wall, from the beach and also, particularly at sunset, from the little promontory at the end of the first street to the right after place Bel Ombra, beyond the Hôtel Sole Mare.

Église Ste-Marie Majeure

Behind the pink exterior of the Baroque church of St Mary the Elder (Santa Maria Maggiore in Corsican), at the heart of the lower town, is an impressive domed ceiling. Built between 1765 and 1838, in testimony, as it were, to the growth of the lower town,

A Calvian Called Columbus?

An ancient house in the Calvi citadel bears a plaque attesting to the birth therein of the obsessed explorer credited with the discovery of the New World. A little 72-page book, *Christophe Colomb, Corse*, written by Joseph Chiara and available for a pittance in the Calvi tourist office and also many shops (but only in French, regrettably), makes the case for Columbus' Calvian birth.

Roger Caratini, however, in his masterly *Histoire du Peuple Corse* (1995) mocks the Corsican 'amateur historians' who have made 'dogma' of Columbus' Calvian origins. All serious scholars and documents agree, Caratini asserts, Columbus was the son of a Genoese weaver; the person first to argue the case for Columbus' birth in Calvi, in the mid-19th century, was a 'credulous churchman'.

But Chiara believes that Columbus' birth in Genoa (distinct from his undisputed Genoese 'citizenship') will itself never be more than a hypothesis. He suggests that when Columbus went looking for underwriting at the Spanish court, he could not very well admit to being of Calvian origin because the Calvians had massacred a Spanish garrison, thus putting an end to Spanish ambitions in Corsica, in 1521. Chiara's arguments, supported by reference to Columbus' name and own recorded use of language, have irresistible romantic appeal.

Moreover, there's actually something at stake for Corsica in the dispute. If Corsica gave the world Napoleon but not Columbus, well, maybe it was just chance. If Corsica gave the world both Napoleon *and* Columbus, then there begins to be a pattern, which could be seen to indicate an inherent Corsican desire to dream more boldly and travel farther than other ethnic groups. It remains true that wherever Columbus himself was born, numerous Calvians figured in his crews, and by the mid-16th century Calvians were living in the New World in numbers out of all proportion to the Corsican population.

the church houses 16th- and 18th-century paintings and a statue of the Assumption that is carried through the town every year during the Assumption Day procession at the end of August.

Beaches

The beach in Calvi stretches 4km from the marina along the bay to the east. To get to it by foot from the town centre follow ave Christophe Colomb south until you reach chemin de la Plage (the beach path), which goes off to the left after the Casino supermarket. There's also a tram along the beach.

Boat Trips

Between April and October Colombo Line (☎ 04 95 65 32 10), whose office is on the harbour, offers various outings on modern glass-bottomed boats that allow you to see into the sea depths. There are tours, costing 240FF and 290FF (and a longer one for 360FF during the high season), which take in the Réserve Naturelle de Scandola and stop in Girolata or Ajaccio. Children aged four to 10 pay half-price; children under four go free. All trips are dependent on good weather so it is wise to check in advance.

Activities

Garage Ambrosini (☎ 04 95 65 02 13), not far from rue de l'Uruguay, hires out **mountain bikes** for 100FF per day and 265FF for three days. It opens 8 am to noon and 2 to 6 pm daily except at weekends in winter. You will be required to leave a deposit of 1500FF.

A Cavallu riding centre (☎ 04 95 65 22 22) offers trail rides and also more modest turns for 120FF per hour. Confident riders can even go swimming with the animals. The centre is 2km from the centre of town in the direction of the airport. Since 1998, Calvi has also been the site of an obstacle-riding competition in April. Contact the Centre Équestre de Balagne (☎ 04 95 60 66 66) for the exact dates.

Altore (☎ 04 95 61 80 09), east of Calvi on the D151 between Montemaggiore and Cateri, offers **paragliding flights** between April and December for 350FF to 400FF. In winter this club, which specialises in extreme sports, organises cross-country skiing and snowshoe-trekking expeditions. The company has a second branch in St-Florent and their Web site is at www.altore.com.

The **Scimia Calvese** is a relatively new attraction, created by Altore, in the pine wood at the northern end of the beach near the restaurant Le Bout du Monde. It's a 700m-long structure of bridges, passageways, ladders, beams, logs, pulleys and cables that you negotiate end to end, up in the air, but not without a harness and a line to keep you from breaking your neck. It costs 100FF (children 80FF) and opens 10 am to 6 pm Wednesdays, Saturdays and Sundays, May to October.

Le Tennis Club de Calvi (☎ 04 95 65 21 13) is by the beach near Camping La Pinède. The six courts cost 70FF/hour in winter and 80FF/hour in summer (with a 50% discount between noon and 4 pm in summer in the most intense heat of the day). There is a 10FF/hour supplement in summer for a floodlit court in the evening. The club opens daily and has a pleasant clubhouse.

See the Diving chapter for details of diving opportunities around Calvi.

Organised Tours

Les Beaux Voyages (☎ 04 95 65 11 35, fax 04 95 65 29 26), place de la Porteuse d'Eau, offers coach trips from Calvi. The various trips cover areas in the Balagne but also as far afield as Bonifacio and last from a half-day to two days. The prices range from 60FF to 550FF and the tours only take place with a minimum of 15 people. The office opens 9 am to noon and 2 to 7 pm, Monday to Saturday from May to October, and Monday to Friday the rest of the year.

Corse Voyages (☎ 04 95 65 00 47, fax 04 95 65 26 71), blvd Wilson, in conjunction with Autocars Mariani, organises similar excursions with comparable prices. The days on which their tours take place vary to Les Beaux Voyages which can be helpful. Corse Voyages opens 9 am to noon and 2 to 7 pm Monday to Saturday.

Both companies offer reduced child fares.

Special Events

Calvi hosts a range of festivals in the months between Easter and October:

La Passion Holy Week is celebrated with a large-scale spectacle retracing Christ's Passion in the Corsican language. For information call ☎ 04 95 65 23 57.

Rencontres d'Art Contemporain Works by contemporary painters and sculptors are exhibited in the citadel between June and September. For details phone ☎ 04 95 65 16 67.

Calvi Jazz Festival Towards the middle of June big names from the international jazz scene come to Calvi for open-air or indoor concerts and jam sessions. Call ☎ 04 95 65 00 50 for more information.

Eterna Citadella This is a *son et lumière* (sound and light) spectacle retracing the history of the citadel in mid-July. For details phone ☎ 04 95 65 16 67.

Rencontres de Chants Polyphoniques Since 1989, this mid-September festival of polyphonic musical expression has been held in Église St-Jean Baptiste, at L'Oratoire St-Antoine at La Poudrière and in place d'Armes in the citadel. Information is available on ☎ 04 95 65 23 57.

Festival du Vent Come October, this last blast in Calvi's annual festival calendar celebrates the role of the wind in the arts, in science and in sport. You can find out more by calling ☎ 01 42 64 37 69 or visiting the Web site www.le-festival-du-vent.com.

Places to Stay

In August especially, Calvi is very crowded and so it's worth booking accommodation several weeks in advance.

Places to Stay – Budget

About 1.5km south of the town centre and close to the beach, ***Camping La Pinède*** *(☎ 04 95 65 17 80, fax 04 95 65 19 60)* has quiet pitches under a canopy of pine trees and a wealth of facilities. It costs 35/45FF per person in low/high season and 14/15FF per tent/car. Caravans and mobile homes are available to rent. The site opens 1 April to 15 October. ***Camping Paduella*** *(☎ 04 95 65 06 16, along ave Christophe Colomb)*, is closer to town and cheaper but not as pleasant. It opens May to mid-October and costs 30/14/13FF per person/tent/car (a little more in July and August).

Auberge de Jeunesse BVJ Corsotel *(☎ 04 95 65 14 15, fax 04 95 65 33 72, ave de la République)*, practically opposite the train station, and with the words Youth Hostel

CALVI & THE BALAGNE

emblazoned across its wide yellow front, is one of the few establishments of its kind on the island. There are 133 beds in simple but clean rooms (with bathroom) for two to eight people. It costs 130/110FF per bed with/without the copious breakfast, which is excellent value if you're travelling on your own in high season. There is no maximum age, you don't have to belong to an affiliated youth hostel network and you'll be warmly welcomed. It opens April to October.

Hôtel du Centre *(☎ 04 95 65 02 01, 14 rue Alsace-Lorraine)*, the most economical lodging after the youth hostel, has decent double rooms with a wash basin for 160FF in low season and 230FF in August. Rooms with a shower cost between 180FF and 250FF, depending on the season, and triples cost 200/320FF. Small studio apartments rent for 1400/2000FF per week. Hôtel du Centre opens June to September. It does not accept credit cards.

Places to Stay – Mid-Range & Top End

Thoroughly renovated in the year 2000, ***Hôtel Belvédère*** *(☎ 04 95 65 01 25, fax 04 95 65 33 20, place Christophe Colomb)*, offers smallish but pleasant doubles, each with bathroom, air-conditioning and TV, for 230FF in low season, 280FF in May and June, 330FF in June and July and 410FF in August and September. Larger rooms go for between 330FF and 590FF according to the season. ***Hôtel Christophe-Colomb*** *(☎ 04 95 65 06 04, fax 04 95 65 29 65, rue de l'Uruguay)*, rents good double rooms with bathroom, TV and telephone for 250FF to 350FF in low season and 450FF to 550F in July and August. The hotel opens April to October.

Hôtel Sole Mare *(☎ 04 95 65 09 50, fax 04 95 65 36 64)*, at the end of a little street north of place Bel Ombra in the direction of the sea, could use a little renovation, particularly in the bathroom department, but for a place with a swimming pool the rates are reasonable. A spacious double with a little balcony costs 240FF to 290FF in low season, jumping to 490FF in July and August.

Hôtel Le Rocher *(☎ 04 95 65 20 04, fax 04 95 65 36 71, blvd Wilson)*, opposite the post office, rents pleasant, functional studios with bathroom, air-conditioning, kitchenette and telephone for 400FF to 840FF, according to the season, for two people. They rent apartments for three or four people and also have weekly rates. Hôtel Le Rocher opens the end of May to September.

Places to Eat

You will find any number of stalls selling sandwiches, *panini* and other snack foods along the harbour and in the touristy streets just above it. Pizzerias and restaurants offering traditional Corsican menus also abound.

Budget Away from the sometimes suspect restaurants near the harbour, ***Le Chalet du Port*** *(☎ 04 95 65 46 30)*, beyond the Tour du Sel on the ferry quay, serves simple but good food at affordable prices in a casual, friendly atmosphere. In July and August, the doors stay open until 2 am daily. If you're not too hungry, ***Le Havanita*** on the harbour offers tapas for between 20FF and 25FF, including peppers stuffed with *brocciu*, pickles, tortillas and Corsican ham. It has a little terrace and opens 5 pm to 2 am daily, May to September. ***La Gelateria Solea*** *(rue Clemenceau)*, opposite Église Ste-Marie Majeure, serves generous portions of excellent ice cream in some unusual flavours. Its open late in summer.

The big ***Super U*** supermarket on ave Christophe Colomb opens 8 am to 8 pm Monday to Saturday and 8 am to 1 pm Sunday in summer; 8.30 am to 12.30 pm and 3 to 7.30 pm Monday to Friday and 8.30 am to 7.30 pm Saturday in winter.

Mid-Range & Top End Open since summer 2000, ***Le Tire-Bouchon*** *(☎ 04 95 65 25 41, rue Clemenceau)* is a wine bistro serving food as well as a broad selection of Corsican wines. It opens daily for lunch and dinner, April to October.

Calellu *(☎ 04 95 65 22 18)*, directly on the harbour, has a reputation for friendly service and good fish. There is a 100FF *menu* and wines start at 90FF. Calellu opens afternoon and evening, March to October except in July and August when it opens evenings only.

Le Chalut *(☎/fax 04 95 65 00 50, 22 rue Clemenceau)* has an indoor restaurant and also an outdoor dining area on the harbour. It serves a 98FF *menu* and a la carte fish dishes. The proprietor is also the organiser of the Calvi jazz festival. The restaurant opens daily for lunch and dinner in high season; weekends only in low season.

Tao *(☎ 04 95 65 00 73)*, in the citadel, has become such an institution over the years that it's even celebrated in song by a leading French crooner. It was conceived by Tao Kanbey de Kerekoff, who had served in a White cavalry regiment in the Crimea and then, defeated, headed west. He got as far as New York, circled back to Paris and, in 1928, found his way to Corsica. He fell in love with the citadel, acquired what was once the palace of the bishops of Sagone and, in 1935, opened Corsica's first cabaret. It was passed on to his children, and although it is still most noteworthy as a piano bar it now doubles as a restaurant offering excellent food and a wonderful view over the bay. Main courses cost from 90FF to 130FF, with desserts for between 40FF and 50FF. Tao opens end of May to September. To get there, take the little road off to the right when you get to place d'Armes.

Entertainment

The vaulted rooms decorated in pastel shades at ***Tao*** (see Places to Eat) are the old cellars of the bishop's palace. Decorated by Toni Casalonga, an artist from Pigna, they open to after-dinner revellers 11 pm to 5 am daily in the high season. Tao-By, one of the founder's sons, begins the evening at the piano with his repertoire of French and Corsican popular song and international standards. Later, a DJ takes over. Cocktails cost between 70FF and 80FF; champagne and spirits start at about 60FF.

La Camargue disco *(☎ 04 95 65 08 70)*, 1.5km beyond Calvi in the direction of Île Rousse, has a restaurant, piano bar, open-air dance floor and a swimming pool. There's a free shuttle service from the harbour. An admission charge of 60FF entitles you to one drink. It opens April to September. ***L'Acapulco*** *(☎ 04 95 65 08 03)*, another disco, is 5.5km from the town centre on the road to Calenzana.

An open-air cinema, ***Airpop Cyrnos*** *(☎ 04 95 65 01 24, ave Christophe Colomb)*, shows a different film every evening in summer at 9.45 pm. A ticket costs about 40FF. Look for it alongside the Casino supermarket.

Getting There & Away

Air The spanking new terminal at Calvi-Ste-Catherine airport (☎ 04 95 65 88 88), 7km south-west of the town centre, seems large in proportion to the volume of traffic passing through it. The runways, moreover, are so close to the mountains that, when winds are high, flights are redirected to Bastia. There is also no ATM or bureau de change at the airport and no way of getting into town except by taxi or rental car (for details on the car rental companies at the airport see Car later).

Bus Les Beaux Voyages (☎ 04 95 65 11 35, fax 04 95 65 29 26) serves Algajola, Île Rousse, Ponte Leccia and Bastia from Calvi daily except Sunday and public holidays (Bastia; 80FF, 2¼ hours). Buses leave Calvi at 6.45 am from in front of the agency's offices in place de la Porteuse d'Eau. In July and August the company also has a service to Galéria (35FF plus 5FF for luggage, one hour) and Calenzana (30FF plus 5FF for luggage, two daily – at 2 pm and 7 pm, 30 minutes). In winter the school bus will take you to Calenzana every weekday except Wednesday. If you're planning to go to Calenzana and want to start walking the GR20 the same day, a taxi is a better option than the bus. (See Taxi under Getting Around.)

From 15 May to 10 October SAIB (☎ 04 95 22 41 99) provides a service to Porto via Col de la Croix, where you find the footpath for Girolata (see the Walking chapter and Girolata in The West Coast chapter). The scenery along this route is spectacular. The bus leaves from the marina at 3.30 pm (110FF, approximately 2½ hours). The bus is quicker and cheaper than the train to Calvi.

Train From Calvi's train station (☎ 04 95 65 00 61), on ave de la République, there are two departures daily to Ajaccio (145FF), Bastia (95FF), Corte (79FF) and Vizzavona (110FF).

Between April and October, Tramways de la Balagne operates a local rail service along the coast between Calvi and Île Rousse. There are five to 10 departures daily with about 20 stops en route: in Lumio, Sant' Ambrogio, Algajola, Davia and so on. The one-way fare between Calvi and Île Rousse is 24FF.

Car There's a Hertz car rental agency (☎ 04 95 65 06 64) tucked away in a corner of place de la Porteuse d'Eau. Avis (☎ 04 95 65 06 74) is in the parking area at the marina. Europcar (☎ 04 95 65 10 35) is on the ave de la République near Auberge de Jeunesse BVJ Corsotel.

The following companies have offices in the air terminal: Avis (☎ 04 95 65 88 38), Budget (☎ 04 95 65 36 67), Europcar (☎ 04 95 65 10 19) and Hertz (☎ 04 95 65 02 96). If no one's at the counter, try the companies' car parks.

Boat SNCM operates a high-speed boat to and from Nice (three hours) daily in high season. Corsica Ferries also operates between Nice and Calvi. SNCM, together with CMN, operates between Marseille and Calvi. The agent for SNCM and CMN in Calvi is Corse Consignation et Représentation (CCR; ☎ 04 95 65 01 38), in the harbour opposite the Colombo Line office. It opens 9 am to noon and 2 to 5.45 pm Monday to Friday during the high season. It also opens for two hours before any departure, regardless of hour. Corsica Ferries sells tickets in Calvi through Les Beaux Voyages (see Organised Tours earlier in this section) and other agencies. Les Beaux Voyages opens windows at the ferry port two hours before departures. For more information on boat links between mainland Europe and Calvi, see Sea in the Getting There & Away chapter.

Within Corsica you can get boats from Calvi to Porto between May and October, but it will cost. Take the Colombo Line launch to Girolata (170FF), then the Nave Va boat the final distance (80FF).

The Road from Calvi to Porto

The D81 between Calvi and Porto (known as the D81B as far as Galéria) traverses some spectacular coastal scenery before plunging into the Parc Naturel Régional de Corse (PNRC). If you're driving and not accustomed to this kind of road your capacity for aesthetic response may be inhibited by a prudent reluctance to keep a date with your maker prematurely. The condition of the road is at once thrilling and scandalous. The curves are unrelenting. Falling rocks have partially destroyed the parapet. The tarmac has been patched up again and again – and still it's ridden with unexpected cavities. The narrowness of the road surface makes passing other vehicles – no, not those in your own lane but those coming *at* you – a very nerve-racking game of dominance and deference of the kind usually associated with male lower mammals in a state of sexual rut.

Despite this the slow climb up to the Col de la Croix, after the turn-off to Galéria, and then from the Col de la Croix down to Porto is a sequence of what must be among the very most spectacular views on the planet. And part of what's extraordinary about the ride is the length of time that the little seashore village of Girolata, utterly inaccessible except by boat or precipitous footpath, remains in sight beneath you as you negotiate hairpin turn after hairpin turn. It's as if you're making no progress at all! If you take this road, and you survive it, it will stay with you for a long time as among the most memorable experiences you'll have had on the island of Corsica – or anywhere.

About 180 berths in the beautiful marina in Calvi are reserved for visiting sailors. There are chandlers, mechanics and sail repairers in the harbour and, of course, fuel and water facilities. Charges to tie up a 9m boat range from 97FF to 160FF, depending on the time of year. A hot shower costs 15FF. The harbour master's office (☎ 04 95 65 10 60), underneath the tourist office, opens 7.30 am to 1 pm and 2 to 7.30 pm in the low season and 7 am to 9 pm in summer.

Getting Around

You will easily be able to get around Calvi on foot.

To/From the Airport There is no public transport service to or from the airport other than taxis (see below). A taxi from the airport to the centre of town costs about 80FF, or 100FF in the evening, at weekends and on public holidays.

Taxi There's a taxi rank (☎ 04 95 65 03 10) next to the local government office on place de la Porteuse d'Eau. A taxi will take you to the Forêt de Bonifatu for about 200FF, to Galéria for 300FF and to Calenzana for 130FF. The rates are the same for one to four people.

AROUND CALVI

Pointe de la Revellata

Its jagged edges sprayed with fine white foam, this cape, just 3km west across the sea from Calvi's citadel, offers a little foretaste of the still wilder and more beautiful coastline beyond it. You'll find a pretty, sandy beach in a little cove here, lapped by gorgeous turquoise waters, but also a Belgian marine biology station. Despite the many maps still pointing to a Grotte des Veaux Marins, what you aren't likely to see are *veaux marins*, or seals. The seals have declined in numbers precipitously, and they no longer make this part of the coast a port of call.

You can get to Pointe de la Revellata on foot or by mountain bike. Take the D81 in the direction of Galéria and Porto until you reach the footpath down to the cape. After 1km there's a turning off to the right, towards the beach. Except with four-wheel drive, it's just as well not to try it in a car.

Notre Dame de la Serra

Five centuries old, this chapel stands on a wild and windswept height. There is also a statue of a shrouded Virgin Mary facing out to sea. Like the statue, you will find yourself gazing out over the Golfe de Calvi, which is particularly breathtaking at the end of the day when Calvi is lit up. The shady pine trees also make it an ideal spot for a midday picnic.

You can get to the Notre Dame de la Serra by going left, away from the sea, not right, at the point at which the track branches off the D81 towards Pointe de la Revellata. A sign cites the distance as 1.5km. You can also reach Notre Dame de la Serra on foot along a somewhat circuitous route from Calvi; ask at the tourist office for information.

ALGAJOLA

postcode 20220 • pop 216

This town on the coast north of Calvi, has been somewhat eclipsed by Île Rousse to its north, but is nevertheless given a new lease of life each tourist season when people flock to its long, beautiful sandy beach. There is evidence that the town was once occupied by the Romans and was also strongly Genoese at one time. The Genoese citadel, which was ravaged by Saracen attacks in the mid-17th century, was the seat of government of the Balagne for several years. It is now under private ownership. Algajola was once famous for its porphyritic granite, a magma rock rich in coloured crystals. The quarry, however, is no longer mined.

There is a post office and a few restaurants and shops. In summer Algajola is linked to Île Rousse and Calvi by train (see the Calvi Getting There & Away section).

Places to Stay

Close to the pretty little train station, ***Hôtel St-Joseph*** *(☎ 04 95 60 73 90, fax 04 95 60 64 89)* has pleasant doubles for between 280FF and 380FF, depending on the season, including breakfast. This is the best of the village's reasonably priced lodgings and opens May to mid-October. Recommended ***Hôtel Beau Rivage*** *(☎ 04 95 60 73 99, fax 04 95 60 79 51, ⓔ beaurivage@hotelscorse.com)*, right up by the beach, is fairly luxurious and the prices reflect this: pleasant doubles with a balcony and sea view cost 380/490FF in low/mid-season and 590FF in high season. The hotel also has 10 less comfortable but lower-priced rooms in an annexe a few hundred metres away in the village. Half-board is an option.

ÎLE ROUSSE (ISULA ROSSA)

postcode 20220 • pop 2350

Its cobbled streets and the plane trees in place Paoli give Île Rousse a certain charm, and the town remains peaceful, even lazy-feeling, despite the influx of tourists drawn to its fine sandy beach; the beach can be reached by a miniature railway along the lovely promenade A Marinella. The town's name comes from the red colour of the granite of the formerly offshore Île de la Pietra, now linked to the town by a jetty. This is where ferries from mainland Europe dock.

History

Some sources suggest that the city of Agilla as mentioned by the 2nd-century geographer Ptolemy once stood hereabouts. It's certain that the Romans had a trading post on the site for a time, but this was abandoned for reasons now uncertain, though probably connected with Saracen invasions.

The town came back to life in 1758 when the visionary patriot Pascal Paoli chose what was then a modest fishing village as a port city to rival the Genoese capital, Calvi. Île Rousse remained a thriving commercial centre until WWI, after which it began to

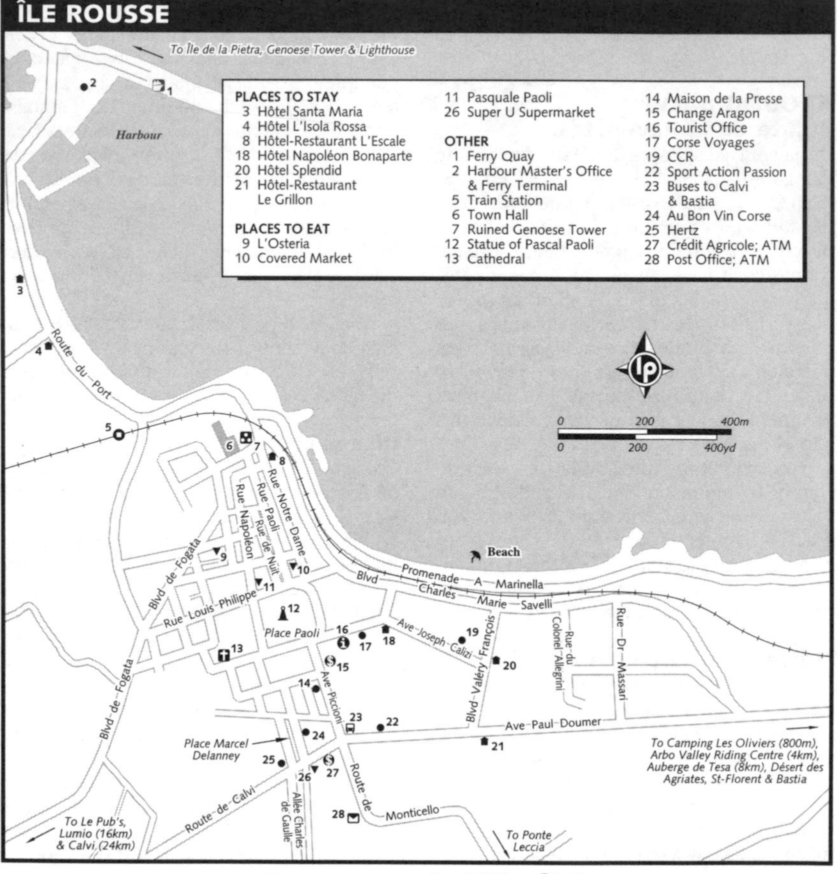

decline; then being given a new lease of life by tourism.

Orientation

Coming from the direction of Bastia, you enter Île Rousse along ave Paul Doumer, which takes you to the diminutive ave Piccioni, which leads on to place Paoli in the centre of town. North of the square are four little streets (rue Notre Dame, rue Paoli, rue de Nuit and rue Napoléon) around which is the covered market and most of the town's restaurants and shops. The ferry quay is on the Pietra peninsula to the north of the town centre, about 500m from the train station. The beach starts to the east of place Paoli and extends to the south-east.

Information

Tourist Offices The tourist office (☎ 04 95 60 04 35, 04 95 60 24 74, ⓔ info@ot-ile-rousse.fr) is on place Paoli, right in the town centre. It opens 9 am to 7 pm Monday to Saturday and 10 am to noon and 3 to 7 pm on Sunday; and 9 am to noon and 2 to 6 pm Monday to Friday in winter. The Web site at www.ot-ile-rousse.fr (French only) provides more information.

Money Change Aragon (☎ 04 95 60 32 38), on ave Piccioni, opens 8.30 am to 8 pm in high season. Société Générale, on the same street, has an ATM and also changes money. Crédit Agricole, next to the Super U supermarket near place Marcel Delanney opens 8.15 to 11.55 am and 2.05 to 5 pm Monday to Friday and has an ATM. There is also an ATM in front of the post office.

Post & Communications The post office (☎ 04 95 63 05 50) is on route de Monticello, which is an extension of ave Piccioni, a few minutes walk from place Paoli. It opens 8.30 am to 5 pm Monday to Friday and on Saturday morning.

For an Internet connection (60FF per hour) try cafe-restaurant Le Caruchettu at the eastern end of the beach.

Bookshops Maison de la Presse (☎ 04 95 60 30 41), ave Piccioni, has a range of books, guides, magazines and foreign-language publications. It opens 6 am to 8.30 pm daily in high season and 6 am to 12.30 pm and 3 to 7 pm daily the rest of the year.

Things to See

Lined with cafes and restaurants, the **beach** here constitutes pleasure number one. Île Rousse, however, is also a great place just to stroll around in – under the trees in place Paoli (don't miss the statue of the great man himself), along **promenade A Marinella,** parallel to the beach, and in and out of the cobblestone streets of the **old town** behind the **covered market**. The market is worth a visit, not only to shop (the stall-holders, who come every morning in summer and are not averse to giving out free samples), but also to see the architecture. The 19th-century building, with its 21 columns, is classed as a historical monument. You can also walk (or take the little tourist train) to the Île de la Pietra, where there is a **Genoese tower** and a lighthouse.

Activities

Sport Action Passion (☎ 04 95 60 15 76), on ave Paul Doumer, hires out mountain bikes for about 100FF per day (less on a daily basis for longer rentals). The shop opens 7 am to 8 pm daily in summer and 9 am to noon and 2 to 7 pm Monday to Saturday, the rest of the year.

For details of Arbo Valley riding centre (☎ 04 95 60 49 49, 06 12 06 34 38), a short distance from town in the direction of Bastia see Horse Riding under Désert des Agriates in the Bastia & the Far North chapter.

See the Diving chapter for details of diving opportunities around Île Rousse.

Places to Stay – Budget

About 800m out on the road towards Bastia, ***Camping Les Oliviers*** *(☎ 04 95 60 19 92, fax 04 95 60 30 91)* is a pleasant (and flowery) site. It costs 30/17/11FF per person/tent/car and opens April to September.

Hôtel-Restaurant Le Grillon *(☎ 04 95 60 00 49, fax 04 95 60 43 69, ave Paul Doumer)*, has unfussy doubles with bathroom for 200/260FF in low/mid-season and 280FF in July. Half-board, at 560FF for two people, is obligatory in August. Singles cost slightly less. The hotel opens March to mid-November and reception is at the bar.

Places to Stay – Mid-Range

In the old town, ***Hôtel-Restaurant L'Escale*** *(☎ 04 95 60 10 53, rue Notre Dame)* has two rooms with a nice view over the sea for 300FF to 400FF, depending on season, and somewhat noisier rooms at the back for 250FF to 300FF. Rooms in another facility closer to the port cost 2600FF per week in July but there are nightly rates out of season.

The beautiful ***Hôtel Splendid*** *(☎ 04 95 60 00 24, fax 04 95 60 04 57, blvd Valéry François)* offers good doubles with bathroom for 240/400FF in low/high season. Singles cost 220/310FF. The hotel opens from the end of March to October and there's a swimming pool.

Hôtel L'Isola Rossa *(☎ 04 95 60 01 32, fax 04 95 60 57 32, route du Port)*, towards the harbour, has comfortable rooms with bathroom, TV and telephone. Doubles cost 250FF to 350FF (depending on floor and view), in low season, 300FF to 450FF in May, June and September and 450FF to 650FF from mid-July to the end of August.

See ***Auberge de Tesa*** under Places to Eat for a further option just outside Île Rousse.

Places to Stay – Top End

With an imposing ochre facade and two crenellated towers in a corner of place Paoli, ***Hôtel Napoléon Bonaparte*** *(☎ 04 95 60 06 09, fax 04 95 60 11 51, place Paoli)* is a monument in itself. This former palace, dating from 1870, served as home in 1953 and 1954 to the exiled Mohammed V of Morocco and his son, the future Hassan II. Although it has seen better days (the rooms cannot really be described as luxurious any more), it has a certain quaint charm. Prices for a double range from 540FF to 900FF, depending on the season and the view (sea or garden). The hotel has a swimming pool.

Hôtel Santa Maria *(☎ 04 95 63 05 05, fax 04 95 60 32 48, route du Port)* is unquestionably the town's most luxurious hotel. The three-star property has 58 rooms with all the predictable amenities. Doubles cost 485/580/785FF in low/mid/high season. There is direct access to both the beach and a swimming pool. Visit the Web site at www.hotelsantamaria.com for more information.

Places to Eat

Budget There are pizzerias, and cafes serving sandwiches along the streets of the old town, in place Paoli and along the beach.

Hôtel-Restaurant L'Escale (see Places to Stay – Mid-Range) has an extensive menu. There's a Cuban bar upstairs, and a billiard room in which tournaments are held on Tuesday evenings in the low season.

The ***Super U*** supermarket on ave Paul Doumer, at the top of ave Piccioni, serves the needs of self-caterers.

Mid-Range & Top End Rustic and somewhat austere, ***L'Osteria*** *(☎ 04 95 60 08 39, place Santelli)* serves an excellent no-nonsense 115FF *menu*. The restaurant opens every evening except Wednesday in July and August; and lunchtimes and evenings except Wednesday in the low season. ***Pasquale Paoli*** *(☎ 04 95 60 39 11, 2 place Paoli)* has a pleasant terrace and several *menus* starting at 70FF. Look out for the thrush terrine (yes, that's right) on the 90FF *menu*. The restaurant opens daily, April to October.

For a serious gastronomic experience, head for ***Auberge de Tesa*** *(☎ 04 95 60 09 55)*, 8km outside of Île Rousse. It claims to be an inn rather than a restaurant, which means you are treated as a guest rather than a customer, and it is not unknown for all the guests to end up at the same table. The 200FF *menu* is incredibly generous, and everything is included; you won't even get charged for an extra coffee. They bake their own bread and most other ingredients come from local producers. No lunch is served, only dinner. The handful of impeccable rooms, with bathroom, cost 300FF. Half-board for two people is 600FF – a bargain. The inn is next to a little stream, and it is wonderfully quiet. Follow the main road for 6km towards Bastia, then turn right at the sign for the Auberge and follow the road for 2km. There are no public transport options.

Entertainment

There's not much going on in Île Rousse after dinner. You can try the open-air disco, ***Le Pub's*** *(☎ 04 95 60 02 58)*, on the way out of town in the direction of Calvi or just take a seat on the terrace of the bar ***Les Platanes*** *(place Paoli)*.

Shopping

A number of craft shops can be found along the little streets of the old town, and Corsican foodstuffs can be found every morning at the covered market.

Au Bon Vin Corse (☎ 04 95 60 15 14), on place Marcel Delanney, sells wines, liqueurs, honeys and olive oil. It's not just a shop but also a wine bar and a good place to stop for a little pick-me-up. It opens until about 8.30 pm daily except Sunday.

Getting There & Away

Air Île Rousse is 25km away from Calvi-Ste-Catherine airport.

Bus Les Beaux Voyages (☎ 04 95 65 11 35, fax 04 95 65 29 26), based in Calvi, links Île Rousse, daily except for Sundays and holidays, with Calvi, Bastia and Ponte Leccia, where a connection can be made to Ajaccio. For travellers heading west the stop is outside Le Sémiramis bar, on the corner of ave Paul Doumer and ave Piccioni, and for travellers going east it is in front of the Super U supermarket.

Train There are two departures daily from Île Rousse train station (☎ 04 95 60 00 50) to Bastia (78FF), Corte (62FF), Vizzavona (93FF), Ajaccio (128FF) and various villages along the way.

Tramways de la Balagne link Île Rousse and Calvi for 24FF each way via Lumio and Davia numerous times daily between April and October.

There's a left-luggage facility at the station, which charges 17FF per item for 24 hours.

Car Hertz (☎ 04 95 60 12 63) is on the corner of place Marcel Delanney and route de Calvi. It opens June to September.

Boat There's a high-speed boat link between Nice and Île Rousse operated by SNCM, a service from Marseille on SNCM and CMN and a service from Savona in Italy on Corsica Ferries. Corse Consignation et Représentation (CCR; ☎ 04 95 60 09 56), on ave Joseph Calizi, is the representative for all these companies. It opens 8.30 am to noon and 2 to 5.30 pm Monday to Friday and Saturday morning. Corse Voyages (☎ 04 95 60 11 19), on place Paoli, next to the tourist office, also sells ferry tickets.

The Interior

GETTING AROUND

Since there are no local bus services to Belgodère, Speloncato or the forests of Tartagine Melaja and Bonifatu, your options are to hire a car, take your chances at hitching, or take a bus part of the distance and then hike or go by taxi.

You can travel between Calvi and Calenzana by bus (see the earlier Calvi Getting There & Away section for details) and by taxi to Calenzana or the Forêt and Cirque de Bonifatu (see Getting Around under Calvi earlier). You could also take a taxi directly from Calvi-Ste-Catherine airport.

BELGODÈRE (BELGUDÈ)

postcode 20226 • pop 371 • elevation 310m

This tiny village high above the olive groves in the Vallée du Prato, at a distance of 15km from Île Rousse, has a richer history than you might expect.

For a long time Belgodère belonged to a rich family of Tuscan origin, the Malaspinas, who lived in the big white building on the way out of the village towards Speloncato. In 1630 one of the Malaspina family, a prior, was put to death by villagers who could not bear his authority. The villagers also expelled a curate in 1847. By way of revenge he wrote a 48-verse poem about everything that was wrong with the village and its people.

The visit of the painter Maurice Utrillo with his mother, artist Suzanne Valadon,

The Balagne Craft Road

Anxious to show that the Balagne has preserved its traditional crafts, the association A Strada di l'Artigiani (☎ 04 95 32 83 00), 3 rue Marcel Paul, 20407 Bastia, and the Chambre des Métiers de Haute-Corse (Haute-Corse Chamber of Trade) have marked out the Route des Artisans de Balagne (Balagne Craft Road). This snakes through the mountain and hill villages between Calvi and Île Rousse and leads you to the doorsteps of traditional cutlers, beekeepers, cabinet-makers, stringed-instrument makers, bookbinders, wine-makers and potters. The artisans' workshops open to the public. The leaflet *Strada di l'Artigiani* is available at the tourist office in Calvi.

between 1912 and 1913, was a less bitter episode. Utrillo painted a portrait of Valadon in the village square a copy of which is kept in the village hall.

The church in Belgodère is worth a visit for its Baroque altarpiece. It's often closed but if you ask at the cafes next door someone will tell you who has the key. Another interesting feature of the village is the fort, partially ruined, from which there is a wonderful view over the surrounding valleys with their numerous olive trees. To get to the fort, go through an archway between the two cafes behind the war memorial in the village square, then follow the little alleyways.

The village has a post office (☎ 04 95 61 30 00).

Places to Stay & Eat

A few hundred metres from the square on the road to Ponte Leccia, ***Hôtel-Restaurant Niobel*** *(☎ 04 95 61 34 00, fax 04 95 61 35 85)* has good *menus* for 75FF to 130FF. A single/double/triple costs 220/260/296FF in the low season and 390/590/625FF in July or August; all have a bathroom and some have a balcony and a superb view over the valley. The owner knows Belgodère history inside out.

There are also ***cafes***, open year round.

SPELONCATO (SPILUNCATU)

postcode 20226 • pop 222 • elevation 600m

Eleven kilometres south-west of Belgodère along a road that snakes up the mountainside, Speloncato is without doubt one of the most beautiful villages in the Balagne. Perched at an elevation of 600m, not far from the site of an ancient Roman encampment, it owes its name to the nearby grottoes (*e spelunche* in Corsican) and its charm to its little streets with their densely packed stone houses. **Église St-Michel**, which is overall Romanesque in style, has a handsome Baroque choir dating from 1755, and it is worth a visit not only for its paintings and sculptures but also for its magnificent Tuscan organ (1810) and 17th-century wooden reliquary. The bell-tower was added in 1913.

Places to Stay & Eat

The only public lodging in the village, ***Hôtel A Spelunca*** *(☎ 04 95 61 50 38, fax 04 95 61 53 14)* is a beautiful building that was constructed in 1850 by Cardinal Savelli, the director-general of the police in Rome under Pope Pius IX and a native son of Speloncato. Its 18 comfortable rooms, around a central staircase, cost 230FF to 250FF in low season, depending on the view, and 290FF to 350FF in high season. Singles cost 200FF. The cheapest accommodations are pleasant attic rooms. Hôtel A Spelunca opens May to September.

Lunch and dinner are available at the bars and restaurants in the village square.

COL DE BATTAGLIA

The Col de Battaglia (1099m), on the D63 on the way from Speloncato to the Forêt de Tartagine Melaja, marks the outer boundary of the Parc Naturel Régional. The contrast between the views in the two directions is striking. On one side, the mountainsides covered with maquis fall off gently to the sea. On the other side, there is a landscape of chestnut trees and the lake formed by the Codole dam. A snack bar opens here in the summer season.

FORÊT DE TARTAGINE MELAJA

Although you'll need some sort of vehicle to get to it, the forest, which covers more than

2700 hectares, makes a pleasant day trip. From the village of Pioggiola, 3km beyond the Col de Battaglia, the road winds through 16km of stunning landscapes before reaching the forest proper. (On the way out of Poggiola, take the time to admire the lovely Église Ste-Marie, whose yellow front rises solitarily in front of the mountains.) Initially, the scenery on the drive into the forest seems a little inanimate (except for the livestock you're likely to encounter on the narrow mountainside road) but then the scattered pine trees begin to cluster more densely. The road reaches the forestry lodge about 3.5km after the sign indicating the start of the forest. A few hundred metres beyond that you can swim in the river, have a picnic or go for a walk along one of the marked paths (including a firewall path) that stretch out along the stream in the shade of the pine trees.

Places to Stay & Eat

In Pioggiola, ***Auberge Aghjola*** *(☎ 04 95 61 90 48, fax 04 95 61 92 99)* is a pretty, ivy-covered house with a little swimming pool and eight pleasant double rooms with bathroom for 320FF to 380FF for two, breakfast included. Half-board (375FF per person) is obligatory in July and August. There are menus at 100/160FF for lunch/dinner. The shepherd's menu – *spuntinu* – for 80FF consists of a *charcuterie* plate, a selection of cheeses and caramelised apple sorbet. Auberge Aghjola opens March to mid-October.

Hôtel A Tramala *(☎ 04 95 61 93 54)*, at the junction of the D63 and the D963, 2km out of Pioggiola in the direction of the forest, is a big stone house with spacious double rooms, with shower, for 380FF, or a little more in high season, breakfast included. ***Auberge La Tornadia*** *(☎ 04 95 61 90 93, fax 04 95 61 92 15)*, next door, is a 30-year-old restaurant, popular among the locals, with a terrace shaded by chestnut trees. *Menus* range in price from 115FF to 150FF. Among other dishes on offer are courgette fritters, young roast suckling pig with chestnuts or suckling lamb. Auberge La Tornadia serves lunch and dinner from mid-March to mid-November.

CALENZANA

postcode 20214 • pop 1722 • elevation 250m

This big village, 13km above Calvi, was once a pocket of opposition to the Genoese occupation. In 1732, during the Corsican uprising, Corsican partisans battled ferociously

Via Ferrata: Climbing with a Handle

During WWI the Italians attached iron bars – in effect, rungs – to some steep mountainsides in the Dolomites in order to facilitate troop movements. As it happens, though, this was only a military adaptation of a feat of engineering that the Austrians had developed for sport in the 19th century. Italian sportsmen were not to be outdone. No sooner did the war end and the Italian army abandon their *vie ferrate* (iron roads) than sportsmen began climbing them there, too.

The first *via ferrata* appeared in France – in the French Alps – in 1988. Now there are 60 of them throughout the Alps. There are two in Corsica – in the Vallée d'Asco and at Chisa. The one in the Vallée d'Asco, specifically in the Gorges de l'Asco, is on the D47 at a distance of 11km from the intersection with the N197. It dates from 1997. It takes 3½ hours to climb, and is considered one of the best in France. You pay 30FF admission, 70FF for equipment and 220FF if you want to be supervised by a guide from In Terra Corsa (☎ 04 95 47 69 48, fax 04 95 47 69 45, ⓔ in.terra.corsa@wanadoo.fr), which manages the facility.

The Chisa via ferrata, dating from July 2000, takes two hours to climb. You pay 35FF admission (those aged under 18, 15FF) and 60FF for equipment. Chisa is at the end of the D645, about 14km inland from the east coast village of Travo. The starting point for the climb (☎ 04 95 56 36 61/57 31 11) is at the edge of the village next to the gîte.

The iron rungs aren't your only security, by the way. You're also secured by a cable so that you couldn't fall even if you wanted to.

against Genoese troops and their German mercenary allies here. Today, the village is a rallying point for walkers, as it is the northern starting point of the GR20 and also on the Mare e Monti Nord (see the Walking chapter for more information).

Work on the Église St-Blaise in the village square began in 1691 and took 16 years to complete. The cornices, decorated with acanthus leaves, were added in 1722 and the high altar in polychrome marble (based on drawings by Florentine architect Pierre Cortesi) in 1750. The splendid Baroque bell-tower was built between 1862 and 1875. The field adjacent of the church is the resting place of 500 Germans killed in the 1732 conflict.

Places to Stay

The ***Gîte d'Étape Municipal*** *(☎ 04 95 62 77 13)*, a few hundred metres along the road to Calvi, past the service station on the right-hand side, has clean, comfortable dormitories for eight people at 60FF per night. You can also pitch a tent nearby for 25FF plus 35FF per person. The shelter opens year round and the showers are hot.

Hôtel Bel Horizon *(☎ 04 95 62 71 72, fax 04 95 62 70 08)*, opposite the church, has clean rooms with shared toilet but en-suite shower, and is popular with weary walkers. It costs 200/230/250FF for a single/double/triple in low season and 230/250/280FF in high season. The rooms at the front have a lovely view over the church, with spectacular mountain vistas in the background. The hotel opens April to September. ***Hôtel Monte Grosso*** *(☎ 04 95 62 70 15)*, about 200m north of the church, offers doubles for about 270FF.

Places to Eat

On the main road behind the church ***La Calenzana*** *(☎ 04 95 62 70 25)*, also known as Chez Michel, serves wood-fire pizzas and a 96FF Corsican *menu* that includes wild boar during the hunting season. It opens April to October. ***A Stazzona*** *(☎ 04 95 65 11 85)*, in a former blacksmith's shop roughly opposite Hôtel Monte Grosso, specialises in fresh pasta for 50FF to 75FF and also offers a 95FF *menu*. Of the other alternatives, ***Pizzéria Prince Pierre***, in front of the church, is worth a mention for its pastas and pizzas for 40FF to 60FF.

Spar, at the edge of the village on the road to Calvi, is a well stocked little supermarket.

AROUND CALENZANA

About 1.5km to the east of the town is the Romanesque **Chapelle de Santa Restituta**, who was martyred hereabouts in the early 4th century. The townspeople originally intended the chapel, built in the 11th or 12th century, to be in a different spot but changed their plans when, as per legend, the building materials were found to have moved mysteriously in the course of each night. Restituta, they concluded, was herself communicating where she wanted the chapel built. Her remains are paraded each year in late May. Ask for the key to the chapel at the nearby tobacconist's.

The village of **Montemaggiore** (elevation 400m) a few kilometres to the north of Calenzana is well worth a detour for the wonderful view and for its 17th-century Baroque church of St-Augustin. You can stop off en route to taste wine at the cellars of **Domaine d'Alzi Pratu** (☎ 04 95 62 75 47), near the former convent of the same name, 2.5 km from Calenzana on the D151. The cellars open 8 am to noon and 2 to 7.30 pm daily and are not far from the **Zilia mineral water spring**, which can be visited by appointment if you call ☎ 04 95 65 90 70.

FORÊT & CIRQUE DE BONIFATU

The word Bonifatu means 'place of good life' and in the early years of the 20th century this area was frequented by convalescents wanting to take advantage of its pure air. This purity is also enjoyed by a considerable population of mouflons, foxes, bearded vultures, Corsican nuthatches and wild boars.

The forest, ranging in elevation from 300m to 1950m, consists of maritime and laricio pines, green oaks and other broad-leafed trees. These different species cover a total area of about 3000 hectares, mostly in the cirque, which is more than just a basin but looks like a series of tangled ridges and crests. At the end of the day the sun paints it brilliantly in bluish-greens, reds and coppers.

At one time the forest and the cirque

The Olive Tree

Since ancient times the olive tree has been considered a symbol of peace, although according to Greek legend it was created from turmoil: it is supposed to have sprung up in the Acropolis after Athena, the goddess of war and wisdom, threw a spear during a battle with Poseidon. Far from ancient Greece, this supposedly eternal tree spread across Corsica in Roman and Genoese times. The Genoese authorities forced every family to plant olive trees in large numbers, along with chestnut trees, cereals and vines.

Olive trees flower in June and can bear up to a million flowers each – they produce so much pollen that locals describe the fine golden powder that spreads across the Balagne as a 'yellow wind' – but only 1% to 5% of the flowers actually produce olives. Throughout Corsica, the absence of frost makes it possible to harvest the fruit simply by waiting until it drops onto the large coloured nets that are set out to receive it. Olives, in other words, remain on the tree until they are completely ripe. This gives them time to soak up all the rich fragrances in the environment, which result in the superior flavour of Corsican olive oils. Long maturation also explains the slow reproduction cycle of Corsican olive trees; they bear fruit only every second year.

After a period of decline following WWII as the result of competition from other oils and later of fires (one in 1971 spared only 500 trees out of the 35,000 in the Balagne), the future of Corsican olive culture is now looking more rosy. Indeed, it has been flourishing since the early 1990s thanks to the professionalism of the producers and the fact that olive oil is becoming increasingly fashionable. In the mid-19th century, olive growing accounted for more than 90% of income in the Calvi area, and the Balagne remains the main centre of production to this day. Although current production levels are lower than in the past, the quality is still as good as it has ever been.

Olive trees like sunny hillsides up to a maximum altitude of 600m. They particularly contribute to the beauty of the scenery in the Balagne. Corsica hosts two annual olive festivals: on the third weekend in July in the hills above Calvi and in Ste-Lucie de Tallano in the Alta Rocca (southern Corsica) in March.

were traversed by shepherds taking their flocks between winter and summer grazing grounds. Now they are mainly frequented by walkers tackling the GR20.

If you're not an ambitious walker you will probably want wheels to get here. From Calvi take the road towards the airport (D251) and continue for about 20km more. There's a sign for the Forêt de Bonifatu 7km after the turnoff for Calenzana. Two kilometres farther on is Col de Rezza (510m), which overlooks a barren landscape sometimes called the Chaos de Rezza. The pass is a little before the forestry lodge, an inn and a car park.

A little footpath known as the Sentier du Mouflon (Mouflon Path) starts from the car park. It's a small and easy forest track (see Bonifatu to the Refuge de Carrozzu under Strolls & Country Walks in the Walking chapter) that takes you along the River Figarella, where you can swim in the hot months. After about 20 minutes this track leads to the paths that take you to the Refuge de Carrozzu (two hours farther) or the Refuge d'Ortu di u Piebu (about three hours further) on the GR20 route. These fairly quick walks are a good way of exploring the cirque, because you can only get a vague impression of it from below.

Places to Stay & Eat

The *Auberge de la Forêt* (☎ *04 95 65 09 98)*, next to the car park, has five comfortable rooms with en-suite bathroom but shared toilet for 300FF double and 240FF per person at half-board. There are also two impeccable dormitories with 16 bunk beds for 75FF. It is also possible to camp and have the use of a hot shower for 38FF.

Auberge de la Forêt is popular with walkers and serves a generous *menu* for 99FF, as well as sandwiches, on a pretty terrace. It opens April to September.

A further option would be to walk to the Refuge de Carrozzu (see Strolls & Country Walks in the Walking chapter for details).

The West Coast

In their numerous scalloped indentations, the great western gulfs of Porto, Sagone and Ajaccio shelter treasures such as the Réserve Naturelle de Scandola, the strange rock formations of Les Calanques de Piana, little resort villages on golden beaches and hamlets with long histories. A few kilometres back into the hinterland, villages in the heights over Porto and the River Liamone hang on to hoary traditions, while Ajaccio, the most populous town on the island, plays at being a little Corsican version of Nice.

Highlights

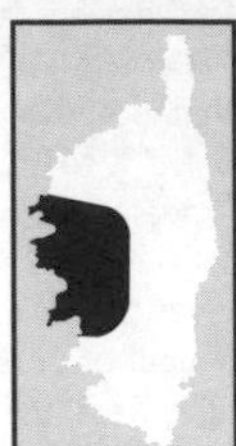

- Observe the multitude of fascinating plant and bird species in the Réserve Naturelle de Scandola
- Explore the eerie rock formations of Les Calanques on the stretch of coast between Porto and Piana
- Buy yourself a Napoleon T-shirt and pay homage in his home-town of Ajaccio

Golfe de Porto

RÉSERVE NATURELLE DE SCANDOLA

Created in 1975, the Scandola nature reserve at the northern end of the Golfe de Porto occupies 920 hectares of land and approximately 1000 hectares of sea. Owing its exceptional ecological richness to a varied geology as well as a particularly favourable climate and regular sunshine, it is home to a variety of plant and animal species, including osprey, cormorant, puffin, coral and seaweed. Scientists come in droves to study this flora and fauna.

Although the reserve was established too late to save the last colonies of monk seal and Corsican deer (now reintroduced around Quenza in the Alta Rocca), Scandola is a unique breeding ground for grouper and osprey (see the boxed text 'The King of the Scandola Nature Reserve' later in this chapter). Another of its curiosities is a type of calcareous seaweed that is so hard it forms pavements on the water's surface.

Nature Reserves

There are almost 120 nature reserves in France, of which five are located in Corsica: Étang de Biguglia south of Bastia, Îles Finocchiarola off the northern tip of Cap Corse, Bouches de Bonifacio, Îles Cerbicale near Porto Vecchio, and finally the Scandola area in the northwest.

Visitors to the reserves must observe a number of regulations. In particular, it is forbidden to pick plants, remove rocks, leave rubbish behind or light fires. Pets are not encouraged and fishing, hunting and camping are prohibited.

The reserve is bound in the north by Punta Palazzu and in the south by Punta Muchillina. Île Gargalo, with its tower, and Île Garganellu at the western edge of the reserve have won renown both for their wildlife and for their volcanic caves and faults. Birdwatchers are usually in luck until around the end of June.

The reserve is managed by the Parc Naturel Régional de Corse (PNRC), whose work the Council of Europe recognised with a special certificate in 1985. A portion of the coastline belongs to the Conservatoire du Littoral, and Scandola is also on the Unesco World Heritage list.

Getting There & Away

There is no motor-vehicle access or footpath to the Scandola nature reserve, which means that the only way to get close is by water. Companies organising boat trips to the reserve operate out of Porto, Cargèse,

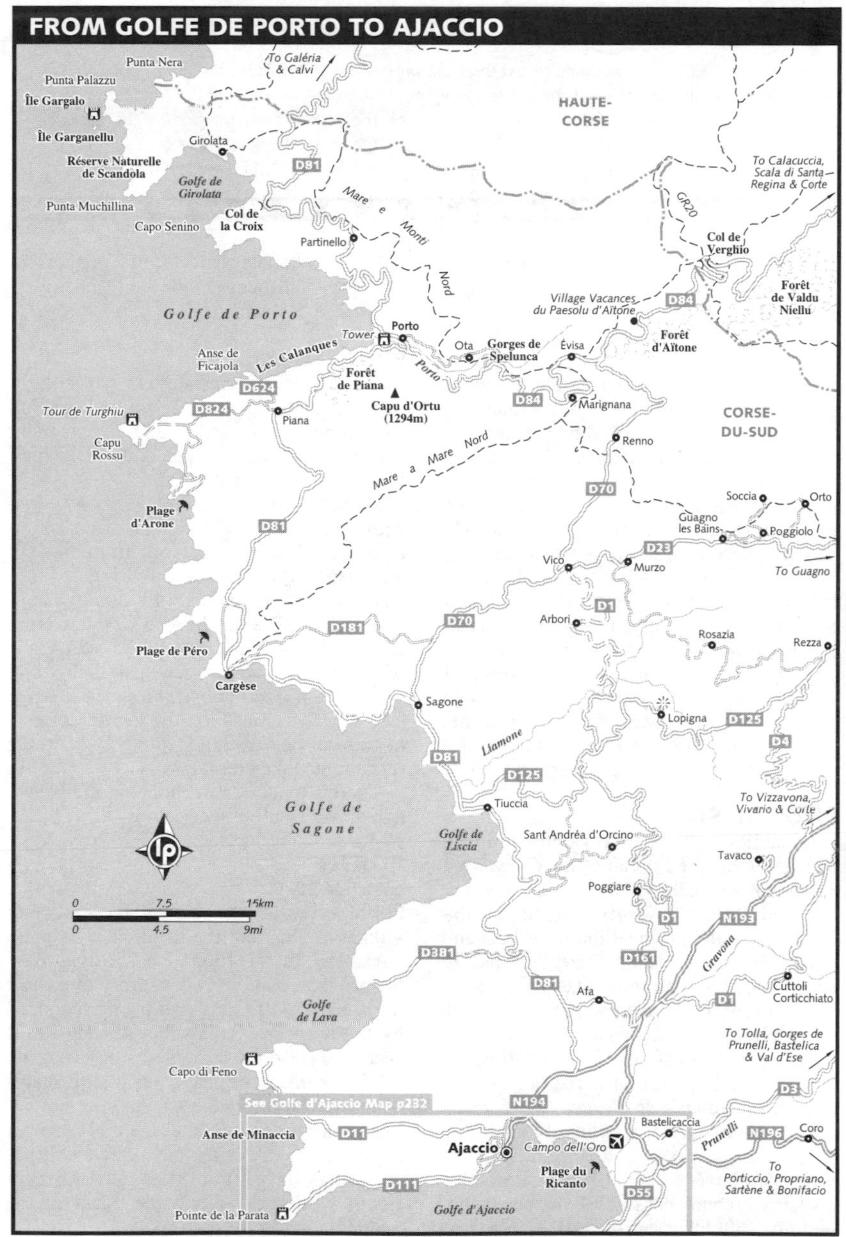
FROM GOLFE DE PORTO TO AJACCIO
Punta Nera
Punta Palazzu
Île Gargalo
Île Garganellu
Réserve Naturelle de Scandola
Punta Muchillina
Girolata
Golfe de Girolata
To Galéria & Calvi
HAUTE-CORSE
D81
Mare e Monti Nord
Capo Senino
Col de la Croix
Partinello
GR20
To Calacuccia, Scala di Santa Regina & Corte
Col de Verghio
Forêt de Valdu Niellu
Village Vacances du Paesolu d'Aïtone
D84
Forêt d'Aïtone
Golfe de Porto
Tower
Porto
Ota
Gorges de Spelunca
Évisa
Anse de Ficajola
Les Calanques
Porto
Forêt de Piana
D624
Capu d'Ortu (1294m)
D84
Marignana
Tour de Turghiu
D824
Piana
CORSE-DU-SUD
Renno
Capu Rossu
Mare a Mare Nord
D70
Plage d'Arone
Soccia
Orto
Guagno les Bains
Poggiolo
D81
D23
Vico
Murzo
To Guagno
D1
Arbori
D181
D70
Rosazia
Rezza
Plage de Péro
Cargèse
Sagone
Lopigna
D125
Llamone
D4
D81
D125
Golfe de Sagone
Tiuccia
To Vizzavona, Vivario & Corte
Golfe de Liscia
Sant Andréa d'Orcino
Tavaco
0 7.5 15km
0 4.5 9mi
Poggiare
D1
N193
D381
D161
Gravona
D81
Afa
Cuttoli Corticchiato
D1
Golfe de Lava
To Tolla, Gorges de Prunelli, Bastelica & Val d'Ese
Capo di Feno
D3
See Golfe d'Ajaccio Map p232
N194
Bastelicaccia
Anse de Minaccia
D11
Prunelli
N196
Coro
Ajaccio
Campo dell'Oro
Plage du Ricanto
To Porticcio, Propriano, Sartène & Bonifacio
D111
D55
Golfe d'Ajaccio
Pointe de la Parata

THE WEST COAST

The King of the Scandola Nature Reserve

The Scandola peninsula was home to just three osprey pairs in 1973. Today there are about 20 pairs, which is more than one-third of the entire osprey population in the whole of the Mediterranean. A large bird of prey with a white body and brown wings, the osprey is a magnificent sight, especially when hunting. It soars in wide circles until it spots a fish moving just below the water's surface, then dives towards the waves. It extends its claws to grab the fish only at the very last moment.

Sagone and Ajaccio (see Boat Trips under these towns later in this chapter), and Calvi (see the Calvi & the Balagne chapter).

GIROLATA

Although not officially part of the Scandola nature reserve, Girolata and the surrounding area are, all the same, outstanding. Although Girolata can be seen from many points on the drive between Calvi and Porto it can't be reached except by boat or on foot from Col de la Croix. The walk (about 1½ hours) is described in the Walking chapter.

Despite its inaccessibility, Girolata, between the Scandola peninsula and Capo Senino, gets quite busy in July and August. Private yachts carrying the kind of people who frequent end-of-the-world beaches pull in at the superb harbour, and some people complain that the beach gets dirty. But this jewel of the Corsican coast, with its Genoese fortress, is definitely worth a visit.

Places to Stay

Girolata lies on the Mare e Monti Nord path and has two gîtes d'étape. ***Le Cormoran Voyageur***, where the village meets the beach, is a red stone house lovingly tended by Joseph Ceccaldi (a sometime fisherman and one of Girolata's leading citizens). It has 20 beds divided among three reasonably comfortable rooms. Obligatory half-board, with an emphasis on fish dishes, costs 180FF; there are no self-catering facilities. It opens April to October. Credit cards are not accepted. ***La Cabane du Berger*** *(☎ 04 95 20 16 98)*, on the beach, is primarily a bar and restaurant, but it has gîte d'étape facilities as well. You have a choice between wooden chalets with bunk beds (70FF per person per night or 180FF for half-board), a camp site (40FF) or a double chalet (100FF per person, 240FF at half-board). Showers and toilets are shared. It opens April to mid-October.

Places to Eat

There are several restaurants particularly well situated above the beach and beneath the Genoese fortress; they all have excellent fish-based menus and open daily in the high season for lunch and dinner.

Le Bel Ombra *(☎ 04 95 20 15 67)*, just above Le Cormoran Voyageur, offers an unrestricted view over the cove from the teak armchairs on its terrace, a 98FF daily special lunch *menu* and a 150FF dinner *menu*. The restaurant opens May to October. Next door, ***Le Bon Espoir*** *(☎ 04 95 10 04 55)* offers the same great view, fish dishes and a Corsican *menu*. ***La Cabane du Berger*** (see Places to Stay), on the beach, offers a la carte dishes for 60FF to 80FF. All three restaurants take credit cards.

There's a public telephone on the beach, and also a small grocery store.

PORTO

postcode 20150

Porto serves as the port for the mountain village of Ota, and the location is its main attraction, at the foot of a lovely square tower erected in the 16th century to protect the superb Golfe de Porto from incursions by the Saracens. This small seaside resort seems to have mushroomed somewhat too suddenly in recent years, yet it still retains a certain charm. Packed in summer but deserted in winter, it makes a good base for exploring the mountainous back-country – as well as for getting a look at the exceptional wilderness along the coast of the Scandola nature reserve.

Orientation

Porto's pharmacy is one of the few buildings visible from the D81, the main road through this part of the coast, and it is a useful landmark because it is at the intersection with the road that leads 1.5km down to the area around the harbour. Between the pharmacy and the harbour lies the quarter known as Vaïta, or Porto le Haut. The harbour area is divided by the River Porto, which is crossed by a footbridge. Those travelling by car to the southern side of the harbour area should take the road signposted 'Porto rive gauche' on the D81 towards Piana.

Information

Tourist Offices The friendly and efficient tourist office (☎ 04 95 26 10 55) in the harbour car park opens 9 am to 7 pm daily, July and August; and 9 am to noon and 2 to 6 pm Monday to Friday, the rest of the year.

Most of the staff speak English, and they can provide you with information on activities and walks in the area. You can check out the Web site at www.porto-tourisme.com (French only).

Money Porto's only ATM is across from Hôtel Cala di Sole in Vaïta. It takes all major credit cards. A bureau de change, near the Spar supermarket on the D81, provides cash advances against credit cards. The post office changes travellers cheques denominated in French francs.

Post & Communications The small post office next to Hôtel Lonza in Vaïta opens 9 am to 12.30 pm and 2 to 4 pm Monday to Friday and 8.30 to 11 am Saturday. The hours are longer in July and August. There are public telephones in front of the post office. The tourist office will send faxes for 5FF per page within France or for 10FF per page to other countries.

Bookshops L'Aiglon (☎ 04 95 26 10 46), at the harbour, sells French and foreign newspapers, beach accessories and camera film. Newspapers are also available from Le Colomba in Vaïta.

Laundry The laundrette in Vaïta opens 8 am to 10 pm; expect to pay 40FF for washing and 25FF for drying.

Genoese Tower

Standing guard over the entrance to the fishing harbour, the Genoese tower is an ideal place from where to watch the sun set over the gulf. It was built in 1549, in the same period as the other 85 towers around the Corsican coast, and it was restored so as to look almost as good as new in 1993.

The tower opens 9 am to 9 pm daily, July and August and 11 am to 7 pm daily, the rest of the year. Admission costs 15FF, and it's worth it for all the information you'll get about how this and the other towers were financed and about the hard life of the tower watchman. You reach the tower via a series of steps starting next to La Tour Génoise restaurant. In fine weather you can see the tower on Capo Rosso (often called the Tour de Piana, because it was used to protect Piana) on the southern side of the gulf from the top of the tower.

Aquarium de la Poudrière

Open since summer 2000 in the town's former powder magazine, this little aquarium (☎ 04 95 26 19 24) is worth a visit if you take the time and effort to read the accounts of the marine species in residence. Admission costs 35FF (children 20FF) and the aquarium opens daily in summer. It's adjacent to Hôtel Monte Rosso.

Boat Trips

Two companies arrange boat trips out of Porto between April and October. Nave Va (information from Hôtel Le Cyrnée, ☎ 04 95 26 15 16) runs three-hour trips along the coast of the Scandola nature reserve in summer which cost 190FF (children aged 6 to 12 half-price). There are two departures daily.

Porto Linea (tickets and information at Hôtel Monte Rosso, ☎ 04 95 26 11 50) organises a similar excursion aboard a yellow 12-seat boat, *Le Mare Nostrum*, which is small enough to explore some very little inlets. Trips to Scandola cost 190FF and to Les Calanques, 100FF.

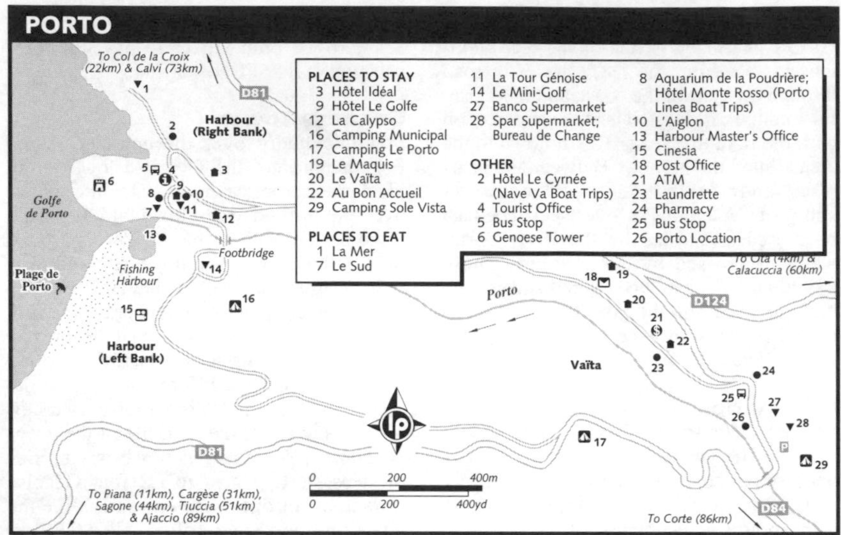

Those wishing to explore the Golfe de Porto on their own can hire inflatable motor dinghies from 450FF for a half-day – ask at the harbour.

Things to See & Do

It is not the most stunning beach in Corsica but the **Plage de Porto** should content those keen on sunbathing and swimming.

Cinesia (☎ 04 95 26 10 49) screens films in the open air in a little eucalyptus forest by the harbour in July and August.

Places to Stay

Like elsewhere in Corsica, it's a good idea to make reservations in advance in the high season.

Places to Stay – Budget

Near the Spar supermarket on the D81 above Porto, ***Camping Sole Vista*** *(☎ 04 95 26 15 71, fax 04 95 26 10 79)* offers pleasant shady pitches that are well separated from one another. The rates are 32/15/12/12FF per adult/child aged under seven/tent/car. ***Camping Municipal*** *(☎ 04 95 26 17 76)*, on the left bank of the river, in the harbour area, is a rather basic camp site charging 28/10/10FF per person/tent/car or a few francs more at the height of the season. To get there by car, take the road signposted 'Porto rive gauche' on the D81 heading towards Piana. It opens mid-June to September. ***Camping Le Porto*** *(☎ 04 95 26 13 67, fax 04 95 26 10 79)*, on the D81 in the direction of Piana, before you come to the intersection towards 'Porto rive gauche', has been recommended by readers.

Hôtel Le Golfe *(☎ 04 95 26 13 33)*, at the harbour, has 10 decent rooms with toilet and shower costing from 180FF. The hotel is a few metres from the path out to the Genoese tower.

Au Bon Accueil *(☎/fax 04 95 26 19 50)*, in Vaïta, offers doubles with bathrooms for 180FF to 300FF, depending on the season.

Le Maquis *(☎ 04 95 26 12 19, fax 04 95 26 12 77)*, about 2km from the sea at the intersection of the D81 and the D124 to Ota, has five very basic, and consequently cheap, double rooms. They cost 240/300FF with washbasin/bathroom. The hotel is renowned, however, for its food, and half-board is compulsory at the height of the season. The restaurant opens year round except for a couple of weeks in November and December and again in January and February.

Places to Stay – Mid-Range

On the D81 in Vaïta, ***Le Vaïta*** *(☎ 04 95 26 10 37, fax 04 95 26 12 81)* has 26 rooms, some with terraces, which cost 200FF to 450FF, depending on the season. There is a pleasant lounge and a restaurant. The hotel opens April to November.

Hôtel Idéal *(☎ 04 95 26 10 07, fax 04 95 26 11 57)*, at the bottom of the slope that leads to the harbour, has clean and pleasant, if somewhat small, double rooms with bathroom for 300FF to 350FF in low season and 400FF to 450FF in July and August. Rooms overlooking the sea have terraces. The hotel opens Easter and to October.

La Calypso *(☎ 04 95 26 11 54, fax 04 95 26 12 17)*, in the harbour area, has doubles with sea views for 270FF in low season, 350FF in July and September and 490FF in August. It costs 320FF to 550FF for three people and 390FF to 610FF for four people, depending on the season. The hotel has a car park and laundry facilities. It opens April to October and advance booking is recommended.

Places to Eat

Budget Lots of restaurants and hotels along the seafront serve pizzas and inexpensive, unsurprising *menus*. ***La Tour Génoise*** *(☎ 04 95 26 17 11)*, with pizzas starting at 40FF and several 'touristy' *menus*, perhaps stands out a bit from the others. ***Le Mini-Golf*** *(☎ 04 95 26 17 55)*, on the left bank, serves particularly generous pizzas in a little green area.

Spar and ***Banco*** supermarkets on the D81, not far from the pharmacy, provide for self-caterers and there's also a little ***grocery*** by the harbour.

Mid-Range & Top End With its superb terrace beneath the Genoese tower, ***Le Sud*** *(☎ 04 95 26 14 11)* has 130FF 'sea' and 'land' *menus*. This is one of the nicest restaurants in Porto and it opens for lunch and dinner daily, April to October.

La Mer *(☎ 04 95 26 11 27)*, at the harbour, serves good fish dishes on its terrace overlooking the gulf and the Genoese tower, which is illuminated at night. The 138FF *menu* includes fresh anchovies and chilled ratatouille, grilled swordfish, cheese or dessert. The lunch *menu* costs 99FF.

Le Maquis (see Places to Stay) is Porto's gastronomic temple. A Corsican *tian* (stew) with *figatellu* (liver sausage) for 100FF and an excellent crusty lobster pastry (135FF) are among the high points. The service is as attentive as the cuisine is refined.

Shopping

Natura Viva, not far from the post office in Vaïta, sells fragrances, and *objets d'art* made from driftwood, shells and pebbles. There's a shop selling Corsican food products midway down the road from Vaïta to the marina.

Getting There & Away

SAIB buses (☎ 04 95 22 41 99) stop in Porto between one and four times daily on their way back and forth between Ajaccio and Ota. Precise frequency depends on time of year and day of the week. The one-way fare from Ajaccio is 70FF. Other towns served, in addition to Ota, are Piana, Cargèse, Sagone and Tiuccia. SAIB also connects Porto and Calvi (110FF, approximately 2½ hours), via Col de la Croix, once daily from 15 May to 10 October.

Autocars Mordiconi (☎ 04 95 48 00 04) runs buses from Porto to Calacuccia and Corte daily except Sunday from July to mid-September. Porto to Corte costs 110FF and the bus leaves at 2pm. This journey is spectacularly beautiful.

Buses stop at the pharmacy and at the harbour; ask at the tourist office for further information.

Sailors should note that space for mooring in Porto harbour is limited due to its size and shallowness. Typically, yachts drop anchor just off the beach. Washroom facilities are at Camping Municipal, a 10-minute walk away. The little harbour master's office (☎ 04 95 26 14 90) is at quayside on the left bank of the river.

Getting Around

Porto Location (☎/fax 04 95 26 10 13) opposite Spar supermarket on the D81 hires out cars for 420FF per day, scooters for 300FF per day, mountain bikes for 90FF per day or 60FF per half-day as well as some two-passenger buggies for 390FF per day or 250FF for a half-day. Rates go down on rentals of two days or longer. Porto Location opens 8.30 am to 9 pm in high season.

FROM PORTO TO COL DE VERGHIO

The D124 leads out of Porto and up through the mountains to Ota, with its superb Genoese bridges. It then connects with the D84, which continues the climb to the marvellous Gorges de Spelunca in Évisa, the Forêt d'Aïtone and Col de Verghio (Bocca di Verghju), above which lies the Niolo (Niolu) region. From here you can continue on to the Forêt de Valdu Niellu, Calacuccia, the Scala di Santa Regina and Corte (see the Central Mountains chapter).

Ota

postcode 20150 • pop 452 • elevation 335m

Perched above its cemetery, the pretty village of Ota clings to a mountainside 5km to the east of Porto. Here you'll find stone houses, a war memorial shaded by palm trees (opposite the village hall) and a peaceful atmosphere. Inexpensive gîtes signal the village's setting along the Mare e Monti Nord path.

The two **Genoese bridges**, about 2km beyond the village centre on the D124, merit a prolonged glance. The graceful Pont de Pianella to the south of the road forms a perfect arch. You can walk down to the river here and go for a swim. The second bridge, a few hundred metres beyond, is equally astonishing. It stands at the confluence of the rivers Aïtone and Tavulella, crossing them one after the other. A footpath off to the right beyond this second bridge gets you back to Ota, along the river, in about 40 minutes.

A lovely walk, from the Genoese bridges into the nearby Gorges de Spelunca, also begins nearby. It's an old mule track that runs up through the Défilé de la Spelunca to the Ponte Vecchju, then climbs up to the overgrown Ponte Zaglia and on to Évisa. This route is described in more detail in the Walking chapter.

Places to Stay & Eat The dormitories at ***Chez Félix*** *(☎/fax 04 95 26 12 92, place de la Fontaine)* each have a bathroom and six bunk beds, which cost 65FF per night. There is a communal kitchen but half-board at 180FF, including breakfast, is a good deal for the home cooking. Visitors not spending the night will pay 110FF for a *menu* that features rabbit 'the way grandma used to make it'. Chez Félix also rents private rooms and studios as well as operating the only local taxi service.

Down the road is ***Chez Marie, Bar des Chasseurs*** *(☎ 04 95 26 11 37)* which has impeccable dormitories at prices identical to those at Chez Félix. There is also one double room for 140FF. Half-board costs 170FF. Chez Félix and Chez Marie are both friendly places with terraces that open out over magnificent mountain scenery.

The grocery shop near the church opens 7 am to 12.30 pm and 3 to 8 pm Monday to Saturday in the high season. Hours are shorter at other times of the year.

Getting There & Away SAIB (☎ 04 95 22 41 99) operates two buses to Ota daily except Sunday and public holidays from Porto, Piana, Cargèse, Sagone, Tiuccia and Ajaccio, and in the period from 1 July to 15 September there is a third bus and Sunday service as well. Buses leave Ota from place de la Fontaine, not far from Chez Félix.

Marignana

postcode 20141 • pop 99 • elevation 750m

This little village, on a mountainside between Ota and Évisa, was famous in the 19th century as the scene of a particularly prolonged and bloody vendetta. Now it's a stop for hikers on the Mare a Mare Nord trail.

Places to Stay & Eat At ***Ustaria di a Rota*** *(☎ 04 95 26 21 21)* gîte beds cost 65FF per night. The *menu* costs 75FF, and the traditional Corsican dishes are quite good. Ustaria di a Rota also provides a home for Corsica Trek, which organises hikes and outdoor sports activities in the area. Studio apartments can be rented in the village as well.

SALLY DILLON

Burnished gold, ochre, copper and bronze: Les Calanques do their best to complement the sky.

TONY WHEELER

Whether you're after balmy days on boats and beaches...

TONY WHEELER

...or walks along the mountain reaches, Porto serves as a tranquil base.

SALLY DILLON

Ota is near some exceptional Genoese bridges.

OLIVIER CIRENDINI

Another balmy day bites the dust near Porto.

NICOLA WILLIAMS

A band of Corsicans gathers in Ajaccio.

FRANCES LINZEE GORDON

Big fish Napoleon was spawned in...

JEAN-BERNARD CARILLET

...colourful Ajaccio.

Évisa

postcode 20126 • pop 265 • elevation 830m

The quiet little village of Évisa, between the Gorges de Spelunca and the Forêt d'Aïtone, is popular with walkers because of its location at the junction of the Mare a Mare Nord and Mare e Monti Nord paths. Its fame, however, arises from its chestnut harvests. 'Evisa Chestnuts' even have their own appellation, and a chestnut festival is held in the village every November.

There is a supermarket and a post office (☎ 04 95 26 20 43).

Places to Stay & Eat The *Gîte d'Étape d'Évisa (☎ 04 95 26 21 88)* near the post office, at the end of a narrow street, is prized among walkers for its warm reception. The dormitory rate is 70FF per night, half-board costs 170FF and it opens April to October.

La Châtaigneraie *(☎ 04 95 26 24 47)*, meaning chestnut grove, at the entrance to the village as you come from Porto or Sagone, offers good double rooms with bathroom for 180FF to 250FF, depending on the season. The reputable restaurant provides a 95FF *menu*, and wines are reasonably priced. It opens March to October, credit cards are accepted, and English is spoken.

U Pozzu *(☎ 04 95 21 11 45)* on the outskirts of Évisa as you head for the Forêt d'Aïtone, opens May to September and has decent rooms for 200FF to 250FF depending on the season. The hotel's restaurant, ***U Mulinu***, serves crêpes and Corsican specialities.

L'Aïtone *(☎ 04 95 26 20 04, fax 04 95 26 24 18)*, opposite U Pozzu, has pleasant double rooms for 240FF to 650FF, depending on the season and the view. There is a swimming pool and the restaurant offers *menus* costing 95FF to 130FF.

Several cafes in the village serve snacks and there are grocery shops as well as a supermarket that accepts credit cards.

Getting There & Away Autocars Ceccaldi (☎ 04 95 20 29 76) operates a bus service from Ajaccio to Évisa via Vico (70FF) daily except Sunday and public holidays.

Forêt d'Aïtone

The Forêt d'Aïtone – 1670 hectares in area, 800m to 2000m high – begins a few kilometres outside Évisa. In the 17th century the Genoese built a path through these trees to Sagone, from where timber from the forest was sent to shipyards in Genoa. Corsican laricio pine is the dominant species, covering around 800 hectares. Beech covers around 200 hectares and you'll also come across maritime pine, fir and larch. The forest has long been famous for its wealth of plant extracts.

Look out for the signs for a tiny waterfall and natural basin serving as a miniature swimming pool on the left-hand side of the road as you come from Évisa. The walk takes only about 10 minutes and the site is cool and peaceful. The waterfall is about 4km from Évisa along a pleasant footpath.

Two kilometres above the waterfall is **Village Vacances de Paesolu d'Aïtone**, a holiday village, and a PNRC information centre (☎ 04 95 26 23 62). The information centre has an interesting exhibition on the fauna and flora of the forest. Unfortunately, it is often closed, but you may be able to borrow the key at the holiday village reception.

A few hundred metres away, the short Sentier de la Sittelle (Nuthatch Path) – watch for the image of the nuthatch on Office National des Forêts (ONF; National Office for Forests) signposts – offers an opportunity to explore the forest close up. The path follows the former Piste des Condamnés (Trail of the Condemned), named in memory of the prisoners who did forced labour in the forest in the 19th century.

There's no public transport service to the forest but you can take a taxi from Ota.

COL DE VERGHIO

About 6km above the Village Vacances de Paesolu d'Aïtone, Col de Verghio (1467m) marks the boundary between Haute-Corse and Corse-du-Sud. As you cross this boundary you'll pass a statue by the sculptor Bonardi; it represents Jesus in a long cloak, his arm outstretched, his palm turned upwards towards the heavens. A vendor of

Corsican produce and drinks in the car park is his constant companion in summer.

There are a number of walking paths from Col de Verghio, which has unobstructed views over the Forêt d'Aïtone on one side and the Forêt de Valdu Niellu on the other. The walk to the Bergerie de Radule on the GR20 is described in the Walking chapter.

The Niolo region and the Forêt de Valdu Niellu stretch eastwards from Col de Verghio. A few parcels of forestry land are used to study the longevity of the Corsican laricio pine. Some of its trees are 300 years old and have grown to a height of 30m.

In addition to hotel and restaurant Hôtel Castel di Verghio (see the Walking chapter), which caters mainly for walkers, accommodation is available in Calacuccia, about 20km from Col de Verghio (see The Central Mountains chapter).

PIANA

postcode 20115 • pop 500 • elevation 438m

Piana overlooks the Golfe de Porto from a small plateau, 68km from Ajaccio and 12km south-west of Porto. Les Calanques (E Calanche), Piana's famous rocky inlets, cast a golden shadow over the village. Many people just pass through Piana, but it is a pleasant village and definitely worth a stop.

In the 15th century Piana was ruled by the hot-headed *seigneurs de Leca*, who governed a vast area on the western coast of the island. Rebelling against Genoa, they were massacred alongside the defenders of the parish. The Genoese then banned anyone from living in Piana, which came to life again only after Genoese influence on the island had begun to wane.

The **Église Ste-Marie**, which contains several exceptional statues, was built between 1765 and 1772.

Orientation

Entering Piana from Porto, you'll first see Hôtel des Roches Rouges, then the path to the Gîte d'Étape Giargalo on a bend in the road just before the Hôtel Mare e Monte. Following that you'll find the tourist office, post office and the village square with its church and restaurants. The Hôtel Continental and a supermarket are on the outskirts of Piana in the direction of Cargèse.

Information

Staff at the tourist office (☎ 04 95 27 82 72), on the main road next to the post office, can supply you with brochures and information on walks in the area. It opens 9 am to 7 pm daily in July and August; and 9 am to noon and 2 to 5 pm Monday to Friday and Saturday morning, the rest of the year.

There are no banks, bureaux de change or ATMs in Piana but you should be able to exchange your travellers cheques at the post office (☎ 04 95 27 89 29), in the building next to the town hall, which opens 9 am to 3 pm in summer.

Places to Stay

Camping de la Plage d'Arone *(☎ 04 95 20 64 54)* is a lovely camp site (but with little shade) 11km from Piana and 600m from the Plage d'Arone. Rates are 30/15/14/13FF per adult/child aged under seven/tent/car. It opens June to September.

The ***Gîte d'Étape Giargalo*** is owned by Le Glacier restaurant, where you'll find its reception. It offers beds in rooms for two to four for 50FF per person or 160FF at half-board. There is also a communal kitchen. To get to the gîte, climb a few hundred metres off the main road from the bend at Hôtel Mare e Monti. Look for a grey stone building.

Hôtel Mare e Monti *(☎ 04 95 27 82 14, fax 04 95 27 84 16)* has immaculate and comfortable, if somewhat fusty, rooms with bathroom, telephone and balcony for 220/240/310FF single/double/triple.

Hôtel Continental *(☎ 04 95 27 83 12)* on the southern outskirts of Piana, offers simple but pleasant singles/doubles with rustic wooden floorboards and shared bathroom for 160/190FF or 270FF in the annexe. It opens April to September.

Le Scandola *(☎ 04 95 27 80 07, fax 04 95 27 80 00)*, also at the southern end of the village, has pleasant doubles which cost 200FF to 380FF depending on the season.

THE WEST COAST

Hôtel des Roches Rouges *(☎ 04 95 27 81 81, fax 04 95 27 81 76)*, below the road on the way into Piana from Porto, occupies a large building which dates from 1912. In addition to a terrace with a lovely view over the Golfe de Porto, it has 30 excellent, traditionally furnished double rooms for 380FF. It opens April to the beginning of November.

Places to Eat

Le Casanova *(☎ 04 95 27 84 20)*, in a pretty stone house with a pleasant little terrace, serves large wood-fire pizzas for about 50FF and *menus*. It opens daily for lunch and dinner from Easter to October.

Le Glacier *(☎ 04 95 27 82 05)* offers tasty food at reasonable prices. It serves excellent pastries and, true to its name (the ice-cream maker), excellent home-made ice cream for 30FF to 35FF. A stone's throw from the main square, it opens for lunch and dinner daily April to September.

The restaurant at the ***Hôtel des Roches Rouges*** (see Places to Stay earlier) gives you the opportunity to settle into a comfortable cane armchair and enjoy superior cuisine, superb decor and an exceptional panoramic view of the gulf. *Menus* are available for 130FF, 160FF and 250FF.

Le Moulin des Calanques *(☎ 04 95 27 84 80)*, 1km outside of Piana in the direction of Porto, was opened in the year 2000 in an old chestnut flour mill to provide a drink, lunch or snacks such as *panini* to visitors to Les Calanques. The proprietors are real enthusiasts of the area and will gladly provide advice on where to walk.

Getting There & Away

SAIB buses (☎ 04 95 22 41 99) stop in Piana on their way back and forth between Ajaccio and Porto. The buses run twice daily Monday to Saturday except public holidays. Between 1 July and 15 September they operate on Sundays as well.

LES CALANQUES (E CALANCHE)

Guy de Maupassant, who visited Corsica in 1880, likened these strange geological formations to 'some fantastic fairy-tale race, petrified by an unknown supernatural force'. In fact, this amazing stone garden – which Unesco has named a World Heritage Site – was formed by wind and sea erosion.

The D81 begins to wind its way through Les Calanques at a distance of about 1.5km from Piana, on the way to Porto; the route then twists and turns through the ochre-red rocks for several kilometres more.

Walks

You can explore the site and surrounding area of Les Calanques on foot. The first three of the routes described below start at the Pont de Mezzanu, approximately 1.5km from Piana in the direction of Porto (halfway between the Chalet des Roches Bleues souvenir shop and Piana). A brochure and a map detailing the paths are available from the tourist office in Piana.

Sentier Muletier This route takes about an hour and follows the mule track that linked Piana and Ota before the D81 was built in 1850. It is signposted in blue.

Forêt de Piana This comprises two alternative routes, taking 2½ and three hours respectively, passing through the pine forests and chestnut groves above Les Calanques.

Capu d'Ortu This starts like the Forêt de Piana walk before ascending to a rocky spur. The walk takes six hours and takes you to the Capu d'Ortu plateau (1294m).

Château Fort Leading to a rocky promontory over the Golfe de Porto and Les Calanques, this walk takes about 40 minutes round trip. See Strolls & Country Walks in the Walking chapter for details.

Sentier du Coeur The name refers to the heart-shaped indentation in the rock to which it leads in a walk of no more than 15 minutes from Le Moulin des Calanques (see Places to Eat under Piana) whose proprietors developed this walk.

Getting There & Away

It is easy to get to Les Calanques on foot from Piana. SAIB buses between Ajaccio and Porto can also drop you off here or at the Chalet des Roches Bleues souvenir shop.

AROUND PIANA

Les Calanques do not exhaust the interest of the area around Piana, but in order to explore farther you may find it useful to have a car.

La Marine de Ficajola

From the church in Piana, follow the D824 towards the Plage d'Arone for 1km, then turn right onto the D624, which winds its way down through superb rocky red mountains for about 4km. Leave your vehicle and walk for about 10 minutes down a path to the marina. This is a spot where, in days gone by, lobster-fishing boats used to take shelter. Along the way you will have opportunities to admire the marvellous views over Les Calanques. At the marina there is a small snack bar in summer.

Plage d'Arone

This long and lovely fine-sand beach is reached by following the D824 for 12km from the church in Piana. The drive takes you along a ridge offering wonderful views over the Golfe de Porto, then cuts through superb wild mountain scenery and maquis to end up south of Capu Rossu.

The beach itself has a special place in Corsican history as it was here that the first weapons for the Corsican resistance arrived on the submarine *Casabianca* in 1943, under the command of Captain L'Herminier (after whom several quays in Corsican harbours are named). A number of bars and restaurants open along the beach in summer.

Capu Rossu (Capo Rosso)

Between the Golfe de Porto and the Golfe de Sagone, this scrub-covered headland with pink-grey rock stands 300m over the sea, and is crowned by the Tour de Turghiu. There is an excellent walk along the headland, and the view over the Golfe de Porto and the Plage d'Arone is breathtaking. To get to the headland, follow the D824 out of Piana in the direction of the Plage d'Arone. The 7km road that turns off to Capu Rossu cuts through a superb wilderness. The walk to Capu Rossu from the D824 is described in Strolls & Country Walks in the Walking chapter.

Golfe de Sagone

CARGÈSE (CARGHJESE)

postcode 20130 • pop 900

This sleepy little town, on a promontory over the sea, was founded in 1676 to house a community of 730 Greeks, who had appealed to Genoa for refuge from the conquering Turks (see the boxed text 'From the Peloponnese to Cargèse' on the next page). There is no longer much to mark the town as Greek, however, other than the Greek Orthodox religious festivals celebrated in the Eastern Rite church (Église Catholique de Rite Grec). The immigrants' descendants are no longer in any significant way distinguishable from other Corsicans. Cargèse's history has created a unique atmosphere but its charm lies simply in its quiet streets and white facades.

Orientation

Most of the hotels and restaurants in Cargèse lie along the main road (D81) while the old town and the churches are to the right as you come from Piana. Several streets lead off the main road down to a small fishing harbour but it is not of great interest. The Plage du Péro is 1.5km north of Cargèse.

Information

The tourist office (☎ 04 95 26 41 31) is below the main road in the direction of the old town. It opens 9 am to 1 pm and 3 to 7 pm daily in summer with shorter hours in winter.

The Banque Populaire Provençale et Corse (☎ 04 95 26 40 43), on the way into town from Piana, exchanges foreign currencies and travellers cheques, except Eurocheques, will provide cash advances against credit cards and has an ATM. It opens 8.30 am to 12.30 pm and 1.30 to 4.45 pm Monday to Friday and Saturday morning. A branch of Crédit Agricole (☎ 04 95 26 41 75) on rue Colonel Fieschi also

From the Peloponnese to Cargèse

In 1663 some 800 Greeks from the southern Peloponnese fled their Ottoman-Turk conquerors and entered into talks with the Genoese authorities to find a new homeland. Twelve years later the Genoese granted them the territory of Paomia, just above what is now Cargèse, at a distance of about 50km north of Ajaccio. In March 1676 the surviving 730 émigrés – those who had not perished en route – set foot on Corsican soil for the first time. Their colony flourished. Some even gave up the '-akis' with which Greek names characteristically end and replaced it with a more Corsican-Italianate '-acci'. But then came the hitch. When the Corsicans rebelled against the Genoese in 1729, the Greeks, true to their pledge to their Genoese benefactors, sided with Genoa, and the Corsicans sacked Paomia. The Greek community moved to Ajaccio, where it then lived unobtrusively for about 40 years.

Relations between Greeks and Corsicans began to improve during the period of Corsican independence but it was only in the first decade of French rule that Cargèse itself was granted to them and they began to build new homes there. This time they were set upon by inhabitants of the neighbouring village of Vico and by Niolo shepherds who had been in the habit of wintering their flocks in the Cargèse area. Until around 1830, the Greeks hesitated between Cargèse and relatively friendly Ajaccio but by then tempers had at last cooled and hostilities had gradually ceased. The Greeks installed themselves in Cargèse and for most of the past two centuries they and their Corsican neighbours have lived together in exemplary harmony – to the point at which nothing in particular distinguishes the two communities but the continuing allegiance of most of the Greeks to the Greek Orthodox church.

changes currency. There are also ATMs at the Shopi supermarket and at the post office.

The post office (☎ 04 95 26 41 97), on the main road at the entrance to the old town, opens 9 am to 4.45 pm Monday to Friday, June to August; and 9 to 11.45 am and 2.30 to 4.45 pm Monday to Friday, the rest of the year. It opens 9 to 11.45 am on Saturday year round.

Église Catholique de Rite Grec

This white-fronted church, opposite the Église Latine Ste-Marie, is worth visiting for its icons (several of which were brought from Greece in 1676), its old paintings and for its interior staircase. The present church dates from 1852, when it replaced the original building, which was no longer large enough to accommodate the entire congregation. The new church took 20 years to build and the parishioners were themselves frequently enlisted to help. Like all Greek churches, this is above all distinguished by the richness of its ornamentation and its iconostasis (a traditional painted wooden partition separating the sanctuary from the nave).

Église Latine Ste-Marie

The history of this church goes back to 1817, when the town's non-Greek families decided that it was time to establish a fund to build a Roman-Catholic sanctuary. Work, in the neo-classical style, began eight years later and continued until 1828. Wind blew the roof off in 1835 and there were no interior fittings until 1845. The square tower was added in 1847.

Boat Trips

Renaldo (☎ 04 95 28 02 66) organises boat trips to Capu Rossu, Les Calanques and the Scandola nature reserve. Boats leave the harbour at 9 am and return at 4 pm May to September. The 225FF fare includes a two-hour stop at Girolata and a half-hour swim in an inlet. Tickets are sold at the shop Chez Fanny (☎ 04 95 26 44 43) on rue Colonel Fieschi. The tourist office also has information on two other local companies offering boat trips.

Places to Stay

Hôtel de France 'Chez Mimino' *(☎ 04 95 26 41 07, rue Colonel Fieschi)* has 12 decent double rooms with bathrooms for 160FF to 230FF, depending on the season.

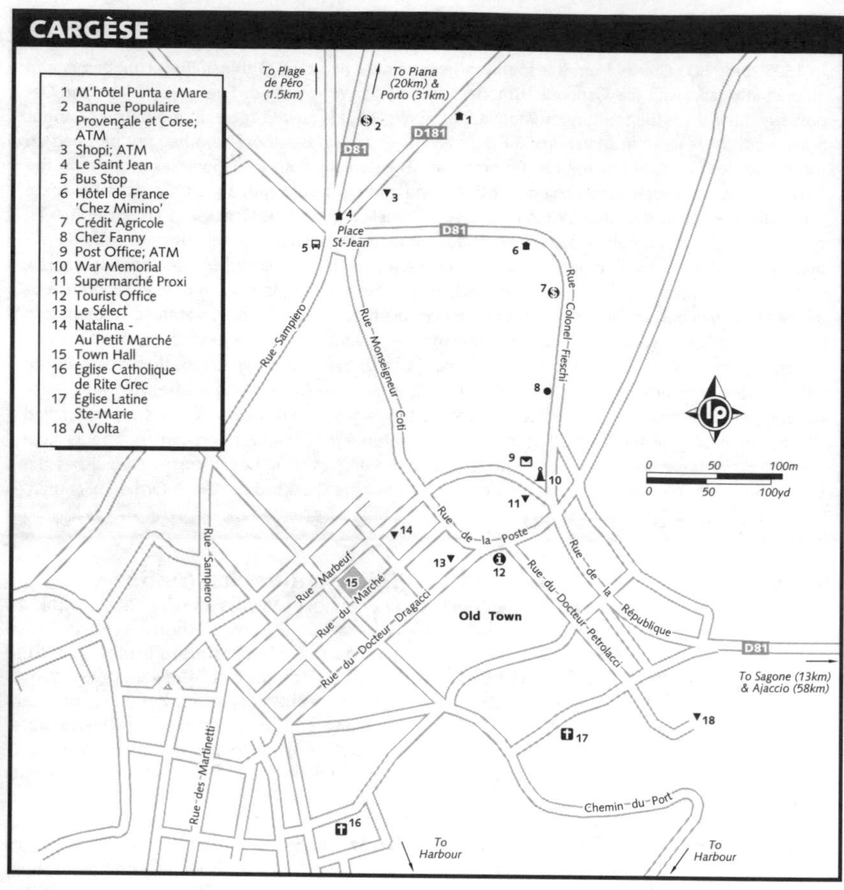

This family business, with a built-in pizzeria, opens April to October.

Le Saint Jean *(☎ 04 95 26 46 68, fax 04 95 26 46 17, place St-Jean)* has utilitarian but comfortable rooms with air-conditioning, TV, terrace and telephone. A double room costs from 245FF to 450FF, depending on the time of year and the view. An extra bed costs 100FF. The hotel's restaurant, with a broad choice of *menus*, is the liveliest in town.

M'hôtel Punta e Mare *(☎ 04 95 26 44 33, fax 04 95 26 49 54)*, a few hundred metres from place St-Jean on the D181 as it begins its ascent into the mountains, has impeccable, quiet double rooms for 200FF to 300FF, depending on the time of year. The little apartments at the front of the building are older and not so pleasant. The hotel rents mountain bikes.

Places to Eat

Cargèse is no great gastronomic destination but there are many quite adequate restaurants along the main road and some pizzerias on the harbour. In the old town, ***Le Sélect*** *(☎ 04 95 26 43 41)* is a pleasant, unpretentious little cafe that serves good daily specials for around 50FF as well as *menus*. The lasagne merits special mention. At ***A Volta*** *(☎ 04 95 26 41 96)*, in a cul-de-sac at the end of rue du Docteur Petrolacci in the old town, your lunch or dinner comes with a splendid view of the sea. The 98FF *menu* might even include fillet of forkbeard (a type of fish).

There are two supermarkets (Shopi on the D81 is one) for self-caterers and ***Natalina – Au Petit Marché***, a small grocery shop in the old town, sells Corsican delicacies.

Getting There & Away

SAIB buses (☎ 04 95 22 41 99) on their way to Ajaccio and Porto stop two or three times daily in place St-Jean or at the post office. The one-way fare from Ajaccio is 50FF.

SAGONE & TIUCCIA

These seaside resorts to the south of Cargèse are renowned for their beaches. Sagone, an old Roman city, had a bishop's palace from the 6th to the 16th century but no trace of it remains today.

Crédit Agricole in Sagone (☎ 04 95 28 19 00) has an ATM that accepts Visa, MasterCard and Cirrus.

You can do Renaldo's (in Cargèse; ☎ 04 95 26 41 31) **boat trips** from Sagone (departing at 8.30 am). Tickets are sold at the souvenir shop next to Le Bowling (an ice-cream shop, not a bowling alley) in Sagone.

There are plenty of bars, hotels and restaurants near the two resorts.

SAIB buses (☎ 04 95 22 41 99) operate between Ajaccio and Ota via Tiuccia and Sagone two or three times daily.

LE LIAMONE

This mountainous green micro-region, also known as Les Deux Sorru, between Sagone and Col de Verghio, takes its name from the river that flows through it to the Golfe de Sagone. Its largest villages are Renno (Rennu) and Vico (Vicu), which has an imposing convent. The villages detailed below lie along the Mare a Mare Nord path.

Guagno les Bains

The road that winds its way up beyond Vico leads to a picturesque cluster of villages perched on the mountainside. Guagno les Bains, the first village you come to, became a popular thermal spa in the 18th century because of its hot springs, and villagers are now once again trying to entice people here to experience the curative powers of Corsica's mineral waters – with minimal success.

Places to Stay & Eat Grand but rather forlorn, ***Hôtel des Thermes*** *(☎ 04 95 26 80 50, fax 04 95 28 34 02)*, offers doubles costing from 440FF to 520FF, depending on the season. Various curative treatments are available and the restaurant has a *menu* of the day for 135FF. The hotel opens May to October.

Soccia & Orto

postcode 20125 • pop 121 & 54

Perched at an elevation of 650m, the pretty village of Soccia is set on terraces on the side of the mountain, 6.5km above Guagno les Bains. A great place to escape from the GR20, it is the starting point for the pleasant Lac de Creno walk (see Strolls & Country Walks in the Walking chapter). The **village church** dates from 1875 and contains a 15th-century triptych. It is supposed to be open 10 am to noon and 4 to 7 pm, but times vary. The war memorial in the picturesque village square is a testimony to the importance of local involvement in WWI – it lists almost 50 names.

Orto, a few kilometres from Soccia, is even more remote, at the bottom of a narrow, steep valley where each house seems to overhang the one below.

Accommodation options and restaurants are detailed in the section on the GR20 (Stage 6) in the Walking chapter.

Guagno

postcode 20160 • pop 139 • elevation 800m

From Guagno les Bains follow the winding road up the valley for 8.5km until you reach Guagno, only a three-hour walk from the GR20. There are several paths from Guagno to this walking route, which you can join either at Col de Soglia or just to the south of the Pietra Piana refuge. The village hosts a gîte d'étape, a small grocery shop and a public telephone.

Getting There & Away

Based in Soccia, Arrighi (☎ 04 95 28 31 45, 40 95 22 20 62) operates a bus service daily (except Sunday) between Ajaccio and Soccia. Buses go via Tiuccia, Sagone, Vico, Guagno les Bains, Poggiola and Orto. Buses leave Soccia at 6.55 am and depart from the Ajaccio ferry terminal at 3.35 pm. The journey between Ajaccio and Soccia costs 75FF.

Golfe d'Ajaccio

AJACCIO (AJACCIU)

postcode 20000 • pop 59,000

Ajaccio is the largest town on the island, the capital of the French department of Corse-du-Sud, the site of the Assemblée Territoriale de la Corse, and famous as the birthplace of Napoleon Bonaparte. It even has a more lively side slightly reminiscent of Nice on the Côte d'Azur some 230km to the north-west. But don't expect more of Ajaccio than it can deliver. Ajaccio is a provincial town with a limited bag of tricks with which to seduce outsiders and it also has a melancholic, or as the French might say *triste*, side.

Some of the town's museums, particularly Musée Fesch, contain collections whose quality cannot be faulted; but they are not guaranteed to appeal to all. The kitsch representation of native son Napoleon I may provoke second thoughts in those dreaming of world conquest and international fame. The more appealing of the two major shopping streets, rue du Cardinal Fesch, is a good place for a stroll.

History

Some sources attribute the town's origins to the mythical Greek hero Ajax, while others claim that its name derives, much more prosaically, from that of a Roman encampment. In fact, modern Ajaccio probably dates from no earlier than 1492, when Genoese families first began moving here from other

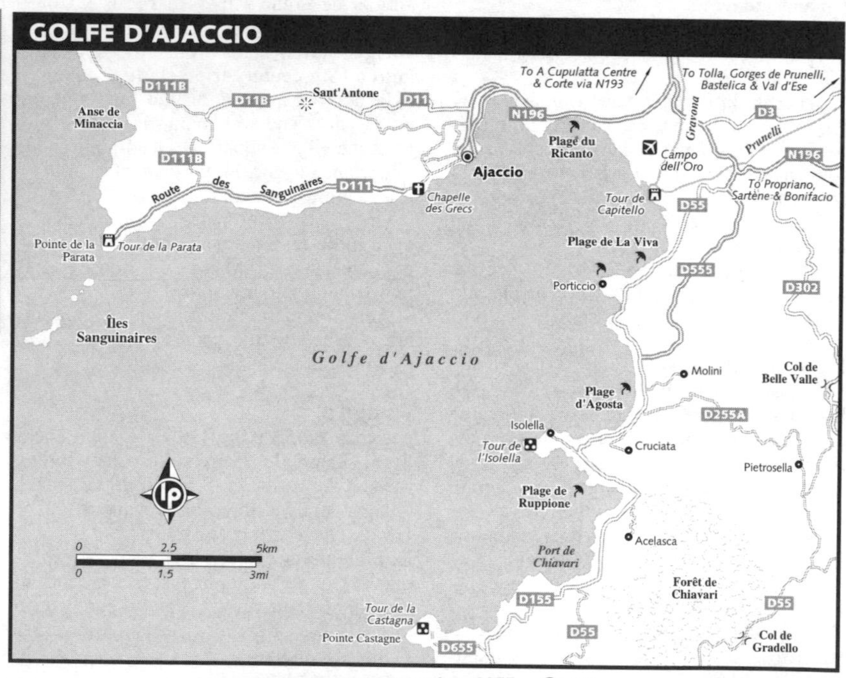

less healthy spots on the island. Indigenous Corsicans were banned from living in the town until 1553, when it was seized by Sampiero Corso and his French allies, assisted by the Turkish privateer Dragut. Shortly afterwards a citadel was built on the foundations of a pre-existing Genoese castle. Recaptured in 1559 by the army of the Republic of Genoa, the town was not truly open to Corsicans until 1592.

The birth of Napoleon on 15 August 1769 was a turning point in the town's history. In accordance with the emperor's later decree, Ajaccio replaced Bastia as the island's capital in 1811 (see the boxed text 'Napoleon's Capital'). From that point forward, the town's prosperity – or at least its relative prosperity – was a foregone conclusion.

Orientation

The main road through the town, cours Napoléon, links place de Gaulle (place du Diamant) with the train station. The old town is bordered by place de Gaulle, place Foch and the citadel. The route des Sanguinaires (D111), which leads to Pointe de la Parata, leads out of town, along the coast, to the west.

Information

Tourist Offices The tourist office (☎ 04 95 51 53 03, fax 04 95 51 53 01), 3 blvd du Roi Jérôme, ⓔ ajaccio.tourisme@wanadoo.fr, has numerous brochures and the staff, who speak English, Italian and German as well as French, can provide lots of information. It opens 8 am to 8.30 pm Monday to Saturday and 9 am to 1 pm Sunday, July and August; and 8 am to 6 pm Monday to Friday and 8 am to 5 pm on Saturday except for a lunch break, the rest of the year.

The Bureau d'Information du Parc Naturel Régional de Corse (PNRC; ☎ 04 95 51 79 10, fax 04 95 21 88 17, ⓔ infos@parc-naturel-corse.com) is the regional park information office. It's at 2 rue Sergent Casalonga and can provide you with all sorts of useful information on walking in Corsica. It opens 8 am to 7 pm Monday to Friday and 8 am to noon and 2 to 7 pm Saturday. Its Web site is at www.parc-naturel-corse.com (French only).

Napoleon's Capital

Ajaccio rose to fame under Napoleon, its most illustrious native son. In 1811 an imperial decree made Corsica a single department, and Ajaccio was made its capital. There was an outcry in Bastia, which lost its status as the island's principal town, but Napoleon justified his decision by asserting that Ajaccio 'should be the capital...since it is a natural harbour that lies across the water from Toulon and is thus the closest to France after St-Florent'. In accordance with the emperor's wishes, Ajaccio went on to spearhead the campaign to Gallicise the island.

Money Banque de France (☎ 04 95 51 72 44), 8 rue Sergent Casalonga, opens 8.45 am to noon and 1.45 to 3.30 pm Monday to Friday. Exchange services are available mornings only. Crédit Lyonnais (☎ 04 95 29 30 01), 59 cours Napoléon, exchanges currency, Eurocheques and travellers cheques, and has an ATM. It opens 8.25 am to 12.20 pm and 1.50 to 4.40 pm Monday to Friday.

You can also exchange travellers cheques at the main post office, and you will find other ATMs at Banque Populaire Provençale et Corse (☎ 04 95 21 49 85), 6 ave Antoine Serafini, place Foch and BNP (☎ 04 95 21 54 90), 33 cours Napoléon.

Post & Communications The main post office (☎ 04 95 51 84 75), at 13 cours Napoléon, opens 8 am to 6.30 pm Monday to Friday and Saturday morning. Poste restante mail should be addressed: Poste Restante, poste principale d'Ajaccio, cours Napoléon, 20185 Ajaccio RT. Mail is kept for two weeks and there must be a return address. The post office also has a fax service.

The bookshop Agora (☎ 04 95 21 08 29), on the very short pedestrian rue Emmanuel Arène, open 2 to 7 pm Monday to Saturday, rents four computers at 40FF per half-hour.

Bookshops The stall opposite the main post office on cours Napoléon sells local, national and foreign newspapers. It opens 6 am to

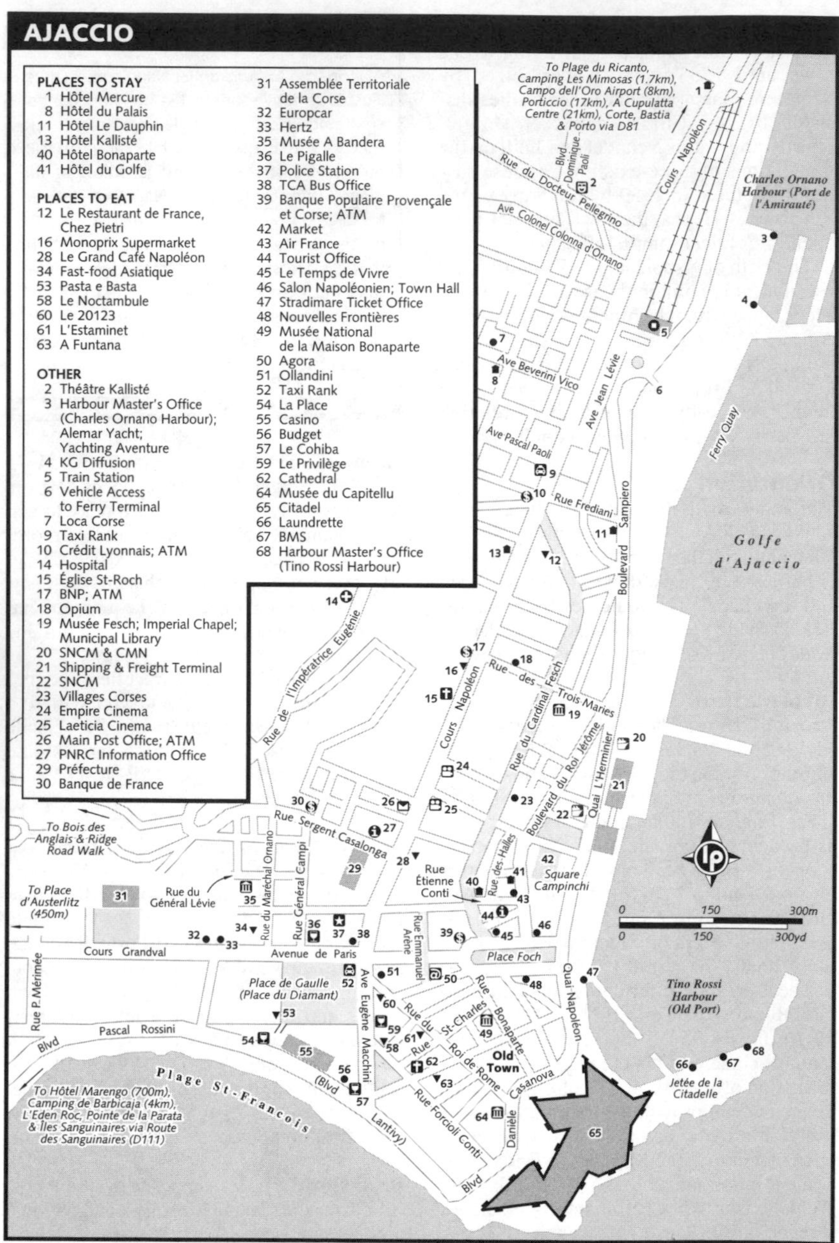
AJACCIO
PLACES TO STAY
1 Hôtel Mercure
8 Hôtel du Palais
11 Hôtel Le Dauphin
13 Hôtel Kallisté
40 Hôtel Bonaparte
41 Hôtel du Golfe
PLACES TO EAT
12 Le Restaurant de France, Chez Pietri
16 Monoprix Supermarket
28 Le Grand Café Napoléon
34 Fast-food Asiatique
53 Pasta e Basta
58 Le Noctambule
60 Le 20123
61 L'Estaminet
63 A Funtana
OTHER
2 Théâtre Kallisté
3 Harbour Master's Office (Charles Ornano Harbour); Alemar Yacht; Yachting Aventure
4 KG Diffusion
5 Train Station
6 Vehicle Access to Ferry Terminal
7 Loca Corse
9 Taxi Rank
10 Crédit Lyonnais; ATM
14 Hospital
15 Église St-Roch
17 BNP; ATM
18 Opium
19 Musée Fesch; Imperial Chapel; Municipal Library
20 SNCM & CMN
21 Shipping & Freight Terminal
22 SNCM
23 Villages Corses
24 Empire Cinema
25 Laeticia Cinema
26 Main Post Office; ATM
27 PNRC Information Office
29 Préfecture
30 Banque de France
31 Assemblée Territoriale de la Corse
32 Europcar
33 Hertz
35 Musée A Bandera
36 Le Pigalle
37 Police Station
38 TCA Bus Office
39 Banque Populaire Provençale et Corse; ATM
42 Market
43 Air France
44 Tourist Office
45 Le Temps de Vivre
46 Salon Napoléonien; Town Hall
47 Stradimare Ticket Office
48 Nouvelles Frontières
49 Musée National de la Maison Bonaparte
50 Agora
51 Ollandini
52 Taxi Rank
54 La Place
55 Casino
56 Budget
57 Le Cohiba
59 Le Privilège
62 Cathedral
64 Musée du Capitellu
65 Citadel
66 Laundrette
67 BMS
68 Harbour Master's Office (Tino Rossi Harbour)
To Plage du Ricanto, Camping Les Mimosas (1.7km), Campo dell'Oro Airport (8km), Porticcio (17km), A Cupulatta Centre (21km), Corte, Bastia & Porto via D81
Charles Ornano Harbour (Port de l'Amirauté)
Golfe d'Ajaccio
Ferry Quay
Tino Rossi Harbour (Old Port)
Jetée de la Citadelle
Old Town
Plage St-François
Place de Gaulle (Place du Diamant)
Place Foch
Square Campinchi
To Bois des Anglais & Ridge Road Walk
To Place d'Austerlitz (450m)
To Hôtel Marengo (700m), Camping de Barbicaja (4km), L'Eden Roc, Pointe de la Parata & Îles Sanguinaires via Route des Sanguinaires (D111)
Cours Napoléon
Blvd Dominique Paoli
Rue du Docteur Pellegrino
Ave Colonel Colonna d'Ornano
Ave Beverini Vico
Ave Jean Lévie
Ave Pascal Paoli
Rue Frediani
Boulevard Sampiero
Rue de l'Impératrice Eugénie
Rue des Trois Maries
Rue du Cardinal Fesch
Boulevard du Roi Jérôme
Quai L'Herminier
Rue Sergent Casalonga
Rue Étienne Conti
Rue des Halles
Rue du Général Lévie
Rue du Maréchal Ornano
Rue Général Campi
Cours Grandval
Avenue de Paris
Rue Emmanuel Arène
Rue P. Mérimée
Blvd Pascal Rossini
Ave Eugène Macchini
Rue du Roi de Rome
Rue St-Charles
Rue Bonaparte
Quai Napoléon
Rue Forcioli Conti
Rue Danièle Casanova
(Blvd Lantivy)
Blvd
0 150 300m
0 150 300yd

8 pm Monday to Saturday and on Sunday morning. There's a second stall on place Foch.

The large book and stationery shop Le Temps de Vivre, 2 place Foch, has a good selection of books, including a decent section of books in English and German. It opens 8.30 am to noon and 2.30 to 7 pm Monday to Saturday and on Sunday morning (except in summer).

Medical Services The hospital (☎ 04 95 29 90 90), 27 ave de l'Impératrice Eugénie, has a 24-hour emergency department.

Laundry The laundrette in the old port opens 7 am to 11 pm. You'll pay 40FF to wash 7kg.

Musée Fesch

Built at the instigation of Cardinal Fesch (see the boxed text 'Cardinal Fesch') to house a collection that he donated to the town in 1839, Musée Fesch (☎ 04 95 21 48 17, fax 04 95 21 80 94, ⓔ fesch@sitec.fr), 50 rue du Cardinal Fesch, has some outstanding 14th- to 19th-century Italian paintings by Titian, Fra Bartolomeo, Veronese, Botticelli and Bellini. On level 1 look out for *La Vierge à l'Enfant Soutenu par un Ange sous une Guirlande (Mother & Child Supported by an Angel under a Garland)*, one of Botticelli's masterpieces. *Portrait de l'Homme au Gant (Portrait of the Gloved Man)* by Titian forms a matching set with another in the Louvre. Level 2 displays yet more Italian works. In the basement there is a rather disappointing Napoleonic collection. Admission costs 35FF (groups of more than 10, students and seniors 25FF).

Admission to the **Imperial Chapel**, next door, where the tombs of several members of the Imperial family are found, costs 10FF. Don't expect, however, to find Napoleon's own remains here – he's buried in Les Invalides in Paris.

Musée Fesch opens Monday afternoons, 9 am to 6.30 pm Tuesday to Thursday, 9 am to 6.30 pm and 9.30 pm to midnight on Friday and 10.30 am to 6 pm at weekends in July and August; and 9.15 am to 12.15 pm and 2.15 pm to 5.15 pm daily except Monday morning from April to June and in September. In winter, the hours are shorter.

Cardinal Fesch

Joseph Fesch (1763–1839) was Napoleon's mother's half-brother; his father was Swiss – a military man in the service of Genoa – which explains Joseph's un-Corsican name. His religious vocation was apparently genuine (he studied in the seminary at Aix and served as archdeacon of Ajaccio), but not his only interest. He left the church for a time to make himself rich and accompanied his warrior nephew to Italy as super-glorified quartermaster. By 1800, Fesch was nevertheless back in clerical garb. In 1802, he was archbishop of Lyon and, the following year, a cardinal, in which capacity Napoleon made him ambassador to Rome, with the leading French Romantic literary figure François-Auguste-René Chateaubriand as his first secretary.

In Rome, Fesch's great achievement was to persuade the Pope to travel to Paris for the purpose of personally crowning Napoleon emperor – not that Napoleon allowed him to do so. Napoleon, the paradigm of the self-made man, took the crown from the Pope's hands and crowned himself. All of this, though, is only to scratch the surface of Fesch's complex career that moved alternately between the ecclesiastical and the secular. Fesch's very large responsibilities did not, moreover, preclude his finding time to amass the large collection of paintings and books that have made Ajaccio the art-pilgrimage town it certainly could never have become in any other way.

Municipal Library

Situated actually inside the Musée Fesch but with its own separate entrance not on the courtyard, but just to the left of it, as you face the courtyard, Ajaccio's municipal library (☎ 04 95 51 13 00) merits a long pause. The two lions decorating, or perhaps guarding, the entrance are modelled on the beasts that stand watch over the tomb of Pope Clement XIII at St Peter's in Rome; Cardinal Fesch donated them. Inside, uniform leather-bound volumes stretching to the ceiling, wooden ladders, and an 18m-long central table are altogether very impressive.

Napoleon's brother, Lucien Bonaparte, commissioned the library as early as 1801 to house the thousands of works piled up helter-skelter under the museum's gables. He added another 12,310 volumes confiscated during the French Revolution from emigre aristocrats and members of the religious orders. Cardinal Fesch made yet further contributions. The library was built in 1868, to plans by the architect Caseneuve. It opens 8 am to noon Monday to Friday. Admission is free.

Musée A Bandera

Tucked away in rue du Général Lévie, the interesting Musée A Bandera, or flag museum (☎ 04 95 51 07 34, fax 04 95 51 39 60, ⓔ abandera@sitec.fr), provides an overview of Corsican history from its origins until WWII. Among the highlights are a diorama of the 1769 battle of Ponte Novo that confirmed French conquest of the island, a model of the port of Ajaccio as it was in the same period, a coat of arms of the short-lived Anglo-Corsican kingdom and some yellowing 19th-century pages from the *Petit Journal* and *L'Illustré*, recounting the arrest of famous Corsican bandits. Attention is also given to the role of women in Corsican society and in particular to the considerable power that they have sometimes wielded.

The museum opens 9 am to 7 pm daily, May to October; and 9 am to noon and 2 to 6 pm daily, the rest of the year. Admission costs 25FF (concessions 15FF). There are plans to move the museum to larger quarters on the route des Sanguinaires.

Musée National de la Maison Bonaparte

The chief interest of this museum (☎ 04 95 21 43 89) on rue St-Charles, one of the narrow streets of the old town, is that it contains the room in which the emperor was actually born. Admission costs 22FF (concessions 15FF, those aged under 18 free). Visitors are asked to dress in a respectful manner. The museum opens 9 am to noon and 2 to 6 pm in summer and 10 am to noon and 2 to 5 pm in winter. It closes on Saturday mornings and Sunday afternoons, year round.

Salon Napoléonien

This ceremonial room (☎ 04 95 51 52 62), just over the entrance chamber of the town hall on place Foch, contains sculptures and paintings of the imperial family, furniture from the 'return from Egypt' period, a Bohemian crystal light and numerous medals. Admission costs 10FF (those aged under 16 free). It opens 9 to 11.45 am and 2 to 5.45 pm daily except Sundays and public holidays, 15 June to 15 September. It closes at 4.45 pm, the rest of the year.

Other Things to See

Small, private **Musée du Capitellu** (☎ 04 95 21 50 57), 18 blvd Danièle Casanova, provides a fascinating glimpse into the town's history. It opens 10 am to noon and 2 to 6 pm daily except Sunday afternoon, 15 March to 15 October. Admission costs 25FF (children aged under 10, 10FF).

The Venetian-style **cathedral** was built in the second half of the 16th century. Inside, you can see the font used for Napoleon's baptism and Delacroix's painting of the *Vierge au Sacré Coeur*. The cathedral, which has an ochre facade and is in the shape of a Greek cross, stands in the old town at the corner of rue Forcioli Conti and rue St-Charles.

About 1km from place de Gaulle, **place d'Austerlitz** contains an immense statue of Napoleon. There's a suggestion Napoleon may have played as a child in the adjacent grotto, which was undergoing restoration at the time of writing.

Boat Trips

Stradimare (☎ 04 95 51 31 31) in the old port organises boat trips to the Îles Sanguinaires (120FF), the Scandola nature reserve via Les Calanques, Piana and Girolata (250FF) and Bonifacio (260FF) from April to September (usually daily at the height of the season). It is a good idea to confirm the times and book ahead; the office opens 9.30 am to 12.30 pm and 4 to 7.30 pm, and also 8.30 to 11.30 pm in summer. Children ride at half-price.

Beaches

Those who like to laze around on golden sand will be in their element in the Ajaccio area. The large Plage du Ricanto lies about 6km east of the town in the direction of the airport. You can reach it on the No 1 bus. Smaller expanses of sand can be found in Ajaccio itself and around Pointe de la Parata, which you can reach on the No 5 bus. The seaside resort of Porticcio, south of the airport (see under Porticcio later) prides itself on its long sandy beach, and there are yet more beaches south of Porticcio.

Activities

The friendly team at Yachting Aventure (☎/fax 04 95 10 26 25, ⓔ yachting.aventure@libertysurf.fr), near the harbour master's office in the Charles Ornano harbour, hire out three-seat jet skis (from 1900FF per day) and five- to 10-seat motor boats (2200FF to 9000FF per day). Rates are lower for rentals of several days. They have a Web site at www.yachting-aventure.com (French only). KG Diffusion (☎ 04 95 20 51 05, fax 04 95 20 70 12) and Alemar Yacht (☎ 04 95 20 92 55, fax 04 95 20 90 08), also near the harbour master's office, both hire out sailing dinghies.

See Strolls & Country Walks in the Walking chapter for the three- to four-hour Ridge Road walk just outside Ajaccio; the Diving chapter provides information about diving in the area. See Motorcycle & Bicycle in the Getting Around chapter for details of hiring motorbikes, scooter and mountain bikes.

Organised Tours

Ollandini (☎ 04 95 23 92 40), 3 place de Gaulle (on the corner of rue du Roi de Rome), runs six coach trips from Ajaccio to various spots around Corsica. It opens 8.30 am to 12.30 pm and 2 to 6 pm Monday to Friday and 9 to 11.45 am on Saturday. Autocars Ceccaldi (☎ 04 95 21 38 06) at 1 route d'Alata, not far from Camping Les Mimosas, also organises tours.

Festivals

Ajaccio's calendar of events includes a dance festival (held in the Théâtre Kallisté) and a Spanish cinema festival in January. Les Journées Napoléoniennes in June includes parades, torch-light processions and firework displays. Les Musicales d'Ajaccio takes place in July, and the town celebrates Napoleon's birthday on 15 August.

Places to Stay – Budget

Close to the beach on route des Sanguinaires, ***Camping de Barbicaja*** *(☎ 04 95 52 01 17)*, about 4.5km from the town centre, tends to get very crowded in the high season. Expect to pay 39/12/14FF per person/tent/car. The camp site opens May to September. To get there catch the No 5 bus. ***Camping Les Mimosas*** *(☎ 04 95 20 99 85, fax 04 95 10 01 77)*, 3km from the town centre along route d'Alata, is small and rather unattractive but it's shady and there's a small grocery shop. It costs 29/12/12FF per person/tent/car. It opens 1 April to 15 October. The No 4 bus comes within 900m of the site.

Hôtel du Palais *(☎ 04 95 22 73 68, 5 ave Beverini Vico)* offers eight comfortable and pleasant rooms. It costs 270/320/380FF for singles/doubles/triples with shower in July and August and you can pay 40FF more for a room with a toilet.

Hôtel Bonaparte *(☎ 04 95 21 44 19, 1 rue Étienne Conti)* is a family-run, two-star hotel in a good location. The 16 rooms, with bathroom, TV, telephone and harbour view, cost 280/320/370FF single/double/triple. It opens April to October.

Places to Stay – Mid-Range

You'll find clean rooms, all with bathroom, satellite TV and telephone at ***Hôtel Kallisté*** *(☎ 04 95 51 34 45, fax 04 95 21 79 00, 51 cours Napoléon)*. The hotel also houses car, motorbike and mountain bike hire (☎ 04 95 51 61 81), a bureau de change and a car park. Rooms cost 240FF to 560FF depending on size and season. An extra 40FF gets you a bathtub. The owner speaks English.

Hôtel Marengo *(☎ 04 95 21 43 66, fax 04 95 21 51 26, 2 rue Marengo)*, just outside the town centre, will appeal to those in search of sun, sand and relaxation. Its 16 lovely rooms have air-conditioning, TV, telephone and balconies, and there are a few parking spaces outside. Doubles cost from

275FF to 350FF, depending on the facilities and time of year. Single rooms cost the same as doubles. Hôtel Marengo opens 16 March to 14 December.

Hôtel Le Dauphin *(☎ 04 95 21 12 94, fax 04 95 21 88 69, 11 blvd Sampiero)* offers pleasant, though in some instances rather old-fashioned-looking, rooms with bathrooms, TV and telephone. Depending on the time year, singles go for 230FF to 250FF, doubles for 260FF to 320FF and triples for 320FF to 410FF, including breakfast, depending on the time of year. Half-board is available at a reasonable supplement. The hotel is opposite the ferry terminal and reception is in the bar.

Places to Stay – Top End

Near the railroad station, ***Hôtel Mercure*** *(☎ 04 95 20 43 09, fax 04 95 22 72 44, 115 cours Napoléon)* has 49 uniform but comfortable rooms particularly suited to business travellers. Rooms have telephones with modem connections and there is free garage parking. Expect to pay 340FF to 450FF for a single room and 390FF to 540FF for a double, depending on the time of year.

Hôtel du Golfe *(☎ 04 95 21 47 64, fax 04 95 21 71 05, 5 blvd du Roi Jérôme)* is a pretty three-star property overlooking the Golfe d'Ajaccio. Basic single/double/triples cost 364/458/672FF in August. Singles/doubles with sea view and balcony cost 424/498FF. In low season prices are 15% to 20% cheaper.

L'Eden Roc *(☎ 04 95 51 56 00, fax 04 95 52 05 03, e edenroc@wandadoo.fr)* is a four-star hotel, 10km from the town centre in the direction of Pointe de la Parata, with an elaborate thalasso fitness centre, a swimming pool and a glamorous lounge area. A standard double costs between 700FF and 2080FF depending on the time of year. You can visit their Web site at www.edenroc-corsica.fr.

Places to Eat

Budget You'll find unbeatable prices at ***Fast-food Asiatique*** *(☎ 04 95 21 23 31, 1 rue du Maréchal Ornano)*. Fried noodles cost 22FF; chicken curry and the daily special both cost 30FF. There are a few tables for those who want to eat in. It opens 11 am to 3 pm and 6 to 11.30 pm daily.

Le Noctambule *(☎ 04 95 50 51 19, 22 rue du Conventionnel Chiappe)* serves delicious wood-fire pizzas (50FF to 60FF) and good crêpes (15FF to 45FF). As its name implies, the restaurant opens all night, daily, and usually there's music.

Paste e Basta *(☎ 04 95 50 18 92, 8 place de Gaulle)* features a wide choice of well-prepared pastas for 50FF to 70FF. Also try the excellent 'Berthier' mussels, cooked in balsamic vinegar, for 60FF. The restaurant has a pleasant terrace with sea view. It opens daily except Sunday.

There's also no lack of supermarkets in Ajaccio. The well-stocked ***Monoprix*** in cours Napoléon opens 8.30 am to 7.15 pm Monday to Saturday; and to 7.45 pm in summer.

Mid-Range At ***Le Restaurant de France, Chez Pietri*** *(☎ 04 95 21 11 00, 59 rue du Cardinal Fesch)*, which is charmingly old-fashioned, there is a 95FF *menu* and an a la carte menu with Corsican specialities. It opens for lunch and dinner and serves until 10.30 pm daily except Sunday.

L'Estaminet *(☎ 04 95 50 10 42, 6 rue du Roi de Rome)* has a pretty dining room and terrace in the heart of the old town. In addition to traditional Corsican fare, you will find Provençale and Lyonnais specialities. The restaurant is friendly and the food good. It opens noon to 2 pm and 7.30 to 10.30 pm except Sunday and Monday lunchtime. It's a good idea to book in advance.

Le 20123 *(☎ 04 95 21 50 05, 2 rue du Roi de Rome)* is renowned for its authentic Corsican cuisine and its copious 165FF *menu*.

Top End At ***Le Grand Café Napoléon*** *(☎ 04 95 21 42 54, fax 04 95 21 53 32, 10 cours Napoléon)* you'll find a seductive candlelit dining room with a grand piano, white tablecloths and lots of green plants. There is a 200FF *menu* and it opens noon to 2 pm and 7 to 10.30 pm daily except Sunday.

A Funtana *(☎ 04 95 21 78 04, fax 04 95 51 40 56, 9 rue Notre Dame)* is the best restaurant in town. Exciting *menus* cost 150FF and 300FF, and the wine cellar is serious and ambitious. It serves until 11 pm daily except Sunday and Monday.

Entertainment

Bars & Discos There are a number of bars around rue du Roi de Rome but you can also try ***Le Pigalle*** *(place de Gaulle)*, or ***Le Cohiba*** on the corner of ave Eugène Macchini and blvd Pascal Rossini. ***Le Privilège*** *(☎ 04 95 50 11 80, place de Gaulle)* is a piano bar that offers more elaborate musical acts.

La Place *(☎ 04 95 51 09 10, blvd Lantivy)*, next to the casino, is the only disco in Ajaccio. It opens nightly from 11 pm.

Casino The municipal ***casino*** *(☎ 04 95 50 40 60, blvd Lantivy)* is rather on the plush side but fun anyway. Its slot machines, bureau de change, restaurant and bar open to anyone over the age of 18 from 1 pm to 5 am year round. The more serious gaming room, with roulette and blackjack, opens at 9.30 pm. Visitors are expected to dress 'appropriately'.

Cinema The ***Empire*** *(☎ 04 95 21 21 00)*, ***Laeticia*** *(☎ 04 95 21 07 24)* and ***Bonaparte*** *(☎ 04 95 51 26 46)* cinemas on cours Napoléon all screen new releases. Tickets cost around 45FF. Programs generally begin at 9.30 pm but the Bonaparte also has screenings at 2.30 pm and 6.30 pm.

Shopping

There is a farmer's market in square Campinchi every morning, and at weekends stalls of clothing and crafts join those of fruit, vegetables, and Corsican cheeses and meat products.

Villages Corses (☎ 04 95 51 08 05), 44 rue du Cardinal Fesch, is packed with Corsican delicacies, including *charcuterie*, cheeses, liqueurs, wine, chestnut flour, and honey. It opens 8 am to 12.30 pm and 2.30 to 7.30 pm Monday to Saturday and sometimes on Sunday. Opium (☎ 04 95 21 12 17), 6 rue des Trois Maries, offers no Corsican products at all. The owner, herself a victim of the travel bug, instead sells magnificent jewellery and crafts, for the most part from Africa and Asia.

Getting There & Away

Further information is contained in the Getting There & Away chapter.

Air The modern terminal building at Campo dell'Oro airport (☎ 04 95 23 56 56), 8km east of town, boasts a bar, souvenir and craft shops, a bookshop and even a precious ATM machine.

Air France (reservations and general information: ☎ 08 02 80 28 02), 3 blvd du Roi Jérôme, opens 8.30 am to noon and 2 to 6 pm Monday to Friday as well as on Saturday morning. Other airline offices can be found in the airport itself. Nouvelles Frontières (☎ 04 95 21 55 55), 12 place Foch, opens 9 am to noon and 2 to 6 pm Monday to Friday and on Saturday morning.

Bus A number of bus companies have offices in the modern ferry terminal on quai L'Herminier and, together, they provide service from Ajaccio to most other parts of the island. Eurocorse (☎ 04 95 21 06 30) goes to Bonifacio (120FF, three to four hours, four daily) at 8 am and 8.30 am and at 3 pm and 4 pm, in summer. On Sundays and pub lic holidays, there are two buses. In summer, there are buses Monday to Saturday to Sartène (70FF, two hours, four daily) and to Zonza and Bavella (100FF, 3¼ hours, twice daily). Buses leave for Bastia (110FF, twice daily) at 7.45 am and 3 pm. It is faster and cheaper to get to Calvi by bus than by train. SAIB (☎ 04 95 22 41 99) goes to Porto (70FF, two hours, three daily). Casanova Buses (☎ 04 95 21 05 17) have several daily departures between Ajaccio and Porticcio (15FF, 20 minutes). There are also services to Vizzavona, Vivario and Corte.

Train Four trains daily leave Ajaccio station (☎ 04 95 23 11 03) for Vizzavona (41FF, plus 5FF tax in summer), Vivario (49FF) and Corte (66FF). There are four trains daily to Bastia (124FF) and two to Île Rousse (128FF) and Calvi (145FF). The left-luggage facility in the station costs 17FF for the first day, 22FF per day thereafter and 6FF at night.

Boat Ferries leave from the modern terminal building (☎ 04 95 51 55 45) on quai L'Herminier, which also houses the ticket windows for intercity buses. The terminal opens from 6.30 am to 8 pm (when the last ship sails).

SNCM Ferryterranée (☎ 04 95 29 66 99, 04 08 36 67 95 00) has two offices in the harbour. The office next to the Compagnie Méridionale de Navigation (CMN) sells tickets for same-day travel; the other, opposite the terminal building, handles reservations. Both open 8.15 to 11.45 am and 2 to 6 pm Monday to Friday and also on Saturday morning.

CMN (☎ 08 10 20 13 20, fax 04 95 21 57 60) also runs crossings and its offices on blvd Sampiero open 8.15 am to 12.15 pm and 2 to 7.15 pm Monday to Friday, except on Tuesday and Thursday when it closes at 5.30 pm.

In summer you can get a boat from Tino Rossi harbour to Porticcio, see Getting There & Away under Porticcio for more details.

Ajaccio has two yacht harbours; the Charles Ornano is bigger but sailors prefer the Tino Rossi.

At the Charles Ornano harbour the harbour master's office (☎ 04 95 22 31 98, fax 04 95 20 98 08, VHF channel 9) opens 7 am to 9 pm in summer and from 8.30 am to noon and 2 to 6 pm, the rest of the year. There are 850 berths, 40 of which are reserved for visitors, and water, fuel, showers, toilets, weather reports, a careening area and a chandlery. The daily rate for a 12m boat varies from 62FF to 294FF depending on the month. Multihull vessels are charged an additional 50%. The harbour used to be known as the Port de l'Amirauté until it was renamed after a former mayor but most of the town's inhabitants use the old name.

At the Tino Rossi harbour (old port) the harbour master's office (☎ 04 95 51 22 72, fax 04 95 21 93 28) opens 8 am to 8 pm. Washroom facilities, showers, shops, a laundrette, a ship's chandler, weather reports, restaurants, mechanics and a sail-repair shop are just some of the services available. The harbour makes more berths available to visitors than the Charles Ornano even though it is smaller. Expect to pay between 90FF and 310FF daily depending on the size of boat and the season. The high season runs from 1 June to 30 September.

Getting Around

To/From the Airport TCA bus No 8 runs between the airport and the town centre 8km away. The trip usually takes around 20 minutes, though it can be longer in heavy traffic. Tickets cost 26FF. Buses leave the airport from 9 am to 10.45 pm daily. They leave from the car park at the far end of the air terminal on the departures side. They leave the ferry terminal every day from 6.25 am to 6.10 pm, approximately every hour.

A taxi from the airport to the town centre costs around 100FF except between 7 pm and 7 am and on Sunday and public holidays, when the fare will be closer to 130FF. Ask whether the 12FF airport tax is included or supplementary.

Bus TCA buses provide service within Ajaccio for 7.50FF per ticket or 59FF for a book of 10. You can get timetables and a network map from the TCA office in ave de Paris (☎ 04 95 51 43 23). The office opens 8 am to noon and 2.30 to 5.45 pm. The main lines are as follows:

No 1 Capitello–town centre–Les Crêtes
No 2 Mezzavia–town centre–Les Crêtes
No 3 Town centre–Pietralba
No 4 Budiccione–town centre–Hôpital de la Miséricorde
No 5 Town centre–Pointe de la Parata (Route des Sanguinaires)
No 6 Station–Castelluccio
No 7 Loretto–town centre–Empereur
No 8 Bus station–airport

Car At the airport, there are car-hire firms in the car park across from the terminal. Theoretically they open 9 am to about 11 pm in summer and 9.30 am to 9 pm, the rest of the year. Rates differ considerably; it's worth the trouble to compare. Their contact details are as follows:

Ada (☎ 04 95 23 56 57, fax 04 95 23 56 58)
Avis (☎ 04 95 23 56 90, fax 04 95 23 56 96)
Budget (☎ 04 95 23 57 21, fax 04 95 23 57 23)
Castellani Sixt (☎ 04 95 23 57 00, fax 04 95 23 56 99)
Citer (☎ 04 95 23 57 15, fax 04 95 23 57 16)
Europcar (☎ 04 95 23 57 01, fax 04 95 23 57 03)
Hertz (☎ 04 95 23 57 04/05, fax 04 95 23 57 06)

In town, Budget (☎ 04 95 21 17 18, fax 04 95 21 00 07), résidence Diamant, 1 blvd

Lantivy, has cars for hire for 490FF per day (including 250km), 1680FF per week (with 1750km) or 2862FF for two weeks (with 3500km). These prices, which are subject to change, include comprehensive insurance cover.

Motorcycle & Bicycle Loca Corse (☎ 04 95 20 71 20), 10 ave Beverini Vico, hires out 125cc motorbikes (350/2078FF per day/week in summer), scooters (from 200/275FF per day to 1100/1319FF per week in low/high season) and mountain bikes (83/455FF per day/week). It opens 9 am to noon and 2.30 to 6.30 pm daily except Sundays. BMS (☎/fax 04 95 21 33 75), on the wharf at Tino Rossi harbour, has mountain bikes for 75FF per day, scooters for 290/1700FF per day/week and motorbikes for 310FF per day with a 10% to 15% discount in low season. BMS opens 7.30 am to 7 pm Monday to Saturday and Sunday morning.

Taxi There is a taxi rank on the corner of cours Napoléon and ave Pascal Paoli and another on the place de Gaulle. You can order a taxi by calling ☎ 04 95 23 25 70.

AROUND AJACCIO

Îles Sanguinaires

These four small islands with their jagged coastlines take their name – meaning Bloody – from their distinctive red rock. They lie just off Pointe de la Parata at the mouth of the Golfe d'Ajaccio and they are a good place for a walk.

Stradimare (☎ 04 95 51 31 31) organises boat trips to the islands from Tino Rossi harbour in town for 100FF. The No 5 bus will take you as far as Pointe de la Parata.

A Cupulatta Centre

A Cupulatta (☎ 04 95 52 82 34, fax 04 95 52 98 93), 21km from Ajaccio in the direction of Corte, is Europe's largest centre for the breeding and preservation of tortoises. It was opened in 1998 thanks to the enthusiasm of Philippe Magnan and his team of volunteers and today shelters approximately 3000 representatives of more than 150 species from all over the world, some of them in danger of extinction. A one-hour visit will cost 30FF (children 15FF). They have a Web site at www.acupulatta.com.

PORTICCIO

postcode 20166

Some people find this nearest seaside resort to Ajaccio devoid of charm; others like it for its long fine-sand beach and its liveliness in summer. Porticcio is just south of Campo dell'Oro airport.

Orientation

The town stretches along the length of its beach. A series of modern commercial developments known as La Viva, Les Marines and Les Marines 2 on either side of the D55 are the focal points. As you come from Ajaccio, the first thing you'll see is the VIP disco on your left. A bit farther along on the right-hand side is La Viva, with its bars and restaurants. There is a turning on the left towards the equestrian centre, a few hundred metres away from Camping Les Marines de Porticcio. You eventually come to Les Marines, which has a tourist office, bookshop, cinema, the Blue Moon disco and a landing stage. Across the road, Les Marines 2 has a petrol station, a taxi rank, banks, a post office and a Champion supermarket.

The Golfe d'Ajaccio south of Porticcio is composed of three beaches: Plage d'Agosta, Plage de Ruppione and Plage de Mare e Sole.

Information

Tourist Offices The small white kiosk (☎ 04 95 25 01 01) in Les Marines opens 8.30 am to 1 pm and 2 to 8 pm daily in summer; and 9.30 am to 12.15 pm and 2.30 to 6.30 pm Monday to Saturday, the rest of the year. Its staff are very helpful.

Money Société Générale (☎ 04 95 53 80 90) next to the post office has an ATM, changes currency, and opens 8.15 am to noon and 1.45 to 4.45 pm Monday to Friday. Crédit Agricole, next door, charges 35FF to exchange currency and foreign travellers cheques and opens 8.30 to 11.45 am and 2.15 to 5 pm Monday to Wednesday (to 4.30 pm Thursday and Friday). It has an ATM.

Post & Communications The post office (☎ 04 95 25 01 92), behind the Elf petrol station in Les Marines 2, opens 8.30 am to 5.30 pm Monday to Friday and to 11.30 am Saturday mornings in summer. Outside the high season hours are shorter.

Bookshops The newsagent in Les Marines (☎ 04 95 25 08 41) sells French and foreign newspapers and a small selection of books; look for the sign that reads 'tabac-presse-lotto'. It opens daily except Sunday afternoon.

Laundry There is a self-service laundrette behind the shops at Les Marines. Expect to pay about 40FF per machine and 1FF per minute to dry. If you need help, ask at Fast Food, next to the souvenir shop.

Things to See & Do

Porticcio's main attraction is its **beaches**. The beautiful Plage de La Viva that fringes the town is the most popular; it boasts bars and restaurants as well as stalls that hire out sailboards and deck-chairs. Plage d'Agosta, Plage de Ruppione and Plage de Mare e Sole, farther south, are less popular, less crowded and therefore often more pleasant.

A kiosk (☎ 04 95 25 94 14) near the tourist office in Les Marines organises **boat trips** on a 20m sightseeing boat from April to October. There are trips to the Scandola nature reserve, Bonifacio and the Îles Sanguinaires. They cost between 120FF and 260FF.

Activities

The Porticcio Nautical Centre (☎ 04 95 25 01 06, fax 04 95 25 04 99), at Plage de La Viva, rents **windsurfing** equipment (70FF to 100FF per hour), kayaks (55FF per hour), sailing dinghies (180FF per hour) and Hobie Cat 16 catamarans (220FF per hour). Beginner and advanced classes in windsurfing are available for children and adults.

Ski Nautique Viva (☎/fax 04 95 25 17 93), near the Maeva Diving Centre, offers **water-skiing** (130FF for a 10-minute spin) as well as beginner- or advanced-level instruction. The centre opens daily 8 am to noon and 2 to 7 pm.

Rive Sud Nautique (☎ 04 95 25 19 89 or 06 09 98 87 56) on Plage de La Viva hires out **jet skis** and organises jet-ski outings from June to September. Loconautique (☎ 04 95 21 70 23), next door, hires out **Zodiac boats** (no permit required) and water skis are also available.

The Porticcio **Yachting Club** (☎ 04 95 25 96 14, fax 04 95 25 05 62), next to the Colisée Brasserie, will make you want to discover Corsica by sea. A good selection of boats to rent is available with or without captain.

For information on **diving** in the area, see the Diving chapter.

Hôtel-Motel de Porticcio rents the use of hard earth **tennis courts** for 60FF per hour; ask at the reception desk.

The Centre Équestre de Porticcio (☎ 04 95 25 11 05) offers **horse riding**; lesson cost 100FF per hour. Turn off the main road at the VIP disco and continue for 1km. The centre is signposted.

The Shell station (☎ 04 95 25 06 64) rents out **mountain bikes** at 80/400FF per day/week against a 1000FF deposit.

Places to Stay – Budget

Porticcio has little accommodation for the independent traveller. ***Camping Les Marines de Porticcio*** *(☎ 04 95 25 09 35, fax 04 95 25 95 11)*, a shady camp site near the beach and the town centre, behind the Elf petrol station, has the virtue of being fairly quiet. Expect to pay 31FF per person (36FF in July and August) and 12FF per car (15FF in July and August). Small prefabricated chalets, available by the week in July and August for 1800FF to 2800FF, depending on the exact date, are suitable for three to four people. The camp site also has a children's play area. It opens June to September. ***Camping de l'Europe*** *(☎ 04 95 25 42 94, fax 04 95 25 59 66)*, near the Plage d'Agosta, 5.5km from Porticcio and 600m from the D55 is a little remote but has a bar and laundry. Rates are 28/30FF per person in low/high season, and 11/12FF per tent/-car. Studios and flats are available for two to five people and it opens May to October.

Places to Stay – Mid-Range

On a bend in the road near Les Marines, ***Hôtel-Motel de Porticcio*** *(☎ 04 95 25 05 77, fax 04 95 25 11 11)*, offers good single/double rooms, with bath and toilet, for 230/290FF in the low season and 340/450FF in August. Five pleasant double rooms with bath but no toilet are cheaper. Studios for four people with kitchenette and covered balcony cost between 360FF and 570FF, depending on the time of year. Rates are reduced for stays of a week or longer.

Hôtel Kallisté *(☎ 04 95 25 54 19, fax 04 95 25 59 25)*, 5km from Porticcio in the hills above Plage d'Agosta, has lovely, light rooms with air-conditioning, TV and telephone. A double costs from 260FF to 540FF, depending on the view and the season. The hotel also offers apartments with a view over the Golfe d'Ajaccio costing from 3360FF per week in high season. Although this hotel will protect you from the perhaps overrated hustle and bustle of Porticcio, you'll need a car to get to it. It opens April to October.

Places to Eat

Porticcio is not one of Corsica's great eating destinations. Fare at its snack bars and restaurants is quite unremarkable. Nearly all the local restaurants, however, have wide terraces overlooking the sea and tables on the beach.

Le Colisée Brasserie *(☎ 04 95 25 00 43)* at Les Marines has a nice terrace and a large selection of pizzas costing from 40FF to 60FF. ***A Marana*** *(☎ 04 95 25 10 56)* in La Viva serves simple hearty fare and opens daily January to October. Next door, ***A Merendella*** *(☎ 04 95 25 08 27)* serves good crêpes for 22FF to 59FF and opens noon to midnight daily during the summer and to 11 pm daily, the rest of the year.

For self-caterers, there is a ***Champion*** supermarket at Les Marines 2.

Entertainment

Bars and Discos Above La Viva, ***Le Pub Saint-James*** opens to 3 am every night and puts on good live blues and rock acts. ***Le Sextan*** *(☎ 04 95 25 54 07)*, also at La Viva, is a new piano bar where you can hear jazz, Cuban and Corsican music until 2 am.

The ***VIP*** is a disco on the main road just before the turning for the equestrian centre. The admission charge of 60FF includes a drink. The club opens 10.30 pm to 5 am. Many people prefer ***Blue Moon*** *(☎ 04 95 25 07 70)*, above Les Marines. Admission charge and opening times are the same as for VIP but the atmosphere is more relaxed. Doors open daily between July and mid-September but only at weekends in winter.

Cinema In Les Marines, ***Les Trois Stars*** *(☎ 04 95 25 91 82)* cinema has two screens showing up to three different films daily. Tickets cost 40FF.

Getting There & Away

Bus There is a bus service (☎ 04 95 25 40 37) between Ajaccio and Plage de Mare e Sole from 1 July to 15 September. Buses leave approximately every 90 minutes from 8.30 am until 6.30 pm from Ajaccio and from 7.30 am until 5.30 pm from Mare e Sole. They stop at Porticcio (15FF) and Isolella. There is a morning and evening shuttle in winter.

Boat In summer, launches are available to Porticcio from the Tino Rossi harbour in Ajaccio. The trip takes around 20 minutes and costs 25/40FF one-way/return, with the first of five daily departures at 8 am and the last at 6.30 pm. Call ahead (☎ 04 95 25 94 14) to make sure they're not taking the day off.

Getting Around

There is a taxi rank in the Elf garage car park in Les Marines 2.

GORGES DU PRUNELLI, BASTELICA & VAL D'ESE

After leaving Ajaccio the D3 winds its way up into the mountains for about 25km until it reaches the village of Tolla on a perch over a lake. The road then continues along the Gorges du Prunelli, which can be seen lower down, at bends in the road, until it gets to Bastelica, with a population of 400.

This rustic mountain village is famous for its charcuterie, made from local *cochons coureurs* (see the boxed text 'Pigs on the

Pigs on the Run

There are no longer any wild pigs (except wild boar) in Corsica: pigs seen at the sides of mountain roads are domestic animals known as *cochons coureurs*, or free-ranging pigs. It is estimated that there are 15,000 free-ranging pigs in Haute-Corse and 30,000 in Corse-du-Sud.

Corsican pork derives its flavour from the free-ranging pigs' diet of acorns and chestnuts (supplemented with other food at certain times of the year). The charcuterie produced in Corsica is excellent but expensive and some of the specialities sold on the island are actually made from imported pork meat.

Run'), and also as the home town of Sampiero Corso (see the boxed text 'Sampiero Corso the Fiery' in the Facts about Corsica chapter). Visitors are greeted by a statue of Corso. A curious plaque, contributed by William Bonaparte Wyse (Napoleon's Irish grand-nephew), on the site of the house in which Corso was born, announces the hero as 'the most Corsican of all Corsicans'. The Val d'Ese ski resort is a farther 16km away along an unimproved road through beautiful mountain scenery. The ski resort (at an elevation of 1700m) has little impact on the environment: there are only two buildings and no hotel or restaurant. You can hire ski equipment in Bastelica.

Places to Stay & Eat

Next to the town hall and opposite the statue of Sampiero Corso is ***Hôtel-Restaurant Le Sampiero*** *(☎ 04 95 28 71 99)*. It has rather old-fashioned but clean and comfortable rooms with TV and telephone. A single costs 260FF. Doubles run from 300FF to 370FF, with bath, in high season.

Auberge Castagnetu *(☎ 04 95 28 70 71, fax 04 95 28 74 02)* has pleasant, neat rooms for 270/310FF per person at half-board in low season/summer. The cuisine has been acclaimed by several gastronomic associations. There are daily 100FF and 150FF *menus*, served in the lovely rustic dining room. The auberge is 1.5km from the Église de Bastelica.

Getting There & Away

The Bernardi bus company connects Ajaccio and Bastelica on Mondays, Wednesdays and Fridays. Buses leave Ajaccio from the Octroi Bar (☎ 04 95 20 55 58) on Cours Napoléon.

The South

Southern Corsica, in the area south of east-coast Porto Vecchio and west-coast Propriano, manages to line up an astonishing variety of human cultures and landscapes, despite tightly cramped quarters. Porto Vecchio and Propriano are the lively nerve-centres of increasingly sprawling beach resorts. In the hills behind Port Vecchio, Alta Rocca harbours fascinating little villages, ancient archaeological sites and numerous footpaths. The Sartenais, the area around the proud old town of Sartène, is home to many of the island's most celebrated complexes of *menhirs* (standing stones), *dolmens* (standing stones capped by a horizontal stone) and *torri* (circular stone formations or towers). The very southernmost tip of the island, meanwhile, boasts a wonderful coastline, a countryside of handsome cork oaks and the cliff-top, fairy-tale town of Bonifacio that looks across the straits to Italian Sardinia. Although the south was initially slower to capitalise on tourism than other parts of the island, it is now quickly catching up.

Highlights

- Marvel at the prehistoric sites of Filitosa, Cauria and Paddaghiu with their carved menhirs, their dolmens and their *torri*
- Dream fantastic dreams of sieges and great rescues in Bonifacio's citadel high atop steep chalk cliffs on the straits opposite Sardinia
- Spread out on a glorious beach somewhere on the outskirts of lively Porto Vecchio or Propriano

Propriano to Filitosa

PROPRIANO (PRUPIÀ)

postcode 20110 • pop 3200

Founded by the Genoese as early as 1640, for a long time Propriano remained a modest hamlet in the shadow of the village of Fozzano.

The town is at the eastern end of the Golfe de Valinco, from where Sampiero Corso led an attempt to liberate the island in 1594. Its belated growth was largely a result of the construction of port facilities early in the 20th century, which made Propriano the centre of maritime activity for the Sartenais region. The arrival of tourists to the Golfe de Valinco's shores did the rest, and Propriano is now a popular seaside resort. Although the area around the harbour is still pretty, this changes rapidly a block or two back from the sea. Propriano. However, it's still a good base for discovering the Sartenais and Filitosa.

Orientation

Avenue Napoléon, which runs alongside the harbour, and rue du Général de Gaulle, which veers off to the south-east, are the main thoroughfares of the town centre and the focus of most activity. If you arrive from the north, you'll come into Propriano along rue de 9 Septembre (the wide coastal road), which comes out at the junction of the above two roads.

Information

Tourist Offices The tourist office (☎ 04 95 76 01 49) is at the marina. It opens 8 am to 8 pm daily in summer; 9 am to noon and 3 pm to 7 pm Monday to Saturday the rest of the year. The office provides photocopy and fax services.

Money An ATM outside the Société Générale (☎ 04 95 76 05 44), 1 rue du Général de Gaulle, changes foreign-currency travellers cheques and cash. The bank itself opens 8.15 am to noon and 1.45 to 5 pm,

Monday to Friday. There's another ATM outside Crédit Agricole, also on rue du Général de Gaulle.

The U Scambiu (☎ 04 95 76 31 02) bureau de change, on rue du Capitaine Pietri, also changes foreign currency and travellers cheques. It opens 10 am to 1 pm and 4 to 8.30 pm daily except Sunday in the summer.

Post & Communications The post office (☎ 04 95 76 02 04) is on route de la Paratella, a little way out of the town centre, but only a few minutes walk from the harbour. It opens 9 am to 6 pm Monday to Friday and on Saturday morning in summer; 9 am to noon and 2.30 to 5.30 pm Monday to Friday and on Saturday morning the rest of the year.

Bookshops La Maison de la Presse (☎ 04 95 76 06 77), on the corner of ave Napoléon and rue du Général de Gaulle, stocks a large range of paperbacks and books about Corsica, as well as French and foreign newspapers. It opens 7 am to 11.30 pm daily in the high season, 7.30 am to 12.30 pm and 2.30 to 7.30 pm, Monday to Saturday and Sunday morning, in the low season.

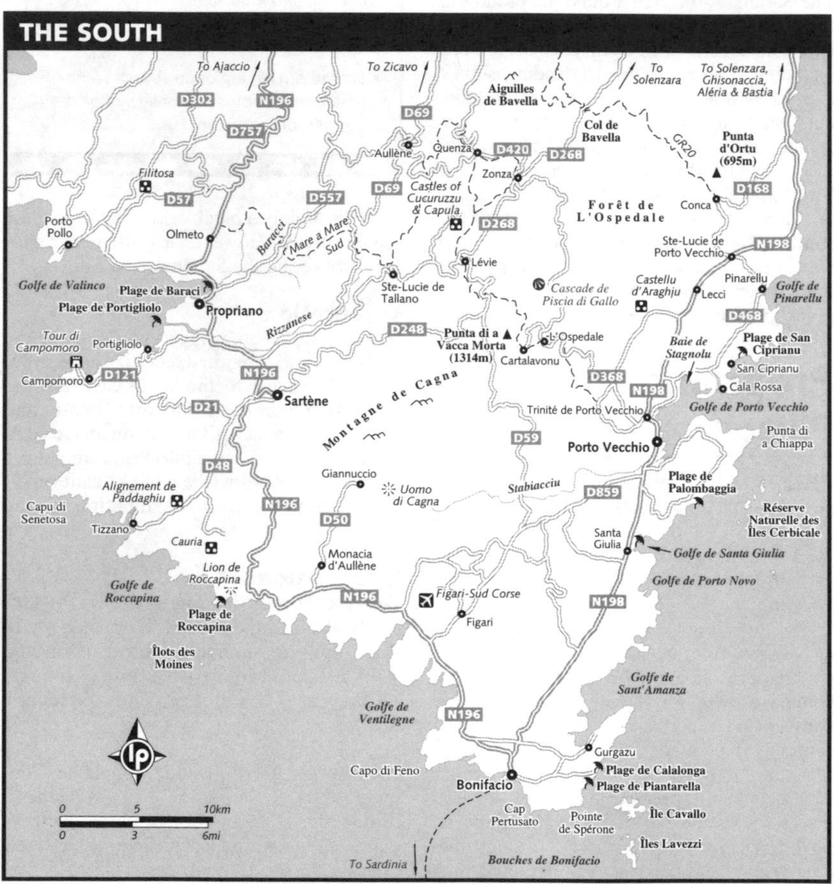

Laundry The laundrette on rue du Général de Gaulle opens 7.30 am to 7 pm daily except Sunday and public holidays, when it closes at noon.

Boat Trips

Boat excursions in the Golfe de Valinco, two hours long, in groups of two to 11 people, are organised by the École de Voile de Propriano (see under Water Sports) aboard a sightseeing vessel or a catamaran. The boat stops at an inlet for swimming and, thanks to an innovative sound system, actually listening to music underwater! Expect to pay 120FF (children 80FF). A picnic stop of three-and-a-half hours, costing 190FF, can also be arranged. Private excursions can be arranged too.

I Paesi di u Valincu (☎ 04 95 76 16 78), close to the tourist office at the harbour, organises outings in an 80- or a 130-seat boat. Both have been specially fitted for close observation of the underwater world. One route, southerly, takes in Bonifacio by way of the Lion de Roccapina (see Roccapina later in this chapter) and Figari Bay, with departure at 8.30 am and return at 6 pm, costing 230FF. Another, northerly, heads for the Réserve Naturelle de Scandola via Les Calanques de Piana, the Golfe de Porto and the Îles Sanguinaires, with departure at 8 am and return at 7.30 pm, costing 280FF. The company also offers a two-hour excursion around the Golfe de Valinco for 90FF, and Corsica-by-night excursions, from 9.30 to 11 pm, for 80FF. Children aged six to 12 pay half-price.

Beaches

The best of the little beaches in town are Plage du Lido, west of the lighthouse, and its extension, Plage du Corsaire. There are better places to swim in the Golfe de Valinco, especially Plage de Portigliolo, 7km south of town.

Water Sports

The École de Voile de Propriano (☎ 04 95 76 04 26/15 23, fax 04 95 76 20 85) is on the wharf 100m beyond the tourist office. It offers private and group lessons in sailing both catamarans and Optimists, and in windsurfing for adults and children at all skill levels. Also available for rental are surfboards (80/120FF per hour), centreboards (140FF), catamarans (240FF), and canoes (40/60FF for a single/double). It opens 8 am to 7 pm in July and August, and 9 am to 12.30 pm and 4 pm to 7 pm in June and September. Check out the Web site at perso.wanadoo.fr/propriano/nautic (French only).

Locanautic (☎ 04 95 76 31 31, fax 04 95 77 17 15), in the harbour, rents boats with or without a captain. Expect to pay 900FF per day for a seven-seat 50HP boat. Boats for which no permit is required are available for 550FF per day.

Mountain Biking

Ventura Location (☎ 04 95 76 11 84), on ave Napoléon near the ferry quay, hires out good mountain bikes at the bargain price of 60FF per day (with a 1500FF deposit) and 125cc trail bikes for 350FF per day (with a 10,000FF deposit). It opens 9 am to noon and 3 to 7 pm daily in the high season, and daily except Sunday out of season. It also organises motorcycle trips in the winter.

Horse Riding

Ferme Équestre de Baracci (☎ 04 95 76 08 02, fax 04 95 76 19 48, ⓔ emmanuel.clinckx@wanadoo.fr), on route de Baracci about 2km north of Propriano, stables 15 Corsican horses, which you can take out riding or trekking with a guide or qualified supervisor. A two-hour ride in the maquis and along the coast will set you back 200FF. The centre puts special emphasis on week-long treks along the sea (3850FF) and outings of up to 17 days to cross the whole island (7800FF), without a guide, with nights spent either camping out or in *bergeries* (shepherd's huts).

The centre, open June to October, has a reputation for high-quality service. There is a Web site at www.corse-equitation.com (French only).

Diving

See the Diving chapter for details of diving in the region.

Places to Stay – Budget

About 1.5km north of Propriano is ***Camping Tikiti*** (☎ *04 95 76 08 32, fax 04 95 76 18 25,* ⓔ *camping_tikiti@hotmail.com)*, overlooking the main road towards Ajaccio. The site is huge, and covered with flowers and greenery; it's not built up like many of the other camp sites in the area. It has spotless new facilities, and, above all, plenty of space. It opens year-round; expect to pay 30/34FF per person in winter/summer and 10/15FF per tent/car. The beach is within walking distance.

Ferme Équestre de Baracci (☎/*fax 04 95 76 19 48)*, a few hundred metres farther along the same road, rents six double rooms at half-board in July and August for 450/360FF with/without private bath and 250/210FF out of season, without meals. The rooms are simple, a little on the small side, but clean.

Places to Stay – Mid-Range

Hôtel Bellevue (☎ *04 95 76 01 86, fax 04 95 76 38 94,* ⓔ *hotel.bellevue@wanadoo.fr)*, near the harbour, has an eye-catching pink facade and blue shutters. It's pleasant, if a little noisy; all rooms are en suite and some have a view over the harbour. A single costs from 200FF to 330FF in August; a double room will set you back between 220FF and 350FF and a triple between 300FF and 440FF, and there are also a few rooms for four costing from 360FF to 500FF depending on the season. Try to book the rooms with balconies (20FF more). Half-board is available. The reception is in the bar.

Le Claridge (☎ *04 95 76 05 54, fax 04 95 76 27 77)*, under the same ownership, is an ochre-coloured building a few streets back from the harbour. Though the setting is somewhat less engaging than that of the Bellevue, the Claridge is much quieter. The en-suite rooms are spacious and comfortable, and the hotel also has a car park. Doubles cost 250FF or 270FF, depending on the room, rising to 400FF or 420FF in the high season. Singles, triples and rooms for four are also available.

Hôtel Loft (☎ *04 95 76 17 48, fax 04 95 76 22 04)*, on rue Jean Pandolfi parallel to ave Napoléon, offers spacious and spotless rooms usually with both a double bed and two bunk beds. The rooms, with sloping ceilings one flight up definitely win on the charm front. A standard double costs 280FF between April and June and in September, 340FF in July and 380FF in August. It has a car park. The hotel opens between March and September.

L'Ibiscus (☎ *04 95 76 01 56, fax 04 95 76 23 88)* is a modern, rather characterless building on the way out of town towards Ajaccio. It has good, functional rooms with terraces, and it opens year-round. Singles/doubles cost 270/310FF in the low season, in high season all rooms cost 410FF. The hotel also offers half-board and parking.

Places to Eat

There are lots of cafes and restaurants along the marina.

Budget The ***Coccinelle supermarket***, rue du Général de Gaulle, opens 7.30 am to 12.30 pm and 3 to 7.30 pm, Monday to Saturday, and until lunchtime on Sunday. In August, there's no midday break.

Au Péché Mignon (☎ *04 95 76 01 71)* is a patisserie by the harbour. It has a few tables and is ideal for a breakfast of hot drinks and pastries. It opens 7 am to 10 pm daily in summer. Out of season, it closes Monday, at lunchtime, and considerably earlier in the evening.

The ***crêperie*** of the Hôtel Bellevue (see Places to Stay – Mid-Range) serves sweet and savoury crêpes costing 13FF to 35FF, plus ice creams and cocktails, on a pretty terrace with a good view of the harbour.

Mid-Range Offering the best-value fresh seafood in the area is ***U Pescadori*** (☎ *04 95 76 42 95, 13 ave Napoléon)*; the 95FF *menu* includes a three-fish terrine and a monkfish à la Proprianese. More elaborate *menus* are also available at 135FF and 185FF. It stays open late.

Le Bischof (☎ *04 95 76 02 05, rue des Pêcheurs)*, is reputed for its meat. The owner's father has a butcher shop and the high-quality fresh ingredients attract a local clientele year round. Three *menus* costing

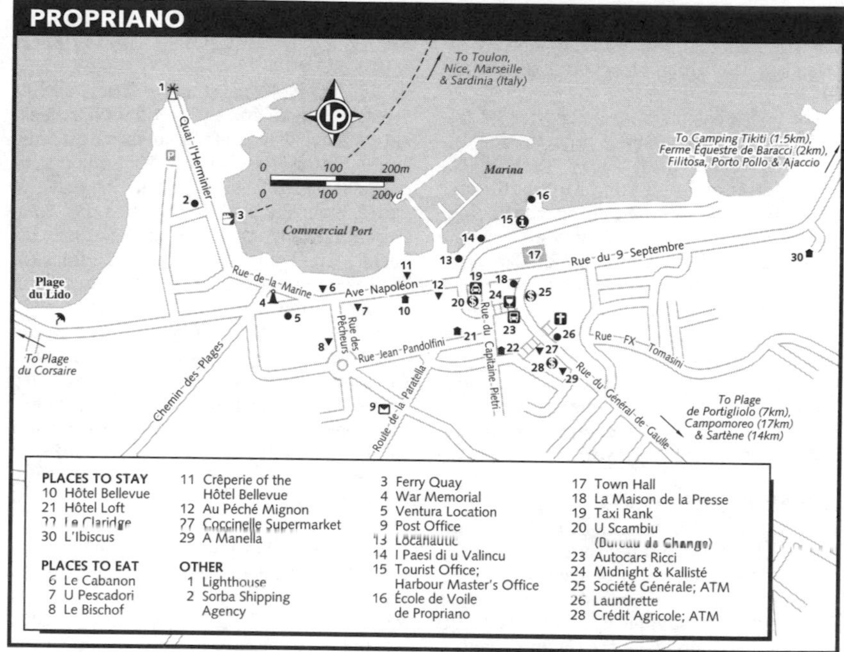

from 88FF to 140FF are offered along with several well chosen local wines.

A Manella *(☎ 04 95 76 14 85, 18 rue du Général de Gaulle)* has a 98FF *menu* from local ingredients, and also serves pizzas and a more sophisticated *menu* for 140FF. It opens for lunch and dinner daily, June to the end of September, and Thursday to Saturday from November to February.

Le Cabanon *(☎ 04 95 76 07 76, ave Napoléon)* has a good reputation for fish, its quiet terrace overlooking the sea and its 85FF *menu*. The restaurant also serves oysters, and elaborate *menus* at 110FF and 160FF. It opens both for lunch and dinner daily, Easter to the end of October. If you want to eat on the terrace, book in advance. Service can be a little slow when the restaurant is busy.

Entertainment

Two clubs, the ***Midnight*** and the ***Kallisté***, face each other across the steps in rue Grosseli in the centre of town.

Getting There & Away

Bus Autocars Ricci (☎ 04 95 76 25 59), on ave du Général de Gaulle, runs buses from Ajaccio (65FF plus 5FF for luggage, one hour 40 minutes) at 4 pm Monday to Saturday year-round and at 3 pm daily in summer. The return service to Ajaccio is at 7.15 am daily except Sunday year-round and at 9.15 am daily in summer. Buses leave from in front of the Autocars Ricci office.

Car & Motorcycle Ventura Location (see under Mountain Biking earlier) represents Citer car hire. A small car costs 488/1750FF per day/week.

Scooters can be rented from TTC (☎ 04 95 76 15 32, fax 04 95 76 15 34), rue Général de Gaulle.

Boat Ferries link Propriano with Nice, Toulon and Marseille as well as with Sardinia. The Sorba shipping agency (☎ 04 95 76 04 36, fax 04 95 76 00 98), quai L'Herminier, represents all the lines. Tickets are sold from 8 to 11.30 am and 2 to 5.30 pm Monday to Thursday. The office closes at 4.30 pm on Friday.

The yacht basin's harbour master (☎ 04 95 76 10 40) shares space with the tourist office. In season, allow 100FF to 165FF to tie up a craft of 9m to 10m. Multihulls pay a 50% premium. In the marina you'll find hot showers for 10FF and also electricity, mechanical help, fuel and supplies. The harbour master's office opens 8 am to noon and 2 to 7 pm daily in the high season.

Getting Around

There is a taxi rank on rue du Capitaine Pietri, which is often called '*rue des taxis*'. Some drivers organise excursions in the summer; ask at the tourist office for details.

GOLFE DE VALINCO

This bay, all the more magical if you approach it for the first time from the open sea, has a little seaside resort on each side of its open mouth – on the north side is Porto Pollo, and on the south is Campomoro. Both are good for diving (see the Diving chapter for details). Seven kilometres south of Propriano, the beautiful **Plage de Portigliolo** stretches out on either side of a little airfield that manages not to spoil the coastline. The beach is 4km long and cut in two by the River Rizzanese.

South of Portigliolo, the road climbs a little before reaching Belvédère. The coast is magnificent and still wild; it is under the protection of the Conservatoire du Littoral. At the end of the road is the pretty little seaside resort of **Campomoro**, where you will find the **Tour di Campomoro**. Built in the 16th century by the Genoese, the tower is one of Corsica's largest, and it is also the only one on the island to have been fortified with a star-shaped surrounding wall. It was lovingly restored in 1986.

To the north of the bay, Plage de Baraci is just one of the beaches you come across before you reach **Porto Pollo**, with its hotels, restaurants and bars. Porto Pollo is the closest village to the megalithic site at Filitosa (see the next section).

THE SOUTH

Places to Stay & Eat

Near Plage de Portigliolo, ***Camping Lecci et Murta*** *(☎ 04 95 76 02 67, fax 04 95 77 03 38)* has isolated, shady pitches, a children's play area and a pizzeria with a pleasant terrace. There are also tarmac tennis courts. Allow 32/12/12FF per person/tent/car (38/16/16FF in July and August); it opens from June to September. By road from Propriano, drive towards Sartène for about 3km, then follow the D121 for 5km until you come to a sign for the site, which is 300m to the left.

At the bottom of the village before the pathway leading to the tower, ***L'Hôtel Campomoro*** *(☎ 04 95 74 20 89/22 68 49)* offers simple, clean rooms with a sea view. In summer, expect to pay 445/580FF for a single/double at half-board (385/530FF in winter). The room alone, without board, costs 250/310FF in winter/summer. The hotel also rents flats.

There are also places to stay in Porto Pollo, on the other side of the bay. ***Camping U Caseddu*** *(☎ 04 95 74 01 80, fax 04 95 74 07 67)* is a large site, not much shaded and rather crowded in summer. But it's right on the edge of Porto Pollo and on the beach. It opens from the end of May to the beginning of October. There are washing machines and a restaurant. Allow 33/15/10FF per person/tent/car.

Hôtel du Golfe *(☎ 04 95 74 01 66)*, the cheapest in Porto Pollo, is near the village's harbour. Its basic but clean double rooms cost 200FF, all with bathrooms. The hotel opens from April to August, and half-board is mandatory in July and August (385/520FF for one/two people).

Hôtel Kallisté *(☎ 04 95 74 02 38, fax 04 95 74 06 26)*, Porto Pollo's best, has comfortable, spotless rooms with bathroom. Allow 320FF for a double in the low season and 400FF in July. Half-board is available in July (300FF/380FF per person in the first/second half of the month) and is mandatory in August (420FF). It has good *menus* for 125FF and 140FF. The Corsican-style kid sometimes on the menu is excellent and the desserts are also very good. The hotel opens between 1 April and 15 October.

Getting There & Away

Casabianca (☎ 04 95 74 05 58) runs a daily bus service between Propriano and Porto Pollo during the summer (25FF, 45 minutes). Buses leave at 7.35 am and 3.50 pm from Porto Pollo and at 11.30 am and 7 pm from Propriano.

Autocars Ricci (☎ 04 95 51 08 19) goes to Porto Pollo from Ajaccio at 4 pm on Monday, Wednesday and Saturday. Buses return from Porto Pollo at 6.30 am on the same days.

FILITOSA

Even though it's the most celebrated prehistoric site in Corsica, there are still many mysteries about Filitosa that remain to be solved. The site was discovered in 1946 by the owner of the land, Charles-Antoine Césari (whose family still runs the reception area), and owes a great deal to the archaeologist Roger Grosjean, who supervised the excavations. What is special about Filitosa is that some of its many monuments date from as far back as the early Neolithic era; others from as relatively recently as Roman times.

The oldest findings on the site suggest a human population living in caves, and remnants of pottery, arrow heads and farming tools point to fixed settlements beginning as early as 3300 BC.

The menhir statues of the megalithic period are even more impressive; the fact that they were erected at all marks a major human advancement. What the purpose was of these granite monoliths 2m to 3m high and carved to represent human faces or entire human figures armed with weapons, is not clear. It's unknown whether they are phallic symbols to encourage the fertility of the land, representations of local horsemen (the Paladini) or monuments to ward off the threat of the Torréen invaders (see the boxed text 'Mysterious People of the Sea').

Researchers are at least agreed that the Torréens arrived at the peak of the megalithic period. The Torréens were more advanced and better armed than the then indigenous communities on the island, and they seem to have driven the creators of the menhirs from Filitosa around 1500 BC. Apparently, they destroyed some of the menhirs and buried others face down, and in their place they erected circular structures, now known as *torri*, of which the central and western monuments in Filitosa are examples. The purpose of the torri is as mysterious as that of the menhirs.

Filitosa is worth a one-hour visit. Admission costs 22FF (children free), you have to go through the little museum (better visited on the way out) to get to the menhir statue known as Filitosa V. This has a distinctive, rectangular head, and is the largest and 'best-armed' statue in Corsica; a sword and a dagger are both clearly visible.

If you continue along the path you come to some caves and the foundations of some huts before you get to the central torre with its six little statues, including the one known as Filitosa IX, the face of which is considered one of the masterpieces of megalithic art.

The western monument, where a pile of stones marks the perimeter of a torre, is a

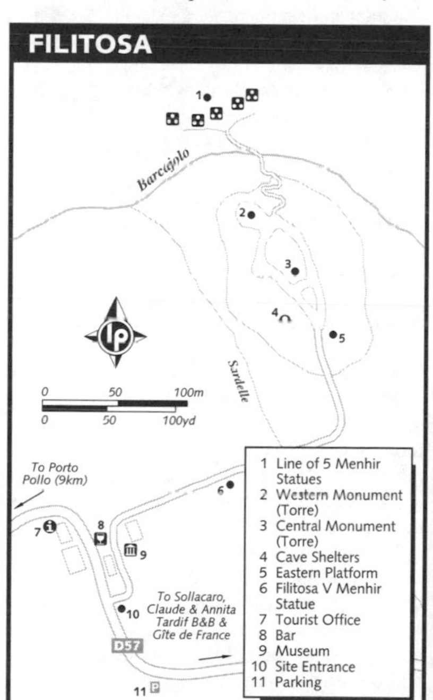

Mysterious People of the Sea

Who were the Torréens, those people who appeared on Corsican shores around 1100 BC, drove out the settled inhabitants of Filitosa, destroyed many of their statues and built the *torri* (circular monuments) in their place? The traces they left are very faint indeed.

According to Roger Grosjean, the archaeological authority on Filitosa, they could actually have been Shardanes, the people enigmatically known to historians as 'sea people', who battled with the pharaoh Ramses III. They probably originated from Anatolia, from Crete or from along the coast of the Aegean Sea.

The Shardanes are first mentioned in around 1200 BC. They were allied with the Libyans and planned to attack the prosperous civilisation in the Nile Valley. It was a mistake: Ramses III succeeded in blocking their advance and sinking the Shardanes' fleet during a battle that is recorded in hieroglyphics carved into the wall of the Medinat Habu temple in Luxor, Egypt. After this defeat, the vanquished Shardanes made their way to Corsica and then to Sardinia, before disappearing back into obscurity.

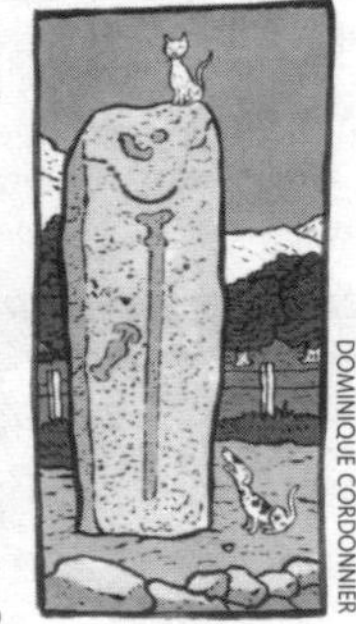
DOMINIQUE CORDONNIER

Corsica's ancient statuary remains a mystery.

few metres farther on, and then the path goes down towards the highlight of the visit: five menhir statues lined up in an arc around the foot of a 1200-year-old olive tree. Behind them is a little granite quarry, from where it's thought the ancient sculptors got their materials.

Visitors who aren't archaeology buffs might want some help from the little 28FF guide, but experts and casual visitors alike will be struck by the peaceful stillness of the atmosphere, especially at the end of the day, and the impressive geometry of the last five statues as seen from the west monument.

It is worth spending a few minutes in the museum before you leave. It houses three more menhir statues, some pottery, some human remains, a few stone tools and information about the Torréens-Shardanes. There is also a bar and a souvenir shop on the site.

Filitosa (☎ 04 95 74 00 91) opens 8 am to sunset daily, April to October. The Filitosa Tourist Office, 100m from the entrance to the site, in the village, opens 10 am to 7 pm daily, May to October. The office is particularly helpful at supplying information on accommodation.

Places to Stay

The nearest camp sites and hotels are in Porto Pollo (see under Golfe de Valinco earlier in this section). To get there by car from Filitosa, take the D57 towards Propriano for 4.5km, then turn right onto the D157 for the same distance.

You can find B&B accommodation and gîtes closer to Filitosa. The B&B belonging to ***Claude and Annita Tardif*** *(☎ 04 95 74 29 48/06 62 43 13 69)* with a magnificent ocean view, offers three clean and pleasant rooms with bathrooms for 350FF including breakfast. The admission fee also entitles you to use the excellent outdoor cooking facilities. It is 2.5km beyond Filitosa along a small side road; it's well signposted.

Paul Luccioni's ***Gîte de France*** *(☎ 04 95 74 00 98)*, 1km beyond Filitosa, to the left of the main road, has well appointed apartments that cost 2700FF per week in the summer, 1700FF in June and September, and 1300FF off-season.

Getting There & Away

There are no real bus services to Filitosa, but Autocars Ricci (☎ 04 95 51 08 19) on its Ajaccio to Porto Pollo line passes 2km from the site.

The Sartenais

In more ways than one, the Sartenais is a reminder of what the whole of Corsica used to be like; the town of Sartène itself fervently perpetuates traditions going back to the Middle Ages, while to the south of the town there are prehistoric remains that bear witness to the way of life of the island's very first inhabitants.

SARTÈNE (SARTÈ)

postcode 20100 • pop 3410

'The whole place breathes war and vengeance', the poet Paul Valéry said about Sartène, and the shadowy town's gaze out over the Rizzanese valley from its high granite walls does seem quite ferocious. In earlier times, Sartène was a bastion for great families of noblemen who didn't want anyone meddling in their business, and even today Sartène seems reluctant to reveal very much about either its past or its present. Nevertheless, history tells that the town was subject to repeated Saracen raids in the 15th and 16th centuries and pirates from Algiers took 400 of its inhabitants into slavery in 1583.

Danger for Sartène didn't always come from the outside, either. The town enjoys pride of place in the chronicles of Corsica's long tradition of vendetta. In the course of the Colomba Carabelli vendetta, a curate protagonist is said to have remained shut up for nine years in his home in the Borgo quarter for fear of reprisals; Colomba Carabelli was the principal inspiration for Prosper Mérimée's romantic tale of Corsican vendetta, *Colomba*. Another famous 19th-century rivalry pitted one family from the Borgo quarter against another from Santa Anna. What was in effect a small-scale civil war ended only with the ratification of a peace treaty in the Église Ste-Marie. And some suggest that all of the bloody confrontations leading up to the treaty of peace were provoked by nothing more than a dispute over a dog.

Undoubtedly it was the tradition of the vendetta and other related exotica that inspired Mérimée's comment that Sartène was the 'most Corsican of all Corsican towns'.

In recent years, the Catenacciu procession, dating from the Middle Ages (see the boxed text 'The Procession du Catenacciu'), has been exploited to attract tourists, so perhaps the town is at last emerging from its immemorial introversion.

Orientation

Sartène is built around place de la Libération, from which cours Sœur Amélie and cours Général de Gaulle, the town's main streets, lead off.

The old quarter of Santa Anna stretches out to the north of place de la Libération. Many of its little streets have more than one name and just as many signs.

Information

Tourist Offices The tourist office (☎ 04 95 77 15 40), 6 rue Borgo, is near to place de la Libération and opens 9 am to noon and 3 to 6 pm, Monday to Saturday, May to October.

Money Crédit Lyonnais, on cours Général de Gaulle, changes travellers cheques and cash. It opens 8.15 am to 12.15 pm and 1.30 to 4.30 pm Monday to Friday.

The only ATM is outside Crédit Agricole, at the bottom of cours Sœur Amélie near the petrol station.

Post & Communications The post office (☎ 04 95 77 70 72) is on rue du Marché, not

The Procession du Catenacciu

On the eve of Good Friday, Sartène is the setting for one of the oldest religious traditions on the island – the Procession du Catenacciu. In a colourful re-enactment of the Passion, the Catenacciu (literally, 'the chained one'), an anonymous, barefoot penitent, covered from head to foot in a red robe and cowl, carries a huge cross through the town; dragging heavy chains at his feet. The Catenacciu is followed by a procession of other penitents (eight dressed in black, one in white), members of the clergy and local notables. As the chains clatter by on the cobblestones, spectators look on in great (if rather humourless) excitement. Needless to say, everyone is curious to find out the identity of the penitent, selected by the parish priest from applicants seeking to expiate a grave sin.

When they are not in use, the chains and cross of the Catenacciu can be seen in the Église Ste-Marie.

far from place de la Libération. It opens from 8.30 am to 12.30 pm and from 2 to 5.30 pm, Monday to Friday, and Saturday morning.

Old Town

The old town is a labyrinth of stone stairways and little streets and alleyways, some of them so narrow that a person can barely pass through them. Yet a virtue of these corridors, particularly on hot summer days, is that they provide the pedestrian with some welcome shade.

The bell tower of the **Église Ste-Marie** rises above place de la Libération, which is still sometimes called place Porta. The church was built in 1766 on the site of an older building that collapsed not long after it was erected. It boasts a superb altarpiece of polychrome marble (formerly in the Couvent St-François) and canvasses of the stations of the Cross dating from 1843. The chains and cross used during the Catenacciu procession are also on display.

Next to Église Ste-Marie is the building that now houses the **town hall** but which, in the 16th century, was the palace of the Genoese lieutenants. Sadly, the anonymous Italian canvasses it shelters have not been maintained properly. It opens 8.30 am to noon and 2 to 6 pm Monday to Friday; admission is free. If you go through the gateway below this former palace, you will come out on the narrow streets of the **Santa Anna quarter**, which is the real jewel of the old town.

An **échauguette**, or watchtower, to the right of the post office, bears witness to the importance the people of Sartène gave to keeping a lookout around the city. It is not open to visitors.

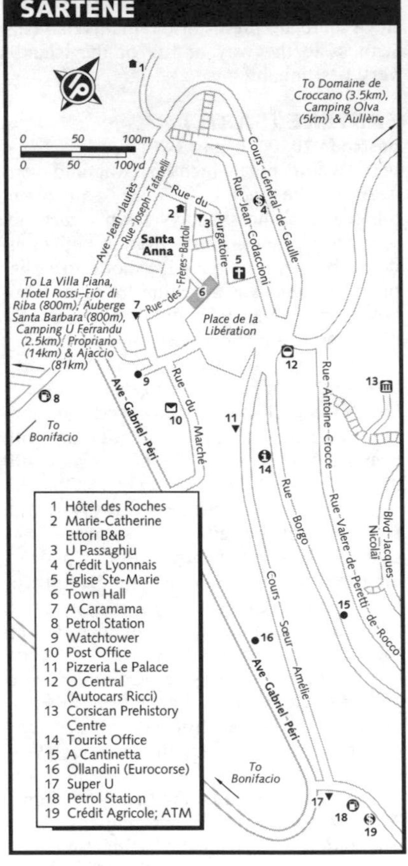

Corsican Prehistory Centre

Perhaps it is to reinforce Sartène's austere atmosphere that the town museum (☎ 04 95 77 01 09) has been established in a former prison with thick walls, sinister-looking hinges and barred windows. The one substantial room and five cells house a diverse collection, some dating back to Neolithic times. The most interesting exhibits are the pottery (especially some beautiful painted pieces from the Middle Ages), jewellery, tools and stone arrow heads.

To get there, follow the steps off cours Bonaparte, to the right, behind place de la Libération. It opens 10 am to noon and 2 to 6 pm daily except Sunday, 15 June to 15 September. Admission costs 15FF (children and group members 10FF). The museum is due to move to larger quarters sometime in the future.

Horse Riding

Le Domaine de Croccano (☎ 04 95 77 11 37, fax 04 95 73 42 89, ⓔ christian.perrier@

wanadoo.fr) offers options both for beginners and advanced equestrians. The basic rate is 120FF per hour, or week-long outings are available for 3300FF to 7000FF, particularly along the still rather wild coastline. The Domaine, magnificent in open countryside, also has rooms to rent (see Places to Stay). It's 3.5km out of town on the road to Granace.

Walking

The Association Nature et Sentiers du Sartenais (☎ 04 95 77 18 21, ⓔ rando.sartene@libertysurf.fr), the nature and trails association, organises theme walks around Sartène and in southern Corsica.

Places to Stay

The closest camp site to the town, ***Camping U Farrandu*** *(☎ 04 95 73 41 69)* is 2.5km north on the right-hand side of the Propriano road. It's clean, the service is friendly and the pitches are private and shady. Allow 33FF per person per day (18FF per child). This little camp site, open April to October, counts among its amenities both a tennis court and mini-golf.

Camping Olva *(☎ 04 95 77 11 58)* is on the other side of town, 5km out on the D69 towards Aullène. It is a quiet eight-hectare park shaded by eucalyptus trees and its amenities include a good tennis court, a swimming pool and a little supermarket. In the summer, it costs 35/16/13FF per person/tent/car. It also rents bungalows for 1600/2800FF (low/high season) per week for four people. If you are on foot, call from Sartène and someone will pick you up.

Hôtel des Roches *(☎ 04 95 77 07 61, fax 04 95 77 19 93)*, at the bottom of ave Jean Jaurès, is the only hotel in the centre of Sartène. Its rooms, with en-suite bathrooms, TV and telephone, are clean but slightly old-fashioned. In August, expect to pay 370/400/490FF for a single/double with a village view, and 470/500/590FF with a valley view. The valley view is worth the extra cost.

Another nice option is the B&B belonging to ***Marie-Catherine Ettori*** *(☎ 04 95 77 05 01)* in the heart of Santa Anna. Clean, new rooms, with private bath, cost 250FF. Excellent B&B rooms can also be rented at ***La Domaine de Croccano***, which is 3.5km from Sartène. Rates run to 150/200FF in low/high season) per person, and 270/320FF at half-board. Expect to pay 100FF more for a single.

Hôtel Rossi – Fior di Riba *(☎ 04 95 77 01 80/09 58)* is noteworthy for its warm, family atmosphere and comfortable, spotless double rooms, which cost from 285/350FF (low/high season) to 340/450FF. On the Propriano road, 800m from town, it opens mid-March to mid-October. There is even a small swimming pool.

La Villa Piana *(☎ 04 95 77 07 04, fax 04 95 73 45 65)* is next to the Hôtel Rossi – Fior di Riba, and has comfortable double rooms costing from 290FF to 570FF and 330FF to 600FF in the low and high seasons. It opens from the beginning of April to the end of September. Guests have the use of both a swimming pool and a tennis court.

Places to Eat

Budget & Mid-Range If you are self-catering, head for the ***Super U***, at the bottom end of cours Sœur Amélie near the petrol station. It opens 8.30 am to 7.45 pm Monday to Saturday.

U Passaghju *(☎ 04 95 77 21 84, rue des Frères Bartoli)* opens for lunch and dinner daily April to September. *Menus* are available for 75FF and 105FF, and a lunch *menu* of, for example, stuffed mussels, fish kebab and dessert is available for 60FF. However, the restaurant is less distinguished for its cuisine than for its pleasant setting in the alleyways of the old town.

A Caramama *(☎ 04 95 77 07 84)*, also in the old town, serves a respectable pizza for between 38FF and 52FF, to eat in or take-away and offers a wide range of *menus* (78FF to 139FF) and daily specials until late into the evening. It has street tables and opens from the end of May to mid-October.

Pizzeria Le Palace *(☎ 04 95 77 02 97, 4 cours Sœur Amélie)* also serves pizzas (costing from 44FF to 58FF) and grilled meats and fish starting at 86FF. The restaurant isn't much to look at, but the dishes are large and tasty, and it's possible to eat on the balcony perched above the street.

Top End Across from La Villa Piana (see Places to Stay), ***Auberge Santa Barbara*** *(☎ 04 95 77 09 06, fax 04 95 77 09 09)* deserves its reputation as one of the region's best restaurants. The mullet salad (80FF) and especially the squab roasted with maquis myrtle over polenta (150FF) are excellent. A Corsican *menu* is available at 155FF.

Shopping

Have a look at the wine, the liqueurs and the honey at A Cantinetta (☎ 04 95 77 08 75), rue Borgo. Marie-Dominique Bartoli will welcome you warmly to the family cellar, established in 1902. The wines here are the Sartenais' best, and the *charcuterie* and the cheeses can make an exceptionally good meal.

Getting There & Away

Autocars Ricci (☎ 04 95 51 08 19) buses leave Sartène for Ajaccio at 7 and 9 am daily (70FF plus 5FF for luggage, 1½ hours). The service is via Propriano, Olmeto and St-Georges. There are also departures at 5 and 6 pm for Ste-Lucie de Tallano, Lévie and Zonza and in summer to the Col de Bàvella. The Autocars Ricci base in Sartène is the O Central bar, on place de la Libération.

Ollandini (☎ 04 95 77 18 41), ave Gabriel Péri, the representative for Eurocorse, has buses leaving for Ajaccio at 6 and 7.55 am and 4 pm daily (except Sunday in the off season). There are also two buses daily (except Sundays in the off season) to Bonifacio and Porto Vecchio (at 10.30 am and 5.45 pm) and one to Zonza (at 5.45 pm). Ollandini opens 7.30 am to noon and 2.30 to 6.30 pm, Monday to Friday, and Saturday morning.

PREHISTORIC SITES OF THE SARTENAIS

Corsica's dolmens and menhirs remain shrouded in considerable mystery. Archaeologists and historians seem to agree at least that the dolmens mark burial sites. But what of the menhirs? Were they meant to represent divinities, or deceased elders, or were they sculpted as a means of stripping enemies of their power? The answers are elusive, and the diversity of the evidence only complicates the problem.

Some of the menhirs are extremely crude, but on others, human faces and weapons can clearly be made out. Yet others, as at Filitosa, are so phallic that they're thought to have been fertility symbols for the land.

In the absence of any conclusive scientific answers, many visitors will be happy simply to let the dolmens and menhirs serve as a rather spooky backdrop to their walks.

The sites of Cauria and Paddaghiu, to the south of Sartène, are not only among the most interesting on the island, but also stand as they have for thousands of years, unfenced, untended, unprotected by guards, and unmediated by guides. Such remoteness means that you will have a hard time getting to them without a vehicle.

Cauria

The desolate and beautiful Cauria plateau, about 15km south of Sartène, is home to three megalithic curiosities: the *alignements* (lines) of menhirs of Stantari and Rinaghiu, and the Funtanaccia dolmen.

To get to the sites, you will have to climb over some barriers designed to keep animals from straying, and this makes the walk somewhat challenging for people with reduced mobility. In any event, do not expect to do this visit in less than an hour.

No admission is charged for any of these sites, and there are no facilities.

From Sartène, follow the road to Bonifacio for 2km before turning off onto the winding D48, on the right. The megalithic site at Cauria is signposted off to the left after another 8km. The next leg, 4.5km along a road that is only casually maintained, leads to a sign riddled with bullet holes. The sign points to the menhirs and the dolmens, along a driveable track to the right, but you can leave your car in the shade here and undertake the last 700m to the **Alignement de Stantari** on foot.

The Alignement de Stantari consists of nine stones: the fourth from the left represents a sword, and its next two neighbours represent faces with their mouths open in muted cry. The **Alignement de Rinaghiu** is

THE SOUTH

OLIVIER CIRENDINI

Strange scale-like rocks protect the idyllic Archipel de Lavezzi.

OLIVIER CIRENDINI

Bonifacio's cliffs are 70m high.

JEAN-BERNARD CARILLET

A stretch of extraordinary coastline is punctuated by Bonifacio's tranquil harbour.

OLIVIER CIRENDINI

Paul Valéry said of stony-faced Sartène, 'The whole place breathes war and vengeance.'

OLIVIER CIRENDINI

Mysterious, evocative complexes of standing stones around Sartène include the Fontanaccia dolmen.

JEAN-BERNARD CARILLET

Larico pine forests abound near Conca.

OLIVIER CIRENDINI

Luminous seas surround Cap Pertusato.

larger and slightly less orderly, and 300m farther on at the edge of a little wood that some say may once have been sacred.

If you retrace your steps to the Alignement de Stantari, you can climb over a barrier made from the two main branches of a cork oak, then follow the path another 350m to the **Funtanaccia dolmen**. This megalithic monument is the largest of its type in Corsica, and is worth the effort more than the lines of menhirs.

Alignement de Paddaghiu

With nearly 260 menhirs, some standing, others lying, the Alignement de Paddaghiu is the largest collection of megalithic statuary in the Mediterranean. Four distinct alignments, each of them four to eight menhirs long, are the highlight.

To get there by car from Cauria, drive the 4.5km back to the D48 and turn left towards Tizzano. The entrance to the site is on the right, 1.3km beyond the Mosconi vintners wine-tasting facility. Follow the arrows for about 1.2km before coming to the car park. Admission is free.

PROTECTED COASTLINE

Marine de Tizzano

This charming little cove, formerly protected by a fort that is now in ruins, lies approximately 5km south-west of the Alignement de Paddaghiu. You'll find a beach, a few little inlets, a grocery, a hotel and restaurants. It is an ideal spot to spend a few nights.

At ***Hôtel-Restaurant du Golfe*** *(☎/fax 04 95 77 14 76)*, the light and pleasant double rooms on the ground floor, all with bathroom, TV and telephone, cost from 430FF to 640FF, depending on the season. The upstairs rooms go for 30FF more but the view is wonderful and the bathrooms come with bathtubs rather than showers. Expect to pay 140FF for a third bed. The hotel opens from the end of March to October, and the restaurant serves sophisticated food at reasonable prices.

Chez Antoine *(☎ 04 95 77 07 25)* is reputed for its grilled fish (130FF menu), its bouillabaisse (240FF) and its stone bower at the edge of the harbour.

Roccapina

The landmark Roccapina site, 20km from Sartène and 30km from Bonifacio, is famous for a geological curiosity: a lion sculpted by nature out of the rock. To find it, look out in the direction of the sea from the neighbourhood of the Auberge la Corralli, on the N196. Although by no means as perfect as the Sphinx in Egypt, the Roccapina big cat is easy enough to make out: two enormous blocks of rock on top of a ridge crowned by a Genoese tower define the basic shape; a few standing rocks suggest the mane. The lion is not the only curiosity at the site. From the snack bar 2km beyond Auberge la Corralli in the direction of Bonifacio, you'll see another rocky configuration whose shape suggests a gorilla's head. If you have a vivid imagination, you may also be able to make out the shape of an elephant in the rocks; it's recognisable by its trunk.

To get to the beach at Roccapina, take the track leading off the main road next to Auberge la Corralli and follow it downhill for 2km. The juniper-covered dunes, damaged by campers in the years prior to 1985, are now protected by the Conservatoire du Littoral. Limpets are also protected; the larger females used to be eaten by mollusc-fanciers, and the species was in danger of extinction before it was added to the protected list.

The beach is an ideal place for a dip. A footpath connects it to the lion rock.

Places to Stay & Eat If you don't mind feeling a little cut off, there are a few places to stay in the area.

Camping Municipal Arepos *(☎ 04 95 77 19 30, fax 04 95 77 10 60)*, at the bottom of the path, charges 17/22FF for a site in low/high season and the same amount again per adult and 12FF for children. Though the facility has few amenities, it is very close to the beach. It opens from May to September.

Auberge la Corralli *(☎ 04 95 77 05 94)* is on the main road and has four good rooms with bathroom, balcony and TV. Doubles start at 280FF in June and September. In summer, rooms are rented by the week with half-board 3500FF for two. *Menus* are offered for 80FF and 120FF.

Getting There & Away Eurocorse buses (☎ 04 95 21 06 30, 04 95 70 13 83) stop at Roccapina on the route between Ajaccio and Bonifacio.

The Far South

A narrow plain separating the coast from the island's rocky foothills, along with abundant cork oaks, gives the extreme southern end of the island its special look. The extraordinary town of Bonifacio is the principal reason for coming to the area, but there are also beaches, boating and water sports.

BONIFACIO (BUNIFAZIU)

postcode 20169 • pop 2700

Bonifacio is a town on two levels. The citadel, with its ancient buildings and its narrow, twisty streets sits up at cloud level. Its walls and buildings are constructed so they appear to be a continuation of the sheer, chalky cliffs on which they're perched. Down below, an inlet, or fjord, about 100m wide, plunges in behind the great cliffs to form the town's fine natural harbour, home to a buzzing port.

This 'Corsican Gibraltar', as Bonifacio is sometimes called, looks across a mere 12km of water to the Italian island of Sardinia.

History

The discovery of the *Dame de Bonifacio*, (Bonifacio Woman) the remains of a young woman who lived near the present town about 8500 years ago, proves that the area was inhabited as far back as the Neolithic period. There is no doubt that there was a sizeable population in the period that we now think of as Classical Antiquity, and some people even suggest that the episode of the Odyssey in which Ulysses meets the Laestrygonians, a race of giant cannibals, at the foot of 'sheer cliffs on either side' could well have taken place at the entrance to the Goulet de Bonifacio (Bonifacio Narrows). The town we know today was probably founded by the Marquis de Toscane Boniface, who gave it its name, in 828.

A few hundred years later, in 1187, the town was taken by Genoa, supposedly while the locals were busy celebrating a wedding. Genoa sent in colonisers, who prospered, and, true to form, Genoa drove the previous inhabitants out.

Genoese Bonifacio nevertheless had to fight for its life on two separate occasions. The first came in 1420, when Alphonse V of Aragon laid siege to the town for five months on the grounds that Pope Boniface VIII had given Corsica to Spain; according to legend, the Escalier du Roi d'Aragon (King of Aragon's Stairway) was carved at this point. Ultimately, a Genoese squadron was dispatched to assist the colony and Alphonse was obliged to retreat.

The second siege took place in 1553. This time it was an alliance between French troops, followers of Sampiero Corso and the Turkish pirate Dragut who aimed to liberate the town. Bonifacio resisted the attack for 18 days, then surrendered on the heels of double-dealing by one of its inhabitants. Together with the rest of the island, it was returned to the Genoese in 1559, however, under the terms of the treaty of Cateau-Cambrésis.

Orientation

Bonifacio can be separated into two main sections: the marina at the bottom of the Goulet de Bonifacio, and the Genoese-built citadel – also known as the Old Town *(Vieille Ville)* or Upper Town *(Ville Haute)* – perched on the cliff-top between the inlet and the sea. There are two ways into the citadel: by the handsome Porte de Gênes (Genoa Gate; pedestrian access only) at the top of montée St-Roch, and the Porte de France (France Gate; vehicle access), which overlooks the ferry terminal.

Information

Tourist Offices The tourist office (☎ 04 95 73 11 88, fax 04 95 73 14 97, ⓔ tourisme.bonifacio@wanadoo.fr), 2 rue Fred Scamaroni, is next to the Porte de France. It opens 9 am to 8 pm daily in summer and 9 am to noon and 2 to 6 pm, Monday to Friday, as well as Saturday morning, during the rest of the year. The organisation has a Web site at www.bonifacio.com.

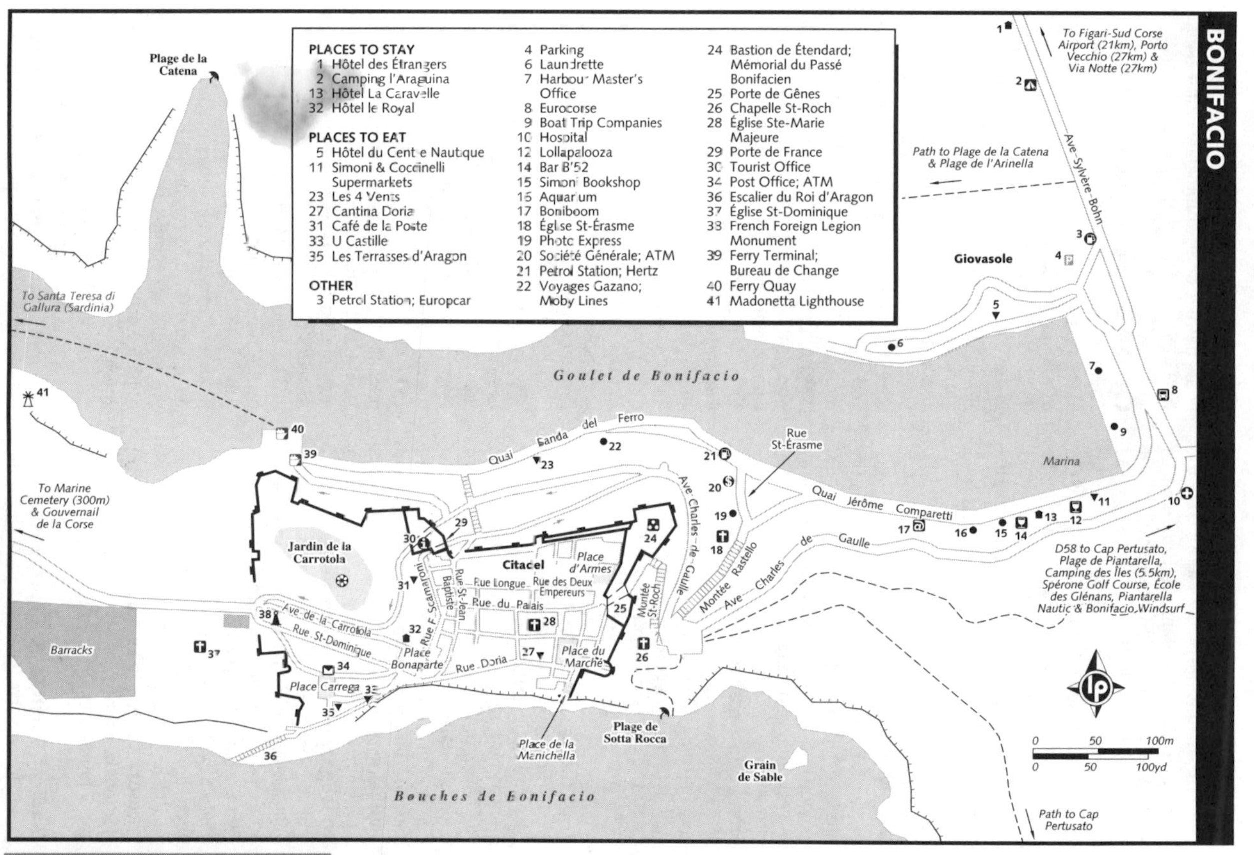
BONIFACIO
PLACES TO STAY
1 Hôtel des Étrangers
2 Camping l'Araguina
13 Hôtel La Caravelle
32 Hôtel le Royal
PLACES TO EAT
5 Hôtel du Centre Nautique
11 Simoni & Coccinelli Supermarkets
23 Les 4 Vents
27 Cantina Doria
31 Café de la Poste
33 U Castille
35 Les Terrasses d'Aragon
OTHER
3 Petrol Station; Europcar
4 Parking
6 Laundrette
7 Harbour Master's Office
8 Eurocorse
9 Boat Trip Companies
10 Hospital
12 Lollapalooza
14 Bar B'52
15 Simoni Bookshop
16 Aquarium
17 Boniboom
18 Église St-Érasme
19 Photo Express
20 Société Générale; ATM
21 Petrol Station; Hertz
22 Voyages Gazano; Moby Lines
24 Bastion de Étendard; Mémorial du Passé Bonifacien
25 Porte de Gênes
26 Chapelle St-Roch
28 Église Ste-Marie Majeure
29 Porte de France
30 Tourist Office
34 Post Office; ATM
36 Escalier du Roi d'Aragon
37 Église St-Dominique
38 French Foreign Legion Monument
39 Ferry Terminal; Bureau de Change
40 Ferry Quay
41 Madonetta Lighthouse
To Figari-Sud Corse Airport (21km), Porto Vecchio (27km) & Via Notte (27km)
Ave Sylvère Bohn
Path to Plage de la Catena & Plage de l'Arinella
Giovasole
Marina
D58 to Cap Pertusato, Plage de Piantarella, Camping des Îles (5.5km), Spérone Golf Course, École des Glénans, Piantarella Nautic & Bonifacio Windsurf
Path to Cap Pertusato
Quai Jérôme Comparetti
Ave Charles de Gaulle
Rue St-Érasme
Montée Rastello
Goulet de Bonifacio
Quai Banda del Ferro
Montée St-Roch
Place d'Armes
Citadel
Rue des Deux Empereurs
Rue du Palais
Rue Longue
Place du Marché
Rue St-Jean Baptiste
Rue Doria
Rue F Scamaroni
Place Bonaparte
Place de la Manichella
Plage de Sotta Rocca
Grain de Sable
Bouches de Bonifacio
Jardin de la Carrotola
Ave de la Carrotola
Rue St-Dominique
Place Carrega
Barracks
Plage de la Catena
To Santa Teresa di Gallura (Sardinia)
To Marine Cemetery (300m) & Gouvernail de la Corse
0 50 100m
0 50 100yd
THE SOUTH

Money Société Générale (☎ 04 95 73 02 49), 7 rue St-Érasme, on the south side of the harbour, is the only bank in Bonifacio; it also has an outdoor ATM. It opens 8.15 am to noon and 2 to 4.50 pm. A second ATM can be found at the post office.

There's a bureau de change (☎ 04 95 73 18 98) inside the ferry terminal, open in the high season from 8 am to 8 pm. Still other bureaux de change crop up along the marina in high season.

Post The post office (☎ 04 95 73 73 73), rather hidden in place Carrega in the citadel, opens 8.30 am to 6 pm Monday to Friday and until noon on Saturday morning in the summer. The rest of the year it opens 9 am to noon and 2 to 5.30 pm Monday to Friday and Saturday morning.

Email & Internet Access Boniboom (☎ 04 95 73 05 89), a very superior Internet cafe, is built into the cliff under the upper town on the quai Jérôme Comparetti. It opens 6 am to 2 am. The rate is 70FF per hour. See the Web site at www.boniboom.com (French only).

Bookshops Simoni (☎ 04 95 73 02 63), on the harbour near the aquarium, is a bookshop and stationers stocking a wide range of French and foreign newspapers, periodicals and books in the summer. It opens 8 am to midnight daily (except from 1 to 4 pm on Sunday) in July and August (8 am to noon and 3.45 to 7 pm Monday to Saturday and until noon on Sunday, the rest of the year).

Photography Thanks to the number of tourists, the price of film can sometimes soar to nosebleed levels in Bonifacio. In summer, for example, it is not unusual for a 100 ASA film to cost 68FF. Try Photo Express (☎ 04 95 73 58 87), 5 place St-Érasme, where the prices are reasonable all year round.

Laundry There is a laundrette on the north side of the marina. It opens 8 am to noon and 2 pm to 8 pm in the high season.

Medical Services & Emergency Bonifacio Hospital (☎ 04 95 73 95 73), on the marina, has an emergency unit open 24 hours daily. For an ambulance call ☎ 04 95 73 95 95.

Citadel & Upper Town

There are two sets of stairs from the harbour to the citadel. **Montée St-Roch**, which starts as montée Rastello, links rue St-Érasme to the Porte de Gênes. The second set ascends to the Porte de France from quai Banda del Ferro, not far from the ferry quay. The montée St-Roch and Porte de Gênes route is undoubtedly the best way to enter the citadel.

The **Porte de Gênes**, which was fitted with a drawbridge in the last years of the 16th century, was the only way of getting into the citadel until the Porte de France was built in 1854. To the north is the **Bastion de l'Étendard**, a remnant of the fortifications built in the aftermath of the siege in 1553. It is home to the **Mémorial du Passé Bonifacien** (Memorial to Bonifacio's Past; admission 10FF) where various episodes in the town's history have been recreated. To the south of the bastion are **place du Marché** and **place de la Manichella**, with their splendid views over the Bouches de Bonifacio (see later in this chapter).

The street that under Genoese supremacy was the citadel's main thoroughfare now bears the name **rue des Deux Empereurs**; the emperors alluded to are Charles V and Napoleon I, both of whom lodged in the town, the former on his way to Algiers in 1541, the latter in 1793 on his way to conquer Sardinia. Commemorative plaques at Nos 4 and 7 indicate the houses the two men stayed in, but neither house opens to the public.

The **Église Ste-Marie Majeure** was built by the Pisans and completed in the 14th century. Although it has been modified on numerous occasions and has gradually lost its original style, it retains its main feature, the loggia, under the arches of which the notables of the town used to gather. Opposite it is the old cistern, in which the town formerly collected rainwater from the many aqueducts running above the streets of the old town. Much of the citadel's stonework was erected for the purpose of solving the town's water-supply problem, and for a long time water supply was by means of mule-powered scoop wheels.

Even the **Escalier du Roi d'Aragon** (10FF) may have been connected with water provision. Legend has it that the 187 steps down from the south-western corner of the citadel to the sea 60m below were carved in a single night by the King of Aragon's troops during the 1420 siege. It is more likely that this impressive scar down the side of the cliff was carved to allow access to a spring discovered by monks.

To the west of the citadel is the **Église St-Dominique**, one of the few Gothic churches in Corsica. It houses an altarpiece made of polychrome marble that dates back to the mid-18th century, as well as the reliquaries carried in processions through the town during a number of religious festivals. The church opens in the summer only and admission costs 10FF.

The **marine cemetery**, with its immaculate lines of tombs, stretches out to the sea a few hundred metres farther to the west. Although the surroundings are far from seductive, there is a spectacular view over the Sardinian coast, about 12km away. An **underground passage** dug by hand during WWII leads to the **Gouvernail de la Corse** (the Rudder of Corsica), a rock about a dozen metres from the shore with a shape reminiscent of the rudder of a ship. The passage opens to the public until around 6 pm in the summer; admission costs 10FF.

Marina

The **É[illegible] St-Érasme**, dedicated to the patron sa[illegible]shermen, was built in the 13th centu[illegible]hurch is at the foot of montée Raste[illegible]

The **Aquarium** (☎ 04 95 73 03 69) is in a natural cave on quai Jérôme Comparetti and features the marine flora and fauna of the Bouches de Bonifacio; admission costs 22FF (students 16FF, children 11FF).

Beaches

A very steep path leads down from the bottom of the montée St-Roch to **Plage de Sotta Rocca**, which nestles at the foot of the cliffs across from the so-called Grain de Sable (Grain of Sand); this is a section of cliff that seems to have escaped erosion a few dozen metres out to sea.

The little **Plage de la Catena** and **Plage de l'Arinella** stretch out at the back of the coves of the same name, on the north side of the *goulet*. There is a path leading to them from the corner of the U Veni snack bar on ave Sylvère Bohn. Unfortunately, both of these beaches tend to collect the rubbish from the goulet. With a car you can reach the beaches at Piantarella, Calalonga and Santa Manza in the Bouches de Bonifacio.

Boat Trips

The beauty of the seascapes on view around Bonifacio means that numerous companies offering boat trips jockey with one another for position and space along the quays of the marina.

A boat trip is an excellent way to see the beauty of the area and is highly recommended. There are two basic itineraries. The first includes the goulet, the *calanques* (deep rocky inlets; *calanche* in Corsican) and the Grotte du Sdragonato (Little Dragon Cave); a 50-minute tour costs about 70FF. The second puts emphasis on the Îles Lavezzi; this costs approximately 120FF. The launches for this second jaunt are about 10m long and they are operated shuttle-fashion, so you can linger on the islands. But, if you do, consider carrying your own food and drink, since you won't find any there. On the way back, the boats pass close to Île Cavallo, the Pointe de Spérone, the calanche and the cliffs.

In summer, the sightseeing boats operate from 9.15 am to 7 pm. The rides are all basically the same, but you may be able to negotiate small reductions in price or, if you're driving, you might also watch for operators who offer free parking.

Walking

There is a sign describing the footpaths along the coast at the foot of montée St-Roch. Don't miss the one that goes to the Pertusato lighthouse (see Strolls & Country Walks in the Walking chapter).

Diving

See the Diving chapter for information on diving in the Bonifacio area.

Water Sports

A branch of the reputed École des Glénans (☎ 04 95 73 03 85, fax 04 95 73 18 84, ⓔ glenansbo@wanadoo.fr), on the Santa Manza road 300m from the port, offers sailing courses for adults and for children aged 13 or over. Beginners learn on a 5.7m boat in the inlets near Bonifacio. More advanced learners take a 13m boat out onto the open sea. One-week programs cost 1980/2370FF (low/high season) for beginners (with lunch) and 2330/2750FF for advanced learners (without lunch). See the Web site at www.glenans.asso.fr (French only).

Windsurfing and kayak fans should head for the magnificent Pointe de Spérone. On the Plage de Piantarella, Bonifacio Windsurf (☎ 04 95 73 52 04, fax 04 95 73 52 07) rents standard and Fun boards (60/100FF an hour) as well as one and two-person kayaks (50/100FF an hour). Private lessons are given for beginners (200FF an hour) and for those who want to hone their skills on the Fun (250FF). A five-day package of group lessons is also available (500/900FF).

Piantarella Nautic (☎ 04 95 73 51 64/06 70 03 69 43), on the same beach, rents Zodiacs (permit required) for 400/600FF for two hours/day with a deposit of 1000FF.

Golf

Spérone Golf (☎ 04 95 73 17 13, fax 04 95 73 17 85, ⓔ golf@sperone.net) on the seaside, before Piantarella beach, is a beautiful 18-hole course. Count on 330/490FF per day in the low/high season, or 1000/1750FF for four days. Golf lessons are available (280FF for a 45-minute session), and so are starter courses (2200FF) and advanced courses (3300FF). Equipment can be rented. See the Web site at www.sperone.net.

Places to Stay

The majority of the hotels in Bonifacio have three stars; however, it is possible to find more reasonable accommodation options nearby.

Places to Stay – Budget

Camping Tightly packed, but close to town, is ***Camping l'Araguina*** *(☎ 04 95 73 02 96, fax 04 95 73 01 92, on ave Sylvère Bohn)*, north of the marina. It's clean, shady, and there's a snack bar and a laundrette. The site also rents out eight pretty and comfortable bungalows, which cost 2300FF to 4900FF a week, according to the season, for four to five people. Allow 35/11/12FF per person/tent/car. The camp site opens April to October, and guests get a deal on boat trips run by Cristina.

Camping des Îles *(☎ 04 95 73 11 89, fax 04 95 73 18 77)*, 5.5km from town on the road to Cap Pertusato, is in a glorious setting and has enough amenities to make some hotels envious. Plage de Piantarella is about 1km away; the Spérone golf course is across the way. The only downside is that there isn't any shade. The site opens April to October and charges 30FF to 43FF per person, depending on the season, 12FF and 16FF per tent and 11FF and 14FF per car. The camp site also rents chalets for two to four people and bungalows for six.

Places to Stay – Mid-Range & Top End

Hotels A few hundred metres north of the marina, ***Hôtel des Étrangers*** *(☎ 04 95 73 01 09, fax 04 95 73 16 97, ave Sylvère Bohn)* is friendly and reasonably priced. Rooms are simple but comfortable, and all are en suite. Prices vary according to the season, room size and appointments: doubles cost 426/260FF with/without AC or TV. The choicest rooms, cool and quiet, are at the rear. The hotel opens April to October.

Hôtel Le Royal *(☎ 04 95 73 00 51, fax 04 95 73 04 68, Place Bonaparte)*, in the heart of the citadel, offers large double rooms for 450/490FF (street/sea view) in July, 600/650FF in August and from 250FF to 350FF in low season. All 14 rooms have AC, TV and bathroom. An extra bed costs 100FF.

Hôtel La Caravelle *(☎ 04 95 73 00 03, fax 04 95 73 00 41, 35 quai Jérôme Comparetti)*, at the marina, is a three-star operation with 28 comfortable rooms, all with air-conditioning, TV and telephone. Allow

526FF to 626FF, depending on the season, for a double overlooking the courtyard, and 700FF to 1200FF for one with a harbour view. Suites, if you want to live it up, cost between 1000FF and 1700FF. The hotel opens from the end of March to 15 October.

Places to Eat

Budget There are many shops and cafes by the harbour where you can get sandwiches, pizzas and *panini*.

The ***Simoni supermarket***, on the south side of the marina, opens 7 am to 8 pm daily in summer and 8 am to 12.30 pm and 3.30 to 7.30 pm Monday to Saturday and Sunday morning in winter. The ***Coccinelli Supermarket*** is right next door.

Les Terrasses d'Aragon *(☎ 04 95 73 51 07, place Carrega)* deserves to be singled out from among the many pizzerias in Bonifacio for its location in the citadel (opposite the post office) and the glorious view from its terrace. In addition to its 42FF to 66FF pizzas it serves fish dishes and *menus*. It closes in January.

Mid-Range & Top End With a sprawling terrace on the citadel's main street is ***Café de la Poste*** *(☎ 04 95 73 13 31, fax 04 95 73 01 47, ⓔ laposte@corsud.com, 5 rue Fred Scamaroni)*. It can satisfy almost every appetite thanks to its wide range of snacks, lunch *menus* for 55FF, pasta, pizzas, grilled meat and fish dishes, and *menus* of Bonifacio specialities for 88FF or 138FF. It opens for lunch and dinner, year-round except January.

Cantina Dora *(☎ 04 95 73 50 49, 27 rue Doria)* is a pleasant little restaurant that brings traditional Corsican mountain cuisine to Bonifacio's citadel. Long wooden benches add to its country atmosphere, and it serves a lip-smacking *menu* (85FF). It opens April to September, daily in the summer, but closes on Sunday and Tuesday evening in the shoulder season.

Les 4 Vents *(☎ 04 95 73 07 50, quai Banda del Ferro)*, near the ferry quay, is popular for its fish in the summer, its Alsatian specialities in the winter, and for its warm welcome year round. A *menu* is available for 110FF. It opens for lunch and dinner daily in the high season (closed on Tuesday the rest of the year).

U Castille *(☎ 04 95 73 04 99, rue Simon Varsi)* is a lovely stone room in the heart of the citadel. There are *menus* for 80FF and 120FF or daily specials for 55FF to 85FF. The restaurant opens daily in summer.

The restaurant in the ***Hôtel du Centre Nautique*** *(☎ 04 95 73 02 11, fax 04 95 73 17 47)*, on the north side of the harbour opposite most of the other restaurants, has a nautical feel. From this side you get the best view of the citadel when it is lit up in the evening. The clientele is classy and maybe even a little snobbish, but the pasta dishes are first-rate. The restaurant opens for lunch and dinner year round and it's a pleasant, if expensive, way to spend the evening.

Entertainment

Concerts are sometimes staged on the terraces of the marina's bars and restaurants in the summer.

Bar B'52 *(quai Jérôme Comparetti)* stays open until 2am. You can enjoy a drink on the terrace or dance in the grotto-like room carved into the rock. ***Lollapalooza*** *(25 quai Comparetti)*, 100m away, is a newer and larger bar.

Amnésia, on the road towards Porto Vecchio, was once *the* club in Corsica as well as the only one in the immediate environs of Bonifacio. The reign is over – in the spring of 2000 Amnésia was blown up, presumably by someone with a score to settle. Now, if you want to dance the night away, you'll have to go up to ***Via Notte***, an enormous open-air club at the south end of Porto Vecchio. It's not that far.

Getting There & Away

Air Figari-Sud Corse airport (☎ 04 95 71 10 10) is in the middle of the maquis, 21km north of Bonifacio, near the village of Figari. Daily flights from Marseille, Nice and Paris, plus charter flights in summer, serve both Bonifacio and Porto Vecchio.

Like most airports in Corsica, this one has neither an ATM or a bureau de change, despite its having been renovated as recently as 1996.

Bus Eurocorse (☎ 04 95 21 06 30, 04 95 70 13 83), whose offices at the harbour open all day, operates services between Bonifacio and Porto Vecchio, Roccapina, Sartène, Propriano, Olmeto, Ste-Marie Sicche and Ajaccio. There are up to four departures daily during the high season (at 6.30 and 8.30 am and 12.30 and 2.15 pm), though only two on Sundays and public holidays (at 8.30 am and 2.15 pm); there are two departures daily in the low season (at 6.30 am and 2 pm). The journey to Ajaccio takes 3½ hours and costs 125FF.

Car There is a Europcar agency (☎ 04 95 73 10 99) on the way into town, near the petrol station. It opens 9 am to noon and 3 to 7 pm Monday to Saturday, April to October (open on Sunday in July and August).

Hertz cars can be rented at the Elf petrol station at the corner of rue St-Érasme and the quai Banda del Ferro.

The airport has the widest choice of car rental companies, many of which, however, open only when flights are arriving and departing. The main ones are:

Avis	☎ 04 95 71 00 01
Budget	☎ 04 95 71 04 18
Citer	☎ 04 95 71 02 00
Europcar	☎ 04 95 71 01 41
Hertz	☎ 04 95 71 04 16

Boat Ferries operated by the Italian Moby Lines sail between Bonifacio and Santa Teresa di Gallura in Sardinia. Moby Lines is represented in Bonifacio by Les Voyages Gazano (☎ 04 95 73 00 29, fax 04 95 73 05 50), which opens at the ferry terminal 7 am to 8 pm every day in summer and 7.30 am to 1 pm and 3 pm to 8 pm the rest of the year. In summer Moby Lines provides 10 daily return services from 7.45 am to 10 pm, with a last return from Sardinia at 9.20 pm; in April, June and September there are four crossings. Tickets cost 50/65FF per person (winter/summer) and it costs 140/210FF for a car.

Another company, Saremar (☎ 04 95 73 00 96, fax 04 95 73 13 37), also at the ferry terminal and cheaper than Moby Lines, operates four crossings daily to Santa Teresa di Gallura in summer and two crossings daily the rest of the year. The offices open 9 am to 10.30 pm in summer and, generally speaking, 8.30 am to noon and 2.30 to 6.30 pm in winter; on Sunday in winter, the offices only open at departure times.

The Bonifacio harbour master's office (☎ 04 95 73 10 07, fax 04 95 73 18 73), by the marina, opens 7 am to 10 pm in July and August, 7.30 am to 8 pm in June and 8 am to noon and 2 to 6 pm the rest of the year. Chandlers, fuel, water and showers are all available. The charge for mooring a 9m to 10m boat ranges between 93FF and 149FF, depending on the season.

Getting Around

Because it is such a popular destination, because it is in a sense the end of the line, and for half a dozen other reasons, Bonifacio does to automobiles what a spider's web does to flies. In summer, traffic sometimes backs up all the way from the town centre to the roundabout on the main road – no short distance. Nor are matters helped by the scarcity of car parks. Your best bet, particularly in the high season, is to find a hotel that provides a parking space and get around on foot.

To/From the Airport Transports Rossi (☎ 04 95 71 00 11) provides a shuttle service between the airport and Bonifacio from the end of June to the beginning of September. The departure times correspond to the arrivals and departures of the flights. The journey to Bonifacio costs 50FF and takes about half an hour. The departures for the airport leave from the harbour car park.

By taxi, the trip from the airport to Bonifacio centre costs a set price of 200/280FF (weekdays/weekends and nights).

BOUCHES DE BONIFACIO

This is the name for the narrow stretch of sea that separates the southern tip of Corsica from Italian Sardinia. It is home to several of the island's natural treasures, and is a protected area (Les Réserves Naturelle des Bouches de Bonifacio).

Archipel des Lavezzi

The Archipel des Lavezzi (Lavezzi Archipelago) is a group of about 10 main islands, a protected paradise between sky and sea. The islands' beauty owes a great deal to the colour palette from which they have been decorated – the turquoise and ultramarine of the water, the bright hues of the granite. The islands' strangeness owes much to the way the rocks have been sculpted by the forces of sand and sea so that, while some have a polished, sensual roundness, others seem reminiscent of the scales of a fabulous sea monster.

The 65-hectare **Île Lavezzi**, which gives its name to the whole archipelago, is the most accessible of the islands. It is the southernmost point of Corsica, and signal-station keepers are its only inhabitants.

The island's savage beauty aside, its superb natural pools make good swimming holes, and the island also has the cemetery for the victims who perished on board the *Sémillante* (see the boxed text 'The Sad End of the *Sémillante*'). In high season, the tour boat operators at Bonifacio harbour make it easy to get to; see Boat Trips under Bonifacio for details.

Île Cavallo, just north of the Îles Lavezzi, is a paradise frequented by, and protected from outsiders by, the very rich. Though it is almost twice the size of Île Lavezzi and even has a small landing strip, it is inaccessible except by private boat.

Cap Pertusato

Recognisable by its resemblance to a sinking ship, Cap Pertusato (also called Pointe St-Antoine) makes a good destination for walkers from Bonifacio. Details of the 4km route along the chalky cliffs can be found in the Walking chapter. By car, take the D58, by the hospital. It would be difficult to describe the panoramic view of cliffs, open water, the Îles Lavezzi and the high citadel. Suffice it to say that the cape is the best place you'll find for a fantastic view of the town without stepping onto a boat.

Pointe de Spérone

Among other things, Pointe de Spérone has become a destination for international celebrities. The golf course that overlooks it was created by importing the fertile soil needed to grow the grass for perfect greens. The course is now one of the most celebrated in Europe. To the north is the little Plage de Piantarella, which opens to the public. You can rent boats, kayaks and windsurf gear (see Water Sports under Bonifacio earlier). There is also a snack bar.

The Sad End of the *Sémillante*

The line of graves in the Achiarino cemetery on Île Lavezzi is a reminder of the tragic events of the night of 15 February 1855. The *Sémillante* had left Toulon the night before with more than 350 crew and 400 soldiers on board. She was bound for Sebastopol with reinforcements for the Crimean War. Heading out through the poorly marked Bouches de Bonifacio in heavy fog, the three-mast frigate caught a sudden gust of wind and ran aground on Île Lavezzi. For weeks, nightmarishly mangled naked bodies washed up onto the shore. The only one who could be identified was the captain; the other victims of the tragedy were buried anonymously. It is still the worst shipping disaster ever in the Mediterranean.

PORTO VECCHIO (PORTIVECCHJU)

postcode 20137 • pop 10,326

Porto Vecchio owes its appeal not so much to what's left of its citadel as to the beautiful coastline stretching out both north and south from this old 'city of salt'. The town is also an excellent base if you want to discover Alta Rocca, the Forêt de l'Ospedale, the Col de Bavella and Aiguilles de Bavella, and the surrounding villages.

History

In a bid to establish itself on the eastern coast of the island, the Genoese republic set its sights on Porto Vecchio in the 15th century. This site, which was inhabited in ancient times, is set at the back of a deep bay, and provided the best shelter between the fortified towns of Bonifacio and Bastia. The

Genoese settled on the heights over the bay, where they created what is now called the Ville Haute (Upper Town), which they fortified with thick ramparts.

Their attempt to wall themselves off from danger did not prove successful, however: the malaria prevalent along the coast decimated the Genoese settlers.

A few years later a second attempt to populate the town, this time with forcibly recruited Corsicans, was no more successful. Porto Vecchio was essentially abandoned before re-emerging in 1564, when Sampiero Corso chose it as base for his renewed efforts to liberate the island. The town was besieged and forced to capitulate a few months later.

The town did not really begin to thrive until the malaria-infested swamps around it were transformed into salt marshes. At last unthreatening to health, the town started out again as if from scratch. The beauty of the beaches stretching away on either side of the bay helped to make it the popular and lively tourist town that it is today.

Orientation

Porto Vecchio has two parts. There is the upper town with its little streets and the ruins of the citadel, and below this the more modern harbour, which stretches along ave Georges Pompidou. Rue de Cavasina, which leads off the first roundabout to the north of the marina, links the two parts. The carrefour des Quatre Chemins, to the north, is the focus for much of the activity in the town.

Information

Tourist Offices The tourist office (☎ 04 95 70 09 58), on rue du Deputé Camille de Rocca Serra, opens 9 am to 8 pm Monday to Saturday and until 1 pm on Sunday in summer. In winter the office opens 9 am to 12.30 pm and 2 pm until 6.30 pm Monday to Friday and until noon on Saturday. The English-speaking staff are helpful and are happy to provide information on gîtes and B&Bs. A small 'learning garden' in front identifies many of the maquis plants.

THE SOUTH

Money Crédit Lyonnais (☎ 04 95 70 94 81) is on the corner of rue du Général Leclerc and rue Scamaroni, not far from the post office. It does not change travellers cheques, but there is an ATM outside the bank.

Société Générale (☎ 04 95 70 10 15), on rue du Général Leclerc, also changes foreign currencies. It opens 8.15 am to noon and 1.45 to 4.50 pm Monday to Friday.

There is an ATM at the post office (see below), which also will change travellers cheques for you. It has better exchange rates than the banks.

Post The post office (☎ 04 95 70 95 00) on rue du Général Leclerc opens 8.30 am to 6 pm Monday to Friday and on Saturday morning, year-round.

Email & Internet Access The tobacconist on the place de la République, 100m from the tourist office, offers Web access at 20FF for a quarter hour and 60FF for a full hour.

Bookshops The Librairie-Papeterie-Presse (☎ 04 95 70 07 71), 12 rue Pasteur, stocks a range of French and foreign newspapers, as well as some books and stationery. It opens 7.30 am to 8 pm daily except Sunday afternoon in summer, and 8 am to noon and 2 to 7 pm Monday to Saturday during the winter period.

Laundry There's a laundrette (☎ 04 95 70 15 62) in the same building as the harbour master's office on ave Georges Pompidou. It opens 8 am to 6 pm Monday to Friday and 10 am to 6 pm at weekends in summer.

Medical Services The Clinique de l'Ospedale, between the Hyper U supermarket and the stadium, close to the carrefour des Quatre Chemins, has a 24-hour emergency unit (☎ 04 95 72 09 76). The nearest hospital is in Bonifacio.

Upper Town

There are still a few vestiges of the old Genoese citadel here, notably the Porte Génoise and the Bastion de France (closed to the public). The beautiful rue Borgo gives a glimpse of what the city was like in earlier days.

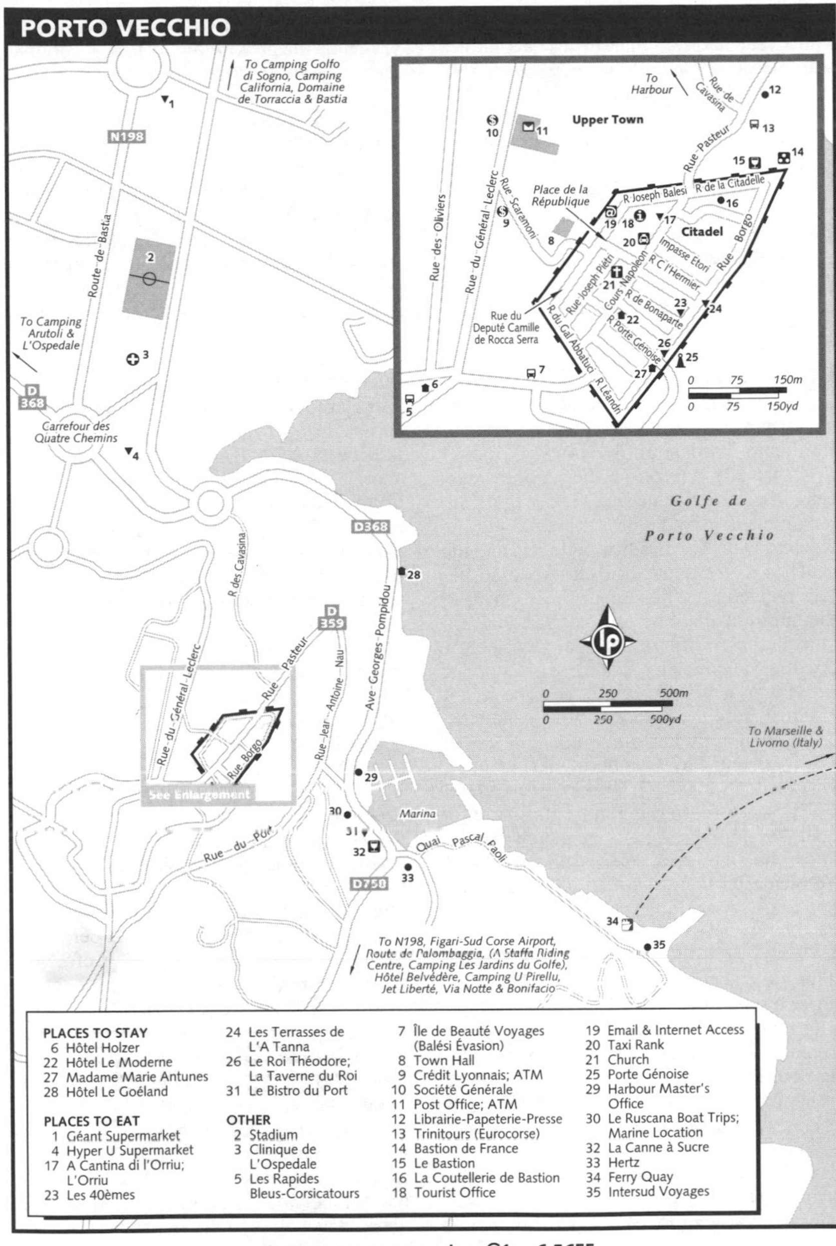
PORTO VECCHIO
To Camping Golfo di Sogno, Camping California, Domaine de Torraccia & Bastia
N198
Route de Bastia
To Camping Arutoli & L'Ospedale
D 368
Carrefour des Quatre Chemins
D368
R des Cavasina
D 359
Rue Pasteur
Rue du Général Leclerc
Rue Borgo
See Enlargement
Rue Jean Antoine Nau
Ave Georges Pompidou
Rue du Port
Marina
Quai Pascal Paoli
D758
Golfe de Porto Vecchio
To Marseille & Livorno (Italy)
To N198, Figari-Sud Corse Airport, Route de Palombaggia, (A Staffa Riding Centre, Camping Les Jardins du Golfe), Hôtel Belvédère, Camping U Pirellu, Jet Liberté, Via Notte & Bonifacio
To Harbour
Rue de Cavasina
Upper Town
Rue Pasteur
Place de la République
R Joseph Balesi
R de la Citadelle
Citadel
Rue des Oliviers
Rue du Général Leclerc
Rue Scaramoni
Impasse Etori
R C l'Hermier
Rue Borgo
Rue Joseph Pietri
Cours Napoléon
R de Bonaparte
Rue du Deputé Camille de Rocca Serra
R du Gal Abbatucci
R Porte Génoise
R Léandri
0 75 150m
0 75 150yd
0 250 500m
0 250 500yd
PLACES TO STAY
6 Hôtel Holzer
22 Hôtel Le Moderne
27 Madame Marie Antunes
28 Hôtel Le Goéland
PLACES TO EAT
1 Géant Supermarket
4 Hyper U Supermarket
17 A Cantina di l'Orriu; L'Orriu
23 Les 40èmes
24 Les Terrasses de L'A Tanna
26 Le Roi Théodore; La Taverne du Roi
31 Le Bistro du Port
OTHER
2 Stadium
3 Clinique de L'Ospedale
5 Les Rapides Bleus-Corsicatours
7 Île de Beauté Voyages (Balési Évasion)
8 Town Hall
9 Crédit Lyonnais; ATM
10 Société Générale
11 Post Office; ATM
12 Librairie-Papeterie-Presse
13 Trinitours (Eurocorse)
14 Bastion de France
15 Le Bastion
16 La Coutellerie de Bastion
18 Tourist Office
19 Email & Internet Access
20 Taxi Rank
21 Church
25 Porte Génoise
29 Harbour Master's Office
30 Le Ruscana Boat Trips; Marine Location
32 La Canne à Sucre
33 Hertz
34 Ferry Quay
35 Intersud Voyages

Salt Flats

Porto Vecchio is not the world's best-known salt-mining site, but it's distinctly in the salt-mining business nevertheless. You can visit the flats close by the ferry dock, quai Pascal Paoli (☎ 04 95 70 23 69), and watch the activity. Visitors are welcome 10 am to noon and 4 to 6 pm daily. Admission costs 40FF.

Beaches

Although there is no beach in the town proper, some of the island's best, and most famous, beaches are close by. See Around Porto Vecchio later in this chapter for details.

Boat Trips

Le Ruscana is an old fishing boat aboard which you can explore the coast as far as Bonifacio. Its ticket office (☎ 04 95 70 33 67/71 41 50) is opposite the harbour master's house at the marina. The excursion, which takes a whole day, passes along the Réserve Naturelle des Îles Cerbicale and the beaches to the south of Porto Vecchio before reaching the Îles Lavezzi, Île Cavallo, the Pointe de Spérone and Bonifacio (weather permitting). The congenial crew provides commentary, and there is a stop for a swim in a lovely little cove. The ticket price of 300FF (children 150FF) includes a picnic. The ticket office opens 8 am to 12.30 pm and 4 to 9 pm during the summer.

Kallisté Plongée (☎ 04 95 72 07 63/06 80 11 71 54), at the harbour, runs glass-bottom boat excursions. You'll be taken to the Pecorella shipwreck site and the depths of Cerbicale, in both of which places you are free to go snorkelling (see the boxed text in the Diving chapter). Figure on 150FF for 1½ hours or 250FF for half a day. Departures are at 9 am and 11 am. Advance booking is a must.

If you would prefer to explore the coast yourself, Locorsa (☎ 04 95 70 12 37), in the harbour master's building, hires out Zodiac inflatable dinghies (no permit required) at prices starting from 700FF per day. Locorsa opens 9 am to 12.30 pm and 4 pm to 8 pm daily in summer. In winter, phone to make arrangements.

Marine Location (☎ 04 95 70 58 92, e caroline.revol@wanadoo.fr), next to the Ruscana ticket window, offers a good selection of motorboats for hire.

Horse Riding

The A Staffa riding centre (☎ 04 95 70 47 51/06 16 56 73 60) opens year round. To get there, take the N198 south and turn off onto route de Palombaggia; the centre will be on your right after about 400m. Rides in the maquis and along the seafront are organised both early in the morning and in the evening (6.45 am and 7 pm). Advance booking is necessary.

Water Sports

The École de Voile San Ciprianu (☎ 04 95 71 61 24/06 03 12 90 42), right on the beach, is without doubt the best place for all water sports. You can rent windsurfing equipment (100FF per hour for a Fun board), catamarans (200FF per hour for a Hobbie Cat 16), canoes (50FF), kayaks (40FF), and pedal boats (50FF). Private and group sailing and windsurfing lessons are offered at reasonable prices.

Jet Liberté (☎ 06 81 02 40 90), on the beach at Palombaggia, rents jet skis from 250FF for 15 minutes. Organised walks (8.30 am to 2 pm) will take you as far afield as Bonifacio and the Lavezzi islands. They cost 1200FF.

Diving

See the Diving chapter for information on diving in the Porto Vecchio area.

Places to Stay – Budget

The camp site closest to the town centre is ***Camping Arutoli*** *(☎ 04 95 70 12 73)*, 1km from the carrefour des Quatre Chemins on the road towards L'Ospedale and Zonza. Watch for the signposts to the site from the D368. The pitches are quiet and shaded, the site is clean, and there is a laundrette and a swimming pool. Allow between 30FF and 35FF per adult, depending on the season, and 13FF to 16FF per tent and per car. The site also rents out bungalows sleeping up to four people for between 1600FF and 3400FF per week, depending on the season.

There are plenty of other camp sites in the vicinity but you will need a car to get to them. See Around Porto Vecchio for details.

If you prefer a B&B, ***Madame Marie Antunes*** *(☎ 04 95 70 37 31, 55 rue Borgo)*, in the citadel, rents two rooms, one with a balcony and a pretty view of the gulf for 200/350FF (low/high season) and the other with a kitchen for 50FF more. Houses with patios, for four persons, adjacent to the harbour, can be rented for 2500/4000FF per week.

Places to Stay – Mid-Range & Top End

Hôtel Holzer *(☎ 04 95 70 05 93, fax 04 95 70 47 82, 12 rue Jean Jaurès)* is near the centre of the upper town (it also has a door on rue Jean Nicoli) and offers comfortable, spotless rooms with air-conditioning, satellite TV and telephone. Singles/doubles/triples cost 280/350/450FF in winter, 300/450/520FF in July and 420/650/750FF in August. Half-board is mandatory in August (480FF per person for two).

Hôtel Le Moderne *(☎ 04 95 70 06 36, 10 cours Napoléon)* is a white building with blue shutters across from the church. Its bright, pleasant double rooms, with shared bathroom, cost 250/350/520FF in April/July/August. Rooms with en-suite bathroom cost 280/380/550FF. Although it's a little noisy, rooms 20 and 21 look out over a large terrace high up over the town and the harbour, and they are relatively quiet. The hotel opens from May to October.

Family-run ***Hôtel Le Goéland*** *(☎ 04 95 70 14 15, ave Georges Pompidou)* owes a great deal of its charm to its waterside location, between the harbour and the roundabout before the carrefour des Quatre Chemins. The atmosphere is relaxed and quiet, and there's a garden. Single or double rooms with shared bathroom, depending on the season, cost from 250FF to 280FF or 280FF to 330FF, and an en-suite double room from 330FF to 440FF. It opens from Easter to November. English and Spanish are also spoken.

Places to Eat

Budget The ***Hyper U supermarket*** *(carrefour des Quatre Chemins)* and the ***Géant supermarket*** on the next roundabout to the north stock everything self-caterers will need. Both are in large shopping complexes with lots of other shops.

Les 40èmes is a crêperie on rue Borgo in the upper town. The house specialities are crêpes with mozzarella. It opens 5 pm to midnight, June to September. The crêpes range from 20FF to 54FF.

Mid-Range In the upper town, ***A Cantina di l'Orriu*** *(☎ 04 95 72 14 25, cours Napoléon)* is a wine bar that serves the same products that are sold for takeaway in the shop, l'Orriu, next door. You can try some excellent Bastelica ham or charcuterie from Évisa and Corsican cheese. The cantina also serves tasters (15FF) to go with a glass of wine (17FF to 28FF). It opens 11 am to 2 pm and 6 to 11 pm daily except Sunday lunchtime from May to the end of September.

Le Bistro du Port *(☎ 04 95 70 22 96, ave Georges Pompidou)* has a good reputation for its fish (from 95FF) and for its 88FF lunch *menu*, or 128FF dinner *menu*. The setting is pleasant and the decor nautical.

In the upper town, rue Borgo is home to a number of restaurants that back on to the ramparts and have attractive terraces facing out over the sea. ***Les Terrasses de l'A Tanna*** *(☎ 04 95 70 04 46)* is one of these. There are pizzas (45FF to 63FF), stuffed mussels (65FF), or a *menu* at 100FF. The stonework and the wood furniture make for a cosy atmosphere.

Top End In the Porte Génoise, ***Le Roi Théodore*** *(☎ 04 95 70 47 98)* offers an appetising 'gastronomic' *menu* at 192FF. The specialty of the house is an old-fashioned Corsican bouillabaisse for 182FF. Book a table in advance.

Entertainment

Le Bastion *(☎ 04 95 70 69 70, ⓔ pbastion@club-internet.fr, 11 rue de la Citadelle)* is the most happening place in Porto Vecchio. As many as 300 beers are available on tap and bottled, and there's often live music. The pub opens 10 pm until to the early hours daily year-round.

La Taverne du Roi at the corner of Porte Génoise and rue Borgo also has a following. The featured entertainment is traditional Corsican music with guitar accompaniment.

La Canne à Sucre *(☎ 04 95 70 35 25)*, on the harbour, allows you to while away the evening over an ice cream or a cocktail. It opens 6.30 pm to 2 am, June to October.

Via Notte *(☎ 04 95 72 02 12, ⓔ contact@vianotte.com)*, on the road out of Porto Vecchio in the direction of Bonifacio, is *the* club. It's big. It's in the open air and there's even a swimming pool. It opens 11 pm to 5 am. See also the Web site at www.vianotte.com.

Shopping

L'Orriu (☎ 04 95 70 26 21), on cours Napoléon, is fragrant with hams hanging from the ceiling, cheeses sitting on the shelves amidst wines and spirits, and jams and pâtés. It opens 9 am to midnight daily except between 1 and 6 pm on Sunday. It also closes in November and mid-February to mid-March.

U Tavonu, at 9 rue du Général de Gaulle, offers high-quality foodstuffs too.

La Coutellerie du Bastion (☎ 04 95 72 06 02), 14 rue de la Citadelle, offers a broad selection of Corsican knives (*coutellerie* is akin to cutlery) from a shepherd's knife to a stiletto to a knife identified somewhat chillingly as a Vendetta. The craftsman whose store this is makes some of the knives he sells himself, and he also offers items from his outstanding collection of antique knives.

Getting There & Away

Air Figari Sud-Corse airport is about 20km from Porto Vecchio. See the Getting There & Away section for Bonifacio for details.

Bus Les Rapides Bleus-Corsicatours (☎ 04 95 70 96 51/52, fax 04 95 70 96 55), 16 rue Jean Jaurès, operates a twice-daily service (daily except Sunday and public holidays in winter) to Bastia via Ste-Lucie de Porto Vecchio, Solenzara and Ghisonaccia (115FF, departures at 8 am and 1.30 pm). They also operate a shuttle service to Santa Giulia in the summer, via Camping Arutoli (15FF, four shuttles daily). The office opens 8.30 am to 12.30 pm and 2.30 to 6.45 pm Monday to Friday, and also on Saturday mornings.

Île de Beauté Voyages (☎ 04 95 70 12 31), 13 rue du Général de Gaulle, represents Balési Évasion, whose buses go to Ajaccio via the mountain towns of Zonza, Bavella, Aullène and so on. Buses depart daily except Sunday and public holidays in July and August, and on Monday and Friday only in winter (110FF to Ajaccio, 35FF to Zonza). The office opens 8.30 am to 12.30 pm and 2.30 to 7 pm Monday to Friday, as well as on Saturday morning.

Eurocorse, represented by Trinitours (☎ 04 95 70 13 83), on rue Pasteur at the Cavasina junction on the way into the citadel, operates a service to Ajaccio along the coast via Sartène and Propriano. In summer there are three departures daily Monday to Saturday (at 6.30 am, 8 am and 2.15 pm) and two on Sunday and public holidays (8.30 am and 2.30 pm). There are also two departures daily in winter, and in summer there is a further bus to Ajaccio at 7 am via the mountain route through Ospedale, Zonza, Bavella and Quenza. It costs around 120FF to Ajaccio. The company also operates four buses in the direction of Bonifacio between 8 am and 7 pm (40FF). A shuttle service to Palombaggia starts at 10 am and ends at 5.30 pm; a return journey costs 40FF. Trinitours opens 8.30 am to noon and 2 to 6.30 pm, Monday to Friday, and on Saturday morning. Buses depart from in front of the offices.

Car Europcar (☎ 04 95 72 13 10) and Citer (☎ 04 95 70 16 96) have car-hire facilities in the building housing the harbour master's office on ave Georges Pompidou; it opens in the summer. Hertz is on the quai Pascal Paoli towards the ferries.

See Getting There & Away in the Bonifacio section for details of car-hire companies at Figari-Sud airport.

Boat The *Monte d'Oro*, with capacity for over 500 passengers, links Porto Vecchio with Marseille on behalf of SNCM, and with Livorno in Italy on behalf of the SNCM subsidiary, Corsica Marittima.

SNCM and Corsica Marittima are both represented by Intersud Voyages (☎ 04 95 70 06 03), whose offices are in the tinted-glass building with the red metal column on top opposite the ferry quay. The agency opens 8.45 to 11.45 am and 2.30 to 5.30 pm.

About 100 moorings in the Porto Vecchio marina are reserved for visitors. Look for the harbour master's office (☎ 04 95 70 17 93) on ave Georges Pompidou. Showers, fuel, water and chandlers are all available. The office opens 8 am to 9 pm during the high season, and 8.30 am to 6 pm, except for lunch, in the low season. It costs between 65FF and 130FF, depending on the season, to moor a 9m to 10m boat.

Getting Around

To/From the Airport Transports Rossi (☎ 04 95 71 00 11) operates a shuttle service between Figari-Sud Corse airport and Porto Vecchio (50FF, 30 minutes) from the end of June to the beginning of September. The times of buses correspond to flight arrival and departure times; they depart from in front of the Bar de la Marine by the harbour.

For a taxi, allow about 240FF (340FF on Sunday, on public holidays and at night).

Taxi There is a taxi rank (☎ 04 95 70 08 49) on cours Napoléon.

AROUND PORTO VECCHIO

Between the Golfe de Pinarellu and the Golfe de Sant'Amanza the jagged coastline is regularly punctuated by stretches of gorgeous, white-sand beach. Sadly, these beaches are no longer a secret; at the peak of the summer tourist season, they are frequently very crowded.

South of Porto Vecchio

The **Plage de Palombaggia** is certainly the most famous beach in south Corsica, and it may be the most beautiful, too. It is a long ribbon of sand edged with pine trees and with a view of the Réserve Naturelle des Îles Cerbicale a short distance offshore.

The road to this beach is well marked, off the N198 just south of town; it is 14km from the turnoff to the beach.

Plage de Santa Giulia, at the back of a bay of the same name, is also accessible from the N198 about 3km south of the turnoff to Palombaggia. Santa Giulia is another contender for honours as the most beautiful beach in south Corsica.

Places to Stay & Eat There's a string of camp sites along the road to Palombaggia, and during the high season bars and restaurants open along the edge of the beach. Santa Giulia is more oriented towards visitors staying in holiday villages and offers few amenities for the independent traveller.

Camping Les Jardins du Golfe *(☎ 04 95 70 46 92, fax 04 95 72 10 28, route de Palombaggia)* is 4km from Porto Vecchio and 10km from the Plage de Palombaggia. It opens year round and has a pizzeria, a supermarket, a swimming pool, children's play areas, mountain bikes (75FF per day), billiards and table-tennis. Pitches cost from 28FF to 32FF per tent and 12FF to 14FF per person and per car. You can also rent chalets.

Camping U Pirellu *(☎ 04 95 70 23 44, fax 04 95 70 60 22, ⓔ u.pirellu@wanadoo .fr)*, about 4km from the Plage de Palombaggia, has a nice pool, a supermarket, good shower and toilet blocks, a bar, a pizzeria, half-size tennis courts (50FF per hour), mini-golf (25FF) and a sauna. Pitches cost from 29FF to 39FF depending on the season plus 13FF to 19FF per car and per tent. It opens from Easter to the end of September.

Intimate, three-star ***Hôtel Belvédère*** *(☎ 04 95 70 54 13, fax 04 95 70 42 63, ⓔ info@ hbcorsica.com)* is 6km from town on the edge of the Golfe de Porto Vecchio. It has 16 rooms with balconies and three suites, all with air-conditioning, TV and telephone. There's also a large swimming pool and lovely gardens. Prices for a double range from 300FF to 1000FF, depending on the season. The hotel's gastronomically ambitious restaurant serves some impressive dishes; half-board costs 250FF per person beyond the room rates. For further details check out the Web site at www.hbcorsica .com.

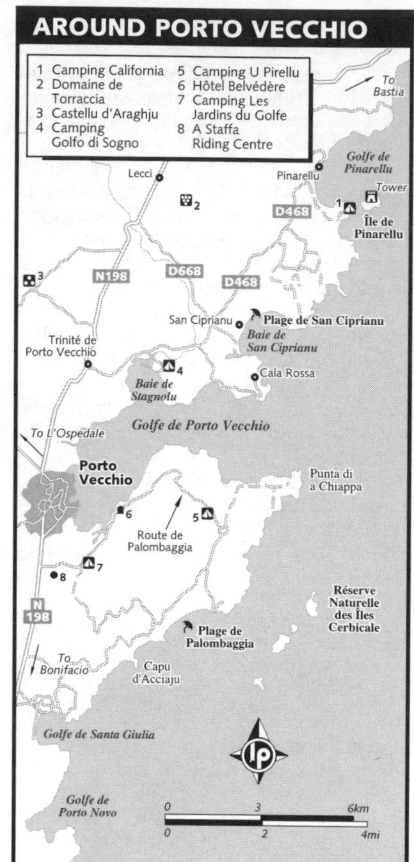

North of Porto Vecchio

At Trinité de Porto Vecchio, a few kilometres north of Porto Vecchio proper on the N198, you can turn east onto the D468 towards the popular beaches at **Cala Rossa** and the **Baie de San Ciprianu**. Farther to the north is the stunning peninsula of **Pinarellu** (Pinaraddu) with its Genoese tower and yet more beautiful stretches of sand.

When the white sand, turquoise sea, warm sun and shady pine trees get to be too much, head for the village of **Lecci**, just before Ste-Lucie de Porto Vecchio on the main road. As you enter the village you will see a sign for the **Domaine de Torraccia** (☎ 04 95 71 43 50), 1.5km away in the direction of the sea. The owners of this 43-hectare estate produce sweet wines, marc brandy, olives and olive oil, but the estate is best known for its red, rosé and white table wines, costing between 30FF and 35FF per bottle.

Higher up the scale, the vineyard's red Domaine de Toraccia really is outstanding, and l'Orriu, a 'prestige' vintage red, is unquestionably one of the best reds produced in all of Corsica (the 1997 sells for 56FF, the 1995 for 65FF). In fact, Torraccia is one of the island's few wine-producers to age its reds at all. In summer the estate opens 8 am to noon and 2 to 8 pm Monday to Saturday. In winter it closes an hour earlier.

Places to Stay & Eat *Camping Golfo di Sogno (☎ 04 95 70 08 98, fax 04 95 70 41 43)* is about 6km north-east of Porto Vecchio via the N198 and then the D468 in the Baie de Stagnolu. If there's such a thing as a luxurious camp site, this is it. Pitches are large and green, and there's a bar, a restaurant, direct access to the beach, two tarmac tennis courts (50FF per hour) and facilities for hiring mountain bikes or windsurfing equipment. A pitch for two people and a car costs 135FF; the charge for each additional person is 34FF. The camp site also rents basic bungalows. It opens 1 May to mid-November.

Camping California (☎ 04 95 71 49 24) is about 10km farther along the D468 on the Pinarellu peninsula and, though the welcome leaves something to be desired, the site itself is excellent. Shower and toilet facilities are just what they should be, there's a tennis court (50FF per hour), a beach on either side, of which one is nudist. The site opens June to September and charges 16/36/10FF per person/tent/car.

Places to eat open along the beach during the high season.

Alta Rocca

Alta Rocca is the name given to one of the regions of foothills to the great mountain range that constitutes the long dorsal spine of the island; it is the region specifically that looks out towards the Golfe de Porto Vecchio. The tranquillity of L'Ospedale, the prehistoric remains in Lévie and the surrounding countryside, the beauty of the little villages clinging to the rocks and the stunning Bavella massif all combine to make Alta Rocca a region not to be missed.

The tourist office (☎ 04 95 78 41 95, fax 04 95 78 46 74) for the Alta Rocca region is in Lévie. It opens 8.30 am to noon and 2 to 5.30 pm Monday to Friday.

Getting There & Away

Autocars Ricci (☎ 04 95 51 08 19) runs a daily bus service between Ajaccio and Zonza (100FF, two hours 50 minutes) via Propriano, Sartène, Ste-Lucie de Tallano and Lévie. Buses depart from Ajaccio at 3 pm and 4 pm, Propriano at 4.30 pm and 5.30 pm, Sartène at 6 pm and Ste-Lucie de Tallano at 6.30 pm; they arrive in Zonza at about 6.50 pm. In the other direction, buses leave Zonza at 6 am and 8 am. In summer, the service extends beyond Zonza to the Col de Bavella.

Balési Évasion (☎ 04 95 70 15 55) operates buses that link Zonza (and Bavella in summer) to L'Ospedale, Porto Vecchio, Quenza and Ajaccio. In summer buses run daily Monday to Saturday, and on Monday and Friday only the rest of the year. Buses from Porto Vecchio leave from the offices of Île de Beauté Voyages. The fare from Porto Vecchio to Zonza is 35FF.

L'OSPEDALE

postcode 20137

L'Ospedale holds a special place in the hearts of the good people of Porto Vecchio. The place takes its name from a former 'hospital', or health spa, and has long been synonymous with relief from the oppressive heat of summer at sea level. About 1km up from the village of L'Ospedale, the **Forêt de l'Ospedale** starts. It covers vast plains above Porto Vecchio, and still bears the scars of fires in 1990 and 1994.

A short way into the forest on the D368 from L'Ospedale, a road branches off to the left for the hamlet of Cartalavonu. After about 2km on this you can turn off onto the **Sentiers des Rochers** (Rock Path), also known as the Sentier des Tafoni.

The path has been well marked out by the ONF and is a good place for an easy, mainly flat walk among the laricio pines and the cavities formed in the rocks by erosion (see Geology in the Facts about Corsica chapter); these cavities are the *tafoni* that give the walking trail one of its names. After about 30 minutes you come to a little grassy plain littered with rocks. The Mare a Mare Sud walk crosses here, too, and the view is wonderful.

If you're feeling energetic you can continue along the path (which is now not as well marked) to the left towards Punta di a Vacca Morta (1314m), from where you can look down over the Golfe de Porto Vecchio and the Lac de l'Ospedale. You can also start the walk at the Refuge de Cartalavonu or the Col de Melu on the Mare a Mare Sud.

The forestry lodge at Marghese (☎ 04 95 70 01 49) organises walks in the forest (40FF) accompanied by ONF guides; these take place at 9 am on Thursdays in July and August. You'll find the lodge at the end of a road 100m off the D368 in the direction of Cartalavonu.

If you continue on the D368 towards Zonza, you will come to the pretty lake formed by the Barrage de l'Ospedale. The walk from there to the **Piscia di Gallo** waterfall is described under Strolls & Country Walks in the Walking chapter.

Things to See

The **Castellu d'Araghju** is less visited than the castles of Cucuruzzu and Capula, but it is better preserved and, though it dates from the 2nd millennium BC, the entrance allows you to guess at the importance the stronghold must once have had. Follow the corridor a dozen metres long to the interior rooms. Then climb to the top of the thick walls for a magnificent view over the Golfe de Porto Vecchio and the mountains. It takes about 25 minutes to get up from the village of Araghju; be sure to carry water and wear a sturdy pair of shoes. Admission is free. The village snack bar, L'Orée du Site, is a good spot for a drink and stocks brochures explaining the site.

The road that leads into Araghju is the D759, 12km from the village of L'Ospedale off the D368.

Places to Stay & Eat

Le Refuge *(☎ 04 95 70 00 39)* in Cartalavonu is popular with walkers tackling the Mare a Mare Sud. It opens year round and has good dormitories (with bathroom) sleeping six people, as well as a large common room, for 60FF per night (160FF at half-board). There are also three lovely double rooms costing 250FF. The restaurant serves good home-cooked food. The refuge is in a pretty stone building right at the edge of the village. By road, leave the D368 before the lake of L'Ospedale and head 3km in the direction of Cartalavonu.

ZONZA

postcode 20124 • pop 2600

This mountain village was briefly home to the exiled Mohammed V of Morocco in 1953 before he moved on to Île Rousse; it's now frequented by walkers and those heading for the famous peaks of Bavella by car. Its excellent location goes some way towards explaining the village's amazing hotels. There's an information stand at the town hall and a bookshop, open daily, that sells detailed IGN (National Geographic Institute) maps, guides and film. The village has several grocery stores. The best one, at the village exit going towards L'Ospedale, sells good Corsican products that are often cheaper than in the centre of town.

Should the stultifying heat make you want to take a dip, head 2.5km towards Ajaccio and Quenza on the D420, park your car just before the bridge and head down towards the river, where a beautiful pool awaits you.

Places to Stay & Eat

Camping Municipal de Zonza *(☎ 04 95 78 62 74)* is a haven of tranquillity in the depths of the forest, 3km east of the village on the D368. Few camper vans come this way. A pitch costs 20/14/14FF per person/tent/car or motorcycle. The site opens from mid-May to the end of September.

Hôtel-Restaurant de la Terrasse *(☎ 04 95 78 67 69/66 03, fax 04 95 78 73 50)* is the least expensive hotel in Zonza, with en-suite doubles from 250FF to 300FF. You can try home-made charcuterie in the restaurant. The hotel opens from April to October.

Hôtel-Restaurant l'Incudine *(☎ 04 95 78 67 71/71 43 11)* has good double rooms with bathroom, with prices starting at 350FF in low season. Half-board rates, obligatory in July and August, run to 340FF per person. The restaurant has a *menu* for 120FF.

Hôtel-Restaurant Le Tourisme *(☎ 04 95 78 67 72, fax 04 95 78 73 23)* has 13 bedrooms with TV, telephone and balcony. Rooms with compulsory half-board cost 490/740FF for one/two people in summer and 420/620FF in low season. The hotel opens from April to the end of October. Its Web site is at www.francehotelreservation.com/hottourisme02.

L'Aiglon *(☎ 04 95 78 67 79, fax 04 95 78 63 62)* is a restaurant with a good reputation for local cuisine. There are three *menus* ranging in price from 115FF to 165FF. The pretty, well maintained rooms of this warm and cosy establishment are available on a half-board basis only, but at 290FF a person, they're good value.

Horse Riding

At Serra di Scopamène, 15km from Zonza, the riding centre of U Paradisu (☎ 04 95 78 68 06) gives you the opportunity to look around Alta Rocca on horseback. The program includes excellent itineraries around the plateau of Cuscionu, with half-day rides costing 250FF and full-day rides, including lunch, for 450FF. Rides of several days, with gîte lodging, are also available.

QUENZA

postcode 20122 • pop 214

This little gem of a village is high up in the mountains a few kilometres to the west of Zonza along the D420, on the way to Aullène. The village, with its numerous sporting options, is dealt with in more detail in the Walking chapter (see the section on the GR20).

CONCA

postcode 20135 • pop 783

Backing onto the mountains but still close to the coast (6km as the crow flies), Conca is a little town nestling at the foot of Punta d'Ortu (695m) and best known to walkers as the end (or start) of the GR20.

Gîte d'étape ***La Tonnelle*** *(☎ 04 95 71 46 55)* is on the road into the village just opposite the cemetery. A night in a room sleeping two/three/four people costs 110/90/80FF per person. Each room has an en-suite bathroom, and there's also a large common room and a kitchenette. It's also possible to camp here for about 30FF per person. Breakfast costs 30FF and lunch or dinner goes for 70FF. The gîte will provide transportation down to Porto Vecchio for 40FF or, for 15FF, to Ste-Lucie de Porto Vecchio, where it's possible to catch the bus to Porto Vecchio proper. You can also change money at the gîte. It opens year-round.

Hôtel San Pasquale *(☎ 04 95 71 56 13, fax 04 95 71 42 10)* charges between 250FF and 350FF, depending on the time of year, for a functional double room with bathroom and 100FF for an extra bed. The setting of the hotel is pleasant. You can also rent studios for 2000FF to 3500FF per week.

There's a choice of snack bars and restaurants in the centre of the village. Conca also has a post office and a well stocked grocery, open daily in summer.

In the absence of public transport services to Conca, ask at La Tonnelle. They'll help you to get around on an informal basis.

AIGUILLES DE BAVELLA

The Col de Bavella (Bavella Pass; 1218m), about 8km north-east of Zonza, is overlooked by the imposing silhouette of one of the most beautiful landscape features in the south of Corsica: the Aiguilles de Bavella. These peaks, which rise to a height of more than 1600m and which are also known as the Cornes d'Asinao (Asinao Horns), are jagged points whose colour ranges from ochre to golden depending on the position [illegible] sun in the sky. Behind these stone [illegible] looms the profile of Monte Incu-[illegible] which the GR20 links to the Col de Bavella. From the pass you can see the statue of Notre Dame des Neiges, Our Lady of the Snows. You may also spot more than a few of the mouflons that frequent the area.

The Bavella massif is a wonderful place for climbing, canyoning and walking (see the Walking chapter). There is indeed a high-mountain spur of the GR20, which splits off beyond Notre Dame des Neiges and allows you to approach the peaks (see the Walking chapter for more details). Bear in mind that the pass is not always open in winter. Some of the guides in the area meet at the ***Auberge du Col de Bavella*** *(☎ 04 95 57 43 87)*; look out in particular for Jean-Paul Quilici and Didier Micheli (see the boxed text 'Organised Walks' in the Facts for the Visitor chapter).

The D268, which descends in the direction of Solenzara via the Col de Larone, is also worth a look. Crossing the Bavella forest, replanted after the 1960 fire, the road scoots along between tall peaks and tall pine. You can also explore the forest with an ONF guide who organises three-hour walks. Just turn up at 9.30 am on a Monday at the Arza Forest Lodge, 6km beyond the pass (☎ 04 95 23 78 21). Particularly winding, the D268 was still not totally asphalted at the time of research but work was in progress to smooth it out.

The challenge of driving here does not take much away, though, from what is in every respect an astonishing 30km descent to Solenzara. About 12km before you reach the coast the D268 begins to run along the wide stony bed of the River Solenzara, which is particularly good for swimming in the summer.

ARCHAEOLOGICAL SITES OF PIANA DE LÉVIE

The *piana* (Corsican for the French *commune*, a small administrative area) of Lévie is home to two remarkable archaeological sites: the *castelli* (castles) of Cucuruzzu and Capula. The Cucuruzzu site was discovered in 1963 and is an interesting example of Bronze Age monumental architecture. Set in a granite wilderness, the remains indicate that this was the site of an enduring and organised community whose activities were originally based on agriculture and animal husbandry but then broadened during the later Bronze Age (1200 to 900 BC) to include milling, pottery and weaving. The Castellu de Capula is somewhat more recent, although it is likely that Cucuruzzu was still in business when it was founded; Capula, it is believed, continued to be inhabited into the Middle Ages.

Besides the wonderful view they provide over the Aiguilles de Bavella, these two castles are worth a detour for the way they've been packaged for consumption by visitors. Individual stereo kits are provided at the entrance to the site, with a recorded commentary backed by traditional Corsican polyphonic chants (see Arts in the Facts about Corsica chapter). The commentary brings the castles to life with mini-lectures on, for example, curiosities of Corsican nature such as the *tafoni* (big rock blocks into which erosion has dug deep cavities) and the ubiquitous chestnut tree.

The archaeological sites (☎ 04 95 78 48 21) are on the right-hand side of the D268, 3.5km after the village of Lévie in the direction of Ste-Lucie de Tallano; the sites are about 4km after the turn-off. They open 9.30 am to 8 pm daily in July and August and 9.30 am to 6 pm, April to October. Admission costs 30FF (children 15FF), which includes the loan of an audioguide. Be prepared to spend a good 1½ hours here. Wear sturdy shoes and carry water.

LÉVIE (LIVIA)

postcode 20170 • pop 781

The peaceful little village of Lévie was a bastion of Corsican resistance during WWII and is now frequented by walkers on the Mare a Mare Sud route. You'll find bars, restaurants, a post office and a tourist office here, and you'll also find a very impressive little **archaeological museum** (Musée de l'Alta Rocca; ☎ 04 95 78 47 98); it is currently housed in the stables of a former Spanish ambassadorial residence behind the village hall, but there are plans to move it into a larger building in 2002.

The museum does a good job of elucidating Corsican geology, climate, flora and fauna. You can see Bonifacio Woman, the oldest human remains ever unearthed on the island; she is thought to have lived on the island about 8500 years ago.

The museum also displays cutting tools made of obsidian, flint and rhyolite, arrow heads, Neolithic vases and some wonderful Bronze Age pottery. The Iron Age is represented by a woman's skeleton that was found at the Capula site, and textiles and jewellery with some remarkable workmanship.

The museum has a scientific seriousness which, at least as regards prehistoric times, frequently seems to be in much shorter supply elsewhere on the island; photography is not permitted. The museum opens 10 am to 6 pm daily, July to mid-October. In the low season it opens 10 am to 4.30 pm daily except Sunday and Monday and at lunchtime. Admission costs 15FF.

Activities

La Ferme Auberge A Pignata organises half-day horse rides for 200FF. You can also rent mountain bikes (from 70FF for half a day) for either of two well marked circuits of 11km and 25km. Advance booking is a must.

Based in Lévie, ***Christophe Pigeault*** (☎ 04 95 78 58 25/06 20 61 76 81) organises beginner and advanced canyoning outings. This certified mountain guide will show you magnificent little-known wilderness canyons around the Bavella massif. It helps to be in good shape physically. It costs 300FF for a full day; groups consist of up to 12 people.

Places to Stay & Eat

The ***Gîte d'Étape de Lévie*** *(☎ 04 95 78 46 41)* is in a stone building above the police station. It opens April to October and charges 75FF per night for a room for four with en-suite bathroom and 160FF for half-board.

La Ferme Auberge A Pignata *(☎ 04 95 78 41 90/49 81, fax 04 95 78 46 03)*, on the road leading to the Cucuruzzu and Cap[illegible] archaeological sites, enjoys a loyal f[illegible] ing for its excellent home coo[illegible] 170FF *menu* is perfect. You [illegible]

THE SOUTH

one of the spacious rooms at half-board for 330FF per person. Advance booking is recommended. To get there, travel 1.4km after the turnoff from the D268 and then take the first left in the direction of the stables.

STE-LUCIE DE TALLANO (SANTA LUCIA DI TALLA)

postcode 20112 • pop 430

Ste-Lucie de Tallano would definitely be a contender if anyone decided to award a prize for the prettiest village in Corsica. Although time has robbed the hamlet of many of its inhabitants, it has taken away none of the charm of its little houses, with their reddish-orange tiled roofs, which nestle tightly together against the deep green, verdant backdrop of the surrounding forest and maquis.

There's a post office (☎ 04 95 78 81 59) on the square. It opens 9 am to 3 pm in summer, Mondays to Fridays, and also on Saturday morning. A welcome centre (☎ 04 95 78 80 13, fax 04 95 78 85 46) is in the village hall. It opens 9 am to noon and 2 to 5 pm, Monday to Friday, June to mid-September; it provides a wealth of information. See also the Web site at www.sainteluciedetallano.com (French only).

The **moulin à huile** (oil mill), which can be visited for the modest sum of 5FF, illustrates the importance of olive culture in the history of the village. It opens 10 am to noon and 3.30 to 6.30 pm daily except Sunday in summer. Ste-Lucie enjoys a reputation not just for its olive oil, however, but also for its deposits of **orbicular diorite**. This is a rare igneous rock with distinctive grey cavities; see it close up on the pedestal of the war memorial in the village square.

The **Église Ste-Lucie** is also worth a visit, as is the Renaissance-style **Couvent St-François**. This is an imposing building, which sometimes stages theatrical events. It's at the edge of the village on the road to Lévie. If it's closed, ask for the key at one of the eateries in the village square.

Another regional curiosity is the **bains de Caldane** (☎ 04 95 77 00 34), a 38°C sulphur spring that's said to have health benefits. The bathing area accommodates 20 people. The baths open 8 am to 8.30 pm in summer, and 9 am to 7 pm in the low season. Admission costs 20FF (10FF for children). To get there, head south out of Ste-Lucie for 5km, then turn left onto the D148 for 2.2km more.

In the spring, a carnival and a masked ball take place after the Festa de l'Olio Novu (the new olive festival), and a craft fair takes place in July. There are also feasts in the nearby hamlets of Bizé and Chialza in August.

Places to Stay & Eat

The *Gîte d'Étape U Fragnonu (☎ 04 95 78 82 56)*, about 300m from the main square in the direction of Zonza, has nine spacious dormitories, each with four beds and a spotless en-suite bathroom. The common room is large and pleasant and the overall level of comfort is – for a gîte – exceptional. The rate is 75FF a night. If you're not a walker eager to get on, take half-board at 175FF; the food is outstanding. The gîte opens year round.

Two Ste-Lucie restaurants serve Corsican specialities: the ***Santa-Lucia***, with its terrace on the square, and the ***Sporting Bar***, which serves pizzas as well as Corsican specialities, on the way out of the village.

MONTAGNE DE CAGNA

This isolated massif overlooks Figari, and is famous for the **Uomo di Cagna**, a huge rock balanced on a block of granite at the summit. Many people think they can make out a human profile in it. The Cagna mountain, with its wonderful views, is a popular place for walking. The climb starts just above the highest house in Giannuccio, a village at the end of the D50 north of Monacia d'Aullène. The path, roughly marked out with cairns, passes through an impressive granite landscape. Make sure you take some water with you if you plan to go as far as the hamlet of Uomo di Cagna; it takes about three hours.

The Eastern Plain

LA CASINCA

Go a few kilometres south-west of Bastia-Poretta airport and you enter La Casinca, the small region along the eastern side of Monte Sant'Angelu (1218m). It's to the north-east of La Castagniccia, between the rivers Golo and Fium'Alto. Here, substantial villages of tall, stone houses, plastered to the hillsides and looking out over the Eastern Plain, seem to burst out from among forests of chestnut and olive trees.

From Torra (on the N198 north-east of Vescovato), follow the D237, if you have a car, as it wends its way through these villages for about 20km. The excursion should not detain you for more than a few hours.

Highlights

- Visit the Jérôme Carcopino Archaeological Museum in the magnificent old Fort de Matra, and roam the adjacent Roman ruins
- Experience the charms of La Casinca and La Castagniccia, exploring their rugged landscape and traditional villages

Vescovato to Castellare di Casinca

Formerly a fortified town, hilltop **Vescovato** (population 2350) got its name from the word *vescovo* (bishop); it was the site of the bishop's palace in the 15th century, before the bishop's seat was relocated to Bastia.

It is best to leave your car at the edge of the village and explore the little alleyways and stairways between the high houses on foot. At the top of the village is a wide square lined with plane trees and several little cafes. The adjacent Baroque **Église San Martino** is on a small terrace overlooking the roofs of the neighbouring houses. If you want to look inside, ask the residents for the keys.

If you carry on past Vescovato cemetery to the south-east you'll come to **Venzolasca** (population 1500). To the north of this village is the picturesque ***Ferme-Auberge U Frangnu*** *(☎ 04 95 36 62 33)*. It is run by a hearty young grandfather who serves a *menu* (180FF at lunchtime, 200FF in the evening) around an olive press inside, or on an outside terrace overlooking the fields. Children's meals are half-price or 50FF, depending on the age of the child. The restaurant opens every evening in summer, and on Thursday, Friday and Saturday evenings and at Sunday lunchtime the rest of the year, except for an October holiday. Bookings are essential.

Brief detours from the D237 will take you to **Loreto di Casinca** and **Penta di Casinca**. Continuing on, pass through **Castellare di Casinca** to return again to the N198. The 10th-century **Chapelle San Pancraziu** is just before the intersection.

LA CASTAGNICCIA

Bordered by the River Golo to the north, the River Tavignano to the south and the central mountains to the west, La Castagniccia owes its name to the Genoese, who planted its first chestnut trees in the 16th century (see the boxed text 'Corsican Manna' later in this chapter). The region's hills and mountains are shot through with streams and rivulets, and the whole is blanketed with a dense vegetation out of which a village will emerge here and there. The villages are linked by small, winding roads and dozens of footpaths.

La Castagniccia was one of the main bastions of Corsican nationalism in the 18th century. In the 19th century, with its inhabitants numbering more than 50,000, it was both the most populous and the most prosperous of the island's several regions, but it suffered severe depopulation after WWI and today its villages are almost deserted. You may want to take some walks to see an authentic Corsica of hospitable warmth and an impressive stone domestic architecture. Accommodation in the area is extremely limited.

La Porta & Around

La Porta, the former capital of La Castagniccia, can be reached via a little road (the D506) that winds through chestnut groves. The **Église St-Jean Baptiste**, with its impressive bell tower, is at the entrance to the town. Built between 1648 and 1680, and recently renovated, it is now among the most beautiful Baroque buildings on the island; it enjoys landmark status. Its hand-crafted organ, which dates back to 1780, was originally destined for the nearby Couvent St-Antoine de Casabianca but was offered to the church at the time of the French Revolution by the Bonapartist Commissioner Antoine-Christophe Salicetti, who closed the convent. A concert of Corsican organ music is held here annually; a CD version (120FF) can be obtained by writing to ⓔ disques.coriolan@wanadoo.fr, or from the little grocery shop on the main street.

The ruins of **Couvent St-Antoine de Casabianca** are at the Col St-Antoine, about 8km north of La Porta on the D515. This community was founded in 1420 and it was here that Pascal Paoli was proclaimed general of the nation (see History in the Facts about Corsica chapter for more details).

Morosaglia, north-west along the D71 (via Quercitello, about 15km from La Porta), is the birthplace of Pascal Paoli and boasts a small museum in his honour. It opens daily except Tuesday, 9 am to noon and 2.30 to 7.30 pm in summer, 9 am to noon and 1 to 5 pm during the rest of the year. Admission costs 10FF.

Heading back east from Morosaglia, the D71 will lead you on to the **Col de Prato**, from where dozens of footpaths spread out in all directions. One, signposted, leads to **Monte San Petrone** (1767m), the highest point in La Castagniccia. Allow two to three hours to reach the peak and as many again for the return journey.

At the Col de Prato, the **Hôtel San-Petrone** (see Places to Stay & Eat) houses an amazing collection of old Corsican furniture, pottery, weapons and tools. The owner has spent 40 years ferreting out these antiques and has created in effect a little ethnographical museum. Admission is free.

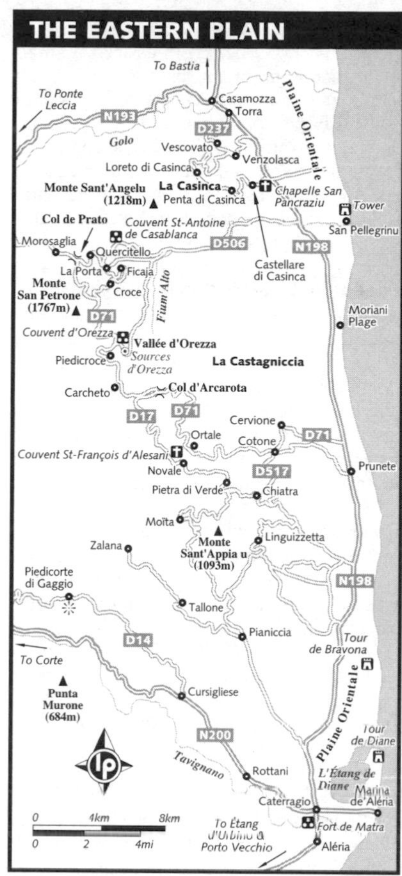

Walking La Porta is the starting point for a number of paths, suitable for most types of walkers (except perhaps GR20 types), across the heights of La Castagniccia. They'll get you to the various mountain passes (the Col de Prato, for example, in about 70 minutes), or to villages such as **Quercitello** (20 minutes), **Croce** (40 minutes) or **Ficaja**. Even in midsummer the paths are cool in the dense forest shade. Yet more footpaths start at Croce and Piedicroce. A small card available in bars, restaurants, and at the Piedicroce information stand (see La Porta to Cervione on the next page) gives details.

Horse Riding The Centre Équestre Soliva (☎/fax 04 95 39 22 92) in Croce (at an altitude of 800m) organises horse riding for people of all abilities; it costs 90FF per hour or 400FF per person per day, lunch included, in groups of 10 to 12. The centre has a restaurant and can offer accommodation (see under Places to Stay & Eat). Be careful, though, of the dog at the entrance – this one is not always a charmer.

Places to Stay & Eat In the absence of hotels, the only way to find accommodation in La Porta itself is to contact ***Felix Taddei*** *(☎ 04 95 39 20 51)*, who rents out five rooms costing around 200FF each (plus another 50FF for modest cooking facilities). If possible, choose one of the two rooms on the way into the village rather than one of the three next to the post office.

Chez Élisabeth *(☎ 04 95 39 22 00)*, on the main road, is the only decent restaurant in La Porta. Its large dining room has bay windows overlooking the gardens of surrounding houses. There are Corsican *menus* (100FF and 150FF), fish and meat dishes starting at 55FF, and pizzas (30FF to 50FF); portions can be large. The restaurant opens daily from mid-March to mid-November; the rest of the year it opens daily except Monday. Booking is recommended. If you can control your appetite, try to arrive after the tourist coaches have left.

L'Hôtel San Petrone, at the Col de Prato, offers clean, quiet doubles/triples for 250/350FF. You can also pitch your tent outside the hotel for 32FF and eat in the restaurant.

Centre Équestre Soliva (see under Horse Riding) has four en-suite bedrooms, each with four bunk beds. Accommodation costs 130FF per person with breakfast, 200FF for half-board.

The Waters of Orezza

Although the English did not discover Orezza until the beginning of the 20th century, Pascal Paoli came to take the cure here every year as far back as the 18th century, and so did much of the then polite society of Bastia and Ajaccio. Orezza spring waters were discovered early on to be very rich in iron, and some enthusiasts claimed that they were the richest in iron in the entire world. In 1866 the water began to be bottled and distributed both locally and on the French mainland, and in 1896 a thermal spa centre with massage rooms, showers and baths was built.

Despite the competition from mainland spas Orezza developed rapidly, but the buildings had to be abandoned in 1934 after a violent storm destroyed the pipes. During WWII the occupying Germans came to believe in the curative properties of the water and set up a small bottling plant; after the war the property changed hands numerous times but the little bottles with green caps continued to be sold. When no buyer could be found for the plant in 1995, production had to stop, but the springs were finally bought by the Conseil Général de Haute Corse, which now, after a complete overhaul, has them back in business again. Look for the pretty blue-labelled bottles and give it a try. It's as good a sparkling water as you'll find anywhere.

La Porta to Cervione

From La Porta the D515 goes through Ficaja and Croce before rejoining the D71 in the direction of the **Vallée d'Orezza**. Here you can visit the old **Couvent d'Orezza**, now in ruins, and natural springs that have recently been restored to proper working order (see the boxed text 'The Waters of Orezza'). In the small village of **Valle d'Orezza**, artisans craft wooden pipes among other curios. Not so long ago, the quarries hereabouts were mined for Vert d'Orezza, a hard emerald-green stone that polishes up almost like marble. It's the stone from which the magnificent Medici Chapel in Florence was constructed. A little information stand in **Piedicroce,** open 9 am to 6 pm daily in summer, will provide guidance on walks and places to visit.

On leaving Piedicroce take the D146 towards the **Col d'Arcarota**. You should make a stop at the small village of **Carcheto** with its pretty stone houses and its impressive church (ask for the keys at the town hall). The waterfall is a good place for bathing.

At the Col d'Arcarota, there is a market of regional produce across from the Auberge des Deux Vallées 10 am to 8 pm every Sunday. To continue, take the D17 towards the old **Couvent St-François d'Alesani**.

To get down to Cervione via Cotone, take the D71 along the north bank of the River Bussu or the D17 through **Novale** and **Chiatra**, then turn north on the D517 when you come to the **Barrage d'Alesani**.

Places to Stay & Eat In Piedicroce, ***Hôtel Le Refuge*** *(☎ 04 95 35 82 05/81 08)* offers a warm welcome in an otherwise characterless modern building. Doubles overlooking the valley cost 280FF; the best rooms, particularly numbers 11 and 12, have a spectacular view. Rooms not on the valley side cost 250FF (with shower and toilet). The restaurant offers a good *menu* at 98FF. It closes 15 November to Easter.

Auberge des Deux Vallées *(☎/fax 04 95 35 91 20)* at the Col d'Arcarota opens from May to September. A pleasant chalet-style building with a terrace facing Monte San Petrone, this walkers' refuge contains 10 beds. A night in the six-bed dormitory costs 60FF; a double room with bunk beds costs 120FF or 150FF, depending on the season. The shelter serves *menus* costing 80FF or 95FF, which include *charcuterie*, fresh cheese fritters, trout stuffed with more fresh cheese, and stuffed meats. The hotel also sells regional products and provides information on walks and places to visit.

At the ***Piedicroce town hall*** (☎ 04 95 35 81 86/82 52), walkers can rent refuge space costing 120FF for two to three people in the heart of the village.

Walkers wanting to enjoy an extended stay in this lovely area might also get in touch with writer ***Jean-Claude Rogliano*** (☎ 04 95 31 29 89/35 82 03). Rogliano has taken an 18th-century edifice at the far end of Carcheto, below the main road, and divided it up into several pleasant and quiet gîtes. They cost 1,400/2,200FF per week in low/high season for four people. A small house for five or six is available for about 1,000FF more. A pretty shared pool is part of the bargain.

Corsican Manna

Pascal Paoli said, 'As long as we have chestnuts, we'll have bread'. For Corsicans, the chestnut tree was indeed for many long centuries 'the bread tree', and the French had no sooner conquered the island in 1771, than the king's council of state recommended restricting the continuing plantation of the tree, and even considered destroying them, for fear it made the Corsicans lazy. 'They dry it, they mill it, even their horses feed on it. The result is that the land is otherwise neglected'.

In the glory days of Corsican chestnut culture, a Corsican wedding dinner typically required 22 different chestnut delicacies. In the region of La Castagniccia (from *castagnu*, meaning chestnut) a single chestnut tree kept a family easy for a month. The people of La Castagniccia, once the single most prosperous and most populous of the island's many regions, traded their chestnuts with the Balagne for olive oil, with the Niolo for cheese, and with Porto Vecchio for salt. Chestnuts and chestnut meal were frequently all that was needed in the way of exchange currency, and casual agricultural labourers were paid in chestnuts.

Chestnut culture began to decline after WWI as the result of massive depopulation, fungal diseases, and an infant chemical industry that used the chestnut wood, and just the wood, for the production of cellulose and tannin. In the 1880s, Corsica harvested some 150,000 tonnes of chestnuts. By 1992, the chestnut harvest was down to a mere 2000 tonnes.

Cervione

This village is home to the **Musée Ethnographique** (☎ 04 95 38 12 83), open 10 am to noon and 2.30 to 6 pm Monday to Saturday. Its rich and varied collection covers a wide range of island traditions and occupations. It's in the community centre in the centre of town.

PLAINE ORIENTALE

Stretching nearly 70km from Bastia in the north to Aléria in the south, this alluvial coastal plain and the narrow ribbon of sandy beach parallel to it constitute the only real flatlands in all of Corsica. Until WWII, malaria made the region effectively uninhabitable, and it was not until the 1960s that repatriates from Algeria introduced modern farming techniques and viticulture. Wine cooperatives developed with the encouragement of the government; and dams were built to improve irrigation (see the boxed text 'Simeoni's Stand'). Today, farmers here also grow citrus fruits such as clementines, citrons and kiwis.

Though the long beach itself is fairly uninspiring, a number of tourist complexes have sprung up, especially along the stretch just south of Bastia (see Around Bastia in the Bastia & the Far North chapter) and in the immediate environs of Aléria.

ALÉRIA

postcode 20270 • pop 1966

In ancient times Aléria, first known as Alalia, was Corsica's capital. Today it is a charmless little town that most travellers will simply pass through on their way between Bastia and Porto Vecchio on the N198. The town's Roman ruins and archaeological museum are nevertheless worth a visit, and L'Étang de Diane and L'Étang d'Urbino (lakes Diane and Urbino) to the north and south, respectively, are excellent places for walking, as are the banks of the River Tavignano.

Simeoni's Stand

On 21 August 1975 Edmond Simeoni and 20 followers barricaded themselves in a wine cellar in Aléria to protest against the French government's financial support of refugees from Algeria, who were – according to Simeoni – 'dispossessing' native Corsicans there (and, in addition, making bad wine and profiting fraudulently from it). The following day, in an extraordinary show of force, the Interior Ministry dispatched eight squadrons of crack law-enforcement officers from Paris and assaulted Simeoni's redoubt. Two of the policemen lost their lives. The sequence of events was not only a first warning to France that the country had a serious 'Corsica problem', it was also the beginning of a full quarter-century of separatist agitation.

Information

Tourist Offices The tourist office (☎ 04 95 57 01 51), on the main road, opens 8 am to 8 pm daily except Sunday afternoon in summer and 8 am to noon and 2 to 6 pm during the rest of the year. Guided tours to the archaeological site are organised for groups. Staff speak English.

Money There are a number of banks with ATMs on the main road. You can change money at Crédit Agricole, open 8.15 to 11.55 am and 1.30 to 4.45 pm Monday to Friday, next to Super U supermarket, and at Marina d'Aléria camp site (see Places to Stay).

Musée Archéologique Jérôme Carcopino & Roman Ruins

The Jérôme Carcopino Archaeological Museum (named after the distinguished historian of ancient Rome) is in the magnificent **Fort de Matra**. Built by the Genoese in 1484, this edifice towers over the Vallée du Tavignano and L'Étang de Diane. The objects on display within were unearthed at the former site of Alalia and bear witness to the town's Etruscan, Phocaean and Roman past. The exhibition rooms open 8 am to noon and 2 to 7 pm May to September and to 5 pm during the rest of the year. Combined admission to the museum and the Roman ruins costs 10FF. An additional 11 exhibition rooms are now in the process of being prepared.

The archaeological site is a 300m walk south-west of the fort. Excavations started in 1921 but were first organised in a methodical way in 1958. The site now boasts the remains of a forum, a citadel, some temples and part of the centre of the Roman town, but the largest part of the city remains to be unearthed.

Activities

The Marina d'Aléria camp site (☎ 04 95 57

06 24; see Places to Stay) has six tennis courts open 7 am to 10 pm daily. They cost 50FF per hour. Lessons are also available.

Fun Orizonte (☎ 04 95 57 33 37/06 13 04 30 95), at the Marina d'Aléria camp-site beach, rents windsurfing equipment/pedal boats/kayaks/catamarans at 60/80/40/150FF per hour. Jet skis are available for 150FF for 10 minutes and 650FF per hour. Water skis go for 140FF for 15 minutes. Walks are also organised as far as Porto Vecchio.

The Centre Équestre de Bravone (☎ 04 95 38 91 00), 9.7km north of Aléria on the N198, offers trail riding in the maquis and rides by the ocean. Rides cost 100FF per hour or 400FF per day. The centre opens 8.30 am to noon and 4 to 8 pm.

Organised Tours

ONF (☎ 04 95 32 81 90), in Bastia, organises trips to the Forêt de Marmano (Tuesday at 10 am; two hours). Meet at the Maison Forestière de Marmano on the D69, 12 km beyond Ghisoni. Tickets cost 40FF either at the site or at the tourist office.

Places to Stay – Budget

The four-star ***Marina d'Aléria*** *(☎ 04 95 57 01 42, fax 04 95 57 04 29)* camp site, stretches for 500m along the edge of the long sandy beach at the eastern end of the N200. Sites cost 30/40FF per person (depending on the season), 8/10FF per tent, and 10/14FF per car. In July and August, advance booking is necessary. The camp site also has bungalows with a double bed and two small bunk beds suitable for children. Expect a charge of 1400FF for a week in the low season rising to as much as 4400FF per week in August.

Several naturist clubs near Aléria provide accommodation right next to the beach. The closest to Aléria proper is ***Riva Bella*** *(☎ 04 95 38 81 10, fax 04 95 38 91 29)*, which has camping facilities. The best-equipped is the ***Domaine de Baghera*** *(☎ 04 95 38 80 30, fax 04 95 38 83 47, e baghera@wanadoo.fr)*, 13km to the north of Aléria; a chalet sleeping two people costs 179/368FF in the low/high season, and 20/34FF per person; or a pitch in the camp site costs 15/30FF per tent and 14/23FF per car. Gîtes are also available for rent. The Domaine has tennis courts and a diving centre, and mountain bikes (100FF per day), windsurfing equipment and catamarans for hire. There is also a restaurant and even a club.

Hôtel Les Orangers *(☎ 04 95 57 00 13, fax 04 95 57 05 55)*, the only one-star hotel in town, is 50m from the junction of the N200 and the N198, in the direction of the beach. Rooms with sink cost 180/200/230FF for a single/double/triple; it costs around 50FF more for a shower and a TV. The hotel is clean and well-kept though sometimes a little noisy.

Hôtel L'Empereur *(☎ 04 95 57 02 13)* is on the N198 but some of its rooms are on an inside courtyard away from the traffic noise. Singles/doubles cost 260/280FF, though better rates can be negotiated for a stay of several days. All rooms are en suite.

Places to Stay – Mid-Range

Right next to the tourist office, ***L'Hôtel Atrachjata*** *(☎ 04 95 57 03 93, fax 04 95 57 05 03)* has been completely renovated. Its comfortable three-star rooms, soundproofed and air-conditioned, are reasonably priced. They go for 280/320/370FF per single/double/triple in the low season and 380/440/490FF in August.

Places to Eat

There are lots of bars and restaurants along the N198 and on the seafront. ***Le Bounty*** *(☎ 04 95 57 00 50)*, on Plage de Padulone, offers pizzas (starting at 40FF) and fish (roasted sea bream with rice, 85FF) on its terrace facing the open sea. You will get over the slightly tacky decor.

Aux Coquillages de Diana *(☎ 04 95 57 04 55)*, a wood-frame, seafood establishment atop pilings on L'Étang de Diane, offers a seafood platter for 130FF, fish from 90FF, or a *menu* at 100FF. The restaurant opens June to September only. But nearby ***Le Chalet*** *(☎ 04 95 57 04 46)*, on the N198, takes up the baton, October to May, when Aux Coquillages de Diana closes, though even it closes on Wednesday and in January. It has the same *menu* at the same prices.

L'Étang de Diane Shells Out

L'Étang de Diane, the lake north-east of Aléria, 600 hectares in surface area and up to 11m in depth, has been famous for its oyster farming since classical antiquity. Back then, most of the product went across the waters to Rome. In the absence of jars or tins, the flesh was extracted from the shells and preserved either in salt or in olive oil and vinegar inside amphorae. Production levels were so great that you can still, today, see a little artificial island of discarded Roman Imperial shells. Oysters, mussels and other shellfish are still farmed and sold here.

Entertainment

There's a club in the Domaine de Baghera (see Places to Stay), 13km north of Aléria. It opens at 9 pm.

Getting There & Away

Aléria is on the Bastia/Porto Vecchio bus line, which is operated by Les Rapides Bleus (☎ 04 95 31 03 79). In summer only, Autocars Cortenais (☎ 04 95 46 02 12) operates a service to Aléria from Corte (55FF, 70 minutes).

Departures from Corte are from in front of the train station at 10.55 am, while in Aléria, departures go from in front of the camp site at 2.50 pm.

The Central Mountains

Corte, the mountain redoubt that was the capital of Pascal Paoli's short-lived Corsican nation, remains today a symbol of the island's distinct and separate cultural identity. In picturesque villages, particularly to the south of the town, islanders attempt to preserve a millennial way of life despite both a dwindling population and the erosive force of more and more of the gadgetry of modern civilisation.

The towns and villages in this part of Corsica are linked by the Chemins de Fer de la Corse (CFC), Corsica's metre-gauge single-track railway, which winds lazily through forests and around mountains. The scenery in this central part of Corsica, above all the Vallée de la Restonica and the Scala di Santa Regina, is spectacular.

Highlights

- Immerse yourself in the fascinating historic town of Corte, home of Corsica's university
- Bathe in the beautiful pools of the Vallée de la Restonica
- Drive the awesome Scala di Santa Regina

CORTE

postcode 20250 • pop 6329 • elevation 486m

At the mouth of the Restonica and Tavignano valleys, surrounded by mountains, Corte (Corti in Corsican) seems rooted to its rocky headland. Its citadel dominates both the upper town *(ville haute)* and the lower town *(ville basse)*. Corte swelters in summer; in winter, strong winds lash it. Home to Corsica's only university (with 3500 students) and the Musée de la Corse (or Musée Régional d'Anthropologie), the town has in recent years attempted to reinforce its position as Corsica's cultural and spiritual heart.

History

Corte was founded in 1419 by the Corsican viceroy Vincentello d'Istria, who built a small fort that became known as the Nid d'Aigle (Eagle's Nest) on the rocky headland. The only fortified town in central Corsica, Corte – halfway between Bastia and Ajaccio – witnessed all of the battles against Genoese rule. Between 1755 and 1769 Pascal Paoli founded the first independent Corsican government in the town and established the voting in of one of the first democratic constitutions in the world (in the Couvent d'Orezza). In 1765 the university was established, and then four years later Paoli was defeated by the French. From then on Corte was a garrison town, and was even used as a base by the French Foreign Legion when it left North Africa in 1962.

Orientation

The main street, cours Paoli, divides the town in two. To the west, steps lead to the upper town and the citadel. To the east, you descend into the lower town and the new quarter, which stretches towards the valley. Rue Jean Nicoli, on which the university is located, leads onto cours Paoli. The train station is about 800m from the town centre.

Information

Tourist Offices The tourist office (☎ 04 95 46 26 70, fax 04 95 46 34 05, ⓔ corte .tourisme@wanadoo.fr) is housed in the Padoue barracks at the entrance to the citadel. It opens 9 am to 1 pm and 3 to 7 pm Monday to Saturday and 10 am to 1 pm and 3 to 7 pm Sunday in summer. It closes at 6 pm weekdays and is not open at all at the weekend, the rest of the year. Staff distribute a small map of the town and the surrounding area and a useful pamphlet, *Parcours Patrimonial*, published by the local historical society, which lists the main points of interest in the town. The office also provides a list of places to stay, though they do not take bookings.

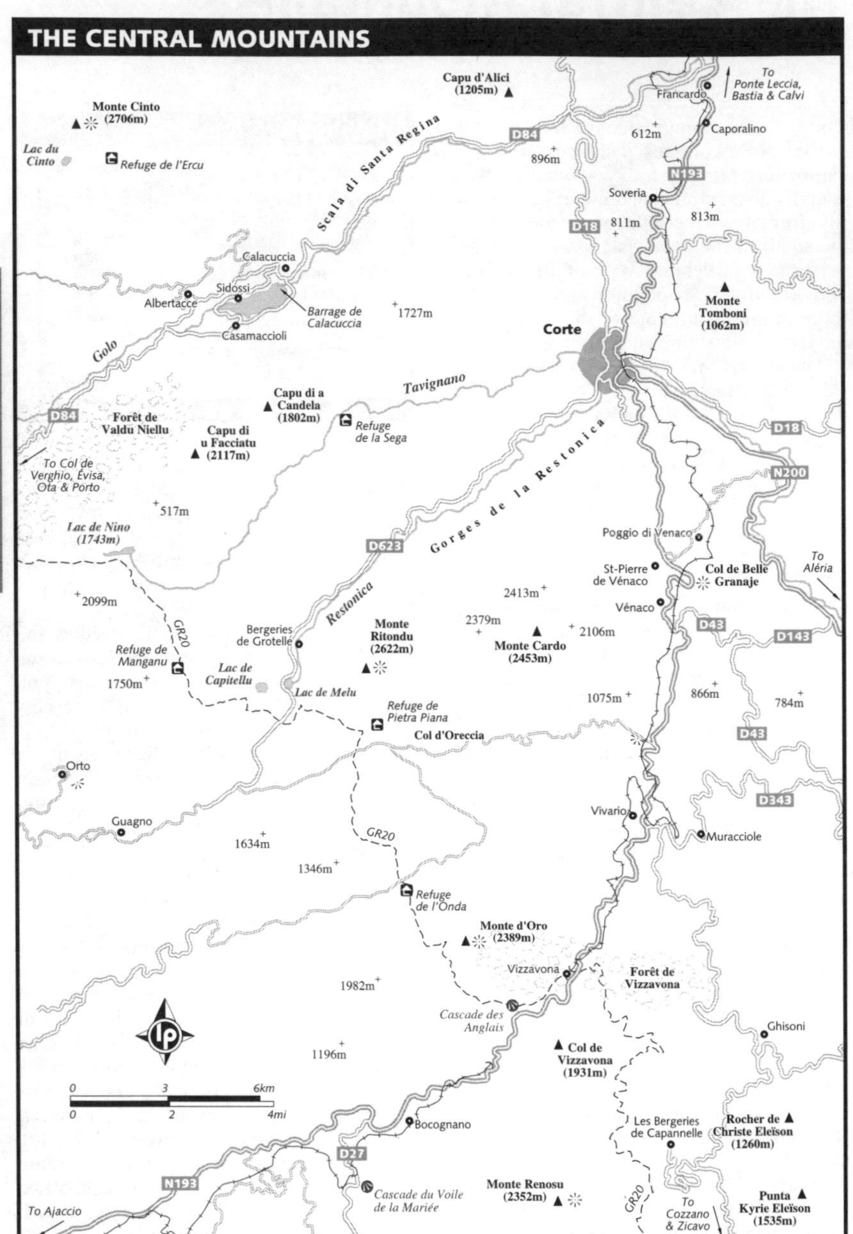
THE CENTRAL MOUNTAINS
Capu d'Alici (1205m)
To Ponte Leccia, Bastia & Calvi
Francardo
Monte Cinto (2706m)
Caporalino
612m
D84
896m
Lac du Cinto
Refuge de l'Ercu
Scala di Santa Regina
N193
Soveria
813m
811m
D18
Calacuccia
Sidossi
Albertacce
Barrage de Calacuccia
1727m
Monte Tomboni (1062m)
Corte
Casamaccioli
Golo
Tavignano
Capu di a Candela (1802m)
D84
Forêt de Valdu Niellu
Capu di u Facciatu (2117m)
Refuge de la Sega
D18
Gorges de la Restonica
N200
To Col de Verghio, Évisa, Ota & Porto
517m
Lac de Nino (1743m)
D623
Poggio di Venaco
St-Pierre de Vénaco
Col de Belle Granaje
To Aléria
2413m
Restonica
2099m
GR20
Vénaco
Monte Ritondu (2622m)
2379m
2106m
Monte Cardo (2453m)
D43
D143
Bergeries de Grotelle
Refuge de Manganu
Lac de Capitellu
1750m
Lac de Melu
866m
1075m
784m
Refuge de Pietra Piana
Col d'Oreccia
D43
Orto
D343
Vivario
Guagno
Muracciole
1634m
GR20
1346m
Refuge de l'Onda
Monte d'Oro (2389m)
Vizzavona
Forêt de Vizzavona
1982m
Cascade des Anglais
Ghisoni
Col de Vizzavona (1931m)
1196m
0 3 6km
0 2 4mi
Bocognano
Les Bergeries de Capannelle
Rocher de Christe Eleïson (1260m)
D27
N193
Cascade du Voile de la Mariée
Monte Renosu (2352m)
GR20
Punta Kyrie Eleïson (1535m)
To Ajaccio
To Cozzano & Zicavo

On the right as you enter the citadel, the Parc Naturel Régional de Corse (PNRC) Office (☎ 04 95 46 27 44/51 79 10) opens daily in summer and autumn. You can obtain walking brochures and advice on itineraries here.

Money North of cours Paoli you will find several banks with both ATM machines and windows for changing money face to face. La Société Générale (☎ 04 95 46 00 81) opens 8.10 am to noon and 1.50 to 4.50 pm Monday to Friday. The Crédit Agricole (☎ 04 95 45 22 00) opens 8.15 to 11.55 am and from 1.45 to 4.50 pm. For cash transactions over 35FF expect to pay a commission of 4.5%. The bank also changes travellers cheques and Eurocheques.

Post & Communications The main post office on ave du Baron Mariani opens 8 am to noon and 2 to 5 pm Monday to Friday and 8 am to noon on Saturday. The post office also has an ATM.

Bookshops The Librairie de Flore at 5 cours Paoli opens 9 am to 8 pm daily except Sunday afternoon, in summer. It sells maps, guidebooks on Corsica and a small selection of English-language books. French newspapers and, in summer, some foreign newspapers as well can be bought from the Maison de la Presse (☎ 04 95 46 01 38), also on cours Paoli.

Library The library in the Centre de Recherches Corses in the Palazzu Naziunale opens 9 am to noon and 2 to 6 pm Tuesdays, Wednesdays and Thursdays but, unlike many other institutions in Corsica, it generally closes during the summer. The library collection contains everything that has ever been written on Corsica in areas ranging from history to flora and fauna. This is also a good place to have a look at the nationalist press, including the famous *Il Ribombu*, the official publication of the A Cuncolta Naziunalista (Nationalist Assembly) party.

Medical Services The Santos Manfredi Hospital (☎ 04 95 45 05 00) is on allée du 9 Septembre near the train station.

Emergency The police station is on the N200, on the outskirts of town, in the direction of Aléria.

Citadel

The high-perched and roughly triangular citadel dominates Corte. Climb the flight of stairs cut from Restonica marble to reach the old **château** at the citadel's southern limit. Prettily restored, this building, which itself resembles a small fort more than anything else, was built in 1419 and extended by the French in the 18th and 19th centuries. The ramparts, in the style of the famous French military engineer Vauban, are impressive, as is the view from the ramparts walkway. There is also a nice view of the citadel and also of the town itself from the Belvedere at the top of the upper town.

After entering the citadel you reach two large buildings facing one another, the **Casernes Serrurier and Padoue** (Serrurier and Padoue, or Padua, Barracks). Built under Louis-Philippe, they have been used for a variety of purposes, including as a prison and later, from 1962 to 1983, as housing for elements of the French Foreign Legion. Today the Caserne Serrurier houses the Musée de la Corse. Since 1981 the Caserne Padoue has been used for teaching by the university. It now also provides space for the Maison du Tourisme et de la Culture.

The FRAC (Fonds Régional d'Art Contemporain), also in the Caserne Padoue, opens 2 to 6 pm Monday to Saturday. It organises four exhibitions a year, one of which is usually dedicated to a Corsican artist. For further information call ☎ 04 95 46 22 18.

Musée de la Corse (Musée Régional d'Anthropologie)

For its inauguration as a museum in December 1997, this building was restored by the Italian architect Andrea Bruno, who kept the long facade and enlarged the windows to allow more light to enter the rooms.

The **Galerie Doozan**, one flight up, exhibits examples from a collection of approximately 3000 traditional Corsican craft objects. The gallery is named for the priest who assembled the collection over nearly three decades, from 1951 to 1978.

The next level up, the *'musée en train de se faire'* (museum under construction), covers more contemporary subjects such as industry, tourism and music. The ground floor is reserved for temporary exhibitions.

The museum (☎ 04 95 45 25 45, fax 04 95 45 25 36, ⓔ museu@sitec.fr) opens 10 am to 8 pm daily. It closes at 6 pm and all day Sunday, all day Monday and holidays in low season. Admission costs 35FF for adults and 20FF for children over 10 years old. Cassette tours can be rented in English or French for 10FF. Tours of 1½ hours can be reserved in advance, but only for groups.

A special edition *Beaux Arts Magazine* featuring the museum is on sale in the entrance hall for 55FF.

Palazzu Naziunale (National Palace)

The large rectangular building to the left of the citadel entrance was once the palace of the local Genoese government, and it subsequently housed Paoli's first and only independent Corsican government. Paoli lived here in this palace, which was simultaneously the principal university facility. Now the building houses some departments of the 20th-century university, as well as a library. The ground floor now serves as an exhibition room for local artists.

Below the palace on place Gaffory is the **Église de l'Annonciation**, built in the mid-15th century. It was transformed and enlarged in the 17th century.

Università di Corsica Pasquale Paoli

One of the demands of the nationalists in the 1960s was that Corsica should have its own university. In 1975, the French government acceded to the demand, and in October 1981, nearly two centuries after Paoli founded his university, doors here were once again opened to students who had completed secondary school. The student body of around 3500 attend classes in subjects such as the social sciences, biology, languages and economics. The main building is on ave Jean Nicoli near the entrance to the lower town.

Student life in Corte is not all a bed of roses. The public transport infrastructure leaves a great deal to be desired and, because housing is in short supply, students are often obliged to take rooms in hotels.

Walking

Valle e Cime (☎ 04 95 48 69 29/33, fax 04 95 48 69 36) organises full-day hikes for small groups for 80FF; picnic lunch costs 40FF more. Other options include two- and three-day hikes (for example, from Vizzavona to Corte, room and board included, for 500FF) and even week-long hikes. Check out the Web site at www.vallecime.com.

Horse Riding

La Ferme Équestre L'Albadu (see Places to Stay later) offers a number of horse-riding packages through the Tavignanu valley. A full-day outing, including lunch, costs 450FF. A half day costs 200FF. A one-hour ride costs 90FF. There are also week-long packages. Further information about horse-riding opportunities in the area can be had from the Association Régionale du Tourisme Équestre en Corse (☎/fax 04 95 46 31 74, ⓔ arte.corse@wanadoo.fr) at 7 rue du Colonel Ferracci.

Organised Tours

A small trackless tourist train (☎ 06 09 95 70 36) makes a circuit of Corte's principal attractions from its terminal in the Tuffeli car park at the lower end of cours Paoli. The tour lasts 30 minutes (or one hour, with stops) and costs 25FF. Tours are in French.

Autocars Cortenais (☎ 04 95 46 02 12/22 89) organises a variety of excursions through the Vallée de la Restonica, including the Bergeries de Grotelle (70FF return) and the Pont de Tragone (60FF return).

Places to Stay – Budget

Open from mid-April to the beginning of October, ***Camping Alivetu*** *(☎ 04 95 46 11 09)* is on allée du 9 Septembre, south of the Pont Restonica, approximately 900m from the train station. It charges 32/15/15FF per adult/tent/car.

TONY WHEELER

Looking over from Vizzavona towards Monte D'Oro, Corsica's fifth-highest peak (2389m).

JEAN-BERNARD CARILLET

A host of golden genêt shrubs

JEAN-BERNARD CARILLET

A shepherd's shelter, near Bassetta on the GR20

TONY WHEELER

How now, making a meal of the GR20...could the Manganello valley be cow heaven?

Corsica was described by Balzac as 'a French island basking in the Italian sun', but the island has a singular character that is entirely its own.

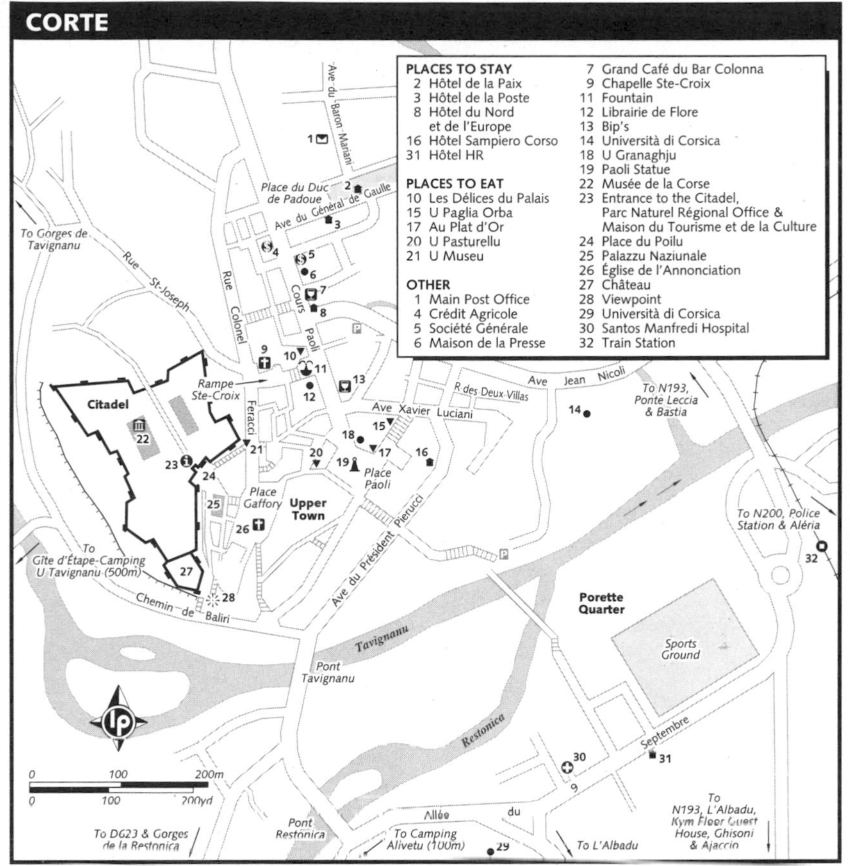

Gîte d'Étape-Camping U Tavignanu *(☎ 04 95 46 16 85)* opens Easter to October. It charges 22/11FF per adult/tent. To find it, head west along chemin de Baliri on the western side of the citadel and look out for signs; the site is at the end of a narrow road 500m after the bridge. U Tavignanu also has rental tents (80FF for two) and dormitory beds (80FF with breakfast or 160FF at half-board). It opens year round and is close to the GR20.

La Ferme Équestre L'Albadu *(☎ 04 95 46 24 55)*, an equestrian centre on the old Ajaccio road (the route du Calvaire), in open country, has a number of small, clean rooms with shower and outside toilet for 200FF for two. Half-board lodging, with tasty meals of local farm products, is billed at a mere 180FF per person. Hikers can also sleep in a dormitory (70FF) or pitch their tents on terraced plots. It costs 50FF per day for two people with a tent plus 10/5FF for a car/motorbike. Owner Jean Pulicani is a knowledgeable enthusiast on local environmental matters. The easiest way to get there is to take the main road to Ajaccio, then turn right after 1km (the facility is signposted). If you are on foot, they will pick you up if you telephone.

Hôtel de la Poste *(☎ 04 95 46 01 37, fax 04 95 46 13 08, 2 place Padoue)* offers 12 basic rooms in a charming old building. Doubles go for 175FF to 200FF depending on size, and 240FF with toilet. Triples run to 230FF or 260FF. Rooms 5 and 6 have balconies and rooms 9 and 10 share a wide terrace. The hotel is open year round and a warm welcome is guaranteed.

Hôtel HR *(☎ 04 95 45 11 11, fax 04 95 61 02 85, 6 allée du 9 Septembre)* is, with its 135 rooms, the largest hotel in Corte, and also one of the cheapest. The hotel building itself, about 150m from the train station, is devoid of any discernible charm, but the rooms are pleasant enough. Doubles start at 145FF (199FF with shower and toilet). Rates are barely more expensive in August and half-board runs to 99FF. The hotel, open year round, has both a sauna (25FF) and a fitness room as well as private parking. Make sure you book ahead, even in low season.

Places to Stay – Mid-Range

At the end of a short, quiet street just off cours Paoli is ***Hôtel de la Paix*** *(☎ 04 95 46 06 72, fax 04 95 46 23 84, ⓔ socoget@aol.com, ave du Général de Gaulle)*. Doubles with toilet, shower and telephone, cost 260/280/300FF, depending on the season. Triples go for 310/330/350FF. Count on about 50FF more for bath and TV and 35FF for breakfast. Recently renovated, its 63 rooms are a good deal.

Hôtel du Nord et de l'Europe *(☎ 04 95 46 00 68, 22 cours Paoli)* is arguably even better. The 13 rooms all have showers and some are studio size. Doubles cost 200FF (270FF with toilet on the courtyard side), rooms with two large double beds cost 260FF (310FF with toilet). The hotel charges 320FF for four people. Though the east-facing rooms are distinctly quieter than those on the street, windows on all sides are double-glazed. The hotel also runs Le Grand Café (left as you come out of the hotel), where breakfast goes for 30FF. Not only are hikers welcome but they can leave their rucksacks in a secure room behind the cafe. The hotel has details of English-speaking guides. It opens year round.

Hôtel Sampiero Corso *(☎ 04 95 46 09 76, ave du Président Pierucci)* is a modern building with double rooms for 270FF and triple rooms for 400FF. A child's cot costs 100FF. Each room has a bathroom, toilet and telephone. The hotel is in a noisy street but the windows are all double-glazed.

Le Kyrn Floor *(☎ 04 95 61 02 88, fax 04 95 46 08 02)* about 3km out on the N193 in the direction of Ajaccio, on your left if you are coming from Corte, on your right if you are arriving, is an attractive large stone house on a height overlooking the roadway. The owners, in addition to distilling oil essences from maquis plants such as rosemary and myrtle, have been taking guests in for more than a decade. The five rooms in the main house, each with shower, toilet and washbasin, go for 300FF (including a generous breakfast). But also consider opting for one of the free-standing studios (350FF) on the same level as the garden, where you can have a barbecue or eat breakfast alfresco. A studio for four (with mezzanine bedroom) costs 550FF with breakfast. The rooms are perfect and you are assured of a hearty welcome. The only problem is the proximity of the N193, worse, unfortunately, in the studios than in the main house.

Places to Eat

Snacks A tiny little bakery, ***Les Délices du Palais*** *(☎ 04 95 46 02 67, 7 cours Paoli)*, sells delicious, freshly baked sweet and savoury pastries. Try out the *gâteau aux châtaignes* (chestnut cake) in season. For eating on the run, stop preferably at the little supermarket on place Paoli for a *fougasse*; this is bread topped with olives or sometimes with onion and bacon.

In the evening two ***pizza vans*** – one in place Padoue and the other at the corner of ave Xavier Luciani and cours Paoli – sell substantial, if somewhat uninspired, wood-fire pizzas for between 30FF and 45FF.

Restaurants An appealing little restaurant, ***U Museu*** *(☎ 04 95 61 08 36, rampe Ribanelle)* is situated just before the entrance to the citadel in the upper town. There's even a shaded terrace. The *menu* at 89FF might include fish soup, trout in *peveronatta* (a sauce of pepper, tomato and wine), cheese and dessert. A 75FF *menu* includes a main course and your choice of starter or dessert. The children's *menu* costs 38FF. A la carte specialities you might want to try include an excellent wild-boar stew with wild myrtle (65FF), *tripettes à la Cortenaise* (tripe with red wine sauce and shallots; 49FF), and *brocciu* and mint omelette (43FF). The restaurant opens daily in summer but closes on Sunday and school holidays in low season. There is a menu in English. It's popular, but doesn't accept reservations, so you may have to eat early or late to get a table.

Au Plat d'Or *(☎ 04 95 46 27 16, 1 place Paoli)* is a small, pretty restaurant where tourists rub shoulders with locals. You can eat in one of two quiet dining rooms or on the shrub-screened terrace. By way of starters, the chef assembles a selection of imaginative salads – one called *marocaine* consists of semolina flavoured with cumin and white grapes, another brings together chicken liver and nuts (49FF for either). The refreshing terrine of brocciu with sweet peppers on a *coulis de tomates* (similar to tomato purée) at 65FF is another tasty treat, as are the brochettes of beef with fresh mushrooms (100FF). There are delicious home-made desserts and three *menus* ranging from 60FF to 110FF. Service is quick and attentive.

U Paglia Orba *(☎ 04 95 61 07 89, ave Xavier Luciani)*, above a busy street, offers two *menus* at 65FF and 85FF. The first includes a plate of Corsican ham, meat cannelloni and a chestnut flan. Appealing a la carte specialities include an escalope of veal rolled and stuffed with mint (80FF) and the *storzaprette* (slabs of herb-flavoured brocciu; 56FF). There are a few pizzas on the menu, starting at 35FF. The restaurant opens Monday to Saturday.

La Ferme Équestre L'Albadu (see Places to Stay) has an extensive menu based on its own farm products: soup, cheese fritters, meat, whole cheeses, fruit tarts, coffee and wine. At 80FF per person, the value cannot be beaten. But you must book in advance. Consider enjoying the meal in conjunction with a day or afternoon of horse riding (for details see Horse Riding earlier in this section).

Entertainment

Bars Although there are a few bars on cours Paoli and in place Paoli (notice in particular ***Le Grand Café*** and ***Bip's***), in summer nightlife in Corte winds down around 1 am. In winter, thanks to the student presence, nightlife is livelier. Locals nevertheless tend to be nostalgic for the good old days when the Foreign Legion kept a good 20 joints alive.

Shopping

In the upper town (between the citadel and place Paoli) several craft shops sell handmade items such as pottery, wooden toys and paintings.

At the two U Granaghju stores (☎ 04 95 46 20 28, fax 04 95 46 19 78), 2 cours Paoli, you can stock up on local produce.

Getting There & Away

Bus Corte is on the Bastia–Ajaccio bus route operated by Eurocorse (☎ 04 95 21 06 30). Buses leave from in front of the bar Majestic. A single to Bastia costs 55FF; a single to Ajaccio 65FF.

Autocars Cortenais (☎ 04 95 46 02 12) runs buses between Corte and Bastia (60FF, 1¼ hours) via Ponte Leccia three times a week (Mondays, Wednesdays and Fridays), year round. The bus leaves from the Corte Voyages agency at 19 cours Paoli. In summer the same company also has departures to Aléria (55FF) on Tuesdays, Thursdays and Saturdays with departures in front of the railroad station.

Autocars Mordiconi (☎ 04 95 48 00 04) has buses going to Porto via Calacuccia and Évisa (100FF) daily except Sunday and public holidays. They leave from place Paoli.

Train From the train station (☎ 04 95 46 00 97) there are four trains daily to Ajaccio (66FF, two hours). There are also five trains to Bastia (59FF, 1½ hours). Yet more trains go off to Calvi (79FF), Île Rousse (62FF) and Vizzavona (31FF). To carry a bicycle

THE CENTRAL MOUNTAINS

costs an additional 76FF. Left luggage costs 17FF per day.

SCALA DI SANTA REGINA

This awesome mountain pass north-west of Corte was, for years, the only way of getting into or out of Calacuccia and the villages in the tiny Niolo region. And what a passageway it was! The deep granite gorges that plunge down to the bed of the River Golo make this one of the island's most dramatic mountain landscapes – and all the more so because of the rock's other-worldly reddish rust colour.

The D84, a narrow road that sometimes seems to be hardly more than a ledge with reinforced verges supported by arches, winds its way through the pass for around 20km, from the outskirts of Calacuccia to close to the junction with the N193. The only blot on the landscape is the chain of rusty electricity pylons following the line of the river.

A dam and hydroelectric power station, which can dramatically alter the water levels, make any descent into the gorges perilous. It's possible to go down a narrow walkway 4km from Calacuccia but the view from the road is just as stunning.

You need a car to get to the Scala di Santa Regina. From Corte, go north on the N193 as far as Francardo, then, at the D84, turn west.

CALACUCCIA

postcode 20224 • pop 320 • elevation 847m

Resplendent above its lake, Calacuccia is a popular haunt of hikers following the Mare a Mare Nord route. There is not much to do in the town, especially now that the lake, managed by the electricity company EDF, is off limits to swimmers. Signs posted around the lake in fact prohibit not just swimming but also sailing and fishing, though not, strangely, the occasional canoeing competition. Locals tend to swim instead in the mountain streams between Casamaccioli and Albertacce.

The town lies in the shadow of Monte Cinto (2706m). But you'll also have a good view of Les Cinq Moines (The Five Monks), a series of five jagged peaks that could be taken to resemble the dorsal spine of some giant prehistoric reptilian.

A memorial plaque in the town pays homage to Gracieux Lamperti, the 1959 French and European boxing champion who came from Calacuccia.

Calacuccia has bars, restaurants, a petrol station, two grocery shops and a post office (behind the town hall).

Information

The tourist office (☎ 04 95 48 05 22, fax 04 95 48 08 80), the Association Sportive et Culturelle du Niolu and the Compagnie Régionale des Guides et Accompagnateurs en Montagne de Corse (☎ 04 95 48 05 22) share quarters 1km before the village as you arrive from the Scala di Santa Regina. These entities, all committed to the promotion of tourism in the Niolo area, can clue you in on a variety of sporting activities. All three open 9 am to noon and 2 to 6 pm daily, July to September. In low season they close at weekends.

Activities

For outdoor sports enthusiasts, the Niolo region, around Calacuccia, is the all but perfect playpen. Guides, some of them skilled in mountaineering, can help both beginners and proficient climbers up the peaks of Cuccia and Calasima (see Information earlier). You can also explore the canyons of the Ruda and the Frascaghju or kayak in the Golo. Organised group hikes to the top of Monte Cinto, Corsica's highest peak, are offered several times a week, and so are hikes to the Lac de Nino peat bogs (see the boxed text 'Highland Lakes & *Pozzines*' in the Walking chapter).

Places to Stay

The ***Gîte d'Étape du Couvent*** *(☎ 04 95 48 00 11)*, 1km south of Calacuccia just above the road, is a favourite port of call among walkers; the convent nuns have moved on. Dorm beds cost 65FF and the six double rooms cost 220FF. The gîte opens year round.

Gîte d'Étape d'Albertacce *(☎ 04 95 48 05 60/48 08 05)*, 2.5km south of Calacuccia on the outskirts of the quiet village of Albertacce, is a handsome stone house with dormitories for four, a room for socialising, a kitchen and clean bathrooms. Expect to pay 65FF per night, 25FF for breakfast and 170FF for half-board.

Hôtel des Touristes *(☎ 04 95 48 00 04, fax 04 95 48 05 92)* is a large grey building not entirely without charm that offers comfortable and traditionally furnished single/double rooms for 200/230FF (with bidet), 270/300FF (with shower) and 300/370FF (with bath). Hikers can sleep in a dormitory for 70FF a night. Bungalows are available from 2100FF per week in August.

Hôtel Acqua Viva *(☎ 04 95 48 06 90, fax 04 95 48 08 82)*, Calacuccia's other, more modern hotel is in the building above the petrol station. Doubles with balconies, bath and TV run from 300FF to 400FF, depending on the time of year (without breakfast).

Places to Eat

The ***Auberge Casa Balduina*** *(☎ 04 95 48 08 57),* opposite the convent offers good home cooking. The 85FF *menu* includes locally produced *charcuterie*, an excellent baked noodle dish, cheese and fruit. The 120FF *menu* includes a cheese pastry starter, veal sautéed with mushrooms, and an assortment of cheeses and fig jam. A cheese platter all by itself costs 50FF.

Le Restaurant du Lac *(☎ 04 95 48 02 73)* at Sidossi, around 2km from Calacuccia on the edge of the lake, enjoys a deserved reputation as the best restaurant in the area, and its fresh produce does it credit. The restaurant has two *menus*, one at 80FF, which includes a salad, sautéed veal with peppers and olives, and cheese or a pastry. A more extravagant *menu*, at 128FF, includes dishes such as a mushroom pastry, grilled free-range veal or quail with wild mushrooms, a julienne of mountain veal with basil or cod with balsamic vinegar, as well as cheese and a dessert.

Getting There & Away

Les Bus Mordiconi (ask at the Hôtel des Touristes; see Places to Stay) provide services, from July to mid-September, to Corte, Évisa, Verghio and Porto. A bus leaves daily except Sunday at 9 am for Porto (65FF) and at 3.30 pm for Corte (45FF).

VALLÉE DE LA RESTONICA

Despite some overcrowding during the summer months, the Vallée de la Restonica is unarguably one of the top highlights of the Corte area. The river, rising in the grey-green mountains, has hollowed out pretty little basins in the rock, and these provide numerous sheltered settings for bathing and sunbathing alike. The D623 winds its way through the gorges from Corte until it gets to the Bergeries de Grotelle, which have made a number of concessions to modern civilisation and tourism.

You can bathe in nearly all the gorges. However, the best spots are between the Auberge de la Restonica and the information stand (near a small chapel with lovely natural swimming pools), and along the last 3km of the road before you get to the Bergeries.

A number of walks are signposted along this road as well; they can take from 30 minutes to several hours. Most visitors come to the gorges to see the **Lac de Melu** at 1711m, an hour's hike, and the **Lac de Capitellu** at 1930m, around 1¾ hours away on foot. The path to the lakes is signposted in yellow from the Bergeries de Grotelle car park (1370m). Be sure to wear good walking shoes if you plan to go on foot, and avoid the midday sun. Bear in mind that the mountains are often still snow-capped in May.

The path to the Lac de Melu follows the right bank of the Restonica for most of the way, before branching into two tracks. The track that continues along the bank is harder going than the one that crosses the river but you are less likely to come across snow in winter and spring.

The huge number of tourists in the Vallée de la Restonica in summer has led to the imposition of new regulations. Along the gorges, for example, you must not park in spots not clearly designated for parking; and in particular, when the road occasionally broadens slightly to allow two cars travelling in opposite directions to pass each other, the extra bit of navigable surface must be respected as the lay-by that it is. Caravans and camper vans are halted at Tuani, 7km from Corte, and not even cars are allowed to pass after 2.30 pm. A free shuttle service, starting 3km before Tuani, has recently been made available at intervals of 30 minutes between 9.30 am and 6.30 pm, but whether this amenity will last it is impossible to say.

The car park at the Bergeries costs 20FF in summer. Fires, bivouacs, camping on unauthorised sites and the dumping of waste in or near the river, which supplies Corte with drinking water, are forbidden.

Information

The information stand for Vallée de la Restonica (☎ 04 95 46 33 92) is at the place called Tuani, opposite the camp site. Theoretically, it opens from mid-June to mid-September from 7.30 am to 7.30 pm daily, but hours may occasionally vary.

Places to Stay & Eat

The following places are listed in the order in which you will find them as you come from Corte. The last is therefore closest to the Bergeries de Grotelle and the start of the trail to the lakes.

Hôtel de la Restonica *(☎ 04 95 45 25 25, fax 04 95 61 15 79)*, less than 2km from Corte, has a nice swimming pool. It is a lovely stone house with six rooms and one little split-level apartment that cost 290FF to 360FF for two people in low season, and 320FF to 420FF in summer. Add 40FF more for breakfast. The hotel opens year round, except for one month in winter. Next door is a restaurant, and a waterfall and natural pools are also close by.

Hôtel Dominique Colonna *(☎ 04 95 45 25 65, fax 04 95 61 03 91, ⓔ restonic@club-internet.fr)*, opposite the Hôtel de la Restonica (and owned by the same family), is named after the current owner's father, a former professional football player. Its three-star double rooms, each boasting a bath, balcony, TV and telephone, cost from 320FF to 620FF depending on their size, the view they offer and the time of year. The hotel, which uses the same swimming pool as Hôtel de la Restonica, closes between mid-November and mid-March.

Hôtel-Restaurant Le Refuge *(☎ 04 95 46 09 13, fax 04 95 46 22 38)*, around 800m beyond Hôtel de la Restonica, has comfortable rooms with bathrooms. The value is outstanding, even with compulsory half-board (600FF to 700FF for two persons, depending on the season). The hotel opens April to September and you can swim in the nearby gorges. But it's a good idea to book in advance, since the accommodation and cuisine have made this hotel a popular destination.

Le Relais des Lacs, Chez César opens noon to 5 pm from June to September. It is renowned for its meat dishes cooked on a wood fire (44FF to 61FF) and for its trout (54FF). *Menus* cost from 69FF.

Camping Tuani *(☎/fax 04 95 46 26 71)*, opposite the Vallée de la Restonica information point, is a vast, shaded camp site with fairly basic facilities; it costs 32/15/14FF per person/tent/car. The ground is very hard, as is often the case in Corsica, but the site is pleasant and you can swim here. It also has a bar and pizzeria. It is 6km from Corte and 5km before the Bergeries de Grotelle, where you can buy cold drinks and snacks. It opens April to September.

Getting There & Away

In summer Rinieri Minibuses (☎ 04 95 46 22 89/02 12) takes passengers from Corte to the Bergeries de Grotelle. Tickets cost 70FF and there's a minimum of 10 passengers. A taxi from Corte (☎ 04 95 46 04 88/61 01 17) will take up to four passengers to the Bergeries and back for 200FF.

VÉNACO

postcode 20231 • pop 620 • elevation 610m

Vénaco overlooks the Tavignano valley. Famous for the trout from its streams and its ewe's milk cheese, this once-bustling village is now, like any number of Corsica's mountain hamlets, rather subdued. Vénaco does, however, still have a post office (at the bottom of the village in a building shared with the town hall, school and fire service), cafes and a grocery shop. The train station is at the foot of the village 600m from the main road.

The D143 drops down into the valley just

as you enter Vénaco from the direction of Ajaccio. The Noceta bridge, across the River Vecchio, 5km farther along, on the Mare a Mare Nord trail, is at the centre of a superb mountain landscape. There is also a lovely view over the village here. The river is a good place to swim.

Places to Stay & Eat

Hôtel U Frascone *(☎ 04 95 47 00 85)* on the southern side of the village is the only hotel here. Double rooms, year round, cost 300FF with breakfast, but the hotel would just as soon you lodge at the half-board price of 220FF per person. The restaurant has *menus* at 80FF (wild-boar terrine, cannelloni with brocciu or grilled trout, and dessert) and 140FF (*figatellu* terrine, roast lamb with local herbs).

Camping-Auberge de la Ferme de Peridundellu *(☎/fax 04 95 47 09 89)*, alongside the D143, 3.5km from Vénaco, is a small and friendly family-run camp site on a headland facing the valley. Open between Easter and October, it charges 30/17/15FF per adult/tent/car. Meals here are first-rate. The *menu* of local farm produce, different every day, costs 90FF.

Other accommodation is available in St-Pierre de Vénaco (Santo Pietro di Venaco), north of Vénaco proper. ***Gîte d'Étape de St-Pierre de Vénaco*** *(☎ 04 95 47 07 29)* is a favourite stopover for people walking the Mare a Mare Nord. This handsome stone house, built in the traditional Corsican style, has large dormitories for four people (160FF half-board) and single/double rooms at 200/250FF. The owner, Charles Hiver, a mountain guide, can organisewalks and help you explore the area. To get to the gîte, go up to the top of the village, passing behind the church, then follow the signs. The gîte is renowned for its friendly atmosphere and good food, and is often full in summer.

Hôtel Le Torrent *(☎ 04 95 47 00 18)*, open July to September, is a rather antiquated but pleasant traditional French inn with double rooms with bathrooms starting at 220FF (250FF with bath) and a half-board rate of 455FF for two. Some of the rooms are a bit uncomfortable. The *menus* are good value at 70FF and 110FF. The hotel is signposted from the N193.

Getting There & Away

Eurocorse (☎ 04 95 21 06 30) runs buses twice daily (except Sunday and public holidays) that stop in Ajaccio, Vizzavona, Vivario, Vénaco, Corte, Ponte Leccia and Bastia. They leave both Ajaccio and Bastia at 7.45 am and 3 pm, one in one direction, one in the other. Expect to pay 55FF for a ticket from Ajaccio to Vénaco (one hour 20 minutes).

CFC also goes to Vénaco: four trains daily link the village with Ajaccio, Corte and Bastia via Vizzavona and Vivario. Departures are usually at 7 am and 9 am and at 2.30 pm and 4.35 pm from Ajaccio, and at 7.15 am, 9.05 am, 2.25 pm and 3.50 pm from Bastia.

VIVARIO

postcode 20219 • pop 500 • elevation 696m

Nestling among mountains in a narrow compass around its church, this pretty village, with its tiled roofs standing out against the green of the surrounding forests, merits at least an extended pause. On an alternative route of the Mare a Mare Nord, the village dates back to Roman times.

One of its curiosities is the bridge that crosses the Vecchio 3km to the north. This small structure, in stone, lies under the towering supports of a great, graceful railway viaduct designed by Gustave Eiffel. Unfortunately, a rather unsightly concrete bridge is currently under construction alongside it, apparently to avoid a bend in the road.

Vivario has a bar, restaurants, two little grocery shops and a post office. The train station is around 500m north of the village.

Places to Stay

Le Macchje Monti *(☎ 04 95 47 22 00)*, near the church, is the only hotel in Vivario. Half-board lodging costs 250FF per person or 340FF if you're alone.

Getting There & Away

Eurocorse (☎ 04 95 21 06 30) runs buses to Vivario from Ajaccio, Vizzavona, Vénaco, Corte and Bastia twice daily except Sunday and public holidays. The ride from Ajaccio costs 50FF and takes 70 minutes.

There are four trains daily from Vivario to destinations such as Ajaccio, Bastia, Corte, Vénaco and Vizzavona. The trip from Ajaccio to Vivario costs 49FF and takes between 1½ and 1¾ hours.

GHISONI

postcode 20227 • pop 180 • elevation 650m

Before WWII Ghisoni boasted three dance halls, 12 cafes and 1800 inhabitants. Its population has since dwindled to about 180. The village lies peacefully at the foot of Punta Kyrie Eleïson, a mountain south-east of Vivario. Robert Colonna d'Istria, in his *L'Histoire de la Corse*, explains where its unusual name came from: In the 14th century members of the Giovannali sect, who were of Franciscan origin but resented secular and church authorities equally, were burnt alive on the mountain. Legend has it that as the flames rose and the priest sang the prayer of the Kyrie Eleïson, a white dove began to wheel above the burning woodpiles.

Ghisoni has a camp site, hotel, pizzeria, grocery shop and post office. Further information can be found in the Walking chapter.

Getting There & Away

There are no buses to Ghisoni. The train to Vivario or the bus to Ghisonaccia are the closest you can get by public transport.

VIZZAVONA

elevation 910m

Beneath the towering 2389m of Monte d'Oro, the fifth-highest peak on the island, Vizzavona is familiar to the many walkers who start or end their GR20 trek there. The small village, with its few dozen inhabitants, consists of a cluster of houses and hotels around a train station 700m from the main road. Places to stay and eat are detailed in the earlier Walking chapter.

The Forêt de Vizzavona, where bandits routinely held travellers to ransom in the 19th century, is now a peaceful haven. It covers 1633 hectares and consists mainly of beech and laricio pine trees, some, it is said, more than 800 years old. Footpaths are numerous. But be careful! Despite the humid climate there have been five major fires in the forest since 1866.

Cascades des Anglais

Two and a half kilometres from the spot where the road from Ajaccio branches off towards the train station, the short path to this sequence of waterfalls is signposted on the right. The path, not just short but also quite easy, wanders down through a superb forest of pine and beech.

After about 15 minutes you come to the GR20, where there is a refreshment stall in summer. The waterfalls are to your left. You can get to Vizzavona station in 30 minutes by taking the GR20 to your right.

In summer, to be sure, you should not expect to find falls at all and still less white-water rapids but rather a series of clear pools ideal for swimming in. You can also sunbathe on the smooth rocks. The pools extend up the mountain for a distance best measured as a relatively easy 15-minute climb. The attraction owes its name to the British holidaymakers who used to flock to Vizzavona, undeterred by the cold water. These relaxing forest pools are really quite idyllic.

Cascade du Voile de la Mariée

Continue south-west along the main road for a few kilometres until you get to the village of Bocognano. The road to the Cascade du Voile de la Mariée (Bridal Veil Falls) is on the left as you leave the village, at the Bar-Restaurant Le Copacabana. The narrow road passes a railway bridge, then comes up on a second bridge, recognisable by its iron guard-rails, 3.5km from the main road. A small wooden ladder on the left allows you to get over the fence. Continue along the path that climbs through the undergrowth, roughly marked out with lengths of rope tied between the trees. After around 10 minutes of rather difficult terrain you come to a tall, broad waterfall. Fast-flowing in winter, it is rather disappointing in summer but allows you to freshen up.

The rocks on the edge of the waterfall are slippery, so be careful.

Getting There & Away

Vizzavona and Bocognano are both on the Eurocorse (☎ 04 95 21 06 30) Ajaccio–Bastia route. There are two departures daily except on Sunday and public holidays. Allow one hour to get to Vizzavona from Ajaccio or Corte. Tickets from Ajaccio are 45FF. There are departures at 7.45 am and 3 pm from the coach station in Ajaccio and at 9.30 am and 4.15 pm from Corte.

There are four trains daily from Vizzavona to destinations including Ajaccio, Bastia, Vivario, Vénaco and Corte. The trip from Ajaccio to Vizzavona costs 41FF (plus 5FF tax in summer) and takes around one hour 20 minutes. Departures are at 7.15 am, 9.05 am, 2.25 pm and 3.50 pm from Bastia; at 7 am, 9 am, 2.30 pm and 4.35 pm from Ajaccio; and at 8.59 am and 11.10 am and 4.13 pm and 5.44 pm from Corte, although times are subject to change.

Language

FRENCH

Pronunciation & Grammar

This guide gives only a basic overview of French. For a more comprehensive guide to the language get hold of Lonely Planet's *French phrasebook*.

Most letters in French are pronounced more or less the same as their English counterparts. Here are a few which may cause confusion:

- **j** as the 's' in 'leisure', eg, *jour* (day)
- **c** before **e** and **i**, as the 's' in 'sit'; before **a**, **o** and **u** it's pronounced as English 'k'. When undescored with a 'cedilla' (ç) it's always pronounced as the 's' in 'sit'.
- **r** pronounced from the back of the throat while constricting the muscles to restrict the flow of air
- **n, m** where a syllable ends in a single **n** or **m**, these letters are not pronounced, but the vowel is pronounced though the nose

Be Polite!

An important distinction is made in French between *tu* and *vous*, which both mean 'you'; *tu* is only used when addressing people you know well, children or animals. If you're addressing an adult who isn't a personal friend, *vous* should be used unless the person invites you to use *tu*. In general, younger people insist less on this distinction, and you will find that, in many cases, they use *tu* from the beginning of an acquaintance.

Gender

All nouns in French are either masculine or feminine and adjectives reflect the gender of the noun they modify. The feminine form of many nouns and adjectives is indicated by a silent *e* added to the masculine form, as in *étudiant* and *étudiante*, the masculine and feminine for 'student'.

In the following phrases both masculine and feminine forms have been indicated where necessary. The masculine form comes first, separated from the feminine by a slash. The gender of a noun is often indicated by a preceding article: 'the/a/some', *le/un/du* (m), *la/une/de la* (f); or a possessive adjective, 'my/your/his/her', *mon/ton/son* (m), *ma/ta/sa* (f). With French, unlike English, the possessive adjective agrees in number and gender with the thing possessed: 'his/her mother', *sa mère*.

Greetings & Civilities

Hello/Good morning.	*Bonjour.*
Good evening.	*Bonsoir.*
Good night.	*Bonne nuit.*
Goodbye.	*Au revoir.*
Yes.	*Oui.*
No.	*Non.*
Maybe.	*Peut-être.*
Please.	*S'il vous plaît.*
Thank you.	*Merci.*
You're welcome.	*Je vous en prie.*
Excuse me.	*Excusez-moi.*
Sorry/Forgive me.	*Pardon.*
How are you?	*Comment allez-vous?* (polite) *Comment vas-tu?/ Comment ça va?* (informal)
Fine, thanks.	*Bien, merci.*
What's your name?	*Comment vous appelez-vous?*
My name is ...	*Je m'appelle ...*
I'm pleased to meet you.	*Enchanté* (m)/ *Enchantée.* (f)
How old are you?	*Quel âge avez-vous?*
I'm ... years old.	*J'ai ... ans.*
Where are you from?	*De quel pays êtes-vous?*
I'm from ...	*Je viens ...*
Australia	*d'Australie*
Canada	*du Canada*

England	*d'Angleterre*
Germany	*d'Allemagne*
Ireland	*d'Irlande*
the Netherlands	*des Pays-Bas*
New Zealand	*de Nouvelle Zélande*
Scotland	*d'Écosse*
the USA	*des États-Unis*
Wales	*du Pays de Galle*

Language Difficulties

I understand.	*Je comprends.*
I don't understand.	*Je ne comprends pas.*
Do you speak English?	*Parlez-vous anglais?*
Could you please write it down?	*Est-ce que vous pouvez l'écrire?*

Getting Around

I want to go to ...	*Je voudrais aller à ...*
I'd like to book a seat to ...	*Je voudrais réserver une place pour ...*
How long does the trip take?	*Combien de temps dure le trajet?*

What time does the ... leave/arrive?	*À quelle heure part/arrive ...?*
aeroplane	*l'avion*
bus (city)	*l'autobus*
bus (intercity)	*l'autocar*
ferry	*le ferry(-boat)*
train	*le train*

Where is (the) ...?	*Où est ...?*
bus stop	*l'arrêt d'autobus*
train station	*la gare*
ticket office	*le guichet*

I'd like a ... ticket.	*Je voudrais un billet ...*
one-way	*aller-simple*
return	*aller-retour*
1st class	*première classe*
2nd class	*deuxième classe*

left-luggage locker	*consigne automatique*
platform	*quai*
timetable	*horaire*

I'd like to hire ...	*Je voudrais louer ...*
a bicycle	*un vélo*
a car	*une voiture*
a guide	*un guide*

Around Town

I'm looking for ...	*Je cherche ...*
a bank/ exchange office	*une banque/ un bureau de change*
the ... embassy	*l'ambassade de ...*
the hospital	*l'hôpital*
the market	*le marché*
the police	*la police*
the post office	*le bureau de poste/ la poste*
a public phone	*une cabine téléphonique*
a public toilet	*les toilettes*
the tourist office	*l'office de tourisme*

Where is (the) ...?	*Où est ...?*
beach	*la plage*
bridge	*le pont*
church	*l'église*
ruins	*les ruines*
square	*la place*
tower	*la tour*

What time does it open/close?	*Quelle est l'heure d'ouverture/ de fermeture?*
I'd like to make a telephone call.	*Je voudrais téléphoner.*
I'd like to change ...	*Je voudrais changer ...*
some money	*de l'argent*
travellers cheques	*chèques de voyage*

Directions

How do I get to ...?	*Comment dois-je faire pour arriver à ...?*
Is it near/far?	*Est-ce près/loin?*
Can you show me on the map/ city map?	*Est-ce que vous pouvez me le montrer sur la carte/le plan?*
Go straight ahead.	*Continuez tout droit.*
Turn left.	*Tournez à gauche.*
Turn right.	*Tournez à droite.*

at the next corner	*au prochain coin*
behind	*derrière*
in front of	*devant*
opposite	*en face de*
north	*nord*
south	*sud*
east	*est*
west	*ouest*

Accommodation

I'm looking for ...	*Je cherche ...*
the youth hostel	*l'auberge de jeunesse*
the camp site	*le camping*
a hotel	*un hôtel*
Where can I find a cheap hotel?	*Où est-ce que je peux trouver un hôtel bon marché?*
What's the address?	*Quelle est l'adresse?*
Could you write it down, please?	*Est-ce vous pourriez l'écrire, s'il vous plaît?*
Do you have any rooms available?	*Est-ce que vous avez des chambres libres?*
I'd like to book ...	*Je voudrais réserver ...*
a bed	*un lit*
a single room	*une chambre pour une personne*
a double room	*une chambre double*
a room with a shower and toilet	*une chambre avec douche et WC*
I'd like to stay in a dormitory.	*Je voudrais coucher dans un dortoir.*
How much is it ...?	*Quel est le prix ...?*
per night	*par nuit*
per person	*par personne*
Is breakfast included?	*Est-ce que le petit déjeuner est compris?*
May I see the room?	*Est-ce que je peux voir la chambre?*
Where is the toilet?	*Où sont les toilettes?*
I'm going to stay ...	*Je vais rester ...*
one day	*un jour*
a week	*une semaine*

Shopping

How much is it?	*C'est combien?*
It's too expensive for me.	*C'est trop cher pour moi.*
Can I look at it?	*Est-ce que je peux le/la voir?* (m/f)

Signs

Entrée	**Entrance**
Sortie	**Exit**
Ouvert	**Open**
Fermé	**Closed**
Chambres Libres	**Rooms Available**
Complet	**No Vacancies**
Renseignements	**Information**
Interdit	**Prohibited**
(Commissariat de) Police	**Police Station**
Toilettes, WC	**Toilets**
Hommes	**Men**
Femmes	**Women**

Do you accept credit cards?	*Est-ce que je peux payer avec ma carte de crédit?*
Do you accept travellers cheques?	*Est-ce que je peux payer avec des chèques de voyage?*
more/less	*plus/moins*
cheap	*bon marché*
cheaper	*moins cher*
bookshop	*la librairie*
chemist/pharmacy	*la pharmacie*
laundry/laundrette	*la laverie*
market	*le marché*
newsagency	*l'agence de presse*
stationers	*la papeterie*
supermarket	*le supermarché*

Time, Dates & Numbers

What time is it?	*Quelle heure est-il?*
It's (two) o'clock.	*Il est (deux) heures.*
When?	*Quand?*
today	*aujourd'hui*
tonight	*ce soir*
tomorrow	*demain*
yesterday	*hier*
in the morning	*du matin*
in the afternoon	*de l'après-midi*
in the evening	*du soir*
Monday	*lundi*
Tuesday	*mardi*
Wednesday	*mercredi*
Thursday	*jeudi*

Friday	*vendredi*
Saturday	*samedi*
Sunday	*dimanche*

January	*janvier*
February	*février*
March	*mars*
April	*avril*
May	*mai*
June	*juin*
July	*juillet*
August	*août*
September	*septembre*
October	*octobre*
November	*novembre*
December	*décembre*

1	*un*
2	*deux*
3	*trois*
4	*quatre*
5	*cinq*
6	*six*
7	*sept*
8	*huit*
9	*neuf*
10	*dix*
11	*onze*
12	*douze*
13	*treize*
14	*quatorze*
15	*quinze*
16	*seize*
17	*dix-sept*
18	*dix-huit*
19	*dix-neuf*
20	*vingt*
21	*vingt-et-un*
22	*vingt deux*
30	*trente*
40	*quarante*
50	*cinquante*
60	*soixante*
70	*soixante dix*
80	*quatre-vingt*
90	*quatre-vingt-dix*
100	*cent*
1000	*mille*

one million	*un million*

Emergencies

Help!	*Au secours!*
Call a doctor!	*Appelez un médecin!*
Call the police!	*Appelez la police!*
Leave me alone!	*Fichez-moi la paix!*
I've been robbed.	*On m'a volé.*
I've been raped.	*On m'a violée.*
I'm lost.	*Je me suis égaré/ égarée.* (m/f)

Health

I'm sick.	*Je suis malade.*
I need a doctor.	*Il me faut un médecin.*
Where is the hospital?	*Où est l'hôpital?*
I have diarrhoea.	*J'ai la diarrhée.*
I'm pregnant.	*Je suis enceinte.*

I'm ...	*Je suis ...*
diabetic	*diabétique*
epileptic	*épileptique*
asthmatic	*asthmatique*
anaemic	*anémique*
I'm allergic ...	*Je suis allergique ...*
to antibiotics	*aux antibiotiques*
to penicillin	*à la pénicilline*

antiseptic	*antiseptique*
aspirin	*aspirine*
condoms	*préservatifs*
contraceptive	*contraceptif*
medicine	*médicament*
nausea	*nausée*
sunblock cream	*crème solaire haute protection*
tampons	*tampons hygiéniques*

FOOD

breakfast	*le petit déjeuner*
lunch	*le déjeuner*
dinner	*le dîner*
grocery store	*l'épicerie*

I'd like the set menu.	*Je prends le menu.*
I'm a vegetarian.	*Je suis végétarien/ végétarienne.*
I don't eat meat.	*Je ne mange pas de viande.*

Starters & Soup

bouillabaisse
Mediterranean-style fish soup, originally from Marseille, made with several kinds of fish, including *rascasse* (spiny scorpion fish); often eaten as a main course

croûtons
fried or roasted bread cubes, often added to soups

entrée
starter

potage
thick soup made with puréed vegetables

soupe de poisson
fish soup

soupe du jour
soup of the day

Meat, Chicken & Poultry

agneau	lamb
bifteck	steak
bœuf	beef
bœuf haché	minced beef
boudin noir	blood sausage (black pudding)
canard	duck
cervelle	brains
charcuterie	cooked or prepared meats (usually pork)
cheval	horse meat
chèvre	goat
côte	chop of pork, lamb or mutton
côtelette	cutlet
dinde	turkey
escargot	snail
foie	liver
foie gras de canard	duck liver pâté
jambon	ham
lapin	rabbit
lard	bacon
mouton	mutton
oie	goose
pieds de porc	pigs' trotters
porc	pork
poulet	chicken
rognons	kidneys
sanglier	wild boar
saucisson	large sausage
saucisson fumé	smoked sausage
steak	steak
tripes	tripe
viande	meat
volaille	poultry

Common Meat & Poultry Dishes

blanquette de veau or *d'agneau*
veal or lamb stew with white sauce

bœuf bourguignon
beef and vegetable stew cooked in red wine (usually burgundy)

cassoulet
Languedoc stew made with goose, duck, pork or lamb fillets and haricot beans

chou farci
stuffed cabbage

choucroute
sauerkraut with sausage and other prepared meats

confit de canard or *d'oie*
duck or goose preserved and cooked in its own fat

coq au vin
chicken cooked in wine

civet
game stew

fricassée
stew with meat that has first been fried

grillade
grilled meats

marcassin
young wild boar

quenelles
dumplings made of a finely sieved mixture of cooked fish or (rarely) meat

steak tartare
raw ground meat mixed with onion, raw egg yolk and herbs

Fish & Seafood

anchois	anchovy
calmar	squid
chaudrée	fish stew
coquille St-Jacques	scallop
crabe	crab
crevette grise	shrimp
crevette rose	prawn
fruits de mer	seafood
gambas	king prawns
homard	lobster

huître	oyster
langouste	crayfish
langoustine	very small saltwater 'lobster'
moules	mussels
palourde	clam
poisson	fish
sardine	sardine
saumon	salmon
thon	tuna
truite	trout

Vegetables, Herbs & Spices

ail	garlic
aïoli or *ailloli*	garlic mayonnaise
anis	aniseed
artichaut	artichoke
asperge	asparagus
aubergine	aubergine (eggplant)
avocat	avocado
betterave	beetroot
carotte	carrot
céleri	celery
cèpe	cep (boletus mushroom)
champignon	mushroom
champignon de Paris	button mushroom
chou	cabbage
concombre	cucumber
courgette	courgette (zucchini)
crudités	small pieces of raw vegetables
épice	spice
épinards	spinach
haricots	beans
haricots blancs	white beans
haricots rouge	kidney beans
haricots verts	French (string) beans
herbe	herb
aitue	lettuce
gumes	vegetables
tilles	lentils
	sweet corn
	onion
	olive
	parsnip
	parsley
	peas
	leek

poivron	green pepper
pomme de terre	potato
ratatouille	casserole of aubergines, tomatoes, peppers and garlic
riz	rice
salade	salad or lettuce
tomate	tomato
truffe	truffle

Cooking Methods

à la broche	spit-roasted
à la vapeur	steamed
au feu de bois	cooked over a wood-burning stove
au four	baked
en croûte	in pastry
farci	stuffed
fumé	smoked
gratiné	browned on top with cheese
grillé	grilled
pané	coated in breadcrumbs
rôti	roasted
sauté	sautéed (shallow fried)

Sauces & Accompaniments

béchamel
basic white sauce

huile d'olive
olive oil

mornay
cheese sauce

moutarde
mustard

pistou
pesto (pounded mix of basil, hard cheese, olive oil and garlic)

provençale
tomato, garlic, herb and olive oil dressing or sauce

tartare
mayonnaise with herbs

vinaigrette
salad dressing made with oil, vinegar, mustard and garlic

Fruit & Nuts

abricot	apricot
amande	almond

ananas	pineapple
arachide	peanut
banane	banana
cacahuète	peanut
cassis	blackcurrant
cerise	cherry
citron	lemon
datte	date
figue	fig
fraise	strawberry
framboise	raspberry
mangue	mango
marron	chestnut
melon	melon
noisette	hazelnut
orange	orange
pamplemousse	grapefruit
pastèque	watermelon
pêche	peach
poire	pear
pomme	apple
prune	plum
pruneau	prune
raisin	grape

Desserts & Sweets

crêpe
thin pancake
crêpes suzettes
orange-flavoured crêpes flambéed in liqueur
flan
egg-custard dessert
frangipane
pastry filled with cream flavoured with almonds or a cake mixture containing ground almonds
galette
wholemeal or buckwheat pancake; also a type of biscuit
gâteau
cake
gaufre
waffle
gelée
jelly
glace
ice cream
tarte
tart (pie)
tarte aux pommes
apple tart
yaourt
yoghurt

Snacks

croque-monsieur
a grilled ham and cheese sandwich
croque-madame
a croque-monsieur with a fried egg
frites
chips (French fries)
quiche
quiche; savoury egg, bacon and cream tart

Basics

beurre	butter
chocolat	chocolate
confiture	jam
crème fraîche	cream
farine	flour
huile	oil
lait	milk
miel	honey
œufs	eggs
poivre	pepper
sel	salt
sucre	sugar
vinaigre	vinegar

Utensils

bouteille	bottle
carafe	carafe
pichet	jug
verre	glass
couteau	knife
cuillère	spoon
fourchette	fork
serviette	serviette (napkin)

DRINKS

Nonalcoholic

mineral water	*eau minérale/ eau de sour*
tap water	*eau de robi*
orange juice	*jus d'ora*
milk	*lait*
(a) coffee	*(un) co*
coffee with milk	*café c*
offee with cream	*café*

expresso coffee	*express*
black coffee	*(petit) noir*
(a) tea	*(un) thé*
tea with lemon	*thé au citron*
white tea	*thé au lait*
(a) herbal tea	*(une) tisane*
(a) hot chocolate	*(un) chocolat chaud*

Alcoholic

beer	*bière*
cider	*cidre*
wine	*vin*
white wine	*vin blanc*
red wine	*vin rouge*
champagne	*champagne*
sparkling wine	*vin mousseux*
brandy	*cognac*
aniseed liqueur with water	*pastis*
whisky	*whisky*
vodka	*vodka*
gin	*gin*

CORSICAN

'Good day' in the Corsican language is *bunghjornu*. 'Thank you' is *grazie*. Bread is *pane*. Dog is *cane*. 'Best wishes!' is *pace i salute!* If this all sounds suspiciously like Italian to you, you're not off the mark. The Corsican language – *Corsu* in Corsican – is descended from and still related to the Tuscan language that also fathered modern Italian. If you think Corsican is Italian or a dialect of Italian, you might nevertheless do well to keep this view to yourself. Though Corsicans are too good-natured to want to punish innocent foreigners for the hasty conclusions they draw on only partial evidence, many Corsicans are committed to the view that Corsican is not a dialect, and still less Italian itself, but a distinct language.

It is not recommended that you make any effort to communicate with Corsicans in Corsican. As Alexandra Jaffe says in her excellent *Ideologies in Action: Language Politics in Corsica*, Corsican is the language of the Corsican heart and hearth. French 'commands the domain of the formal, the authoritative, the instrumental and intellectual'. You may think you are being ingratiating if you attempt a few words of Corsican. More likely, however, you will be perceived as patronising or condescending, as if the person you are addressing did not speak French perfectly well. You may be perceived to be baiting the person you are addressing on what is in Corsica a heavily charged political issue. Finally, again Corsican being the language of the Corsican heart and hearth, you may be perceived as intruding on personal and private space – as if, invited into a stranger's living room, you proceeded immediately into the stranger's bedroom. Another way to put it is to say that presuming to address a stranger in Corsican is akin to the liberty you take in addressing a stranger in the familiar pan-Mediterranean 'tu' form rather than in the more respectful 'vous', 'lei' or 'usted' form.

If you speak French or Italian, stick with that. Dedicated Corsophiles can enrol in language courses at the Università di Corsica Pasqual Paoli in Corte or as offered by the association Esse (☎ 04 95 33 12 00) in Bastia.

Glossary

The following abbreviations are used:

(F) French
(C) Corsican

AGENC – Agence pour la Gestion des Espaces Naturels de Corse; Office for the Management of the Natural Areas of Corsica
aiguille (F) – rock mass or mountain peak shaped like a needle
anse (F) – cove
appellation d'origine contrôlée (F) – mark of quality for wines and cheeses
ATM – automated teller machine; cashpoint
auberge (F) – inn
auberge de jeunesse (F) – youth hostel

baie (F) – bay
bain (F) – bath
barrage (F) – dam
bastiglia (C) – fortress
bergerie (F) – shepherd's hut, often used as accommodation for walkers
bocca (C) – mountain pass
bouches (F) – straits
brèche (F) – breach, gap
brocciu/bruccio (C) – Corsican goat or ewe's milk cheese
bruschetta – toasted bread rubbed with garlic and topped with any of a number of salads, roasted vegetables or other treats

calanques (F), calanche (C) – rocky inlets
cap (F), capu/capo (C) – cape
carrefour (F) – crossroads, intersection
cascade (F) – waterfall
casgili (C) – cheese cellar
castagnu (C) – chestnut
castellu, castelli *pl* (C) – castle
chapelle (F) – chapel
charcuterie (F) – cooked pork meats
cignale (C) – wild boar
cirque (F) – a semicircular or crescent-shaped basin with steep sides and a gently sloping floor, formed by the erosive action of ice
clos (F) – vineyard
col (F) – mountain pass
commune (F) – smallest unit of local government in rural areas/districts
Conseil Général (F) – General Council; implements legislation at local level
Conservatoire du Littoral (F) – Conservatoire de l'Espace Littoral et des Rivages Lacustres; Organisation for the Conservation of Coastal Areas and Lakeshores
Corse (F), Corsu (C) – Corsican language
couloir (F) – deep gully on a mountain side
couvent (F) – convent
crête (F) – ridge

défilé (F) – gorge, narrow pass
démaquisage (F) – scrub clearance
département (F) – unit of French regional administration
désert (F) – desert
dolmen – megalithic standing stones capped by a horizontal stone, thought to be tombs
domaine (F) – estate, especially one that produces wine

écobuage (F) – cultivation on land covered in burnt stubble
église (F) – church
étang (F) – lake, pond

fiadone (C) – flan made with *brocciu*, lemon and eggs
figatellu (C) – type of liver sausage
fola (C) – folk tale
forêt (F) – forest
FLNC – Front de Libération Nationale de la Corse; Corsican National Liberation Front

gîte d'étape (F) – mountain lodge, more comfortable than the basic *refuge*
golfe (F) – bay, gulf
goulet (F) – narrows; bottleneck at entrance to a harbour

île (F) – isle, island

lac (F) – lake

laricio (C) – type of pine native to Corsica
lauze (F) – type of stone found only in the area around Bastia
libeccio – south-westerly wind

maison (F) – office, house
maquis (F) – scrub vegetation
marché (F) – market
menhir – single standing stone, often carved, dating from the megalithic era
mouflon (F) – wild sheep native to Corsica

névé (F) – mass of porous ice; also called a firn

ONF – Office National des Forêts; National Office for Forests
optimiste (F) – coracle

panini – filled bread rolls
phare (F) – lighthouse
pieds-noirs (F) – repatriated French from Algeria
pieve (C) – small region; parish
pinzuti (C) – settlers from the French mainland
place (F) – square
plage (F) – beach
plongée (F) – diving
PNRC – Parc Naturel Régional de Corse; Corsican Nature Reserve
port de plaisance (F) – marina
pozzi (C) – pits
pozzines (C) – interlinked water holes
préfecture (F) – unit of regional administration in France
priorité à droite (F) – give way to the right
prisuttu (C) – Corsican raw ham
pointe (F), punta (C) – point; headland

randonnée (F) – walk
refuge (F) – mountain accommodation, from a basic hut to a simple hostel

sanglier (C) – wild boar
Saracen – Moor; Moorish
sec (F) – shallow (diving); dry (climate, wine, etc)
Sécurité Civile (F) – civil defence department
sémaphore (F) – coastal signal station
Shardanes – 'sea people'; ancient nautical race
son et lumière (F) – night-time presentation at a historic site using lighting, sound effects and narration
source (F) – spring

tafoni/taffoni (C) – cavities (geology)
torre, torri ***pl*** **(C)** – circular stone formation or tower
Torréens – invaders who conquered Corsica around 1100 BC; possibly the Shardanes
tour (F) – tower

vallée (F) – valley
vendetta – blood feud

Guides by Region

Lonely Planet is known worldwide for publishing practical, reliable and no-nonsense travel information in our guides and on our Web site. The Lonely Planet list covers just about every accessible part of the world. Currently there are 16 series: Travel guides, Shoestring guides, Condensed guides, Phrasebooks, Read This First, Healthy Travel, Walking guides, Cycling guides, Watching Wildlife guides, Pisces Diving & Snorkeling guides, City Maps, Road Atlases, Out to Eat, World Food, Journeys travel literature and Pictorials.

AFRICA Africa on a shoestring • Cairo • Cape Town • Cape Town City Map • East Africa • Egypt • Egyptian Arabic phrasebook • Ethiopia, Eritrea & Djibouti • Ethiopian (Amharic) phrasebook • The Gambia & Senegal • Healthy Travel Africa • Kenya • Malawi • Morocco • Moroccan Arabic phrasebook • Mozambique • Read This First: Africa • South Africa, Lesotho & Swaziland • Southern Africa • Southern Africa Road Atlas • Swahili phrasebook • Tanzania, Zanzibar & Pemba • Trekking in East Africa • Tunisia • Watching Wildlife East Africa • Watching Wildlife Southern Africa • West Africa • World Food Morocco • Zimbabwe, Botswana & Namibia
Travel Literature: Mali Blues: Traveling to an African Beat • The Rainbird: A Central African Journey • Songs to an African Sunset: A Zimbabwean Story

AUSTRALIA & THE PACIFIC Auckland • Australia • Australian phrasebook • Australia Road Atlas • Bushwalking in Australia •Cycling New Zealand • Fiji • Fijian phrasebook • Healthy Travel Australia, NZ and the Pacific • Islands of Australia's Great Barrier Reef • Melbourne • Melbourne City Map • Micronesia • New Caledonia • New South Wales & the ACT • New Zealand • Northern Territory • Outback Australia • Out to Eat – Melbourne • Out to Eat – Sydney • Papua New Guinea • Pidgin phrasebook • Queensland • Rarotonga & the Cook Islands • Samoa • Solomon Islands • South Australia • South Pacific • South Pacific phrasebook • Sydney • Sydney City Map • Sydney Condensed • Tahiti & French Polynesia • Tasmania • Tonga • Tramping in New Zealand • Vanuatu • Victoria • Watching Wildlife Australia • Western Australia
Travel Literature: Islands in the Clouds: Travels in the Highlands of New Guinea • Kiwi Tracks: A New Zealand Journey • Sean & David's Long Drive

CENTRAL AMERICA & THE CARIBBEAN Bahamas, Turks & Caicos • Baja California • Bermuda • Central America on a shoestring • Costa Rica • Costa Rica Spanish phrasebook • Cuba • Dominican Republic & Haiti • Eastern Caribbean • Guatemala • Guatemala, Belize & Yucatán: La Ruta Maya • Healthy Travel Central & South America • Jamaica • Mexico • Mexico City • Panama • Puerto Rico • Read This First: Central & South America • World Food Mexico • Yucatán
Travel Literature: Green Dreams: Travels in Central America

EUROPE Amsterdam • Amsterdam City Map • Amsterdam Condensed • Andalucía • Austria • Baltic States phrasebook • Barcelona • Barcelona City Map • Berlin • Berlin City Map • Britain • British phrasebook • Brussels, Bruges & Antwerp • Budapest • Budapest City Map • Canary Islands • Central Europe • Central Europe phrasebook • Corfu & the Ionians • Corsica • Crete • Crete Condensed • Croatia • Cycling Britain • Cycling France • Cyprus • Czech & Slovak Republics • Denmark • Dublin • Dublin City Map • Eastern Europe • Eastern Europe phrasebook • Edinburgh • Estonia, Latvia & Lithuania • Europe on a shoestring • Finland • Florence • France • Frankfurt Condensed • French phrasebook • Georgia, Armenia & Azerbaijan • Germany • German phrasebook • Greece • Greek Islands • Greek phrasebook • Hungary • Iceland, Greenland & the Faroe Islands • Ireland • Istanbul • Italian phrasebook • Italy • Krakow • Lisbon • The Loire • London • London City Map • London Condensed • Madrid • Malta • Mediterranean Europe • Mediterranean Europe phrasebook • Moscow • Munich • Norway • Out to Eat – London • Paris • Paris City Map • Paris Condensed • Poland • Portugal • Portuguese phrasebook • Prague • Prague City Map • Provence & the Côte d'Azur • Read This First: Europe • Romania & Moldova • Rome • Russia, Ukraine & Belarus • Russian phrasebook • Scandinavian & Baltic Europe • Scandinavian Europe phrasebook • Scotland • Sicily • Slovenia • South-West France • Spain • Spanish phrasebook • St Petersburg • St Petersburg City Map • Sweden • Switzerland • Trekking in Spain • Tuscany • Ukrainian phrasebook • Venice • Vienna • Walking in Britain • Walking in France • Walking in Ireland • Walking in Italy • Walking in Spain • Walking in Switzerland • Western Europe • Western Europe phrasebook • World Food France • World Food Ireland • World Food Italy • World Food Spain
Travel Literature: Love and War in the Apennines • The Olive Grove: Travels in Greece • On the Shores of the Mediterranean • Round Ireland in Low Gear • A Small Place in Italy

INDIAN SUBCONTINENT Bangladesh • Bengali phrasebook • Bhutan • Delhi • Goa • Healthy Travel A… & India • Hindi & Urdu phrasebook • India • Indian Himalaya • Karakoram Highway • Kerala • Mu…

LONELY PLANET

You already know that Lonely Planet produces more than this one guidebook, but you might not be aware of the other products we have on this region. Here is a selection of titles that you may want to check out as well:

Index

Text

Bold indicates maps.

Bold indicates maps.

Boxed Text

MAP LEGEND

BOUNDARIES

International
Regional
Suburb

HYDROGRAPHY

Coastline
River, Stream
Lake
Swamp

ROUTES & TRANSPORT

Motorway
Primary Road
Secondary Road
Tertiary Road
Unsealed Road
City Motorway
City Primary Road
City Road
City Street, Lane
Pedestrian Area
Path Through a Park
Tunnel
Railway & Station
Cable Car or Chairlift
Walking Track
Walking Tour
Bus Route
Ferry Route & Terminal

AREA FEATURES

Park, Gardens
Urban Area, Building
Forest
Market
Beach or Desert
Cemetery

MAP SYMBOLS

Bastia City or Large Town
St-Florent Town
Vizzavona Village
Point of Interest
Place to Stay
Camp Site
Chalet, Shelter
Place to Eat
Pub or Bar
Airport, Aeroplane Wreck
Ancient or City Wall
Archaeological Site
Bank
Beach
Bus Stop, Station
Castle or Fort
Cathedral or Church
Cave
Cinema
Cliff or Escarpment
Dive Site, Centre
Embassy or Consulate
Fountain
Hospital
Internet Cafe
Lighthouse
Lookout
Monument
Mountain, Range
Museum
Parking
Pass
Petrol Station
Police Station
Post Office
Ruins
Shipwreck
Spot Height
Theatre
Tourist Information
Transport
Vineyard
Walking Route
Waterfall

Note: not all symbols displayed above appear in this book

LONELY PLANET OFFICES

Australia
Locked Bag 1, Footscray, Victoria 3011
☎ 03 8379 8000 fax 03 8379 8111
email: talk2us@lonelyplanet.com.au

USA
150 Linden St, Oakland, CA 94607
☎ 510 893 8555 TOLL FREE: 800 275 8555
fax 510 893 8572
email: info@lonelyplanet.com

UK
10a Spring Place, London NW5 3BH
☎ 020 7428 4800 fax 020 7428 4828
email: go@lonelyplanet.co.uk

France
1 rue du Dahomey, 75011 Paris
☎ 01 55 25 33 00 fax 01 55 25 33 01
email: bip@lonelyplanet.fr
www.lonelyplanet.fr

World Wide Web: www.lonelyplanet.com *or* AOL keyword: lp
Lonely Planet Images: lpi@lonelyplanet.com.au